STUDIES IN CONTEMPORARY JEWRY

The publication of *Studies in Contemporary Jewry* was made possible through the generous assistance of the Samuel and Althea Stroum Philanthropic Fund, Seattle, Washington.

INSTITUTE OF CONTEMPORARY JEWRY
THE HEBREW UNIVERSITY
OF JERUSALEM

ART AND ITS USES
The Visual Image
and Modern Jewish Society

STUDIES IN

CONTEMPORARY

JEWRY

AN ANNUAL

VI

————————— 1990 —————————

Edited by Ezra Mendelsohn
Guest Symposium Editor: Richard I. Cohen

Published for the Institute by
OXFORD UNIVERSITY PRESS
New York • Oxford

Oxford University Press

Oxford   New York   Toronto
Delhi   Bombay   Calcutta   Madras   Karachi
Petaling Jaya   Singapore   Hong Kong   Tokyo
Nairobi   Dar es Salaam   Cape Town
Melbourne   Auckland
and associated companies in
Berlin   Ibadan

Copyright © 1990 by Oxford University Press, Inc.

Published by Oxford University Press, Inc.,
200 Madison Avenue, New York, New York 10016

Oxford is a registered trademark of Oxford University Press

ISBN 0-19-506188-8
ISSN 0740-8625
Library of Congress Catalog Card Number: 84-649196

2 4 6 8 10 9 7 5 3 1
Printed in the United States of America
on acid-free paper

STUDIES IN CONTEMPORARY JEWRY

Reuven Rubin, *The Artist's Family*, 1927. Tel-Aviv Museum.

Preface

The sixth volume of the annual publication *Studies in Contemporary Jewry* retains its traditional format: a symposium, essays, review essays and a large number of book reviews (now arranged by subject). The symposium itself, however, represents a new departure, an attempt to illuminate aspects of modern Jewish history and society through the study of what one of our contributors calls "a new text." The use of this "new text," the visual image, is well established in the historical profession in general but rather uncommon in the field of modern Jewish studies. The eight essays included in this volume reveal the many levels of meaning present in the different types of visual material they discuss–ranging from high art by Jewish artists to Judaica, caricatures and political propaganda. Providing the reader with the tools necessary for "translating" the iconography, they make the important point that the illustrations under review must be understood in their proper social and political contexts. I believe that the essays yield new insights and shed new light on such topics as Jewish nationalism, Jewish identity and Jewish-gentile relations, thereby effectively demonstrating the utility of this particular approach. I am likewise confident that the symposium will help place the serious investigation of the various "Jewish images" on the agenda of modern Jewish studies.

Dr. Richard I. Cohen, a modern Jewish historian with a special interest in the field of art history, has served as the guest symposium editor. This volume owes much to his expertise. I am also grateful to my colleagues in the Department of Art History at The Hebrew University for their willingness to contribute to this volume and to advise its editors. As always, the work of our managing editor, Dr. Eli Lederhendler, and our book review editor, Ms. Hannah Koevary, has been exemplary.

Now in its sixth year of existence, *Studies in Contemporary Jewry* remains faithful to its original conception, first articulated in 1984. It presents to those interested in modern Jewish studies an interdisciplinary, innovative approach to the study of the recent Jewish past, attempting through its book review section to survey the large and ever-growing literature in the field. In this challenging work, its editors are supported by the Institute of Contemporary Jewry at The Hebrew University and by Oxford University Press in New York. As for future plans, the reader is referred to p. 417, where the contents for Volume VII are presented.

E.M.

Contents

Symposium:
Art and Its Uses:
The Visual Image and Modern Jewish Society

Essays

Review Essays

Book Reviews (arranged by subject)

Antisemitism, Holocaust and Genocide

Communal History

Demography, Economics and Sociology

Language, Art and Literature

Religion, Thought and Education

Zionism and Israel

Symposium

Art and Its Uses:
The Visual Image
and Modern Jewish Society

An Introductory Essay:
Viewing the Past

Richard I. Cohen
(THE HEBREW UNIVERSITY)

Contemplating the uses and implications of visual sources for the study of the past, one is reminded of the classic work of Johan Huizinga, *The Waning of the Middle Ages,* and especially of his remarkable concluding chapters. Convinced that the various modes of artistic creation reflected the prevailing tendency of the age toward magnificence, Huizinga went so far as to characterize even the contemporary festivals and spectacles as applied literature. It was clear to him that "art was subservient to life. Its social function was to enhance the importance of a chapel, a donor, a patron, or a festival, but never that of the artist."[1] As such, its social reception was inevitably associated with the religious sentiment it intended to arouse, limiting the possibilities of appreciating beauty in its own right. But Huizinga was also intrigued by the creative force of the artistic material in relation to the literary genre of the period, remarking both on its strength in the expression of depth and detail and on its weaknesses in communicating sardonic and comical intention. Art was thus not an isolated domain within Huizinga's cultural study of France and the Netherlands, but an integral part of that history, both refining and extending it long before Fernand Braudel pronounced that art and literature are "the true witnesses of every worthy history."

Today, more than sixty years since the publication of Huizinga's pathbreaking study, historians seem to be addressing themselves with increasing interest to the issues that lay at the heart of his analysis: the degree to which art can represent and illuminate a given historical period and help reconstruct its internal ethos; the impact and importance of patrons of art, secular or ecclesiastical, on artists and their creations; the public's reception and response to works of art; the social, commercial and even political implications of public criticism; and the study of style within the framework of actual social situations and experience. Underlying these issues is the interrelationship between visual and written material. Some scholars, in the pursuit of a social history of art, have begun to look at art within the context of ideology, science, technology, class, race and gender. Motivation, causation, images and symbols have been scrutinized to widen the interpretive context of the visual material.

The historian's visual sources bring together "high" and "low" culture, established masterpieces and knickknacks, archival records and photographic albums.

3

We see an unending effort to date or attribute objects with unclear provenance and to unravel hidden patterns, practices and preoccupations of former generations. Art assumes an ever-wider meaning as the social historian turns to paintings that hung in Catholic and Protestant homes in seventeenth-century Metz to help determine aspects of religious belief in those communities, or studies the sea of paintings, woodcuts and lithographs produced in seventeenth-century Holland to explain the tension in that society between wealth and religious teachings. Art historians have not lagged behind. Ranging from the ingenious study of Michael Baxandall on fifteenth-century Italian painting, which declares, "a fifteenth-century painting is the deposit of a social relationship,"[2] to the highly original and controversial studies of T. J. Clark, in which French art of the nineteenth century is understood through the prism of political developments,[3] one can ascertain a shift from pure iconographic examination to a closer scrutiny of the social matrix often revealed in the creation of works of art.

True, we are not always provided with the necessary clues or references to penetrate beyond the iconographic inquiry, and the social context often remains unclear. Nonetheless, one need not deduce that particular objects or fields of creativity lie outside the realm of the historian's concern. In such cases the historian can appropriate a semiotic approach whereby objects of art, like all products of human activity, are perceived to have a certain organizing principle and are informed by a unified intention. Treating objects in this manner may help transmit a cultural reality pertinent to our understanding of the past and present.[4] The study of culture, especially among non-literate societies, has, indeed, been greatly advanced by research guided by the above premise, and it would appear that an appreciation of its potential has enriched various historical studies on modern and developed societies.

With this in mind, it is well to recall Leopold Zunz's call for the study of the Jewish past in his classic essay of 1819 on rabbinic literature. After noting the virtual non-existence of Jewish research, Zunz laid before the *Verein für Kultur und Wissenschaft der Juden* an ambitious outline of desiderata that covered almost all walks of Jewish life. Interestingly, he specifically mentioned the arts in the context of the need to inquire into the ways in which Jews were able to master nature— through crafts, archaeology and art itself. He believed that such studies would demonstrate a greater involvement of Jews in these areas than had previously been believed, while illuminating unknown aspects of Jewish life.

In this field, as in many others, generations passed before Zunz's call was taken up, and only toward the end of the nineteenth century did various individuals turn their attention to aspects of Jewish artistic creativity. Some were motivated by Zunz's desire to prove to the "liberal" world that Jews had made a significant contribution to the visual arts, but they also had in mind the positive self-image such studies would provide for Jews in Central and Western Europe, in particular among the more integrated Jews. Jewish art, instinctively associated with the internal Jewish experience, was construed to have meanings and implications far beyond the purely artistic. Consider the remarks of Dr. Hermann Adler, the chief rabbi of England, on viewing one of the first exhibitions of Jewish art in London in 1887: "Had there been less mystery about our religious observances, there would perhaps have been less prejudice, certainly greater freedom from foul aspersions. It is the object [of a section of the exhibition] to remove something of the mysteriousness which, in the mind of the outer world, seems to encompass everything relating to our observances."[5] Or, as one of the initiators of the exhibition commented, "It would serve to promote among our countrymen a lasting interest in the history of the British Jews; it would vindicate the past in their eyes."[6] Indeed, the immediate communicative possibilities of Jewish art were manifest at the turn of the century although a more reflective, research-oriented approach to Jewish art was already beginning to emerge.

From the late nineteenth century to the present, the attitude toward Jewish art, however defined, has changed radically. Both in its functional possibilities and in its incorporation into the body of Jewish research, Jewish art has been integrated into the Jewish experience, epitomizing the break with traditional society and affirming the modern spirit. For example, by transplanting the sacred into the profane, Jewish ritual artifacts were no longer regarded solely as functional pieces to be used in ritual observances, but were studied in their own associational context as a historical phenomenon, outside the purely religious framework. Jewish museums, which began to flourish at the turn of this century, became the new repositories of Judaica, competing with the synagogue and constituting a cultural presence that celebrated objects of interest and beauty and promoted reflection and attachment. Their founders were often motivated by a desire to preserve a "vanishing past" and were preoccupied with the educational effect of such an enterprise. To improve the image of Jews and Judaism was another goal of these museums, which were founded in Vienna, Danzig, Frankfurt, Prague and elsewhere in Europe. One finds among the founders of these museums art enthusiasts, collectors and educated laymen, almost always non-observant Jews, each with his own special attitude to the Jewish past and present. Christians were also involved in some of these undertakings, as they were in helping to promote Jewish artists of the time.

Not incidentally, we find at about the same time a crucial breakthrough in the study of Jewish art: the elaborate and learned publication of the *Sarajevo Haggadah* (1898). Here a window was opened to the iconography of medieval Jewish art and to the study of illuminated Jewish manuscripts. Thus, on two fronts—the collection and preservation of Jewish ritual objects and the systematic analysis of Jewish art— the study of Jewish art took a major step forward.

As Jewish art was being institutionalized, a growing number of modern Jewish artists were confronting their Jewish identity, treating Jewish themes and expressing their predicament in their work. A group of them—Maurycy Gottlieb, Artur Markowicz, Josef Oppenheimer, Camille Pissarro and Lesser Ury—were brought together for the first time in a special exhibition of Jewish artists, held in Berlin in 1907, whose organizers, to judge by the introduction to the catalogue, were well aware of its historic significance.[7] They pondered the ability of Jewish artists to overcome a tradition that tended to downgrade the visual arts, asked whether their "race" endowed them with any particular originality and wondered to what extent their work was consciously infused with a desire to create Jewish art. By this time a Jewish presence in the visual arts was certainly becoming apparent, and it was soon to be bolstered by the efforts of the Bezalel Academy of Arts and Design in Jerusalem, which was bent on emphasizing the interrelationship between Zionist ideology and the decorative arts. In pre–First World War Palestine a new recognition of the integral nature of the arts was being formed, heralded as a significant breakthrough in the process of the normalization of the Jewish people in its historic homeland.

Considering, from our vantage point, the developments in Jewish life since the Emancipation, one cannot overlook one of its most remarkable features: the intense participation of Jews in the cultural ambience of contemporary society. In the visual arts, which is the concern of this symposium, their involvement touched on many aspects of the interrelationship between art and society. We find Jews actively engaged in the patronage, collection and dealership of European art, art publications, art criticism and the actual creation of art. Indeed, their espousal of the arts was to become a source of growing tension with the surrounding society in several countries. These points aside, a proper understanding of Jewish society in the post-Emancipation period and its relationship within the surrounding society requires a consideration of the many-faceted Jewish preoccupation with the arts.

The present symposium brings together a number of essays on the visual dimension of post-Emancipation Jewish society. Adopting as a working definition that "Jewish art is art which reflects the Jewish experience,"[8] each author's starting point is a particular body of visual material that relates either to a single artist or to a specific theme. Each essay reveals the potential inherent in the artistic material to expand our perspective on the internal developments and *mentalité* of the Jewish community and on its relationship with the surrounding society.

The symposium opens with Michael Berkowitz's treatment of art in the service of a political movement. He discusses artistic material of diverse nature and quality— ranging from Ephraim Moses Lilien's lithographs to Zionist postcards and cigarette wrappers—and interprets its significance for building a committed nationalist consciousness among European Jewry. Here we are encouraged to treat seriously mundane objects and souvenirs and to focus on their symbolic and mythic character, recognizing that their import resides in a didactic effort to rejuvenate the Jewish world.

Milly Heyd's iconographic exploration into the art of Reuven Rubin, an artist who worked in Palestine/Israel, reveals a different aspect of the interrelationship between the Zionist experience and art. Intrigued by the sources of his art, Heyd discovers them in a time and place far removed from the political context of the evolving Jewish settlement in Palestine. Her findings point to the long-lasting impact of the artist's return visit to his native Romania during the First World War. Residues of Romanian neo-Byzantine art were later appropriated by Rubin and integrated into his Oriental scenes. Moreover, Rubin resorted to a primitivistic style to cope with the Palestinian reality. Heyd's study thus offers an insight, not readily available from written sources, into the process of cultural integration in interwar Palestine—withdrawal from the recurrent collective tensions while preserving and reconstituting one's own individual past.

The question of what constitutes modern Jewish art has intrigued and baffled art critics and commentators since the earliest exhibition of Jewish artists in Berlin, and it has given rise to profound disagreements. Entering into the fray, where extreme opinions abound, Irit Rogoff breaks new ground in her essay on the early works of Max Liebermann. Using as her starting point Jürgen Habermas's theory of the "public sphere," Rogoff argues that Liebermann's early oeuvre needs to be considered in light of his particular social situation in post-unification Germany and his conflict with dominant trends in German society. Rogoff maintains that various paintings, with apparently very different themes, constitute a coherent cycle and illuminate Liebermann's misgivings about contemporary middle-class German society. These include works that she links to his marked feelings of alienation as a Jew in antisemitic Wilhelminian Germany. Liebermann's "Jewishness" is thus linked to his art, despite the absence of overtly Jewish subject matter.

Focusing on the impact of the Second World War on a group of European artists, Ziva Amishai-Maisels shows how they incorporated the dramatic events of the period into their art and dealt with both their individual crises and the tragic fate of the Jewish people. For some, like Marc Chagall, the new existential situation elicited a penetrating reevaluation of the interrelationship between Judaism and Christianity, expressions of which sharpen our perception of the ways historical memory was infused in the imagination of the day. Amishai-Maisels's essay records a profound artistic response to the political and human maelstrom that continued to reverberate with no less intensity after the war. Furthermore, as Vivianne Barsky shows in her study of the contemporary Jewish artist R. B. Kitaj, past historical events left a troubled heritage for subsequent generations of artists. Unlike many of his predecessors, Kitaj is concerned that his work be construed as the product of a Jewish artist who grapples with the dilemmas of the modern Jew. Indeed, the paintings discussed in the essay incorporate references and responses to seminal cultural and historic moments of contemporary Jewry that are synthesized in a fashion that thrives on ambiguities and contradictions. Barsky's reading of Kitaj's work shows him to be an important interpreter of these situations, one who includes in his interpretation traditional and modern images. Kitaj may not provide evidence for one historical argument or another, but he demonstrates a fascination with things Jewish that cannot be ignored by the scholar of contemporary society.[9]

The symposium also contains essays on other aspects of Jewish visual art. Chone Shmeruk's inquiry into the adaptation of non-Jewish visual and written children's material in Yiddish publications continues his research into the sources of Yiddish book illustration. Here he concentrates on well-known children's stories whose Yiddish renditions, published in the 1920s, Judaized the text and illustrations, turning non-Jews into Jews by virtue of a skullcap or a beard, changing their names and eliminating references to the Church. In his discussion of these adaptations, Shmeruk mentions that in several Hebrew editions of these particular stories and in all Hebrew versions published after 1950, the original, non-Jewish illustrations were left intact. His research raises several cultural questions: whether the later Hebrew editions reflect a greater trust in the openness of the potential audience and an ability to achieve a secular rendition; or whether the traditional Jewish figures were now seen to be anachronistic and less appropriate to the social context of modern-day Israel and were thus replaced by the original characters. These questions indicate the potential insights that can be gleaned from the study of the sources of illustrations in Hebrew and Yiddish texts.

The study of Jewish ceremonial art is represented by an analysis of Italian majolica plates—attributed for decades to seventeenth-century Italy. Vivian Mann questions the veracity of the provenance, finds it wanting and proceeds to locate its source in late nineteenth-century Italy. Forgeries of art objects require a market and a nostalgic public, two preconditions that aptly describe the social and cultural situation of West and Central European Jewry of the late nineteenth century. In revealing this particular forgery and associating it with the growing trend to collect tangible objects of Jewish interest, Mann cautions us as to the authenticity of early Judaica, while expanding our knowledge of the ways in which post-Emancipation Jewry repossessed its past.

Modern historical events are often accompanied by a large amount of visual material, as was the case with the Dreyfus affair. My own essay deals with various aspects of the voluminous visual material relating to the affair.

Jewish ceremonial art, printed books, modern Jewish painting and sculpture, antisemitica and Jewish memorabilia constitute only a few examples of the Jewish interaction with visual material. Many dimensions of this interaction are not examined: the collection of, and dealing in, art; art criticism; synagogue architecture; commemorative medals; Jewish monuments; portraits of Jewish families and individuals; and so forth. Moreover, though the geographic range of our symposium is extensive, too little is said about East European and American Jewish art. Nonetheless, we have here the first serious attempt of any Jewish historical journal to address the visual sphere and reflect on its implications for the study of Jewish history. By bringing together contributions from diverse disciplines, with various approaches to the visual material, we have tried to sensitize the modern Jewish historian to a world of associations and messages that are communicated in nonwritten texts. Stored in these texts, in their style and content, is invaluable material that can be assimilated to the vast body of written material. We also hope that art historians will find value in the attention our studies have paid to the social and political contexts of their respective subject areas of interest.

Notes

1. Johan Huizinga, *The Waning of the Middle Ages* (New York: 1956), 258.

2. Michael Baxandall, *Painting and Experience in Fifteenth-Century Florence: A Primer in the Social History of Style* (London: 1972), 6.

3. T. J. Clark, *Image of the People: Gustave Courbet and the 1848 Revolution* (London: 1973); *The Absolute Bourgeois: Artists and Politics in France, 1848–1851* (Princeton: 1982). See also the comments by Svetlana Alpers, "Is Art History?" *Daedalus* 106 (Summer 1977), 1–13.

4. Jan Mukařovský, "The Essence of the Visual Arts," in *Semiotics of Art: Prague School Contributions,* ed. Ladislav Matejka and Irwin R. Titunik (Cambridge, Mass.: 1977), 229–244.

5. *Jewish Chronicle* (London), 22 April 1887, 8.

6. Isidore Spielman, *Jewish Chronicle* (London), 1 April 1887, 8.

7. Prior to the exhibition in Berlin, Jewish artists were viewed together in the framework of several Zionist congresses and in an all-encompassing exhibition of Judaica held in London in 1906, but never before had there been a special exhibition of Jewish artists. See *Ausstellung jüdischer Künstler* (Berlin: 1907).

8. Vivian Mann and Gordon Tucker (eds.), *The Seminar on Jewish Art: January–September 1984: Proceedings* (New York: 1985), 10.

9. See R. B. Kitaj, "Passion," *European Judaism* 21 (1988), 33–34.

Art in Zionist Popular Culture and Jewish National Self-Consciousness, 1897–1914

Michael Berkowitz
(UNIVERSITY OF JUDAISM)

The first generation of European Zionists waved flags, sang songs, hung portraits of their leaders, sent picture postcards to their families and friends and pasted Jewish National Fund (JNF) stamps on their correspondence. These were conscious forms of identification with, and participation in, the Zionist movement. Yet such phenomena have only occasionally been the concern of historians of Zionism.[1] In particular, there has been little investigation of the visual imagery that summarized, transmitted and symbolized the Zionist project.[2] The images appropriated or created by the early Zionist movement are usually taken as assumptions that need not be qualified or studied. This attests to the ultimate success of these symbols, but it leaves an important gap in the historical comprehension of Zionism.

Zionism was born into a highly visual age when advances in graphic technology, coupled with the rise of the popular press, made possible a profusion of photographic and artistic representations.[3] The development of photography coincided with the increasing prevalence of cartoon and caricature; this extended politics into the personal realm at an unprecedented level. In urban concentrations, at least, great masses of people had access to similar depictions of places, policies and personalities, ranging from realistic photographs to the most exaggerated caricatures.[4] Even if we assume that Jews tended to be more literate than the surrounding populations,[5] it is still crucial to examine not only what European Jews read about Zionism, but also what they saw as Zionism.

This paper explores the role of art in Western and Central European Zionist popular culture during the period 1897–1914 as an expression of national self-consciousness, as a means of propagating the aims of the movement and as an indicator of less apparent biases in Zionism. In its totality, the Zionist movement strove to establish an important Jewish presence in Palestine and to do away with Jewish subordination to European national cultures. It also aspired to preserve the cultural assets that Jewry had inherited from contact with the non-Jewish world.[6] An attempt was made to replace the Jews' exilic condition with a respectable, dignified, self-assured, autonomous and cohesive Jewry, united by a common vision of a

9

present and future Jewish national life in Palestine. Artistic images in Zionist popular culture, from the advent of Theodor Herzl to the First World War, assisted in establishing paradigms for Western Jewish perceptions of the Zionist project. They helped sustain beliefs in a Jewish national regeneration and in a unified Jewry—despite the reality of divisions within Zionism and the fragmented character of Jewish existence. Such images contributed to sustaining Zionist ideas in the European Jewish imagination at a time when the movement was making few material gains. In the context of a loose polity beset with vehement disagreements, national myths and symbols—no matter how banal or sentimental—were the manifestation of ideals that kept those who called themselves Zionists on common ground.[7] Most important, within the framework of the discourse of Zionism, these images created a mythical Palestinian homeland and national landscape in the mind of European Jewry as alternatives or supplements to those put forth by the familiar European nationalist ideologies.

Our analysis necessarily begins with Theodor Herzl's initiation of political Zionism. Herzl founded the movement in order to assemble and activate all of Europe's Jews as a distinct Jewish nation intent on regaining and resettling its ancestral homeland. It was the first appeal to the masses of acculturated European Jewry to subscribe to a coherent, secular and politicized Jewish ideology. Herzl was the archetype of the "new Jew" that the movement aspired to create as well as its leading theoretician. He maintained that subjects that fell into the vague realm of "Jewish culture" were best left to develop organically after the establishment of the Jewish state.[8] His most urgent concern was obtaining a charter from the Turkish sultan for mass Jewish settlement in Palestine. Nonetheless, when he approached the rostrum of the First Zionist Congress in Basel, on August 29, 1897, central elements of a Jewish national culture had already been established, almost single-handedly, by him. He held definite ideas about the role of myths and symbols in Zionism, and he recognized the need for an aesthetic dimension to the new mass movement he wished to forge.

"There is a wall," Theodor Herzl wrote in June 1895, "namely, the demoralization of the Jews. I know that beyond it lies freedom and greatness."[9] For Herzl, art and aesthetics would be a vehicle for the absorption of national ideas; "the simple and moving form of symbols" would be employed as a means to breach the wall.[10] Herzl believed it crucial to "think in images" because people were moved largely by "imponderables, such as music and pictures." But this was not just to reach the unwashed masses—Herzl was well aware of the impact of such phenomena as Wagnerian opera on the middle class.[11] Concurrently, he recognized the tremendous efficacy of traditional Jewish symbols that were held in common by all Jews. He knew that "dreams, songs, and fantasies" that were "floating in the air"[12] must be harnessed to practical politics. "In all of this," Herzl wrote, prescribing a Jewish national festival with an elaborate backdrop and costumes, "I am still the dramatist."[13] Art was to be part of the stage setting for the theater of politics that, he hoped, would transform the Jewish world.

The first products of Herzlian Zionism that used art to arouse Zionist sentiments were the postcards and delegates' and visitors' cards designed for the First Zionist Congress (fig. 1).[14] The quality of this work is amateurish; indeed, it was drawn by Carl Pollak, a university student who helped run the daily operations of the Zionist

Fig. 1. (*a*) Postcard and (*b*) delegate card from the First Zionist Congress (Basel, 1897), drawn by Carl Pollak and designed by Heinrich York-Steiner (Central Zionist Archives, Jerusalem [hereafter cited as CZA], Printed Materials File for the First Zionist Congress [hereafter cited as PMF I; roman numerals correspond to congress number]).

office in Vienna.[15] The quality of the pictures, however, did not diminish the delegates' enthusiasm in seeing and possessing their first Jewish national artifacts. The London *Jewish Chronicle* made special note of the appearance of the Congress postcard and included a reproduction of it in its report. At the final session of the Congress there was "a brisk sale of commemorative postcards."[16]

The postcard shown in figure 1 has two framed narrow images at the ends, with the heading "Zionisten-Congress 1897" and a Star of David in the center. Beneath is the proclamation: "Who will bring from Zion the redemption of Israel?"[17] The left panel shows three pious Jewish men and one woman praying at the Western (Wailing) Wall in Jerusalem. The right panel has a bearded man in peasant garb engaged in sowing the land. This duality between the religious traditional Jew and the pioneer peasant-farmer Jew persisted as the most frequently employed generic Zionist image. It proclaims that both the religious Jew at the wall and the farmer will bring redemption.

The Star of David, which was appropriated for the Zionist flag and lapel pins, appears in nearly every visual representation of Zionism. Gershom Scholem has pointed out that for the early Zionists, the Star of David "possessed two qualities which recommended it as a new symbol: it was well known because of . . . its appearance on many new synagogues in Western and Central Europe and on the seals of communities, the philanthropic societies and the like, and it lacked any clear connection with religious conceptions and associations."[18] As for the picture of the Jewish farmer, it also had little significance in Jewish historical memory, but it looked ahead to a future order where true emancipation would be attained through the Jews' labor on their own soil. This was an appropriate image for nearly every variety of Zionist thought at that time. Each faction of the movement—political, cultural, religious or labor—shared the notion that the regeneration of the Jews could only be attained "by the sweat of their brow," by physical labor tied to agriculture or crafts.[19]

The official postcard from the Second Zionist Congress (Basel, August 28–31, 1898), drawn by Menahem Okin, also shows Jews praying at the Western (Wailing) Wall and an agricultural scene (fig. 2).[20] A Star of David is near the center, enclosing a Lion of Judah, and a quotation from Ezekiel, in large Hebrew characters, occupies the bottom-right corner. It reads, "Behold I will take the children from amongst the nations and bring them to their land."[21] A Moorish arch, a classical column and a nun reading the Bible are included, presumably to symbolize the universal relevance of Zionism. Erwin Rosenberger, a young delegate to the Congress who also helped staff the Zionist Organization office in Vienna, explained that the Congress postcard displayed "the new life burgeoning out of the ruins— workers in the field, a man sowing seed who vaguely resembled Herzl, dancing children, peacefully grazing cattle, and in the background . . . a hill . . . intended to suggest Mount Zion."[22] Reinforcing the image from the First Congress postcard, the top illustration showed "Jewish" Palestine in a pastoral, Central European, preindustrial setting. The symbol of the sun's rays emanating from the horizon was meant to intimate the divine presence called forth by the Jews' return.

The scenes of Jewish farmers, working under the sun on a vast expanse, were a conspicuous attempt to parry the stereotype of Jews as an innately urban people, averse to nature and agricultural pursuits.[23] The farmers share the scene with mourning or praying Jews; religious Jewry is thus recognized as a potential mass of followers for Zionism. But Orthodoxy is presented as a condition of the past, to be transcended by the new ideal, illustrated in the contrasting scene. Another possible interpretation is that in this vision of the future, the worlds of secular and religious Jews could peacefully and fruitfully coexist. The national landscape visualized for the Jews of Europe almost always contained Jews farming and praying. This utopian imagery was complemented by a proliferation of "Jewish" Palestine photographs

Fig. 2. (*a*) Postcard and (*b*) delegate card from the Second Zionist Congress (Basel, 1898), by Menahem Okin (CZA, PMF II).

and texts that ranged from children's tales and travelogues to serious scientific studies, all disseminated through the Zionist movement.[24]

After the Second Zionist Congress, reproductions of a number of pen-and-ink drawings by Menahem Okin appeared in *Die Welt,* the official Zionist organ (fig. 3).[25] Okin also contributed to the institutionalized memory of the event by painting Theodor Herzl shaking hands with Max Nordau, a scene from the opening ceremony. This was distributed to Zionist reading rooms as a framable picture; it was also reduced to postcard size for personal use (fig. 4). It shows the leaders surrounded by the delegates, whose eyes are transfixed on them. All of the men are clad in the obligatory white tie, starched shirt and black formal wear, highlighting

Fig. 3. Max Nordau at the Second
Zionist Congress, by Menahem Okin (*Die
Welt*, 9 September 1898).

the quintessentially bourgeois and respectable tenor of the Congress. The painting
was intended to be the equivalent of European and American state-founding portraits, but its indifferent artistic value doomed it to oblivion shortly after it was
introduced.[26] Probably the most popular group representation from the earliest
years of Zionism was the portrait of participants in the First Zionist Congress, done
in cameos, with an enlarged Herzl in the center (fig. 5).

The commemorative postcard from the Third Zionist Congress (Basel, August
15–19, 1899) is notable because it combines, in a single scene, motifs from formerly distinct pictures in Zionist iconography (fig. 6). Okin's drawing shows an old,
bearded, tallith-clad man with his arms outstretched, his pious wife behind him. He
is blessing two pioneer-farmers, one of whom has his arm around his youthful

Fig. 4. Opening scene of the Second Zionist Congress, by Menahem Okin (CZA, PMF II).

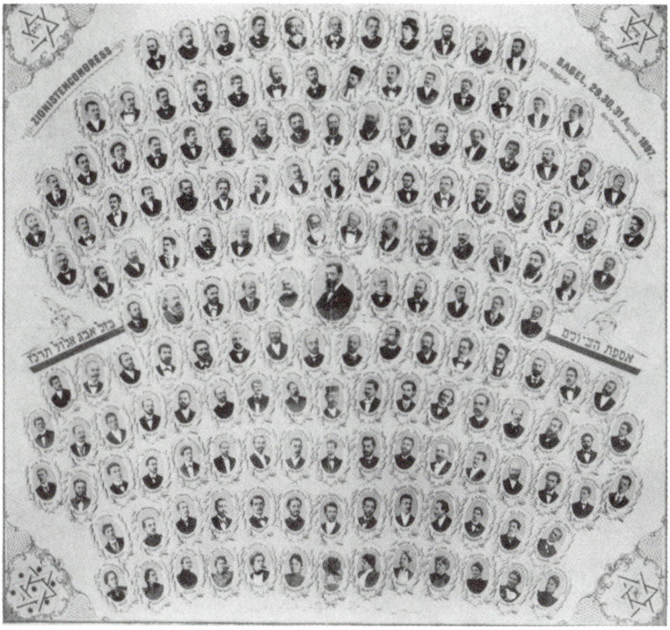

Fig. 5. Group portrait of the First Zionist Congress (CZA, PMF I).

son.[27] We have here a clear portrayal of harmony between generations. A trend that will continue, especially in drawings and etchings of Jewish Palestine, is the depiction of religious Jews as belonging to the older generation. It is a manifestation of what may be termed a division of labor in the imagery of early Zionism: the elderly do the praying, the young do the plowing. Young religious Jews appear only rare-

Fig. 6. Postcard from the Third Zionist Congress (Basel, 1899), by Menahem Okin (CZA, PMF III).

Fig. 7. Postcard from the Fourth Zionist Congress (London, 1900) (CZA, PMF IV).

ly in Zionist representations; religious Jews are portrayed as sages or grandfatherly figures. Such unanimity and harmony, of course, was far from being an accurate reflection of Jewish-Palestinian reality. An accommodation of sorts between Orthodox Jews and Zionist immigrants did not occur until later, at the time when Abraham Isaac Kook assumed the post of the chief rabbi to the Ashkenazi Jews of Jerusalem in 1919.[28] At the very least, such scenes obscured the vehement opposition to the Zionist project voiced by many Orthodox Jews.

The youth/old age dichotomy is again employed for the official picture of the Fourth Zionist Congress (London, August 13–16, 1900), but in this case the exilic state of the elderly is emphasized (fig. 7). Recalling the notion of the Wandering Jew, a small bundle and a cane lie on the ground near the central figure, who wears a *shtraymel* (Hasidic fur hat); behind him is a trail of shtetl Jews. Directly in back of him is a weary or despondent woman with her head resting on her hand. The counterimage, to the right, shows a group of small, indistinct, darkish figures placing bushel baskets into a cart; a tropical tree is in the background before what appears to be the walls of the Old City of Jerusalem. Mediating between these scenes is a hazily drawn woman in a flowing white robe and angel's wings, with a Star of David as her halo, hovering above the wandering Jews. She points to the Palestinian harvest scene, directing the old Jews to the new Jewish society.

Reminiscent of Germania, Britannia and Marianne,[29] this female symbol was a familiar one in Zionist postcards. After Herzl's death in 1904, she is employed as a bridge between Herzl and the Jews' march to Zion (fig. 8). A more distinct female image was featured in the postcard for the Sixth Congress (Basel, August 23–28, 1903). In figure 9 she rises out of the ground before a farmer, accompanied by the Biblical injunction: "Those who sow in tears will reap in joy."[30] This generic female symbol, an agent of change from the wretched Jewish past to the happy,

Fig. 8.   Postcard of Theodor Herzl, by S. Roukhomovsky (CZA, Herzl "Personality" File).

healthy future, did not persist past 1914 as a Zionist motif, possibly owing to its lack of grounding in Jewish mythology.

The souvenir postcard of the Fifth Zionist Congress (Basel, December 26–30, 1901) is of much greater artistic value than its predecessors. Here Ephraim Moses Lilien makes his debut as a leading artist in the Zionist camp (fig. 10).[31] Before the

Fig. 9.   Postcard from the Sixth Zionist Congress (Basel, 1903) (CZA, PMF VI).

Fig. 10. Postcard from the Fifth Zionist Congress (Basel, 1901), by E. M. Lilien (CZA, PMF V).

Congress, the Zionist organ *Die Welt* lavishly praised the books *Juda* and *Lieder des Ghetto,* poetry anthologies illustrated by Lilien.[32] Illustrations from *Juda* and *Lieder des Ghetto* were used repeatedly in Zionist publications. Israel Zangwill praised the accessibility of Lilien's pictures, noting that "by contributing not to galleries but to books, magazines, and bookplates, [he] has brought art nearer to everyday life. Restricting himself to black and white he has minimized the difference between his original touch and its mechanical reproduction." For Zangwill, a writer who geared his novels to the Jewish masses of London's East End, "a Lilien postcard was more valuable than many a pretentious oil painting."[33]

Executed in a *Jugendstil* or art nouveau style and surrounded by a floral pattern, Lilien's pen-and-ink drawing recalls the dichotomies of youth and old age, exile and redemption, the Diaspora and Palestine. As usual, the figure at the left-bottom corner is an old, stooped, white-bearded Jew who leans on his cane; he is encircled by barbed wire—a further example of his bondage. Above him, standing sturdy and upright, is a male angel with huge, finely feathered wings who wears a large Star of David on the front of his white robe. The angel's right hand grasps the shoulder of the old man; his left hand points to the image on the right: against the background of a radiant sun, a man plows a field behind a team of oxen. Disproportionately large stalks of wheat sprout in the right corner, below the man and oxen. The Hebrew inscription beneath the picture, flanked by the Star of David, reads, "Let our eyes witness Your loving return to Zion,"[34] a verse from the '*Amidah,* a central prayer in Jewish liturgy. This became one of the most reproduced Zionist works, adorning the JNF's appeal pamphlets for the Purim and Hanukkah holidays.[35]

Unlike his forerunners, Lilien was a well-known member of the Zionist Organization. The Zionists' admiration of Lilien's work was undoubtedly influenced by the respect accorded the artist. Lilien embodied a strange blend of fin-de-siècle antitypes. His art resembled that of Aubrey Beardsley, whom most Zionists would classify as a model of degeneracy, but Lilien's goal was Jewish national health and regeneration.[36] He came from Galicia and though he appeared to be the very antithesis of the stereotypical pale, sickly, unkempt, unaesthetic Eastern Jew, he nevertheless maintained a commitment to many elements of traditional Judaism.[37] The fact that Lilien spoke Yiddish and seemed to remain "a Jew through and through"[38] lent integrity to his overtly sentimental drawings.

Ten of Lilien's works were featured together with the works of Jozef Israëls, Jehuda Epstein, Alfred Nossig, Hermann Struck and Lesser Ury, among others, in an exhibition concurrent with the Fifth Congress, held in the Congress hall.[39] The First Zionist Congress had hung portraits of proto-Zionists in the hallway of the Basel Stadtcasino,[40] but the 1901 exhibition was clearly the first time that the works of Jewish artists were presented in a Jewish national context in Central Europe. At the very least, most delegates probably shared the impression that the exhibition was "modest but promising" and portended "the beginnings of a national art."[41] These and other shows during the congresses were open to the public, and they usually ran several days prior to, or after, the Congress dates.

The exhibition at the Fifth Congress was a prominent manifestation of Zionist ideals upon which nearly every Zionist could agree, stressing biblical heroism and affirming Jewry's place as a contributor to European high culture. Complementing the show, Martin Buber delivered a very long speech on Jewish art. The talk focused on the plastic arts, but it included developments in Jewish literature and music within the framework of the speaker's theory of Jewish national regeneration.[42] Buber introduced Lilien as the most consciously Jewish artist of the group; this initiated a tremendous ovation by the delegates.[43] The tribute to Lilien was part of Buber's attempt to trace the course of the Jewish revival, which he regarded as a prelude to a full-fledged cultural flowering that could only take place after the attainment of Jewish sovereignty in Palestine.

In his talk, Buber referred to a recently published assertion by Nordau that art could only be used for didactic purposes in furthering Zionism's political aims. Nordau did not comment on the role of art in fashioning a national soul for Jewry, which was Buber's theme.[44] This relatively minor conflict between Buber and Nordau was part of the larger debate on the *Kulturfrage* in Zionism. The fact was that Zionism simply had no central policy on art and aesthetics; individuals in the organization continued to pursue their own dogmas and designs. There was never any overall program with power to influence all that was produced or promoted in the name of the movement. Nonetheless, Buber, despite feeling that he was out of line with the recognized leadership of Zionism, had already established himself as a de facto head of the movement concerned with the advancement of Jewish art.

This was due to Buber's participation in the "Democratic *Fraktion*," which advocated a more deliberate concentration on culture, in the sense of aesthetic and scientific education, as a central and obligatory component of Zionism.[45] The publishing house, Juedischer Verlag, more than any of the *Fraktion*'s projects, was the most effective means of spreading its concept of Jewish culture. Buber, along with Lilien and Berthold Feiwel, was a founding editor of this venture. After Herzl, who had determined that Zionism would largely conform to bourgeois tastes while utilizing techniques of mass politics, these men were among the principal shapers of the aesthetic dimension of Zionism. But it should not be forgotten that along with their sincere intent of cultivating the national soul of the Jews, the Zionist political program was ever present, and art also constituted "propaganda in the grand manner" (Buber) and "a beautiful and valuable means of agitation" (Feiwel).[46]

Among the first group of works published by the Juedischer Verlag in 1902 was the *Juedischer Almanach,* consisting of poetry, prose and artistic reproductions. The artistic section was edited by Lilien, with Feiwel as the general editor.[47] The next year's selection included *Juedische Kuenstler,* edited by Martin Buber, an anthology of biographies and reproductions of six Jewish artists.

Feiwel hoped that the *Juedischer Almanach* would become a "noble document"[48] of the cultural awakening of Jewry under Zionism. The reviews of the book indicate that it impressed its audience very favorably, proving convincingly that there was now an incipient, but positive relationship between Jewry, culture and art.[49] The very name was meant to be revolutionary and provocative—to show pride in Jewry and Jewishness[50]—reminiscent of Herzl's attempt to turn the phrase *Juden-Blatt* into a badge of honor for *Die Welt.*[51] Indeed, the fact that the *Fraktion* saw a work such as the *Juedischer Almanach* as a primary instrument for nation building, with its success or failure to be gauged by its evaluation in the arts and literary section of the press, tells much about the variety of nationalism they espoused. The Juedischer Verlag was far from a mere ornament; it was an integral part of the *Fraktion*'s program. Their quest for recognition and respectability was greatly abetted because they were able to include works by Jewish artists who were well known in Europe, especially Jozef Israëls and Max Liebermann—mingled with much less celebrated and more overtly Jewish and Zionist artists.

The *Juedischer Almanach* published a number of Biblical scenes, most of which attested to the imagined heroism, vitality and romance of ancient Israel. The contemporary subjects reflected everyday bourgeois life, with which their Central and West European readers could easily identify. Consistent with the tradition of postcard pictures, there are numerous depictions of traditional Jews, and the division of Zionist labor (cited earlier) is also paralleled in this product of "higher" culture. Most often, East European or traditional Jewry is represented by etchings of old men removed from any landscape; they possess an air of wisdom and rich character but are afflicted by misery (fig. 11).[52] Only rarely are there younger men or women in religious garb, and such youths are also passive and non-threatening, belonging more to the past. The *Almanach*'s treatment of the Zionists' vision of their future home in Palestine was of a higher quality than the earliest postcards, but it appealed to similar sentiments. Palestine was usually shown through etchings; the antiquity of the Land of the Bible was the point of emphasis.

One of the artists who contributed a number of the Palestine pictures, Hermann Struck, also drew what proved to be the most popular and enduring single image of Zionism during the years 1897–1914—a profile-portrait etching of Theodor Herzl (fig. 12).[53] It is interesting to recall that Struck, who was one of the most prominent artists to attempt to define a Zionist aesthetic, was a loyal and outspoken member of Mizrachi, the Orthodox section of the Zionist movement, which was founded in 1902. In large part, the impetus for the consolidation of Mizrachi was to combat the "cultural Zionists," especially those of the "Democratic *Fraktion,*" who hoped to engender a secular national culture in order to replace what they saw as an ossified Orthodox hegemony over the Jewish world. Struck's party contended that there was no need for the Zionist movement to concern itself with secular Jewish culture because Orthodox Judaism combined with the return of the Jews to Palestine provided the real solution to the Jewish question. Evidently, Struck had no problem in combining these ostensibly dissonant roles.[54]

Struck, though mentioned by Martin Buber in his Fifth Congress address, did not merit a place in *Juedische Kuenstler,* which Buber edited for the Juedischer Verlag in 1903. In the introduction to this volume, Buber begins his summary of Jewish artistic accomplishments in a defensive manner. In this instance, though, his adversary is a genuinely bitter foe—Richard Wagner. Even *Juedische Kuenstler,* a product of the so-called cultural regeneration of Zionism, took antisemitic assertions as its starting point.[55] Wagner's theory was well known. The Jews, he claimed, did not possess an inner life capable of original creative artistic expression. Buber's response was rather apologetic. How, he asked, could Jews be expected to attain the cultural level of other peoples if they live on soil that is inherently alien or even hostile to them, where they are excluded from national traditions and history. Buber concluded that the current work represented an admirable beginning since Jews had only recently left the ghetto and gained access to the world of Western art.[56]

Even before his appearance in the gallery at the Seventh Zionist Congress (Basel, August 14–21, 1905), Jozef Israëls was repeatedly represented in displays of Zionist art (fig. 13).[57] Was Israëls a "Jewish" artist according to the new Zionist criteria?[58] The problem was that no one knew how to define exactly what a "Jewish" artist was, including Buber himself.[59] Israëls was unusual in the group of artists used in the *Almanach* and in Buber's anthology because he did, eventually, publicly express sympathy for the Zionist movement. Ironically, it was Max Nordau, the paragon of political Zionism, who delivered the brief eulogy for Israëls at

Fig. 11.   *Polish Jew,* by Hermann Struck (*Juedischer Almanach,* vol. II, ed. Berthold Feiwel [Berlin, 1904], 28).

A

Fig. 12. (*a*) *Theodor Herzl,* by Hermann
Struck (*Juedischer Almanach,* vol. II, ed.
Berthold Feiwel, 107); (*b*) postcard from
the Ninth (Hamburg, 1909) and (*c*) Elev-
enth (Vienna, 1913) Zionist congresses
(CZA, PMF IX and XI, respectively).

B

C

the Tenth Zionist Congress in 1911. "Israëls shows a Jewish artist's temperament, whether or not he himself was aware of it," claimed Nordau, whom Buber and others had accused of extreme insensitivity to the need to nurture Jewish national creativity. "We find in his drawings the intensity of feeling, the energy of expression, the high moral dedication, and the emotional nature" that embodied the great characteristics of his people.[60]

Most of Buber's Jewish artists chose not to say anything about their feelings about Zionism; the only member of the group to place his works squarely in the category of "Zionist art" was Lilien. The text of *Juedischer Kuenstler* never went so far as to claim that the others were Zionists. Nonetheless, they allowed their works to be seen and reproduced in the framework of a Zionist project. This was similar to the appropriation of Jewish literature by the *Almanach* and Juedischer Verlag; most of the writers were not Zionists, but they authorized their works to be included under the banner of the movement.

Until the First World War, Juedischer Verlag along with the Libanon and Phoenix companies, was a major producer and distributor of Zionist pictures and postcards.[61] Although Juedischer Verlag styled itself as the custodian and disseminator of "high" culture in Zionism, it was not averse to this function. The vast majority of these postcards could be classified as fin-de-siècle iconography and, overwhelmingly, Theodor Herzl was the most popular subject. One cannot overestimate the extent to which Herzl's image figured in the self-definition of Zionism and in the media concerning Zionism that was presented to the Jewish world. The profusion of Herzl portraits, in many cases copies or imitations of the Struck etching, is startling. Besides existing as pictures that could be framed or simply tacked to walls, they adorned the trademarks of candy made in Palestine, canned milk, cigarette boxes, rugs and numerous household articles as well as Jewish ceremonial objects.[62] From 1897 to 1914, a Zionist office, meeting hall or reading room without the Struck etching or a photograph of Herzl was simply not to be found.

Fig. 13. *Torah Scribe* and *A Son of an Old People,* by Jozef Israëls
(*Juedischer Almanach,* vol. II, ed. Berthold Feiwel, 94, 68).

For most Zionists, the representations of Herzl were much more than a matter of
kitsch for the masses. It was something to be taken very seriously, especially after
Herzl's death in 1904.[63] To almost everyone who wrote on early Zionism, including
his chief critic, Ahad Ha-Am, Theodor Herzl was the personification of the incipient Jewish State.[64] Herzl's physiognomy, to most Zionists, was the purest symbol
of Zionism's aspirations. One might say his was the specific countenance of the
movement. Herzl was presented as serious, proud, intelligent, noble, attractive,
unique and at the same time—recognizably Jewish. He was eminently respectable

and manly. Summarizing the whole of Zionist imagery, the Herzl portraits looked both forward and backward. His beard and visage placed him squarely in the context of traditional Judaism while his gaze was directed toward the future.[65] His manliness and handsome looks consciously rebuked the antisemitic stereotype of Jewish effemininity and ugliness[66] while his dark complexion and face were perceived and extolled as the perfect face in which the Zionist movement and the Jews could take great pride.[67]

One of the most reproduced pictures of Herzl was a photograph taken by E. M. Lilien. It shows Herzl leaning over the balcony of his hotel room in Basel, overlooking the Rhine (fig. 14). It placed Herzl in the present—in Basel, the site of the early Zionist congresses, the temporary hub of the national life of the Jews—but he was undoubtedly thinking of the future.[68] Herzl himself expressed great satisfaction with the picture.[69] After his death, this image was super-imposed on a Jerusalem scene, with Herzl looking toward the Tower of David rising above the walls of the Old City as a team of Jewish pioneers march to work in the valley between Herzl and the walls (fig. 15). This variation was used for pictures and JNF stamps, which, along with photographs from Herzl's journey to Palestine in 1898, helped associate Herzl with the Jewish national landscape of Eretz Israel.[70]

Theodor Herzl's image helped bridge the gap between secular/national aspirations and traditional Jewish hopes. A joke among Zionists, told in several variations, claimed that the success of the movement was directly related to Herzl's beard—because it recalled traditional Judaism and the Jews' image of the prophets.

Fig. 14. Postcard of Herzl overlooking the Rhine in Basel; photograph by E. M. Lilien (CZA, Herzl "Personality" File).

Fig. 15. Promotion for a Theodor Herzl
JNF stamp (CZA, JNF Stamp Collection).

This messianic or prophetic perception of Herzl, especially in the Congress
postcards, was often merged with the twin images of the old, pious East European
type of Jews and the muscular pioneer farmers in a Europeanized Palestine landscape (fig. 16).[71] Such images were not marginal; they should be examined in the
light of the attitudes they elicited at the time. Berthold Feiwel, Stefan Zweig, Robert
Weltsch and Gershom Scholem, among others, have written on the tremendous
impact the figure of Herzl held for them in their youth. "In our earliest youth,"
Feiwel wrote, Herzl signified "the embodiment of all beauty and greatness. We, the
young, had been yearning for a prophet, for a leader. We created him with our
longing." A common element in their recollections is that Herzl's picture was an
essential part—if not the essence—of the total world they saw encompassed by
Zionism; the words and pictures were part of a complete Weltanschauung.[72] The
acceptance of Herzl's image was also influenced by his standing as a member of the
German-speaking cultural establishment, both as a playright and as a correspondent
and feuilletonist of the *Neue Freie Presse* of Vienna,[73] one of the leading newspapers in fin-de-siècle Central Europe. Some of the settings of postcards and portraits highlight this dimension of Herzl as a culture hero (fig. 17).[74]

  Max Nordau, the second most recognized leader of the Zionist movement, had a
wider international reputation than the movement's founder. Nordau's was the second most frequently employed portrait in Zionist representations (fig. 18), and it

Fig. 16. Postcards from the Seventh Zionist Congress (Basel, 1905), by Carl Pollak (CZA, Herzl "Personality" File).

was common for Nordau and Herzl to appear in the same medium (fig. 19).[75] The idealization of Herzl and Nordau's friendship, the focus of the First Congress portrayal by Okin, was consistent with the notion of men coming together as friends in the framework of the nation. Along with other aspects of early general European nationalism, Zionism adopted the concept of the nation engendering a cult of sincere male friendships.[76] Nordau, like Herzl, was a journalist and litterateur; his

Fig. 17. Postcard of Herzl, Hermann Schapira, Max Nordau, Israel Zangwill and Leon Pinsker (CZA, Herzl "Personality" File).

Fig. 18. Postcard of Max Nordau (CZA, Nordau "Personality" File).

Fig. 19. (*a*) Herzl and Nordau New Year's postcard (CZA, Nordau "Personality" File); (*b*) JNF cigarette box (*Herzl in Profile: Herzl's Image in the Applied Arts,* ed. David Tartakover [Tel-Aviv Museum, 1978–1979], 27).

authority as a physician and scientist enhanced his position as a best-selling author. Nordau's books transversed the boundaries of politics, philosophy, science and social criticism. His *Conventional Lies of Our Civilization* (1883) went through at least seventy-three printings and was translated into more than fifteen languages. As a featured journalist for such newspapers as the Budapest *Pester Lloyd,* Berlin's

Vossische Zeitung, the *Frankfurter Zeitung,* and the *Neue Freie Presse* of Vienna, he enjoyed an even larger audience.[77]

Although Nordau did not often deal with specifically Jewish topics in his books and articles before 1897,[78] his traditional Jewish background—he was the son of a rabbi—constituted part of the mythology that formed his public image. This fact lent itself to the appropriation of Nordau as a Zionist icon. Many Jews identified Nordau as a teacher and as an exemplar of distinctively Jewish characteristics;[79] after he appeared at the First Zionist Congress, there was, of course, much more substance for such claims. He was esteemed for his mastery of many different fields, and he was thought to be a sincere, honest and bold critic of his environment while upholding wholesome values such as hard work and self-restraint. As a Jew and celebrated figure of German Kultur, Nordau provided a tremendously attractive force.[80]

These factors were complemented by Nordau's appearance. He had a full white beard and a robust countenance; numerous comparisons were made between Nordau and the ancient sages or prophets.[81] Thus, Nordau was also able to serve as a symbolic mediator between the world of secular European culture and traditional Judaism. His immense popularity was reflected in the variety of postcards and portraits that appeared until the First World War.[82] This was true even after he became alienated from the movement's other leaders and sharply curtailed his Zionist activities.[83] The perception of Nordau as a "culture hero"[84] was underscored in the numerous depictions of Nordau writing at his desk, intently reading a book or amidst scientific instruments (fig. 20).[85] One postcard uses a Hebrew translation of the introduction to *Conventional Lies of Our Civilization* for a traditional micrographic portrayal of Nordau (fig. 21).[86]

Fig. 20. Max Nordau (CZA, Photography Collection [hereafter cited as PC] 13.792).

Fig. 21. Postcard of Nordau, done in micrograph (CZA, Nordau "Personality" File).

The diffusion of the iconography of Theodor Herzl and Max Nordau intensified under the auspices of the JNF (Keren Kayemet le-Israel), often in conjunction with Juedischer Verlag.[87] The JNF, founded in 1901, was the component of the Zionist movement that reached the greatest number of Jews living west of the Pale of Settlement by 1914. The fund-raising activities of the JNF for the purpose of purchasing land for collective Jewish settlement and agriculture developed a bureaucratic apparatus and even myths and symbols of its own. All of the previously discussed iconographic themes were employed by the JNF in postcards, stamps,[88] pamphlets, certificates for specific donations and medals—with one notable addition. Cultural institutions in Palestine that were in some way related to the JNF were featured incessantly in its materials. Most popular were images of the Herzliya Gymnasium and the Bezalel Academy of Arts and Design; these gained currency in the Zionist discourse around 1907 (fig. 22).[89] The JNF supplied land and funds for these and other institutions, thereby styling itself as the main instrument for endowing Palestine with the cultural amenities that might attract mass Jewish settlement.[90]

The JNF was the institutionalized connection to the Jewish "native landscape" that the Zionists wished to impress on European Jews; this was part of the attempt to make Jews identify the territory and incipient Jewish society in Palestine as their true homeland. One of the main functions of the JNF was planting forests; these forests were not simply a means of agricultural reclamation or aesthetics, they personalized Jewish integration into the imagined Jewish-Zionist nation. The certificate one received as a donor of a tree included a romanticized pastoral scene with a portrait of Herzl in the center.[91] The fund-raising literature and certificates in recognition of larger donations usually reproduced pictures that appeared on Congress postcards and in the *Juedischer Almanach*. Some of the postcards and medals displayed the concept of *ẓedakah,* the giving of charity, with a typically European child putting a coin into a JNF box (fig. 23).[92] The movement invented the story

Fig. 22. Herzliya Gymnasium medal (CZA, Medals Collection, box 2).

Fig. 23. Jewish National Fund medal for children (CZA, Medals Collection, box 2).

that the JNF box was imagined in a dream by the originator of the fund, Hermann Schapira, who was enshrined as a Zionist hero upon his death.[93] It was commonly known, though, that the JNF boxes were modeled after the boxes into which Jews had deposited alms for *yeshivas* and charitable societies for at least a century (fig. 24).[94]

The promotions of the JNF shared many of the trappings of charity,[95] but the line between the givers, Western Jews, and the objects of their donations, Eastern Jews, was obscured by the Western Jews' integration in the movement by way of the fund's iconography. Indeed, it was through the JNF's mass mailings and inexpensive postcards and pictures that Jewish art seems to have achieved its widest audience. Because the Zionist Organization was constantly in need of funds, charity became a part of the movement's matrix of culture and Jewish nationalism (fig. 25).[96]

The next most significant institution that combined Zionism and Jewish art on the level of popular culture was the Bezalel Academy of Arts and Design in Jerusalem, founded by Boris Schatz in 1906. Bezalel was an ultra-conservative arts-and-crafts school—influenced by the theories of Walter Crane and John Ruskin—that aspired to produce an artist-craftsman type that had long been pushed to the margin of industrial society. Nonetheless, in the eight years from its inception to the First World War, Bezalel played a large role in providing a visual dimension to Zionism

Fig. 24. Jewish National Fund box (CZA, Nahum Sokolow papers).

Fig. 25. (*a*) *By the Waters of Babylon,* by Eduard Bendemann, from
Leaflet no. 8 of the JNF (CZA, A2/6/7/1); and (*b*) JNF postcard, by
S. Roukhomovsky (CZA, Nahum Sokolow Archive).

for European Jewry. The school spawned picture books and pictures for Zionist
meetings and reading rooms, with reproductions of the works produced in its
workrooms. It also released a flood of postcards, but its most effective means of
disseminating its spiritual and material fare was through European exhibitions.
These were usually held concurrently with the Zionist congresses,[97] but many more
shows were put on between congresses in a number of European cities;[98] the goals
were to spread information about Bezalel's existence and achievements, to sell its
goods and to solicit contributions.[99]

Bezalel, too, took part in spreading icons of Theodor Herzl. Second to Herzl was not Nordau, but the institute's mentor, Boris Schatz. A main subject of paintings was the Jerusalem landscape and Palestinian flora, and there were also numerous reliefs, paintings and sculptures on Biblical themes. Most plentiful, though, were the Jewish ceremonial objects created by the institute, such as menorahs, kiddush cups, spice boxes, lamps, Holy Arks and Bible bindings. The style and quality of these pieces varied greatly.

There was, of course, nothing new about these objects. But, like the pictures of Orthodox Jews, the Bezalel items served to recast the Jewish religious experience as a national experience. It was part of the larger effort to alter the Jews' allegiance to Judaism into Jewish nationalism. Pictures of Bezalel objects were scattered in the pages of the Zionist press, adorning articles about Palestine or the institute, or sometimes randomly placed within the text.[100] These were meant to be taken as evidence that the creation of things Jewish and beautiful was already underway in Palestine through the Zionist movement.

Visitors to the Bezalel exhibitions and viewers of its media were exposed almost as much to the processes of creating the Bezalel products as to the products themselves. Scenes of filigree, damascene, textile workrooms and studios filled with art students were among the most prevalent picture and postcard subjects (fig. 26).[101] Bezalel styled itself as an institution actively and publicly training its charges and building a new national culture. The premise behind Bezalel was that it was a prodigious nucleus for Jewish settlement in Palestine, and its propagandists wildly exaggerated its significance. Nonetheless, it provided European Jews with images of the Jewish artist-craftsmen as central figures in the new, emerging Jewish society. It affirmed that there was such a thing as Jewish art, with its nucleus in the Holy City of Jerusalem. Representations of Bezalel concretized the notion that Jewish productivity and the innate creativity of Jewish manual laborers was synonymous with Zionism's ideological goals. The buildings that housed the institute were shown repeatedly as sturdy Oriental structures of Jerusalem stone, symbolizing its permanence (fig. 27).[102] Furthermore, it supplied a secular national framework for symbols and objects that were already familiar to most Jews although they had been previously encountered in an exclusively religious setting. In some respects, the intention and effect of the Bezalel pictures and shows was similar to that of the *Juedischer Almanach:* to shake the alleged complacency of European Jewry by confronting it with manifestations of a blatant and proud Jewish national consciousness and to strengthen the commitment of those who were already sympathetic (to some degree) to Zionism.

Jewish art in Zionist popular culture was an important force in the effort to concretize and personalize a Jewish national ideology for European Jewry. It is extremely difficult to assess the degree to which Zionism succeeded in inculcating a sense of belonging to a Jewish nation by such means. Zionist culture underscored the Jewish attempt to reevaluate the Jewish past and present in hopes of restructuring a radically different future course for the Jews. In its images, Jews were manly and heroic; they fulfilled every traditional, productive function in society, especially agricultural work and craft industries. Here was a world in which secular and religious Jews shared a common space in the Holy Land, where Jews remained unique while undergoing a transformation from the old to the new. In this utopian

Fig. 26. Postcards of (*a*) picture-frame making and (*b*) drawing studio at the Bezalel Academy of Arts and Design, Jerusalem (CZA, Bezalel File).

scheme, previously disparaged "Jewish characteristics" could be celebrated as an aspect of national liberation. Thus, Zionism made Jews free to appreciate the diversity of Jewish appearances and culture.[103] The Jewish people constituted, according to Zionist popular culture, a coherent cultural order—including all of the Jewish people—and this helped sustain the myth of a like-minded Jewry that would eventually fulfill the Zionist mission.

The Zionists' ultimate goal—to win Jews over to the idea of Jewish nationalism—certainly was not realized on any vast scale for the Jews of Central and Western Europe before 1914. What Zionist popular culture did achieve, though, was to create a form of expression for a supplementary nationalism that could be activated in the event of a crisis within the conventional Jewish allegiance to the European nation-states. Zionism was largely unacceptable to most Western Jews by

Fig. 27. The Bezalel Academy of Arts and Design, Jerusalem (CZA, PC 451).

the outbreak of the First World War. Nonetheless, a new, specifically Jewish nationalism was beginning to take form, not least of all in the mind's eye.

Notes

Research for this work was conducted primarily at the Central Zionist Archives in Jerusalem while the author was a Lady Davis fellow of The Hebrew University and a doctoral dissertation scholar of the Memorial Foundation for Jewish Culture. I would like to acknowledge the assistance of the director of the Central Zionist Archives, Dr. Michael Heymann, and record special thanks to Reuven Koffler and Pinchas Selinger, members of the professional staff, for their invaluable aid and support in many facets of this project. Professor George L. Mosse of the University of Wisconsin and The Hebrew University of Jerusalem, Professors Steven E. Aschheim and Richard I. Cohen of The Hebrew University and Andrew N. Bachman of the University of Wisconsin offered essential insights and critical comments. All photographs are reproduced courtesy of the Central Zionist Archives.

1. The historiography of Zionism has been slow to assimilate newer methods of historical inquiry. A predictable consequence is the neglect of Zionist cultural history: see Paula Hyman, "The History of European Jewry: Recent Trends in the Literature," *Journal of Modern History* 54, no. 2 (June 1982), 305; David Vital, "The History of Zionism and the History of the Jews," *Studies in Zionism* 6 (Autumn 1982), 159–170.

2. Among the small number of works in this category are *Bezalel, 1906–1929,* ed. Nurit Shilo-Cohen (Jerusalem: 1983); *Herzl in Profile: Herzl's Image in the Applied Arts,* ed. David Tartakover (Tel-Aviv: 1978–1979); Mark H. Gelber, "The *jungjuedische Bewegung,*" *Leo Baeck Institute Year Book* 31 (1986), 105–119; Milly Heyd, "Lilien and Beardsley: 'To the pure all things are pure,' " *Journal of Jewish Art* 7 (1980), 58–69.

3. George L. Mosse, *Myths of the World Wars* (New York: 1988); see also Carl E. Schorske, *Fin-de-siècle Vienna. Politics and Culture* (New York: 1980), xx–xxvii, *passim.*

4. See the recent catalogue of the exhibition, *The Dreyfus Affair: Art, Truth, and Justice,* ed. Norman L. Kleeblatt (Berkeley, Los Angeles and London: 1987), 1–24, *passim.*

5. See Marshal L. Rozenblit, *The Jews of Vienna: Assimilation and Identity, 1870–1914* (Albany: 1983) 4–5, 99, 113.

6. Theodor Herzl, "Eroeffnungsrede zum ersten Kongress," in *Theodor Herzls Zionistische Schriften* (Berlin-Charlottenburg: 1908), 223.

7. Shmuel Almog contends that inspired by Zionism a new Jewish consciousness had come into being by 1906. *Zionism and History: The Rise of a New Jewish Consciousness* (New York and Jerusalem: 1987).

8. Herzl's view is summarized by his remark in a conversation with Ben-Ami (pen name of Chaim-Mordechai Rabinovich), "The child is not yet born, nonetheless they quarrel over its education," cited in "Errinerungen an Theodor Herzl," *Die Welt,* 3 July 1914, 691.

9. *The Complete Diaries of Theodor Herzl,* vol. I, ed. Raphael Patai, trans. Harry Zohn (New York: 1960), 116.

10. *Ibid.,* 27, 165.

11. *Ibid.,* 33, 236.

12. *Ibid.,* 27.

13. *Ibid.,* 67.

14. The Congress is the quintessential institution of Herzlian Zionism; see David Vital, *The Origins of Zionism* (Oxford: 1975), 354–375; Central Zionist Archives (hereafter cited as CZA), Printed Materials File for Zionist Congresses, First Zionist Congress (hereafter cited as PMF I; Roman numerals correspond to congress number).

15. Heinrich York-Steiner designed the card: *Die Welt,* 10 September 1987, 16.

16. *Jewish Chronicle* (London), 3 September 1897, 10; *Die Welt,* 10 September 1897, 16.

17. Psalms 14:7.

18. Gershom Scholem, *The Messianic Idea in Judaism* (New York: 1971), 280–281.

19. See Herzl, "Eroeffnungsrede zum ersten Kongress," 227; Leon Simon, *Ahad Ha-Am* (Philadelphia: 1960), 105; CZA, medals collection, box 2, Mizrachi buttons.

20. CZA, PMF II.

21. Ezekiel 37:21.

22. Erwin Rosenberger, *Herzl as I Remember Him,* ed. and trans. Louis Jay Herman (New York: 1959), 141–142.

23. George L. Mosse, *The Crisis of German Ideology* (New York: 1964), 126–145.

24. See Davis Trietsch, *Bilder aus Palaestina* (Berlin: n.d.); *idem, Palaestina Handbuch* (Berlin: 1912); Adolf Friedemann and Hermann Struck, *Palaestina: Reisebilder* (Berlin: 1904); J. H. Kann, *Erez Israel: Das Juedische Land* (Cologne and Leipzig: 1909); Jean Fischer, *Das heutige Palaestina* (Antwerp: 1907); Josef Gerstman, *Kultur- und Bildungsfortschritte unter den Juden Palaestinas* (Munich: 1909); *Palaestina: Zeitschrift fuer die Culturelle und Wirtschaftliche Erschliessung des Landes* (1902–1903); *Altneuland: Monatsschrift fuer die wirtschaftliche Erschliessung Palaestinas* (1904–1906); *Jung Israel* (1905, 1910–1914); *Der zionistische Student* (1912–1914).

25. There is very little information concerning Menahem Okin's background or career after he ceased submitting work to the Zionist Movement; see *Die Welt,* 9 September 1898.

26. Reproductions of this picture—for hanging in reading rooms and as postcards—were not among the Zionists' favorites.

27. CZA, PMF III.

28. Arthur Hertzberg, *The Zionist Idea: A Historical Analysis and Reader* (New York: 1977), 418; see Israel Kolatt, "The Organization of the Jewish Population of Palestine and the Development of its Political Consciousness Before World War I," in *Studies on Palestine During the Ottoman Period,* ed. M. Ma'oz (Jerusalem: 1975), 211–243.

29. George L. Mosse, *Nationalism and Sexuality: Respectability and Abnormal Sexuality in Modern Europe* (New York: 1985), 90–100; see Maurice Agulhon, *Marianne into Battle: Republican Imagery and Symbolism in France, 1780–1880,* trans. Janet Lloyd (Cambridge: 1981); Lynn Hunt, *Politics, Culture, and Class in the French Revolution* (Berkeley: 1984), 93–94.

30. CZA, PMF VI; quoted from Psalm 126, the "Song of Ascents" or "Song of Returning Exiles"; the symbol was also used for the certificate given to donors to the JNF Golden Book, PMF VI; see pl. 189, reproduction of Edouard Debat-Ponsan's painting, *She Is Not Drowning* or *Truth Leaving the Well*, in Kleeblatt, *The Dreyfus Affair*, 258.

31. See Rosenberger, *Herzl as I Remember Him;* CZA, Adolf Pollak, *Die Welt Index—Zionistische Chronologie (vom Juni 1897 vis Juli 1914)* (Tel-Aviv), 1–24. Up to this point the choice of illustrations seems to have been made in the Vienna office by the university students under the guidance of Herzl.

32. Alfred Werner, "The Tragedy of Ephraim Moses Lilien," *Herzl Year Book* 2 (1959), 100; see Gelber, "The *jungjuedische Bewegung,*" 108ff.

33. Israel Zangwill, "Introduction" to a portfolio of heliogravures by E. M. Lilien, *The Holy Land* (Berlin and Vienna: 1922), no pagination.

34. CZA, PMF V.

35. CZA, A2/6/7/1.

36. Lilien's relationship to Beardsley was consciously antithetical, yet he selectively appropriated many of Beardsley's techniques and motifs; Heyd, "Lilien and Beardsley."

37. Zangwill, "Introduction;" Almog, *Zionism and History,* 169.

38. Alfred Gold, "E. M. Lilien," in *Juedische Kuenstler*, ed. Martin Buber (Berlin: 1903), 87.

39. CZA, PMF V.

40. Moses Montefiore (1784–1885), Moses Hess (1812–1875), Hirsch Kalischer (1795–1874) and Leo Pinsker (1821–1891) were among those represented; this was part of an effort to make political Zionism seem continuous with proto-Zionist thought; CZA, H VIII/226, David Farbstein to Theodor Herzl, Zurich, 29 July 1897.

41. *The Letters and Papers of Chaim Weizmann,* vol. V, ser. A, gen. ed. Meyer Weisgal (London and Jerusalem: 1974), 44.

42. *Stenographisches Protokoll der Verhandlungen des V. Zionisten-Congresses,* 152–170.

43. *Ibid.,* 162.

44. Max Nordau, "Der Zionismus der Westlichen Juden," in *Max Nordaus Zionistische Schriften* (Cologne and Leipzig: 1909); orig. in *Israelitische Rundschau* (1901), 316–317; see Nordau, *Von Kunst und Kuenstlern* (Leipzig: n.d.); Nordau was one of Europe's most outspoken opponents of the notion of "art for art's sake."

45. *Programm und Organisations-Statut der Demokratisch-Zionistischen Fraktion* (Heidelberg: 1902).

46. Martin Buber quoted in *Stenographisches Protokoll der Verhandlungen des V. Zionisten-Congresses,* 168; and Berthold Feiwel to Theodor Herzl, CZA, H VIII, 7 April 1902. Retrospective accounts have cast doubt on the degree of unanimity between the "Democratic *Fraktion*" members and the political Zionist leadership; see Maurice Friedman, *Martin Buber's Life and Work: The Early Years, 1878–1923* (New York: 1981), 48, 53–54; and Jehuda Reinharz, *Chaim Weizmann: The Making of a Zionist Leader* (New York: 1985), 86–90.

47. Gelber, "The *jungjuedische Bewegung,*" 112ff.

48. Feiwel to Herzl, CZA, H VIII, 7 April 1902.

49. "Juedische Renaissance"; Press-Stimmen ueber den *Juedischen Almanach* (Berlin: 1903), CZA H VIII, 124.

50. *Almanach 1902–1964* (Berlin: 1964), 7.

51. Theodor Herzl, founding statement of *Die Welt,* 4 June 1897.

52. Hermann Struck, *Polnischer Jude, Juedischer Almanach,* vol. II, ed. Berthold Feiwel (Berlin: 1904), 28.

53. *Idem, Juedischer Almanach,* vol. II, 107; CZA, PMF IX and XI; see Nathanja Sahuwi, "Vor Hermann Strucks Herzl-Portraet," *Ost und West* (9 September 1903), 709–714.

54. Hermann Struck, "As an Artist Saw Him," in *Theodore Herzl: A Memorial,* ed.

Meyer Weisgal (New York: 1929), 36; *Radierung von Hermann Struck: Mit einem Essay von Max Osborne* (Berlin: 1904), 2.

55. In the polemics and historiography of Zionism "political" Zionism is often singled out for being primarily motivated by antisemitism; see Jacques Kornberg, "Theodore Herzl: A Reevaluation," *Journal of Modern History* 52 (June 1980), 227.

56. Martin Buber, "Introduction," in Buber (ed.), *Juedischer Kuenstler* (Berlin: 1903), no pagination.

57. Jozef Israëls, (*a*) *Der Thoraschreiber (Skizze)* and (*b*) *Ein Sohn des alten Volkes,* in Feiwel, *Juedischer Almanach,* vol. II, 68, 94.

58. See Fritz Stahl, "Josef Israëls," in Buber, *Juedische Kuenstler,* 12, 14.

59. Harold Rosenberg, *Rediscovering the Present* (Chicago: 1973), 223–231; Avram Kampf, *Jewish Experience in the Art of the Twentieth Century* (South Hadley: 1984), 7–10.

60. *Stenographisches Protokoll der Verhandlungen des X. Zionisten-Kongresses* (Berlin and Leipzig: 1911), 159.

61. See the advertisements in the back pages of *Die Welt,* 7 January 1910, for example, and the *Juedische Rundschau* and advertising supplements of Juedischer Verlag, CZA A6/77.

62. Tartakover, *Herzl in Profile;* and M. Narkess, "The Arts Portray Herzl," in Weisgal, *Theodore Herzl: A Memorial,* 119–120.

63. *Prelude to Israel: The Memoirs of M. I. Bodenheimer,* ed. Henriette Bodenheimer, trans. Israel Cohen (New York: 1963), 117–118.

64. Ahad Ha-am, quoted in Tartakover, *Herzl in Profile,* 51.

65. See Sahuwi, "Strucks Herzl-Portraet," 712–713.

66. See, for example, Georg Hecht, *Der Neue Jude,* "Herzl serves the exemplar of a new Jewish ideal of manliness" (Leipzig: 1911), 113, 124.

67. See Stefan Zweig, *The World of Yesterday,* trans. Harry Zohn (Lincoln and London: 1964), 105; Dr. Ch. Lippe, "Theodor Herzl"; Oskar Marmorek, "Herzl als Freund"; Emma Nuestadt, "Die Wehklage der Zionisten"; Daniel Pasmanik, "Dr. Theodor Herzl" all in *Die Stimme der Wahrheit: Jahrbuch fuer wissenschaftlichen Zionismus,* ed. Lazar Schoen (Würzburg: 1905), 129–143; *Verbindung Kadimah, 1933,* 82; J. Silberbusch, "Herzl—Eine legendaere Erscheinung," in *Zeitgenossen ueber Herzl,* 185.

68. CZA, PMF, Herzl "Personality" File.

69. Werner, "Tragedy of Ephraim Moses Lilien," 92.

70. CZA, Herzl "Personality" File; JNF Stamp Collection, Photography Collection (hereafter cited as PC), 17001.

71. JNF Tree Certificate, reproduced in Tartakover, *Herzl in Profile,* 24; CZA, PMF, Herzl "Personality" File; PMF VIII and IX.

72. Berthold Feiwel, memoir of meeting with Richard Beer-Hoffmann, CZA, K11/147; Zweig, *World of Yesterday;* Robert Weltsch, "Theodor Herzl and We," in Martin Buber and Robert Weltsch, *Theodor Herzl and We,* trans. Chaim Arlosoroff (New York: 1929), 26–27; Gershom Scholem, *From Berlin to Jerusalem,* trans. Harry Zohn (New York: 1980), 28; David Biale, *Gershom Scholem: Kabbalah and Counter-History* (Cambridge, Mass.: 1979), 53.

73. See *Festschrift zu Feier des 100, Semesters der akademischer Verbindung Kadimah, 1933,* 82; Zweig, *World of Yesterday.*

74. CZA, Herzl "Personality" File; CZA, PC 17, 196.

75. *Ibid.;* and Tartakover, *Herzl in Profile,* 27; CZA, Nordau "Personality" File.

76. Oskar Marmorek, "Herzl als Freund," in *Die Stimme der Wahrheit: Jahrbuch fuer wissenschaftlichen Zionismus,* ed. Lazar Schoen (Würzburg: 1905), 132–133; see Mosse, *Nationalism and Sexuality,* 67–70.

77. For the *Neue Freie Presse,* Max Nordau wrote the annual political review for several years.

78. When Nordau dealt with specifically Jewish topics, he was not very sympathetic. This was used against him in the controversy over Herzl's utopian novel, *Altneuland;* see "Die Juden von gestern" (eine Erwiderung), *Ost und West,* 4 (April 1903), 225–226.

79. Milton P. Foster, *The Reception of Max Nordau's Degeneration in England and America* (Ph.D. diss., University of Michigan, 1954), 2, 40; *Jewish Chronicle* (London) 9 February 1923, 10; *Palestine Weekly* (Jerusalem), 26 January 1923, 53; the latter points out that his decline in popularity was sometimes due to antisemitism.

80. See Steven E. Aschheim, *Brothers and Strangers: The East European Jew in German and German Jewish Consciousness, 1800–1923* (Madison: 1982), 84. Nordau was not, however, an intellectual of the first rank; his deep-seated hatred of modernist literature, art and social thought reveals not only misjudgments of significant cultural trends, but also fears of change that later would be associated with paranoia. In 1891 Sigmund Freud found Nordau "vain and stupid and did not cultivate his acquaintance"; Ernest Jones, *The Life and Work of Sigmund Freud* (New York: 1966), 124; Desmond Stewart, *Theodor Herzl* (Garden City: 1974), 322–323; P. M. Baldwin, "Liberalism, Nationalism, and Degeneration: The Case of Max Nordau," *Central European History* 13 (June 1980), 99.

81. See Meir Ben-Horin, *Max Nordau: Philosopher of Human Solidarity* (New York: 1956).

82. CZA, PMF, Nordau "Personality" File.

83. CZA, H VIII 614/15, no. 162, Max Nordau to Theodor Herzl, 28 December 1903; Chaim Weizmann to Richard Lichtheim, no. 84, 1 December 1920, Weisgal, *Letters and Papers of Chaim Weizmann*, vol. X, ser. A, 107; Weizmann and Lichtheim were perturbed that Nordau was so popular; they considered him a troublesome anachronism.

84. Stanley Nash, *In Search of Hebraism: Shai Hurwitz and his Polemics in the Hebrew Press* (Leiden: 1980), 170–171, 188.

85. CZA, PC 13, 792.

86. CZA, Nordau "Personality" File.

87. See *Die Welt*, 31 March 1911, 301.

88. Jay L. Kaplove, *Stamp Catalogue of the Jewish National Fund* (Youth and Education Department of the JNF and the Educational Society of Israel Philatelist, Jerusalem: 1973).

89. CZA, JNF Stamp Collection, Medals Collection, box 2. It is difficult to date precisely the appearance of these images because many of the postcards and pictures are undated. The Herzliya Gymnasium was originally the Jaffa Schule; it received financial support from the Zionist movement starting in 1898, but it became important as a Zionist symbol only after Jacob Moser of Bradford, England, made a contribution for a new building in Herzliya in 1907; *Beschluesse und Resolutionen der Zionisten-Kongresses I–VIII*, ed. Hugo Schachtel (Vienna: 1906), 13; *Stenographisches Protokoll der Verhandlungen des VIII, Zionisten-Kongress im Haag vom 14 bis inklusive 21 August 1907* (Cologne: 1907), 349; see *Herzliya Hebrew Gymnasium: Memorandum* (Tel-Aviv: 1927), 4. The Bezalel Academy of Arts and Design was officially founded in 1906.

90. Adolf Boehm, *The Jewish National Fund* (The Hague: Head Office of the JNF, 1917), 27.

91. There were some editions of the JNF Tree Certificate without Herzl's portrait; it was certainly on the majority of designs until 1914.

92. CZA, Medals Collection, 2; *Die Welt*, 21 January 1910, 64.

93. CZA 14.205, Simon Neumann, *Der Traum von der Nationalfondsbuechse: Ein Maerchen fuer Kinder* (Cologne: n.d.).

94. JNF Box from CZA, Nahum Sokolow Archive.

95. Boehm, *Jewish National Fund*, 15, 26.

96. Reproduction of *By the Waters of Babylon* by Eduard Bendemann, from Leaflet no. 8 of the JNF, CZA, A2/6/7/1; see Franz Landsberger, *A History of Jewish Art* (Cincinnati: 1946), 277; CZA, Nahum Sokolow Archive.

97. Zionist congresses were held annually from 1897 to 1901, and biennially from 1903 to 1913, eleven in all before 1914.

98. For example, between 1910 and 1913, there were two exhibitions in London and Vienna, and major shows were held in Amsterdam, Karlsbad, Zurich, and Berlin.

99. For a typical article on a Bezalel show, see "Bezalelausstellung in Wien," *Die Welt*, 11 February 1910, 124.

100. See "Aus dem Geschäftsbericht des 'Bezalel,' " *Die Welt,* 14 January 1910; 17 October 1910; 19 January 1912; 28 March 1913; 25 April 1913 for some of the numerous examples.

101. CZA, PC 1635, 415; PMF "Bezalel" File.

102. Fischer, *Das heutige Palaestina,* 97; CZA, PC 451, 15.683, 15.600. In fact, the buildings, bought from a Turkish effendi, were intended to house an orphanage; Gideon Ofrat-Friedlander, "The Periods of Bezalel," in Shilo-Cohen, *Bezalel 1906–1929,* 49–51.

103. "Zionistisches Gartenfest," *Die Welt,* 18 August 1911, 876.

The Uses of Primitivism:
Reuven Rubin in Palestine

Milly Heyd
(THE HEBREW UNIVERSITY)

Modern art is characterized by a series of artistic revolutions occurring over a short period of time and at a pace previously unknown in art history. Since the establishment of the Bezalel Academy of Arts and Design in 1906, Jewish art in Eretz Israel has gone through a parallel process. Yet, rather than formulating various styles of their own, artists in Eretz Israel borrowed from the already established European artistic languages and adapted them to local purposes. Since artists did not use the whole spectrum of the styles available, the questions of choice emerge: Why were certain modes of expression chosen? What does the choice signify? Certain European styles and iconography were more suitable to the needs of the newly emerging art in the Jewish state-in-the-making since they expressed the artist's struggle to adapt to the new environment. The transposition of style from one context to another also raises the question of novelty: Is there any uniqueness in the local scene? How do form and content from different milieus coexist? In what way does a given style in the art of Eretz Israel differ from its source?

In the 1920s, part of the reaction to the academic style of Bezalel led to the use of a primitivistic-naive style whose source of influence, it has been claimed, was the French artist Henri Rousseau.[1] The selection of elements from Rousseau was typical of the period: artists were inspired by his naive, childlike qualities and ignored the dark, sinister aspect of his art. But why was the naive style suitable for this period? What was there in naive primitivism that was relevant to this stage of development of art in Palestine?

The answer can be given on three levels: ideological, psychological and perceptual. On the ideological level, both the awareness of the need to establish a new art in an as yet non-existent state and the utopian view of the character of this future state turned the artist's quest toward a style that stressed the positive nature of a reality that the artist wanted to believe in rather than the actually existing reality. Thus, from the psychological perspective, we have an example of how art serves as a defense against crude reality and employs a naive, childlike style to build up a new imaginary reality. In his autobiography *My Life, My Art,* Reuven Rubin suggests that art functions as an escape from local political events both for the artist and for the public:

In 1936 there was yet another outbreak of Arab riots, which started in Jaffa and spread throughout the country. Again bloodshed and violence. Nonsensical as it seemed at that particular time, I decided that I would hold an exhibition in Jerusalem. It was my way of fighting the gloom created by the situation. . . . Depressed Jerusalem welcomed the event like an unexpected gift. In spite of the general situation the show was well received, with many visitors and good sales.[2]

Rubin's description of his reaction to the War of Independence also shows that art served as a mechanism of escape:

But the U.N. resolution was the signal for the most violent Arab attacks the country had known. They started to kill, burn, destroy, loot. The street where we lived became part of the front line; we became accustomed to the sound of bullets and bombs. One side of the house was constantly exposed to the bullets of the snipers from Jaffa. We had one room with a partition and behind this I took my easel and, strangely enough, found I was painting with renewed vigor.[3]

There is a contrast between the events of the period and Rubin's stylistic interests. When events became grim, Rubin withdrew into the world of art he had originally created as a non-existent dreamworld, a naive environment that could not accommodate the events of real life.

Fig. 1. Reuven Rubin, *Jaffa,* 1925. Oil on canvas. Collection Mr. & Mrs. Lawrence Hamilton, Claremont, California.

On the perceptual level, the naive style also gives the artist a tool for studying the new environment in a childlike manner. By depicting every detail of a flower in a linear way–as in Rubin's 1925 painting of *Jaffa* (fig. 1) —flattening it out and bringing it forward to the spectator in such a primordial way, so that nothing is missing, the artist is viewing the world afresh. He, thus, interiorizes his surroundings while mastering it. He has a need to familiarize himself with, and to become part of, the new land, its scenery and the inhabitants with whom he identifies. The mode of perception accords with the psychological and ideological needs. Whereas Henri Rousseau can be content with a depiction of a *Bouquet of Flowers* (fig. 2) in an interior, Rubin, in a conglomeration of sources of inspiration, places a variation on Matisse's aquarium next to the Rousseauesque flowers, but he situates the cultivated world on a balcony parallel to the city of Jaffa and its Arab inhabitants who are passively smoking the narghile. There are parallel lines between the flower's stalk and Jaffa's tower; the personal, European and cultivated world is externalized on the balcony and is seen as an analogy to the Oriental world of Jaffa. The two entities, the private and the social (or local), cannot be separated. Rubin utilizes the naive-primitive style in a broader sense than does his European predecessor, whose world of dream and fantasy is unconcerned with the national aspects

Fig. 2. Henri Rousseau, *Bouquet of Flowers*, 1895–1900. Oil on canvas. Tate Gallery, London/Art Resource, New York.

Rubin wished to stress. This *raison d'être* for Rubin's linear naive style can also account for the later change in Rubin's art. Once he had interiorized his surroundings, so that mastery of the objects was no longer necessary, he could let go of the precise line and become immersed in the landscape, creating the atmospheric, hazy scenes that are typical of his later style. Therefore, in late works such as *Mimosa and Black Iris* (1961), the flowers on the windowsill unify the external and internal world into one entity.

A naive dreamworld is depicted in the 1923 work *Arab Rider on a Donkey* (fig. 3) in which the wife is disproportionately reduced in size, for she is riding behind in accordance with the traditions of the Orient. Yet the Arab is also carrying a disproportionately enlarged bouquet of cultivated flowers wrapped in cellophane, thus signifying the West. A dreamlike atmosphere that unites East and West prevails. Rubin is either giving the Arab rider a token of his goodwill or is receiving such a token from him. Equality and harmony are emphasized between Jews and Arabs, East and West, man and artifice, man and nature. In a parallel manner, in the artist's *Self-Portrait* (c. 1924) an analogy is drawn between the artist's brown, tanned skin and the color of the land viewed from the window behind him—the same kind of analogy to be seen in the Arab figure in *Arab Rider on a Donkey*. Thus, Rubin

Fig. 3.   Reuven Rubin, *Arab Rider on a Donkey,* 1923.
Oil on canvas. Collection Horace Richter, New York.

shows the affinity between the land and its inhabitants, Jews and Arabs. The stylistic qualities of the naive style, which stress equality by (among other things) ignoring differences of texture, also become an ideological tool for presenting a harmonious idealized view of reality. Rubin's dream in the 1920s, in which he paints the Arab with a bouquet of flowers, relates to the country and its people, whereas Rousseau's *The Dream* (1910) is a private and erotic juxtaposition of the natural and the artificial. In Rousseau's dream-jungle, a naked woman reclining on a stylized velvet couch is surrounded by wild beasts as she listens to sensuous music. Rousseau's "artistic unity" is expressed by "the elements best able to exteriorize a vision that was wholly personal"—to quote Ardengo Soffici's comment on the painting.[4]

Rubin's 1927 group portrait entitled *The Artist's Family* (fig. 4), done sometime after the arrival of his mother and two siblings in Eretz Israel, is also partially influenced by Henri Rousseau: it resembles the latter's 1905 work *The Country Wedding* (fig. 5). In both cases, we have a group portrait of a family accompanied by an animal displayed in nature. In Rousseau's painting, the animal is a little dog, which suggests urban life; in Rubin's work, it is a goat, which represents the village—and for his family the continuity between the old and the new. The leaf

Fig. 4.   Reuven Rubin, *The Artist's Family,* 1927. Oil on canvas. Tel-Aviv Museum.

Fig. 5. Henri Rousseau, *The Country Wedding*, 1905. Oil on canvas. Musée de l'Orangerie, Paris. Collection Jean Walter et Paul Guillaume.

offered to the goat is a repeated motif in Rubin's art (see *The Dancers of Meron*). The groups in both paintings seem to be confronting a camera; in each case the artist, through his positioning of the figures, emphasizes the family resemblance. Yet there are basic differences between the two paintings. Rousseau's landscape is depicted by the same technique as that of his human figures, that is in a linear, flat style. In Rubin's case, the landscape differs from the four figures in the background. They are linear and flat to such an extent that they suggest paper cutouts, but the green foliage in the background is painterly and hazy. This stylistic duality already suggests Rubin's late style, which expresses his complete absorption in the land. Interestingly, this dual style was chosen in a transition period both for his family and for himself. It is obvious from Rubin's pose, clothes, footwear and chair that, in contrast to his relatives, he belongs to the environment he depicts.

In Rousseau's painting, the formality of the ceremony almost borders on caricature; Rubin's outlook is diametrically opposed to this—his family's solemnity and contemplative mood is a means of enhancing his and their importance. In terms of composition, three figures are seated while the fourth is standing behind the group laying her arm on the central figure, thus forming a diagonal. The artist characterizes the four as he sets them within a parallelogram. Thus, we can look comparatively at the painting's four sides: on the right are the two women, on the left the two men. Mother and daughter demonstrate the difference between old age, orthodoxy, severity and strength vis-à-vis youth, modernism, softness and a dream-like expression—black versus rose. The two men, Reuven Rubin and his brother, Isaac Zelikovich, represent antipodal modes of life: the formal European suit of the brother contrasts with the bohemian non-formal clothes Rubin is wearing. The entire painting is built on comparisons such as the European chair the mother is sitting on and Rubin's Oriental straw one. There is also a humorous touch—the goat's calves and body are analogous to the sister's legs and dress.

Not only does each figure in the painting represent unique characteristics, but the heads of the four vary in style. The mother bears the most realistic features; the sister's head is naturalistically depicted; the brother's head, elongated with thick lips, is slightly African. But this special stylistic attribute is reserved by the artist for himself. Unlike his brother's brows, Rubin's form one continuous line and his thick mouth is in the primitivistic style of African masks, a style that has so greatly influenced modern art through the works of Picasso, Matisse, Derain and Vlaminck.

Much has been written about the expansion of the concept of primitivism to include African art.[5] The most significant comment on this development relevant to Rubin is Jack D. Flam's:

> African art was also removed in time . . . for the beginning of the century its historical development was unknown, so that it seemed to exist in a kind of temporal vacuum. Its anonymous creators and their uncharted cultures had thus been able to escape the tyranny of nineteenth-century historicism—although in popular evolutionary thought they were nevertheless believed to represent the "beginning" of man's development.[6]

It is the artist, the new creator in a new land who in Rubin's case acquires the African features. Bearing the most primitive features is his way of associating himself with new beginnings. The transition from the employment of one style to another in portraying the four figures (realistic, naturalistic, slightly African and African) is another way of suggesting that the subjects themselves are in a period of transition.

While the influence of Rousseau and African art is clearly felt, we must ask whether the French style to which the artist had been exposed during his stay in Paris (1913–1914) was the only primitivistic source of his art. Rubin, who was born in Romania, had studied at Bezalel (1912–1913) and then at the École des Beaux-Arts in Paris. After spending some time in Italy, he returned to Romania for a period of three years (1916–1919). For part of this time (1917–1918), he moved to Czernowitz (Cernăuti; now Chernovtsy, USSR), which was annexed to Romania after the First World War. He often visited Fălticeni, his late boyhood town, since his family was still living there.[7]

What type of artistic languages, other than Rousseau's, could Rubin have been exposed to either in his childhood or during his second sojourn in his native country?

Romanian art in the beginning of the twentieth century, led by Nicholas Grigorescu, Stefan Luchian and Ion Andrescu,[8] was very much under the influence of Parisian art of the second half of the nineteenth century—a style reflecting a mixture of realism and impressionism. This artistic "revival," manifested by Rubin's contemporary Romanian artists, did not leave any traces on Rubin's own art. His paintings after his reimmigration to Palestine show that his native country inspired him through the art of earlier periods—that of the neo-Byzantine style. Rubin was exposed to fifteenth- and sixteenth-century Romanian art both through the art of the monasteries and the icons displayed in the Bucharest Museum.

Monasteries in Moldavia bear a unique feature: their exteriors are covered with neo-Byzantine mural paintings executed by anonymous artists. In monasteries such as Probota, Rîşca and Piatra Neamţ (within the pre-First World War borders of Moldavia) as well as Suceava, Suceviţa, Voroneţ, Humor, Arbore, Dragomira and Moldoviţa (annexed to Romania after the war), Christian iconography in a neo-Byzantine style blends with the beauty of the mountainous landscape.[9] The intensity of the murals' vibrant colors waxes and wanes according to the light. The Romanian art historian Georges Oprescu compares the painted churches

> to a flower-filled garden or to the precious carpets from Asia Minor—the churches are relatively small. . . . The comparison to carpets is understandable since the artists, like wonderful carpet-weavers of the Near East, really meant an entire wall . . . to give an impression of harmony in both color and composition. The dominating color, sometimes green and sometimes intense, brilliant shades of blue, encourages comparison with the splendid fabrics of Asia Minor.[10]

The harmonious blending of man and nature in Rubin's paintings and his use of nuances of blue and green to form the freshness of the atmosphere may be seen as his modern variation on the neo-Byzantine murals. There is a didactic purpose to the painted walls, which resemble an illustrated Bible. It has been claimed that

> the presence of frescoes on the outside of the church of Voroneţ [or other churches with painted exteriors] may certainly be explained by the desire of the leaders of religious life to make the teachings of the Bible more accessible to the multitude. . . . The church walls thus become a kind of screen upon which scenes from the lives of the saints succeeded each other, or such deeply-stirring compositions as *The Last Judgment,* with Paradise and Hell.[11]

Rubin, inspired by the frescoes, also used a didactic style. Typical of his optimistic message, he could paint paradise without pointing for contrast to any contemporary hell.

One has to bear in mind that the monasteries are located near Fălticeni, the town where Rubin (who was born in Galaţi [formerly Galatz]) lived during late childhood.[12] Rîşca and Piatra Neamţ are monasteries south of Fălticeni: Rîşca is fifteen kilometers from Rubin's hometown. Probota is twenty-two kilometers east of Fălticeni, and Voroneţ is thirty-five kilometers west of it. Whereas Rîşca, Piatra Neamţ, and Probota were within the borders of Moldavia, Voroneţ was part of Bukovina and was annexed to Romania only following the First World War. All the monasteries mentioned include painted external murals as well as internal ones.

In his memoirs, Rubin mentions, *en passant,* that the family owned a horse and a wagon (which obviously made traveling possible, including to the monasteries). He also tells that his job was to take the goat and cow to graze; when he had time he read and painted. Reuven's arrival at Fălticeni was preceded by a short visit to the art school at Iaşi, which he described with enthusiasm in his memoirs, namely, that it was then that his awareness of an interest in art was clearly manifested.[13] Since the church murals are outside, one could see them without violating the Jewish custom of not going into a church, a restriction that could have been relevant to Rubin, the child of a hasidic family.

Romanian neo-Byzantine art blends stylistic features that can be called proto-primitivistic. Its iconic treatment of the face, which stresses enlarged eyes; the non-realistic sense of scale according to the importance of the protagonists; the elongated flat figures; the inverse perspective and the disproportion between man and nature are all features that are found both in neo-Byzantine art and in Rubin's primitivist paintings.

Iconographically, there is a disguised Christian element concealed in many of Rubin's paintings. It is evident as late as his return to primitivism in the 1950 *First Seder in Jerusalem,* which is his version of *The Last Supper.*[14] Rubin's 1926 *Hasidim* (fig. 6), shows a youngster and an elderly hasid, each holding a lulav and

Fig. 6. Reuven Rubin, *Hasidim,* 1926. Oil on canvas. Rubin Museum Foundation.

etrog, thus echoing the images of the saints in a row, each holding his attribute (a scroll, either rolled or unfurled; a book; etc.)—here exemplified in the saints from the exterior of Voroneţ (fig. 7). Stylistically, the iconic treatment of the face is typical of many of his figures in the 1920s such as *The Milkman* (1923) and *The Girl with Pomegranates* (1922). The treatment of the figures in Rubin's 1924 *Family in Jerusalem* (fig. 8), for instance, focuses on the large dark eyes and schematization of the face; despite obvious differences, this painting can be compared to the depiction of *Our Lady of Mercy* from Voroneţ.

In Rubin's *Jaffa* (discussed earlier), the table on which the objects are placed is depicted in an inverse perspective that is not found in Rousseau, but it is the common perspective used in Moldavian neo-Byzantine art—for instance, in the table of the *hetimasia* (the seat prepared for judgment), in *The Last Judgment* in the monastery of Probota; in the Church of St. Nicholas, where the uplifted base of the table brings the objects of the ritual forward.[15]

Arab Rider on a Donkey bears the same type of scale relationship as do the many scenes that depict Saint George and the dragon. In the seventeenth-century, the Romanian icons on this theme (e.g., fig. 9, Museum of Romanian Art, Bucharest) express historical concretization through the image of the crowned king carrying a goblet, thus signifying a ritual. The ruler, however, is riding behind the saint and is

Fig. 7. Moldavian murals, *Saints*, sixteenth century. Voroneţ, Romania.

Fig. 8.   Reuven Rubin, *Family in Jerusalem,* 1924. Oil on canvas. Rubin Museum Foundation.

disproportionately reduced in scale. In Rubin's painting, the relationship between the Arab rider and the minute figure behind him echoes the neo-Byzantine code of depiction. Furthermore, in order to aggrandize the function of the figures (both human and animal) there is a similar disproportion between them and the landscape in both paintings. The non-equal scale in Rubin's paintings can also be compared to *The Offering Scene* from the Church of Saint Nicholas in the monastery of Probota or to a parallel scene in *The Tree of Jesse* in Voroneţ. But the most interesting Moldavian influence can be traced in Rubin's 1926 painting, *The Dancers of Meron* (fig. 10). The painting shows a group of nine hasidim, tightly grouped together, dancing in ecstasy. The tenth member of the minyan is riding on a donkey, an allusion to the Messiah. Stylistically, the figures are elongated, completely flat, suggesting Moldavian figures. Even their faces bear a similar expression, with the emphasis on the eyes. Through the stylization of the face, stressing the essential, an iconic effect is achieved and the hats in various brown and yellow shades around their heads, which resemble petals, replace the Christian halos. The theme itself suggests traditional Jewish beliefs interwoven with a cult of nature. Human beings and the landscape echo one another: the plant on the left has ten distinct leaves corresponding to the figures, and the group resembles a tree trunk.

Fig. 9. *St. George Slaying the Dragon,* seventeenth century. Tempera on wood. Museum of Romanian Art, Bucharest.

In the Moldavian murals, there are many examples of people grouped together bearing similar features with expressive eyes and flat, elongated figures. They appear in *The Last Judgment* in Rîşca and in the west facade of *The Last Judgment* in Voroneţ, the row depicting the *Prophets* (fig. 11). The gestures of the arms and palms are another means for unifying the group, both in the mural and in Rubin's Meron dancers. In both the Byzantine prototype and Rubin's depiction—in spite of the recurrent facial type—there are slight differentiations that signify individuality. In both examples, the eldest person is in the center and has the longest beard, and there are also beardless faces such as the second figure from the left in Voroneţ and the second young man from the right in Rubin's painting. In the scene from the life of Saint John, another group bears similar features and all the participants have covered heads. Large groups also flank the two sides of the scene representing *St. George Received by the Empress* from the church at Arbore.

Fig. 10. Reuven Rubin, *The Dancers of Meron,* 1926. Oil on canvas. Rubin Museum Foundation.

From Rubin's ideological and iconographical point of view, however, the most significant groups are those in which Romanian artists depicted the Jews. Thus, for instance, in *The Last Judgment* from Voroneţ Jews are portrayed among the damned (fig. 12). A sneering comment against the Jews is also expressed in the scene of the *Jews Departing from Egypt* from Suceviţa, the Church of the Resurrection of Notre Seigneur. Here there is an inscription "au plecat cu caţel şi purcel" ("they have left while taking dogs and pigs"), and these animals are depicted in the lower row.[16] The inclusion of pigs, of all animals, in relation to the Jews, is obviously meant to be derogatory.

A number of problems emerge regarding the Moldavian influences on Rubin. When was he exposed to it? In his late childhood, when the family moved to Fălticeni? During his return to Romania? Or was he able to digest and externalize the impact of the primitivistic aspect of the Moldavian murals only on his return to Palestine when the need for a new style emerged? Moreover, what do these Moldavian works contain that Rousseau could not provide? And last, how could Rubin be influenced by a style that bears anti-Jewish features? Or rather, how did he deal with these features?

It seems likely that Rubin was exposed to the neo-Byzantine style in his late childhood and that the early imprints were reinforced during his second Romanian

Fig. 11. Moldavian mural, *Prophets,* sixteenth century.
Voroneţ, Romania.

period after his exposure to Rousseau. Owing to the change in borders that occurred
during his second sojourn in Romania, he obtained easy access to the complete
range of monasteries. Yet the awareness of the need for a new style emerged only on
his arrival in Palestine. Moreover, Rousseau's impact did not manifest itself on a
tabula rasa, but on earlier impressions of Moldavian art. Thus, either consciously, or
possibly without Rubin being fully aware, iconic Moldavian art was metamorphosed into his naive art.

As already noted, Rubin differs from Rousseau in his concern for the community,
in his national involvement. The naive painter's individuality could not have been a
sufficient answer to Rubin's need for a vision of a new land and its inhabitants. On
the other hand, his "old country" paradoxically provided him with an artistic
language he needed: it embodied national features with the typical Byzantine
themes. The Moldavian murals were a stylistic solution for Rubin. As art historians

Fig. 12.   Moldavian mural, *The Last Judgement,* sixteenth
century. Voroneţ, Romania.

such as Georges Oprescu have shown, Moldavian art interweaves its religious
themes with local historical events and, thus, reflects the fate of the nation. For
instance, in the church of Moldoviţa there is a depiction of the siege of Constantinople by the Persians in the seventh century. The city is saved by the miraculous icon
of Mary carried by the clergy as they confront the enemy. The recurrent votive
themes, in which the miniature of the church is given to the Virgin, commemorate
her help against the attacks of the Turks.[17]

In the painting *The Dancers of Meron,* Rubin adopts the theme of involvement
with the community, but he also utilizes his variation on the Moldavian style as a
means to reverse the attitude to the Jews. No longer are they damned, but they are
now free to dance ecstatically in their own environment. In this respect, his art
serves as a restitution for the treatment of his people in Moldavian art. We should
bear in mind that Rubin was of a hasidic family and that his attraction to this sect in
Meron was closely related to his roots in Romania. Paradoxically, it was Christian

art (the Moldavian murals) that helped Rubin to familiarize himself with the aspect of Eretz Israel that reflected his roots. Thus, in spite of his conscious rebellion against the Orthodox way of life, the encounter with the hasidim in the Galilee became one of the means for acclimatization in the new surroundings, a meeting ground between childhood and the present that emerged during a period of transition.

Reverting to one's reminiscences of childhood is not an uncommon phenomenon among immigrant artists. Consider the case of Mordecai Ardon. Michele Vishny describes Ardon's abrupt move from Berlin to the barren hills of Jerusalem as a change "which must have been traumatic for the thirty-seven-year old artist" who moved from "Cosmopolitan Berlin" to "the provinciality of Jerusalem." Ardon remembers that he had difficulty painting during the first year in Palestine, for he was "unable to see color—everything looked gray." He overcame his sense of alienation in Mea Shearim, the Orthodox quarter of Jerusalem, which brought him back to his native town (Tuchów, Poland) and Orthodox family. This experience enabled him to relate to the landscape and return to painting.[18] For Rubin, the landscape of Safed could also have been a link to the mountains of Moldavia where he grew up.

Parenthetically, analogies can be drawn between the beginnings of American art and art in Eretz Israel—the foundation of Israeli art. We are dealing with the art of the pioneers, with people moving from one culture to another. The problem of cultural transition in American art has been dealt with by James Thomas Flexner,[19] who refutes the assumption that "nationalistic thinking postulates that as they [the pioneers] stepped on American soil they should have sloughed off the Old World as a snake sloughs off its skin. In their eagerness to have a unique culture, writers have misunderstood the evidence."[20] It is wrong to expect a complete break with tradition. In Flexner's words, "The first Americans wanted to forget forest and savage; they wanted to imagine themselves at home."[21] Being at home for Rubin meant creating pictures that would connect him to his past.

One of the aspects in Rubin's art in Eretz Israel that might be misunderstood as a new departure is his attitude toward the Orient. But the exposure to the Orient is also a feature found in Moldavian murals, as in scenes of "The Last Judgment," where the Turks, like the Jews, are among the damned. It seems, therefore, that for Rubin, who in the 1920s depicts the East in a positive way, there is an equation between the Orientals (the Turks) and the Jews, both of whom are represented negatively in Romanian art. Rubin reversed his native country's value judgment of both Jews and Arabs; there is actually a physical identification in Rubin's depiction of his own skin, the color of the land and the color of the Arab.

When dealing with the political reality in Palestine in the 1920s, Rubin deviates from the Moldavian model in which many war scenes are depicted and where, in the *Siege of Constantinople* in the church of Moldoviṭa, firing cannons are seen. Rubin portrays *The Port of Jaffa* in a year of riots (1929) as if it were Eden, the cannons resembling toys. He, therefore, adds his own dimension to the already-existing fairy-tale quality that the Bezalel artists had attributed to the Orient. Rubin's *The Port of Jaffa* bears the same legendary qualities as Nahum Gutman's *Turkish Police* (1926), in which the police station takes the form of a dollhouse. The Turkish soldiers themselves, in their miniaturized dimensions and colorful uniforms, look like dolls. Their legendary quality is apparent in the differences among the subject, the reality behind the Turkish soldiers and Gutman's depiction. For both artists, art served as an escape mechanism.

Rubin's 1926 *Self-Portrait* (fig. 13) is another link between the new land and his past. Here we see the artist as a creator. The unusual setting for such a self-portrait, more commonly portrayed in an interior, should be noted. The landscape is heavily stylized, flat to an extent that makes one feel that the artist is on a stage. Vegetation grows out of plant pots, giving the ground an air of artificiality. The artist is the creator not just of the painting in front of him, but of the whole setting of his make-believe world. Does this allude to the scene of *Genesis* in Sucevița (fig. 14)? In that mural, the conventional finger-pointing gesture symbolizes Creation and the stylized plants and trees portray a similar sense of creation. In his *Self-Portrait*, Rubin creates a new artistic language in which he amalgamates African influences (for the

Fig. 13.   Reuven Rubin, *Self-Portrait*, 1926. Oil on canvas. Rubin Museum Foundation.

Fig. 14. Moldavian mural, *Genesis,* sixteenth century.
Suceviţa, Romania.

depiction of his head) with those of his native country, adapting them to the needs of
the new land. While the influences of Rousseau and African art are clearly felt, the
Moldavian murals also provide the source for the artist's simultaneous use of
the linear and painterly in *The Artist's Family.* In Rîşca's Église Sainte Nicholas, in
the *Paradise* scene (fig. 15), which is one of the scenes of *The Last Judgment,* Mary
is prominently seated in a separate and circular seat of honor. Three saints are seated
consecutively on the bench, while Christ, behind them, is bearing a cross and forms
a diagonal. The personages portrayed have similar features and are depicted in a
linear style, whereas the green vegetation in the background is painterly. The
composition (with obvious differences) and part of the details are echoed in *The
Artist's Family* (the diagonal, the standing figure, the feminine rounded chair that
emphasizes the mother's importance). But the main relevance of the scene to *The
Artist's Family* is the simultaneity of the linear and painterly as part of the duality
between man and nature. In a state of transition in Eretz Israel, Rubin recalls the
paradise within *The Last Judgment* in the Moldavian monastery nearest his
hometown.

It is interesting that although Rubin became acquainted with primitivism before
his arrival in Palestine in the 1920s, the style was irrelevant to his work during the
First World War years in Romania. Since there are no oil paintings by Rubin that
depict Moldavian art and his writings do not provide any statements about his
sources, we must turn to his sketchbook. Not many drawings from Rubin's second
stay in Romania have remained, but one of them (fig. 16) shows an elongated icon
of Christ with an inscription that echoes the use of captions in Moldavian icons—

Fig. 15. Moldavian mural, *Paradise,* sixteenth century. Rîşca, Romania.

"Predică fără cuvinte," ("A sermon without words"). Two words are either emphasized or crossed out—"Către pămănt" ("Against the earth"). The dejected image of Christ with his drooping features, a Christ who has something against the earth during the years of the First World War, is later metamorphosed into the image of the hasidim who are integrated into the landscape of the Galilee.

During Rubin's second Romanian period, the artist was engaged in illustrating Zionist magazines such as the Yiddish quarterly *Likht* and *Hatikvah,* published in Romanian. These illustrations, which have been completely ignored, demonstrate his links with various artistic languages used in the Bezalel Academy of Arts and Design. Although Rubin left Bezalel disappointed and did not give the school any credit in his writings, it is obvious that E. M. Lilien's Jewish *Jugendstil* became relevant when Rubin needed a language to convey Zionist aspirations in the Diaspora and the fate of the Jewish people during the First World War years. The frontispiece to *Hatikvah* (fig. 17), which was used throughout 1915–1916, is a variation of Lilien's 1901 postcard for the Fifth Zionist Congress (fig. 18). Lilien's work, which alludes to the reversal of the expulsion from paradise, is divided into two foci: Galut (Diaspora) versus Zion. It portrays a young angel who points toward Zion in order to awaken the national identity of a bearded Orthodox Jew in a withdrawn, *Vita Contemplativa* pose. *Vita Activa* is represented by an Orthodox Jew plowing the land.[22] Rubin preserves his predecessor's conception (even the trees echo the position of the pointed figure as the feathers in the angel's wings echo the pointing finger). Yet Rubin demystifies Lilien's black-and-white drama both graphi-

Fig. 16. Reuven Rubin, *Christ, a Sermon Without Words.*
Drawing. Rubin Foundation.

cally and ideologically. A young woman replaces the angel, and a secular *halutz*
(pioneer) takes the place of the Orthodox plowman. Thus, the two artists' images
create a sequence of "before" and "after": Lilien's vision preceded his arrival in the
Land of Israel and Rubin's followed his own *aliyah* (immigration). Rubin's version
reflects not only a conflict between Orthodoxy and secularization, but places new
emphasis on the rebellion of the young. It is also Rubin's personal dilemma, as he
was in revolt against his Orthodox family It seems that the way in which Rubin
adapted Lilien's Basel postcard was not accidental—it revealed his own individual
condition. However, a synthesis between Lilien's utopia and Rubin's conflict is
found in Rubin's art of the 1920s once he returned to Palestine. As shown earlier, he
turned to the dancers of Meron and integrated them in the landscape—they cannot
be separated from the land.

The angel in Rubin's frontispiece to *Likht* (fig. 19), which drew its inspiration

Fig. 17.   Reuven Rubin, frontispiece, *Hatikvah,* 1915–1916.

Fig. 18.   E. M. Lilien, Postcard from the Fifth Zionist Congress, 1901.

Fig. 19.   Reuven Rubin, frontispiece, *Likht,* 1915.

from Lilien's 1904 *Fathers and Sons* (fig. 20), is an intriguing image in the new context. Lilien's illustration, which appeared in *Ulk,* a newspaper in Berlin, portrays a scene representing the Russo-Japanese War in which young Jewish soldiers were sent to the front (eastward) and their fathers were expelled in the opposite direction (westward). The angel of death, seen from a distance, is aiming at both groups, and the angel of light, whose torch is directed downward, covers his head in mourning. Rubin's iconography is ambivalent. On the one hand, an angel of light is an appropriate concretization of *Likht,* the name of the magazine, especially since the position of the angel's hand is altered so that he now raises the torch, which becomes the letter *lamed* and lights seven flames, transforming the image to symbolize a menorah. On the other hand, the position of the covered face remains: the condition of the Jews in one war (the Russo-Japanese War) suggests their position in another (the First World War).

Rubin was not the sole artist in the first quarter of the twentieth century to use iconic primitivistic language as a way to overcome ambivalences by integrating the past and present. The revival of the icon in Russia was a dominant feature in the art of the avant-garde during the first two decades of the twentieth century. A short detour into Russian developments will enable us to view Rubin's primitivism in a

Fig. 20.   E. M. Lilien, *Fathers and Sons,* 1904. Illustration in *Ulk.*

wider context. The impact of icons on the emerging modern culture in Russia was exemplified in the large exhibition of ancient Russian icons in 1913, the three hundredth anniversary of the Romanov dynasty, which displayed treasures from various collections.[23] At the same time, Aleksander Shevchenko published his booklet *Neo-Primitivism: Its Theory, Its Potentials, Its Achievements,* in which the credo of the Russian neo-primitivists is declared, "For the point of departure in our art we take the *lubok,* the primitive art form, the icon, since we find in them [*sic*] the most acute, most direct perception of life—and a purely painterly one, at that."[24] Shevchenko expressed national ideas also formulated by Natalya Goncharova, "Neo-Primitivism is a profoundly national phenomenon."[25] Goncharova takes national ideas even further in the preface to her 1913 exhibition, "The West has shown me one thing: everything it had is from the East."[26]

Natalia Goncharova, Mikhail Larionov, Kuzma Petrov-Vodkin, Vladimir Tatlin, Kazimir Malevich, Ilya Mashov, David Burliuk, Marc Chagall as well as artists of the *Blaue Reiter* such as Wassily Kandinsky and Alexey von Jawlensky all express in their art the impact of the icon. It has been pointed out that the most distinctive characteristic of Russian art is "that it is always inwardly connected to the destiny of the nation."[27] Margaret Betz has shown that the Russian icon "was a paragon of collective art"[28] and that its reemergence coincided with the nationalistic ideas of the prewar period. The icon conveyed a sense of "a security of belief and firmness of purpose."[29] Betz quotes from I. S. Ostroukhov's manuscript, probably written around 1913:

> The icon takes us into an absolutely special world, one which has nothing in common with the world of painting—into the world beyond, a world created by faith and filled with representations of the spirit.
>   This world is unreal and therefore it is implausible to approach the icon with demands that it embody real problems of earthly phenomena.[30]

Among these artists there is a consciousness of new beginnings: "rebirth of Russian painting," "rebirth of life," "Russian Renaissance," "a new era of creation," "the beginning of a new culture."[31] Similar metaphors were expressed by Jewish artists in Palestine in the 1920s. In October 1926 Rubin wrote the following in an essay published in *Menorah:*

> Here in Jerusalem, Tel Aviv, Haifa and Tiberias I feel myself reborn. Only here do I feel that life and nature are mine. The grey clouds of Europe have disappeared. My sufferings and the war too are ended. All is sunshine, clear light and happy, creative work. As the desert revives and blooms under the hands of the pioneers, so do I feel awakening in me all the latent energies.[32]

Furthermore, according to the Russian neo-primitivists, the East served as a means of rejecting French influences.[33] In like manner, before returning to Palestine in the 1920s, Rubin wrote; "Now I was leaving Paris because I felt I must escape from the pressures imposed by the French culture and French tradition. Beautiful and invigorating as they were, I would not allow them to envelop me."[34] Could Rubin have been aware of the national primitivistic trends occurring in Russian art? The impact of the icon on his work, his need to expand beyond Rousseau's individualism, his dissatisfaction with the West as well as his feeling at home with the simple peasants or farmers living in nature, all these qualities in his work have their parallels in Russian avant-garde art. He might actually have seen Goncharova's works, as she and Larionov had an exhibition in Paris in June 1914 at the Galerie Paul Guillaume.[35] In Rubin's memoirs, we have evidence that he stayed in Paris during that period:

> June and July were wonderful months. I did not even want to leave the city because of the heat as did many people, but felt as they left for the sea or countryside that Paris became more and more *my* city. Days I spent at the art schools and the evenings were passed mostly in libraries or in feasting my eyes on the city at night.[36]

According to Gordon, fifty-five of Goncharova's works were exhibited in the 1914 show, and the list of these works shows that she exhibited various styles. Works on Gordon's list that are relevant to Rubin's iconic language are no. 24, *The Madonna* (1904); no. 49, *The Harvest* (1910); no. 55, *The Reapers* (1907); two works, nos. 27 and 28, showing *Jewish Women* (1910); and no. 29, *A Jewish Woman* (1909).[37] A common feature of Goncharova's works of this period is the iconic, ritualistic monumental style that elevates the peasant beyond the narrative or genre scene. Goncharova was fascinated by the Jewish-Russian peasants, by "the solemnity of their bearing."[38] In her 1910–1911 painting *The Jewish Family* (fig. 21), she turns them into monumental icons with large, dark eyes. This iconic dignity can be compared with Rubin's *The Family in Jerusalem* of 1924. His 1923 triptych *The First Fruit* retains the ritualistic monumentality of expressive iconlike figures.

Other Russian neo-primitivistic influences on Rubin derive from Marc Chagall.[39] In 1923 Rubin published an album of black-and-white woodcuts, *The God-Seekers.* Here distinguished Christian symbolism lurks behind the scene describing *Immigrants in Repose,* which echoes the theme of the repose in the flight to Egypt in Christian iconography. There is an expressive quality to the woodcuts that in the scene of *The Dreamers* borrows from Chagall's upside-down head. In 1921 A. Efross and J. Tugendhold published a book on Chagall's art[40] in which his major works were represented, and Rubin might have seen it through his contacts with Jewish circles in Paris. The book contains the painting of the poem *Half-Past Three* which is Chagall's classic example of a topsy-turvy head.

It can also be briefly suggested here that several other artists in Palestine in the 1920s display parallel tendencies: Nahum Gutman's oil paintings *The Sheaf-Carrier (1926)* and *Goatherd* (1926) are even closer to Goncharova's works in their iconic

Fig. 21. Natalia Goncharova, *The Jewish Family,* 1911– 1912. Oil on canvas. Private collection, Paris. Copyright 1990. ARS N.Y./ADAGP.

quality, color scheme and spiritual, mythical features that aim at transcending time. Gutman lived in Europe between 1920–1926 (two years each in Vienna, Berlin and Paris)[41] and may have been exposed to Russian art there. Pinchas Litvinovsky went back to Russia after a year at Bezalel in 1913 and studied at the Academy of Petrograd, where he was exposed to Russian neo-primitivism. He returned to Palestine in 1924, where his work conveyed a similarity to the Russian avant-garde (e.g., see *Arab with a Flower,* which can be compared to Rubin's *Arab Rider on a Donkey*).

Actually, the roots of the influences of Russian primitivistic ideology on the art of Eretz Israel can be found in Boris Schatz's thought.[42] Schatz believed in national art and in drawing the sources of inspiration from the folklore of the people and, therefore, placed great emphasis on crafts. He also believed in the existence of communities of artists and succeeded in building a commune in Ben Shemen in which Yemenite silversmiths lived and worked. The establishment of a school of arts and crafts in Bulgaria in 1895 with its focus on Bulgarian national art, integrating folk elements with those of the church, represented Schatz's first experiment with these ideas.

Camilla Gray opens her book on Russian art by declaring that "the cradle of the modern movement in Russian art can be traced to the colony of artists which was brought together by Savva Mamontov, the Russian railway tycoon of the 1870's."[43] She shows that this colony of artists was determined to create a new Russian culture. One of the people in this group was the Jewish sculptor, Mark Antokolsky,[44] who was Schatz's teacher. In Antokolsky's exchange of letters in the 1870s and 1880s with Vladimir Stasov,[45] he discussed the question of the need for Jewish folk art. It is in "the rediscovery of the national artistic heritage" [that Gray sees] . . . the starting-point of a modern school of painting in Russia.[46] Schatz, under the impact of these ideas, searched for the national artistic heritage of the Jewish people in what he considered to be Jewish folk art. His establishment of an arts and crafts school laid the basis for the development of modern art in Palestine/Israel. Since almost all the primitive artists in the 1920s, including Rubin, studied at Bezalel before going to study abroad, they were exposed to this ideology through Schatz. As shown earlier, the impact of Bezalel was felt in Rubin's illustrations during his second Romanian period. However, discontented with Schatz's artistic language, artists went abroad to find alternative styles and returned in the 1920s, a period when primitivism flourished in Palestine.

Finally, it is important to note that they chose this style because none of the artistic languages prevalent in Europe at the time could have answered the needs of the artists in Eretz Israel. The pessimism of the expressionists, the nihilism of Dada and the nightmarish dream quality of the surrealists as well as the elimination of subject matter in the Bauhaus and de Stijl all took place in societies with a long history and tradition of visual representation and did not fit in with the dreams of becoming integrated in a new land. Primitivism for its own sake, without its national component, could also not have been sufficient. Rubin created a new artistic language in which he amalgamated French influences with those of his native country and those of Russian avant-garde, adapting them to the needs of a new country.

Rubin's primitivistic style has been shown to consist of a number of layers, the individualistic style of Rousseau being only one of them. Rubin's neo-Byzantine style metamorphosed to a Jewish context, and the broader influence of Russian avant-garde icons serve as a counterpoint to Rousseau's individualistic style. Christian artistic language is lurking behind Rubin's style in the 1920s. Although there is a rebellion against Bezalel during that period, it is only partial—a typical situation of conflict between generations. Rubin is one of the founders of a style of a generation resisting the authority of Boris Schatz, the founding father of art in Eretz Israel. Yet he has created a style to which his artistic predecessor aspired. Can George S. Hellman's 1928 view of Rubin as "Palestine's Gauguin"[47] be endorsed? Rubin's national aspirations show that, attractive as this formulation may sound, his main concern lay elsewhere.

Notes

1. Sarah Wilkinson, *Rubin Reuven* (New York: 1975), 46–47. Wilkinson mentions that Rubin "emphatically denied having seen any of Rousseau's works at that time. That there is a resemblance cannot be gainsaid." It is characteristic of Rubin that he does not mention artists who have inspired him.

2. Reuven Rubin, *My Life, My Art* (New York: 1969), 199.

3. *Ibid.*, 210.

4. Ardengo Soffici, "The Dream," quoted in *Henri Rousseau* (New York: 1985), 251.

5. Robert Goldwater, ed., *Primitivism in Modern Art* (New York: 1938, rev. 1965); William Rubin, *Primitivism in 20th Century Art* (New York: 1984).

6. Jack D. Flam, "Matisse and the Fauves," in Goldwater, *Primitivism in Modern Art,* 212.

7. Rubin, *Primitivism in 20th Century Art,* 119–121.

8. Ion Petrescu, *Pictura Romînească Contemporană* (Bucharest: 1964).

9. For reproductions of the Moldavian murals see Vasile Dragüt, *La Peinture murale de la Moldavie* (Bucharest: 1983).

10. Georges Oprescu, *Rumania: Painted Churches of Moldavia* (New York: 1962), 11.

11. Petru Comarnescu, *Voroneţ* (Bucharest: 1959), 16.

12. Rubin, *My Life, My Art,* 38.

13. *Ibid.*, 37–38.

14. *The First Seder in Jerusalem* (1950) is a rare example of a melancholic painting done by Rubin in Israel. Here the Christian allusion to *The Last Supper* is related to the fact that Old Jerusalem, depicted from a distance, is lost and betrayed.

15. For other examples of inverse perspective, see Christ's seat in *The Votive Scene* from the monastery of Humor, the table of *The Holy Communion* from the monastery of Moldoviţa, and Mary's chair in *Paradise* from the monastery of Rîşca.

16. V. Vătăsianu, *La Peinture murale roumaine* (Bucharest: 1965), 32.

17. Oprescu, *Rumania,* 14.

18. Michele Vishny, *Mordecai Ardon* (New York: 1973), 23–26.

19. James Thomas Flexner, *First Flowers of our Wilderness: American Painting, the Colonial Period* (New York: 1969).

20. *Ibid.*, 2.

21. *Ibid.*, 3.

22. This illustration was previously analyzed in a different context by Milly Heyd, "Lilien and Beardsley: 'To the pure all things are pure,'" *Journal of Jewish Art* 7 (1980), 58–69.

23. Margaret Betz, "The Icon and Russian Modernism," *Artforum* 15 (Summer 1977), 38.

24. Aleksander Shevchenko, *Neo-Primitivism: Its Theory, Its Potentials, Its Achievements* (Moscow: 1913); quoted in J. Bowlt, ed., *Russian Art of the Avant-Garde* (New York: 1976), 46.

25. *Ibid.*, 48.

26. Natalia Goncharova, "Preface," *Catalogue of One-Man Exhibition* (Moscow: 1913); quoted in Bowlt, *Russian Art,* 58.

27. Betz, "The Icon," 39.

28. *Ibid.*, 38.

29. *Ibid.*, 42.

30. I. S. Ostroukhov manuscript, reprinted in *Mastera iskusstve* (Moscow: 1970), 223–232. Quoted in Betz, "The Icon," 39.

31. Statements taken from Bowlt, *Russian Art,* 5, 8, 11, 108, 113.

32. Quoted in Rubin, *My Life, My Art,* 162.

33. Goncharova, "Preface," quoted in Bowlt, *Russian Art,* 57.

34. Rubin, *My Life, My Art,* 162.

35. Donald E. Gordon, *Modern Art Exhibitions,* vol. 2 (Munich: 1974), 850.

36. Rubin, *My Life, My Art,* 85.

37. Gordon, *Modern Art Exhibitions,* vol. 2, 850.

38. Mary Chamot, *Goncharova* (London: 1979), 40.

39. On the iconic feature in Marc Chagall, see Ziva Amishai-Maisels, "Chagall's Jewish In-jokes," *Journal of Jewish Art* 5 (1978), 87; and Mira Friedman, "Icon Painting and Russian Popular Art as Sources of Some Works by Chagall," *Journal of Jewish Art* 5 (1978), 94–107.

40. A. Efross and J. Tugendhold, *Die Kunst Marc Chagalls* (Potsdam: 1921).

41. Nahum Gutman and Ehud Ben-Ezer, *Bein ḥolot ukeḥol shamayim* (Tel-Aviv: 1980), 203.

42. On Schatz's ideology, see his aphorisms in Boris Schatz, *Bezalel Exhibition Palestine Arts and Crafts* (New York: 1926), 13. On his biography and ideology, see Yigal Zalmona, *Boris Schatz* (Jerusalem: 1985). Zalmona, however, does not discuss Russian influences in this context. I would like to thank Ziva Amishai-Maisels for suggesting this line of thought to me. On the beginning of the revival of Russian Jewish art, see Miriam Rajner, *Journal of Jewish Art* (forthcoming).

43. Camilla Gray, *The Great Experiment: Russian Art, 1863–1922* (London: 1962), 9.

44. *Ibid.*, 11.

45. Mark Antokolsky, *Zikhronot uzeror mikhtavim* (Jerusalem: 1951–52).

46. Gray, *The Great Experiment,* 10.

47. George S. Hellman, "Palestine's Gauguin," *The New Palestine* xv (1928), 467–469.

The Visual Dreyfus Affair—A New Text? On the Dreyfus Affair Exhibition at the Jewish Museum, New York

Richard I. Cohen
(THE HEBREW UNIVERSITY)

Virtually no event in France's contemporary history has rivaled the Dreyfus affair in its attraction to the mind and imagination of writers and scholars. And now, just as the appearance of a recent comprehensive book[1] had seemingly put the affair to rest, at least for the time being, one encounters the exhaustive exhibition on the Dreyfus affair at The Jewish Museum in New York (September 1987–January 1988), which stuns even the most voracious reader of Dreyfusiana. A whole new world, a visual one, which has only barely been assimilated into historical analysis, is revealed. Neglected or simply overlooked, the extensive graphic work assembled in the recent exhibition and its catalogue jars, provokes and humors our sensitivies while raising new questions on the nature of the affair and the interrelationship between the visual and the literary texts.[2] In the service of social history in its true sense, a wealth of perceptions and responses has been assembled, reflecting "high" and "low" culture, tangential to the affair and directly related to it. The art of Degas, Pissarro and Toulouse-Lautrec is placed alongside postcards, fans, children's games and other ephemera, revealing a cross-section of society's responses to the affair and, what may be even more significant historically, how society's outpouring of expression helped create the affair and maintain interest in it through the latter years of the 1890s. Indeed, the complete picture certainly challenges the thesis, proposed by Michael Burns[3] and supported by Eugen Weber,[4] that the affair was, in essence, a highly localized issue that did not stir French society in a significant way.

The accepted dimensions of the affair, based on the chronology of the dramatic events and literary eruption that accompanied them, may be arranged into three main periods: the first, from the imprisonment of the Jewish captain until the publication of Emile Zola's "J'accuse" in Georges Clemenceau's *L'Aurore* on January 13, 1898; the second, in which the public controversy turned from a simmering case of suspicion of miscarriage of justice into a major political event that threatened the very fabric of French society, extending from Zola's bombshell until Dreyfus's retrial and second condemnation at Rennes in September 1899; and the concluding period, the denouement, which ended with the reinstatement of Dreyfus as a captain

(1901) by a parliamentary vote and a presidential pardon.[5] These parameters seem to be clearly upheld within the framework of the visual material, which shows an intensive manifestation of public involvement in the interim period 1898–1899.[6]

As we turn to the visual material itself, it seems necessary to emphasize that the historian need not be distressed by the lack of cold historical facts embedded in these sources; rather, one should be sensitive to their visceral character, immediate contact with the culture concerned and non-elite attributes.[7] What does the visual material communicate? In looking first at the work of "vanguard artists" (the term is Linda Nochlin's),[8] one comes across a series of drawings by Camille Pissarro entitled *Les Turpitudes sociales* (1889 or 1890), which were executed for the education of his two nieces (fig. 1). Linda Nochlin's sensitive and persuasive essay, in which the drawings are alluded to, carefully discusses the attitudes of Degas, Pissarro and Toulouse-Lautrec to antisemitism, the Dreyfus affair and to each other. Her findings and perspicacious analysis leave no room for quarrel. However, in the case of Pissarro and his social context, some remarks are in order. Nochlin endeav-

Fig. 1. Camille Pissarro, *The New Idolator,* illustration for *Les Turpitudes sociales,* c. 1890. Brown ink on glazed paper. Denver Art Museum. Courtesy of The Jewish Museum, New York.

ors to explain how this Jewish artist could use "stereotypically Jewish figures to personify capitalist greed and exploitation" and then later become a staunch Drey-fusard. She concludes, "It was simply that no other visual signs worked as effec-tively and with such immediacy to signify capitalism as the hook nose and pot belly of the stereotyped Jews." Yet other graphic artists of the period (e.g., Franz Kupka), were able to vent their rage against capitalism without resorting to the antisemitic slur.[9]

By placing these few drawings in a wider social network, they will possibly assume a less mysterious quality. Pissarro reveals both how deeply anti-Jewish symbols had penetrated in the modern period, and how predominantly they figured in the French socialist movement. Jews and Judaism had been associated with capitalism and anti-social activity in France for more than two generations, and the anarchist movement—Pissarro's political environment—was certainly not immune to such tendencies. Moreover, the parallel with the contemporary preoccupation of a fellow Parisian anarchist and Jew, Bernard Lazare, is very striking. As is well known, Lazare's earliest writings on Jewish life were in the form of scathing criticism of the "juifs," who refused to integrate into the host society and assimilate into its lifestyle. These Ashkenazic Jews, clearly portrayed in Pissarro's drawings, were driven by an alleged egoism that knew no bounds; they could be distinguished instantly by their anti-social behavior. Motivated by greed at the expense of others (as depicted in Pissarro's *Capital,* p. 98 of the catalogue), Lazare's Ashkenazic Jews were the source of society's mockery and hatred of the Jews.[10] Both Lazare and Pissarro had next to no Jewish education and their adult encounter with the Jews was clearly through the prism of prevalent anarchist conceptions of Jewish behavior in modern society and, at least in the case of Lazare, through the writings of Edouard Drumont.[11] But this negative image of the Jew would come under scrutiny by both of these anarchists, and within several years their support of Dreyfus and negation of antisemitic arguments were complete. Both had come to recognize that the use of antisemitic imagery, literary or visual, was misplaced, and Lazare's open campaign to refute the Drumont thesis and vindicate Dreyfus received the spirited support of Pissarro the Jew and the anarchist.[12] Although Pissarro's renunciation of his fleeting adoption of antisemitic imagery was not accompanied by any further intensification of his Jewish association, and despite the fact that no later painting or drawing can be used as a basis of comparison with Lazare's total immersion in Jewish affairs, the similar initial positions of Pissarro and Lazare illuminate their personal develop-ment.

Interestingly, Lazare's revolution came full circle. After having basically aligned himself with the imagery that Pissarro portrayed, namely, the rejection of the physical appearance and the cultural world of Ashkenazic Jewry, he rapturously and nostalgically hailed Alphonse Lévy's series of drawings illustrating the religious life and mores of the Jews of Alsace. Lévy's drawings, already known in the late 1880s, attempted to recapture the internal world of Alsatian Jewry as a "homage rendered by a son of Alsace to simple ways and rustic customs that are falling by [*s'égrenent*] the wayside and disappearing."[13] Depicting the Jew in the context of his normative religious behavior, Lévy's drawings recall the series executed by Moritz Oppenheim in Germany in the 1860s in that he returns the Jew to the home, to prayer, to the study of religious texts and to the performance of religious acts. Lévy did not remove the Jew completely from worldly concerns, but his was a world markedly distant from the rugged urban setting that Pissarro assailed.[14] Warmth and contentment reign in Lévy's pictures: the elderly and the young (as in *La Promenade du samedi*) graciously encounter each other in a spirit of undivided satisfaction. For Lazare, writing around 1900, Lévy's strength lay in his recognition that Jews are not simply millionaires, and this, in turn, derives from the "conscience of a man who knows that to reach the true Jew [*le juif véritable*] and not that of antisemitic legend, one should not go to the Opéra, to a gala evening, where one meets him with an archduchess on his arm." Lazare's affirmation of Pissarro's antisemitic imagery, followed by his inner satisfaction with Lévy's rustic illustrations, demonstrates the communicative possibilities of the visual imagery. In this case, the chain of Lazare's revolution is condensed and telescoped. Here the visual text buttresses the literal.

It was not the "vanguard artists" who stood at the forefront of the Dreyfus affair. As Phillip Cate points out in his authoritative and comprehensive catalogue essay

Fig. 2.   Henri-Gabriel Ibels. Top: "It was bound to happen!" Bottom: "There is a sequel": *Le Sifflet* 2, no. 11, 14 April 1899. Photomechanical print. Collection of Mr. & Mrs. Herbert Schimmel. Courtesy of The Jewish Museum, New York.

"The Paris Cry," that honor went to a group of talented graphic artists who in the 1880s gravitated to Paris and established a formidable presence in Montmartre.[15] It was they who were largely responsible for the popular iconographic representation of the affair. Deeply concerned with social criticism, these artists exploited a wide range of themes (from capitalism to anti-clericalism) and left few areas of society untouched in their various journals and magazines. Cate identifies the significant imagery of the Dreyfusards and the anti-Dreyfusards, as epitomized, respectively, in the illustrated publications *Le Sifflet* (fig. 2 by Henri-Gabriel Ibels, 1899) and *Psst . . . !* (fig. 3 by Jean-Louis Forain, 1898). Both sides searched diligently for appropriate image and symbols that could easily catch the attention of the public by conjuring up associations with the past. Their creations bear out Ernst Gombrich's assessment, "Cartoonists at all times have claimed the right to invent their own comparisons or similes and to characterize new events in terms of familiar situations whether or not language had preceded them."[16] For the historian of modern European Jewish history, the collection of caricatures assembled in the exhibition, bril-

Fig. 3. Jean-Louis Forain, "A Success." *Psst . . . !* no. 9, 2 April 1898. Photomechanical print. Courtesy of The Jewish Museum, New York. Gift of Charles and Beth Gordon, Connecticut.

liant and pungent as they often are and rich in content and commentary, is indeed a veracious text. Yet one cannot overlook the fact that only rarely do these caricatures break the bounds of previous iconographic treatments of the ideologies they espouse; attention must be drawn to some of the precedents.

Phillip Cate is correct when he claims that Adolphe Willette's *Les Juifs et la semaine sainte* (*The Jews and Holy Week,* p. 65 of the catalogue; see fig. 4) "not only expresses Drumont's basic arguments, but also establishes essential iconographic elements for anti-Jewish and eventually anti-Dreyfus imagery of the following fifteen years."[17] This pre-Dreyfus illustration is a singular effort worthy of a momentary excursus. Willette has here attempted to merge the major ingredients of anti-Jewish iconography and accusations of previous generations. As an artist attracted to symbolic meanings, Willette offered a unique characterization of the presence of Jews in modern society.[18] Set within the genre of Christian antisemitic caricatures, and preceding Eduoard Drumont's *La France juive,* the print shows a motley cavalcade of human beings and animals, leaving behind several magisterial buildings, including one designated the Bourse (Stock Exchange). The procession is led by a figure with a hooked nose, who carries an open book with the inscription "Table De Pythagore" ("Pythagora's Table"). He wears a hat with the

Fig. 4. Adolphe Willette, *The Jews and Holy Week. Le Courrier français,* 5 April 1885. Photomechanical print. Jane Voorhees Zimmerli Art Museum. Courtesy of The Jewish Museum, New York.

partially identifiable inscription "L'Or XX" ("Gold XX"[?]). Following him are several trumpeters announcing the coming of the procession. They are, in turn, followed by a graceful, semi-nude woman in chains, adorned with a headpiece (jewelry?), who gazes upward to the sky. Four persons, carrying on their shoulders the Golden Calf hoisted atop an altar, follow suit. One of the figures with "semitic" features carries an umbrella in his hand; another, holding a leash tied to two dogs, seems to bear a facial resemblance to a pig. They are followed by a horse-drawn carriage that tramples a young boy. The carriage is driven by a corpulent Jew whose feet are placed on a tablet in the form of the Tablets of the Law, upon which "La Loi Par l'Argent" ("The Law Of Money") is inscribed. The wealthy Jew's vest bears the inscription "Baron De"; he also holds a staff with a devil's hand at its end as he turns to the calf. On the side of the carriage a seal is affixed with the letter "R" beneath a crown. The carriage is followed by peasants (?), rakes in hand, a flock of birds and more men, some of whom seem to have animal appearances. Alongside the carriage, another figure, outwardly fatigued, gawks at the Golden Calf while he holds a skull partially covered by a top hat. Two guardsmen holding shields proceed in front; one is serious and conscientious; the other, with a hooked nose, holds a cigar in one hand and seems to be enjoying himself. In the lower right corner above Willette's autograph, a youthful-looking character, holding a rod in one hand and a playing card bearing an ace of spades in the other, looks on, bewildered. In the background, above the procession, another less realistic procession is in progress between two crosses. At the head of it a nude woman holds high a nude baby while other, less distinct figures tread their way up the hill haltingly toward a large cross. A printed text appearing above this scene partially explicates sections of the visual text, and a further text (a prayer) in the lower left corner informs us of the eternal resilience of the Jew.

The contrasting processions that Willette presents in this large illustration appear to signify a symbolic enactment of Pythagoras's Table—an interaction of opposites or, perhaps, even a kind of metempsychosis: a state in which the Christian soul (or possibly even Christian Messiah) has been taken over by the Jew in the form of a wealthy entrepreneur. Apparently, the strange figure on the right-hand side of the illustration is intimating this interaction of opposites as he holds a skull underneath a top hat. The skull was the commonly used symbol for the unidentified place known as Golgotha (*kranion*—see Mark 15:22),[19] where, according to the New Testament, Christ was crucified; the top hat certainly refers to capitalism. Let us recall that the processions were taking place during Holy Week, the week before Easter, which is devoted to the Passion of Christ. In a reenactment of the last moments of Christ's life, a nude woman lifts her child and brings him to the Cross in heaven. Christ, as the upper text notes, had been crucified by the Jews for having expelled them from "la Bourse de Jérusalem" (the Stock Exchange of Jerusalem—i.e., the Temple).[20] Now the eternal Jew (as the longer text, the prayer, notes) conquers all the stock markets of the world, tramples over people, brings workers to his service and even enchains France, allegorized by the semi-nude woman. The eternal Jew follows only one law—that of the golden calf, the symbol of Jewish materialism, as so often depicted in nineteenth-century caricatures of the Jews. This new reigning law has also an overseer in the person of Baron de Rothschild, whose name is alluded to in the seal of the wagon ("R"), adroitly replacing the appropriate RF (République Française).

Willette has quite brilliantly illustrated Richard Wagner's notion that the Jews relinquished the King of the Jews in order to become the Jews of the kings. Moreover, in order to emphasize the eternal wanderings of the Jew, he has placed a Jew in a procession with a shawl (tallith?) and an umbrella, a common contemporary depiction of the Wandering Jew. The umbrella replaces the more conventional trapping of the Wandering Jew (the staff) and is not to be seen as merely an attribute of the bourgeoisie.[21] Thus, Willette has not only focused on central antisemitic iconography (the golden calf, crude physiognomic features, the Wandering Jew), but has imaginatively united the presumed Jewish control over European finance with the Jews' abuse of Christ and Christian tradition. Indeed, he has capsulized in this visual portrayal the essence of Drumont's analysis in *La France juive*. The crude, corpulent Jew, whom four years later Willette depicted with a crown on his head (a plastic expression of the noted antisemitic phase "les juifs les rois de l'époque) and whom he identified as S. M. Rothschild, king of France (p. 67 of the catalogue; see fig. 4) becomes a clear guide to decode Jewish character: the external physiognomy is an authentic reflection of his internal nature.[22]

Willette's antisemitic caricatures persisted through the 1890s. As late as 1902 (see *L'Assiette au beurre*), Willette had not forsaken his crude physiognomic portrayals of the Jew, lampooning him and his Talmud along with other "foreign" elements[23] (fig. 5 by Willette, 1889). And his efforts in graphic criticism of the Jews had many followers. Other fine graphic artists participated in the attempt to decry the Jewish presence in France as being outside the fabric of French society, and they exploited themes developed by Willette and others. Some followed his lead and exhibited the Jew (as personified by Dreyfus) as both anti-Christian and anti-French—devious, untrustworthy and a betrayer. Historians will find in the revival by them of Judas Iscariot, as a symbol of the treacherous Jew, a cogent reminder of the staying power of historic archetypes.[24] Judas, who in medieval iconography only intermittently portrayed the symbolic Jew (usually through his red hair)[25] was seldom chosen iconographically as the optimal figure to symbolize the confrontation with Judaism. But in this case, in making Dreyfus out to be the modern-day Judas, one could assimilate several themes at once: the treacherous nature of the Jew, his love for money at all costs and his disrespect for Christianity (see pp. 156, 160, 161 in the catalogue). Dreyfus was like Judas—an alien, a betrayer, unworthy of the trust bestowed in him by the French Republic; those who took up his cause were guilty by association. Dreyfus, like Judas, could be seen as a pariah, responsible for his crimes and deserving of his horrible end. Once again, the visual material offers a vivid testimony of the way the allegations against Dreyfus could be easily accepted and integrated into commonly maintained preconceptions.

Why so easy? Certainly, in part, because of traditional forms of French antisemitism, but also thanks to the special artistic tradition of depicting the Jew in racial terms dating back to the eighteenth century. As the catalogue does not address this issue, attention must be drawn to the formative precedents of this stereotyping. Representation of the Jews with "semitic" features can be found here and there in medieval iconography, but by no means did this constitute a distinct genre. As

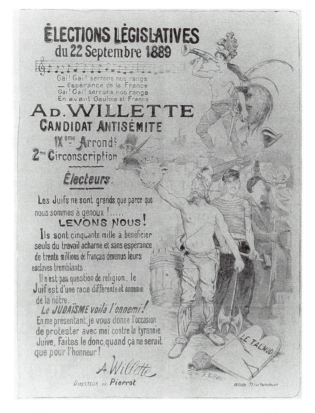

Fig. 5. Adolphe Willette, poster for the *Anti-Semitic Candidate,* 1889. Lithograph. Courtesy of The Jewish Museum, New York.

Isaiah Shachar has shown,[26] it was not until the "Jew Bill" in England in 1753, in the midst of the public denunciation of the Liberals' attempt to naturalize the Jews of England, that caricaturists seized upon a medium to depict the Jews as "others," to stereotype them and point to their alienation from the rest of society.[27] In that age of Hogarth, when political caricature with a sharp edge was emerging and physiognomic theories were in vogue, caricaturists seized on the "Jewish nose" and turned it into the identifying characteristic of "the Jew." An underlying "racial" characterization of "the Jew" was embedded in this new effort, long before Gobineau's theories on race became commonplace. This was a definite break with traditional forms of anti-Jewish representation, and from that point onward—with peaks and valleys—there was no turning back; "the Jewish nose" (at times aligned with unpleasant-looking eyes and a shabby appearance) became a constant accoutrement of the anti-Jewish litany. Repeated *ad nauseam* throughout the nineteenth century, this new persona had definite contours that later caricaturists developed, as is well documented in the works of Caran d'Ache, Hermann Paul, Forain, Léandre and Willette himself. Yet, as pungent as the physical characterization could be, it was often supplemented by a linguistic slur: the corruption of the Jew's speech revealed his foreign associations, unmasking him. Here, too, the caricaturists in *Psst . . . !* were less than innovative—one finds precedents as early as the seventeenth century. In all these cases, language is used to stigmatize the speaker as "other." Thus, when these well-rehearsed attributes were ultimately directed at Dreyfus, they intended to conjure up in the minds of the beholder an image of "the Jew," whose roots were alien to French society and who could never be assimilated into that culture.

As opposed to the antisemitic imagery that abounded during the affair—and was definitively associated with one side of the warring camp—the Dreyfusard-republican imagery was utilized by both camps. Antisemitic imagery could be counteracted only through universal images, just as literary protests against antisemitism focused on universal principles and not on a particularistic defense of the Jews against the attacks of their antagonists. Thus, the Dreyfusard artists, like their opponents, looked for historical precedents to dramatize their cause. In the visual sphere, the most compelling and consistent Dreyfusard image was the allegorical figure of Truth, usually in the form of a nude or semi-nude woman, often emerging from a well (fig. 6 by Edouard Debat-Ponsan, 1898). The choice would seem to be self-evident, both within the context of French republican iconographic development ever since the Revolution and the symbolic portrayal of Truth in Western civilization. Maurice Agulhon has argued that throughout the nineteenth century, republican elements sought ways to infuse their rationalist ideals with some sort of deification and constantly tried to nurture their female representation of the Republic—Marianne—with appealing symbols in order to confront its detractors.[28] As with Marianne, the allegory of Truth in the affair did not remain a monopoly of the republicans, for its unswerving identification with the Dreyfusard position evoked the power of the image even in the eyes of the anti-Dreyfusards. Other accepted republican allegories were apparently found to be too controversial and were hardly ever portrayed by the Dreyfusard artists. An example is the Phrygian cap, the hallowed symbol of liberty, which had been a source of constant controversy in nineteenth-century French society owing to its association with the Revolution. The cap was shunned by the Dreyfusard artists, for the lingering debate over crowning Marianne with the Phrygian cap necessitated the use of less provocative symbols. Indeed, anti-Dreyfusard artists (e.g., Jean-Louis Forain and Bob [Comtesse Sibylle Martel de Janville]) took up the public opposition to the Phrygian cap and mockingly employed it, effectively showing the Republic's submission to dangerous evils (fig. 7 by Bob, 1896). In this battle of symbols that was being waged, the use of a female, not specifically connected with Marianne and not necessarily associated with as clear a libertarian image as the Phrygian cap, was more readily adopted. It was apparently necessary in combating the vicious and ugly antisemitic imagery to create less controversial images that could find popular justification and support. Dreyfusards found the figure of the nude or semi-nude woman, by virtue of its universal culture and religious associations, more useful in their struggle. Marina Warner has persuasively argued that in Western society the nude figure came to represent innocence and possessed a redemptive quality capable of freeing society of its constraints; it also personified Truth.[29] "Truth shall spring out of the earth" (Ps. 85:10–11) had its clear parallel in our context, with Truth emerging from the well or from the depths, offering an illuminating vision (often holding a mirror—

Fig. 6. Edouard Debat-Ponsan, *She Is Not Drowning* (Latin: *Nec Mergitur*), 1898. Oil on canvas. Musée de l'Hôtel de Ville, Amboise. Courtesy of The Jewish Museum, New York.

see fig. 8 by Ibels, *Truth,* 1898) and comfort to the victims of repression and falsehood. The visual image of Truth seems to invoke a classical affirmation of the primordial being, almost foreshadowing Charles Péguy's famous dictum that for some Dreyfusards the fight for Dreyfus had turned into a *mystique* that refused to be degraded into *politique*. Truth, in these portrayals, took on a sublime appearance. The contrast between this classical (and republican) image and the tremendous emphasis on physiognomy in the antisemitic iconography illustrates the complicated uphill battle Dreyfusards had to undertake, reflecting the Third Republic's constant confrontation with reactionary forces. Rational principles were much harder to preserve, defend and visualize than the anti-republican, antisemitic and militaristic arsenal hurled at them.

The visual material relating to French Jewry, in general, in the nineteenth century

Fig. 7. Bob (Comtesse Sibylle Martel de Janville), *History of the Third Republic* in *Le Rire*, 14 November 1896. Photomechanical print. Jane Voorhees Zimmerli Art Museum. Courtesy of The Jewish Museum, New York.

is understandably not at the heart of the exhibition and catalogue, but several objects deserve mention. A painting by Georg Emanuel Opiz (ca. 1828; p. 30 of the catalogue) depicts the dedication of a synagogue in Alsace (fig. 9 by G. E. Opiz).[30] Here, crowded between three village houses, a large assembly of Jews and non-Jews gather to dedicate a synagogue in an Alsatian village. While children play and villagers converse, as if they were oblivious to the ceremony, the dedication takes place with the participation of local dignitaries. The confined setting—with its many contrasts in dress, activities and interest—lends to the dedication a commonplace and carefree quality. Thus, the public visibility of the Jews seems to be neatly woven into the fabric of Alsatian society, as Michael Burns convincingly shows in his essay on the Dreyfus family.[31] Set within the context of an often-tense relationship between Jews and Alsatians, the painting is a reminder of the pendulumlike relationships between them. Moreover, the externalization and festive dedication reflects the growing tendency within Jewish communities in Western and Central Europe to show a visible pride in their being "at home." Consecration ceremonies tended to be scrupulously prepared.[32] Often including public officials, the processions became more numerous and ostentatious, and it became the custom

Fig. 8. Henri-Gabriel Ibels, *Truth*. Illustration for *Le Sifflet,* 14 July 1898. Ink and crayon on paper. Musée de Bretagne, France. Courtesy of The Jewish Museum, New York.

to have medals struck to commemorate the event. This painting offers us a window into the yet unexplored world of Georg Emanuel Opiz.

Opiz, who was born in Prague (1775) and died in Leipzig (1841), is not a well-known artist, and his oeuvre has attracted almost no historical research in general and almost no attention on the part of researchers into Jewish iconography.[33] His objective and realistic painting of the dedication scene is one example of his interest in the life and ways of people in the streets and squares of Vienna, Paris, Leipzig and many other cities in the 1820s and 1830s. His attraction to lively scenes in which a host of individuals engage in various activities, sometimes extraneous to the central theme of the painting, is widely apparent. Full of humor and exaggeration, both of physiognomic features and cultural mores, Opiz offered a panoramic approach to life in which "foreigners" merged comfortably with the local folk. Among the "foreigners," alongside the Turks, Greeks, Russians, Poles and English, Jews recurrently appear. Opiz, in the congenial style of Biedermeier, has Russian

Fig. 9. Georg Emanuel Opiz, *Dedication of a Synagogue* (in Alsace), c. 1828. Oil on canvas. Courtesy of The Jewish Museum, New York. Gift of Mr. & Mrs. Henry Moses.

Jews coming to the Leipzig market and selling their wares in his enchanting series on the Leipzig markets (1825); he places Polish Jews in a Polish street scene and has Jews performing various functions (as translators and middlemen) in Turkey.[34] In all of these examples, the Jewish presence in society, even as *Ostjuden* in Germany, seems to be a natural part of the diversity of life, arousing no particular objection. Placed within this framework, the *Dedication* scene is not a unique creation of Opiz, but one that fully complements the genre work he was engaged in during those years.

In widening the context in which the *Dedication* was created, mention must be made of the broader cultural phenomenon of which Opiz was a part: the romantic and "realistic" interest in depicting the regional and provincial way of life in art and literature. In this he antedated the appearance of Moritz Oppenheim and others by more than a generation. Opiz was joined in this objective depiction of economic and religious Jewish activities by other European artists (inter alia, Norblin, Hollaenderski and Jonkowsky), attesting to a certain awareness and even acceptance of Jewish involvement in European society. His work, and that of his just mentioned contemporaries, may provide a missing link to the development of Jewish "genre" painting in the nineteenth century, since it made dealing with such topics a legitimate concern.

In contrast to Opiz's "public document," the catalogue and exhibition present interesting artifacts from the private domain—especially with regard to Dreyfus himself. The Dreyfus artifacts, which include family photographs and a photograph of Dreyfus with his fellow classmates from the École de Guerre (August 1891; cat. p. 145) also relate to his Jewish heritage. According to family tradition, Dreyfus and his wife had hung in their bedroom a cloth with Hebrew inscriptions, commemorating the Jewish pilgrimage festivals (Sukkoth, Passover, Shavuoth). The possession of such a fabric and its position in the home encourages speculation as to whether the accepted image of the assimilated Dreyfus is entirely in order. However, as is often the case with material culture,[35] we are in the dark when it comes to determining how the family felt about this object and what value it attached to it. Another artifact of specific Jewish content relating to Dreyfus—his wife's marriage contract—provides contrasting but inconclusive evidence. On the one hand, it attests to his marriage according to Jewish tradition; however, it also attests to his total acculturation to French society. Dreyfus's name appears in the text of the contract as Alfred, implying that he had no Jewish name, while his signature on the contract is in Latin characters alone, apparently suggesting his inability to sign his name in Hebrew characters as was customary on the *ketubah*. Moreover, the decorated menu for the marriage celebration gives no indication of any "Jewish content," but every indication that the festivities were held outside the confines of the synagogue in a wealthy setting. Taken together, the tangible artifacts relating to Dreyfus's life (and they are sparse) cannot themselves help us determine the level of acculturation that prevailed in the Dreyfus family; but they clearly transmit an image of a man ostensibly associated with Judaism, though perhaps basically removed from it. Indeed, it would seem, as Michael Burns claims, that "the two faiths of family and Fatherland sustained him" (p. 14 of the catalogue)—not, I would add, the hallowed faiths of the Central Consistory: religion and Fatherland.

Aside from the lampooning of the dramatis personae of the affair, the work of the caricaturists, the catalogue offers a rich portrayal of the trials themselves by several graphic artists. As Norman L. Kleeblatt, the editor of the work, points out (catalogue p. 9), it was the highly skilled work of Paul Renuard that produced a vivid image of the trials. Since photographs were not allowed in the courtroom, Renuard's drawings take on an added historical value. Illustrative of his efforts are his drawings of Dreyfus in the Rennes trial of 1899, which provide a remarkable affirmation of Dreyfus's steadfastness. Serious and reserved, proud and unassuming, Dreyfus maintains himself with total composure. Even as he leaves the court, as the guards turn their backs on him, his eyes do not turn to the side but gaze forward (fig. 10 by Renuard, 1899[?]). The exactness of Renuard's depiction of Dreyfus in this scene of dishonor is borne out by a photograph taken by Julliard[36] that captures the unflinching gait of Dreyfus through the gauntlet of guards.

Photography as a source of documentation emerges vividly in the Dreyfus affair, from the rare photograph of Dreyfus's degradation (fig. 11, 1895), through his reinstatement (fig. 12, 1906), but especially as captured by the camera lens of Gerschel, whose work is well represented in the catalogue. Gerschel's two hundred photographs of the Rennes retrial show the involvement of distinguished person-

Fig. 10. Paul Renuard, *Exiting the Lycée,* Paris, 1899(?). Lithograph. Jewish Theological Seminary of America, New York. Courtesy of The Jewish Museum, New York.

Fig. 11. The degradation of Dreyfus at the military school, 5 January 1895. Photograph. Collection of J. Robert Maguire. Courtesy of The Jewish Museum, New York.

Fig. 12. E. Le Deley, *The Reinstatement of Dreyfus*, 1906. Postcard. Collection of J. Robert Maguire. (Dreyfus chatting with French officers after his decoration). Courtesy of The Jewish Museum, New York.

alities in the outcome of the case (from Maurice Barrès to Max Nordau), while offering a sensitive glance at the pained face of Mrs. Lucie Dreyfus. But probably the most historically relevant of Gerschel's photographs do not appear in the catalogue. Two large photographs transmit the attention given the affair by the French and the international press: Dreyfusard and anti-Dreyfusard journalists and photographers posed willingly for group photographs, overcoming their particular points of view and expressing their sense of involvement in a most historic moment. It was as if these journalists and photographers recognized their distinct role in contributing to the affair's international character and by so posing desired to leave historical testimony of their self-importance. The press was a central force at the time of the affair and it was well aware of this fact.[37]

As one takes stock of the diverse visual outpourings that accompanied the affair, one recognizes the many levels on which the affair proceeded, only some of which have been addressed here.[38] Combined, they widen our grasp of its significance for French society and urge us to recognize that in an age in which visual material became so much more accessible to the wider public, its proliferation expanded the level of society's involvement. Images and symbols that celebrated well-worn ideas and conceptions of the past were invoked to provoke and goad the respective camps and to mobilize support. This "new" material suggests that to "read" the Dreyfus affair is no longer sufficient—one must also "see" it. *The Dreyfus Affair: Art, Truth, and Justice* opens up a new text for reading the affair, one that may not change basic attitudes to it but will undoubtedly expand our understanding of it.

Art in this essay reproduced courtesy of The Jewish Museum, New York, in connection with the
exhibition "The Dreyfus Affair: Art, Truth, and Justice," Sept. 13, 1987 to Jan. 14, 1988.

Notes

1. Jean-David Bredin, *The Affair: The Case of Alfred Dreyfus.* trans. Jeffrey
Mehlman (New York: 1986).
2. Norman L. Kleeblatt (ed.), *The Dreyfus Affair: Art, Truth and Justice* (Berkeley,
Los Angeles and London: 1987). The catalogue contains several essays that relate to wider
historical and literary issues that will not be discussed in this article. These issues include two
broad historical overviews (1) on the French-Jewish community during the nineteenth century
(Paula Hyman) and (2) on popular antisemitism (Michael Marrus) as well as a portrait of the
Dreyfus family (Michael Burns); an essay on the French legal system during the 1890s
(Benjamin F. Martin); and a most enlightening inquiry into the significance of the affair for
French literature (Susan Rubin Suleiman). The essays that deal with visual material will be
mentioned in the course of the discussion.
3. Michael Burns, *Rural Society and French Politics* (Princeton: 1984), and see
Stephen Wilson, *Ideology and Experience: Antisemitism in France at the Time of the Dreyfus
Affair* (Rutherford: 1982). I am of the opinion that Wilson's extensive evidence has not been
sufficiently taken into consideration.
4. Eugen Weber, "Introduction," Kleeblatt, *The Dreyfus Affair,* xxviii.
5. Michael Marrus, *The Politics of Assimilation* (Oxford: 1971); Richard Cohen,
"The Dreyfus Affair and the Jews," in Shmuel Almog, ed., *Antisemitism Through the Ages*
(Oxford: 1988), 291–310.
6. The exhibition contains more than five hundred objects, of which less than a tenth
stemmed from the first period. According to Kleeblatt, "The Dreyfus Affair," this represents
only about ten percent of the available material.
7. I am pursuing here a line of thought developed by Jules Prown in relation to
material culture. See his "Mind in Matter: An Introduction to Material Culture Theory and
Method," *Winterthur Portfolio* 17 (Spring 1982), 1–19.
8. Linda Nochlin, "Degas and the Dreyfus Affair: A Portrait of the Artist as an Anti-
Semite," in Kleeblatt, *The Dreyfus Affair,* 96–116; quote 109.
9. I mention Franz Kupka because he was extremely critical of the capitalist way of
life and depicted the wealthy capitalist in ways that resemble antisemitic portrayals of Jewish
wealth, yet to my mind, he refrained from antisemitic allusions. See his series on the wealthy
capitalist in *L'Assiette au beurre,* no. 41, January 2, 1902. I, therefore, disagree with the
interpretation offered in Elie Kedourie, ed., *The Jewish World* (New York: 1979), 286, which
sees Kupka's caricature as an example of an antisemitic depiction.
10. See Nelly Wilson, *Bernard Lazare* (Cambridge, Eng.: 1978); Marrus, *Politics of
Assimilation,* chap. 7; Cohen, "The Dreyfus Affair," 294–297.
11. On Lazare's background, see N. Wilson, *Lazare, passim;* on Pissarro see Ralph E.
Shikes and Paula Harper, *Pissarro: His Life and Work* (New York: 1980). An earlier biog-
rapher of Pissarro, Adolphe Tabarant, who was sensitive to Pissarro's Jewishness and was
close to the anarchist circles, has left us an almost-forgotten critique of the socialist position
on antisemitism at the height of the affair. See Tabarant, *Socialisme et antisémitisme* (Paris:
1898). In this context another personality who certainly deserves mention is the symbolist
poet and anarchist Gustave Kahn. Part of this circle of politicized and highly integrated Jews,
Kahn was also at this period extremely critical of the Jewish bourgeoisie "which had shame-
lessly enriched themselves" at the hands of others. See Eugenia Herbert, *The Artist and
Social Reform: France and Belgium 1885–1898* (New Haven: 1961).
12. "Inutile de vous dire combien je partage vos idées sur le mouvement antisé-
mitique et combien je suis heureux de voir un sémite défendre si éloquemment *mes* [ces?]
idées, il n'y avait du reste qu'un Juif anarchiste et savant capable d'élever la voix avec
autorité! Vous avez été courageux et vous avez fait votre devoir." Quoted in N. Wilson,
Lazare, 315, n. 12. See also Shikes and Harper, *Pissarro,* 304. Interestingly enough, I
encountered remarkably few iconographic references to Lazare in this collection. He is

depicted visually only three or four times (not even in a Dreyfusard game where the object is to reach Justice emerging from the well [191]), but his name is mentioned in two other caricatures. This seems to me a most telling indication of Lazare's public visibility during the affair, particularly after it broke in 1898.

13. Alphonse Lévy, *Scènes familiales juives* (Paris: 1902?).

14. Lévy (1843–1918) had originally done an extensive series of illustrations for Léon Cahun, *La Vie juive* (Paris: 1886). Several of his drawings have since been used to illustrate recent works on Alsatian Jewry. See Freddy Raphaël and Robert Weyl, *Juifs en Alsace: Culture, société, histoire* (Toulouse: 1977); *idem, Regards nouveaux sur les juifs d'Alsace* (Strasbourg: 1980). Again, Gustave Kahn's life and development provide an additional perspective. Within a decade he had significantly reversed himself from his withdrawal from the Jewish community and became involved in various Jewish endeavors. In 1926 he published a volume of short stories with a clear nostalgic strain for the more traditional Jewish way of life. See his *Contes juifs* (Paris: 1926). I have yet to determine what occasioned the distinct change in the course of his life and whether the Dreyfus affair had a role to play in it. No work to this date adequately covers his Jewish development. Paula Hyman has touched on aspects of his earlier period in *From Dreyfus to Vichy: The Remaking of French Jewry, 1906–1939* (New York: 1979).

15. Phillip Denis Cate, "The Paris Cry: Graphic Artists and the Dreyfus Affair," in Norman L. Kleeblatt, ed., *The Dreyfus Affair: Art, Truth and Justice* (Berkeley, Los Angeles and London: 1987), 62–95.

16. E. H. Gombrich, "The Cartoonist's Armoury," in *Meditations on a Hobby Horse and Other Essays on the Theory of Art* (London: 1963), 132.

17. Cate, "The Paris Cry," 65.

18. See especially his caricatures on general themes in *Le Courrier français* in the 1880s.

19. See also Matthew 27:33; John 19:17. In Luke 23:33 the name Golgotha does not even appear and "The Skull" is the common substitute.

20. For the description of the banishment of the Jews from the Temple owing to their financial handlings, see Mark 11:15–19 and Luke 19:45–48.

21. See also Willette's illustration for *La Libre parole* (cat., 77). The Wandering Jew motif, which was popular in French lithographs in the nineteenth century, did not always carry with it an antisemitic connotation. Moreover, as is so common with symbolic images, the original design undergoes extensive transformations both in meaning and visual adaptations. Such was the case of the Wandering Jew, who a decade and a half later would be celebrated by the Zionist theorist and sculptor Alfred Nossig as the epitome of the homeless Jew who wandered through lands and centuries with his ever-present *Sefer Torah*. Not incidentally, the German-Jewish journal *Ost und West* illustrated its first issue—immediately after its editorial call for a Jewish renaissance—with Nossig's sculpture. See *Ost und West*, 1(1901), 5–6. A study of this visual motif within its historical development is sorely needed. See Beatrice Farwel, *French Popular Lithographic Imagery*, 5 vols. (Chicago and London: 1981). For the literary and folkloristic aspect of this motif see G. Hasan-Rokem and A. Dundes, eds., *The Wandering Jew: Essays in the Interpretation of a Christian Legend* (Bloomington: 1986).

22. Judith Wechsler, *A Human Comedy: Physiognomy and Caricature in Nineteenth Century Paris* (London: 1982).

23. It is interesting to note that very few antisemitic caricatures of this period are directed at Jewish women or portray them as representative of Judaism. Seemingly, the association of the Jew with financial affairs is at the root of this phenomenon and female participation in Jewish high finance was not common at this time. Possibly, the abusiveness with which the Jewish male was treated carried with it sexual connotations relating to the fear of Jewish manhood. However, Pierre Birnbaum (*Une Mythe politique: la "République juive": De Léon Blum à Pierre Mendès France* [Paris: 1988], 196–236) has made a convincing argument for the presence of a strong association between antisemitism and anti-feminism in the Third Republic, however, the interesting selection of caricatures in the book shows only a few such examples. A parallel situation, emphasis on males, is claimed to exist in the

case of anti-black caricatures. (My thanks to participants in the Yale Judaic Studies Seminar, April 1988, for raising some of these issues, in particular to Oliver W. Holmes and Ze'ev Mankowitz).

24. See Wayland Hand, "A Dictionary of Words and Idioms Associated with Judas Iscariot," *University of California Publications in Modern Philology* 24, no. 3 (1942), 289–356.

25. Ruth Mellinkoff, "Judas's Red Hair and the Jews," *Journal of Jewish Art* 9 (1982), 31–46.

26. Isaiah Shachar, "The Emergence of the Modern Pictorial Stereotype of 'The Jews' in England," *Studies in the Cultural Life of the Jews in England: Folklore Research Center Studies* 5 (1975), 331–365.

27. Compare the efforts made to stigmatize others, as in the case of insanity. See Sander L. Gilman, "What Looks Crazy? Towards an Iconography of Insanity in Art and Medicine in the Nineteenth Century," in Gerald Chapple and Hans H. Schulte, eds., *The Turn of the Century: Literature and Art, 1890–1915* (Bonn: 1981), 53–86.

28. Maurice Agulhon, *Marianne into Battle: Republican Imagery and Symbolism in France, 1789–1880.* trans. Janet Lloyd (Cambridge: 1981); see Ouriel Reshef, *Guerre, mythes et caricatures* (Paris: 1984), 151–184.

29. Marina Warner, *Monuments and Maidens: The Allegory of the Female Form* (London: 1985), esp. chap. 13.

30. The catalogue specifically mentions that the painting is "attributed to Georg Emanuel Opitz"[!] (cat., 30, 270, 271), however, as will be seen, one can with little doubt regard Opiz as the artist.

31. Michael Burns, "The Dreyfus Family," in Kleeblatt, *The Dreyfus Affair,* 140–152.

32. Another cause for such public manifestations was the bringing of a new *Sefer Torah* into the synagogue, as can be seen in the case of another Alsatian community, Reichshoffen, in 1857. See the photograph in Raphaël and Weyl, (facing 320).

33. See Hansjorg Krug, "Georg Emanuel Opiz (1775–1841)," *Philobiblion* 16 (1972), 227–259. Krug seems to be unaware of the *Dedication of a Synagogue* painting and mentions only one painting of Jewish content. Alfred Rubens, *A Jewish Iconography* (London: 1954) lists and illustrates two aquatints, c. 1800, which he notes questionably were "designed by" Opiz. They were, in fact, designed by Opiz as part of an extensive series on Vienna in the early nineteenth century, which includes a further Jewish scene: a group of Jewish merchants. Historical Museum of Vienna, lnv. no. 20569. Rubens held to this identification in the revised edition (1981) and registered three more aquatints from the Leipziger Messe, but he confused their identification. See nos. 1340–1342.

34. Walther Scheidig, *Die Leipziger Messe: Mit bildern von Georg Emanuel Opiz* (Leipzig: 1938); *Original Aquarelle von G. E. Opiz (Prag 1775–Leipzig 1841),* catalogue 69, Neberhay (Vienna: 1980); *Liste 111 George Emanuel Opiz: Aquarelle,* Neberhay (Vienna: n.d.).

35. See John Demos, *A Little Commonwealth: Family Life in Plymouth Colony* (London, Oxford, New York: 1970), 20–22.

36. See Bredin, *The Affair,* between 362–363; photo 29b.

37. *L'Affaire Dreyfus: cinq semaines à Rennes. Deux cent photographies de Gerschel. Texte de Louis Rogès* (Paris: n.d. [c. 1899–1900]).

38. One such issue which requires further study is the extensive anti-Zola material. "J'accuse" catapulted Zola into the center of the public arena and it offered caricaturists a wide range of possibilities.

Max Liebermann and the Painting of the Public Sphere

Irit Rogoff
(UNIVERSITY OF CALIFORNIA, DAVIS)

Traditionally, Max Liebermann has been discussed either within the framework of such stylistic characterizations as naturalism or German impressionism or within the historical institutional context of secessionist politics and later, those of the Prussian Academy of Arts, which he headed during the Weimar years.

These approaches do not, however, yield a great variety of insights beyond those relating to culture as reflective of its social conditions, as of the general social order. Instead, I propose that another notion of culture and its social and political grounding (as suggested by the work of several historians) be applied here. According to this new perspective, culture is constitutive, a signifying system through which, necessarily, a social order is communicated, reproduced, experienced and explored.[1]

The main difference between the more traditional approach and the one advanced here can be seen in the relations they set up between representation and reality. On the whole, analyses that view culture as reflective put forward readings that trace direct lines between social, political and historical realities and their visual representation. These representations, then, serve as visually codified documents of dynamics occurring outside the work of art. The divergent approach, that in which culture is deemed constitutive, holds that representation, in fact, *constructs* meaning and serves to introduce and articulate discourses into the culture that have so far been absent in this form. It opens up possibilities for reading certain works as having political implications that are not directly self-evident in the iconography of the work. Rather, they articulate their political significance through the discursive dimension of their production—for example, to which they are exhibited; how do they relate to other work being produced and displayed simultaneously; what is the critical response to them; and so on. The chief implication of this category of analysis for my purposes is that it introduces culture as a whole and visual representation in particular as a form of political enactment functioning within a political arena rather than relegated to a more marginal realm of cultural activity.

All reproductions are from *Max Liebermann in Seiner Zeit,* ed. Matthias Eberle and Sigrid Achenbach (Berlin: Nationalgalerie, 1979), except figures 3 and 17.

Thus, I shall attempt to situate the work of Max Liebermann in an alternative framework from that of stylistic movements as well as cultural, institutional practices—namely, that of the bourgeois public sphere. As defined by Jürgen Habermas, the public sphere is both a basic forum of political enactment and a complex and autonomous political entity:

> By the "public sphere" we mean first of all the realm of our social life in which something approaching public opinion can be formed. A portion of the public sphere comes into being in every conversation in which private individuals assemble to form a public body. . . . This process marks an important transition from mere opinions (i.e., cultural assumptions, normative attitudes, collective prejudices and values) to a public opinion which presupposes a reasoning public, a series of public discussions concerning the exercise of power which are both critical in intent and institutionally guaranteed.[2]

In this model, the public sphere is conceived of as a discursive space in which certain forms of political debate can be carried out. Habermas has designated this space historically as the forum in which the European bourgeoisie of the seventeenth and eighteenth centuries carved out for themselves an autonomous discourse founded on rational judgment and an enlightened and informed criticism. This forum was located between the absolutist state of the earlier period on the one hand, and the rising political organization of the urban proletariat on the other. Within this space, we find a body of informed, enlightened and liberal opinion that is above all else independent of political parties, national interests or institutionally formulated power hierarchies.

This distance from governing institutions or organized forms of political activity does not, however, imply that the thought of its participants was apolitical. The contrary is the case because, within this alternative space of the bourgeois public sphere, it is not social power, privilege and tradition that confer on individuals the right to speak or judge, but the degree to which they are constituted as discoursing subjects by sharing in a consensus of universal reason and a common language. Language, therefore discourse, construct political space, determine the participation within it and signify its activity. In the analysis that follows, I propose to examine imagery and its role in constructing culture in a similar manner to the way discourse has been seen to function in constructing political space, particularly alternative political space.

The three dominant strains in Liebermann's life—his self-identification as Prussian, bourgeois and Jewish—suggest the public sphere as an appropriate model through which to analyze his work as a painter, cultural politician and polemicist. In the context of such a process of situating, one of the most interesting aspects of both the man and his work is the presence of massive internal contradictions within all three stances, or strands, of his identity and in their political expressions. It is precisely this lack of "coherency" and its potential for yielding discourses working at cross-purposes and disrupting one another that has prompted me to look at his early work. By that, I mean the paintings Liebermann produced between his graduation from the Weimar Academy in 1872 and his return to Berlin in the late 1880s. Compared with this early period, the following two phases of Liebermann's activities as cultural politician at the Berlin Secession and the Prussian Academy of Art can be far more directly identified with clearly formulated policies, institutional politics and recognizable vested interests. During the first two decades of his activity, however, it is the imagery he was formulating that served as his social and political voice, which can be discussed as a form of constitutive visual ideology.

Max Liebermann was born in Berlin in 1847 to a family of immensely wealthy textile manufacturers. His was the third generation of the family in the Prussian capital. When writing of his grandfather, Joseph, who had moved to Berlin in 1824 and had founded the family's wide-ranging business concerns, Liebermann described him in terms of family folklore. In these descriptions he established not only the family's wealth and social standing, but also the progressive nature of their industrial enterprises. Their major contribution seems to have been that they adopted a wide range of technical innovations that had been pioneered in England. Family legend had it that when Joseph Liebermann had an audience with King Karl Friedrich III of Prussia, he introduced himself by saying, "I am the Liebermann who pushed the English off the continent."[3]

The family was extremely proud, not only of its financial and industrial achievements at a time when there were still restrictions on the financial and commercial activities of Jews, but also of its upward social mobility and its standing in both the Jewish community and Berlin society at large. This pride and sense of success was manifested by the building of a large town house for the entire family in 1856 (fig. 1) and by allowing one of its sons to attend university and branch away from commerce.

Liebermann himself took great pains to emphasize the deeply bourgeois nature of his background, "I am as bourgeois, as upright and as predictable as a clock tower," he said in a letter of 1911:

Fig. 1. Photograph, Liebermann house on Pariser Platz, 30 January 1933, p. 16.

Am I to be considered lacking in spirit if all I can paint well is a head? It is of course far easier to write about an artist who bolts with a different woman every year or is to be found rolling in the gutter every evening or behaves with an extroverted and calculated geniality. Need I however elaborate all sorts of fake and nonexistent sensitivities in order to qualify as an artist?[4]

Viewed through the model being examined here, this statement can be read not simply as a rejection of the anecdotal and the trivially pleasing qualities that so dominated *Gründerzeit* art, but also as an insistence that this middle ground of bourgeois existence–neither aristocracy nor bohemia—provided a genuine, legitimate platform for significant cultural activity.

The emphasis on effort, industry and hard work, qualities on which his upbringing and milieu constantly insisted, was reinforced by his perception of his Prussian heritage. Because his family was largely mercantile rather than cultural in its orientation, it seems that Liebermann's perception of Prussian culture was determined by two influences. First, by his teacher Carl Steffeck; second by his contact with the art collections of various assimilated Jewish family friends who collected works by the Nazarenes, especially by such specifically Prussian artists as Franz Kruger and Edward Gartner as well as by Adolph von Menzel.[5] (The Nazarenes is the collective name given to the painters of the Brotherhood of Saint Luke who lived and worked in Italy in the early years of the nineteenth century.) Liebermann identified these works as a preimperial form of authentic culture in which sobriety, modesty and the more universal spirit of the Enlightenment provided the dominant values. They stood in direct contrast to the pomp and circumstance of the early Reich and its somewhat desperate and operatic attempts to formulate a vocabulary of national unity and glory.

Fig. 2. Max Liebermann, *Geesepluckers*, 1872. Nationalgalerie, Staatliche Museen zu Berlin (East), p. 27.

The first work that Liebermann, then a twenty-five-year-old student at the Weimar Academy, exhibited publicly was the *Geesepluckers* of 1872 (fig. 2). Its bold composition of a semicircle of peasants sitting within a cramped and dimly lit space and plucking the feathers from geese relates directly to Mihàly Munkácsy's slightly earlier (1871) *Lintmakers* (fig. 3), with which Liebermann was well acquainted, having visited the Hungarian artist's studio in Düsseldorf while it was being painted. The formal execution of Liebermann's composition is, however, far more brutal and uncompromising, the space darker and more confined. The figures are rough, poorly clothed and bent over their work, and the task itself is of a far more demanding and less aesthetic nature. Bent over their task of plucking the live geese, there is a dimension of a contained personal struggle in the work that each of these peasants is executing.

What is interesting about the comparison between the two works is not so much the set of formal influences that are apparent but rather the way in which Liebermann sets up a critical dialogue with the earlier painting, using its form in order to illuminate and codify the profound conceptual differences between two sets of values. As we can see from his 1872 painting entitled *Vegetable Cleaners* (fig. 4), he has done this in two stages, dispensing first with the narrative dimension of the work and then breaking up the orderly composition. By eliminating the figure of the soldier recounting tales of the Franco-Prussian War (who appears in Munkácsy's painting), Liebermann has cut across several layers of narrative: the anecdotal one in which the scene is represented around an artificially constructed dramatic event and the historical one in which the activity is situated within the context of the needs of a

Fig. 3. Mihàly Munkácsy, *Lintmakers,* 1871. Hungarian National Gallery, Budapest.

Fig. 4. Max Liebermann, *Vegetable Cleaners,* 1872. Private collection, Winterthur, Switzerland, p. 163.

specific historical moment, thereby translating the activity of the workers into a commodity that can be clearly read by the viewers of the painting. Instead, Liebermann makes the abstract concept of *work* the subject of the painting, positing it as the main unifying element in the making of a community governed by principles of mutuality and shared enterprise. By eliminating the voice of the narrator, Liebermann removed far more than the narrative and the anecdotal voice–he substituted the notion of work for that voice and presented a conceptual as well as physical representation of a very large group of people (in the 1860s, eighty percent of Germany's population was living on the land) with neither political voice nor visual representation.

Although other artists, Ludwig Knaus and Wilhelm Leibl, for example, did paint the peasantry, they did so either with an eye for the cozy and anecdotal that pleased and disarmed the urban bourgeois public or with a concern for the loss of regional, folkloric traditions and the redefinition of the relationship between peasant and land brought about by the land reform bills of the 1870s. Liebermann was the first German artist to define these peasants in terms of a far more modern concept of work, attempting simultaneously both to establish that this work community had an autonomy—a voice and a visual identity to which it was entitled—and to criticize the existing social and political order.

The contrast between his origins and situation and his subject matter was not lost on the critics, who asked "Where does a painter who lives in Pariser Platz find the ugly, dirty peasants who inhabit his paintings?"[6] Nor was the work's confrontational intention ignored. One critic wrote, "Although taken from reality, the subject is nevertheless particularly brutal. Those poor creatures, who are plucking feathers from live geese, are the epitome of ugliness. In fact the whole group is so thoroughly common and distasteful that one shudders with horror just standing in front of them."[7]

Likewise, Liebermann's attempt to set up a dialogue with other painters of similar themes was equally clear to the critics, as can be ascertained by the comparison they made with Ludwig Knaus's *Vesperbrot* (*Vespers Bread*) and the resulting caricature published in the satirical journal *Kladderadatsch* in August 1872 (figs. 5 and 6).

Fig. 5. Ludwig Knaus, *Vespers Bread*, 1872. Present whereabouts unknown, p. 27.

Fig. 6.   Caricature, *Kladderadatsch,* August 1872, p. 27.

Here the dreamy and sentimental figure of Knaus's geese girl, who is feeding her charges as though going through a religious ritual of charity (indicated by the work's title), is superimposed over Liebermann's rough, working peasants. The caption reads, "The geese that have been fed by Knaus are being ripped apart by Liebermann." With this first publicly exhibited, work Liebermann was labeled "the smut painter," "the prophet of ugliness" and "the socialist painter."[8]

A series of works that followed throughout the 1870s and 1880s continued to explore the visual codification of these concerns. As in Liebermann's 1876 *Workers in a Turnip Field* (fig. 7), the references to earlier works by admired artists such as Jean-François Millet's *Gleaners* and Gustave Courbet's *Burial at Ornans* are more than obvious gestures of homage and serve as partners in a dialogue concerning the change in the representational status of the subjects. Again and again, the issues of work, community and autonomy are explored, in the case of *Workers in a Turnip*

Fig. 7. *Workers in a Turnip Field,* 1876. Niedersächsisches Landesmuseum, Hannover, p. 189.

Field by an increasing emphasis on the lack of eye contact with the spectator, whose *socially* dominant gaze is negated and denied. The workers arranged in a semicircle, exchange a variety of looks among themselves, while only one of the figures (the woman on the left) levels an extremely unaccommodating look at the viewer. Instead of the usual interplay between protagonists and spectators—so common in this genre of painting in which the norm is representations of peasants constructed out of the expectations and interests of the bourgeois viewing public—here we find an internal mutuality and cohesion founded on internal visual contact and on a coordinated gestural code.

Although the scope of this particular discussion does not allow for an extended elaboration of the way in which Liebermann represented peasant and working-class children, this subject must be mentioned. It was often the case that representations of the peasantry by such painters as Knaus, Theodore Hussmann and Franz von Defreger put images of children prominently in the foreground. By doing so, an added dimension of sentiment and a process of transforming the images into the realm of folklore could be achieved. Furthermore, images of children were more pliant, less resistant, less belligerent and, therefore, less threatening than the fully grown peasant capable of making social, political and economic demands or simply of invading the genteel space of the bourgeois urban salon. The fact is that most of the representations of peasant children are of girls, often separated from a protective family environment, thus shown in the fields or orchards in "nature"—an allusion to a state of naturalized sexual availability. This is an important dimension of the totally proprietorial attitude of the urban bourgeoisie toward the rural peasantry enacted through visual representations.

Here, too, Liebermann took up a position entirely different from that of his German contemporaries. In such works as his 1875 *Potato Pickers* (fig. 8), he

Fig. 8. *Potato Pickers,* 1875. Kunstmuseum der Stadt Düsseldorf, p. 175.

anchors the figure of the small peasant girl in the working family and through the family in the working community. She is not defined through the charms and sentiments she exerts on her middle-class viewers but rather through her place and role in the family and in relation to others like herself. The smaller realm, that of the family, is, in turn, located in the larger one indicated by the distant working figures; as with the earlier works, the figures turn their backs on the spectator, intent on their work and defying the proprietorial gaze.

In this work, we find several stratas of a process of self-definition of the protagonists by other protagonists and by their labor, so that, increasingly, the outside referents can be dismissed. The way in which representations of both gender and of age are incorporated as equal constituents within the depictions of work communities, as in the *Potato Pickers,* was another aspect of Liebermann's effort to establish a translucency and internal redefinition for the space these peasant figures inhabit. All this stands in contrast to the way the women of haute bourgeoisie households are depicted; they loll passively about in a state of cultural reverie, reading books, providing an audience for male cultural activity and being defined by that activity alone. This can be seen in Liebermann's 1902 *The Artist's Studio* (fig. 9).

Although much of the subject matter of this series of early works is usually rural agricultural labor, the impact of the Industrial Revolution on the rural economy is also explored. In the 1886 *Spinner* (fig. 10) and the 1897 *Weavers in Laren* (fig. 11), Liebermann looks at the transformations taking place in the countryside. The fact that the earlier scene is gendered female, whereas the later, more industrialized

Fig. 9. *The Artist's Studio,* 1902. Kunstmuseum, St. Gallen, Switzerland, p. 297.

Fig. 10. *Spinner,* 1886. Private collection, p. 239.

Fig. 11.   *Weavers in Laren,* 1897. Collection George Schäfer, Schweinfurt, West Germany, p. 279.

scene is gendered male is both a commentary on the erosion of forms of economic continuity, of labor divisions and of the roles that these played in small, closely knit communities as well as an observation of the increasing presence of industrial technology in rural communities.

Given Liebermann's set of concerns and his reputation for practicing what Ottmar von Leixner in 1875 termed a "Socialist Democratic aesthetic," why am I then trying to locate him within the bourgeois public sphere rather than within the cultural wing of the emergent German socialist movement? This is a particularly pertinent question given Liebermann's admiration for both the political work and personality of Ferdinand Lassalle, who combined radical activity on behalf of the proletariat with romantic maverick legal activities on behalf of his clients, many of them women protesting against legislative inequality under marital and property laws. One of the reasons for doing so is related to Liebermann's concerns for issues of continuity—continuity in Prussian culture or in communities—sentiments typical of the liberal bourgeoisie who were at odds with the foundations of socialist beliefs founded in revolutionary class struggles against exploitation.

There is also the extremely important issue of antisemitism, which played a fairly central ideological role in the early days of the German socialist movement. The 1870s were, in fact, a demarcating line in the development and articulation of political antisemitism. But even earlier, throughout the period of so-called emancipation—between the Napoleonic campaigns of 1812 and the founding of the Reich in 1870—antisemitism had been a common and familiar companion of antiliberalism. Civil and political emancipation for the Jews symbolized for conservatives the absurdities of the liberal political doctrine; at the same time, the urban commercial activities of the Jews symbolized for a large segment of the German population all the corrosive atrocities of the new industrial system and of the modern state. When both unification and industrialization were rapidly followed by an economic crash in 1873 and a severe, prolonged economic depression, anti-liberalism and antisemitism joined hands (both conservative and socialist) in various irrational outbursts. In these flare-ups, the real issues affecting the new urban industrial proletariat—the concentration of modes of production, criteria of time-value efficiency and their costs, capital distribution, increasingly marked class differentiation—were not considered. Rather, innovation and modernity were viewed as culturally and racially determined, defying either classical models for dealing with change or revolutionary rupture. Even Ferdinand Lassalle, an assimilated Jew and Liebermann's political hero, founder of the General German Workers Union (1863) and ceaseless champion of universal suffrage, was himself profoundly anti-liberal and both Jews and Judaism were repeatedly condemned by him as part and parcel of liberal hypocrisy and capitalist exploitation.[9] In most aspects of Lassalle's public and private political work, however, Liebermann must have seen a model of independent informed thought, determined to win representation for the excluded from public discourse and with an uncompromising sense of his own autonomy. Although Liebermann strongly identified with his Jewish background, he was subject to the classic dilemma of liberal German Jewry, the desire to integrate within the culture as a whole while maintaining certain cultural differences.[10]

By locating Liebermann within the discursive space of the public sphere, we are better able to understand the internal contradictions that inform his work. In the public sphere, universal reason and the spirit of the Enlightenment served equally to work against the darker irrationality of traditional racial prejudice and against its fear of change, of modernity and of the introduction of different perspectives into the culture.

Liebermann himself experienced the full blast of antisemitic prejudice when he exhibited his *Jesus in The Temple* (fig. 12) at the Munich international exhibition of 1879. The subject is a pictorial and thematic convention to be found in Dutch and German painting from the seventeenth and eighteenth centuries; for example, one painted by Menzel among numerous others. Liebermann's version of this theme is executed with naturalist verve using Italian models (the painting was done in Venice). It employs pictorial conventions that emphasize the Mediterranean features and coloring of the protagonists—unlike other versions of this theme that tend to depict the protagonists as North Europeans—and subjects the pictorial space in which the figures are located to unconventional and non-hierarchical revisions. Although originally accepted with enthusiasm for the Munich exhibition and allocated a central hanging position, the painting's public reception was virulently hostile, predominantly for "racial" rather than artistic reasons. While this is not the place to provide the substantial documentation that exists for this sorry episode, suffice it to say that Prince Regent Luitpold demanded that the painting be hung in a less central position and that it was debated in the Bavarian Landestag, where it was characterized as a representation of "ungodly misery, lowliness and outright blasphemy which cannot but offend the profoundest sentiments of the Christian viewer."[11] Judging by letters

Fig. 12.   *Jesus in the Temple,* 1879. Private collection, Hamburg, p. 30.

he wrote at the time as well as over the next fifty years to such close friends as
Alfred Lichtwark and Max Lehrs, this episode had a profound effect on Liebermann. He wrote to Lichtwark:

> I have already told you how, on account of this painting, which at 10 A.M. defeated the
> jury of the exhibition (i.e., The Prince Regent's demands defeated the Jury), by evening
> had made me famous—how I was invited that evening to sit with the gods of the
> Allotria, Gedon, Lenbach, Wagmuller, etc.—how Zugel exclaimed that in 50 years no
> such masterpiece had been painted in Munich—that the Prince Regent Luitpold wanted
> the work removed from the exhibition—that there ensued a two-day debate on the
> matter at the Bavarian House of Representatives (and it was only due to the Center
> leader that I was not crucified)—how, through the fracas around this picture, I made the

acquaintance of Leibl—how Lenbach advised me to flee from the fury of Pobels by leaving Munich and how I made the discovery of Dachau for painting as a result of fleeing Munich. Stöcker maintained that the painting provoked a form of Jew-baiting for which I had to pay a bitter price, since my fellow-believers (in their hyper-sensitivity) would not buy any of my paintings for the next 15 years. The loathsome newspaper feud added to all of this and I, disgusted with the racket around this painting, which today seems inconceivable, resolved never again to attempt to paint a biblical subject matter. . . . In any case, I became the lord of the oppressed in the local pub, as well as for a time to a section of the artists' community.[12]

Through this episode, Liebermann experienced a firsthand acquaintance with and became conscious of the contradictory nature of his position within German culture: he was simultaneously both insider and outsider.[13]

In order to understand Liebermann's art, we must understand his strong social identity as a Jew and his commitment to the concept of a collective enterprise founded in a community. Out of these grew his criticism of the Wilhelminian Reich and its rhetoric of cohesion and unity. Liebermann saw German culture as a host culture in which certain substantial exclusions were practiced, and he was critical of the increasing bureaucratization and divisive strategies of the state in its attempt to replace the community. Liebermann's painting, therefore, took an extremely programmatic turn in which such issues were visually codified and alternative forms were proposed. The source of the model he propounded was a community that traditionally took care of its own needy through a set of institutions such as orphanages, homes for the aged, communal child care, rabbinical courts, arrangements for marriage that ensured the dignity of all parties concerned, and so on. The artist was deeply struck by the Reich's bureaucratization of the organization of social welfare without the granting of any rights to its subjects. Since he could not put forward alternative models for welfare programs from within Jewish communal culture—because the Jewish community did not function as a state and because he was uncertain of the possibility of successfully combining both German and Jewish perspectives within one culture—he proceeded to locate an alternative model in Holland. Long an admirer of both Dutch art and of Dutch republican political culture as well as a close friend and collaborator of the Dutch painter Jozef Israëls, he proceeded to paint a series of orphanages and old peoples' homes in Amsterdam and Leiden, which he imbued with all the qualities of ideal autonomous communities serving the needs of their members and devoid of authoritarian regimentation. In works such as his 1881/1882 *Free Hour at an Amsterdam Orphanage* (fig. 13) or his 1880 *Old Men's Home, Amsterdam* (fig. 14), we find him setting up models of introverted, autonomous communities similar to those he previously created in the early paintings of working peasants. The scenes are set outside, thereby defying the concept of the enclosing, separating institution that removes these welfare and charity clients from any kind of organic social setting. Not only are the figures depicted in natural, comfortable poses, but they are dappled with sunlight and surrounded with trees and other vegetation; they inhabit nature rather than some deviant social realm.

When comparing Liebermann's renditions of such subjects with the standard representations of state orphanages, work colonies, and so on (see the 1904 pho-

Fig. 13. *Free Hour at an Amsterdam Orphanage,* 1881/1882. Städelscher Museumsverein Frankfurt, p. 221.

Fig. 14. *Old Men's Home, Amsterdam,* 1880. Private collection, p. 215.

tograph of the Orphanage in Amsterdam, fig. 15), what becomes apparent is that in each case the source of authority and control of the group depicted has been removed or marginalized and the group has been represented as autonomous and self-governing. Charity, welfare and their institutions are not, therefore, a mode of exclusion that places beneficiaries outside society and robs them of representation but rather they deal with groups whose needs differ from the dominant norm and who need to be satisfied in dignified and accepting ways. In an 1877 work, *Amsterdam Orphanage Sewing Class* (fig. 16), removal of the controlling figure of institutional authority is even more apparent. The scene takes place in a classroom in which the sewing girls are seated behind desks; they are focused entirely on their work and maintain virtually no visual contact with the supposed figure of the teacher. In fact, the teacher's desk is only hinted at the margins of the work, for it has been cut out of the composition by the frame. While this could be viewed as a pictorial device borrowed from the French impressionists whom Liebermann so admired, it seems to me to play a far more substantive and polemical role. This conviction is strengthened when one compares this image to any number of photographic or other images of similar institutions such as the photograph of a Berlin children's soup kitchen of 1904 (fig. 17), a fairly standard representation of its genre, in which the controlling figures of the organizers loom large and dominant.

It appears that Liebermann exploited the late nineteenth-century vogue in Germany for Dutch art and Dutch culture, one that he shared, but for reasons diametrically opposed to Volkisch celebrations of the Netherlandic spirit. He did so in order to put forward a set of critical challenges stemming from a Jewish perspective but couched in terms that were culturally acceptable to all. As Peter Hohendahl has written,

Fig. 15.   Photograph, courtyard of Amsterdam orphanage, 1904, p. 35.

Fig. 16. *Amsterdam Orphanage Sewing Class*, 1877. Von Der Heydt-Museum, Wuppertal, p. 199.

Fig. 17. Photograph, children's soup kitchen. Reproduced from *Berliner Leben,* 8, no. 14, 1905.

"The emergent modern public sphere renegotiates the previously distinct home, family and its activity and the common political activity and concern for public welfare, thus revising traditional notions of state and society as an area negotiating between the two."[14] Not only do these paintings insist on the incursion of private interests into public opinion, but they seem to demand a critical examination of existing institutions by putting forward alternative models. Their anonymous subjects are surrounded by light and air and portrayed in reflective attitudes that were then not deemed appropriate since they were not perceived as playing any significant social role or as possessing an autonomous, reflective voice.

The images conveying these alternatives, which circulated in galleries, museums, exhibitions, the salons of the cultured and educated and the dining rooms of those seeking cultural legitimation, served as a visual counterpart to discussion couched in language. As Habermas has stated, "The public sphere's uniqueness lies in its *medium*—public discussion. It posited the notion of supervision, the principle which demanded that proceedings be made public, against the existing order."[15] I would like to suggest that this early body of work by Liebermann, this painting as a social program, constituted the visual dimension of public sphere culture in its emphasis on equal participation, social transparency and the need to examine, supervise and criticize the existing order. In fact, these works of Liebermann created a constant stir and elicited vitriolic criticism from the center and the right of the cultural establishment.

Although in later years Liebermann was a far more prominent public figure on which a great deal of critical attention as well as support was focused, such attention had to do entirely with his efforts to establish a liberal institutional opposition to the imperial court's domination of public culture, to his galvanization of the wealth and power of the emergent Jewish bourgeoisie to promote these activities, to his ceaseless championing of French and Dutch art and his insistence on a cosmopolitan and international milieu for culture—not to mention his high bourgeois style of life in Pariser Platz surrounded by the work of French impressionist painters. But it was the early paintings that elicited the most direct criticism because they insisted on their power to challenge and to set themselves up in a declamatory political mode.

Notes

A version of this paper was given at the College Art Association meetings in Houston, February 1988. I am grateful to Françoise Forster-Hahn for inviting me to give this paper at her session on German Modernism. A discussion of the respondent's comments to this paper and of the issues of paradigms of inquiry and politics within art history that were raised on this occasion will appear in another version in *Art History*.

1. Terms adapted from Raymond Williams, *Towards a Sociology of Culture* (London: 1983), 13.

2. Jürgen Habermas, *Strukturwandel der Öffentlichkeit,* 2d ed. (Neuwied/Berlin: 1965).

3. Max Liebermann, "Autobiographisches" in *Die Phantasie in der Malerei— Schriften und Reden,* ed. Gunther Busch (Frankfurt: 1978), 12.

4. Letter to Gustav Pauli, 1911. Quoted in Matthias Eberle, "Max Lieber-mann . . . ," in *Max Liebermann in Seiner Zeit*, ed. Matthias Eberle and Sigrid Achenbach (Berlin: 1979), 12.

5. These collections, which were disbanded through several financial crises and two world wars, can be reconstructed, in part, through the notes for Karl Schwarz's uncompleted catalogue of Jewish collectors in Germany and Austria. These notes are now part of the Schwarz estate at the Leo Baeck Institute, New York.

6. Eberle, *Max Liebermann*, 25.

7. *Ibid*, 16.

8. Critics quoted by Erich Hancke, *Max Liebermann—Sein Leben und seine Zeit*, 2d ed. (Berlin: 1923).

9. Shulamit Volkov, "Socialist Democracy's Immunization against Anti-Semitism in Imperial Germany," in *Ferdinand Lassalle*, ed. Shlomo Na'aman (Tel-Aviv: 1983).

10. This is apparent in the interviews conducted with him by Hans Ostwald during the late 1920s and early 1930s which were published as *Das Liebermann Buch* (Berlin: 1930). Similar statements are quoted by Peter Gay in *Freud, Jews and Other Germans* (New York: 1979), 101–108.

11. Minutes of the Bavarian Parliament quoted in Hancke, *Max Liebermann*, 2d ed. (Berlin: 1923), 139–142.

12. Correspondence with Max Lehrs is part of the Liebermann files, Archives of the Leo Baeck Institute, New York; correspondence with Lichtwark reproduced in *Kunstlerbriefe Aus der 19 Jahrhundert*, ed. B. Cassirer (Berlin: 1914).

13. Peter Hohendahl, "Jürgen Habermas—the Public Sphere," *New German Critique* 3 (1974), 45–48.

14. Hohendahl, "Habermas," 55.

15. *Ibid*.

The Artist as Refugee

Ziva Amishai-Maisels
(THE HEBREW UNIVERSITY)

In 1933 the National Socialists ascended to power in Germany and declared war on Jews, Communists and Modern Art more or less at the same time.[1] As a result, a growing number of artists who either were Jewish, had left-wing affiliations or simply refused to abandon their adherence to Modern Art began to leave the country and seek refuge elsewhere. This tendency spread to Austria, Italy, Eastern Europe and France as the Nazis extended their power and ideology over most of Europe, more or less closing the gates against further escape by late 1941.[2] The problem of refugee artists has recently been discussed either as part of the larger problem of intellectuals who were refugees from the Nazis or as part of a study of those persecuted by the Nazis as "degenerate artists."[3] However, the question of the artists' response to their status as refugees has not been adequately analyzed. Thus, no distinction has been made between artists who left Europe to pursue their artistic freedom, many of whom continued with their art as though no major displacement had occurred in their lives,[4] and artists who became refugees either because they were Jewish or because they were left-wing opponents of fascism. It is the artists in these last two categories, as will be seen, who were most likely to stress their feelings as refugees in their art. Moreover, the extent to which their place of refuge made a difference in the way these refugees responded to their condition has not been investigated. The present study will deal with a limited number of Jewish and non-Jewish refugee artists as examples of those whose work *did* demonstrate the influence of their refugee status, and it will attempt to discover by means of an analysis of their art just what kinds of reactions they experienced. These artists fled for the most part to the United States, England, Belgium, Holland and Palestine; they belonged to different schools of art, to different generations, and they came from different countries and backgrounds. What they had in common was their adherence to Modern Art, their refugee status and their opposition to fascism. Since they worked in a variety of styles and media, the connection between them is best seen through their choice and development of subject matter.

One of the most obvious subjects that unites many of these artists is that of the refugee, either in descriptive or symbolic form. Although this is, indeed, a common subject among such artists, it was also popular during the 1930s and 1940s with non-refugee artists who were affected by both the idea and the sight of the refugees streaming out of Germany and later out of occupied Europe.[5] Many refugee artists who dealt with this theme did not wait for their own wanderings to begin before taking up the subject: Marc Chagall and Jacques Lipchitz had been depicting refugees and the need to escape from 1933 onward, although they were safely residing in Paris; Lea Grundig, a Jewish Communist active in Germany, began working on the theme in the mid-1930s, although she did not leave Germany until 1939. However, when these early examples are investigated and compared to the development of the image of the refugee once the artist himself was on the run, his new personal association with the subject will become clear. As Chagall put it, "Here in the harbor . . . close to the ship, I discovered hundreds of my Jews with bag and baggage. I have never experienced such a sad event as when an author and his heroes take the same trip."[6]

Actually, Chagall had been portraying his main refugee type, the traditional Wandering Jew with a pack on his back, since his youth, and he sporadically returned to this figure whenever he himself was on the move, as in 1914–1915 and in 1923.[7] But the Wandering Jew became prominent in his works only in the years following Hitler's rise to power, and he was soon joined by another traditional Jewish refugee who clutches his Torah scroll as he flees, trying to save his spiritual possessions as well as his physical being.[8]

In an illustration (dating from c. 1937–1938) for Abraham Valt's poem "Fear not, my servant Jacob," Chagall depicted the Wandering Jew as the archetypal refugee, Jacob fleeing Esau.[9] The poem, written during the Ukrainian pogroms of 1920, describes how Esau planned the first pogrom and how Jacob thought of a plan that has saved the Jews to this day: threatened, they scatter, so that if one is killed, the others will be saved. The words of the title are not only those God spoke to Jacob, but the eternal reassurance that God will not forsake the Jews in times of strife. Chagall was struck by the applicability of this poem to contemporary events and illustrated Jacob's plan in two works. In *Jacob Wrestling with the Angel* (of this period), the background depicts the burning shtetl, from which two Wandering Jews escape, each heading in a different direction.[10] In *White Crucifixion* of 1938 (fig. 1), Chagall replaced Jacob with a Christian image that would become his prime symbol of the Holocaust, but the Jews fleeing the pogrom in the background—including a Wandering Jew, a Jew with a Torah, a mother and child, two old Jews, one of whom was originally labeled "*Ich bin Jude*," and a group of Jews escaping by boat—scatter in different directions as Valt had suggested.[11]

After Chagall's flight to America in 1941, the Wandering Jew often joins other refugees, as he had in Chagall's earliest renderings of this theme.[12] From this time onward, either singly or as part of a group, alone or set beside the fleeing Jew with a Torah, this figure not only maintains his identity as the Wandering Jew, but also often carries with him an association with the Holocaust.[13] However, he has another meaning as well that accounts for the obsessive recurrence of this image in Chagall's work: The Wandering Jew symbolizes Chagall himself in his wanderings, especially after his flight to the United States. This experience left him with the feeling that he was the eternal wanderer, "The man in the air in my paintings . . . is me. . . . It used to be partially me. Now it is entirely me. I'm not fixed anyplace. *I have no place of my own. . . .* I have to live *someplace*."[14] Chagall spoke these words in 1950 after he had resettled in France. Although he loved France, his wartime poems

Fig. 1. Marc Chagall, *White Crucifixion,* 1938. Oil on canvas, 154.3 × 139.7 cm. Gift of Alfred S. Alschuler. 925. © 1989 The Art Institute of Chicago. All rights reserved.

show his resentment at her betrayal of him; his later letters to Abraham Sutzkever reveal that he continued to feel himself an alien Jew in a Christian environment.[15]

This concept of personal identity also pervades Chagall's other refugee images. For instance, the Jew carrying the Torah became prominent in his art while he was working on his own series of Bible illustrations. At the same time, this figure's development is paralleled by that of a static Jew clutching his Torah, unable to flee, a figure who will soon become a victim of the Holocaust. These two figures—the static victim and the fleeing refugee—were featured in 1933 (the year Hitler assumed office) in two related paintings, *Solitude* (fig. 2) and *The Falling Angel,* both of which Chagall has listed as expressing his presentiments of the coming catastrophe.[16] On the one hand, the fleeing figure represented his wish that the Jews would run, carrying their scroll—the symbol of their religion—to safety. On the other hand, he understood that they would not do so and that a major part of religious Jewry, the upholders of the Torah, were in danger of being destroyed.[17]

Chagall's other major refugee figures, the fleeing mother and her child, joined the other two images in 1934 and became a constant in his works of the late 1930s and

Fig. 2.   Marc Chagall, *Solitude*, 1933. Tel-Aviv Museum.

1940s. In *White Crucifixion* of 1938 (fig. 1), refugee mothers and children appear several times: fleeing on foot at the bottom of the painting and in a boat on the left, among the Russians who come to save the Jews on the upper left, and seated with a family on the ground in the burning village, unable to move. Here, again, a parallel is drawn between the fleeing mother and the one trapped in the village by the pogrom, and it is this latter figure who will dominate several of the works of 1938–1940 such as *Fire* and *The Martyr*.[18]

Once Chagall was safe in America, the image of the mother and child fleeing on foot, horseback, wagon or sled became his dominant symbol of the refugee, taking on overtones of the flight into Egypt. Thus Chagall adapted a Christian theme for the refugee to parallel the Crucifixion, symbol of the Holocaust martyr. In *Harlequin Family* of 1942–1943, also called *Flight into Egypt,* the mother and child ride out of the deserted snow-covered village on the traditional, albeit blue, ass, with "Joseph"—the Harlequin—perched precariously behind them. The same motif appears in the foreground of *Yellow Crucifixion* of 1943 (fig. 3), where, in a sketch, the Wandering Jew replaced the Harlequin in the role of Joseph. In *Christmas 1943* (fig. 4), a drawing done for *Vogue*'s Christmas issue of 1943, Chagall depicted a terrified woman carrying a worried child, fleeing under the direction of an angel, instead of the serene Madonna and Child one would expect.[19] In these works, Chagall attempted to call the Christian world's attention to the plight of the Jews in Europe by addressing them in their own visual language.

But Chagall also made a personal identification with this theme, as is clarified in *Obsession* of 1943 (fig. 5).[20] Here the mother and child are in a wagon hitched to a

Fig. 3. Marc Chagall, *Yellow Crucifixion,* 1943. Private collection. Copyright 1990 ARS N.Y./ADAGP.

blue horse, and escape from a burning building in Russia, which is symbolized by the green-domed church and the men bearing a red flag on the upper right. This image is based on two illustrations from Chagall's autobiography: visually it derives from the drawing of a cart driving away from a house; thematically, it was inspired by the story of Chagall's mother being removed on her bed from the house that burnt down at the moment the artist was born.[21]

The connection of the fleeing mother and child with Chagall's birth—and hence with his own fate as a refugee—also explains his Russification of the theme at this time by the introduction of a sleigh instead of a cart: in the large painting *War* of 1943, the mother and child flee in a sleigh from a snow-covered village alight with flames and inhabited only by a corpse. They abandon both the Wandering Jew, who escapes in a different direction, and the horse and wagon, which seem to have become bogged down in blood.[22] The mother and child also flee in *The Flying*

Fig. 4. Marc Chagall, *Christmas, 1943*, drawn for *Vogue*. Private collection. Copyright 1990 ARS N.Y./ADAGP.

Sleigh in 1945, which is now drawn by a creature, half horse and half rooster, that will have no difficulty in taking off. Although the painting is very dark, certain aspects hint at a relaxation of tension with the end of the war. The houses are dark and empty, but only the yellow strokes on the left still suggest flames. Instead, friendly smoke comes from the chimney and a samovar and cup are set out on the roof in welcome. Above the sleigh a dancing flutist appears and only the two sad, gray faces peering out from behind him like ghosts recall the tragedy of the past years.[23]

Fig. 5. Marc Chagall, *Obsession,* 1943. Private collection, France. Copyright 1990 ARS N.Y./ADAGP.

One needn't go far in seeking the reason for Chagall's obsessive interest in the fleeing mother and her child after 1941, since it derives from his own status at that time. After arriving in New York, he searched for a self-image as a refugee and recalled the story of his mother fleeing the burning house with him at his birth. He, thus, found an autobiographical precedent for his present state in an image that clearly suggested the fact that he had been *saved*. This was, for him, a more comforting symbol than the two other refugee types with which he identified.

The identification of the refugee artist with the refugee theme is not unique to Chagall. Other artists expressed this, either by introducing a personal note, as Chagall had done, or by adding details that strip the theme of its generalizations and relate it to events taking place in mid-twentieth century Europe; this is particularly true of these artists' works once they themselves became refugees.[24] Such a personal approach is even evident in the more symbolic works of Jacques Lipchitz, whose refugee themes formed a major part of his work from 1933 to 1948 until the creation of the State of Israel turned his thoughts in a more optimistic direction.

Lipchitz began working on the theme of flight in 1933 as part of a series of sculptures that expressed his personal reactions to Hitler's rise to power. In the earliest of three small *bozzettos* of the *Rescue of the Child,* the child is lifted out of harm's way by a pair of hands. In the two other sculptures, the reasons for this action become clear: a woman holds the child aloft to protect it from those who try unavailingly to drag her down. In one version, the mother marches resolutely forward, pushing past both the snakes that attack her and the father who "struggles vainly to free them."[25] Lipchitz explained these works, "The child is really my sculpture, all that was in danger. . . . This was a time when, with the spread of fascism, I had a terrible fear that everything I had done would be destroyed."[26]

The fear that both he and his art were in danger grew with the worsening of the political situation and the outbreak of the war in 1939. At this time, Lipchitz sketched another theme entitled *Rescue* (fig. 6) that stressed a more pessimistic view of the refugee's plight. He explained that these drawings depict a man rescuing a woman and that it was "an instance of wishful thinking, a desire to escape from the nightmare in which I felt I was involved." Yet, since the woman's legs have been cut off and she is suffering from her wounds, she is unable to flee: her mutilated legs appear in mid-air while her hands and hair hang down behind her. She turns face upwards toward the man, her large breasts stressing her femininity, and he grasps her around the waist, dragging her along with him. Despite the optimistic title, whether the man will really succeed in escaping with his burden is highly debatable.[27] This desperate image, made at a time when Lipchitz was obsessed with the war, may have been influenced by his wife's reluctance to leave France.

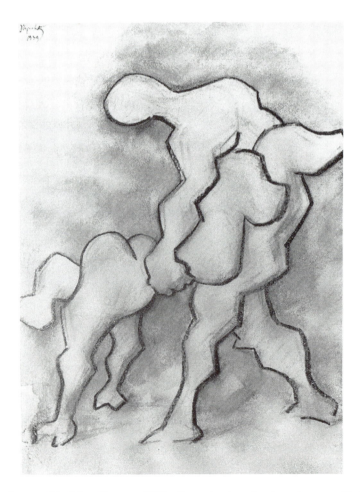

Fig. 6. Jacques Lipchitz, *Rescue*, 1939. Present whereabouts unknown. © Jacques Lipchitz/VAGA New York, 1990.

In May 1940, however, with the Nazis at the gates of Paris, they had no choice. Once Lipchitz and his wife succeeded in escaping, he expressed their attempts to flee in a more optimistic, albeit still anxious, vein. *Flight,* executed in Toulouse in 1940, shows a fleeing man and woman who blend together in their haste, united in their attempt to get away. The woman twists around to look back, but the man holds her about her waist, bearing her forward. *Arrival* (fig. 7), the first statue Lipchitz executed after landing in New York in 1941, was inspired by a burst of energy and a feeling of a return to life.[28] Although based on *Flight,* the entire motion of the figures in *Arrival* moves forward in the direction indicated by the man, and the woman now holds the rescued child aloft. In the sketches, the child resembled that of the 1933 *bozzettos;* in the statue itself, the child bears a striking similarity to Lipchitz's *Mother and Child* of 1939–1945, which he began sketching in Europe

Fig. 7. Jacques Lipchitz, *Arrival,* 1941. Des Moines Art Center, Rose F. Rosenfield Purchase Fund, 1959. © Jacques Lipchitz/VAGA New York, 1990.

but sculpted in New York. The child is, thus, the still unborn statue of the *Mother and Child;* it was not emphasized when Lipchitz himself was in flight, but on arrival, however, it is held out in front, the first to reach safety.[29] This relatively small statue is the basis for one of Lipchitz's large stone carvings, the 1941–1943 *Return of the Child* (fig. 8), which celebrates the sculptor's return to his work after a year's absence.[30] All here is stability rather than motion: the mother sits firmly, catching the child she had tossed playfully in the air, while the child, waving his winglike hands, kisses her in a gesture that merges the two bodies together.

Not all refugee artists felt as joyful about their arrival in a haven of safety as did Chagall and Lipchitz. Faced with establishing a new life, they often felt insecure and

Fig. 8.   Jacques Lipchitz, *Return of the Child,* 1941–1943. Guggenheim Museum, New York. © Jacques Lipchitz/VAGA New York, 1990.

depressed, unsure of their welcome and of their ability to adapt, and haunted by the world they had left. One of the earliest expressions of these feelings and of the deep pessimism they evoked is found in the works of George Grosz, who emigrated to the United States in 1932 from Germany and became an American citizen in 1938. A Communist and antifascist since the early 1920s, Grosz discovered in 1930 that his caricatures of the monstrous evils rampant in Germany had become a reality.[31] Despite a wish to forget politics after arriving in America, the land of which he had dreamed for many years, Grosz—bravado aside—continued to feel insecure, haunted by nightmares of a war that would destroy Germany.[32] In *1932*, executed c. 1933, Grosz depicted his arrival in the United States: he climbs out of the water toward New York's skyscrapers, leaving behind him a Europe ablaze with the war that he foresaw.[33] In comparison to Lipchitz's joyful *Arrival*, Grosz's watercolor is somber and pessimistic. This mood is echoed in his *Self-Portrait no. 2* of 1936, in which Grosz depicts himself calmly painting an exploding city that stretches like a vision behind him, as well as in *Remembering* of 1937 (fig. 9) in which he sits hunched over and dejected among the ruins, with a destroyed city and a man supporting a victim behind him.[34] This last painting is a compound image. It is a self-portrait, but the pose parallels his description of his Jewish friend, Hermann (Hans) Borchardt, whom Grosz went to welcome at Ellis Island after the latter had been freed from Dachau, "He had been asked to wait . . . but he knew no word of

Fig. 9. George Grosz, *Remembering*, 1937. Estate of George Grosz/VAGA New York, 1990.

English. So he sat there, bewildered and frightened, without a jacket, in a raincoat over a shirt, a conspicuous figure under the scorching sun."[35] Grosz—the old Christian refugee—thus identified here with Borchardt—the new Jewish refugee— at the moment of his arrival.[36]

After the outbreak of the Second World War, Grosz painted a symbolic self-portrait, *The Wanderer c. 1940–1943*, in which he wades through a swamp against a background of flames accompanied only by ravens.[37] He explained this painting in a letter written at the end of 1940, "I painted a little picture—*The Wanderer in the Rain*—myself of course. . . . The resonance of explosions and destruction often shakes me bodily." Two years later he wrote of himself as a "disillusioned former fighter," but through it all, he stated, "I shall survive" although there was "a certain horror in me which could not be banished."[38] This "resonance of explosions," which he paints in his refugee pictures, haunted Grosz despite his will to survive and would not allow him to develop freely.

There are several different elements at work in the reactions of refugees such as Grosz, and they can be clarified by studying the way these elements appear in the art of other refugees. The first problem involves the feeling of identification with other refugees. Although safe, the refugee artist was only too aware that others were trying to follow in his footsteps and were in need of help. This is clearly demonstrated in Grosz's identification with Borchardt and in the way many other refugees developed the image of the immigrant boats on which they had made their voyage to salvation.

We have already noted the various types of refugee figures surrounding Christ in Chagall's *White Crucifixion* of 1938 (fig. 1). On the left, Chagall depicted a large rowboat filled with refugees who lean over the side or cry for help. The boat floats on a white river that merges with the snow-covered bank of a village in which a pogrom has just taken place. In contrast to the refugees who flee on foot, the boat has no apparent direction: it has neither sails nor rudder, and the attempts of one figure to guide it with a stick, or an oar, appear fruitless. A similar hopeless condition appears in Marcel Janco's version of this theme: here, too, a rowboat without oars or sails is overloaded with people, including a mother and child.[39] Some of the refugees are sunk in melancholy; others raise their arms to heaven to beseech God for help. Despite the motion engendered by its diagonal position, the boat has no clear direction.

On the other hand, shortly after his arrival in New York, Chagall affirmed his belief in ships as a means of escape. In *Yellow Christ* of c. 1941, he places a steamship opposite the burning village: the refugees who flee the village pass before the figure of Christ and head for the safety of the ship.[40] This relative optimism is also echoed by Peretz Mayer, who was evacuated by the Germans to Mauritius by boat in 1939, and by Lasar Segall, in his large painting *The Immigrant Ship* of 1939–1941. Both depict large ships packed to the gills, as were the rowboats in the works of Chagall and Janco. Segall stresses the overcrowded condition by using a masthead view of the deck passengers who try to lead some sort of life while crammed together among the crates. Many lean over the side of the ship, sick or watching the surging gray waves; others sleep sitting up or lying down in cramped positions; still others stare off into space. Although there are no life-affirming activities here—people do not converse, eat, or play with children—and the dreadful conditions under which refugees traveled are emphasized, they are at least on their way toward a safe haven.[41]

However, not all would make it. In February 1942 the refugee ship *Struma* struck a mine outside Istanbul, after the passengers were denied entry into Palestine and Turkey and were set adrift without adequate fuel. All 769 passengers were killed. This event shocked the world, but it brought no clear changes in immigration policies.[42] It did, however, inspire several artists who had fled Europe by ship and who, therefore, identified personally with the tragedy. Thus, for instance, in Chagall's *Yellow Crucifixion* of 1943 (fig. 3)—a variant on his earlier, more optimistic painting—a village still burns on the right, but, on the left, the *Struma* sinks and drowning refugees reach out for help in vain.[43] Mordechai Ardon, who fled from Germany to Palestine in 1933, also planned a painting around this theme, but all that survives is a series of monotypes—one showing a woman's head, with sorrowful eyes and mouth open in an ineffectual scream; another, more poignant and more clearly connected to the catastrophe, depicting hands reaching up above the water and slowly sinking into it as the refugees drown; and a third (fig. 10) in which he added to the hands a half-skeletal survivor, one leg eaten away to the bone, who hobbles away on crutches—an even more pessimistic symbol of the refugee as a wounded survivor than anything Grosz had envisaged at the time.[44]

Fig. 10. Mordechai Ardon, Sketch for the *Struma*, 1942. Mordechai Ardon Collection, Jerusalem.

Abraham Rattner, an American Jew who fled France by boat shortly before the Germans entered Paris, echoed this theme in his *Survivors* of 1942 (fig. 11), a rather ironic title, as not only were there no survivors from the *Struma,* but there is not much hope that there will be any in this fiery painting. Rattner portrayed sailboats sinking in the background, their masts protruding above the waves, while in the foreground, drowning figures on a blazing ship raise their arms in a futile attempt to attract attention, one of them grabbing hold of a mast in an attempt to save himself. The futility of their efforts is stressed by the composition: the sea rises almost to the top of the painting, and an upside-down face at the bottom reinforces the feeling of sinking into the waves.[45]

In these works, the artists use the immigrant boat as an expression both of their own escape and of their identification with the tribulations and tragedies of all the

Fig. 11.   Abraham Rattner, *Survivors,* 1942. © The Metropolitan Museum of Art, New York, gift of David M. Solinger, 1951 (51.162).

refugees. The importance of the *Struma* as a theme in their works points out to what extent they not only expressed their own plight, but also identified with other refugees. This is clear as well in Oskar Kokoschka's *The Crab* of 1940–1941 (fig. 12). Here, a gigantic crab stands guard on the shore, facing the sea, ready to pounce on the refugee who has escaped the ship and is swimming toward land. Kokoschka has explained that this was a parable of the times: the crab is the unreceptive host of the refugee and may refuse him entry to his country and send him back to his death or—at best—may intern him in a camp for enemy aliens. The crab is thus a personification not of the Nazis, but of the nationalistic and corrupt nations whose treatment of the refugees struck Kokoschka as cruel and filled him with anxiety. Though safe in England, he remained concerned over the fate of other refugees and took his country of refuge to task for its attitude toward others like him.[46]

The concern for the fate of other refugees returns after the war in depictions of boats carrying the camp survivors, now refugees in their turn seeking a place to rest and recover. Myron Sima and Jakob Steinhardt took a tragic view of this situation in 1945–1947, expressing the political realities they faced in Palestine where the British kept the door firmly shut against Jewish immigration. Sima's *Refugees* (fig. 13) seem to be located in a rowboat adrift on the sea, perhaps trying to run the

Fig. 12. Oskar Kokoschka, *The Crab*, 1940–1941. Tate Gallery, London/Art Resource, New York.

Fig. 13. Myron Sima, *Refugees*, 1945. Museum of Art, Ein Harod, Israel.

British blockade.[47] They sleep or huddle exhausted on the floor, green-faced and so ill that the one on the right, whose skeletal body is exposed under the garments, seems to be dying. Sima holds out no hope for these refugees: they are static and only the blue-green overall color of the painting suggests that they are on the high seas—there is no clue that they will survive long enough to arrive at their unstated destination. Steinhardt's 1945 *Refugees* and the figures in his 1947 woodcut on this theme also seem to be in a boat on the open sea with no port in sight.[48] They, too, are completely exhausted, but they show some life and are generally less emaciated than Sima's survivors. In the painting, their static quality is broken by an old couple who attempt a short walk on deck. They have nowhere to go, but even the attempt at motion generates some hope. In the woodcut, three of the figures are asleep, but the man in the foreground and the child in the background look out over the sea in search of land. This particular type of flight ended after 1948, its successful conclusion usually depicted by portraying the refugees on dry land. But the boat would remain a basic symbol in the works of several refugee artists, in particular Naftali Bezem, who constantly uses it both as a symbol of his own escape from Europe and as a symbol of the postwar emigration of the survivors to Israel.[49]

Grosz's works indicate, however, that the need to identify with other refugees was far from being the only problem of those who had found a safe haven before or during the war. Another was their feelings of insecurity, which could take many different forms, depending on where the artist landed. Thus, for instance, Lipchitz, safe in New York, concentrated on the hard road the refugee had to take to adjust himself to a new world in time of war. Whereas in *Arrival* (fig. 7), he expressed his joy on landing safely in New York, *The Exile's Path* of 1941 (fig. 14), created several months later, reveals a different reaction to events. Lipchitz explained that although arriving in New York was like coming "from death to life," living and working there were very hard for him: he didn't speak the language and it was difficult to find the money and materials he needed in order to devote himself to sculpture. In short, he underwent all the hardships faced by a refugee arriving almost penniless in a foreign land. His narrow escape from Europe (leaving just before his passport was invalidated); the harrowing passage on a small Portuguese boat, herded together with other refugees; and an almost fatal mishap when he tried to climb down the ladder on the wrong side of the boat and nearly landed in the

Fig. 14. Jacques Lipchitz, *The Exile's Path*, 1941. Present whereabouts unknown. © Jacques Lipchitz/VAGA New York, 1990.

sea—all of these traumatic experiences continued to prey on his mind.[50] These are the feelings he expressed in *The Exile's Path*, emphasizing the hardships of the refugee's life, both in name and content. In this drawing, a man, moving toward the left, carries a woman on his back, catching her arm over his shoulder while her leg drags behind her. It is thus closer in feeling to *Rescue* (fig. 6) than to his *Flight* or the exultant *Arrival*. The refugees may have arrived, but the long, hard road of exile still stretches before them, and they move slowly down it, heavily burdened.[51]

Lipchitz also expressed his ambivalent feelings as a refugee in several works of 1941–1943 that are related to his life on two different levels. He stated that one of the series of statues he made at this time was inspired by his love for a very difficult woman, which explains the full-bosomed woman who stands in the center of these works.[52] Yet this series is, on another level, an expression of the artist's problems of acclimatization in America and led to his symbolization of himself in *The Pilgrim* of 1942.

Fig. 15. Jacques Lipchitz, *Blossoming*, 1941–1942. Museum of Modern Art, New York.

In the earliest of the series, *Blossoming* of 1941–1942 (fig. 15), the human–plant rises like a primitive fertility goddess from her cactuslike cocoon whose shell and legs bristle with sharp thorns.[53] Arms outstretched, she holds her protective shell in such a way that it is unclear whether she is opening it or retaining her hold on it to cover herself up in case of emergency. Like Lipchitz himself in New York, she is emerging but not emerged, a parable of the refugee in a new haven, unsure of his welcome. However, instead of gaining confidence as time advances, this blossoming figure is the most exposed in the entire series. The works of 1942 have optimistic titles, for example, *The Promise* and *Spring*, but they either reaffirm the ambiguous emerging/imprisoning action or they completely incarcerate the figure. This is particularly evident in the sketch for *Spring* in which Lipchitz experimented with various ways of reclosing the spikelike bars around the buxom woman, finally tying the openings with wires threaded through holes in the cactus bars.[54] Meanwhile, changes were taking place in the woman herself. Whereas *Yara I* resembles *Blossoming*, the appearance of *Yara II* is forbidding: spikes cover her legs, arms and breasts as the figure becomes more skeletal.[55] This skeletal symbolism is stressed in the relief *Album Page* of 1942, in which the cavities of a pelvic cross-section are tied with wires, and in *Myrrah* of 1942–1943, a frightening apparition of spike-covered bones—the effect is heightened by its feminine name.[56] No longer is the thorny shell inhabited by the full-bosomed female with her promise of the future. It is void and desolate, haunting in its associations with a desecrated human body.

The reasons for this development are complex. It obviously parallels the vicissitudes of Lipchitz's relationship with a "difficult" woman. On the other hand, *Blossoming* was begun before America's entry into the war in December 1941, whereas most of the other statues were done during the dark days of 1942 when Japan and Germany were advancing on all fronts. As far as Lipchitz was concerned, even the Allied landing in North Africa at the end of 1942 was depressing, as it led to the German occupation of southern France, which had been a temporary haven for the Jews and for Lipchitz himself. Thus, the statues also reflect the artist's growing depression during the war, notwithstanding his own safety.

As such, they prepare the way for *The Pilgrim* of 1942 (fig. 16) in which, Lipchitz explained, he portrayed himself "blooming" after recovering from the numbness he had felt on arriving in America.[57] This accounts for the similarity to *Blossoming* in the leafy forms on the legs and neck as well as the flowering pilgrim's staff and the sunlike head. However, it does not explain the devastating effect of the statue with its blasted body nor the ambiguity of even its positive aspects, signified by Lipchitz's own words, "His head is like an exploding bomb."[58] This feeling of destruction had not been evident in the sketch, wherein the accent is more on blossoming.[59] In the statue, the former naturalistic leaves of the legs become flamelike and drooping and the pilgrim's flowering branch hardens into a spiked club. The most important change occurs in the flower that had symbolized the pilgrim's body in the sketch: in the statue it becomes a gaping hole surrounded by jagged, wilting petals and filled with battling forms. Lipchitz explained that *The Pilgrim* "is disembowelled, with something like a snake entangled with a rose within his bowels" but that the snakelike intestines seem rather to suggest a fighting couple. Lipchitz admitted that these exploding, fighting forms contradict the opti-

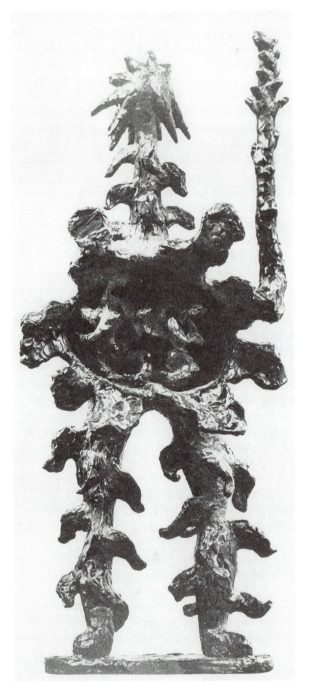

Fig. 16.   Jacques Lipchitz, *The Pilgrim,* 1942. Private
collection. © Jacques Lipchitz/VAGA New York, 1990.

mism of the image, but he claimed that the ambiguities are caused by the statue's affirmation that there is "hope within this period of disaster."[60] The spectator, however, receives the opposite message: *The Pilgrim* may be blooming and still holding on to his budding staff of hope, but he is also a gutted figure of death, carrying within himself a struggle revealed by his dreadful wound. His ambiguous symbolism clearly expresses the mixed feelings of a rescued refugee living in a war-torn world and echoes the "resonance of explosions" that Grosz had mentioned apropos his own paintings of himself as a refugee in this period.

Whereas the problems of the refugee expressed by those who found haven in America were severe enough, they were minor compared to those of artists who remained in Europe. Even England, free of Nazi occupation though it was, did not seem overly secure to many of the refugees, as can be seen by an examination of the works of Jankel Adler. Having originally fled Germany for Paris in 1933, Adler joined the Free Polish Army in 1939 and was evacuated with it to Scotland. He settled in London in 1943.[61] In 1941 Adler began depicting figures confined in a small, dark room as though in hiding, either staring at the viewer or occupied with some activity such as the priestly blessing, which they hope will save them. They seem afraid to venture out-of-doors for fear of being cut to pieces and turned into the type of lifeless sculpture that often occupies the outdoor region in these paintings.[62] The reason for these feelings becomes clear from a series of drawings Adler did in 1943, three of which narrate a story in a straightforward manner. One of them (fig. 17) portrays two scenes: above, a group of Jews hides in a small, dark room, the women turning their fearful gaze toward the spectator; below, a couple leave the safety of their home whose door, with its protecting mezuzah, is clearly delineated at the left, and they are caught in a Nazi searchlight. In a slightly later sketch, they are shown naked, as though stripped to be shot, and their bodies have become fragmented as they undergo abstraction.[63] Another sketch of this series is also divided into two scenes: on top, a woman in a dark room (found in many of the paintings of this period) bursts through the door in exactly the same position as that of the bearded Jew leaving his hiding place in the first sketch. As she leaves, she begins to be fragmented into geometric planes in a way that suggests that she will soon turn into the abstracted image that stands outside her room. Below, a reclining figure has been broken up in this manner—the suggestion is that the figure is dead and dehumanized.[64] The anxiety so openly rendered in these scenes shows a different kind of insecurity in a place of refuge: Adler identifies not only with other refugees, but also with those Jews in hiding in occupied Europe. Safe in England, he still remains "in hiding."[65]

The reasons for his insecurity are clear since he eventually developed this theme of hiding and broken figures into the painting *Destruction* of 1943, which shows both the effect of the blitz on him and his fear of being trapped by the flaming strands of "barbed wire" that encircle the "legs" of his semi-abstract figures.[66] London was obviously not the ideal refuge, and the blitz, with its concommitant need to hide below ground in a shelter, exacerbated anxieties of capture and death rather than calming them.

Perhaps this is why it was so easy for Adler to identify with his friend, Josef Herman, when the latter received word in 1942 from the Red Cross that his whole

Fig. 17.   Jankel Adler, *Jews in Hiding,* 1943. Present whereabouts unknown.

family in Poland had perished. To console Herman, Adler painted *Two Orphans* (fig. 18), representing both artists.[67] The picture depicts two bald children, seen through a fog, who carry the usual refugee bundles. They stand before a dark gray background bordered by a black band, symbolic of mourning. Their eyes stare out of their grayish faces in horror at the spectator, but they are kept from entering the viewer's space by a bright pink-and-black bar that cuts across the entire painting, including the border at the right. Thus, they seem cut off from the horror they view beyond this barrier, a horror that occupies the spectator's space and that has turned

Fig. 18.   Jankel Adler, *Two Orphans,* 1942. Herman Collection, London.

them into orphans. Safe in their blacked-out refuge, they find neither solace nor relief from the horrors of the Holocaust.

The problem was, of course, especially severe for those refugees who were trapped in occupied Europe, as Max Beckmann was in Holland and Felix Nussbaum in Belgium. Beckmann, a German Christian, knew he had a good chance of surviving and could move about with a fair degree of freedom. However, despite his portrayal of himself in 1937 as *The Liberated One* released from his chains, before and during the war he showed himself alone or with friends hiding in a closed room, usually lit only by a candle.[68]

Nussbaum, a German Jew, had been expelled from the Prussian Academy of Art in Rome in 1933 and had found refuge in Belgium. He was interned for several months at Saint Cyprien, France, in 1940, but he escaped back to Belgium only to be caught once more in 1944 and sent to Auschwitz where he met his death. The four years during which Nussbaum remained in hiding after having spent the previous five years as a refugee in prewar Belgium decisively affected his choice of subject matter. He took an increasingly dim view of his situation, occasionally expressing it with sharp irony. During the time he was a refugee, he hid his worries under a smiling carnival mask and constantly painted himself with a variety of masklike expressions, costumes and personalities. At the same time, his interest in boats and harbors from 1933 onward suggests a wish to escape farther afield, away from Europe, a wish he never realized. His paintings begin to deal with death in the early 1930s, and his depictions of destroyed buildings from 1933 onward demonstrate his awareness of the underlying threat to his existence.[69] From mid-1939 on, a stronger feeling of anxiety pervades his work: the boats are replaced by close-up shots of his hiding place and the view from the attic window. He portrays himself, his wife and his friends as increasingly consumed by anxiety, hiding in the street or behind a window, often marked by a yellow star.[70] In *The Dispossessed* of 1941 (fig. 19), he depicts a group of refugees—including himself and his wife on the left—standing still rather than being on the move as other artists tended to show them. Cut off—by the hanging tree on the right and the lightning on the left—from the roads at the far sides of the painting, they stand massed one behind and above the other, some turning toward heaven, others in despair. Only the boy at the left displays a clear element of hope: jeered at by the man directly to his right, he blows on a dandelion as he makes a wish. This painting—executed shortly after Nussbaum had escaped a transport back to Germany from the Saint Cyprien camp and returned to Brussels to go into hiding—is a clear statement of the feelings of helplessness of the refugee who has no place to go and fears that his arrest is only a matter of time.[71]

In a *Self-Portrait* dating from 1943, Nussbaum portrayed himself outdoors, boxed in by the walls behind him, furtively presenting his identity card that marks him as a Jew and emphasizing the large yellow Star of David on his coat. The details in

Fig. 19.   Felix Nussbaum, *The Dispossessed,* 1941. Private collection, Osnabrück.

Nussbaum's *Self-Portrait* are especially significant as he had no such identity card and, since he was in hiding, did not wear a yellow star. He was thus stressing both his identification as a Jew and his fears of being caught out in the open because of it. Rather than presenting himself in hiding (as Beckmann had done, despite his ability to move around freely), Nussbaum—deprived of this ability—shows himself in a moment of danger moving from one hiding place to the next.[72] In a work dating from the same period, he depicted himself painting but labeled the bottles of paint thinner between his easel and palette with a skull and crossbones and the words "nostalgia" and "suffering"; the bottle at the far left, beneath a mask, is labeled "humor," the ingredient needed by the artist to survive, which is also perceptible in his ironic smile.[73] It was, however, a black humor that he began to portray in his work, which concentrated increasingly on the subject of death, the capture of the dispossessed refugees and their extermination.[74]

This deeply pessimistic view of the situation is echoed in a drawing Avigdor Arikha composed as a boy in a camp in Transnistria. He depicted an emaciated mother and two children in rags carrying a pail to beg for food. They try to get into a house while a well-fed man peers unobtrusively out the window, pretending not to be home. The title tells the story, "Starving refugees knock on the door of a house belonging to Ukrainians. They [the Ukrainians] usually denounced them [the refugees] and they were shot."[75]

Strangely enough, given the situation at the time, the place where Jewish refugee artists apparently felt safest and least disturbed by anxiety was Palestine. Werner Haftmann has even gone so far as to exclude this refuge from his book on persecuted artists because these Jewish artists did not feel as though they were refugees since entirely identified with the developing state.[76] Although this was not entirely the case (as we have seen from the discussions on the depictions of the boats of refugees [e.g., fig. 13]), the Palestinian phenomenon *is* fairly unique. Most of the artists turned their backs resolutely and often successfully on their former lands and lives, especially if they came from Germany. Very few of them returned to Germany. The exception to this rule is Lea Grundig, who is also not normative in having concentrated during the entire time she was in Tel-Aviv on refugees and the Holocaust, a subject her fellow refugee artists shunned as far as possible, trying to ignore and block out the events taking place in Europe.[77] Still conscious of their refugee status and often of their inability to speak Hebrew, they tried to replace the past with the present. Steinhardt and Ardon concentrated on painting landscapes and adjusting to the strong local sunlight. Steinhardt also sought a replacement for the Eastern European Jewish milieu he loved—which he knew was about to be destroyed—by constantly depicting the Old City and the other religious quarters of Jerusalem, which reminded him of the shtetl.[78] Yet every now and then, the outside world did intrude: as in the grotesques Steinhardt drew while listening to the hated voice of Hitler over the radio and in his constant stress on blind beggars; or in Ardon's *Struma* series and his *Masks* of 1938, a painting in which he caustically commented on the Anschluss of Austria.[79] Thus, although they devoted proportionately fewer works either to their refugee status or to the Holocaust, the difference between them and the artists who emigrated to the United States was more one of willed forgetfulness than of an altogether different experience.

If the life of the refugees was not difficult enough in the various places to which they fled, an added element was provided by their feelings of guilt and mourning as the war came to an end. Such feelings seem logical in an artist such as George Grosz, who as a German antifascist felt he had failed in his war against the Nazis. Revolted by his countrymen's deeds, nonetheless, he mourned the ruin of his fatherland. He could portray both the evils the Germans perpetuated and the punishment exacted from them, but he could also state in despair, "My mother died in one of those last air raids over Berlin. . . . That was, maybe, the only tie which existed between me and Berlin or Germany. We survivors have to survive, and that is all. Surviving up to the next holocaust."[80] The word "holocaust" here refers to the destruction of Germany rather than to that of the Jews, and it is this picture of a destroyed Germany, symbolic of a destroyed world, that he depicts in his ironic *Peace II* of 1946 (fig. 20). Here, haunted by his mother's death, he painted a "self-portrait" as a survivor emerging from the ruins of a hopelessly devastated, still burning world, one in which peace is synonymous with death.[81]

Such mourning over a destroyed Germany is somewhat more startling when it is found in the works of a German Jew. However, Lea Grundig, returning to East Germany in 1948 to rejoin her husband and to take up a position as a major Communist artist, did just this in her portrayal of a thin woman, aged by suffering, who stands mournfully before the ruins of Dresden in *O Germany, Pale Mother!* The title adds another dimension to the scene as it is taken from a prewar poem by Bertolt Brecht—a paraphrase of *Lamentations*—which castigates Germany for oppressing and murdering the best of her sons.[82] Whereas Brecht wished to express the plight of the proletariat exploited by the capitalists, Grundig applied his poem to the Holocaust she had barely escaped and to the moral as well as the physical state of the Germany to which she returned.

Although Jews usually did not experience the kind of nightmarish reality in which Grosz lived, they, too, felt guilty, but *their* guilt was evoked by the very fact that they had survived while others died and that their art and deeds had been unable to save their loved ones. Indeed, Chagall had begun to express his sense of guilt at the beginning of the war, shortly after arriving in New York. In the final version of *Between Light and Darkness* of 1943, a bird-headed mother and her child do not flee the burning village in the sled at the right, but they stay, appealing to the artist and telling him what is happening behind him—in the painting and in reality—in the Europe and Russia he had left. *Between Light and Darkness*—or in French *Entre chien et loup* (literally, *Between Dog and Wolf*)—suggests Chagall's feelings as he stood between Europe's fearsome experiences and the safety he found in New York.[83] Standing before his easel, his head joined to that of his wife Bella in a way that highlights both their union and his split identity, he tries to put down on canvas the scenes taking place behind him.

However, his faith in his art's ability to render this reality was soon brought into question. In 1944, well aware of what was really happening in Europe, Chagall made a speech in which he expressed an ambivalent attitude toward his art, "Today is a time when there is no room for art. There is a war. But still in the fire, people come to talk about culture, poetry and art, because all this is also our weapon. . . . We, the Jewish artists today, are like grass, maybe nice grass, but grass on

Fig. 20. George Grosz, *Peace II*, 1946. Whitney Museum of American Art, New York. ©
Estate of George Grosz/VAGA New York, 1990.

a cemetery."[84] He stated these ideas even more clearly in 1950 in a poem "To the Martyred Artists":

> They call me. They drag me into their
> pit—me, the innocent—the guilty.
> They ask me: "Where were you?"
> I ran away . . .
> They were taken to the death baths . . .
>
> How can I, how shall I shed tears?
> They were long since soaked in salt—
> from my eyes. . .
> How shall I weep
> when every day I heard:
> the last plank is being torn from my roof,
> when I am too weary to wage war
> for the bit of ground on which I've been left standing,
> in which later I'll be laid to sleep.[85]

These ideas also surface in two paintings. In the 1944 *My Village—Homage to the Past,* Chagall turns from his easel to look at the wintry village and to converse with its female spirit, and reappears above to lean mournfully on a tombstone.[86] In 1947 he reworked the *Apparition of the Artist's Family* (fig. 21) that he had begun in 1936 after visiting Poland and sensing the danger facing the Jews.[87] In both versions, the artist, sitting before his easel, turns to discover his family, who appear behind him accompanied by an angel. While they cry out to him and entreat him in alarm, he can only respond by painting them: he "saves" them by immortalizing them in his art. Several differences between the two versions reflect the events of the intervening years. For instance, Chagall now added an image of his wife Bella as a bride on the right, as she had died in 1944, and he changed the colors of the background from a night sky to a flaming red. Furthermore, he altered his own position: he no longer actively paints, although the colors on the canvas are those of the scene behind him; instead, he holds his hand to his heart in a gesture that combines heartache with a pledge to remember. The fact that in 1936 he could respond to the apparitions who haunted him only through his art and that in 1947 he is *not* painting parallels his ambivalent words: artists are like "grass on a cemetery"—decorative, commemorative and providing hope for the future, but helpless in averting death. Thus, in 1947, Chagall reverted to a prewar premonition of disaster in order to express his feelings of futility and his guilt over having survived while his family was destroyed.

Similar feelings were expressed by Lipchitz in his postwar works in which he developed two prewar themes in a conscious attempt to perpetuate and resolve his earlier ideas.[88] *Rescue I* of 1945 is a straightforward development of the drawings: the man runs forward, clutching the woman around her waist, below her full breasts; her hair streams out behind her and her arms fall to the ground merging with his legs while her mutilated legs dangle in the air behind him.[89] Despite this similarity, the whole feeling of the work has changed. Using round Arplike forms,

Fig. 21. Marc Chagall, *Apparition of the Artist's Family,* 1936–37, 1947. Marc Chagall estate. Copyright 1990 ARS N.Y./ADAGP.

Lipchitz has created a light, joyous statue unrelated in mood to the desperation of the drawings. The couple are united in a lyrical dance of love, expressed in the smooth, harmonious shapes and aided by the joining of the arms and legs at the base to create a light, rocking motion reminiscent of that of a child's cradle or hobbyhorse. The artist explained that although he had wanted to strike a serious note, the lyrical feeling resulted from his joy at the war's end, a joy that dissipated the anger that had inspired the original drawings.[90]

This joy was, however, short-lived: in 1946, in an advertisement for his *Drawings* portfolio, Lipchitz published a new sketch of *The Exile's Path* (fig. 22), significantly different from the original.[91] The two figures, now united into one, totter on weak legs, their arms hanging down helplessly as they topple over. Instead of celebrating the end of the war and a new start to life, the refugees have no more strength to continue, and they fall victim to the despair and exhaustion that have overtaxed them physically and spiritually.

Rescue II of 1947 (fig. 23) also changes the meaning both of *Rescue I* (1945) and of the 1939 drawings (fig. 6), a change already evident in a transitional *bozzetto*.[92] In the latter, the man holds the woman up with one hand, clutching his head with the

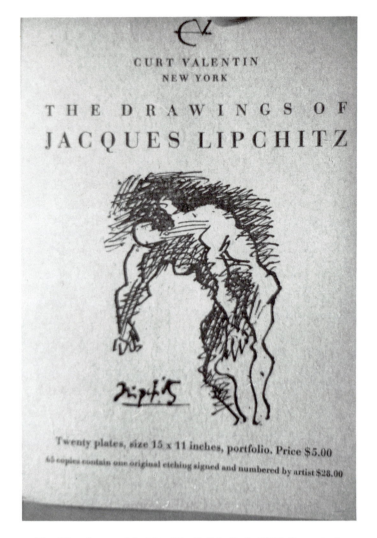

Fig. 22. Jacques Lipchitz, *The Exile's Path,* 1946. Present whereabouts unknown. © Jacques Lipchitz/VAGA New York, 1990.

other. Her arms no longer merge with his legs in a melodic line as in *Rescue I,* but
create a tense situation: leaning on her elbows, the woman grasps her partner's legs
firmly, preventing him from moving forward and rescuing her. The lines here are
still relatively fluid; they become heavier and more angular in the finished statue in
keeping with the feeling of desperation expressed there, a term Lipchitz constantly
repeated in speaking of this work.[93] In *Rescue II,* the woman halts the motion in
another way: her hands are set firmly on the ground, and she merges with the man,
her mutilated leg appearing to grow like a tail from his buttocks. The main change,
however, is in the man, who is cleft in two. Instead of carrying the woman, he

Fig. 23. Jacques Lipchitz, *Rescue II,* 1947. Norton Gallery of Art, West Palm Beach, Florida.

stands over her clutching his split head in despair as he turns it heavenward, his mouth open in a scream.

All these changes can be understood by examining what happened to Lipchitz during 1945–1947. The new version of *The Exile's Path* was done after the enormity of the Holocaust became known in New York. The period of joy was replaced by one of mourning, especially as Lipchitz blamed himself for not rescuing his niece Irene from Warsaw.[94] *Rescue II* was created following his trip to France in the spring of 1946. In Paris, Lipchitz felt haunted by the past and by his own feelings of guilt, to the point that he could not bear to be alone in his old home in Boulogne-sur-Seine (now Boulogne-Billancourt). He was desolated to find that several old friends,

Chaim Soutine and Max Jacob among them, had died during the war because they were Jews.[95] Although he was greeted joyously by Picasso and all his friends who had remained in France, he felt himself separated from them by a subtle barrier: they had gone through a war that united them, whereas he had spent the years in relative comfort in New York. This estrangement was heightened by the fact that Lipchitz had become acclimated to New York's art scene. Unable to readjust to life in Paris, he left his wife, who refused to go with him, and returned to New York at the end of 1946.[96] It was at this time that he created *Rescue II* (1947), which expressed his mourning over what he had found in Europe and his self-reproach over his own escape.

The refugee situation, compounded of alienation, anxiety, attempts to survive and adjust and, for those who managed to do so, a sense of guilt at having succeeded, strongly influenced the works of the artists discussed here. Not all of them responded in the same way or used the same images, but enough similarities can be found among them to enable us to discuss categories of reaction that can also be found in other refugee artists' works. Most of them depicted or symbolized the various shades of their refugee status and expressed anxiety and guilt. However, these leitmotifs varied not only according to the personal characters of the artists, but according to the countries in which they found refuge. The possibly surprising feature is that these reactions were shared by non-Jewish German left-wing anti-fascists and Jews from all sorts of backgrounds and that, despite all of the variations in their reactions, they show a unity of thought and purpose, of feeling and of the ways to express these feelings in their art.

Notes

1. The persecution of Jews and Communists had actually begun before 1933, the year in which the concentration camps at Dachau and Oranienburg were opened and in which the boycott against Jewish stores and other antisemitic actions began. The war on Modern Art was clearly launched by Hitler's speech at the opening of the Haus der Kunst exhibition in 1937 and the opening of the exhibition of Decadent Art that directly followed it, but it had been preceded by the ousting in 1933 of most modern artists from the Academy of Arts and their teaching posts, along with the closing of the Bauhaus.

2. Although Italy had more advanced ideas about art than Germany, the imposition of antisemitic restrictions in 1938 had caused certain artists, such as Corrado Cagli, to emigrate to Paris and later to the United States (Enrico Crispolti and Giuseppe Marchiori, *Corrado Cagli* [Turin: 1964], 133). George Kars, Hans and Sophie Arp, who escaped in 1942 to Switzerland, are among the few artists who managed to get away after the end of 1941 (Miriam Novitch, Lucy Dawidowicz and Tom L. Freudenheim, *Spiritual Resistance* [Philadelphia: 1981], 106; Herbert Read, *Arp* [London: 1968], 58).

3. See, e.g., Anthony Heilbut, *Exiled in Paradise* (New York: 1983), and Werner Haftmann, *Banned and Persecuted* (Cologne: 1986).

4. Such seemingly unaffected artists included the Bauhaus architects and artists— Ludwig Mies van der Rohe, Walter Gropius, Wassily Kandinsky, László Moholy-Nagy and Josef Albers (the last two despite the fact that Moholy-Nagy had Jewish ancestors and that Albers's wife, Anni, was Jewish)—Piet Mondrian, Fernand Léger, Salvador Dali and Hans Hofmann. Other artists, such as Kurt Schwitters and André Masson did not react to their status as refugees but did express their abhorrence of the Nazi regime in their wartime works.

Paul Klee, who returned from Germany to his native Switzerland in 1933, cannot actually be considered a refugee, although he clearly identified with them in his art of this period and depicted their worsening condition (John Elderfield, *Kurt Schwitters* [London: 1985], 210–211 and pl. XXXI; William Rubin and Carolyn Lanchner, *André Masson* [New York: 1976], 174; Erhard Frommhold, *Kunst im Widerstand* [Dresden: 1968], nos. 93, 102; G. Di San Lazzaro, *Klee, His Life and Work* [London: 1957], 202; Kunsthalle, Bremen, *Paul Klee,* 8 October–26 November 1967, 33, no. 186; *The Busch–Reisinger Museum* [New York: 1980], 21; and Jurgen Glaesemer, *Paul Klee—Handzeichnungen* [Berne: 1979], vol. 3, 301, no. 777).

5. My forthcoming book on the influence of the Holocaust on art will discuss the full range of depictions of this theme.

6. Walter Erben, *Marc Chagall* (London: 1957), 115.

7. For an early example, see Franz Meyer, *Marc Chagall* (New York: 1963), classified catalogue (CC) 33. For examples of 1914–1915, paralleling Chagall's return to Russia, see *ibid.,* 232–233; for a 1923 work paralleling his return to Western Europe, see *ibid.,* CC 370.

8. E.g., *ibid.,* 392, 408, and CC 369, 608, 613; and Hans Martin Rotermund, *Marc Chagall und die Bibel* (Lahr: 1970), 24.

9. Abraham Valt (Liesin), *Lider un poemen* (New York: 1938), vol. 2, 284–286. Jacob's archetypal character is made clear in the second line of Valt's poem, "He was the first Jew who took the first road to Exile."

10. Yvan Christ, *Chagall Dessins* (Paris: 1953), no. 43. This connection reappears as late as 1969–1972 in the *Fight of Jacob and the Angel* (National Museum of Modern Art, Tokyo, *Chagall,* 21 August–23 September 1976, no. 58).

11. For the original state of this picture, see *Cahiers d'art* 14 (1939), 152. For a discussion of Chagall's symbolic use of Christ, see Ziva Amishai-Maisels, "The Jewish Jesus," *Journal of Jewish Art* 9 (1982), 85–86, 101–104.

12. E.g., Albertina, Vienna, *Marc Chagall,* February–March, 1953, 17, no. 216; Meyer, *Chagall,* 457, CC 693, 696, 700, 829.

13. For instance, *The Falling Angel* of 1923–1947 (Meyer, *Chagall,* 491); *Jew with a Sack* of 1950 (*ibid.,* CC 822); *Exodus* of 1964 (Ziva Amishai-Maisels, *Marc Chagall at the Knesset* [New York: 1973], 33–34); *The Refugee* of 1976 (Pitti Palace, Florence, *Marc Chagall a Palazzo Pitti,* 5 June–30 September 1978, 69); and *The Traveller* of 1978 (Pierre Matisse Gallery, New York, *Marc Chagall,* May 1979, no. 24).

14. Israel Shenker, "Art Editorial—Paris Dispatch 316," March 1950 (typescript, Museum of Modern Art Library, New York, 3). Emphasis added.

15. Concerning his resentment toward France, see Jean-Paul Crespelle, *Chagall* (New York: 1970), 228, and Chagall's poems, e.g., "The Blue of the Air":

> Silent country
> You wish that I be broken,
> That I implore my life on my knees,
> That the fire burn me,
> That I abandon what I have.

and "Departure":

> A wall is growing between us
> A mountain covered with grass and graves . . .
> I sought my star among you . . .
> You ran away, afraid . . .
> I have no longer a space on earth
> To go, towards which to travel.

(Marc Chagall, *Poèmes* [Geneva: 1975], 64, 109; corrected according to the original version, Marc Chagall, "Fun meyn liderbukh," *Di goldene keyt* 60 [1967], 97, where "Departure" is dated 1941 at Lisbon, Chagall's point of embarkation for New York). See also his 1950 poem

"To the Martyred Artists," quoted later in the text (p. 138); and "On the Sea" of 1941–1942 (Chagall, *Poèmes*, 113). For an example of his letters to Sutzkever, see Sidney Alexander, *Marc Chagall: A Biography* (New York: 1978), 471, 474.

16. Jean Cassou, *Chagall* (London: 1965), 243; Meyer, *Chagall*, CC 613; and the chronology Chagall prepared for the Museum of Modern Art in 1946 (typescript, Museum of Modern Art Library, New York, 3).

17. Chagall himself only left France after he was stripped of his French citizenship and arrested in Marseilles (Alexander, *Chagall*, 326–327).

18. Meyer, *Chagall*, CC 695; Lionello Venturi, *Marc Chagall* (New York: 1945), pl. 49.

19. Erben, *Chagall*, pl. 42; Meyer, *Chagall*, 457; Jacques Lassaigne, *Chagall—dessins inédits* (Geneva: 1968), pl. 73; and *Vogue* 102 (1 December 1943), 66. The *Vogue* drawing appeared opposite an appeal to give to various charities at Christmas.

20. Meyer, *Chagall*, 447.

21. Marc Chagall, *My Life* (New York: 1960), 1 and illustrations opposite p. 138; see also figure 4. The latter combines this personal story with a group of fleeing figures, including the Wandering Jew, and seems to depict the aftermath of a pogrom.

22. Cassou, *Chagall*, 189. Crespelle states that in New York Chagall became a Russian Jew again, establishing contacts with Jewish circles and keeping close watch on the German-Russian front (Crespelle, *Chagall*, 228–229).

23. Meyer, *Chagall*, 471.

24. See, for example, George Kars's *Help the Refugees* of 1943, done in Switzerland after his escape from France (Novitch et al., *Spiritual Resistance*, 107); Lea Grundig's sketches of refugees en route to Palestine and at the detention center in Atlit (Wolfgang Hütt, *Lea Grundig* [Dresden: 1969], 41–42, 47; and works in private collections, Israel); and Frans Masareel's depictions of the stories of both Jewish and non-Jewish refugees in his *Destins-1939-1940-1941-1942* (Zurich: 1943), *passim*. Masareel, himself a refugee, spent most of this period evading the Germans in southern France. Grundig's etchings of refugees done before she left Germany in 1939 (e.g., Landgalerie, Berlin, *Lea Grundig*, 1973, nos. 19, 72, 91) are much more brutal and despairing than those she did after she herself had escaped.

25. H. H. Arnason, *Jacques Lipchitz: Sketches in Bronze* (London: 1969), nos. 89–91; Jacques Lipchitz, *My Life in Sculpture* (New York: 1972), 131. The "vainly" in this quotation is not evident in the statue. It may be Lipchitz's postwar comment on the futility of trying to escape, a feeling he certainly did not have at the time.

26. Lipchitz, *My Life*, 131; and author's interview with Lipchitz in August 1971. His gut reaction to Hitler's rise was, "Something catastrophic is going to happen. And who will be the first to suffer?—the Jews of course!" (Irene Patai, *Encounters: The Life of Jacques Lipchitz* [New York: 1961], 260).

27. Lipchitz, *My Life*, 140; and interview, August 1971. From the start, Lipchitz intended to develop *Rescue* into a sculpture and drew it from different angles (Jacques Lipchitz, *The Drawings of Jacques Lipchitz* [New York: 1944], pl. 5; The Israel Museum, Jerusalem, *Jacques Lipchitz at Eighty*, August–September, 1971, nos. 89, 93).

28. Lipchitz, *My Life*, 143 and figs. 130, 131a; Bert Van Bork, *The Artist at Work: Jacques Lipchitz* (New York: 1966), 3, 15; and Jacques Lipchitz and Katherine Kuh, "Conclusions from an Old Cubist," *Art News* 60 (November 1961), 48.

29. Parke-Bernet Galleries, New York, *Modern Paintings, Drawings, and Sculptures*, 11 April 1962, no. 52; Lipchitz, *My Life*, figs. 133–134. See his comment on this child, "Is it symbolic of my desire to beget a child?—or is it perhaps my sculpture which I feel must be saved?" (Henry R. Hope, *The Sculpture of Jacques Lipchitz* [New York: 1954], 17).

30. Lipchitz, *My Life*, 151 and fig. 132. While fleeing the Germans, Lipchitz had done only sketches and a few small statuettes. The statue, *Return of the Child*, was dated 1941–1943 when first exhibited (Buchholz Gallery, New York, *Jacques Lipchitz*, 12 April–1 May 1943, no. 3). See also the 1941 sketch (Arnason, *Sketches in Bronze*, no. 125), which is close in treatment to *Flight*.

31. Hans Hess, *George Grosz* (London: 1974), 173.

32. "Introduction," Museum of Modern Art, New York, *George Grosz*, circulating exhibition, 7 October–2 November 1941; George Grosz, *A Little Yes and a Big No* (New York: 1946), 294–299; *idem, Briefe 1913–1959* (Reinbek near Hamburg: 1979), 192–193, 223, 269–270.

33. Hess, *Grosz*, 180.

34. *Ibid.*, 208–209.

35. *George Grosz: An Autobiography,* trans. Nora Hodges (New York: 1983), 292–293.

36. The interrelationship between the two men is more complex than it appears, as the sketch for this painting, *Self-Portrait as an Old Warrior,* is from the end of April 1936, whereas Borchardt arrived at the beginning of June 1937 (Grosz, *Briefe,* 244, 259–261). Thus, he apparently made the identification after the fact and described Borchardt as he had portrayed himself rather than vice versa. Grosz had been trying to help Borchardt escape from Germany since 1936 and continued to help him once he arrived in New York (*ibid.*, 232, 253, 261–262). See also Grosz's comment in December 1937 that he is doing studies of refugees, "slightly symbolic of my own characteristic theme" (*ibid.*, 266) as well as his remarks on the bitterness and "ghost world" of the emigrants and on his own feeling of being haunted (*ibid.*, 195, 269–270, 306, 316).

37. Hess, *Grosz*, 210. This picture is usually dated to 1943, but the letter quoted below that discusses it is from 1940, and the sketch on which it is based dates from 1936 (Herbert Bittner, ed., *George Grosz* [New York: 1960], pl. 81). The figure here is a paraphrase of the traditional Wandering Jew, although Grosz carefully avoids the traditional sack, beard and Jewish costume. The idea of the wanderer in the swamps is paralleled in his drawing of *Refugees with Pigs* of 1937 (Heckscher Museum, Huntington, New York, *George Grosz,* 1 July–4 September 1977, no. 33). In both pictures, Grosz, although safe in America, shows no goal for the refugee; the emotion pervading these works is one of hopelessness.

38. Hess, *Grosz*, 217–218 (trans. from Grosz, *Briefe,* 291 and 298); John I. H. Baur, *George Grosz* (New York: Whitney Museum of American Art, 14 January–17 March 1954), 37. Grosz, a Dadaist who never lost his joy in shocking people, revealed the other side of the coin in 1943, "The darkness that surrounds me is not just fear and terror. . . . It is very sustaining." (Quoted in Richard O. Boyer, "Artist—I—Demons in the Suburbs," *New Yorker* 19 [27 November 1943], 41).

39. Marcel Janco, *Kav hakeẓ* (Tel-Aviv: 1981), last picture in book. Janco did this drawing after fleeing from Romania to Palestine in 1941.

40. Meyer, *Chagall,* CC 696.

41. Janet Blatter and Sybil Milton, *Art of the Holocaust* (London: 1982), no. 170; P. M. Bardi, *Lasar Segall* (São Paulo: 1959), 129. Segall had emigrated to Brazil by ship in 1923. Although he calls his painting *Immigrant Ship,* which could relate to his own experiences, the date 1939–1941 and the details in the painting suggest that he is dealing with refugees from the Nazis, a subject that struck him as it had the refugees we are discussing for exactly the same reasons. Segall, who had been depicting immigrants since 1910–1911 (*Lasar Segall, 50 Xilogravuras* [Brazil: 1966, 2 ed.], nos. 1, 10, 25; Bardi, *Segall,* 97), derived his series of *Emigrant* etchings of 1928–1930 directly from his own experience. There he treated the subject in a more orderly and positive way: his somewhat sad figures sit and wait on deck in small groups (Bardi, *Segall,* 128), instead of being massed together as in his later painting.

42. *New York Times,* 25 February 1942, 7; *ibid.,* 21 March 1942, 16.

43. Meyer, *Chagall,* 457. Chagall had begun sketching this theme in 1942 (Lassaigne, *Chagall,* 73), and his identification with the theme can be seen in the sketch for the painting in which he wrote his name and that of Vitebsk on the open Torah in Hebrew (Léon Degrand, *Chagall—Peintures, 1942–45* [Paris: 1947], pl. 4).

44. Michele Vishny, *Ardon* (New York: 1973), nos. 308–309; and a sketch in the artist's collection. According to the artist's son, the third drawing was the original first sketch (information kindly conveyed, July 1987). Since there were no survivors, Ardon seemingly referred to his own escape: the man on crutches will recur in several paintings of the

mid-1940s in an autobiographical context, e.g., *The Prodigal Son* (Michael Ardon Collection, Jerusalem). For the projected painting, see Politzer's description of a seascape, inspired by the sinking of the *Struma,* in which dark sheets of water meet a jagged sky, but the tragic event itself is omitted (Heinz Politzer, "Two Artists and the Hills of Judea," *Commentary* 6 [December 1948], 540). The artist stated to me that although he had done many sketches on this subject, he decided that it was beyond his powers of expression and changed the painting not into a seascape, as Politzer claims, but into a portrayal of the Mount of Olives (interview with Ardon, April 1983). This is an interesting switch: the Mount of Olives is the site of a large Jewish cemetery and could, thus, symbolize the disaster rather than depict it.

45. Abraham Rattner, "An American from Paris," *Magazine of Art,* 38 (December 1945), 311; Allen Leepa, *Abraham Rattner* (New York: 1981), pl. 50 and p. 45. The *Struma* exploded in flames before sinking. Rattner does not mention the *Struma* in his diaries, but he had been obsessed with the sinking of boats throughout 1942, especially that of the *Normandie* on which he had sailed in 1939 (Archives of American Art D204, frs. 438, 452, 473). However, as opposed to the *Struma* and the situation in Rattner's painting, the *Normandie* sank as a result of an accident, only one man died, and the reports describe smoke rather than flames (*New York Times,* 10 February 1942, 1, 7–8). He may have begun work on this painting in May and calls it by name in October (Archives of American Art D204, frs. 506, 556).

46. Edith Hoffmann, *Kokoschka: Life and Work* (London: 1947), 232–233 and color-plate 2; J. P. Hodin, *Oscar Kokoschka: The Artist and His Time* (Greenwich: 1966), 25–26, 199. Two other paintings have symbolism related to that depicted here. In *Private Property* of 1939–1940, a cat-headed woman, symbolizing the phlegmatic English, watches both the fish who die on her shores, possibly symbols of the refugees, and the native mice, symbols of decadence from within (Hoffmann, *Kokoschka,* pl. 75; Hodin, *Kokoschka,* 27–28; and Oskar Kokoschka, *My Life* [New York: 1974], 161). *Lorelei* of 1942, painted after the fall of Singapore, forecasts the fall of the British Empire: Queen Victoria does not save the ship-wrecked victims—possibly foreign refugees en route to be interned in Canada—who perish at sea. Stuffing a sailor (her navy) into the mouth of the shark she rides, she allows the fascist octopus to make off with her trident (Hoffmann, *Kokoschka,* pl. 79; Hodin, *Kokoschka,* 23–24; and Kokoschka, *My Life,* 164).

47. Benjamin Tammuz, Dorit LeVité and Gideon Ofrat, *Sipur haomanut beyisrael* (Jerusalem: 1980), 100. Sima began work on his *Refugees* in 1940, did a second version in 1945 and another in 1950. He associated the first versions with the refugees fleeing Hitler: "Boats lost on the high seas. On these boats—lost human beings, closely packed together, striving towards one aim [Palestine], but without hope of ever gaining it . . . blocks of apathy, of despair, of pity." However, the final version was inspired by the refusal of the British to allow the ship *Exodus 1947,* which carried camp survivors, to land in Palestine, a refusal that Sima termed "the revolting final act of a cruel tragedy" ("Introduction," Bezalel National Museum, Jerusalem, *Miron Sima—Refugees,* 2 September–7 October 1950). Sima had himself emigrated from Germany to Palestine in 1933.

48. Tel-Aviv Museum Collection; Leon Kolb, *The Woodcuts of Jakob Steinhardt* (Los Angeles: 1959), no. 261.

49. E.g., Naftali Bezem, *Naftali Bezem* (Ramat Gan: 1972), 26–35, 38–49, 58, 60–61, 91–92, 96–97, 99, 106–107.

50. Heilbut, *Exiled in Paradise,* 213; Lipchitz interview, August 1971.

51. Lipchitz, *Drawings* (1944), pl. 8. Although Lipchitz stated to me that the child was also present here, its location is not clear. Lipchitz did a painting and an etching of this theme in 1944 (*Lipchitz at Eighty,* 1971, no. 106; Buchholz Gallery, New York, *Jacques Lipchitz,* 26 March–20 April 1946, no. 32), at the time the original drawing was reproduced in Lipchitz, *Drawings* (1944), pl. 8. The later versions are ambiguous: they seem to represent not a rescue, but a flight. The forms remain, but by 1944, the bitterness behind the first sketch (1941) had subsided and the meaning is blurred.

52. Lipchitz, *My Life,* 159; and Lipchitz interview, August 1971.

53. Hope, *Sculpture,* 72. The dating is from Hope and seems more correct than the date 1942 given it when it was first exhibited (Buchholz Gallery, *Lipchitz,* 1943, no. 14).

54. Hope, *Sculpture*, 70–71; Lipchitz, *Drawings* (1944), pl. 11.

55. Lipchitz, *My Life*, no. 144; Lipchitz, *Drawings* (1944), pl. 10; *Twelve Bronzes by Jacques Lipchitz* (New York: 1943), pl. VIII. *Yara* is a siren from the Amazon River area (M. R., "Jacques Lipchitz," *Art Digest* 17 [1 May 1943], 14).

56. Lipchitz, *Twelve Bronzes*, pls. IX–XI. Both *Album Page* and *Myrrah* were dated to 1942 when they were first exhibited (Buchholz Gallery, *Lipchitz*, 1943, nos. 11–12), but *Myrrah* seems later. Henry Hope ("Un sculpteur d'hier et d'aujourd'hui," *L'Oeil* [May 1959], 36) suggests that *Myrrah* is a Hebraic theme influenced by the Second World War. The name seems rather to be simply the name Myra, which means she who weeps or laments.

57. Lipchitz, *Twelve Bronzes*, pls. XV–XVI; and Lipchitz interview, August 1971.

58. Lipchitz, *My Life*, 159.

59. Lipchitz, *Drawings* (1944), pl. 12.

60. Lipchitz, *My Life*, 159. For another example of the ambiguous and lonely position of the refugee artist in a new world, see Max Ernst's *Napoleon in the Wilderness* of 1941 (Uwe M. Schneede, *The Essential Max Ernst* [London: 1972], no. 333), painted shortly after Ernst arrived in the United States.

61. For a discussion of the development of Adler's art during his period as a refugee in Paris and his later development, see Ziva Amishai-Maisels, "The Iconographic Use of Abstraction in Jankel Adler's Late Works," *Artibus et Historiae* 17 (1988), 55–70.

62. *Ibid.*, 56–61; and Städtische Kunsthalle, Düsseldorf, *Jankel Adler*, 1 November–8 December 1985, nos. 85–88, 92, 98, 101, 108–109, 111–112. See also Adler's worried mothers and children, *ibid.*, no. 107; Stanley W. Hayter, *Jankel Adler* (London: 1948), pl. 13.

63. Michael Hasenclever, Munich, *Jankel Adler*, 22 September–22 October 1977, nos. 24 and 23, respectively.

64. *Ibid.*, no. 26; see also Amishai-Maisels, "Adler," 58.

65. Adler also did sketches of refugees at this time, e.g., Galerie Wolfgang Ketterer, Munich, *Jankel Adler*, c. 1969, no. 38.

66. Düsseldorf, *Adler*, 1985, no. 95. For the development of *Destruction* and its interpretation, see Amishai-Maisels, "Adler," 60–62.

67. Düsseldorf, *Adler*, 1985, no. 89.

68. E.g., Saint Louis Art Museum, *Max Beckmann*, 7 September–4 November 1984, 63–66, 267, 272–273, 286–287, 289; Haftmann, *Banned and Persecuted*, 60–61. See also the left wing of his *Perseus* of 1940–1941 and the dismal monstrous world he depicts in these years such as *Dream of Monte Carlo* of 1939–1943 (Friedheim W. Fischer, *Max Beckmann* [London: 1973], 61, 67. Beckmann had left Germany for Holland in 1937 immediately after the opening of the exhibition of Decadent Art. He was trapped in Holland by the war, having unsuccessfully tried to arrange for his entry into the United States.

69. Peter Junk and Wendelin Zimmer, *Felix Nussbaum, Leben und Werk* (Cologne: 1982), 90–99, 109–142; and nos. 65–66, 106–108, 110–119, 123, 129, 135–136, 138–141, 144–146, 148–165, 175–188, 190–193, 197, 200–203, 207, 209, 221, 224–227. Nussbaum had painted both masks and boats before this period (*ibid.*, nos. 38, 40, 48–49, 61, N5, N7) but not with the obsessiveness he now displayed. For his portrayal of ruins, see Emily D. Bilski, *Art and Exile: Felix Nussbaum 1904–1944* (New York: 1985), 35, 37.

70. Junk and Zimmer, *Nussbaum*, nos. 228–246, 253–255, 257–262, 264, 267–275, 278–283.

71. *Ibid.*, 179.

72. Bilski, *Nussbaum*, 18; Junk and Zimmer, *Nussbaum*, 186, 191, 253.

73. Junk and Zimmer, *Nussbaum*, 155–157.

74. Bilski, *Nussbaum*, 63–64, 67.

75. Avigdor Arikha, *Boyhood Drawings Made in Deportation* (Paris: 1971), no. 2.

76. Haftmann, *Banned and Persecuted*, 365.

77. Lea Grundig, *Begai haharegah* (Tel-Aviv: 1944).

78. Vishny, *Ardon*, 30–31, 222–224, and pls. 41–42, 44–45, 47–48, 50, 52–55; Ziva Amishai-Maisels, "Where Past Meets Present: The Art of Ardon," in Tel-Aviv Museum, *Ardon—a Retrospective*, 1985, unpaged; Kolb, *Woodcuts of Steinhardt*, nos. 145–146, 149–

152, 178–189, 204–214, 221–225, 231–232, and Steinhardt's landscapes in private collections in Israel.

79. Kolb, *Woodcuts of Steinhardt,* nos. 232, 242, 251–252; Tel-Aviv Museum, *Ardon,* 1985, no. 12; Amishai-Maisels, "Art of Ardon," unpaged. Steinhardt also executed works dealing with the Holocaust (e.g., Kolb, *Woodcuts of Steinhardt,* nos. 235, 254 and 256) but only on commission.

80. Hess, *Grosz,* 227. See also Grosz's comments on his feelings of failure as an antifascist (Richard O. Boyer, "Artist, III," *New Yorker* 19 [11 December 1943], 40–41) and on not having succeeded in becoming an American (Beth Irwin Lewis, *George Grosz, Art and Politics in the Weimer Republic* [Madison: 1971], 233).

81. Hess, *Grosz,* 227–228. See also *Homeward* of 1947, in which the German survivor, an alter ego of the artist, returns to his home on crutches to find only ruins (*ibid.,* 237).

82. Hütt, *Grundig,* no. 61; Bertolt Brecht, *Gesammelte Werke* (Frankfurt on the Main: 1967), vol. 9, 487–488.

83. Meyer, *Chagall,* 445.

84. Marc Chagall, "Di kunst fun 'glaychlinikayt un klorkeyt,' " *Naylebn* (June 1944), 5 [speech made on 30 April 1944]. Chagall was described at this time as "timid" and "fearful . . . dominated by the persistent remembrance of humiliations, blows, pogroms" (Venturi, *Chagall,* 10).

85. Chagall, *Poèmes,* 99–104, trans. Moshe Kohn and corrected according to Chagall, "Liderbukh," 99–100. Similar guilt feelings were expressed by former camp inmates, e.g., Shmuel Bak, who said: "Personally, the fact that prevented me from cultivating any traditional religious feeling is precisely the fact of my survival: that out of a community of 80,000 souls, only 150—and I among them—should have survived the monstrous evil of those times" (Paul Nagano and A. Kaufman, *Bak, Paintings of the Last Decade* [New York: 1974], 34).

86. Meyer, *Chagall,* CC 736.

87. *Ibid.,* CC 626, 782. Although Chagall later dated it 1935–1947, thus connecting the original version with his visit to Poland, Meyer states that the first version was signed 1936–1937 (*ibid.,* 756).

88. Lipchitz interview, August 1971.

89. Maurice Raynal, *Lipchitz* (Paris: 1947), unpaged.

90. Lipchitz interview, August 1971.

91. Curt Valentin Gallery, New York, *Lipchitz,* 1946, inside back cover.

92. Robert Goldwater, *Lipchitz* (Amsterdam: 1959), pl. 27; Buchholz Gallery, New York, *Lipchitz,* 23 March–17 April 1948, nos. 14–15. See also the intermediate sketch between the *bozzetto* and the finished work, no. 29.

93. Lipchitz interview, August 1971.

94. Patai, *Encounters,* 349.

95. Chaim Soutine died in 1943 of a ruptured ulcer that was not cared for properly because he had been hiding from the Germans (Maurice Tuchman, *Chaim Soutine,* Los Angeles County Museum of Art, 1968, 48). Max Jacob, despite his conversion to Catholicism and entry into a monastery, was shot in a concentration camp. Lipchitz must have felt that this death was especially bitter as Jacob had written him in 1940 that he did not want to die a martyr (Patai, *Encounters,* 289).

96. Patai, *Encounters,* p. 350; and A. M. Hammacher, *Jacques Lipchitz—His Sculpture* (New York: 1960), 63.

"Home Is Where the Heart Is": Jewish Themes in the Art of R. B. Kitaj

Vivianne Barsky
(THE ISRAEL MUSEUM)

R. B. Kitaj is an expatriate American artist who has lived and worked mainly in London for the past thirty years. An absorbing painter and outstandingly sensitive draftsman, Kitaj enjoys considerable prestige both in his adopted country and internationally. From the outset of his artistic career, Kitaj's highly sophisticated pictures—executed in a consciously and deliberately eclectic style, often forming a kind of latter-day allegory—have conveyed an uncommonly wide range of subjects nourished by the artist's keen and shrewd scrutiny of the most disparate aspects of modern life, copious reading and personal experience. One of the strands of that experience is Kitaj's Jewishness, a fact that, ever since the early 1970s, has come to preoccupy him more and more and that has had a significant thematic impact on his art.

Kitaj, whose original name was Ronald Brooks, was born in Cleveland, Ohio, in 1932. His mother, Jeanne Brooks, was the daughter of Russian-Jewish emigrants; the father, who was Hungarian, left town when his son was still a toddler. The artist refers to him as "a nice guy, I'm told, who loved books and horses."[1] The mother supported herself and the boy, working first as a secretary and later teaching school. In 1941 she married Dr. Walter Kitaj, a young Jewish refugee from Vienna. Kitaj describes the home of his childhood as an "agnostic, left–liberal milieu,"[2] which did not foster his Jewish identity. "I've had no [Jewish] training or background, unlike most Jews I know," he writes.[3] The home atmosphere may be sensed through Kitaj's rather vague reference to "political and literary instincts and turmoil which colored and overwhelmed more stable and traditional absolutes."[4] One early impression that excited his imagination was the departure of some of his mother's friends to fight in the Spanish civil war.[5] Later, during the Second World War, even as young Kitaj devoted himself to "baseball, basketball and boxing"[6] (like many typical American boys), "the distant storm in Europe" became a major component in a formative "confluence of art and books and political life."[7] In Kitaj's private life, the most manifest evidence of that storm was the arrival of his stepfather, who had been fortunate enough to escape it. He describes the refugees who flocked to the safe haven of America as "very much *in* our lives."[8] They must have awed the young boy with their life stories and alien ways.

149

From the beginning, Kitaj's art reflected the political instincts he had absorbed in his youth. In several early works, he contemplated and commented on the ideas and lives of revolutionary socialists; as a matter of course some of these were Jewish. However, he did not seem to relate specifically to this fact, just as, for many years, he was capable of not mentioning his Jewish background to people to whom he was otherwise quite close.

When Kitaj eventually referred publicly to his ethnic origins, he did so not only deliberately, but almost demonstratively. American writer Frederic Tuten, a long-time friend and admirer of the artist, describes how, in 1980, "after dinner one evening in London he said he wanted me to read an interview with him in *London Magazine*. 'There are things about me there that you may not know,' he said."[9] Kitaj was referring to an article entitled "A Return to London: R. B. Kitaj Replies to Some Questions Put to Him by Timothy Hyman."[10] This illuminating interview probed Kitaj's view of various aspects of his artistic development and how they linked up with certain experiences and stations along the road (such as his childhood impressions of artworks at the Cleveland Museum of Art or his studies at the Vienna Art Academy in the early 1950s). Referring to the fact that Kitaj's artistic production over the preceding years included "works about Jews, travelers, exiles," Hyman suggested a connection with the artist's "early experiences of wandering— as a seaman, etc." But he laid particular emphasis on the question of Kitaj's sense of identity after more than twenty years of living in London, "Have you come to feel your Jewish birth more significantly? Do you identify yourself as an American? (A Russian? A Jew?) Or do you feel you've become strongly Anglicized and Euro-peanized?"[11] Kitaj responded:

> In recent years I guess I feel more of a Jew. . . . I'm not a *believer* and I'll always be a suspicious reader but a central condition for me has been the murder of the European Jews. Out of that maelstrom I've begun a meditation on historical *Remembrance* and its attendant sense of exile and survival. . . . I've been mulling for years the possibility of representing the Jewish tragedy under the Nazis.[12]

Tuten's article also investigated Kitaj's interest in Jewish matters and the artistic significance of what Tuten called "this new impetus." Kitaj disclosed to him that, his initial ignorance of Judaism notwithstanding, he had always been emotionally involved in the Jewish "condition." This inherent interest eventually prompted him to embark on "a real education and a real journey." Encountering "the great poetry for the first time—Isaiah, Job, Psalms [he particularly immersed himself in] . . . the period which begins with the (relative) liberation of the Jews in Europe and the enormous implications of the questions of assimilation and exile."[13]

In a lecture to a Jewish congregation in the synagogue of Oxford on November 25, 1983,[14] Kitaj traced his preoccupation with these questions to his own sense of homelessness, existential as well as artistic. This amounted to a manifesto for a new kind of expression of Jewishness in art. Kitaj related his quest for a "pictorial synthesis" through which his unfolding Jewish awareness would be adequately reflected to a constellation of two aspects of art history: the problematic issue of Jewish art, on the one hand, and the cardinal influence of the great European turn-of-the-twentieth-century artists on the other. He started off by recalling the Biblical prohibition against idolatrous image making, contemplating its obvious historical implications, which boils down to the question, "Why is there no Jewish art of real consequence?" Citing masters and masterpieces of world art of various periods, Kitaj lamented the fact that no Rembrandt or Picasso had ever "arisen among us, a people gifted way beyond our small number," speculating that the second commandment "*could* account for the thousands of years of mediocre adorning, the results of which may be seen in the well-meaning museums of Jewish art . . . full of . . . liturgical . . . *chachkelahs*" [*sic*] (bric-a-brac) which, with few exceptions, fall short of Christian masterpieces in the corresponding media.

The dearth of great Jewish art was also—he believed—the result of "exile, dispersal and relentless persecution." Even emancipation had not been conducive to a Jewish art of great stature. True, there had been artists "of great interest and brilliance," but they had lacked a proper milieu—unlike, for example, the "dozen world masters . . . and two dozen minor masters who arose in Paris within about half a lifetime (1850–1900)." The "Jewish painters just didn't have enough *time* (as dubious guests) to invent a tradition, like the French or the Italians had time *and* a place!" In any case, Kitaj could find no master to emulate among Jewish artists of earlier generations.[15] Jewish art, he claimed, had not even interested him particularly during the earlier part of his career, "My own dialogue with modernist practice, though quite polemical,[16] did not transgress the common disdain for ethnic representation, even in the expressionist and cubist disguise Jewish art so often assumed."[17] However, his growing absorption in Jewish history eventually began to affect his artistic aims:

> I began with the critical moment in which I found myself, the moment of my art, and from there instinct led me, through reading and thinking and meeting with people, not to the rumoured *origins* of the Jews, but to something that has proved far more seductive for my art—a rumour of Jewishness. The famous phrase ringing in my mind—the Englishness of English art—became, for me, the Jewishness of Jewish art.

In the end, a question of far-reaching consequence crystallized in his mind: "What could a Jewish art be that it had never been before?"

The insight that Kitaj reached during this "critical moment" was that the great turn-of-the-century artists he so admired—Degas, Cézanne, Matisse, Picasso—lacked a basic ingredient: "their condition was not the condition of a Jew."[18] Conversely, when he delved into the same period in the history of his people, he discovered a fascinating gallery of outstanding personalities whose lives and work bore the imprint of their Jewish birth. Although these men were not visual artists, he came to identify strongly with them, seeing in their work a stimulus for his own artistic creation: "I was very moved by the lonely few who saw the future in terms of creative negation of their exile. In the lives of people like Ahad Ha-Am, Franz Rosenzweig, Gershom Scholem, Walter Benjamin and in Kafka's great solution, I could begin to test the ground for a pictorial synthesis of my own making and choosing."[19] Speaking to a Jewish audience, Kitaj felt the need to express himself on this issue more fully than he had in dialogues with gentile interviewers. "Like these [other creative] Jews, I have always felt displaced, as a person, as a painter, as a Jew." This fundamental sense of estrangement expressed itself in an ambiguity of artistic aims: "Like secret Jews, from the Marranos to Benjamin and Kafka, I would perform in the art situation and also practice my refusals of that situation by instinct."[20]

Although, stylistically, his pictures were nourished by "Symbolism, Surrealism, Stream-of-Consciousness and, always, by the great art of Christian Europe which has entered the blood of every western artist worth his salt," their content was another matter. Indeed, long before his conscious decision to create "Jewish art," Jewish themes were not lacking in Kitaj's work. But, as he put it, "Jewish thematic stuff appeared in some of my earlier paintings by stealth, usually wearing the masks of the socialist dramas to which Jews had so often given themselves." The works he mentions as "examples of these first incursions" are *The Murder of Rosa Luxemburg* and *Isaac Babel Riding with Budyonny*.[21]

Kitaj painted *The Murder of Rosa Luxemburg* (fig. 1) in 1960 while still a student at the Royal College of Art in London. Although this picture may be placed within the general framework of Kitaj's political interests at the time ("the roots of Socialism and the themes of political martyrdom"),[22] Kitaj, writing a "preface" twenty years after the completion of the work, revealed that it

Fig. 1. R. B. Kitaj, *The Murder of Rosa Luxemburg,* 1960. Oil and collage on canvas, 60 × 60 in. (152.5 × 152.5 cm). Tate Gallery, London. Art Resource/New York. (Photograph, Marco Livingstone, *R. B. Kitaj* [Oxford: Phaidon Press, 1985], pl. 30.)

arose out of a meditation upon two of my grandmothers. . . . It is about an historic murder but it is really about murdering Jews, which is what brought my grandmothers to America. . . . In the great Spartacist Rosa, in her life and in her death, I'd found an ikon for the dark times I associated with my grandmothers. I didn't paint it because I identified with her revolution (or its failure) but . . . for other oblique reasons.[23]

These reasons were personal: he painted it as a Jew and as an American.

The stream-of-consciousness method of composition that Kitaj employed in *The Murder of Rosa Luxemburg,* as in numerous other works, contributed to its abstruseness as long as the real message was concealed.[24] On the face of it, the artist was obliging: the murder is described in written notes glued onto the upper right part of the canvas (a throwback to the Cubist collages, which, however, were never primarily informative). But several of the details scattered around the painting only become intelligible in retrospect when one reads the preface. The sepulchral monument at the lower left, we are told there, is meant as an illustration of the "bonding of Fascism and a degenerated Romanticism," which culminated in National Socialism; the upper left pyramid "prefigures certain pyramidal monuments deliberately created in some Jewish cemeteries in Eastern Europe after the war out of fragments of gravestones"; and the top left profile represents one of the grandmothers as Rosa's "veiled *wraith.*" The significance of the Statue of Liberty becomes obvious in the context of the two grandmothers who made it to America.

About forty years earlier, very shortly after the actual murder of Luxemburg and Karl Liebknecht, the German expressionist Max Beckmann depicted the event in plate 3 of the graphic portfolio *Hell.* Entitled *Martyrdom* (fig. 2), it connotes the Passion of Christ and the martyrdom of the saints. Indeed, it was Beckmann's intention to impart "religious significance to these deaths. The woman's figure . . . portrays the traditional posture of the crucified."[25] Her index fingers point downward—toward hell—and the crescent moon and stars in the sky imply the cosmic dimensions of this human and political tragedy. The cypresses in the background and the baldachinlike structure above the murdered woman's head have funerary connotations. In the upper left corner, Beckmann included a pyramidal shape; this and other details—Rosa's outstretched arms and boot-clad feet—seem to find their echo in Kitaj's picture, although he denies having been aware of Beckmann's lithograph when he painted his version of the murder.[26] Stylistically, the two works do not have much in common. Beckmann's composition is crowded and nervous, with an emphasis on intersecting diagonals, whereas the juxtaposed images in Kitaj's painting are more loosely combined, with the dreadfully battered corpse in sharp focus. In any case (as we have seen), Kitaj's associations and message were uniquely his own, even if he did quote Beckmann in particular details. Rosa's black boots, for example, were of the kind that his Austrian-born grandmother, Helene Kitaj, continued to wear for decades after emigrating to America.[27]

"Some books have pictures and some pictures have books" was one of Kitaj's mottoes for a solo exhibition at the Kestner-Gesellschaft, Hanover in 1970. *Isaac Babel Riding with Budyonny* (fig. 3), painted in 1962, exemplifies his idiosyncratic manner of transferring books into pictures. Kitaj had read an English edition of

Fig. 2. Max Beckmann, *Martyrdom*, pl. 3 in the portfolio *Hell*, 1919. Transfer lithograph, 25-1/2 × 29-1/2 in. (54.5 × 75.0 cm). Private collection, New York. (Photograph, Carla Schulz Hoffmann and Judith C. Weiss, eds., *Max Beckmann—Retrospective*, Saint Louis Art Museum [Munich: Prestel Verlag; New York/London: W. W. Norton, 1984], 403–405, fig. 250.)

Babel's *The Collected Stories,* with an introduction by Lionel Trilling, who (the artist feels) "catches the complexities of the Babel conundrum."[28] Trilling's discussion pinpointed for Kitaj "the place of violence [in the mind] of a thinking man, creative artist and much else." His rendering of Babel as cavalryman is a collagelike conjoining of seemingly disparate images, some of which are hard to decipher. In the foreground, to the right, against an abstract backdrop, Kitaj painted a horse in full gallop, seen from the rear. The horse is mounted by a uniformed rider whose head looks as if it has been dissolved or liquefied by the swift movement. Another possibility is to read its blurred shape and details as another horse's head—conveying Babel's intense experience of the physical contact between the rider and his mount. The picture comprises several other images of horses, one of which, in the left foreground, has the appearance of a cutout of an abstracted rider donning a flat-topped Cossack cap who is physically fused with the rearing steed.[29] A conspicuous detail in the middle ground, to the right, is an overturned, proplike house on a stick attached to large wheels, like a cannon to its cart—also bringing to mind a Potemkin front. The painting has been interpreted as referring "to Babel . . . and the Revolutionary circumstances from which he drew his inspiration" and as "a portrait

Fig. 3. R. B. Kitaj, *Isaac Babel Riding with Budyonny,* 1962. Oil on canvas, 72 × 72 in. (182.9 × 182.9 cm). Tate Gallery, London. Art Resource/New York. (Photograph, R. B. Kitaj, *Pictures with Commentary, Pictures without Commentary,* Marlborough New London Gallery, 1963, cat. no. 17.)

or . . . an icon of Kitaj's own standpoint as a young leftist and a Jew" rather than as "an illustration of a literary text" (the *Red Cavalry* stories).[30] Nevertheless, it seems to me that the overturned house on the stick alludes to one of Babel's most poignant tales, "The Story of my Dovecot." In this gruesome account of a pogrom, the main protagonist is a Jewish boy (Babel himself), who has just scored the success of being admitted to the local gymnasium, one of two Jews among forty Russian boys—according to the quota. His proud father gives him money to buy some pigeons for his dovecot. But a pogrom erupts on the very day he gets the treasured birds; he himself is beaten up and a pigeon is smashed against his face. All that is only a preamble to the grim scene awaiting him at home where he is met by the mangled corpses of his grandfather and granduncle. The grass around the dovecot has been trampled, as are the Jewish boy's illusions of having been accepted into Russian society.

Isaac Babel (1894–1941?), caught in the quandary of wanting to be a ruthless, unreflecting Cossack while at heart knowing himself to be a perplexed Jewish intellectual, represents but one variety of the agonizing existential and moral dilemmas faced by so many emancipated but essentially alienated Jews. Babel's reflective communism was not orthodox enough, and eventually he was destroyed.[31] Walter Benjamin (1892–1940), whom Hannah Arendt has described as "probably . . . the most peculiar Marxist ever produced by this movement, which God knows has had

Fig. 4. R. B. Kitaj, *The Autumn of Central Paris (After Walter Benjamin),* 1972–1974. Oil on canvas, 60 × 60 in. (152.5 × 152.4 cm). Mrs. Susan Lloyd, New York. (Photograph, John Ashbery et al., *Kitaj: Paintings, Drawings, Pastels* [London: Thames & Hudson, 1984], pl. 6.)

its full share of oddities,"[32] would surely have met a similar fate had he been a Russian rather than a German Jew or had he chosen not to return from his visit to Russia in 1926–1927. Kitaj "discovered" Benjamin in the 1960s,[33] and in 1972–1974 he created two large paintings inspired by the life and writings of this intriguing and tragic personality: *The Autumn of Central Paris (After Walter Benjamin)* (fig. 4) and *Arcades (After Walter Benjamin).*[34] In both these works, he assembles figures and images by what he himself refers to as a "montage practice" consonant with Benjamin's "method of pressing together quickening tableaux from texts and from a disjunct world."[35] Benjamin, Hannah Arendt wrote, dreamed "of producing a work consisting entirely of quotations, one that was mounted so masterfully that it could dispense with any accompanying text," an idea she compared to "the contemporaneous surrealistic experiments."[36] Benjamin was, in fact, fascinated by surrealism, which particularly preoccupied him around 1927 when, disappointed with Russia, he went to Paris. Gershom Scholem explained that the surrealists "embodied much of what had erupted in him during the years just past. What he sought to penetrate and master in intellectual discipline he found noteworthy precisely in the antithetical forms of an untrammeled surrender to the explosions of the unconscious, and it stimulated his own imagination."[37] The surrealist inspiration prompted him to start work on "his projected study of the Paris Arcades," which he conceived of as a "historical–philosophical physiognomy" of Paris.[38] Kitaj, the "grandchild of Surrealism,"[39] found here a truly kindred spirit.

The imagery of *The Autumn of Central Paris (After Walter Benjamin),* although elusive in many of its details, offers itself to a partial interpretation with the help of Kitaj's "preface" to the picture. The title obviously refers to Benjamin's romance with the French capital (where he felt less estranged than in Berlin, his native city) and his immersion in French literature and culture. Kitaj provides some clues to an understanding of the images: the café setting, for example, represents "café life as an *autumnal reverie* of bourgeois society" or as "*open-air interior past* which the *life of the city* moves along." The man with the hearing aid (a recurrent image in Kitaj's work) relates to the function of the artist: "Benjamin thought that the artist is compelled to assume roles that look subversive but are, in fact, harmless: *poet-beggar-detective-flâneur-police spy-secret agent* and above all, *bohemian.*" The painting is conceived as a *diorama/tableau* (based on a line by Benjamin relating to the social performance of the worker in the class struggle). It incorporates the image of "the barricade" (which also derives from Benjamin's writing, in this case his citing of "barricade metaphors" from *Les Misérables*), and the entire composition is a "pile-up (barricade)" of figures as in "A Movie Poster" (alluding to Benjamin's famous essay "The Work of Art in the Age of Mechanical Reproduction"). The cast of café frequenters represents Kitaj's imaginative recreation of Benjaminesque figures and images.[40]

In the middle background, to the right, appears that central figure in Benjamin's life and art: the flâneur.[41] He is depicted from the back, a lone wanderer, moving away from the café crowd and facing an expanse of sky. This figure is linked by Kitaj to Benjamin's suicide—"the flâneur's last journey: death"—and to a line from Charles Baudelaire's *Flowers of Evil (Les Fleurs du mal)* as well as to Benjamin's touching metaphor of the "angel of history" in the ninth of his "Theses on the Philosophy of History," the last essay he wrote, in the spring of 1940, under the influence of the Hitler-Stalin pact.[42] Only a few months later, having fled from Paris and despairing of reaching safety beyond the reach of the Nazis, Benjamin committed suicide on the Franco-Spanish border. The metaphor represented Benjamin's interpretation of Paul Klee's watercolor *Angelus Novus* (1920), which he had purchased in 1921:

> His face is turned towards the past. Where we perceive a chain of events, he sees one single catastrophe which keeps piling wreckage upon wreckage and hurls it in front of his feet. The angel would like to stay, awaken the dead, and make whole what has been smashed. But a storm is blowing from Paradise; it has got caught in his wings with such violence that the angel can no longer close them. This storm irresistibly propels him into the future to which his back is turned, while the pile of debris before him grows skyward. This storm is what we call progress.[43]

"In this angel," Hannah Arendt wrote, "the *flâneur* experiences his final transfiguration." The flâneur image per se, she pointed out, is utterly irreconcilable with "Marxism and dialectical materialism," and so is the angel, who "does not dialectically move into the future. . . . . That such thinking should ever have bothered with a consistent, dialectically sensible, rationally explainable process seems absurd." But then, as she also noted, Benjamin was blessed with "the gift of *thinking poetically.* "[44] Kitaj, whose leftist stance defies dogmatism (to him, socialism is a synonym for compassion) appears to share this gift.[45] The painting's representation of the flâneur–angel does not tally visually with Benjamin's image: the man has his back turned both to the piled-up café crowd and to the architectural wreckage in the center.[46] He seems to move forward, toward the void, rather than being thrust backward into the future by a storm from paradise (though there is a suggestion of windiness in the hair of the solitary redhead seated next to one of the café tables, in the branches of the tree to the left and in the drifting clouds of the autumn sky). In general, a rational and exact interpretation of *The Autumn of Central Paris (After Walter Benjamin)* image by image—to the extent that it is possible—would not account for the painting's poetic, evocative beauty. As in any major work of art, what the picture conveys is beyond the sum of its parts; it reflects Kitaj's intense involvement with Benjamin's life story and the selection of his writings—available in English at the time—as well as his emotional response to the poignancy of Benjamin's ever-vacillating loyalties and the tragedy of his willy-nilly flâneur existence—the epitome of the Wandering Jew.

Another Jewish figure to attract Kitaj's attention was Franz Kafka, a writer who also greatly interested Benjamin. Kitaj first read Kafka as a young sailor in the early 1950s,[47] and Kafka has been a focal point of his discussion of the Jewish aspects of his art:

> Kafka was the *only* artist . . . I know who assumes the condition of Jewishness in
> forms which speak to me. . . . Kafka encourages me to know myself and to puzzle out
> my own Jewishness and to try to make that over into an art of picture-making. . . . He
> did what no painter has been able to do really clearly ([Chaim] Soutine may have been
> an exception). . . . The uncanny disclosures of his great and strange parables were what
> he called "rumors about the true things." Those true things about which he rumored in
> his art—the perplexities and dangers of a pariah people—were to turn more hellish and
> unspeakable than even he could guess within a few years of his early death. . . . His art
> was a kind of prologue to disaster and now, thirty-five years after that disaster, I feel
> fearful, like he did about things, and would like to paint an epilogue.[48]

Although Kitaj has not expressly devoted any of his pictures to Kafka's stories, he maintains that the iconography of some of his paintings derives from them.[49] This inspiration seems to be reflected in a work like *The Listener (Joe Singer in Hiding)* (fig. 5) of 1980.[50] This large pastel-and-charcoal drawing depicts Kitaj's archetypal Galut Jew in a dark underground space listening into the void with a large, pricked-up ear. His eyes are blank and unseeing, the right, disjointed hand gropes in the dark, and the left, strangely immaterial arm extends downward like a shaft into the depth of the cavern. The background is a sterile landscape with low structures whose entrances lead into other dark voids. A faintly outlined woman stands by the leftmost entrance.[51] This setting vaguely recalls surrealist depictions of wasteland scenery and deserted cities. On a hillock to the right, a young boy is engrossed in reading. It is tempting to see in this enigmatic representation an allusion to Kafka's

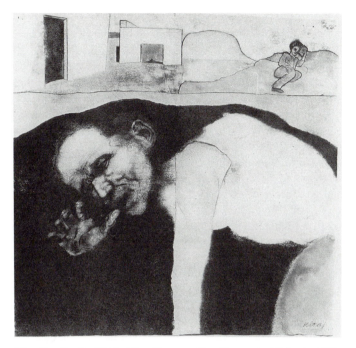

Fig. 5. R. B. Kitaj, *The Listener (Joe Singer in Hiding),* 1980. Pastel and charcoal on paper, 40-5/8 × 42-5/8 in. (103.2 × 108.2 cm). Nelson Blitz, Jr., New York. (Photograph John Ashbery et al., *Kitaj: Paintings, Drawings, Pastels* [London: Thames & Hudson, 1984], pl. 104.)

story "The Burrow," whose unidentified animal protagonist, forever involved in devising ways of increasing his underground safety, is disturbed by threatening noises, presumably from other burrows or subterranean passages that he cannot see. I do not intend to suggest a strict thematic analogy between the story and the picture but rather refer to a correspondence of atmosphere—the uncertainty, the intent listening, the condition of knowing and yet not knowing. One is reminded, too, of Benjamin's observation that Kafka

> listened to tradition, and he who listens hard does not see. . . . The main reason why this listening demands such effort is that only the most indistinct sounds reach the listener. There is no doctrine that one could absorb, no knowledge that one could preserve. . . . Kafka's work preserves a sickness of tradition.[52]

Joe Singer, the assimilated, insecure Galut Jew, hiding away from the world, may well be listening to the indistinct sounds from the past. The reading boy in the background is perhaps informed of the past by the book he reads. In Judaism, after all, tradition has always been preserved through a combination of listening and reading—the oral and written tradition.

One of Kitaj's pictures with a Jewish theme that undoubtedly alludes to Kafka's

experience is *Yiddish Hamlet (Y. Löwy)* (fig. 6), painted in 1985. This work, an
outgrowth of a series of Hamlet studies Kitaj did in the same year, was shown with
these studies at an exhibition that Kitaj entitled "A Passion." At the center of this
exhibition were a number of pictures devoted to Jewish themes, particularly the
Holocaust. *Yiddish Hamlet (Y. Löwy)* depicts a man who is confined within a
cagelike structure, complete with barbed wire, that is shaped as a chimney and
through which a plume of smoke rises. The background is a blank space, turbulently
brushed. "The physical dimensions of Kitaj's 'single figure' paintings," writes a
commentator on his later work, "are frequently the literal dimensions of a human
space."[53] In *Yiddish Hamlet (Y. Löwy)*, the curtailed inner space is contrasted with
the implied cosmic dimensions of the surrounding space. The protagonist-actor, a
swarthy man with accentuated features and a large mouth, distorted in a grimace,
represents Yizchak Löwy, the leader of the Polish Yiddish Musical Drama Company that visited Prague in 1911–1912.[54] Kafka's enthusiastic interest in the actors
and their performances is well documented in his diary entries from this period.
What particularly struck him about their bearing was the amazing fact that these
people "were not self-conscious about being Jews."[55] He developed a warm friendship with Löwy, who awoke in Kafka a sympathetic curiosity about the *Ostjuden*. In
general, Kafka's encounter with the Yiddish troupe and with the plays they staged
sparked his preoccupation with Jewish tradition, history and culture as well as
Yiddish literature.

Löwy's company would have been a surreal cast for performing *Hamlet*. But by
casting Löwy as a Yiddish version of the Shakespearean hero, Kitaj brings out the
utter pathos of the inability of both to become masters of their fate. The famous
soliloquy in act 3, scene 1 of *Hamlet* becomes chillingly relevant in this changed
existential setting:

> To be, or not to be, that is the question:
> Whether 'tis nobler in the mind to suffer
> The slings and arrows of outrageous fortune,
> Or to take arms against a sea of troubles
> And by opposing end them. To die: to sleep;
> No more; and by a sleep to say we end
> The heart-ache, and the thousand natural shocks
> That flesh is heir to
>
> . . . .
>
> For who would bear the whips and scorns of time,
> Th' oppressor's wrong, the proud man's contumely
>
> . . . .
>
> When he himself might his quietus make
> With a bare bodkin?

The cross-shaped object that the Yiddish Hamlet holds in his hand may also represent a dagger. Löwy himself, however, when he was eventually caught up by the
events of the Second World War, put up another kind of resistance: facing the end in
the Warsaw ghetto, he is reported to have "recited Hebrew poetry to keep up the
spirits of his fellow prisoners."[56]

Fig. 6. R. B. Kitaj, *Yiddish Hamlet (Y. Löwy),* 1985. Oil on canvas, 48 × 24 in. (122 × 61 cm). (Photograph, *R. B. Kitaj,* Marlborough Fine Art, London/Marlborough Gallery, New York, 1985–1986, cat. no. 74, p. 73.)

A counterpart to *Yiddish Hamlet (Y. Löwy)* is the anonymous *Bather (Frankfurt)* (fig. 7), also of 1985. It depicts a nude, bespectacled male with a hearing aid plugged into his ear. The nervous delineation of his face and body, one line annulling the other, adds to the sense of tension that is conveyed through the man's harried expression, contorted mouth (which closely resembles the grimacing mouth of Löwy) and posture. The scene takes place in some hellish underworld, and the distressed bather raises both arms above his head in a gesture of surrender, not even trying to avert the knife brandished by the arm of an unseen attacker. In the lower right part of the picture appears the arm of a sinking victim, its inclination echoing that of the arm with the knife.

The bespectacled Frankfurt bather with the hearing aid is the "secret agent" best equipped to expose the crimes of Nazi Germany (cf. fig. 8, *The Jew, Etc.*).[57] The bather represents those assimilated and intellectual German Jews who met the same fate as all other Jews in the Nazi hell. This bather wades the Styx, not the Main. Kitaj heightens the tragedy by linking the haunting scene with the bather theme that preoccupied many European artists at the turn of the century. It was Cézanne who probed this theme most exhaustively, and Kitaj is fascinated by his renderings of it, "not only for the usual formalist reasons, which have guaranteed their place in twentieth-century art, but also for their expressive awkwardness."[58] In 1978–1980, Kitaj did a series of weird and disturbed single-figure bathers; one of these works portrays a psychotic boy.[59] But it was with *Bather (Frankfurt)* that he realized his plan to do Cézanne "over again, after Auschwitz."[60] By doing so, he demonstrated the impossibility of "simply" reconnecting with Cézanne's period, a period that in retrospect looks so much more innocent than that in which we live, two world wars later. Indeed, when compared to Kitaj's frenzied naked victim, eons seem to have passed since Cézanne depicted his *Bathers* (c. 1900), even those of his old age, which impress Kitaj with their "grand" pessimism.[61] As always in Kitaj's art, it is not form but content that carries the painting's message—but the form fuses with the content. The body of the Frankfurt bather appears to be about to dissolve (see the right arm and chest section). Kitaj represented the optical effects of a body in contact with water, but, in the context of the Holocaust, the dissolution acquires added connotations. In contrast, Cézanne's *Bathers,* awkward as they may be, seem intact, despite the broken forms and numerous outlines by which he gropingly described their movements (fig. 9).

If *Bather (Frankfurt)* is a relatively simple image of the Holocaust, conceived in the single-figure format that Kitaj increasingly uses in his work, *Cecil Court, London WC 2 (The Refugees)* (fig. 10), painted in 1983–1984, takes the form of an intricate allegory. Kitaj considers this large canvas as his major painting of the early 1980s,[62] and it was referred to as one of the key works at the Tate Gallery's 1984 exhibition "The Hard-Won Image," subtitled "Traditional Method and Subject in Recent British Art."[63] The setting here is a real-life location: a West End alley with a concentration of antiquarian bookshops that Kitaj, the self-avowed bibliomaniac, would often visit; and as indicated by the names written on the signs, the bookshop owners were mostly Jewish refugees. Kitaj's alley is a kind of paraphrase of two paintings by the French painter Balthus, both entitled *The Street* (fig. 11).[64] On this stage, Kitaj enacts a surreal drama in which the artist himself plays a leading role.

Fig. 7. R. B. Kitaj, *Bather (Frankfurt),* 1985. Pastel and charcoal on paper, 50 × 22-1/2 in. (127 × 57.2 cm). (Photograph, *R. B. Kitaj,* Marlborough Fine Art, London/Marlborough Gallery, New York, 1985–1986, cat. no. 71, p. 72.)

Fig. 8. R. B. Kitaj, *The Jew, Etc.,* 1976–1979 (unfinished). Oil and charcoal on canvas, 60 × 48 in. (152.4 × 121.9 cm). Collection of the artist. (Photograph, *R. B. Kitaj, Fifty Drawings and Pastels: Six Oil Paintings,* Marlborough Gallery, New York, 1979, cat. no. 28.)

He is represented in the immediate foreground, reclining on a Le Corbusier chaise lounge and dressed in the outfit he had worn at his recent wedding to artist Sandra Fisher—like himself, an American Jew.[65] A book lies toppled on the ground below the couch. Behind the contemplative artist is an absurdly stretched-out figure whose dwarfed arm is distorted into an awkward gesture. Two blond children, a protective big sister and her kid brother, dressed in lederhosen, make their exit to the left. Behind the gesticulating man, a seated male figure looks out of the picture as if in anticipation, shielding his eyes with one hand. He is flanked by two standing figures: to the left, an old, gentle-looking man who holds a bouquet of flowers; to the right, a tall, younger man, viewed in semi-profile from the back, with a thick bound volume behind his left arm, which is wrapped in phylacteries.[66] The middle background is occupied by the grotesque figure of a prostitute, who sprawls uncomfortably on the ground. A homunculuslike figure seems to issue miraculously from her body. Behind the "fallen woman" a shopkeeper sweeps the entrance to his store and, in the far background, a girl calls a taxi.

The separate images may be interpreted in this way: Kitaj on the Le Corbusier

Fig. 9. Paul Cézanne, *Seven Bathers,* c. 1900. Oil on canvas, 14-5/8 × 17-3/4 in. (37 × 45 cm). Private collection. (Photograph, *Cézanne: The Late Work,* Museum of Modern Art, New York, 1977, pl. 202.)

couch is the artist, molded by the modernist tradition, who, on the occasion of his second marriage, recollects the past—his own life and that of the Jewish refugees by whom his life has been so deeply touched. The man with the book and the phylacteries is a portrait of Dr. Walter Kitaj—the most important refugee in Kitaj's life, who had died shortly before he painted this allegory.[67] The two children were inspired by a picture in a Nazi publication.[68] The man with the flowers is Seligmann, "one of the refugees who ran an art bookshop" and whose name appears on the shopwindow behind him.[69] The gesticulating man with the theatrical expression is a Yiddish actor—perhaps a symbolic portrait of Yizchak Löwy (the name Löwy appears on one of the signs). The prostitute, too, may have been inspired by the Yiddish theater. In Jacob Gordin's play, *Der vilder mentsh,* for example, prostitution is one of the elements of a family melodrama. Gordin was Kafka's favorite Yiddish playwright;[70] the name Gordin appears in the picture opposite that of Löwy. The man gazing out of the picture may be meant as another, symbolic self-portrait of the artist in the role of a "Messiah watcher," as Kitaj had represented himself in 1978 (fig. 12).[71] The figure of the homunculus suggests a golem (the theme of his major painting of 1980, *The Jewish School [Drawing a Golem]*).[72] Perhaps the man

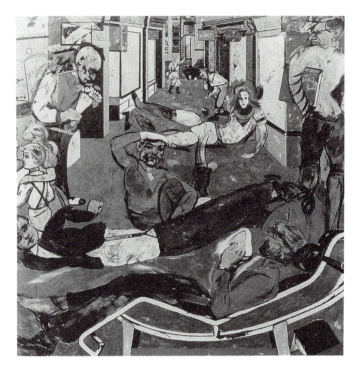

Fig. 10. R. B. Kitaj, *Cecil Court, London WC 2 (The Refugees),*
1983–1984. Oil on canvas, 72 × 72 in. (182.9 × 182.9 cm). Tate
Gallery, London. (Photograph, Marco Livingstone, *R. B. Kitaj*
[Oxford: Phaidon Press, 1985], pl. 143.)

with the broom is making a "clean sweep" of the past (one also recalls documentary
photographs of Jewish shopkeepers in Nazi Germany among the debris of their
vandalized shops); the girl in the background may be embarking on a symbolic ride
of remembrance into the past ("Remembrance" is a frequent expression in Kitaj's
discussions of his Jewish themes).

The names on the signs, as we know, were not chosen arbitrarily; another example is the abbreviation "Sig," standing for the name of Kitaj's biological father,
Sigmund.[73] Possibly the three letters also allude to one of the most famous London
refugees, Sigmund Freud. Freud, in an article by Gershom Scholem that Kitaj had
read, was named along with Walter Benjamin and Kafka as a German-Jewish author
notable for his frank appraisal of his inherently false position within German
culture. Seen in this context, the image of the artist on the couch assumes added
dimensions, presenting psychoanalysis (a Jewish art of introspection) as a means of
summoning memories of the past—on the personal as well as the collective level—
that, by giving free rein to the subconscious, releases the artist's creative imagination (a process propagated by the surrealists).

In the earlier-mentioned Oxford lecture, Kitaj, noting his admiration for sur-

Fig. 11. Balthus, *The Street,* 1933. Oil on canvas, 76 × 92-1/2 in. (193 × 235 cm). Museum of Modern Art, New York. Bequest of James Thrall Soby. (Photograph, *Balthus,* Centre Georges Pompidou, Musée national d'art moderne [Paris, 1983], pl. 8, p. 129.)

realism and other modernist trends as well as for the great precursors of modern art, also acknowledged his debt to "the great art of Christian Europe." Having absorbed that tradition, he can use it at his own discretion. And, so, he draws a symbolic parallel between the Christian Passion and the tragedy of the Jews, "our Crucifixion—at least as searing as *that* has been for Christian life and Christian art,"[74] suggesting that the visual representation of this Jewish Passion may lead to "catharsis." Two years after the lecture, he presented the results of this program in the earlier-mentioned exhibition he rather provocatively named "A Passion." He wrote an introduction to the exhibition catalogue, for which he chose two mottoes. The first, a quotation from Ralph Waldo Emerson's "Divinity School Address," expressive of an essentially American self-sufficiency, is used to support Kitaj in his quest for a Jewish art, created on his own terms: "That is always best which gives me to myself. The sublime is excited in me by the great stoical doctrine: obey thyself." The second motto, more directly connected with the Jewish Passion theme, cites Arnold Schoenberg who, drawing his conclusions from the bitter experience of having had a brilliant career cut short by the Nazis and becoming an exile, announced, "I have long since resolved to be a Jew. . . . I regard that as more

Fig. 12. R. B. Kitaj, *The Messiah Watcher,* 1978. Pastel on paper, 38-5/8 × 15-1/8 in. (98.1 × 38.4 cm). Private collection, Connecticut. (Photograph, *R. B. Kitaj, Fifty Drawings and Pastels; Six Oil Paintings,* Marlborough Gallery, New York, 1979, cat. no. 21.)

important than my art." Kitaj's catalogue introduction amounts to an apology for his thematic choice—the depiction of "Jews in trouble, or Jews in danger," reiterating its conceptual source in Christian art. "It was the Christian Passion of the painter Rouault," he reveals, "which helped me embark on a Passion (1940–1945)."[75] The measure of Kitaj's artistic ambition is demonstrated by his clear sense of being a pioneer: unlike Christian representations of the Crucifixion, which appeared only four hundred years after the event, *his* works approach the Jewish Passion from the historical perspective of a few decades.[76]

An illuminating example of Kitaj's method of quoting the great art of Christian Europe is *The Jewish Rider* (fig. 13), painted in 1984–1985—one of the major works in the "Passion" exhibition. Here he paraphrases the enigmatic painting entitled *The Polish Rider*[77]—hitherto attributed to Rembrandt and dated c. 1655 (fig. 14)[78]—the iconography of which has still not been conclusively resolved. Scholars have claimed that the rider was meant to portray a foreign soldier, a regular Polish cavalry officer or, in view of the "strange and emaciated horse"[79] and the sense of impending danger, "a latter-day *Miles Christianus*, the mounted soldiers who were still defending Eastern Europe against the Turks in the seventeenth cen-

Fig. 13. R. B. Kitaj, *The Jewish Rider,* 1984–1985. Oil on canvas, 60 × 60 in. (152.4 × 152.4 cm). (Photograph, *R. B. Kitaj,* Marlborough Fine Art, London, November–December 1985/Marlborough Gallery, New York, March 1986, cat. no. 56, p. 56.)

Fig. 14. *The Polish Rider,* formerly attributed to Rembrandt Harmensz van Rijn and dated to c. 1655. Oil on canvas (lined), 46 × 53-1/8 in. (116.8 × 134.9 cm). Frick Collection, New York. (Photograph, *Frick Collection, an Illustrated Catalogue,* vol. 1, *Paintings,* New York, 1968, ill. facing p. 258.) Copyright The Frick Collection, N.Y.

tury."[80] It has even been suggested that the painting was intended as "a naturalistic counterpart of Dürer's engraving, *Knight, Death and the Devil.*"[81] Another possibility that has been raised is that *The Polish Rider* is a "spiritual portrait" of the leader of "the Socinians, a Polish anti-Trinitarian sect whose beliefs in tolerance, in particular, had a powerful effect on Dutch nonconformist thought."[82] The Socinian leader adopted the pseudonym "Equus Polonus" and was, in turn, addressed as the "Poolisch Ridder."[83]

Let us now consider what Kitaj has made of all this in his modern Jewish adaptation of *The Polish Rider.* There are several direct quotations. Thus, while the Jewish rider is actually a train passenger, not only does his posture echo that of the Polish rider, but Kitaj even brought the horse into the compartment, partly hidden behind the passenger (who neither rides nor really sits on the seat but seems to be rather uncomfortably suspended within the compartment). The horse's head and rump closely resemble that of the horse in Rembrandt's painting. The awkwardness of the Jewish rider's posture is emphasized by another almost exact quotation from the depiction of the rider on horseback, namely, the bent right arm and the turned-up palm. In the original painting, the rider holds a "war hammer" that intersects "a black quiver full of arrows,"[84] while the Jewish rider's hand is empty. He carries no weapons and travels without baggage (the luggage rack above his head is empty)— except for the book placed conspicuously on the windowsill. The view through the large window echoes and elaborates on the sinister landscape in *The Polish Rider,* the rather obscure details of which include a "flat-domed building which crowns the steep rocky brown hill," other structures, "a square tower . . . beyond the horse's head at right, and a distant fire which glimmers at the water's edge."[85] Kitaj integrated the various parts of this scenery into a single image: a brown, rocky landscape, all barren but for two green trees. Ingeniously, he transformed the fire in Rembrandt's painting into a symbolic image of the Holocaust: a blazing chimney emitting a gust of black smoke. The smoke is blown in the direction of a cross placed on the edge of the steep cliff. The chimney is an extension of the stumplike shape appearing on the same plot in *The Polish Rider.*

The Jewish passenger, with his "thinker's forehead" and inward-looking, speculative expression (actually a portrait of the philosopher Richard Wollheim, a friend of Kitaj's),[86] represents what one critic, referring to Kitaj's Jewish protagonists, calls "the Jewish intellectual, perhaps the bearer of European culture."[87] It is easier to establish his identity than that of the Polish rider. Whoever the latter may be, however, Kitaj may have responded to the implied Christian connotations of *The Polish Rider* in the light of earlier research that interpreted him as a Christian knight advancing toward the infidels—the Turks, in this case—but in principle any non-Christians, not least the Jews. In any case, the juxtaposition of chimney and cross in *The Jewish Rider,* particularly the inclination of the smoke, pointing in the direction of the cross like an accusing finger, suggests an unholy alliance between the Church and Nazism.

The painting's right-hand section, partitioned off from the main scene, depicts the aisle of the train, receding into the background, where a long-legged conductor, standing by the WC sign on the wall, raises his right arm threateningly, ready to strike with his baton. The thrust of the baton forms a visual echo of the smoke issuing from the chimney. This embodiment of the "Banality of Evil" (Hannah Arendt), a concept which Kitaj often evokes in reference to his Jewish pictures, is not connected to the iconography of *The Polish Rider* (although it may perhaps be perceived as an antithesis to the military chivalry that lingers on in the seventeenth-century depiction of the mysterious cavalryman). The conductor represents a stock figure in the nightmarish saga of "European trains which play no small part in our Jewish Demonology" (see fig. 8).[88]

Although (as we have seen) Kitaj quoted or manipulated several details from *The Polish Rider,* he was clearly not adopting or paraphrasing its style. He rather worked in a self-consciously neo-expressionist manner, characterized by strong color contrasts and vigorous brush strokes. (Neo-expressionism burst onto the art scene in the early 1980s, a painterly reaction to the cerebral post-modernist styles of the previous decade.) Some of the foremost exponents of neo-expressionism are German, and Kitaj's appraisal of their significance is markedly ambivalent (not surprising considering the nihilistic decadence of several of them). In the introduction to the "Passion" exhibition, he refers rather sourly to the "New 'German' art," which, he comments "has appeared with a big bang, has it not?"[89] More recently, when a critic suggested a connection between his work and that of Anselm Kiefer—an important and profound German artist (whose work cannot be restricted to categories such as neo-expressionism or any other "ism," just as Kitaj's cannot, and who also shares with him a pressing need to probe the past)–Kitaj reacted more favorably, albeit with a degree of wariness:

> You're not the only one who has recently coupled me with Kiefer. I agree with, it seems *everybody;* he looks very good to me. To put it bluntly, the new German art intrigues me, and I answer it as a Jew, in a Jewish art. If the Germans can have an art of some substance after 50 years of nothingness, then their pals the Jews can, too, I daresay. We can rake over the same rotten earth and see what we find.[90]

His interlocutor expressed reserve about such a clear-cut delimitation:

> "German art," "Jewish art," that bothers me. The Germanness of Kiefer's art has little to do with what it says on his passport. . . . Kiefer is taking German history and experience as the subject of his work, you take Jewish history and experience as the subject of yours. But both of you are making translations into the same culture—that is, the European culture of High Art. From this argument it makes little sense to speak of German art and Jewish art, except to mean an art concerned with German or Jewish experience.[91]

In response, Kitaj seems to relent somewhat, explaining that his statement represents a twofold "quest" (a favorite expression of his), "a quest to lay some ghosts to rest, and a quest which may have to do with things like goodness and reconciliation, brotherhood even." Still, he insists:

> If you agree to a 'Germanness of Kiefer's art,' I wonder why you are bothered by what I called a 'Jewish' art—surely Germans and Jews have things to say to each other. . . . Home is where the heart is, but more often than not, it is also what it says on one's passport—Kiefer's for sure, no? And me? My heart is sort of divided into three: America, London and Jewishness itself. . . . For some reason, probably boredom with internationalism and its slogans in art and life, I'm very tempted to look at questions of nationality, peoplehood, identity and roots—things that seem richly veined and attractive, unlike national*ism,* to make that distinction.[92]

Kitaj's dialogue with Kiefer, within the framework of the European culture of High Art, is demonstrated by *Germania (The Tunnel)* (fig. 15), painted in 1985, one of the major works shown in the "Passion" exhibition. The dark tunnel at its center, enveloped, like the foreground, in a radiant yellow light, has a dual source: van Gogh's *A Passage at St. Paul's Hospital, Saint Rémy* of 1889, and a painting by Kiefer entitled *Shulamite* (fig. 16), done in 1983, the cryptlike setting of which is based on Wilhelm Kreis's design for a "mausoleum for the great soldiers of Germany" in Berlin. In Kiefer's canvas, painted in the characteristic drab shades he employs to convey his tragic vision (whereas Kitaj's *Germania (The Tunnel)* exhibits a contrastingly brilliant color scheme), a seven-flamed fire burns at the back of the crypt. The image has been interpreted as a symbol of mourning and as Kiefer's message that "in murdering the Jews, we Germans . . . have murdered part of ourselves."[93]

Fig. 15. R. B. Kitaj, *Germania (The Tunnel),* 1985. Oil on canvas, 72-1/8 × 84-1/4 in. (183.2 × 214 cm). (Photograph, *R. B. Kitaj,* Marlborough Fine Art, London, November–December 1985/Marlborough Gallery, New York, March 1986, cat. no. 68, p. 69.)

In *Germania (The Tunnel),* Kitaj answers Kiefer as a Jew, first of all with the title of his painting, which embraces multiple allusions. *Germania* is the Hebrew word for Germany ("I am very tempted to look at questions of nationality, peoplehood, identity and roots"); the three last syllables of the word (. . . *mania*) also signify the insanity of that country's past (the dark tunnel). The image of the passage in the mental asylum at Saint-Rémy alludes to van Gogh's mental illness, which was of quite another order and yielded such great and moving art. The imagery of *Germania (The Tunnel)* combines into a Jewish allegory of remembrance and of hope. Four figures occupy the foreground: to the left there is a graying, potbellied, infirm-looking man who supports himself on a stick and rubs a sore spot on his back. The blotches of red on his throat, chest and anterior leg suggest blood and injury, and a strange chimney-shaped contraption seems to obstruct his limping gait. The rear leg ends in what looks like the charred remains of a foot. In front of this pathetic figure, a blond and rosy toddler moves toward the edge of a narrow, elevated structure on which several flames flare—recalling the seven-flamed memorial fire in the funeral hall of Kiefer's painting. The toddler is absorbed by an open book he holds in his outstretched hands.

Fig. 16. Anselm Kiefer, *Shulamite,* 1983. Oil, acrylic, emulsion, shellac and straw on canvas, with woodcut, 114-3/16 × 145 in. (290 × 370 cm). Saatchi Collection, London. (Photograph, *Anselm Kiefer,* Städtische Kunsthalle Düsseldorf/ARC Musée d'art moderne de la ville de Paris/The Israel Museum, Jerusalem, 1984, cat. no. 53, pl. 87, p. 131.) The title and full details of the painting taken from Mark Rosenthal, *Anselm Kiefer* [Art Institute, Chicago/Philadelphia Museum of Art: 1987], pl. 63, p. 118.

I see the infirm man and the bouncing toddler as symbolic portraits of the artist and his infant son, Max, born in 1984. The limping figure connotes the proverbial Wandering (Galut) Jew, particularly that generation of Jews whose lives were lost, destroyed or in some way affected by the Holocaust—as Kitaj's was.[94] The toddler may signify the miraculous survival of the Jewish people and the book in which he is absorbed, the Judaic tradition. The flames seem to represent Kitaj's answer ("as a Jew") to the flames in the crypt—perhaps they allude to the Feast of Lights, Hanukkah, with its rejoicing over being saved from destruction.

The right-hand part of *Germania (The Tunnel),* delineated by a red path that recedes toward a sepulchral opening, shows in the foreground a nude woman, depicted from behind and holding an infant whose head peeps out above her left shoulder. The mother and child are about to enter a pitch-black, tomblike vault. Painted in muted blue shades (except for the woman's sickly yellow legs), they recall the melancholy figures of Picasso's Blue Period (1902–1904) and, more specifically, his allegorical painting *La Vie* (fig. 17) of 1903, which Kitaj first saw

Fig. 17. Pablo Picasso, *La Vie,* 1903. Oil on canvas, 77-1/2 × 50-4/8 in. (197 × 127.3 cm). Cleveland Museum of Art. Gift of Hanna Fund. (Photograph, Timothy Hilton, *Picasso* [London: Thames & Hudson, 1975], fig. 36, facing p. 36.)

as a boy at the Cleveland Museum of Art and singled out as one of his favorite works of art.[95] *La Vie* is a "Symbolist cycle-of-life painting which makes dramatic how that cycle can be cut short" (it had been inspired by the suicide of Picasso's painter-friend Carlos Casagema). The right-hand section of *La Vie* depicts a mother holding a sleeping infant; and both this and other Blue Period works contain "vague suggestions of cloistered architecture."[96] The quotation from *La Vie* links up with the theme of *Germania (The Tunnel):* the cutting short of millions of lives in the Holocaust. All those mothers and children who met their deaths in the gas chambers are here commemorated by the nude woman and her infant entering the dark void.

Several small unfinished oils of 1985, all entitled *Passion,* and each with a different subtitle, epitomize Kitaj's programmatic use of the chimney image in what he describes as his "very primitive attempt at an equivalent symbol, like the cross, both having, after all, contained the human remains in death."[97] One of these works, the stark *Passion (1940–45) Girl/Plume* (fig. 18), shows a scantily dressed girl huddling within the narrow confines of a transparent geometric structure with a pentagonal base and upward-converging sides. A plume of smoke rises through this chimney-cage in front of the girl, blotting out parts of her body and face, its spiraling movement echoing the undulating outlines of the girl's body and contrasting with the stiff geometry of the contours of the chimney-cage. This latter image is

Fig. 18. R. B. Kitaj, *Passion (1940–45) Girl/Plume,* 1985 (unfinished). Oil on canvas, 18 × 10-1/2 in. (45.7 × 26.7 cm). (Photograph, *R. B. Kitaj,* Marlborough Fine Art, London, November–December 1985/Marlborough Gallery, New York, March 1986, cat. no. 65, p. 66.)

a variation of the transparent geometric structures employed by Francis Bacon (b. 1909) in his searing existential portraits. John Russell, contemplating the strange constricted settings of some of Bacon's earlier post-Second World War depictions of "the human condition," relates these to contemporary literary representations of "the extreme situation." "Camus with *L'Étranger,* Sartre with *Huis Clos,* Koestler with *Darkness at Noon,"* he writes, "had all seen the small, enclosed, windowless space as a metaphor for our general predicament; and since a great many Europeans had lately been in captivity of some sort or another, the view had a certain circumstantial validity, quite apart from its metaphorical interest."[98] In *Passion (1940–45) Girl/Plume,* the circumstantial validity is self-evident.

This is also one of those works in which Kitaj answers his German colleague, Anselm Kiefer, "as a Jew." In the early 1980s, Kiefer created a group of paintings inspired by Paul Celan's famous poem "Death Fugue," written in 1944. The titles of Kiefer's paintings, alternately named *Your Ashen Hair, Shulamite* and *Your Golden Hair, Margarete,* are verbatim quotations from the poem, which recurrently juxtaposes these contrasting images. In Kiefer's canvases, the "golden hair" of the archetypal Aryan girl is represented by straw, glued onto the painted surface, which depicts an expanse of field (one of Kiefer's characteristic images). In the paintings dedicated to Shulamite, the archetypal Jewess, a nude woman is depicted in three-quarter profile, her black hair drooping to the ground in lifeless, disheveled strands. The golden straw has been interpreted as an image of life against a background of death (the "rotten earth" to which Kitaj referred in the already-mentioned interview).[99]

The posture of the unnamed girl in Kitaj's painting is similar to that of Shulamite. But her hair is not ashen but blond and, as mentioned, the setting is a symbolically constrained existential space. The plume of smoke recalls the bitter lines in Celan's poem: "and as smoke you/shall climb to the sky/then you'll have a grave in the clouds it is ample to lie/there."[100]

In several of the *Passion* pictures, the chimney image is juxtaposed with a cross or several cross shapes. One of these paintings, *Passion (1940–45) Landscape/ Chamber* (fig. 19) of 1985, is divided into two parts, like a diptych—a traditional format for altarpieces. In Kitaj's diptych, the left side consists of a large cross in a semi-abstract landscape with agitated forms, whereas the right part depicts a geometrically outlined, sinister entrance to the "chamber," which is flanked by two symbolic "pillars of smoke."[101]

Kitaj's preoccupation with the "Jewish Tragedy Under the Nazis" extends into pondering a new anguished dilemma. Although his Jewish identity (as we have seen) remains within the category of the "divided" heart—the foci of his awareness being "America, London and Jewishness itself"—he is also keenly interested in, and concerned with, the problems of Israel. Not incidentally, the published version of his correspondence with Andrew Brighton ends with the following admonition, "Don't forget, I'm a Diaspora Jew, American Jew, London Jew and maybe some other things. If I don't make *aliyah* . . . then my 'geography' is up for grabs."[102] In the interview with Timothy Hyman (1980) Kitaj expressed his concern with the tragic repercussions of the establishment of the Jewish state: "And now the agony of the Palestinians confounds the historical Jewish agonies and those two battered

Fig. 19. R. B. Kitaj, *Passion (1940–45) Landscape/Chamber,* 1985 (unfinished). Oil on canvas, 11 × 20 in. (28 × 50.8 cm). (Photograph, *R. B. Kitaj,* Marlborough Fine Art, London, November–December 1985/Marlborough Gallery, March 1986, New York, cat. no. 67, p. 67.)

peoples embrace in a deathly lock step. I intend to confront these impossible things . . ." and he added, "I want to try and pretend in another picture, a poetic reconciliation between Arab and Jew."[103] A good five years later Kitaj indeed produced a large oil entitled *Arabs and Jews (Jerusalem)* (fig. 20), just in time for its inclusion in the "Passion" exhibition.[104] The picture shows two small boys, hardly more than toddlers, but with precocious expressions and gestures, facing each other on a low couch. Although young enough to cuddle the teddy bears thrown in front of them on the floor, they are depicted in the aspect of little "thinkers," symbolizing the young generation of Palestinians and Sabras who, in order to survive and prosper, will have to consider their common future in a spirit of mutual acceptance and reconcilement. This is, to my mind, Kitaj's boldest—and most risky—attempt to create what Meyer Schapiro, referring to van Gogh, calls "a communication of the *good.*"[105] The risk he takes, knowingly, is to be accused by highbrow critics of sheer sentimentality.

Sometimes Kitaj seems to be quoting himself—not surprising in the case of such an eminently verbal artist. A painting such as *The Divinity School Address* (fig. 21) of 1983–85 could illustrate one of his reflections in the interview with Timothy Hyman: "I am quite taken with the idea that forbidding events in the world can be taken up by a person like myself, who may never have experienced those events,

Fig. 20. R. B. Kitaj, *Arabs and Jews, (Jerusalem),* 1985. Oil on canvas, 36 × 72 in. (91.4 × 182.9 cm). Marlborough Fine Art, London. (Photograph courtesy Marlborough Fine Art, London, November–December 1985.)

except in the mind, and in a quiet room filled with English daylight, pretend to mark the passage of a horror or of a fantasy."[106] In the background of *The Divinity School Address* a dark-haired man rests in a folding chair by the open window in precisely such a light and airy room while the foreground represents a sinister fantasy. To the left, once again, a combination of crosses and a chimney-shaped structure, which here comprises three forbidding faces. The title in combination with the crosses and the red headgear of the upper head brings to mind a priestly confraternity. The implication of antisemitism is underscored by the right-hand cross, whose horizontal beam assumes the appearance of an accusing finger or pen (bringing to mind the confrontation of smoke and cross in *The Jewish Rider*). Not incidentally, the painting's title recalls one of the mottoes of the "Passion" exhibition, taken from Emerson's "The Divinity School Address." This is another instance of Kitaj's position vis-à-vis the Christian tradition within which he grew up and that could not but affect him. But, as a Jew, he is extremely ambivalent about this tradition, absorbing whatever wisdom it may contain, yet constantly on his guard against the ever-present threat of antisemitism.

Thus Kitaj, creating for decades "under English skies," in London, where he believes he will "live and die,"[107] has settled down to the life of the voluntary exile. His sense of belonging, artistically, to that city, is evidenced by the term he coined for a group of prominent artists, who (except one) live and work there and share certain assumptions about their art—the School of London.[108] The most famous artist in this unofficial community is Francis Bacon. Four (Kitaj included) are Jewish; two of them, Frank Auerbach and Lucien Freud, were born in Berlin and came to London as children in the 1930s. The fourth Jew, Leon Kossof, is a "true Cockney."[109] While these artists all exhibit a preoccupation with content and with existential issues, working in more or less figurative styles, Kitaj remains alone in

Fig. 21. R. B. Kitaj, *The Divinity School Address,* 1983–1985. Oil on canvas, 36 × 48 in. (91.4 × 121.9 cm). (Photograph, *R. B. Kitaj,* Marlborough Fine Art, London/Marlborough Gallery, New York, 1985–1986, cat. no. 49, p. 68.)

his quest for a Jewish art. He tells us that they often discuss the risks in this endeavor, and he is aware of the pitfalls—the potential deterioration into a literary or merely illustrative depiction.[110] On the other hand, his immersion in Jewish themes offers him the advantage of staking out his own artistic ground. He quotes Flaubert's quip, "Not to resemble one's neighbour; that is everything."[111] But no doubt his persistent confrontation with Jewish themes stems from a genuine involvement, from an urge to understand, from compassion, from a resolve to remember and from a need to hope. It is the combination of these intense emotions that results in the contemporary Jewishness—and stirring authenticity—of Kitaj's Jewish art.

Notes

1. Marco Livingstone, *R. B. Kitaj* (Oxford: 1985), 8.
2. *Ibid.,* 9.
3. Frederic Tuten, "Neither Fool, nor Naive, nor Poseur-Saint: Fragments on R. B. Kitaj," *Artforum* (January 1982), 65.
4. Livingstone, *Kitaj,* 9.
5. Timothy Hyman, "A Return to London," in John Ashbery et al., *Kitaj: Paintings, Drawings, Pastels* (London: 1983), 41.

6. Livingstone, *Kitaj*, 10.

7. *Ibid.* Kitaj participated in art classes at the Cleveland Museum of Art that he describes as his "happiest childhood memories."

8. *Ibid.*

9. Tuten, "Fragments," 61.

10. "A Return to London: R. B. Kitaj Replies to Some Questions Put to Him by Timothy Hyman," *London Magazine*, n.s. 19 (February 1980), 15-27. Reprinted in Ashbery et al., *Paintings, Drawings, Pastels*, 39–47.

11. *Ibid.*, 42–43.

12. *Ibid.*, 44.

13. Tuten, "Fragments," 65.

14. The quotations that follow are from the unpublished manuscript of the lecture that the artist kindly sent me. Hereafter cited as Oxford lecture. See Livingstone, *Kitaj*, 45.

15. Oxford lecture. Kitaj's ambivalent relationship to earlier (and contemporary?) Jewish artists is beyond the limits of this essay but merits a separate investigation.

16. Oxford lecture. Kitaj probably alludes here to the polemics that surrounded his ardent championing of a new figurative art in conjunction with the 1976 exhibition "Human Clay" (Hayward Gallery, London), which he had been asked to select.

17. Oxford lecture. Here Kitaj seems to refer to Chagall, the Russian-Jewish avant-garde and the Jewish School of Paris. His initially rather contemptuous opinion of the "ethnic representation" of Chagall was modified in later years. See Andrew Brighton, "Conversations with R. B. Kitaj," *Art in America* (June 1986), 100–101.

18. Tuten, "Fragments," 67.

19. Oxford lecture. Kitaj here cites a sentence in an article on Walter Benjamin by Gershom Scholem. See n. 33.

20. Oxford lecture.

21. *Ibid.*

22. Livingstone, *Kitaj*, 13.

23. Note to *The Murder of Rosa Luxemburg*, written in 1980 at the request of the Tate Gallery when it purchased the painting. See Livingstone, *Kitaj*, 42, n. 10. The note was kindly sent to me by the artist in June 1984.

24. An early reference to this picture, supplemented with bibliographical references, is found in the catalogue accompanying Kitaj's first solo exhibition in 1963. The only image referred to specifically in the catalogue is the "profile in the car window," which Kitaj links to Field Marshal Count Helmuth von Moltke (as a symbol, one assumes, of German militarism). See R. B. Kitaj, *Pictures with Commentary, Pictures without Commentary*, Marlborough, New London Gallery, 1963, cat. nos. 1, 5.

25. Carla Schulz Hoffmann and Judith C. Weiss, eds., *Max Beckmann—Retrospective*, Saint Louis Art Museum (Munich, New York and London: 1984), 403–405, fig. 250.

26. Personal communication to author, July 1984.

27. Note to *The Murder of Rosa Luxemburg;* see n. 23.

28. Quoted in Livingstone, *Kitaj*, 43, n. 28.

29. In R. B. Kitaj, *Pictures with Commentary*, in which *Isaac Babel Riding with Budyonny* is illustrated (cat. no. 17), Kitaj refers specifically to the "upright rider in the upper center of the painting" as having been "based on the design of embossed covers of the sixth volume of *South Africa and the Transvaal War*" by L. Creswicke (London: 1901)—an interesting example of his wide frame of reference as well as his working method. The bibliographical references he provides as source material for the painting are no less illuminating: a book entitled *Riders of Many Lands*, written by a colonel in the U.S. Army (London: 1894) and illustrated with drawings. Another important source (for unspecified images) is an article by the renowned art historian Rudolf Wittkower, "Marvels of the East," published in 1942 in the fifth volume of the *Journal of the Warburg and Courtauld Institutes* (159–197), a publication over which Kitaj was wont to pore during his first years in England, finding stimulation for his art in the intriguing iconographic studies it comprised (see

Livingstone, *Kitaj,* 12–13). Wittkower's paper is an iconographic survey of the "monstrous races and animals" said to live in faraway Eastern lands and through which the ancient Greeks rationalized their "many instinctive fears" in a "non-religious form" as against sublimating them by the creation of mythological monsters ("Marvels of the East," 159). The monsters included figures with human bodies and animal heads—a fact that may substantiate my tentative interpretation of the horse's head of the rider.

30. Livingstone, *Kitaj,* 17.

31. Perhaps the strangely muffled creature with the sadly staring eyes in the upper left part of *Isaac Babel Riding with Budyonny,* placed atop yet another horse, refers to the gradual silencing and stifling of Babel by the communist machinery. The image seems related to Kitaj's depiction in other works of the early 1960s of the "late medieval figure of Nobody, represented as a man with padlocked mouth, a symbol of Society's tendency to create a scapegoat on which to blame its ills" (Livingstone, 13; 42, n. 8). Kitaj had come across this image in another paper in the issue of the *Journal of the Warburg and Courtauld Institutes* that features Wittkower's article (Livingstone, 13; also *Pictures with Commentary,* 5).

32. Walter Benjamin, *Illuminations,* ed. Hannah Arendt (New York: 1968), "Introduction," 11.

33. Kitaj read Gershom Scholem's beautiful article on his friend Walter Benjamin in *Leo Baeck Institute Year Book* 10 (1965), 117–136; and *Illuminations,* which was the first English selection of Benjamin's writings.

34. See Livingstone, *Kitaj,* pl. 46.

35. "Preface" to *The Autumn of Central Paris (After Walter Benjamin),* reprinted in Livingstone, *Kitaj,* 149–150.

36. *Illuminations,* see "Introduction," 38–51.

37. Gershom Scholem, *Walter Benjamin, the Story of a Friendship* (London: 1981), 134.

38. *Ibid.,* 135.

39. Livingstone, *Kitaj,* 11.

40. "Preface" to *The Autumn of Central Paris.*

41. *Illuminations,* "Introduction," 21–22.

42. *Ibid.,* "On Some Motifs in Baudelaire," 157–202.

43. *Ibid.,* "Theses on the Philosophy of History," 9; 259–260.

44. *Ibid.,* "Introduction," 12–13; 50.

45. Ashbery et al., *Paintings, Drawings, Pastels,* 44–45.

46. Cf. Benjamin's metaphor of the "pile of debris," "Theses on the Philosophy of History," in *Illuminations,* 259–260.

47. Livingstone, *Kitaj,* 10.

48. Kitaj quoted in Tuten, "Fragments," 67–68.

49. Livingstone, 13; 42, n. 11.

50. Joe Singer was the name of a Cleveland friend of Kitaj's mother; later Kitaj found out that this vaguely remembered man might have become his stepfather. See Livingstone, *Kitaj,* 34.

51. The image faintly echoes the awkward farewell scene in another representation of the fictionalized life of the modern Wandering Jew, tellingly entitled *Bad Faith (Riga) (Joe Singer Taking Leave of His Fiancée)* (1980), reproduced in Livingstone, pl. 117.

52. *Illuminations,* "Max Brod's Book on Kafka," 146–147.

53. Robert Creeley, "Ecce Homo," *Art International* (March 1979), 28.

54. *The Diaries of Franz Kafka,* ed. Max Brod (Harmondsworth: 1982), "The Yiddish Theatre Troupe," 64 ff., *passim;* see also Ronald Hayman, *Kafka, a Biography* (London: 1983), 108–120; and Ritchie Robertson, *Kafka, Judaism, Politics and Literature* (Oxford: 1987), *passim.* Kafka specifically mentioned Löwy's "contorted mouth" in his diary entry dated 30 October 1911.

55. Robertson, *Kafka,* 16.

56. *Ibid.,* n. chap. 1, 288. In 1942 Löwy was killed at Treblinka. See Evelyn Tornton Beck, *Kafka and the Yiddish Theater: Its Impact on His Work* (London: 1971), 219; *passim.*

57. Livingstone, in his discussion of the man with the hearing aid in *The Autumn of Central Paris* (*Kitaj*, 28), suggests that it "could be taken as an image of the artist himself . . . in the guise of an intruder who listens in on the life of others." Here, as in *The Jew, Etc.* (fig. 8)—a painting begun in 1976 and left deliberately unfinished—is depicted, as described by Kitaj, "a lone, pondering, suited fiction of a figure in a European train compartment" (Oxford lecture), the hearing aid is carried by the single existential actor, suggesting a disability or affliction compensated for by an added awareness or insight.

58. Livingstone, *Kitaj*, 36.

59. *Ibid.*, pl. 103.

60. Kitaj paraphrases Cézanne himself, who "said something that's become very famous: he said he'd like to do Poussin over again, after nature" (Oxford lecture). I am reminded in this context of what Michael Hamburger, the English translator of Paul Celan's poems, writes in reference to the "Death Fugue": "the impossibility of writing poems after Auschwitz, let alone about Auschwitz, has become a critical commonplace" (*Paul Celan: Poems; a Bilingual Edition,* trans. Michael Hamburger [New York: 1980], 16), see n. 100.

61. *The Artist's Eye, an Exhibition Selected by R. B. Kitaj* (National Gallery, London: 1980), "Introduction" (by Kitaj).

62. Livingstone, *Kitaj*, 40.

63. Richard Morphet, *The Hard-Won Image: Traditional Method and Subject in Recent British Art* (London: 1984), 44.

64. Livingstone, *Kitaj*, 40, 46 n. 82. Livingstone, 40, 46 n. 82. Kitaj sees Balthus as one of the few "survivors," albeit "mannered," of the "older mode of representation" which he is not willing to relinquish (see Ashbery et al., *Paintings, Drawings, Pastels,* 39). Pierre Loeb has aptly described the peculiar and disturbing ambience of Balthus's street scene: "On croit voir quelque songe étrange dont les acteurs sont des somnambulistes, et une atmosphère angoissante émane de cette parfaite composition" (*Balthus,* Centre Georges Pompidou, Musée national d'art moderne, Paris, cat., 37). Kitaj transposes this unspecified malaise into an allegorical tableau of Jewish experience in the modern world, the experience of an unfathomable nightmare.

65. Livingstone in *Kitaj* writes that this self-portrait "was based on the cover illustration of a pulp novel"—a source in tune both with Kitaj's eclectic tastes and his knack for irony.

66. This observation was confirmed by Kitaj during one of our two meetings in London in July 1984.

67. Morphet, *The Hard-Won Image,* 45.

68. Kitaj in July 1984 meeting with the author.

69. Livingstone, *Kitaj*, 40.

70. Hayman, *Kafka, a Biography,* 115.

71. Kitaj's self-portraits through the years express various aspects of his sense of Jewish identification and merit a separate study.

72. See Livingstone, *Kitaj*, pl. 114. Richard Morphet has remarked on the close relationship between these two paintings. The symbolism of the "fallen woman" and the homunculus figure needs further investigation.

73. Morphet, *The Hard-Won Image,* 45.

74. Oxford lecture.

75. *R. B. Kitaj,* Marlborough, London and New York: 1985–1986, iii.

76. Kitaj's sense of being an explorer of this theme results, one feels, from his critical or, at best, ambivalent estimation of the art of other contemporary Jewish artists. In fact, the Holocaust has been confronted by others before Kitaj; it would be enlightening to compare his bold endeavor with their renderings of the theme.

77. William Feaver, "Bacon Hangs His Favourites," unidentified review of Kitaj's 1985 London Marlborough exhibition and of his National Gallery exhibition, the latter selected by Francis Bacon.

78. Svetlana Alpers, *Rembrandt's Enterprise: The Studio and the Market* (Chicago: 1988), 5–6.

79. *Frick Collection an Illustrated Catalogue,* vol. 1, *Paintings* (New York: 1968), 262.

80. *Ibid.,* 262–263.

81. *Ibid.,* 262.

82. *Ibid.,* 265.

83. *Ibid.* For recent research on *The Polish Rider* see: J. Bruyn, in *Oud Holland* 98 (1984), 146–159.

84. *Frick Collection,* 258. Note, however, Colin Campbell's observation that the rider's gesture traditionally distinguished an equestrian portrait as "non-military" and was associated "less with martial subjects than with persons at leisure to cultivate an elegance of bearing" ("Rembrandt's 'Polish Rider' and the Prodigal Son," *Journal of the Warburg and Courtauld Institutes* 33 (1970), 302).

85. *Frick Collection,* 258.

86. Feaver, "Bacon"; Oxford lecture.

87. Brighton, "Conversations with R. B. Kitaj," 99.

88. Oxford lecture.

89. *R. B. Kitaj,* Marlborough, 1985–1986, ii. The "Passion" exhibition, it is worth noting, coincided with the major Royal Academy show "German Art in the 20th Century."

90. Mark Rosenthal, in his comprehensive survey of Kiefer's artistic evolution, clarifies the latter's preoccupation with Germany's guilt-provoking recent past:

Sensing the presence of World War II everywhere in contemporary Germany, Kiefer found its resonance powerful and inescapable, and felt compelled to confront this reality almost daily. Although he was born in the year the war concluded [1945], he accepted and embraced the event as a touchstone of the inherently German cosmography, a framework that he, regardless of inclination, must accept. . . . Kiefer is, in fact, an anti-hero, incapable of throwing off the chains of his countrymen and their memories. His painful feelings of guilt are not diminished through these endeavors, he explains, but his knowledge about the period is increased.

See Mark Rosenthal, *Anselm Kiefer,* Art Institute, Chicago/Philadelphia Museum of Art, 1987, 17.

91. Brighton, "Conversations with R. B. Kitaj," 100.

92. *Ibid.*

93. *Anselm Kiefer* (Städtische Kunsthalle Düsseldorf, ARC/Musée d'art moderne de la ville de Paris/The Israel Museum, Jerusalem, 1984), 22.

94. A striking resemblance exists between the portrait of Seligmann in *Cecil Court* and the man in *Germania (The Tunnel).* Kitaj is indeed wont to cultivate such similarities between seemingly unconnected figures appearing in different contexts, not least in the "Passion" pictures. Thus, the posture of Dr. Kitaj in *Cecil Court* (fig. 10) is strangely duplicated in Kitaj's fantastic *Self-portrait as a Woman* of 1984 (reproduced in the 1985–1986 Marlborough catalogue, pl. 51) that depicts a nude woman with a placard on her chest, meant to commemorate the gentile women who in Nazi Germany were publicly shamed for having had sexual relations with Jews (Kitaj in an interview in *Times* [London], Thursday, 7 November 1985, 10). Purely compositional considerations aside, Kitaj, by repeating postures in this way emphasizes the fact that the figures are not simply individuals, but characters in the ongoing Jewish drama in the pictures he creates and reflects on.

95. Livingstone, *Kitaj,* 9.

96. Timothy Hilton, *Picasso* (London: 1975), 36.

97. *R. B. Kitaj* (Marlborough, London and New York: 1985–1986), iii.

98. John Russell, *Francis Bacon* (London: 1979), 35–36.

99. Wolfgang Max Faust and Gerd de Vries, *Hunger nach Bildern, deutsche Malerei der Gegenwart* (Cologne: 1982), 78. See also Rosenthal, *Anselm Kiefer,* 95–104.

100. *Paul Celan: Poems;* see n. 60.

101. Other pictures juxtaposing the chimney and cross imagery are *Passion (1940–45)*

Writing and *The Painter (Cross and Chimney)*, which, although very interesting cannot be included here. See *R. B. Kitaj* (Marlborough, 1985–1986) cat. nos. 64, 58.

102. Brighton, "Conversations with R. B. Kitaj," 106.

103. Ashbery et al., *Paintings, Drawings, Pastels,* 43; 44.

104. It was finished too late to be included in the exhibition catalogue (Marlborough— London staff, personal communication, December 1985).

105. Meyer Schapiro quoted in Tuten, "Fragments" (n. 3), 68.

106. Ashbery et al., *Paintings, Drawings, Pastels,* 44.

107. *Ibid.,* 43.

108. Michael Andrews now lives in Norfolk, England.

109. *A School of London: Six Figurative Painters* (British Council, 1987), 8. Limited space precludes specific reference to these artists in this context. Suffice it to mention that critics have sometimes related the work of Frank Auerbach and Leon Kossof to their Jewish background, although neither of them considers himself a specifically Jewish artist.

110. Kitaj in various discussions on his Jewish art; also in July 1984 meetings with the author.

111. Oxford lecture.

Yiddish Adaptations of Children's Stories from World Literature

Chone Shmeruk
(THE HEBREW UNIVERSITY)

Did the girl called Little Red Riding-Hood also have a real name?

In the original German prose version in the famous collection by the Brothers Grimm, no name other than Red Riding-Hood is mentioned.[1] But in the rhymed Yiddish version, entitled "Royt mentele" ("Little Red Coat"), the girl is given a name to rhyme with the title: Yentele. In this version of the tale, the story takes place on Purim. Yentele is on her way to bring grandma the traditional basket of Purim treats: a *homentash*, a strudel, a Purim-cake and a fruit layer cake. There is no hunter as there is in the original; instead, the hero who saves Yentele and grandma is Yehiel, the water carrier.

This adaptation of the story for Jewish children was published in Warsaw in 1921 when the creation of Yiddish literature for children was at its height. It was part of an early childhood series called "For Small Children," produced by the *Kultur lige* (Culture League). Among ten items from this series that I have been able to obtain, six are self-declared adaptations from non-Jewish stories. Moreover, we may assume that the other stories in the series were based on similar sources even when no details are given. Nowhere does the booklet about "Royt mentele" mention the Brothers Grimm.[2]

This testifies first of all to the sorely felt dearth of original children's literature in Yiddish. The lack of suitable Yiddish stories became a pressing issue in the modern Jewish kindergartens established in Poland during the First World War. The efforts of Y. L. Perets to establish such a kindergarten in Warsaw in March 1915 are well known. He planned a collection of songs and stories for children—a plan that was never implemented.[3]

The demand for something to fill the gap grew more pronounced during the final years of the First World War and in the first postwar years in Soviet Russia and independent Poland, where school systems were established with Yiddish as the language of instruction. That is why the first three decades of the twentieth century might be regarded as the heyday of Yiddish children's literature. Unfortunately, this is a body of literature that has not yet been properly studied even though it surely merits serious examination in view of its high level of qualitative and quantitative achievement. This literature was aesthetically produced, with work by some first-

186

rate Jewish artists and illustrators. Their contribution has not received adequate attention either.[4]

It was only natural that the choice of suitable material should fall to those works that were considered classics at that time: the stories of Hans Christian Andersen and the Brothers Grimm, for example. It should perhaps be pointed out, too, that these stories were rarely adapted directly from their original versions, but often reached Yiddish by way of Russian and Polish translations.[5]

The first Yiddish adaptations of children's stories from world literature were done about ten years before the First World War. From the very first, we can detect two opposing tendencies: (1) the attempt to convey in Yiddish stories that were as true as possible to the original and that did not tamper with the stories beyond what was necessary for "adequate" translation; (2) an approach that involved the reworking of the story, at times quite radically, so as to fit not just the language of the target audience, but also its cultural ambience. In the latter instance, the child's ability to identify details of the stories with everyday experience took precedence over the textual integrity of the original tale.

The version of Red Riding-Hood that I have mentioned is obviously an example of the second type of translation, one that sought to supply familiar details even where the original provided no details at all. But there was another Yiddish version of Red Riding-Hood, this one called "Royt haybele," published in Berlin in 1922 by Yashar as part of a series of translations from *Grimms' Fairy Tales*.[6] This furnishes us with a case of the other type of translation. Thus, the same story was likely to be available in Yiddish in various versions, each reflecting a different mode of cross-cultural literary transmission.

The adaptation of the story in "Royt mentele" was based, as I have noted, on the rather daring attempt to transplant the story into a Jewish setting in order to make it more accessible to the young listener or reader. No inherent objection to the story as it was presented in the original was involved. Yet, in many cases, the motive for reworking a story may be said to have stemmed from more complex difficulties arising out of the original version. We may illustrate this phenomenon with some examples from Yiddish translations of Hans Christian Andersen.

The first Andersen story that we know was translated into Yiddish was called "Big Fayvl and Little Fayvl." It was published as a supplement to an issue of the Saint Petersburg daily *Der Fraynd* shortly before Purim in 1904. It was, as the cover announced, a kind of Purim present from the newspaper to Jewish children. The adaptation was done by the Russian-Jewish writer, Chaim-Mordechai Rabinovich, whose pen name was Ben-Ami. On the cover Ben-Ami wrote, "A story by Andersen retold for Jewish children."[7] The same tale, translated by Der Nister in 1919, was called "Big Klaus and Little Klaus," as in the Danish original.[8]

Der Nister's faithfulness to the original—as mediated by a Russian translation—becomes evident at the beginning of the story in a passage describing a typical Danish Sunday, "The bells summoned people to morning worship, everyone was dressed in their Sunday best and clasping their prayer books as they made their way to church to hear the preacher's sermon" (p. 3).

In the Ben-Ami version, there is no trace of bells or of a church for that matter.

Gone are the churchgoers along with the preacher. Instead, the story opens on a Friday and involves only Jewish characters: "The two Fayvls, though they lived in a village, were not shopkeepers, but used instead to plow and to sow the fields, for this was a village of Jewish farmers."

Although Ben-Ami would reintroduce the theme of the Jewish farmer later in the story—modern writers favored farming as a preeminently productive pursuit for the Jew and liked to hold it up as a model for emulation—the rest of his depiction of a typical village Friday could have been modeled on any East European Jewish shtetl:

> The housewives of the village had already put the *cholent* in the ovens and were scrubbing the children. The very pious ones already had their minds on lighting the candles in time for the Sabbath. The menfolk were on their way back from the baths. Young lads were rushing hither and thither with bottles to bring home wine or brandy for the Sabbath benediction. The old beadle had already placed candles in the chandelier of the synagogue and was about to go on his rounds to summon the village to prayers (p. 4).

In this way, Andersen's Danish setting was completely transformed and his characters became bona fide Jews. All Christian references were excised. For example, the treacherous church sexton who appears in the Der Nister translation was turned into "Jonah the Stoolie" in Ben-Ami's version. An omitted passing reference to the church was the occasion to mention a Jewish tavern.

One may conclude, then, that Ben-Ami's Judaizing version was based on a desire to strip from the story, as Jewish children would hear it, any Christian content. Indeed, similar motives prompted the same sort of intervention in stories that seem at first to be only straightforward translations, without any particular attempt to reset the plot in a Jewish context.

A translated collection of Andersen stories was published in Warsaw in 1910 by L. Bromberg. The five stories selected include "The Little Match Girl." In the original, one of the scenes that the little girl imagines as she shivers in the freezing darkness of New Year's Eve is that of a brilliantly illuminated wealthy home with a decorated Christmas tree. Bromberg, who apparently worked from a Polish translation, faithfully noted that the story took place on New Year's Eve, but omitted the Christmas tree.[9] The details missing in Bromberg's translation do appear, of course, in the version by Der Nister.[10] Nevertheless, it is clear that Bromberg did not Judaize the story. He merely removed the overt symbols of Christmas, which he considered to be inappropriate for his target audience.

As a result, this version of the story became religiously neutral, unconnected to any denomination. Sometimes, however, the same underlying reticence with regard to Christian references produced more active interventions in folk tales. We may cite, for instance, the Hebrew version of "The Little Match Girl" by David Frishman, written in 1896.[11] Bromberg was apparently unfamiliar with it. That the Hebrew "Little Match Girl" is a Judaized version is immediately apparent from the subtitle, which calls the story a Hanukkah tale. As we might expect, the Christmas tree is replaced by a menorah.[12] Such a change, which may seem like a minor departure from the original, in fact alters the story's character considerably. By introducing an item as specifically Jewish as a menorah, Frishman evokes a Jewish setting for the story.

It is not always easy to establish a firm definition of what indicates Judaization in literary texts and what constitutes a less substantive emendation. We have, for example, two different translations of the Grimm brothers' "Hans im Glueck."[13] One was prepared by Falk Halperin before the First World War; it is called "Lucky Hans."[14] The second, part of an anthology published in Berlin in 1922, is called "Hans the Lucky."[15] These are two completely independent versions, both of which strive to remain faithful to the German original. But both depart from the original in the passage involving the goose that is brought to the christening. In both cases, the baptismal feast is replaced by a circumcision celebration—an event strictly identified with a Jewish milieu. Halperin wrote, "He brings the goose as a gift for the circumcision"; and in the second translation, once again, we find, "He takes the goose to a circumcision party." Nevertheless, we would not be warranted in regarding either translation as a Judaization of the tale. This one single alteration, which affects neither the characters nor the plot, does not indicate substantial reworking of the original to create a Jewish story.

It may be assumed that omitting references to Christian ceremonies and their simple replacement by Jewish equivalents, without other significant additions, was quite common in the retelling of non-Jewish stories; but this proposition deserves detailed study.

The 1914 Yiddish version of Andersen's story "Olye-Lok-Oye"[16] once again draws our attention to the nature of Judaization and its indicators in a story, either taken as a whole or as affecting its component parts. Andersen's tale involves a boy called Hjalmar,[17] who reappears in Yiddish as Chaiml, a Jewish schoolboy who, naturally enough, is occupied with studying Torah. In the original, the seven chapters of the story–corresponding to the days of the week—begin with Monday. In Yiddish, the story begins on Friday night. Right from the start we get a description of the kind of home you would expect with a boy named Chaiml: "The next day was Friday, and Olye-Lok-Oye came for dinner. The Sabbath candles had burned down, the table was still covered with its white cloth, father and mother had gone to look in on a neighbor, and Chaiml lay in bed" (p. 8). Similar references are scattered throughout the story, leaving no doubt that the action takes place in a Jewish home. This, despite the strange figure with that strange name, Olye-Lok-Oye, which has no connection at all to Jewish life.

Children's books are commonly illustrated, and Yiddish translations or adaptations from foreign-language material were no exception. Often we find a note concerning the source of the illustrations. Thus, the Yiddish selection from *Grimms' Fairy Tales* published in Berlin in 1922 not only bears the name of the translator, but also the information that the illustrations are those of Ludwig Richter. Richter was a nineteenth-century German artist and illustrator whose illustrations for the Grimm stories were reproduced in the 1922 Yiddish edition without alteration. Indeed, this version had little cause to alter the illustrations since it attempted to remain faithful to the original text—apart from a few isolated instances involving Christian symbols or motifs, which hardly affected the stories or the characters.

We may suppose, then, that unchanged renditions were routinely accompanied by illustrations from foreign-language sources–in general, without stating their provenance. The same is true of stories that were only slightly altered, without significantly changing their original characters, and where no incongruity resulted between illustrations and the Yiddish text.

As an example, we may take the Yiddish translation of *Max and Moritz,* the story by Wilhelm Busch, produced by J. Krasnianski in 1921.[18] Despite the fact that explicitly Jewish expressions found their way into the otherwise "adequate" translation, these departures did not actually alter the original story in any substantive way, certainly not with regard to the characters or the setting.[19] The changes, which may be defined as stylistic or linguistic, did not require any alterations in Busch's original illustrations, which were faithfully reproduced.[20]

But what of Judaized stories? How were they illustrated? As we shall see, the publishers had only a few options:

1. From a professional point of view, a new set of illustrations ought to have been commissioned to fit the new version with its Jewish setting and characters. But I have not found any examples before the early 1920s in which this course was taken.

2. It was possible to omit illustrations that clearly no longer fit the text. Thus, both the "Big Fayvl and Little Fayvl" version of Andersen's story and "Royt mentele" were published without any illustrations.

3. One might use illustrations from the original and simply disregard the fact that the Yiddish version had considerably changed the story.[21] This was done for the Judaized Yiddish version of "Olye-Lok-Oye" published in Warsaw in 1914. It included two illustrations from foreign-language editions, despite the fact that the character depicted clearly did not represent little Chaiml.

4. It was also possible, it seems, to alter the existing illustrations slightly in accordance with the new text. This method was chosen for two Wilhelm Busch stories that were adapted and Judaized. Between 1920 and 1923, the popular Jewish humorist, Joseph Tunkel—famous as Der Tunkeler—published five stories by Busch.[22] He considered them as adaptations; indeed, he stated that they were "freely adapted into Yiddish"[23] or "Yiddishized"[24]—a term that embraces both the linguistic and the Jewish cultural aspects.

Der Tunkeler permitted himself a great deal of poetic license with the Busch material and transposed all five stories into Jewish settings. The most obvious indicators of this are the typically Jewish names assigned to the characters. The notorious Max and Moritz became Motl and Notl; as such they also appear in the story "The Robin's Nest," although in the German original we read only of "two lads." Heinrich becomes Kopl, in "Kopl and the Geese"; Fritz, Franz and Konrad are renamed Leybl, Yosl and Moyshe in "The Paper Snake." And Busch's prose story, "Little Pepi and His New Trousers" is entirely transformed into rhymed verse, with the title "Naughty Moyshl."

The Jewish characters had to be provided with a Jewish story, of course, and Der Tunkeler improvised freely from the original texts. Yet the stories remained reasonably close to the Busch version, except for those aspects with explicitly Christian overtones. Thus, *Motl and Notl* is missing the fourth chapter of the German original, the one in which Max and Moritz play a cruel prank on their teacher while he is in church practicing on the organ. It is difficult to determine whether the chapter was omitted due to the streak of cruelty and the unedifying treatment of the teacher, whose pipe was filled with gunpowder, or to the fact that a church figures in the story. Undoubtedly, both factors played a role here. It is interesting, in this regard, that the church organ is not mentioned in all four Hebrew renditions of *Max und Moritz*, even in those that do include the chapter about the teacher.[25]

Beyond the matter of names, Der Tunkeler's Judaization of elements in the stories was obviously guided by the original text itself, insofar as it presented problematic aspects. Max and Moritz's first prank involved their hanging the widow Bolte's hens, as a result of which the hens die. The widow Bolte removes the dead chickens—"die Verstorbenen"—and proceeds without compunction to roast them for dinner. Max and Moritz themselves enjoy the feast.

Now, in the Hebrew versions of the story nothing is changed. The "victims" or the "corpses" in the rather accurate translation by Hava Carmi go directly from the gallows to the frying pan or the oven. Uri Sela, who allows Max and Moritz to retain their German names, nevertheless, does provide some of the characters with Hebrew names. The widow Bolte becomes Aunt Sima. But Aunt Sima when she finds the dead fowl proceeds just as did the widow in the German story:

> No use now in bitter crying,
> she fetched her knife, sadly sighing.
> What's dead is dead.
> And so, instead,
> she'll roast the hens as well as she's able
> and set them upon her dinner table.[26]

Joseph Tunkel, however, chose to handle this matter of the unkosher feast differently. How, after all, could a good Jewish widow called Chaye-Soreh prepare a meal from such an abomination—a meal, moreover, destined to be shared by Motl and Notl, the Jewish pranksters? Der Tunkeler's Judaized adaptation provides a fitting solution to this problem. Coming upon the hanged chickens, the widow Chaye-Soreh:

> Quickly grabs her knife,
> cuts the string, *saves their life.*
> The birds gasp and shudder,
> try to stir, but barely flutter.

And here is what a good Jewish woman does in such a situation:

> "But enough tears shed, I must decide
> what else to do before they've died.
> The only solution left, I feel,
> is to make them into a Sabbath meal.
> Off to the *shoychet*'s stall!" she cries.
> She grabs them up and off she flies.
> Soon hens and rooster are no more.
> She quickly returns through her kitchen door,
> to pluck, salt and soak them as she ought,
> and drain them well as she was taught.

Tunkel, as we see, did not miss a single step in the process of turning this into the proper kosher meal that potential readers of the Motl and Notl adventures would expect.

Apart from providing such solutions to issues of Jewish propriety, Der Tunkeler also managed to convey stylistically a sense of his stories' Jewish setting by using a vocabulary with specifically Jewish referents. His flowing, rhythmic style also deserves notice, but that is another matter.

Tunkel had developed an early talent for drawing; his humoristic literary pieces and parodies were accompanied by his own caricatures.[27] It may be supposed that Wilhelm Busch's success as both a writer and an artist was what first drew Tunkel's interest and inspired him to combine writing and illustration. Certainly, Der Tunkeler was not the only one to have been captivated by Busch's effective integration of text and wonderfully expressive artwork. Every Busch story adapted and published by Der Tunkeler was accompanied by reproductions of the original illustrations. But in two cases, Tunkel decided to Judaize the illustrations in line with the new version of the story. Although it is not explicitly stated, it is more than likely that the alterations were executed by Tunkel himself. There is, in any event, no statement to the contrary.

I will mention several examples.

In *Max und Moritz,* one character is a tailor named Boeck. In Tunkel's version, his name is Aaron, Shloyme's son, and his picture is altered accordingly by giving the tailor a beard and a Jewish hat (fig. 1). This new pictorial image is used throughout the illustrations in this chapter (fig. 2).

In chapter 5 of *Max und Moritz,* we encounter Uncle Fritz. In the Yiddish version this is Uncle Khone-Beyrach, whose picture is, once again, altered to fit the new character. In place of the tufted *Zippelmuetze* originally sported by Fritz, the uncle now wears a yarmulke and he, too, is bearded (fig. 3).

Der Tunkeler also Judaized Busch's anonymous baker, calling him Tsale the Baker, and replaced the German lettering on the sign advertising his wares with the word *bekeray* in Yiddish (fig. 4).

The owner of the granary in the Yiddish version, Sholem, looks different from Bauer Mecke of the original German text (fig. 5). Likewise, Reb Yisroel the miller is depicted as a Jewish figure (fig. 6).

Fig. 1. A and B

Fig. 2. A and B

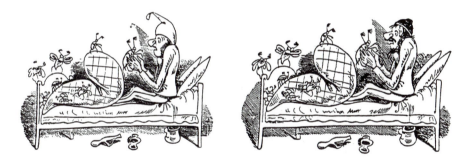

Fig. 3. A and B

Fig. 4. A and B

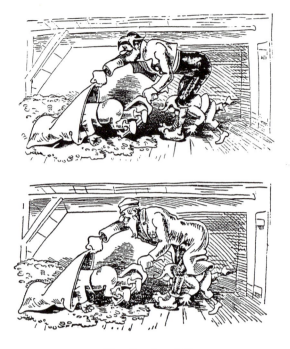

Fig. 5.   A and B

Fig. 6.   A and B

In three Hebrew translations of *Max und Moritz* published in Palestine/Israel, the original illustrations by Busch were retained. Anda Pinkerfeld's 1939 edition, however, included some of Joseph Tunkel's Judaized illustrations as well. For some reason, these were omitted from the 1950 edition in which the illustrations are once again those of Busch.[28]

Another story in which Tunkel matched the illustrations to his text was "Naughty Moyshl." Pepi, as the boy is known in Busch's original, receives a new pair of trousers from his godparent. This religious link is missing, of course, from the relationship between Moyshl and the Jewish tailor. In the Yiddish version, the tailor is simply another Jew and that is how he appears in the story's first illustration. The entire series of Busch drawings for the story appear here, with appropriate alterations. The story concludes with Moyshl receiving his just desserts: a whipping from his father. The Jewish ambience and details are represented in the illustrations, which serve to complete the Judaizing process (figs. 7, 8).

In this discussion, I have only dealt with the absorption and Judaization of children's literature from non-Jewish culture within a brief span of twenty years in the early part of this century. Of course, the phenomenon cannot really be examined in isolation. At least in outline form, I would like to sketch the broader framework for this kind of cross-cultural transference.

Fig. 7. A and B

Fig. 8. A and B

In Yiddish literature, we can point to examples of the exact same process as far back as the fourteenth century. A copyist working on "Dukes Horant"—in a manuscript now in the Geniza Collection at Cambridge University—substituted for the Christian *Kirche,* the Yiddish derogatory *tifleh* in the text he was transcribing into Hebrew letters. He thereby underscored his reluctance to place a word with Christian content into a Jewish manuscript. Similar omissions and neutering of terms may be encountered in numerous texts copied from German into Hebrew characters right through the eighteenth century and beyond. This is well known.[29] In *Bove D'Antona,* adapted from the Italian by Eliyohu Bochur, we find not only neutralization of references to other religions, but also Judaization of elements that were particularly sensitive matters, so that Christian nuptials turn into Jewish weddings, baptisms into circumcisions, and so forth.[30]

In the nineteenth century, this became commonplace in Yiddish adaptations of drama[31] as well as in so-called *shund* (trashy) novels.[32] This would continue right through the 1930s.[33] Thus, the adaptations of children's literature discussed here fit right into an existing pattern.

It should be stressed that the phenomenon of reworking original materials for their reception within Jewish culture is not limited to Yiddish literature alone. It is also a well-known pattern in Hebrew translations of drama in the nineteenth century,[34] and, as we have seen, is a common element shared by Hebrew and Yiddish children's literature. Moreover, the problems of cross-cultural transference apply not just to texts, but to their illustrations as well.

The problem as a whole is not specifically or exclusively a Jewish one, either. Indeed, the adaptation of literature to fit a different cultural milieu is practiced in other languages and cultures, and it has been regarded in certain periods as a perfectly legitimate aspect of translation.[35] Understandably, this is particularly true of what we know as folktales and helps to explain their wide international appeal. Thus, it has been shown that "Little Red Riding-Hood" as we know it from *Grimms' Fairy Tales* is based on a French source, not a German one; nor were the two traditions identical.[36]

Nevertheless, the essential difference between such parallel phenomena and the one we have been discussing is the particular challenge that Christian references posed for Jewish translators. This was clearly the chief motivation behind most deviations from non-Jewish sources, at least within Christian Europe; this factor was not operative in other cultures.

To return to our point of departure, I would like to draw attention to a play for children, "The Purim Bear," which was written by Der Tunkeler and seems to have been first published in Warsaw in 1919.[37] This, too, may serve to illustrate our point about the absorption of non-Jewish children's literature. The play is an original and fascinating construction based on Jewish life in Eastern Europe that involves a rabbi, his wife, their small son, a bear and its gypsy owner. There are resonances here of the traditional Jewish dramatizations at Purimtime of the sale of Joseph, as well as distinct echoes of Red Riding-Hood. The action takes place on Purim, and the child encounters the bear while walking through the woods carrying a basket of Purim treats. This appears to be a direct antecedent of the Judaized "Royt mentele" with which we began. But in "The Purim Bear," the plot is more complex and develops on various levels. I would only add that a set of original illustrations accompanied the text of the play, and these leave no question as to the specifically Jewish setting of the story.

Notes

This essay appeared in Hebrew in *'Iyunim besifrut* (in honor of Dov Sadan on his eighty-fifth birthday), a special publication of the Israel Academy of Sciences and Humanities (Jerusalem: 1988), 59–87. It was translated by Eli Lederhendler.

1. "Rotkäpchen," *Kinder- und Hausmärchen,* gesammelt durch die Brüder Grimm (Darmstadt: 1985), 174–180.
2. *Far kleyne kinder: zibete maysele: "Royt mentele"* (Warsaw: 1921). On the verso of the title page there is a notation in Yiddish and in Polish, "Retold by Sh. Gitelis." Gitelis was a kindergarten teacher in the Soviet Union in the interwar years. See B. Cohen, *Leksikon fun yidish-shraybers* (New York: 1986), 156–157.
3. Sh. Niger, *Y. L. Perets* (Buenos Aires: 1952), 510–511. It should be noted that similar requirements in modern Hebrew education at the end of the nineteenth century prompted Sholem Aleichem to rewrite one of his stories for Hebrew translation; subsequently, following a visit to a primary girls' school, he wrote such stories in Yiddish. See Chone Shmeruk, "Sholem Aleichem un di onheybn fun der yidisher literatur far kinder," *Di goldene keyt* 112 (1984), 39–53, esp. 43–45.
4. Featured prominently at the exhibition mounted by The Israel Museum, Jerusalem, in 1987, "Tradition and Revolution—the Jewish Renaissance in Russian Avant-Garde Art," was work done by E. Lissitzky, Y. Chaikov, Y. Ribak and M. Chagall for Yiddish children's books published in Kiev and Berlin. Children's books from that period formed an obvious, essential part of the exhibition, although the catalogue editors did not point out this connection.
5. See, for example, Y. Ravin, *Royt hitele—instsenizirte maysele in tsvey aktn, baarbayt fun poylish (nokh Or-Ot)* (Lodz: 1917); also see nn. 9, 16.
6. *Royt haybele. Brider Grimm, oysgeklibene mayselekh,* trans. Yashar, 2d booklet (Berlin: 1922), 20–23. The copy at the National and University Library in Jerusalem is bound together with booklets one through four. All share identical title pages; all were published in

1922. Each booklet contains forty to forty-eight pages. I have been unable to discover the identity of Yashar.

7. *Fayvl der groyser un Fayvl der kleyner, a mayse fun Andersenen ibergemakht far yidishe kinder,* Ben-Ami (Saint Petersburg: n.d.). The date of the censor's permit is 12 February 1904. The title page bears the Russian note, "Supplement to issue no. 39 of *Der Fraynd.*" And in Yiddish, "Purim treat from *Der Fraynd* for Jewish children." The same adaptation appears in the fourth issue of the series, *Far unzere kinder* (Vilna: 1913; 2nd ed., 1914). Another edition appeared in New York as part of the *Rozhinkes mit mandlen* series in 1918. See Y. Steinbaum, "Di yidishe kinder-literatur in amerike," *Shriftn* (Fall 1919), 14 (last pagination).

8. Der Nister's translation is cited from the series entitled *Andersens mayselekh. Yiddish: Der Nister,* booklets 1–12 (Warsaw: 1921). The Warsaw edition was reproduced from single booklets that appeared earlier in Kiev between 1918 and 1920 in a somewhat different numerical order. For full bibliographical details on the Kiev edition, see Z. Ratner and Y. Kvitny, "Dos yidishe bukh in f.s.s.r. far di yorn 1917–1921," *Bibliologisher zamlbukh* 1 (1930), 371–486 (see index). The Warsaw edition, *Der groyser Kloys un der kleyner Kloys,* was booklet no. 10.

9. *H. Ts. [sic] Andersen, geshikhten un legenden,* booklet 1, trans. L. Bromberg (Warsaw: 1910), published by *Der Shtrahl. Der Shtrahl* was a Yiddish literary journal that appeared in Warsaw from 1910 to 1911. A second edition of the collection was published in Warsaw in 1914, with the translator's name omitted. The "Ts." as Hans Christian Andersen's middle initial proves that the translation was not done from the Russian and was most likely from a Polish version. This is implied by the use of the word "Sylvester" for the Christian New Year's Eve, which is usual for Catholic countries.

10. See the Warsaw edition cited in n. 8, booklet 2, 20–21.

11. *H. Andersen, hagadot vesipurim,* trans. D. Frishman (Warsaw: 1896), 81–85.

12. E. Ofek, "Agadot Andersen bilevushan ha'ivri," *Sifrut yeladim vano'ar* 2, no. 1 (1976), 21; M. Regev, " 'Al shtei yeẓirot meyuḥadot," *Sifrut yeladim vano'ar* 11, no. 2–3 (1985), 43–46.

13. Edition cited in n. 1, 419–427.

14. The Brothers Grimm, *Der gliklekher Hans,* trans. F. Halperin (Vilna: n.d.). According to the details given in Russian, the story most likely appeared in 1915. It was translated from German in *Kinderbibliotek* no. 6.

15. See edition cited in n. 6, booklet 4, 29–33.

16. G. *[sic]* Andersen, *Olye-Lok-Oye (oder di zibn teg fun der vokh)* (Warsaw: 1914). Judging by the initial "G" in Andersen's name, the Yiddish translator worked from a Russian version.

17. Cf. Der Nister's adequate translation (n. 8), 4.

18. W. Busch, *Max und Moritz,* trans. J. Krasnianski (Odessa: 1921). Three thousand copies of the booklet were published. I would like to thank Professor Shlomo Avineri for his efforts to acquire a photocopy of this rare edition from the Lenin Library in Moscow. See his account of the matter, "Max u-Morits Beyadeinu," *Maariv,* 4 September 1987.

19. A few outstanding examples of Jewish expressions: the chickens are referred to as "those who look at *bnei odom*" [people] (p. 6), "*kapores*" [a Yom Kippur eve ritual] (p. 8), "unkosher necks" (p. 11). *Osterzeit* is altered to Passover eve (p. 25). See also n. 25.

20. The Yiddish translator did not use all of Busch's illustrations. Quite a few that were not essential for fleshing out the story were omitted, probably to economize on paper that was then at a premium.

21. On examples of borrowing illustrations from non-Jewish sources for Yiddish books in earlier periods, see Chone Shmeruk, *Haiyurim lesifrei yidish bameiot ha-XVI-XVII* (Jerusalem: 1986). As in our case, some of these earlier illustrated works were intended for children.

22. Texts and illustrations by Busch are cited from Wilhelm Busch, *Sämtliche Werke und eine Auswahl der Skizzen und Gemälde in zwei Bänden* 1: *Und die Moral von der Geschichte* (Munich: 1959). The booklets by Joseph Tunkel are: *Notl un Motl, zeks shtifer-*

mayselekh (1920) = *Max und Moritz*, 18–69; *Der roben-nest* (1921) = *Das Rabennest*, 174–178; *Kopl un di genz* (1921) = *Der hinterlistige Heinrich*, 261–265; *Di papirene shlang* (1921) = *Die Drachen*, 434–497; *Der shtifer Moyshl* (1923) = *Der kleine Pepi mit der neuen Hose*, 132–137. All the stories were published in Warsaw by the Levin-Epstein Bros. In 1928 new editions of all the stories appeared in modern Yiddish orthography but without alteration in text or illustrations. See also, Wilhelm Busch, *Max und Moritz, eine Bubengeschichte in sieben Streichen in deutschen Dialekten, Mittelhochdeutsch Jiddisch*, ed. and introduced, with bibliographical notes, by Manfred Gorlach (Hamburg: 1982)—*Motl un Notl* appears in transliteration on pp. 147–153.

23. Thus, "freely adapted into Yiddish" on the title pages of *Notl un Motl, Der roben-nest, Kopl un di genz* and *Di papirene shlang*.

24. Thus, "Yiddishized" on all covers for *Der shtifer Moyshl*.

25. In chronological order of publication, these editions were:

1. A. Leibutshitsky, *Shimon ve-Levi—ma'asiyah* (Warsaw: 1913), which includes a note (p. 3) citing the original author and German title. The story appeared in *Biblioteka leyeladim* 5, no. 100. The teacher is named Tarniel (see pp. 15–18).

2. *Gad ve-Dan—shishah ta'alulim shel shnei shovavim, be'ikvot Maks u-Morits* meet *Wilhelm Busch*. Retold by Anda Pinkerfeld (Tel-Aviv: 1939), which omits the entire chapter (see n. 28).

3. *Maks u-Morits—zomemei hamezimot,* meet *Wilhelm Busch,* trans. Hava Carmi (Tel-Aviv: 1939), in which the organ is transformed into a piano in the house (p. 26).

4. *Maks u-Morits,* meet *Wilhelm Busch.* Original illustrations, trans. Uri Sela (Tel-Aviv: 1971). The teacher's name is Yohanan, the organ and church are missing (pp. 32–38) as well as the original picture of the teacher seated at the organ. That picture appears in the Carmi translation (p. 3), with the piano!

On these four versions and their character, against the background of the history of translations for children from German to Hebrew, see G. Toury, *German Children's Literature in Hebrew Translation—The Case of* Max und Moritz. *In Search of a Theory of Translation* (Tel-Aviv: 1980), 140–151, esp. the discussion on Judaized names (150–151).

In the Krasnianski translation, the story opens with a thoroughly Jewish couplet, "Yes, the 'merchandise' of Torah is peerless / those who study it are fearless" (p. 17). Despite this opening, the words are attributed to a Christian teacher and the story takes place, as in the original, in church. The teacher plays a Psalm (*Shir hama'alot*, of all things) on the organ. Krasnianski, apparently, felt free to insert overtly Jewish references but hesitated to introduce any real changes in the story. Was Joseph Tunkel familiar with Krasnianski's translation? There is no solid evidence of that; but we may define Tunkel's work in Judaizing the story as the logical extension of Krasnianski's rendition of it in a free Jewish idiom.

26. Cf. the version by Leibushitsky, (pp. 7–8) as well as the one by Pinkerfeld, (pp. 8–9).

27. Cf. Der Tunkeler, "Dos kapitl vilne in mayn lebn," in *Lite*, vol. 1 (New York: 1951), 1279–1290; Y. Sheintukh, "An araynfir tsu der sugye-humor in der yidisher literatur un Der Tunkeler," *Shnaton hasefer hayehudi* 44 (1987–1988), 94–105.

28. Tunkel's illustrations appeared again in a 1941 edition. Tunkel's version adheres closely to Anda Pinkerfeld's text. She, too, for example, omitted the chapter that had been left out of *Motl un Notl* (see n. 25).

29. Ch. Shmeruk, *Sifrut yidish—perakim letoledotehah* (Tel-Aviv: 1978), 24–39.

30. *Ibid.*, 89–100.

31. Dalia Kaufman, *Tirgumei maḥazot le'ivrit uleyidish (1798–1883)—meḥkar hashvaati* (Jerusalem: 1983), 134–244; *idem*, "Ha'ibud habimati hemeyuḥad leyidish shel 'revisor' le-Gogol," *Bamah* 100 (1985), 19–29.

32. Ch. Shmeruk, "Letoledot sifrut hashund beyidish," *Tarbiẓ* 52 (1982–1983), 325–354.

33. *Ibid.*, 338–340; Ch. Shmeruk, "Te'udah nedirah letoledotehah shel hasifrut halo-kanonit beyidish," *Hasifrut* 32 (1983), 13.

34. Kaufman, *Tirgumei maḥazot; idem,* "'Naval haẓadik o hamitḥased,'—ha'ibud ha'ivri hamaskili shel 'Tartuffe' le-Molière," *Bamah* 105–106 (1986), 38–49.

35. Kaufman, *Tirgumei maḥazot,* 11ff.

36. R. Darnton, *The Great Cat Massacre and Other Episodes in French Cultural History* (New York: 1985), 9–27.

37. *Der purim-ber—a teater-shtik far kinder in dray aktn, fun Tunkeler,* illus. Z. Nekhamkin (Warsaw: n.d.). Z. Reyzen, in his *Leksikon fun der yidisher literatur presse un filologye,* vol. 1 (Vilna: 1928), 1170, notes a "2nd edition, 1919." He also noted the connection with Red Riding-Hood.

Forging Judaica: The Case
of the Italian Majolica Seder Plates

Vivian B. Mann
(THE JEWISH MUSEUM, NEW YORK)

The attempt of the art historian to understand a given work reverses, to an extent, the creative process of the artist and seeks the sources of forms, iconography and compositions. Only by discerning what was common currency in the period when the work was created can the scholar perceive its uniqueness and only by reversing the creative process can the modern observer fully understand the import of a work for the artist's contemporaries.[1] In the case of an undated or unsigned work, the search for sources becomes even more important. Iconographic, compositional and formal models establish a historical context that indicates the approximate date of a work's creation. Occasionally, an investigation of sources may lead the art historian to conclude that a work, even a dated or signed one, is not what it appears to be since one or more of its constituent elements is out of context, inappropriate to its alleged age and provenance. If this is the case, then social historians may ask a further question: Were there any specific circumstances, beyond the obvious motivation of financial gain, that led to the fabrication of a false work?

Since the spread of printing technology in the second half of the fifteenth century, among the sources considered by art historians are prints and printed books.[2] In 1931 Rachel Wischnitzer-Bernstein published a pioneering study on the use of printed sources by artists creating Judaica.[3] She traced many of the engraved scenes accompanying the text of the Amsterdam Haggadah of 1695 back to their sources in the publications of Matthaeus Merian, particularly his *Icones Biblicae,* which first appeared in 1625. By making slight alterations in some of the plates to accommodate Jewish sensibilities concerning graven images, the engraver Abraham Ben Jacob, a convert, was able to adapt complete scenes that had originally been created for Christian purposes. He also adapted individual motifs from various Merian publications to Jewish iconographic needs.[4]

The Amsterdam Haggadah of 1695, in turn, had a significant impact on works created after its publication. It not only set the pattern and standards of many subsequent printed editions of the Haggadah,[5] but also served as a model for works in other media. Numerous illuminated manuscript Haggadot produced by artists/scribes from Germany, Moravia and Austria during the eighteenth century include title pages stating that they were made "with the letters of Amsterdam"[6] and even "with the famous letters of Amsterdam."[7] These artists' imitation of the Amsterdam Haggadah extended beyond the text to its engraved illustrations, which were copied, more or less faithfully, in ink and paint on folios of parchment and vellum.[8] Other products of this school of illumination (books of blessings, *mohel* [circumcisor's] records and the record books of benevolent and burial societies) were likewise modeled on the Amsterdam Haggadah, though less extensively because of their differing texts. Most often it is the title pages of these works, with their monumental figures of Moses and Aaron set against an architectural framework and roundels enclosing narrative scenes, that recall their Amsterdam model.[9]

In the course of the eighteenth century, the pictorial imagery of the Amsterdam Haggadah inspired the decoration of ceremonial objects, like the pewter and silver Passover plates created to hold symbolic foods at the seder.[10] By 1720 the Amsterdam title page with its full-length figures of Moses and Aaron or similar frontispieces in other seventeenth-century Hebrew books served as the model for a new type of Torah shield. On these shields, repoussé (relief) depictions of the two Biblical figures flank the box for plaques indicating the section to which the scroll was turned.[11] The use of printed models for Judaica continued into the nineteenth and twentieth centuries. The popularity of Moritz Oppenheim's *Bilder aus dem altjüdischen Familienleben* (first published in portfolio in 1866 and in four later book editions, the last in 1913) inspired the decoration of numerous porcelain and pewter plates.[12]

Given the demonstrable impact of printed books on the decoration of Jewish ceremonial art in other media, one may reasonably turn to an investigation of printed sources when seeking the date and origin of problematic works. Cecil Roth published a group of such works in a 1964 article entitled "Majolica Passover Plates of the XVI–XVIIIth Centuries."[13] He described a group of plates that were identical in function and similarly formed and decorated. Each consists of a wide rim surrounding a central cavetto (concave molding) inscribed with a text, either the prayer of sanctification over wine (the kiddush) together with the order of the seder service (fig. 1) or a passage from the Haggadah together with the same order of the service (fig. 2).

The decoration of the rim is always elaborate. Raised moldings frame two series of cartouches (ornate frames). The larger ones enclose paintings of Biblical scenes drawn from Genesis and Exodus or a representation of the rabbis' Passover at Bene-Berak (a third-century episode that is incorporated into the text of the Haggadah), one of two variant depictions of a seder, flowers or landscapes. The smaller cartouches are decorated with portraits of Biblical heroes, generally Moses, Aaron, David and Solomon. With two exceptions, all of the plates belonging to the group bear four large cartouches, of which at least two enclose figurative scenes, and four small cartouches.[14] The remaining area of the flanges (rims) is filled with molded vegetal decoration, except for two large examples on which putti (young children) occupy the interstices between the cartouches.[15]

Information exists on twenty-eight majolica Passover plates (including those discussed by Roth) that form a coherent group. The table in figure 3 lists all the examples alphabetically. Museums are cited by city; private holdings according to the name of their last-known owner.[16] The table indicates what scenes appear in the

Fig. 1. Passover plate, Savona or Albisola, 1864–1900, majolica. Formerly Kramarsky Collection.

large cartouches and what text is inscribed in the cavetto. Any information as to signature on the reverse of the plates appears in the last column (e.g., see fig. 4).

The earliest inscription date is 1532, the latest 1889. Roth dated most of the plates on the basis of the painted Hebrew inscriptions appearing on the reverse of several examples: Jacob Azulai, Padua, 1532; Moses Fano, Urbino, 1552; Isaac Cohen, Pesaro, 1613–1614; Jacob Azulai, Pesaro, 1652; and so forth.[17] He recognized that some of the plates appear to be copies, as in the case of the plate that came to The Jewish Museum, New York, from the Benguiat Collection. This plate's overglaze English inscription reads, "Hadji Ephraim ben Abraham Benguiat 20 May 1889"; and in Hebrew it reads, "Hadji Ephraim ben Abraham Benguiat S[ephardi] T[ahor] . . . [5] 649."[18] Roth thought the Benguiat plate was a copy of a plate by the same maker responsible for a plate formerly in the collection of The Jewish Museum, Vienna, which was likewise decorated with six large oval car-

Fig. 2. Passover plate, Savona or Albisola, 1864–1900, majolica.
The Jewish Museum, Budapest, no. 64.445.

touches instead of the four large cartouches appearing on all the other examples.[19] Roth also mentioned other plates he thought were copies because they lacked signatures, depended on later printed models or their stylistic features were incompatible with an early date. He also noted the hexagram or Jewish star that appears as a maker's mark on many of the plates, and he pointed out that some of the signatures such as that on the plate from the Danzig collection now in The Jewish Museum, New York, are painted over the glaze "perhaps as an after-thought," although the maker's mark appears beneath the glaze.[20] Roth offered no solution to the problem of the overglaze signatures and underglaze marks.

For Roth, these majolica plates were evidence of Jewish participation in the artistic flowering of Renaissance Italy, a topic for which he displayed a lifelong enthusiasm.[21] Furthermore, the plates proved to him the existence of Jewish pottery workshops in Pesaro, Urbino, and Ancona during the sixteenth, seventeenth and eighteenth centuries,[22] although he could cite no independent corroborative evidence or relevant stylistic comparisons.[23] The unusual composition and decoration of the plates was ascribed to their function. The form of the plates, Roth wrote, was dictated by their purpose, that is, to hold the symbolic foods displayed at the seder.

Nineteen years before the appearance of Roth's article, Rachel Wischnitzer-Bernstein had described some of the majolica plates inscribed with seventeenth-century dates in connection with the use of printed sources as models for the decoration of pottery and pewter plates.[24] Ironically, her mention of the Passover

Collection	Abraham's Hospitality	Binding of Isaac	Blessing of Jacob	Joseph Sold into Slavery	Joseph Greeting His Brothers	Naming of Moses	Slavery of Moses	Slavery of Israelites I	Passover Meal in Egypt II	Rabbis at Bene-Berak	Beginning of Seder	Grace After Meals	Flowers	Landscapes	Text/Kiddush	Text/Text of Haggadah	Text/Order of Seder	Text/Plaques	Signature
Private								x				x		xx		x		x	1664
Budapest I				x	x									xx					Jacob Azulai, Pesaro 1652
Budapest II					x					x					xx			x	Jacob Cohen, Ancona 1654
Caracotch				x								x		xx	x				Jacob Cohen, Ancona 5414
Floersheim								x	x						x				Jacob Azulai, Padua 1532
Jerusalem I							x					x		xx	x		x		Isaac Cohen, Ancona 1673
Jerusalem II										x		x		xx	x		x		
Jerusalem III		x										x		xx			x		
Kramarsky	x					x								xx	x		x		Isaac Cohen, Pesaro 5373
Lemler					x	x									x		x		
London I				x							x			xx					
London II					x							x		xx	x			x	
Lvov				x								x		xx	x		x		
Mannheimer				x	x												x	x	Ancona 1693
Moriah	x											x		xx			x	x	Isaac Cohen, Pesaro 5377
Mullet								x	x					xx	x		x		Ancona 1616
Nancy I					x							x		xx			x	x	
Nancy II				x							x			xx	x		x		
Nancy III				x							x			xx	x		x		
Nauheim				x						x				xx		x	x		Jacob Cohen, Ancona 5414
New York I						x						x		xx	x		x		Isaac Cohen, Pesaro 5374
New York II								x	x	x		x				x		x	Hadji Ephraim ben Abraham Benguiat, 1889
Prague												x							Jacob Azulai, Pesaro 1532
Toronto					x							x		xx			x	x	
Vienna I												x							Moses Fano, Urbino 1552
Vienna II				x								x		xx		x	x		
Warsaw	x										x			xx	x				
Location Unknown					x							x		xx			x	x	

Fig. 3. Chart of known majolica Passover plates.

plates occurs in the context of a discussion of forgeries and the use of printed sources as a means of solving this "most difficult problem." Since Professor Wischnitzer-Bernstein believed that the narrative scenes on the majolica plates were based on the Venice Haggadah printed in 1609 and on the decoration of the Vatican *loggia* (galleries) for Biblical scenes not appearing in the Haggadah, she accepted their seventeenth-century inscription dates as valid. Roth later found her com-

Fig. 4.   Reverse of Passover plate, Savona or Albisola, 1864–1900, majolica. Formerly Kramarsky Collection.

parisons to the Vatican frescoes superficial and suggested instead contemporary Bible illustrations without specifying an exact model.[25]

A survey of the twenty-eight plates whose appearance is known shows that the decoration of the 116 large cartouches[26] is confined to a limited group of similarly rendered scenes: Biblical subjects, "the rabbis at Bene-Berak," two versions of a home seder, assorted landscapes and variations on a dense floral arrangement.

The Biblical scenes are all drawn from Genesis and Exodus and are labeled with quotations from the Biblical texts.[27] They are Abraham's hospitality to the angels (Gen. 18:2; fig. 1); the binding of Isaac (Gen. 22:11; fig. 5); Isaac blessing Jacob (Gen. 27:22; fig. 2); Joseph sold into slavery by his brothers (Gen. 37:28; fig. 2); Joseph revealing himself to his brothers (Gen. 45:4; fig. 6); two versions of the slavery of the Israelites, both of which are accompanied by the same inscription (Exod. 1:13; figs. 7, 8); the naming of Moses (Exod. 2:10; fig. 1) and the eating of the Passover meal in Egypt (Exod. 12:11; fig. 6). In one version of the slavery scene (fig. 7), the laboring Israelites and their Egyptian taskmasters form two distinct compact groups. All the Israelites, with the exception of the figure bending over in the direction of the taskmasters, stoop under their burdens. In the second version (fig. 8), there are several figure groupings consisting of both Israelites and Egyptians spread across the space. Their actions take place before an imposing stone building set in a hilly landscape.

Fig. 5. Passover plate, Savona or Albisola, 1864–1900, majolica. Musée historique Lorrain, Nancy (Nancy II).

The final scene with an inscription is drawn from the text of the Haggadah. It shows the rabbis of Bene-Berak still seated at the seder table recounting the story of the Exodus as their pupils approach from the right to announce that the time for morning prayers has arrived (fig. 9).

Two scenes of a seder appear on the plates. They differ from the depictions already discussed in that the participants are dressed in more modern garb. The first scene is noteworthy for the placement at right of the head of the household (seated in a more elaborate chair than those furnished the other participants) and by the gesture of the man at far left who grasps a decanter in his raised right arm, holding it away from the table (see fig. 7). The accompanying titulus (short description) is from Psalms 116:13, "I will lift up the cup of salvation." In the second scene, which

Fig. 6. Passover plate, Savona or Albisola, 1864–1900, majolica. The Jewish Museum, New York, D114.

occurs on only two plates, the head of the house is seated at left, the figure raising the decanter is absent and a tall mullioned window appears in the wall behind the table (fig. 9). The example shown here (in the collection of The Jewish Museum, New York) lacks an inscription, whereas on the related work in The Israel Museum, the quotation from Psalms 116 appears again (see fig. 3, Jerusalem II).

A comparison of any two representations of the same subject reveals that both are based on the same model. For example, in Abraham's hospitality to the angels (figs. 1 and 10), the three bearded angels at left are parallel to the front plane of the composition and Sara and Ishmael are seen in the tent behind Abraham. Although many of the details such as the tent are identical, subsidiary elements like trees are treated rather freely. Despite the similarities between these two examples of the same subject, the plates on which they appear differ from one another in many ways:

Fig. 7. Passover plate, Savona or Albisola, 1864–1900, majolica. Private Collection, New York.

in their texts, in the order of the figures in the small cartouches and in the subject of the second scene in the large cartouche. A similar comparison could be made between two versions of Joseph sold into slavery (figs. 2 and 11). The number and disposition of the figures within the scene, their gestures and their treatment are clearly derived from the same source, yet the plates as a whole are not identical, displaying the same divergent elements noted before: text, small figures and the second major scene. Individual elements of one or the other of these two plates might be compared to other plates in the series. The scene of the rabbis at Bene-Berak on the plate in Nancy (fig. 11) is clearly based on the same model underlying the depiction of the scene in figure 10, as can be seen from the number of the figures, their disposition, the placement of objects on the table and details such as dress.[28]

The similar representation of all versions of any single subject and the varying combinations of the same elements indicate a common model for the imagery on these plates. The presence of tituli within many of the cartouches and the extent of the cycle suggest that the model was a manuscript or printed book. As noted previously, two printed Haggadot, the Amsterdam Haggadah of 1695 and the Venice Haggadah

Fig. 8. Passover plate, Savona or Albisola, 1864–1900, majolica. The Israel Museum, Jerusalem, no. 134/15.

of 1609 influenced the decorators of ceremonial objects. However, their pictorial cycles could not have served as the basis of the majolica plate illustrations. Only two of the scenes appearing on the plates occur in the Amsterdam Haggadah—the first Passover meal and the rabbis at Bene-Berak—and their treatment is dissimilar.[29] In the case of duplicate narratives, a different moment is chosen, the drawing of Moses from the water in the Amsterdam Haggadah (p. 8) rather than the naming scene on the plates. The Venice Haggadah of 1609, on the other hand, does include similar, although not identical, figure groupings for those Biblical subjects, which also appear on the plates: Abraham's hospitality, the binding of Isaac, the naming of Moses, the scenes of the slavery in Egypt and the first Passover meal. The Venice Haggadah also includes the same composition for the rabbis at Bene-Berak and for the first seder scene as on the plates. However, the other Biblical scenes do not occur in the 1609 Haggadah or in the subsequent editions based on it.[30]

Fig. 9. Passover plate, Savona or Albisola, 1864–1900, majolica. The Jewish Museum, New York, no. S78.

In 1864 Colombo Coen, a Trieste publisher, produced two new editions of the Haggadah, one with a single Hebrew text and a second accompanied by an Italian translation, the work of Abraham Vita Morpurgo.[31] Both editions were lavishly illustrated with engravings by C. Kirchmayr, whose signature appears at the bottom of the title page. At the time of publication, Kirchmayr was only sixteen years old according to the information given by Bénézit.[32]

A comparison of the narrative scenes on the majolica plates with the same subjects in the Trieste Haggadah clearly demonstrates that this printed book served as the model for the decoration of the group of Passover plates under discussion. The entire cycle of Biblical and extra-Biblical episodes depicted on the plates appear among the Haggadah illustrations; in all cases, the plate illustrations are faithful, although reduced renderings of the printed compositions. Only the tituli are differ-ent.[33] Compare, for example, the rendering of Isaac blessing Jacob from the Trieste

Fig. 10.   Passover plate, Savona or Albisola, 1864–1900, majolica. Collection Moriah Art Gallery, New York.

Haggadah, (a scene not appearing in the earlier Italian editions) with that on the plate in Budapest (figs. 2 and 12). The dramatic use of draperies, the placement of the main protagonists in the right and center foreground, with Esau emerging from behind the wall at left, clearly illustrate the dependence of the majolica decoration on the engraving.

Even in scenes occurring in prior printings of the Haggadah that might argue for an earlier source for the iconography of the plates, individual details indicate the close relationship between the plates and the Trieste Haggadah. The second version of the slavery in Egypt is based on a composition that already appeared in the 1609 Venice Haggadah and in later editions printed in Venice.[34] However, in the Trieste Haggadah version (fig. 13), the scene is expanded by the addition of two figures in the middle ground and the whole composition is Orientalized in accord with nine-

Fig. 11. Passover plate, Savona or Albisola, 1864–1900, majolica. Musée historique Lorrain, Nancy (Nancy I).

teenth-century taste. Straight-sided monolithic pillars replace the columns of the earlier version and Ottoman garb substitutes for the Roman tunics and helmets worn by the Egyptian oppressors in the Venetian version of the early seventeenth century. It is the Orientalized composition that appears on the plates (fig. 8). Similar exotic details occur in other Haggadah scenes and then repeat themselves on the plates such as the fan of palm leaves in the naming of Moses or the recumbent Sphinx on a plinth in Joseph revealing himself to his brothers (figs. 1 and 6).[35] These comparisons could be multiplied. The exact form of the tent in the scene of Abraham's hospitality on the plates (fig. 1) is that appearing in the Trieste Haggadah rather than in earlier printings; the landscape of Jerusalem (fig. 7) derives from that on page 23 of the Trieste printing rather than from the more schematic rendering of earlier Venice printings.[36] The flower arrangements on the plates that fill the remaining

Fig. 12.   "The Blessing of Jacob," Trieste Haggadah, 1864.

large cartouches are variations on the ornament of page 11 in the Haggadah, whereas the four Biblical figures of the small cartouches are extracts from the title page.

The Trieste Haggadah thus provides a *terminus post quem* for the majolica plates.
Since one of the plates—formerly in the Mocatta Collection, London, and subsequently in the Kramarsky Collection (formerly in New Rochelle, New York)—was
shown in the Anglo-Jewish Historical Exhibition of 1887 held in London's Royal
Albert Hall,[37] the Benguiat plate was dated 1889 and The Jewish Museum's plate
from Danzig (fig. 3, New York I) entered a private collection before 1904,[38] we
may establish a *terminus ante quem* ca. 1900.

Two questions remain to be answered. Where were the plates made? Who was
responsible for the forged inscriptions?

The composition of the plates and their decoration most closely resemble the
majolica manufactured in Savona and neighboring Albisola from the early seventeenth century through the twentieth century.[39] The factories of Savona began producing plates whose rims are subdivided into four large cartouches surrounded by
raised moldings, each painted with an individual motif, in the early seventeenth
century; their composition is a marked departure from the single scenes and unified
decoration of most Italian majolica of the sixteenth and seventeenth centuries.[40] An

Fig. 13.   "The Slavery of the Israelites," Trieste Haggadah, 1864.

example is a late seventeenth-century plate bearing the arms of Vicenzo Maria Durazzo Vescova di Savona (fig. 14). The areas between the cartouches on this plate are filled with molded forms as on the later Passover plates.

Similar compositions formed of relief or painted elements were created in Albisola and Savona through the twentieth century. Angelo (or Andrea) Levantino, who was active in the mid-eighteenth century, signed a plate now in the Galleria di Palazzo Rosso, Genoa, bearing the six painted cartouches in an arrangement similar to that on the Benguiat plate (fig. 9).[41] A nineteenth-century example now in Turin, with raised decoration that is based on molds in use a century or more earlier, includes the motif of angels' heads flanked by wings similar to the relief decoration above the small cartouches on the plates in the Floersheim and Prague collections.[42] A late seventeenth- or early eighteenth-century precursor of the Turin plate is decorated with landscape scenes, a staple of Ligurian ceramics that also appears on the Passover plates (figs. 8 and 15).[43] Plates whose flanges are decorated with a series of raised, molded cartouches were still produced in Albisola in the twentieth century.[44]

The closest parallels to the cartouche moldings that surround the full-length Biblical figures on most of the Passover plates are found not on other plates from these two pottery-producing communities, but on the eighteenth- and nineteenth-

Fig. 14. Plate with arms of Vicenzo Maria Durazzo Vescova di Savona, Savona, late seventeenth century (after Giuseppe Morrazoni, *Maiolica antica ligure,* pl. 80).

Fig. 15.   Large plate with sirens, Albisola, second-half of the seven-
teenth- beginning eighteenth century, majolica. Museo del Castell
Sforzesco, Milan (after Federico Marzinot, *Ceramica e ceramisti di
Liguria,* pl. 257).

century majolica *acquasantini* (holy water stoups), whose principal decoration is a
single figure like the Madonna della Misericordia (fig. 16). Finally, the combination
of large and small cartouches on the flanges of the seder plates appears on a
nineteenth-century Savonese plate in the Pinacoteca Civica, Savona, whose cavetto
bears "The Triumph of Neptune" (fig. 17).

The Savonese and Albisolese pottery industry began to flourish at the end of the
sixteenth century, reaching its height in the seventeenth and eighteenth centuries.[45]
Majolica from Savona is distinguished by its affinity to silver work in both form and
decoration.[46] The surface is formed of low relief akin to repoussé silver and plastic
ornament is applied to both cavetto and rim. A comparison of the majolica
acquasantini with those rendered in silver clearly demonstrates this relationship.[47]
It is interesting in this regard that there is a series of silver Passover plates closely
related to the majolica group in composition and decoration (although some of the
narratives are based on different models) that have been published as eighteenth
century(?) and nineteenth century.[48] A thorough investigation of the marked examples is needed to establish their dating relative to the majolica.

The majolica Passover plates clearly appear to have been made in Savona or
Albisola between 1864 and 1900. The Star of David, or hexagram, appearing on the

Fig. 16. Acquasantini, Savona, eighteenth century, majolica. Museo Luxoro, Genoa–Nervi.

back of many of the plates was the mark of the Salamone factory active in Savona and Albisola from the sixteenth century on.[49] The Salamone, a family of Jewish origin, had migrated to Italy from Spain and were already active in the ceramics industry in 1494.[50] By the sixteenth century, they were responsible for two-fifths of all ceramics exported from Savona.[51] Occasionally, other Savonese artists and factories not associated with the Salamone adopted the hexagram mark.[52] Those who produced the seder plates of the group we have discussed continued the use of this traditional Savonese-Albisolese mark, occasionally modifying it by placing the

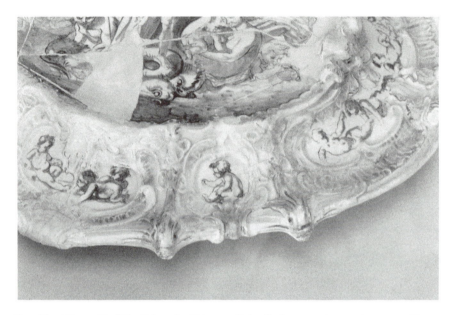

Fig. 17. Plate with "The Triumph of Neptune" detail, Savona, nineteenth century. Pinaco-teca Civica, Savona.

name Pesaro in the middle to harmonize the mark with the fictitious Hebrew inscriptions painted near the edge.

As Isaiah Shachar has remarked, "The similarity in these plates of design, technique, style and scripts—as well as the similarity of the makers' names—seems too acute to exclude doubts concerning their dating."[53] Roth himself noted, "The spelling of the place-names, Ancona and Pesaro, is unusual—suggesting either the relative illiteracy or else the foreign extraction of the manufacturers."[54] The unease displayed by these writers arose from attempts to reconcile all of the evidence presented by the plates: artistic, historical and inscriptional. However, when the plates are placed within their proper stylistic and iconographic contexts, the true character of the inscriptions is revealed. They are false attempts to date the Passover plates some two hundred to three hundred years prior to their manufacture and decoration. The forged inscriptions indicate that the making of Judaica fakes was already underway in the second-half of the nineteenth century. In the article cited earlier, Rachel Wischnitzer-Bernstein examined another nineteenth-century fake, a doctored depiction of the medieval Regensburg synagogue.[55] In the light of these forgeries, we might well ask: What was the nature of the social context that encouraged this phenomenon? It appears that the answer lies both in the nature of Judaica collecting and in the growth of a market for artifacts of Jewish content.

Prior to Emancipation, Jews collected objects of artistic value and beauty in their homes, although no mention is made of a special collection of Jewish ceremonial objects with the one exception of the case of Alexander David (1687–1765).[56] David, who served the dukes of Braunschweig as *Kammeragent* from 1707 until his death, seems to have possessed the first private collection of Judaica. As a court Jew, David was able to purchase land from the ducal holdings on which he built a house with its own synagogue and study, in the fashion of elite Jews of the period. According to a contemporary account, David's collection, in the service of the synagogue, formed a veritable museum (*beit nekhoto*).[57] Twentieth-century descriptions mention the collection of ceremonial art and illuminated manuscripts that David acquired for his synagogue. These later became the nucleus of a community museum of Judaica in 1865 and eventually the core of the Judaica collection of the Braunschweigisches Landesmuseum.[58]

While David's acquisition of Judaica was carried out within the context of a traditional Jewish life (no doubt, influenced by the ambience of the court he served), the collections of the nineteenth century were by and large motivated by other, more secular concerns. True, Philip Salomons's (1796–1867) collection served the private synagogue in his house, but his seems to have been the exception to the rule in the nineteenth century.[59] Toward the latter part of the century, the period in which we begin to encounter Judaica forgeries, we find collectors driven by "a true passion for art" as well as by a sense of nostalgia for a past culture.[60] This was clearly the source of Isaac Strauss's passion for collecting Judaica. The exhibition of Strauss's collection at the International Exposition in Paris in 1878—the first of its kind—led to a greater interest in Judaica and the market for Judaica grew proportionately.

Strauss was not alone in combining the love of art with Jewish historical consciousness. Similar feelings probably drove Lesser Gieldzinski of Danzig to form his collection of Judaica in the late nineteenth century. Like Strauss, Gieldzinski was an avid collector of all kinds of art; his home, full of antiquities and fine art— some acquired on holiday trips to Italy—was visited by connoisseurs, including Kaiser Wilhelm II and the Kaiserin Augusta.[61] But as we learn from Gieldzinski's own writings, the collector was also motivated by a keen historical sense, heightened by an awareness of the extensive loss of Jewish material culture through persecutions.[62] For Gieldzinski, unlike David and Salomons, feelings of filial piety and nostalgia for a religious past were intertwined with historical appreciation and contributed to his search for Jewish objects.[63] In 1904 he donated his collection to the Danzig Synagogue to serve as the nucleus of a Jewish museum. Yet, characteristic of the time, Gieldzinski's collection also fell prey to forgeries; in addition to one of the majolica plates, it included a few other works of dubious origin.[64]

Forgeries are connected with various social and economic processes. They point, in our case, to the existence of a Jewish bourgeoisie in Western and Central Europe that sought after, and had the means to purchase, objects with sentimental Jewish value. This Jewish bourgeoisie was well integrated into the surrounding culture, but not totally alienated from the Jewish community or from the Jewish past. In their desire to preserve some form of attachment to that past, these Jews embarked on diverse projects that provided them with an immediate connection to a forgotten or abandoned past. The purchase and collection of material objects was one such project. Consider the marketing success of Moritz Oppenheim's series on the Jewish family in late nineteenth-century Germany—reproduced in several editions and in various forms for sale to a burgeoning market within the highly integrated Jewish community.[65] Acquisition of such objects by bourgeois Jews was indicative of their effort to hold on to a rapidly disappearing past—a perspective that was exploited by dealers and entrepreneurial types.

Interestingly enough, the Benguiat family was also troubled by the paucity of Jewish material objects. In a statement entitled "A Jewish Museum in America" written by Mordechai Benguiat (the son of Hadji Ephraim) in 1931, an illuminating account is provided of the formation of his family's collection in the nineteenth century:

> A collection of Jewish Antiquities differs from all other collections in more than one way. Most art collections are generally formed ethnographically, or they come into being by preserving treasured heirlooms and gathering art works for the adornment of private homes . . . [but] the Jew could not preserve his treasures because . . . he has been practically always with a travelling bag on his shoulders and without knowing where he would go the very next day. Therefore any antiquities saved from the repeated catastrophes and diaspora are of the greatest value.[66]

Hadji Ephraim ben Abraham Benguiat differed from all the other nineteenth-century collectors of Judaica in that he alone was also a dealer in antiquities, whose clients included Prince Arthur, Duke of Connaught, William Randolph Hearst and public museums. With his knowledge of the general market for antiques and with obvious recognition of the enthusiastic response to the first public exhibitions of Judaica (Paris, 1878; London, 1887), Benguiat may have realized that amid the general desire to collect beautiful objets d'art of the past, lay a more specific market for Judaica.

Among the entire collection of majolica plates that surfaced at the end of the nineteenth century, only one carries an authentic inscription contemporaneous with the dating of the plates according to style and iconography—it bears the name of Benguiat and the date 1889. The inscription appears on the plate that remained in Benguiat's personal collection until its sale to The Jewish Museum, New York, in 1924. Despite its inscribed date, Benguiat had described the plate in the Smithsonian's catalogue of his collection (1901) as having been made in the thirteenth century and glazed in Italy in the sixteenth century.[67] He was able to present this false information because the plate was then encased in a wooden frame.[68]

Benguiat and his immediate family resided in Italy prior to their immigration to the United States in 1882.[69] Some of the larger Benguiat family remained in Italy and were active as collectors and dealers into the twentieth century. They were thus in a favorable position to capitalize on a growing Judaica market. The collectors expressed, through their collections, ties to a pious past that was slowly receding into the distance as they themselves were embracing modernity.

Notes

Research for this paper was supported by a grant from the National Endowment for the Arts.

1. Recent examples of the recovery of lost meaning are Leo Steinberg's *The Sexuality of Christ in Renaissance Art and Modern Oblivion* (New York: 1983); *idem,* " 'How Shall This Be?' Reflections on Filippo Lippi's *Annunciation* in London Part I," *Artibus et Historiae* 16 (1987), 25–44.

2. Concerning the impact of printing on the creation of art and on its historiography, see Elizabeth L. Eisenstein, *The Printing Press as an Agent of Change* (London, New York, Melbourne: 1979), 83ff.

3. Rachel Wischnitzer-Bernstein, "Von der Holbeinbibel zur Amsterdamer Haggadah," *Monatsschrift für Geschichte und Wissenschaft des Judentums* 7 (1931), 269–286.

4. For example, Wischnitzer-Bernstein cites the transformation of a Hannibal figure from a history of Rome into the youngest of the Four Sons in the 1695 Haggadah ("Von der Holbeinbibel," 277–278). See also Rachel Wischnitzer-Bernstein, "Studies in Jewish Art," *Jewish Quarterly Review* 36, no. 1 (1945), 54–55; and Yosef Hayim Yerushalmi, *Haggadah and History* (Philadelphia: 1975), 43–45, pls. 59–62.

5. Yerushalmi, *Haggadah and History,* 45–46; Abraham M. Haberman, "The Jewish Art of the Printed Book," in *Jewish Art: An Illustrated History,* 2d ed., ed. Bezalel Narkiss (Greenwich, Connecticut: 1971), pl. 173; Haviva Peled-Carmeli, *Illustrated Haggadot of the Eighteenth Century,* The Israel Museum, Jerusalem, exhibition cat., 1983, 15–17 (English). See also Cecil Roth, "The Illustrated Haggadah," *Studies in Bibliography and Booklore* 7 (1965), 37–56.

6. For example, Peled-Carmeli, *Illustrated Haggadot,* fig. 41; *Lessing's 'Nathan' und jüdische Emanzipation im Lande Braunschweig,* Lessing-Akademie, Wolfenbüttel, West Germany, exhibition cat., 1981, no. 145.

7. For example, on the title page of a prayer book written and illuminated in Vienna by Aryeh Judah Loeb ben Elhanan Katz. Norman L. Kleeblatt and Vivian B. Mann, *Treasures of The Jewish Museum,* (The Jewish Museum, New York, exhibition cat., 1986, 96–97.)

8. Ernest M. Namenyi, "The Illumination of Hebrew Manuscripts after the Invention of Printing," in Narkiss, *Jewish Art,* 156–157. Also Kurt Schubert, "Die Weisen von Bne Braq in der Haggadaillustration des 18. Jahrhunderts," *Artibus et Historiae* 17 (1988), 71–81.

9. For an example in a circumcision book, see David Altshuler, ed., *The Precious Legacy: Judaic Treasures from the Czechoslovak State Collections* (New York: 1983), no. 257, fig. 193.

10. Such works exist in every major collection of Judaica. For examples, see The Israel Museum, Jerusalem, *Illustrated Haggadot,* 17 (English); R. D. Barnett, ed., *Catalogue of the Permanent and Loan Collections of the Jewish Museum, London,* The Jewish Museum, London (London: 1974), no. 358.

11. Stephen S. Kayser and Guido Schoenberger, eds., *Jewish Ceremonial Art* (Philadelphia: 1955), no. 50. The appearance of sculpted human forms on a Torah shield raised anew the issue of idolatry. It was discussed by Rabbi Moses Sofer (1762–1839) of Pressburg (Bratislava) in a responsum dated 1811. In his reply, the Hatam Sofer observes that the figures on the shield could not be considered potential objects of worship since the clothes in which they were dressed indicated their identities as Moses and Aaron. In other words, the iconography of the two figures was well established at the time the Hatam Sofer was writing. Nevertheless, with the strictness with which Jewish law has usually regarded idolatry, he recommended removing the tips of the noses of Moses and Aaron, thereby rendering them unfit to serve as idols. (Moses Sofer, *Sefer Hatam Sofer. Ḥelek shishi* (New York: 1958), no. 6 (Hebrew).

12. Ismar Schorsch, "Art as Social History: Moritz Oppenheim and the German Jewish Vision of Emancipation" in *Danzig, Between East and West: Aspects of Modern Jewish History,* ed. Isadore Twersky (Cambridge, Mass.; London: 1985), 141–142.

13. Cecil Roth, "Majolica Passover Plates of the XVI–XVIIth Centuries," *Eretz-Israel* 7 (1964), 106–111, pls. xl–xli.

14. The exceptions are a plate in the collection of The Jewish Museum, New York, that was formerly in the Benguiat Collection (fig. 3, New York II) and a plate formerly in The Jewish Museum, Vienna, now in the Floersheim Collection, Zurich.

15. These are the plates in the Floersheim Collection and in The Prague Jewish Museum.

16. Roth mentions two additional plates in private collections in Paris, but he gives only the information that one was signed Joseph Capriles, Ancona, 1584 ("Majolica Passover

Plates," 107, 109). Because it is possible that these two plates are identical to others for which no inscription information is available or because they changed hands since 1964, they have not been included in the chart of known plates (fig. 3).

17. Roth, "Majolica Passover Plates," 106.

18. A photograph of this inscription was taken after the plate entered The Jewish Museum's collection. Portions of the wording were already missing at the time of photography; today the inscription is completely erased. The ink used was probably easily soluble and disappeared during cleaning or perhaps it was deliberately removed in the belief that it was a later addition to an earlier plate.

19. Vienna I, fig. 3. See Roth, "Majolica Passover Plates," 107–110, for a discussion of various copies.

20. Roth, "Majolica Passover Plates," 108, n. 8.

21. See Cecil Roth, *The History of the Jews of Italy* (Philadelphia: 1946), 193–227; idem., *The Jews in the Renaissance* (Philadelphia: 1959).

22. Roth, "Majolica Passover Plates," pl. 106. This assertion has been repeated by other historians writing on the cultural life of Italian Jewry. See, for example, Moses Shulvass, *The Jews in the World of the Renaissance* (Leiden: 1973), 146.

23. In fact, Roth quotes a letter dated 1950 from Mr. E. A. Lane, Keeper of the Department of Ceramics at the Victoria and Albert Museum, "In the whole of our collection of Italian pottery (which numbers nearly fifteen hundred specimens) we have nothing resembling the plate about which you enquire, and it certainly cannot be regarded as a common Italian type" ("Majolica Passover Plates," 107.) On the Victoria and Albert's collection, see Bernard Rackham with additions by J.V.G. Mallet, *Catalogue of Italian Majolica* (London: 1977).

24. Rachel Wischnitzer-Bernstein, "Studies in Jewish Art," 52–59, esp., 58–59.

25. Roth, "Majolica Passover Plates," 107–108.

26. Twenty-six of the known plates are composed of 4 large and 4 small cartouches. Two examples have 6 large cartouches for a total of 116 large cartouches. (See nn. 14, 15 for the plates with 6 large cartouches as well as pp. 205.)

27. The textual references are for the quotations on the plates and do not comprise the entire episode depicted.

28. On the whole, the Nancy plate most closely resembles a plate in The Jewish Museum, London. (See Barnett, *Permanent and Loan Collections*, no. 339.)

29. For example, in the scene of the rabbis at Bene-Berak in the Amsterdam Haggadah, the figures sit around a table set diagonally in space within a richly furnished interior, but on the plates the figures are arranged about a table parallel to the picture's plane.

30. See Yerushalmi, *Haggadah and History,* 42–43, for a discussion of later editions based on the Venice Haggadah of 1609. Some of the scenes already mentioned are published by Yerushalmi: the binding of Isaac (pl. 45, wherein the figure grouping is similar to that on the plates but in reverse); the second slavery scene (pl. 50) and the naming of Moses (pl. 51, wherein the number of figures is fewer than on the plates but the essential composition is similar).

31. Abraham Yaari, *Bibliografiah shel hagadot pesah mireshit hadefus ve'ad hayom (Bibliography of the Passover Haggadah from the Earliest Printed Edition to 1960)* (Jerusalem: 1960), nos. 898–899; Yerushalmi, *Haggadah and History,* 47–48, pls. 102–105; and Tovia Preschel, *The Trieste Haggadah of 1864* (New York: 1979).

32. E. Bénézit, *Dictionnaire critique et documentaire des peintres, sculpteurs, dessinateurs et graveurs,* vol. 6 (Paris: 1976), 223.

33. The quotations on the plates are drawn from the Bible and do not match the tituli presented below each scene in the Trieste Haggadah. For example, the scene of Abraham prepared to sacrifice his son is labeled "The Binding of Isaac" in the Trieste Haggadah, but it is accompanied by the quotation, "Abraham, Abraham" (Gen. 22:11) on the plates.

34. Yerushalmi, *Haggadah and History,* pl. 50.

35. These two Orientalizing details also appear in Gustave Doré's engravings of the same subjects, but the compositions differ. (See *Die Heilige Schrift der Israeliten,* trans. Ludwig Philippson, illustrations by Gustave Doré [Stuttgart: 1874], 108, 124.)

36. Yerushalmi, *Haggadah and History,* pl. 55.

37. Joseph Jacobs and Lucien Wolf, *Catalogue of the Anglo-Jewish Historical Exhibition, Royal Albert Hall, London, 1887* (London: 1888), no. 1697.

38. This plate was owned by Lesser Gieldzinski who donated it to the Danzig Synagogue along with the rest of his Judaica collection in 1904. (Vivian B. Mann and Joseph Gutmann, *Danzig 1939: Treasures of a Destroyed Community,* The Jewish Museum, New York, exhibition cat., 1980, no. 52.)

39. A study of Ligurian ceramics is found in Federico Marzinot, *Ceramica e ceramisti di Liguria* (Genoa: 1987).

40. See Marzinot, *Ceramica,* fig. 208, for an early seventeenth-century example.

41. Constantino Barile, *Antiche ceramiche liguri. Maioliche di albisola* (Milan: 1965), pl. CVIII.

42. *Ibid.,* pl. CXIX; Roth, "Majolica Passover Plates," pl. xli, fig. 4. The Floersheim plate appears identical to that published by Roth as formerly in the collection of The Jewish Museum, Vienna.

43. Barile, *Antiche ceramiche liguri,* pl. LXXXIX.

44. For example, a plate in the Palazzo Rosso, Genoa (M.V. 1841), bearing the mark of "La casa dell'arte albisola capo" is dated to the twentieth century.

45. Giuseppe Morazzoni, *La maiolica antica ligure* (Milan: 1951), 18ff.; Bernhard Rackham, *Guide to Italian Majolica,* (London: 1933), 78.

46. Morazzoni, *Maiolica antica ligure,* 26; M. R. Salon, *A History and Description of Italian Majolica* (London, Paris, New York, Toronto and Melbourne: 1908), 182.

47. Compare, for example, fig. 16 with pl. 88–89 in Giuseppe Morazzoni, *Argenterie genovesi* (Milan: n.d.).

48. Roth, "Majolica Passover Plates," pl. xli, fig. 3; *Monumenta Judaica,* Kölnischen Stadtmuseum, Cologne, exhibition cat., 1963–1964, no. 558 is attributed to the "18th century(?)" although bearing a late nineteenth-century Austrian mark. The following are some unpublished examples: The Israel Museum, Jerusalem, no. 134/25, described as English, nineteenth century; no. 134/20, described as English, 1925; Joods Historisch Museum, Amsterdam, no. 2421, described as German, nineteenth century; an example in the collection of Congregation Emanuel of the City of New York, described as German, nineteenth century; and a similar example in the collection of The Jewish Museum, New York, F 5502.

49. Carlo Varaldo, "I Salamone ceramisti savonesi. Note storiche," in *Centro ligure per la storia della ceramica albisola. Atti VII convegno internazionale della ceramica,* Albisola, 1974, 203–204.

50. *Ibid.,* 205, n. 16.

51. *Ibid.,* 204.

52. For example, the Siccardi factory used the same mark in the seventeenth and eighteenth centuries. (Morrazzoni, *Maiolica antica ligure,* 50; Barile, *Antiche ceramiche ligure,* 66–67.) The same mark appears on a plate painted by Giovanni Augustino Ratti (1699–1775) and on another of Ratti's works that is attributed to the Chiodo factory of Savona. (Saul Levy, *Maioliche settecentesche pietmontesi, liguri, romagnole, marchigiane, toscane e abruzzesi* [Milan, 1964], pl. 34.)

53. Isaiah Shachar, *The Jewish Year* (Leiden: 1975), 20.

54. Roth, "Majolica Passover Plates," 109. It is ironic that Cecil Roth was misled to establish fictitious dynasties of Jewish potters and painters by works that could have led him to bona fide potters and painters of Jewish origin: the Salomona families of Savona and Albisole who were active from the sixteenth century on. There is also documentation on the activities of Jewish majolica makers in the Duchy of Mantua: Shlomo Simonsohn, *History of the Jews in the Duchy of Mantua* (Jerusalem: 1977), 281, and n. 276.

55. Wischnitzer-Bernstein, "Studies in Jewish Art," 52–54.

56. Rolf Hagen, "Die Entstehung der Judaica-Sammlung des Braunschweigischen Landesmuseums," in *Tora-Wimpel. Veröffentlichungen des Braunschweigischen Landesmuseums* 17, 2d ed., (Braunschweig: 1984), 7.

57. Rabbi Samuel ben Elkanah, *Sefer mekom shmuel* (Altona: 1738). The author of this

work was patrionized by David and lived on his premises. The listing of the contents of David's "treasure house" is largely a paraphrase of 2 Kings 20 and cannot be considered accurate. What is interesting are the divergences from the Biblical text: the mixed list of books and objects and the name given to the chamber, which means treasure house or museum. In the great collections of the sixteenth and seventeenth centuries, no distinction was made between books and objects. All were gathered in one *Kunstkammer,* a term parallel to the *beit nekhoto* of Rabbi Shmuel. (On the ducal collections of Braunschweig and the mixing of object types in one collection, see "Barocke Sammellust. Die Bibliothek und Kunstkammer des Herzogs Ferdinand Albrecht zu Braunschweig-Luneburg (1636–1687)," *Wolfenbutteler Bibliotheks-Informationen* 13, no. 1/2 [1988], 2.)

58. Hagen, "Entstehung der Judaica-Sammlung," 9ff.; G. Rulf, "Das Museum der israelitischen Gemeinde Braunschweig, *Mitteilungen zur jüdischen Volkskunde* 19, no. 3 (1906), 89–94.

59. Cecil Roth, "Introduction," in Barnett, *Permanent and Loan Collections,* xiii.

60. [George Stenne], *Collection de M. Strauss. Description des objets d'art religieux hébraïques exposés dans les galeries du Trocadéro, à l'Exposition Universelle de 1878* (Poissy: 1878), xi.

61. Mann and Gutmann, *Danzig 1939,* 44.

62. *Ibid.,* 43–44. Gieldzinski also owned one of the Passover plates under discussion, it came to The Jewish Museum, Danzig, on a brass stand of Ottoman origin, a type of metalwork also found in Benguiat's collection. (Mann and Gutmann, *Danzig 1939,* no. 287; *Sammlung jüdischer Kunstgegenstände der Synagogen-Gemeinde zu Danzig,* Danzig, 1933, no. 114; I. M. Casanowicz, *Collections of Objects of Religious Ceremonial in the United States National Museum. Smithsonian Institution United States National Museum Bulletin* 148 (Washington, D.C.: 1929), 12: no. 30, pl. IV.)

63. See Gieldzinski's handwritten notes on items in his collection. Mann and Gutmann, *Danzig 1939,* nos. 38, 73, 103, and the memorial plaques for Gieldzinski's parents (44).

64. Mann and Gutmann, *Danzig 1939,* nos. 211, 214.

65. Schorsch, "Art as Social History," 141–172. Originally published in Elisheva Cohen, ed., *Moritz Oppenheim: The First Jewish Painter* (Cat., The Israel Museum, Jerusalem: 1983), 31–61.

66. This statement is in the archives of the Judaica Department, The Jewish Museum, New York.

67. C. Adler and I. M. Casanowicz, *Descriptive Catalogue of a Collection of Objects of Jewish Ceremonial Deposited in the U.S. National Museum by Hadji Ephraim Benguiat* (Washington, D.C.: 1901), no. 78 and pl. CXXXIV.

68. Roth, "Majolica Passover Plates," p. 109*, n. 9.

69. Information in the files of The Jewish Museum, New York.

Appendix

List of Known Majolica Plates

1. Private Collection, New York; ex. coll. Mira Salomon.
   Bibliography: New York, Parke-Bernet Galleries, *Jewish Ritual Silver and Other Hebraica Belonging to Mrs. Mira Salomon,* sales catalogue, 1949, no. 120; Roth, "Majolica Passover Plates of the XVI–XVIIth Centuries," *Eretz-Israel* 7 (1964), 109.
2. Budapest Jewish Museum (no. 64.445=Budapest I).
   Bibliography: Wischnitzer, "Studies in Jewish Art," *Jewish Quarterly Review* 36, no. 1 (July 1945), 58–59; idem., 24 (April 1958), 10; Roth, "Majolica Plates . . . ," 107; Egyházi Gyüjtemények Kincsei, *Az Iparmüvészeti Múzeum,* Kiállításának Katalógusa, Budapest 1979, no. 394; Ilona Benoschofsky and Sándor Scheiber, *A Budapesti Zsidó Múzeum* (Budapest: 1987), no. 119.
3. Budapest Jewish Museum (no. 64.427=Budapest II).
   Bibliography: Egyházi Gyüjtemények Kincsei, *Az Iparmüvészeti Múzeum,* no. 394; Benoschofsky and Scheiber, *A Budapesti Zsidó Múzeum,* no. 118.
4. Collection M. A. Caracotch, Paris.
   Bibliography: Isaiah Shachar, *The Jewish Year* (Leiden: 1975), 36, pl. XLC.
5. Collection Michael Floersheim, Zurich.
   Bibliography: Roth, "Majolica Plates . . . ," 109.
6. Jerusalem, Israel Museum (no. 134/15=Jerusalem I); ex. coll. Cecil Roth.
   Bibliography: Roth, "Majolica Plates . . . ," 107.
7. Jerusalem, Israel Museum (no. 134/82=Jerusalem II); ex. coll. Sholem Asch, Victor Carter.
   Bibliography: Roth, "Majolica Plates . . . ," 109.
8. Jerusalem, Israel Museum (no. 134/56=Jerusalem III); ex. coll. Sholem Asch, Victor Carter.
   Bibliography: Roth, "Majolica Plates . . . ," 106 n. 2.
9. Collection Felix Kramarsky, New Rochelle (formerly); ex. coll. F. D. Mocatto.
   Bibliography: Joseph Jacobs and Lucien Wolf, *Anglo-Jewish Historical Exhibition,* no. 1697, pl. 18; New York, Parke-Bernet Galleries, *The Notable Collection of Felix Kramarsky,* sales catalogue, 1959, no. 79.
10. Collection Ferdynand Lemler, Cracow; unpublished.
11. London, Jewish Museum (no. 340=London I); ex. coll. P. A. S. Phillips.
    Bibliography: R. D. Barnett, *Catalogue of the Jewish Museum London,* no. 340; Roth, "Majolica Plates . . . ," 108.
12. London, Jewish Museum (no. 339-London II); ex. coll. P. A. S. Phillips.
    Bibliography: Barnett, *Catalogue of the Jewish Museum London,* no. 340; Roth, "Majolica Plates . . . ," 109.
13. Lvov, Muzeum Przemyslowe.
    Jakób Schall, *Przewodnik po zabytkach żydowskich m. Lwowa i historja Żydów lwowskich w zarysie* (Lvov: 1935), 27.

14. Collection Mannheimer.
    Bibliography: Attilio Milano, *Storia degli ebrei in Italia* (Turin: 1963), pl. 64.

15. Collection Moriah Art Gallery, New York; ex. coll. Marcetto Morpurgo; unpublished.

16. Collection Mullet (Palma de Mallorca).
    Bibliography: F. Cantera and J. M. Millas, *Inscripciones hebraicas de España* (Madrid: 1956), 393–397; José M. Millás Vallicrosa, "Nuevos epígrafes hebraicos," *Sefarad* 10 (1950), 343–347A; Mulet Gomila, *Un plato de ceramica con inscripcion hebraica* (Palma de Mallorca: 1944), pamphlet.

17. Nancy, Musée Lorrain (Nancy I); ex. coll. Wienes; unpublished.

18. Nancy, Musée Lorrain (Nancy II); unpublished.

19. Nancy, Musée Lorrain (Nancy III); unpublished.

20. Collection S. Nauheim (formerly), Frankfurt.
    Bibliography: I. Posen, "Katalog der erscheinenen Abbilddungen zur jüdischen Kunst- und Kulturgeschichte," *Notizblatt der Gesellschaft zur Erforschung jüdischer Kunst- denkmäler,* 30 (1932), 12; E. Toeplitz, "Sedergerat," *Frankfurter Israelitisches Gemein- deblatt* 8 (1931), 246; R. Wischnitzer, "Studies in Jewish Art," 58; idem., "Art and the Italian Renaissance," 9–10.

21. New York, Jewish Museum (D114=New York I); ex. coll. Lesser Gieldzinski, Jewish Community of Danzig.
    Bibliography: New York, The Jewish Museum, *Danzig 1939: Treasures of a Destroyed Community,* no. 52, for older literature.

22. New York, Jewish Museum (S78=New York II).
    Bibliography: C. Adler and I. M. Casanowicz, *Descriptive Catalogue of Objects of Jewish Ceremonial Deposited in the United States National Museum by Hadji Ephraim Benguiat," U.S. National Museum Annual Report* (1899), 555, pl. 17; Roth, "Majolica Plates . . . ," 109.

23. Prague, Jewish Museum (61.596); unpublished.

24. Toronto, Beth Zedek Museum (CR103); unpublished.

25. Vienna, Jewish Museum (formerly= Vienna I).
    Bibliography: Roth, "Majolica Plates . . . ," 109.

26. Vienna, Jewish Museum (formerly= Vienna II).
    Bibliography: F. Landsberger, *Einführung in die jüdische Kunst* (Berlin: 1935), pl. 28.

27. Warsaw, Bersohn Museum (formerly).
    Bibliography: Encyclopaedia Judaica (Berlin: 1932), vol. 9, 1202.

28. Location Unknown. *Bibliography: Jüdisches Lexikon* (Berlin, 1930), vol. 4, no. 2, pl. CLVI.

Essays

Thomas Mann's Attitudes Toward Jews and Judaism: An Investigation of Biography and Oeuvre

Alfred Hoelzel
(UNIVERSITY OF MASSACHUSETTS, BOSTON)

Thomas Mann (1875–1955), one of Germany's finest novelists, ranks securely among the giants of twentieth-century literature. However, Mann's significance extends much beyond his fiction. As an intellectual whose career traversed seven fateful decades of German history and culminated in American and Swiss exile during a cataclysmic war and its controversy-filled aftermath, Mann, unlike such men as Rainer Maria Rilke or Hermann Hesse, never chose to stand aloof from the hurly-burly of his time. On the contrary, Mann's intimate engagement with his sociopolitical environment—from Wilhelminian imperialism to Weimar republicanism, from Nazi dictatorship to the Rooseveltian New Deal, from McCarthy paranoia to European reconstruction—constitutes a distinctive dimension of his legacy. By the time Mann was living in the United States, journalists seeking an interview often had to specify whether their interest was literary or political. In one of his letters, written on the eve of the Second World War, Mann defended his indefatigable public crusade against Nazi tyranny by quoting Goethe, "What now counts is how much one weighs on the scale of humanity; everything else is insignificant."[1]

Such exemplary concern for humane values in a German—and non-Jewish—man of letters who had fled Hitler and National Socialism arouses a special curiosity in the Jewish world, ever sensitive to the attitudes of prominent gentiles. How does Mann's record add up in terms of his position on matters of Jewish concern? How does Mann treat Jews and Jewish themes in his fiction? Mann's long marriage to a woman of Jewish descent and his monumental tetralogy based on the book of Genesis endow such questions with special significance. And Mann's popular image as a moral paragon in the days of Nazi shame makes such questions vitally important for an accurate assessment of the fateful German Jewish relationship in the first half of this century.

Strangely, Mann's relationship to Jews and the Jewish realm has, to this point, stimulated relatively little scholarly interest. Not only does no book exist on this topic, but a perusal of the critical literature reveals no more than two substantial articles,[2] one chapter in a book[3] and a few small articles that either treat a very limited aspect of the subject or, if more general, deal with it very superficially. But even two of the significant items—Flinker and Loewenstein—suffer the handicap of having appeared prior to the publication of Mann's diaries and much of the immense corpus of his letters, two indispensable sources of information and perspective. The other and more recent item of significance benefits from these sources, but limits its time frame to the early Mann years (up to the advent of the Weimar Republic), thus omitting the major part of Mann's life and work, including the all-important Nazi period. A much fuller, although unfocused and regrettably undocumented account of Mann's relationship to Jews and Judaism during these years lies scattered about the pages of Peter de Mendelssohn's mammoth and virtually definitive biography of the young Thomas Mann.[4] In short, then, this topic constitutes a genuine lacuna in Mann scholarship.

The present study cannot claim to do more than trace the contours of this large, complex and largely uncharted territory. This essay attempts to offer only the quintessential elements of what a book-length study would put forward in greater detail. It takes into account, apart from Mann's biography, all of the published Mann: the fiction, the essays, the speeches, the interviews, the diaries and the correspondence as well as unpublished material in the most important of the Mann archives located in Zurich.

Mann's childhood in his native Lübeck, the Hanseatic city on the Baltic, permitted little contact with Jews. This was the result, essentially, of two factors: the city's long-standing restrictive policy on Jewish settlement, which even by Mann's time, in the late nineteenth century, kept the Jewish community down to about six hundred to seven hundred souls;[5] and the restrictive policy of Mann's nanny, whose vigilance ensured only "appropriate" playmates for the Mann children, namely, children from the "best" homes.[6] No Jewish child, of course, could qualify for such company. Yet, in school, away from his governess's snobbish eye, Mann did encounter Jewish children, and he has left a detailed and candid account of such associations in a revealing "letter-article,"[7] written in 1921, that for various reasons (see p. 236) did not surface publicly until 1966, more than a decade after Mann's death. Mann's reminiscences about his Jewish schoolmates reflect quite accurately (as we shall see) his attitudes toward Jews generally: strong admiration for Jewish creative genius and ethnic vitality tinged with supercilious condescension toward Jewish appearance, manners and style. Thus, while Mann readily recalls the superior intellect of his classmate Simson Carlebach,[8] he feels obliged to comment on Carlebach's slovenly looks (*"nicht sehr reinlich"*) and his adroit skill at sneaking correct answers orally to him (Mann) right under the teacher's nose. Or again, while favorably remembering another Jewish classmate of Hungarian origin for his exotic charm and theatrical talent, Mann seems compelled to call attention, quite irrelevantly, to the boy's physical ugliness and his clever mercantile acumen.

Such snide reference to negative Jewish traits should come as no surprise. Let us keep in mind that Mann grew up in a patrician Lübeck environment that regarded Jews as an alien and inferior element and as a popular target of coarse humor. Hostility toward Jews vied in these circles with a grudging respect for their artisan and entrepreneurial skills. Mann's father, scion of a thriving business family and a prominent city elder, seems to have conducted relatively open and unprejudiced business relationships with several Jewish merchants, but none of them could ever expect to gain entry into the Manns' exclusive social circle. Hence, it is hardly astonishing to discover that Heinrich Mann, older brother of Thomas and later a leading figure among left-wing intellectuals, briefly assumed, in the 1890s, the editorship of an ultra-conservative journal (*Das Zwanzigste Jahrhundert*)[9] with, inter alia, a blatantly antisemitic agenda. During his tenure as editor, Heinrich enlisted Thomas's services as an occasional book reviewer, but this somewhat embarrassing episode in the brothers' lives, one which the Mann family and reverent Thomas Mann scholars like to pass over in silence, reflects badly on Thomas mainly for his association with a journal of this stripe rather than for the content of his few contributions.[10]

Much more significant and problematic than his minor pieces in *Das Zwanzigste Jahrhundert* are Mann's characterizations of Jewish figures in that prolific first segment of his oeuvre, which encompasses most of his famous novellas as well as his first novel, *Buddenbrooks* (1901).[11] As Jacques Darmaun's inquiry has demonstrated, Jewish characters in Mann's early works, although mostly in minor roles, do not generally project a wholesome image. From the banker's wife in "The Will to Happiness" ("an ugly little Jewess") and the obsequious storekeeper Blüthenzweig in "Gladius Dei" to the banker's son in *Tonio Kröger* ("bow legs and slit eyes") and the impresario in "The Infant Prodigy"[12] ("a businessman with a hooked nose"), Jews invariably share one common attribute: physical unattractiveness in face and body.

But beyond unappealing looks and ungainly carriage, Mann's early Jewish characters often display a crass aggressiveness that they use to "rudely elbow their way in where they do not belong."[13] Mann employs this negative stereotype of nineteenth-century German literature particularly for the members of the Hagenström family in *Buddenbrooks,* a novel that deserves special attention since, in its numerous autobiographical parallels, it comes so close to being an autobiographical *roman à clef.* As the Buddenbrooks' archrivals in business, whose ever-increasing family vitality and financial success serve as an ironic counterpoint and inverse parallel to the Buddenbrooks' decline, the Hagenströms—actually a German family that has intermarried with Jews—clearly represent the triumph of the dynamic parvenu Jews over the old established German "Bürger." Their purchase of the palatial, ancestral Buddenbrook home in the course of the novel symbolizes that triumph unequivocally. Most of the Buddenbrook family members maintain a restrained and condescending attitude vis-à-vis their successful competitors, but Mann allows Tony Buddenbrook, whose two failed marriages accelerate the Buddenbrook decline, to vent recurrent anti-Jewish sentiment, ranging from sly to venomous, even to the point of calling the Hagenströms "*Geschmeiss*" ("scum" or "vermin"). Tony may not be Mann's own mouthpiece in the novel, but in a character so calculated to elicit the reader's sympathy, such derogation must at least raise suspicions about the author's own sentiments.

But these small examples in Mann's early works pale into insignificance compared to the so-called "*Wälsungenblut*" affair."[14] In February 1905, after a one-year courtship, Thomas Mann married Katia Pringsheim, the attractive and gifted daughter of a prominent mathematician at the University of Munich. The father, Alfred Pringsheim, a non-practicing Jew, had proudly refused baptism, although it would have accelerated his climb up the academic ladder.[15] Baptized in infancy as a Protestant, Katia was halakhically Jewish by virtue of an unbroken Jewish maternal line of nominal Protestants going back to an apostate Jewish great-grandmother. Katia had a twin brother, Klaus, with whom she maintained a close sibling friendship. Shortly after his marriage to Katia, Mann wrote a novella entitled *The Blood of the Walsungs*[16] for *Die Neue Rundschau*. But at the eleventh hour—galley proofs had already been issued—Mann withdrew the story. Although a small run of copies circulated privately in 1921, it took a French translation, *Sang Reservé*,[17] to bring the story into the public domain in 1931, more than a quarter of a century following its composition.

Blood of the Walsungs recounts a tale of sibling incest that concludes with a climactic scene of lovemaking between brother and sister on a bearskin rug. But it was certainly not the story's bold sexual theme that accounted for Mann's difficulties. The last line of the story's original version confirms dramatically that its protagonists, the Aarenhold family, who provoke extreme antipathy to the point of contempt, are assimilated, self-hating Jews. In this story, Mann employs the usual negative stereotypes, but this time pushes them to a point perilously close to coarse antisemitism. Herr Aarenhold acknowledges that his own financial success comes from having behaved like a "worm" and a "louse," the result of "persistent . . . never-satisfied striving"; Frau Aarenhold is an "ugly" and "shrivelled" woman; one of their children, Märit, possesses a "hooked nose" and a "bitter contemptuous mouth"; and the twin siblings not only exhibit vain and vulgar personalities, but also despise their own ethnic origins, as yet unidentified. But that last revelatory line of Mann's original version, "Beganeft haben wir ihn—den Goy" ("We put one over the dumb goy"), spoken by Siegmund Aarenhold after he has just made love to his sister Sieglinde (thereby cuckolding her native German fiancé)—that final moment of malicious sarcasm is a touch a Julius Streicher might well have envied. Fully cognizant of the rank provocation attached to the Yiddish expressions— supplied unwittingly by Mann's father-in-law—Thomas consulted his brother Heinrich as to whether he ought not substitute the more circumspect comment, "His existence will be a little less trivial, from now on." As it turned out, Mann kept the more offensive Yiddish after his brother counseled its inclusion as a matter of artistic integrity,[18] and it appeared thus, with full brutal force, in the 1931 French translation. However, the posthumous inclusion of the original German story in the Mann canon brought with it the euphemistic alternative Mann had considered a half-century earlier. It stands today as the standard text.

But alongside the racist overtones in *Blood of the Walsungs*, other equally compelling reasons prompted Mann's second thoughts, namely, the story's all-too-obvious parallels to actual facts: the assimilated German Jewish Pringsheims, Katia and her close relationship to her twin brother Klaus, Katia's marriage to a native German and, finally, Alfred Pringsheim's fanatical devotion to the music of Richard Wagner. Is it any wonder that when an apprentice at *Die Neue Rundschau* fortuitously discovered the withdrawn galley proofs, the whole of literary Munich buzzed with rumors of a sharply satiric story, now withdrawn from publication, in which the recently married author of *Buddenbrooks* had taken his revenge on his father-in-law for humiliations he had allegedly suffered while courting Katia Prings-heim? Whatever the truth of these and other rumors[19] that surfaced, the fact remains that the vicious lampooning of the Aarenhold family marks the nadir of Mann's Jewish characterizations. *That* remains beyond challenge.

By dramatic contrast, *Royal Highness*,[20] (1909) Mann's next novel, contains his first wholly attractive Jewish figure in Dr. Sammet, the royal physician at the Bavarian court. Possessed of an admirable professional expertise, a discreet manner and a quiet dignity, Dr. Sammet remains free of those belittling touches we have previously encountered in Mann's writing. Nor does it come as any surprise that Mann saved this favorable characterization for a man who practices medicine: throughout his life he preferred the care of Jewish physicians. Even so, the author's condescension toward Judaism still penetrates the text. Not only does the narrator identify, at one point, the circumstance of Jewish birth as a "misfortune," but the grand duke at the court presumes as much when he asks Dr. Sammet, "Have you ever found your origin to stand in your way, a drawback . . . ?" The clear reflection of Mann's own mind in the grand duke's presumptuous question preempts the appropriately proud but respectful response one might want to hear. Sure enough, Dr. Sammet responds with proper humility, saying in effect: no, the "abnormal" circumstance of being Jewish has simply spurred him on to greater effort in order to succeed.

In this first segment of his career, Mann's attitudes to Jews and their world are expressed not just in the indirect testimony of his fiction, but quite explicitly in the direct statement of essays. The best example of such direct statement comes in a response Mann contributed in 1907 to a symposium published in the *Münchner Neueste Nachrichten* under the title, "The Solution of the Jewish Problem." After denying the claim of Adolf Barthels that the Mann family was Jewish—a mistaken notion that still persists in some quarters—while asserting himself to be "a Phil-osemite of conviction and without reservation," Mann goes on eventually to pre-scribe assimilation as the best solution to the "Jewish Problem." Two words stand out in Mann's brief discussion: "*Europäisierung*" (the process of becoming Euro-pean) and "*Nobilisierung*" (the process of becoming noble). The ghetto Jew, the traditional Jew, the clearly identifiable Jew—especially in terms of physical fea-tures—must make way for the assimilated type who, with qualities of "elegance" and "wholesomeness," looks and acts German. For such Jews, Mann advocates intermarriage and baptism as ways to complete their integration into German soci-ety. Then, "it will no longer seem impossible to be a Jew and still a fine human being in body and soul." In venting such ideas, Mann reiterates, essentially, the assimilationist agenda of Theodor Mommsen,[21] one that many German Jews of the nineteenth and twentieth centuries—including the maternal line of Katia Prings-heim's family—eagerly adopted. Mann's essay echoes the patronizing comment he had once written to Heinrich after his first visit to the Pringsheim home, "No hint of Jewishness comes through where these people are concerned; you only sense culture, nothing else."[22]

Still, Mann's feelings of superiority and ambivalence toward Jews in these earlier years do not seem to have compromised or inhibited his professional or social relationship with them. Quite the contrary. With the advent of maturity in Munich, Mann cultivated the social and intellectual company of many Jews. No doubt such relationships developed with accelerated pace after his marriage to Katia, but even earlier, as a rising literary star, Mann traveled in sophisticated cosmopolitan Munich circles where Jews and non-Jews mixed comfortably. In fact, Mann had his first real meeting with Katia, a meeting he himself maneuvered, at the dinner table of mutual Jewish friends.[23] Bruno Walter and his wife, neighbors of the Manns in Munich, became their closest friends. Among the writers of his time, Mann held in esteem such Jews as Artur Schnitzler, Jakob Wassermann, Richard Beer-Hofmann, Stefan Zweig, Bruno Frank and Franz Werfel. He also perceptively recognized and acknowledged the significance of Kafka's work years ahead of the critics. The close personal friendship that developed between Mann and his Jewish publisher, Samuel Fischer, whose firm remained his exclusive German publisher from *Buddenbrooks* on, went far beyond an ordinary business relationship. Mann rarely forgot what his career owed to Jews and he paid tribute to them publicly, first in the 1921 letter-article ["On the Jewish Question"] in which, aside from crediting Jews for his early climb to fame, he also acknowledged that "when I travel in the world to various cities, it is almost without exception Jews—and not only in Vienna and Berlin—who receive me, host me, feed me and coddle me." Decades later he repeated the tribute, "I recall my own youth; I recall my own first steps out into the world. I cannot do so without gratitude for a welcome, an understanding, a furthering of aims, which I found far more among Jews than among the so-called 'Aryans' " (GW13:505-E).[24]

On the other hand, there were also bitter conflicts with adversaries who happened to be Jewish, but whom Mann always identified as *Jewish* adversaries. In the 1921 letter-article, he candidly acknowledged the bad blood that sometimes prevailed between him and Jews, "The most malicious stylizations of my being (*Stilisierungen meines Wesens*) have come from Jews, the most venomously witty negation of my existence came from that direction." Most certainly Mann is alluding here to the prominent Berlin critic Alfred Kerr, who had dismissed *Buddenbrooks* as the work of an unimaginative drudge, had snidely disparaged *Royal Highness,* and, this the unkindest cut, had held Mann up to ridicule in a viciously derisive poem.[25] Katia's memoirs, however, reveal a compelling personal reason for the deep animosity between the two men: Kerr had unsuccessfully courted her before she gave her hand to Mann.[26] In a fine irony, Kerr, a Jew by birth, actually followed the advice of Mann's 1907 essay by formally converting to Christianity.

But Kerr was not Mann's only Jewish antagonist in these years. Another Jew—also briefly an apostate—with whom he became embroiled in a bitter *Schriftfehde* (battle of words), was the philosopher and critic Theodor Lessing (1877–1953). Significantly, Mann's battle with Lessing—and this reveals much about Mann's loyalty to a friend or intellectual kinsman, regardless of ethnic affiliation—developed out of his gallant defense of another Jewish intellectual, Samuel Lublinski. Lublinski had been one of the first critics to recognize in print the greatness of Mann's first novel, a service Mann never forgot. Thus when Lessing cruelly attacked Lublinski's book *Der Ausgang der Moderne* (1908) with a spiteful polemic full of Jewish self-hatred, Mann hastened to Lublinski's side with a stiff counter-polemic in which, inter alia, he even defended Lublinski's Jewish persona against Lessing's odious insults. The details of the ensuing Mann–Lessing imbroglio, waged in the pages of Germany's leading intellectual journals, remain relatively unimportant.[27] Its true significance lies in Mann's genuine outrage over crude vilification of Jewish character and his impulse to speak out courageously and forcefully on a matter of conscience. It presages the new Thomas Mann about to emerge on the scene: the politically engaged man of letters.

Mann's life and career fall rather neatly into three distinctly demarcated segments, with two major political events—the First World War and the Nazi attainment of power (1933)—constituting the two caesuras. If the controversy with Theodore Lessing had provided Mann with an opportunity to hone his polemical skills in a relatively limited and personal arena, the catastrophic Great War became the catalyst that forever transformed Mann as a writer, turning him into a frequent and impassioned commentator on the contemporary scene. Just as Mann had rallied to Lublinski's defense, so too—but now on the scale of national and international issues—did he enter the lists on behalf of his native country to defend its honor against its detractors, both native and foreign. As a result, Mann was forced to confront directly his brother Heinrich, on whom the war had acted with no less catalytic force—however, with diametrically opposite results: his transformation into a fierce and outspoken critic on the Left.

Mann's role as an apologist for the political Right elicited from him, almost predictably, further *ressentiment* against Jews, the more so as so many of that period's liberal voices (protesters against German conduct in the war, pacifists, intellectuals on the Left) were Jewish. On occasion Mann disparages Jews of this type explicitly; more frequently he employs a code that leaves no doubt just whom he has in mind. Thus, Mann's political magnum opus of this period, the lengthy and repetitive *Reflections of a Nonpolitical Man*[28] (a misnomer if ever there was one!), avoids direct attack on Jewish targets. But in a statement such as:

> It is not just patriotic prejudice when one imagines and perceives in the strangely organic, unforced and poetic word combination, *deutsches Volk,* something not only national, but also essentially different, better, higher, purer, yes, holier than in the expression, "English people," or "French people." *Volk* is a truly holy sound. But does it not in any event still have a living meaning just by its connection with the word, *deutsch?* (p. 267),

a sensitive reader cannot help but feel that Mann's concept of "*deutsches Volk*" did not include Jews.

Anti-Jewish sentiment in the *Reflections* appears in indirect ways, often attached gratuitously to some other point. Thus, in the course of whipping up anti-French feeling—Francophobe hysteria abounds in the book—Mann writes, "It was a French general—he signs his name Levy, moreover—who stated that after he had touched a Boche he would consider it a purification to put his hands into a pot of manure." That "moreover" after the Jewish name speaks volumes. Nor does it speak well of Mann's political judgment of that time that he celebrates the virtues of none other than Houston Stewart Chamberlain, a man recognized today as a spiritual progenitor of Nazi racism. The *Reflections* may be regarded as Mann's comprehensive response to Heinrich's attack on the endemic political elitism of German intellectuals, notably Goethe. But it should remain equally clear that when Mann disparages "civilization's literary man (*Zivilisationsliterat*),"[29] he most certainly has in mind a host of contemporary writers standing behind Heinrich, especially the expressionists and activists of that period, a large number of whom were Jewish— Rudolf Herzog, Ludwig Rubiner, Kurt Hiller, Ernst Toller, to name just a few. Elsewhere Mann refers to these writers as a *"Lumpenpack"* (riffraff) and *"Ungeziefer des Geistes"* (vermin of the spirit) (GW13:532).

Not surprisingly, given his political allegiances at the time of the First World War, Mann detested the short-lived and ill-fated Räterepublik, which local socialists attempted forcibly to establish in Bavaria at the end of the war under the leadership of intellectuals such as Kurt Eisner and Ernst Toller. Mann's diary entries during this period leave no doubt that, in his mind, he equates the Socialist Revolutionaries with Jews. Thus he muses, "Both Munich and Bavaria governed by Jewish scribblers. How long will the city put up with that? . . . Our own co-regent a slimy literary racketeer like Herzog, who let himself be kept for years by a movie-star, a money-maker and profiteer at heart, with the big-city piss-elegance of the Jewboy. . . . That is the Revolution! The ones involved are almost exclusively Jewish."[30] This may be the most embarrassing of Mann's anti-Jewish entries, but it by no means stands alone. If a citizen such as Thomas Mann could harbor such views, one need wonder no further about the quick acceptance of that postwar canard in Germany making Jews and Communists the chief culprits, the backstabbers, in Germany's military defeat.

Still, despite such negative private exclamations, the Weimar years also found Mann expressing himself very positively on Jewish matters, primarily so in a long letter of 1921 to his friend Jakob Wassermann (GW13:463–465)—following the publication of the latter's *My Path as a German and Jew*—and, in the same year, in a response to an inquiry from the Jewish editor Efraim Frisch asking him to state his views on Judaism. Interestingly, Mann challenges—but in polite, even friendly terms—Wassermann's plaints about the special difficulties a German Jewish writer faces with the counterassertion that *all* German writers face similar difficulties. As proof against Wassermann's contentions, Mann holds up the Jewish writer's own great successes. Invoking Goethe—Mann frequently repeats this reference in other contexts—he cites his revered predecessor's alleged remark about Jewish intellectual superiority and superior sensitivity as readers. Therefore, Mann continues, Wassermann need have no qualms about his own acceptance. Finally, in a rhetorical question that must have haunted him just over a decade later, Mann asks: Can such a cosmopolitan and heterogeneous society as Germany be "a soil in which the weed of antisemitism could ever truly take deep root?"

Mann's response to Frisch's inquiry—the essay ["On the Jewish Question"] mentioned earlier—an item that did not appear in print for some forty-five years, remains, like the *Wälsungenblut* affair, the focus of continuing debate. Indeed, parallels abound in the circumstances surrounding the writing and publication of both pieces: sensitive Jewish subject matter, last-minute withdrawal from publication, controversy over the reasons for such withdrawal and publication only after a hiatus of many years. The details of the controversial elements need not detain us;[31] what counts are the contents. After a disclaimer of antisemitism on his part—gratuitous really, since no one had accused him of anything—and professing himself as philosemitic (*judenfreundlich*), Mann launches into those recollections of childhood encounters with Jewish children I have already reviewed. Thereafter, Mann goes over old ground, repeating sections of his letter to Wassermann, that is, the Goethe quotation, acknowledgment of both the trouble he has suffered at Jewish hands and the enormous debt his career owes them and his denial—for the umpteenth time—of Adolf Bartel's claim about his Jewish ancestry.

But the last section of this piece invites special attention. Here we find Mann's first repudiation—in 1921!—of the Nazis ("the swastika silliness") at a time when he still stood squarely in the camp of the extreme Right. We also find some foreshadowing of his next major novel, *The Magic Mountain,*[32] in a fleeting reference to German youth's search for a path that would lead between "Rome," on the one side, and "Moscow," on the other. Finally, and most important for this discussion, Mann concludes with a typically ambivalent judgment: Jews may never really have amounted to much as a people, but their great redeeming feature, their native love of "Geist" (that untranslatable word combining intellect with moral virtue) will always place in their debt artists, poets and intellectuals and thus always bind him inseparably to them. In comparing this statement with the one written fourteen years earlier, we find, then, the same profession of sympathy for Jews, the same rejection of antisemitism, but also the same condescension—indeed, in even more derisive terms. However, not a word this time of Jewish assimilation or "nobilization."

For all of Mann's declared appreciation of Jewish intellect, the record during the Weimar years indicates continuing ambivalence toward Jewish character, sometimes even outright antipathy. Nowhere does this become clearer than in *The Magic Mountain,* often considered Mann's greatest novel. Begun after the war and published in 1924, Mann's third novel, a bildungsroman in the finest German tradition, does not simply trace the education of Hans Castorp, a young German; it dresses up in fictional clothes some of Mann's *Reflections.*[33] When Mann writes in his response to Frisch that German youth seek a path between Rome and Moscow, he surely has in mind Castorp's search for *German* values that avoid what Mann sees as Scylla–Charybdis alternatives offered in the democratic West (England, France, Italy) and the mysterious totalitarian East (Russia). Much of Castorp's intellectual education in the novel takes place during long and sometimes heated debate between the loquacious, liberal Settembrini and the mercurial, brilliant Jesuit-Marxist radical, Naphta. Though both represent political-intellectual poles that Castorp must ultimately learn to reject, Mann by no means limns their characters in equally balanced terms. Despite his garrulousness, Settembrini projects a likable, sunny personality, whereas something sinister always lurks behind the explosive Naphta. When their academic disputations ultimately degenerate into bitter personal invective, setting the stage for a duel, the rational Settembrini cannot bring himself at the critical moment to fire at his opponent, whereas the fanatical Naphta, in a frenzy of frustration, fires the fatal bullet—into his own head. Settembrini is an Italian; Naphta, a convert from Judaism.[34]

Let us look a bit more closely at Mann's characterization of Naphta, a major figure in a major novel. As with so many of Mann's Jewish characters, Naphta is physically repugnant, possessing a "piercing . . . corrosive ugliness" marked by a "hooked nose," a "narrow pursed mouth," thickly bespectacled eyes and a slight build. His voice is "reminiscent of a cracked plate tapped on by the knuckle." As though to underscore the nexus between ugliness and Jewishness, Joachim Ziemssen—Castorp's cousin and fellow patient at the sanatorium—observes following their first meeting with Naphta, "And did you see the big Jewish nose he had? Nobody but Jews have such puny figures." Now Mann's earlier Jewish characters (such as the Hagenströms or the Aarenholds), while certainly unattractive or ungraceful, are not so readily identifiable as Jews, the clues placed discreetly enough so as to elude the casual reader. Not so in the case of Naphta. Here Mann makes his Jewish origins a key point, as he devotes several pages to Naphta's shtetl background. Here the young boy learns from his father's "solemn mercilessness" the idea that piety and cruelty go inseparably hand in hand, and from his father's occupation as village *shohet*—this a swipe at kosher slaughtering—the concept that the sacred and the spiritual belong inextricably together with the sight and smell of spurting blood.

Naphta's entire person, his looks, character and personality, radiates a thoroughly alienating image, impressive at first for its intellectual brilliance but then humanly repellent for its adamantine espousal of intellectual and political extremism. Most likely Mann conceived the character type while observing the Jewish socialist intellectuals at the head of the Räterepublik. A diary entry from 1919, recording a conversation with Katia about the contemporary political scene, indicates as much, "We talked also about the type of Russian Jew, the leader of the world movement, this explosive combination of Jewish intellectual radicalism and Slavic Christ-zealotry. A world which still possesses an instinct for self-preservation must combat this type of person with all available energy and legal concision."[35] Mann would surely not have attacked with such severity the Settembrinis of that day.

But even while engaged in the writing of *The Magic Mountain,* a novel with conservative political overtones, and even while observing with great distaste the brief effort to establish a socialist government in Bavaria in the immediate postwar period, Mann's political thinking was undergoing a moderating change. Two specific factors certainly played a major role: the raucous emergence of National Socialism (in Mann's eyes "the Swastika silliness") and the reconciliation in 1922, after several years of bitter intellectual strife and deep personal animus, of the brothers Thomas and Heinrich.[36] In any case, Thomas Mann's speech "The German Republic"[37] for an occasion honoring Gerhart Hauptmann in 1922, signals Mann's recoil from the political Right and his endorsement of democratic principles of government as embodied in the new Weimar Republic.

What did this change in political philosophy and allegiance mean for Mann's relationship with the Jewish world? In the early Weimar years not a great deal. The response to Frisch, with its snide undercurrent, dates after all from 1921. A diary entry from slightly earlier (July 1919) disparages Jews encountered on a train that day in the most contemptuous terms, the emphasis again on appearance and manners, "During the first half of the day I was alone with a Jewish couple, whose female half represented, as an example of the female species, the most disgusting thing imaginable: nauseatingly fat and short-legged, hook-nosed with a pale sensuous-melancholy face, overpoweringly perfumed. . . . The Jews ate constantly, bringing coffee from the dining-car and buying of everything offered despite their own plenteous supplies."[38] Even in that bench mark speech of 1922, Mann cannot resist an occasional anti-Jewish phrase, as when he says, while exhorting Germans to accept the Republic, "There is no ground in the world for imagining the Republic to be a concern of keen-witted young Jews. Do not leave it to them! Take the wind out of their sails."

But by the mid-1920s, Mann had embarked on an ambitious new project that would eventually span almost two decades and be completed (in 1943) in American exile: an epic based on the vicissitudes of the Biblical Joseph, his brothers and ancestors; an enormous tapestry of individuals, events and reflections requiring, as it turned out, the space and structure of four novels. This extraordinary tetralogy, yoked together with Mann's flight from Nazi Germany, mark a major turning point in Mann's relationship with the Jewish world. Ironically, Mann did not set out originally—as his letters of that period indicate—to write a Biblical novel from a Jewish perspective or calculated to elicit Jewish sympathy. On the contrary, he was much more interested in the mythical dimensions of the ancient Canaanite-Egyptian world in which Joseph was to play the role of a "mythic confidence man."[39] But events in Germany conspired to change drastically the course of Mann's life, thrusting upon him an entirely new set of circumstances that compelled major shifts in outlook and agenda, and stimulating a vibrant new period of literary creativity and energetic political involvement.

One might easily infer that Thomas Mann's exile from Germany, almost immediately after the Nazi takeover, was a noble act of conscience. The facts are somewhat different—although, in the final analysis, they still reflect well on Mann. Mann left Germany with Katia on February 11, 1933, taking on tour a Wagner lecture[40] he had just delivered to a packed university auditorium in Munich. The Manns had planned an absence of a few weeks, but the political climate in Germany deteriorated so rapidly that just a month later Erika and Klaus, the two oldest children, warned their parents, then vacationing in Switzerland, to stay away.[41] Why should Thomas Mann, not so many years earlier a leading conservative, need to have worried about his safety so early in the Nazi regime? Because in the meantime Mann's several public denunciations of National Socialism,[42] his thinly veiled caricature of Fascism in the short story "Mario and the Magician"[43] (1930), his writing about the Jewish patriarchs, and now his unflattering comments about Wagner in an otherwise long appreciation, made him a suspect quantity in the Nazis' eyes. Indeed, they had already planted a spy in his household (his chauffeur).[44] Nor did it help matters when Mann courageously withdrew his membership in the Prussian Academy of Art and then in the Association of German Authors (both in mid-March, 1933).[45] Even so, and even despite his growing awareness that he might be facing a long-term exile, Mann was still expecting to return home to Munich when a public attack against him dashed all such hopes. An aggressive, accusatory letter appeared in the *Münchner Neueste Nachrichten,*[46] signed by most of the major figures of the

Munich musical world, calling on Mann to recant his criticism of Wagner. This Mann proudly refused. Shortly thereafter, the Nazis impounded the Manns' house, their property and bank accounts. The rupture was now an open one and a reconcilement improbable.

With the battle lines between Mann and the Nazis clearly drawn and with the alarmingly rapid implementation of the Nazis' avowed antisemitic agenda, one would expect the development of closer bonds between Mann and the Jewish community, both now victims of Nazi persecution. Such bonds did, in fact, develop. Nevertheless, anti-Jewish slurs reaching at times appalling levels of bad taste and distemper erupt now and then in the diaries. Thus, the entry for the Mann's first Christmas celebration in exile (1933) shows Mann reporting unabashedly, "Upon being asked late last night what was nicest about Christmas, the children declared: when Daddy imitated a Jew at the table."[47] If this might pass as harmless ethnic sport, earlier entries made in April of that year commenting on the systematic curtailment of Jewish civil rights permit no benign interpretations. At the very time he himself is feeling the wrath and vindictiveness of Nazi terror, Mann finds it possible to write, "It is no calamity after all that Alfred Kerr's brazen and poisonous Jewish-style imitation of Nietzsche is now suppressed, or that the domination of the legal system by Jews has been ended."[48] And a little later, "I could have a certain amount of understanding for the rebellion against the Jewish element were it not that the Jewish spirit exercises a necessary control over the German element, the withdrawal of which is dangerous; left to themselves the Germans are so stupid as to lump people of my type in the same category and drive me out with the rest."[49]

As disturbing as such private reflections may be—and, in all fairness to Mann, these are more than matched by expressions of sympathy for Jewish suffering—they should not obscure Mann's increasing anti-Nazi and pro-Jewish activity. In mid-1934 he was reluctant to take public stands, for fear of harming family members still under Nazi jurisdiction,[50] but also surely because the Nazis had not yet officially closed the door to him. However, as events in Germany took on a more ominous profile, and especially after his 1935 visit to the United States to accept an honorary degree from Harvard, during which time he had an audience with President Roosevelt at the White House, Mann began to speak out forcefully. Leaping into a dispute between Leopold Schwarzschild and Eduard Korrodi over Schwarzschild's assertion that the flight or expulsion of virtually all the country's significant writers had reduced the contemporary German literary scene to a wasteland,[51] Mann wrote an open letter to Korrodi (February 3, 1936)[52] that seems at first to exhibit considerable circumspection. While rejecting Schwarzschild's thesis and also applying correctives to Korrodi's spirited rebuttal,[53] Mann gallantly defended those German writers who opted to remain under the new regime and—this transparently self-referential—"do not wish to destroy all bridges to their country and all possibility of their influencing it." But then, as though he had been wrestling with himself all along and at last decided to vent his true feelings, the consequences be damned, Mann proclaimed in his final paragraph:

> Countless human, moral and aesthetic observations support my profound conviction that nothing good can possibly come of the present German regime, not for Germany

and not for the world. This conviction has made me shun the country in whose spiritual traditions I am more deeply rooted than the present rulers who for three years have vacillated, not quite daring to deny me my Germanism before the eyes of the world.

With that last sentence Mann demolished whatever remnant of a bridge still stood between him and his native land. Within weeks the Nazis revoked Mann's citizenship; within months the University of Bonn revoked his honorary doctorate.[54] Germany had ceased to be Mann's home—for good.

Just over a year later (March 1937)—the Manns were residing in Switzerland—Mann prefaced a reading from his most recent novel (*Joseph in Egypt*) for the Swiss Zionist organization Kadimah with a lecture on antisemitism. Entitled "On the Problem of Antisemitism" (GW13:479–490), it was his first major *unsolicited* public statement on the subject, and the contemporary political scene lent his views a special significance. Seeking to address antisemitism as a social phenomenon, Mann's analysis included several distinctive nuances. For one thing, Mann saw German antisemitism being fueled by an "aristocracism of the mob," by a feeling in the lower classes that "OK, I'm nothing . . . but I'm no Jew." Mann also believed that antisemitic persecution reflected an atavistic German need to shed the civilizing restraints of Christianity in order to give license to ancient pagan-Germanic instincts. In fact, Mann argued—reiterating a point from his letter to Korrodi—Judaism represented a purer distillation of an ancient Mediterranean–Christian element in the German tradition, one of humane and universalizing tendencies, which Germans wanted to purge—with disastrous results for the Jews. In this discussion Mann invoked Goethe yet again—as he had years earlier in his responses to Moses and Frisch—not only to celebrate Jewish striving for intellectual excellence but, now going further, to demonstrate how, in many ways, Germans and Jews possess a similar character and mission. It was an idea that Mann had enthusiastically adopted from the eminent Princeton intellectual historian Erich Kahler, whose manuscript of *Israel unter den Völkern*[55] he had read a year earlier.

This third of Mann's major attempts to address the question of Jews in German society does differ in one very noteworthy way: it is, for once, completely free of condescension and snide disparagement. Not that Mann had finally overcome that deep-seated antipathy toward Jews that finds its way into his writing with such frequency. Just two months after the Kadimah lecture, he noted in his diary that he had written a letter to Bruno Frank complaining "about the infamous Jewish clique at the *Tagebuch* [i.e., Schwarzschild's journal]."[56] De Mendelssohn's editorial note on the letter, full of paraphrases and direct quotations, reveals Mann at his petulant worst. Enraged by Hermann Kesten's effusive praise for Alfred Döblin as the creator of the "epic myth in the German language" (thereby ignoring Mann's Joseph novels), Mann lashed out at Jewish critics, who had allegedly always treated him badly—an egregious contradiction of his own repeated assertions to the contrary—and had now ignored his accomplishments "by ostentatiously raising on his shield a blood-brother and clique-intimate against me, the dumb goy."[57] Mann himself must have recognized his behavior here as a temper tantrum, for he continued to publish in Schwarzschild's journal.

Mann's immigration to the United States in the spring of 1938 launched a period of intense political activity in the form of lecture tours, radio speeches, interviews, articles and letters and, not least, private efforts on behalf of refugees from Nazi persecution. But if the Nazi regime was the chief target of this energetic activity, its chief beneficiaries were undoubtedly the Jewish community and many Jewish individuals. To judge by Erika's report of audience reaction to his name and telegram at a mass Jewish rally in New York in May 1937,[58] Mann had already enjoyed considerable favor in American Jewish circles before his immigration; but now, in the years of American residence, he became identified as a sympathetic philosemite, staunch ally and—the more so because of his non-Jewish status—effective spokesman for the Jewish cause. Mann's major lecture tours of 1938 and 1939 addressed the general public, but over and above such appearances Mann was also frequently addressing—in spite of his difficulties with English—Jewish audiences in all parts of the United States, from New York to San Francisco, from Tulsa to Detroit, from Cincinnati to Birmingham, from Mobile to Chicago. Mann's diaries and correspondence in these years testify eloquently not only to his generous response to such invitations, but also to the genuine warmth of the Jewish reception on these occasions. The correspondence reveals a no less remarkable generosity in Mann's numerous efforts to help Jewish writers and artists gain a haven in the United States and to get work and subsidies after they had arrived.[59] Mann's magnanimity even extended to writing letters of support for individuals—such as Oskar Goldberg and Alfred Döblin—with whom he had his differences.

As a refugee from Nazi Germany living in the United States, Mann became *nolens volens* a member of a substantial subculture of émigrés, located mainly on the East and West coasts, a group bonded by their native language—and overwhelmingly Jewish. Now, more than ever, Mann traveled and socialized in predominantly Jewish circles. For the most part, Mann accepted this distinct change in his social life gracefully, but on occasion flashes of the old anti-Jewish animus flare up in his diaries. For example, after a party at the Horkheimers on the West Coast, to which the Manns moved in 1941, he records, "Then to Horkheimer . . . to a house-warming party, with many '*Vogerln*,' which turned into a late-evening buffet-dinner and a really excruciating historical-political-philosophical orgy of talk. These Jews have a sense of Hitler's greatness which I cannot take." (An editorial note identifies the term "*Vogerl*"—in Austrian dialect, "birdie"—as Erika's "playful-derogatory expression . . . for the unpleasant immigrant crowd."[60] Mann it seems appropriated it.) On the other hand, Mann also proclaimed his solidarity with his fellow émigrés through occasional articles for *Aufbau*, the New York-based German-language weekly, established for the refugee community and strongly oriented toward Jewish concerns. Klaus Mann quite justifiably observed—this also recorded in Mann's diary[61]—that the German refugees constituted virtually a nation unto themselves with Thomas Mann as their elected ambassador.

With the publication of *Joseph the Provider* in Stockholm (1943), Mann completed the Biblical tetralogy begun seventeen years earlier in Munich. In recounting much of Genesis and recreating the lives of the Jewish patriarchs, this cycle of novels dealt with the wellsprings of Jewish tradition at the very time the Jewish people were facing the cruelest assault on their very survival. But it would be a mistake to infer, as did both Nazis and Jews, that Mann chose his topic as a pointedly defiant gesture. Few could have predicted in 1926, when Mann began to work on his first novel—he did not yet realize his subject would extend to four novels—the extraordinary and disastrous turn of events a decade later in Germany. As noted earlier, Mann did not intend a *"Judenbuch"* at all—he repeatedly denied such notions—and originally wanted to portray Joseph as a kind of "mythic confidence man" (*"Hochstapler"*).[62] But by the time of his Kadimah speech (1937), and in light of the new political scene, he had changed his characterization of Joseph from the pejorative "confidence man" to the much more admirable "artist" (*"Künstler"*).

Limitations of space preclude even a summary, let alone a nuanced discussion, of the nearly two thousand pages Mann devoted to ancient Jewish history and tradition. But there is no denying that the first novel of the cycle, *The Tales of Jacob*,[63] written in the pre-Nazi years, often portrays the Jewish patriarchs in harsh terms: the cowardly Jacob groveling before Eliphaz (Esau's son); the bloodthirsty brothers, led by Simon and Levi, brutally massacring Schechem and his kinsmen. One description of Jacob and his sons is particularly revealing, "Strangers and wanderers—not such very agreeable or harmless ones either, rather vain and dictatorial, indeed, boasting of their superior spirituality, and at the same time capable of looking after their own interest in the wool and cattle trade in a way that made one's self-esteem suffer in comparison."[64] One cannot escape the strong suspicion that this passage encapsulates much of how Mann viewed Jews generally prior to the Hitler era.

But the next three novels, written in exile, adopt a different tone entirely. The second chapter of *Young Joseph* captures Abraham's "discovery" of God—an extraordinary feat of the imaginative intellect—in reverential and non-ironic terms. And though he does not spare his readers the murderous intent of Jacob's sons as they vent their jealous rage on Joseph, this time—in dramatic contrast to the first novel's comparable massacre scene—Mann interjects an authorial note of caution, "But I am not anxious that the reader be finally disgusted with the sons of Jacob . . . ,"[65] and later adds a mitigating, if somewhat patronizing, apologia for their behavior. Far from the "confidence man" of Mann's original conception, Joseph emerges finally, for all his colossal vanity and egocentricity, as a hero on the grand scale whose brilliant economic strategy to save Egypt from ruinous famine mirrors, *mutatis mutandis*, Roosevelt's New Deal.

In any case, the Jewish community, with just a few dissenting voices, bestowed on Mann's "super-midrash"—thus Ludwig Lewisohn[66]—a warm welcome. Reflecting retrospectively on his completed cycle for a Washington audience, Mann came close to claiming polemical motives for his tetralogy, but on the whole his talk remained consistent with his repeated contention from first to last that this immense work was not a *"Judenbuch,"* but a *"Menschheitsbuch."*[67]

Mann's vigorous political activity and denunciations of the Nazis included increasing expressions of shock and outrage over the gradually emerging details of what we now call the Holocaust. The diaries and correspondence register much private disgust over mistreatment of Jews from the 1930s on, an abhorrence that translated into Mann's active and frequent participation in anti-Nazi demonstrations. But as reports of atrocities and mass slaughter trickled through, Mann raised his voice in public outcry, particularly on his regular (approximately monthly) Radio

Free Europe broadcasts over the BBC. Holocaust research has attempted in recent years to pinpoint just when the Allies became privy to "the terrible secret."[68] As early as 1941/1942 Mann was reporting the many thousands of Jewish corpses, victims of typhus, cholera and consumption, piled up in the Warsaw ghetto. Already in January 1942, Mann began his broadcast message by announcing the deaths of four hundred Dutch Jews in an experiment to test the effectiveness of poison gas in mass extermination,[69] surely one of the earliest public alerts about the Final Solution. In the ensuing months, Mann followed this up with regular references to Nazi atrocities leading up to the climactic broadcast of September 27, 1942, devoted entirely to an outraged and moving condemnation of the systematic slaughter of Europe's Jews, complete with specific and accurate detail (GW11:1050–1053). Should anyone think today that the American public, including its Jewish community, had no inkling during the war of the Nazis' intentions with the Jews—a claim still sometimes made—let him read Mann's speech, "The Fall of the European Jews," delivered at a San Francisco rally in June 1943—almost two full years before the camps were liberated—which begins, "Other races at the mercy of Nazi ruthlessness face humiliation, demoralization, reduction, emasculation, slavery. For the Jews it is plain extermination that has been decided upon, and this extermination has begun on a large scale" (GW13:494-E).

In view of such public anguish over Jewish suffering, Mann's radio speech of May 8, 1945, entitled *"Die Lager"* ("The Camps") (GW12:951–953), is truly astonishing for its total omission of the word "Jew" or "Jewish" or any reference whatsoever to the Jews as the primary target of Nazi bestiality. This perplexing lacuna is attributable either to explicit instructions from the Office of War Information,[70] or—the more likely case—to Mann's specific source of his speech, *Time* magazine's report of April 30, 1945, on the camps.[71] That report, covering the revelations from the Erla, Belsen and Buchenwald camps, contained not a single reference to a Jewish victim.

No less questionable was a private comment of Mann's a few years later (after his first return to Germany in the Goethe bicentennial year of 1949), when, in the context of defending his visit to East Germany, he asserted that people died at Buchenwald "only" of hunger and disease but not of "beatings, torture, gassing and sadistic humiliation."[72] Apparently, an environment created to kill people by starvation and disease did not qualify as torture and humiliation.

Having completed his mammoth Joseph project, Mann set out in 1943 to write "nothing less than the novel of . . . [an] era"[73] that would address the Nazi phenomenon in the context of German cultural history. The result, *Doctor Faustus* (1947),[74] is certainly one of the most ambitious and complex novels ever written, one that ingeniously mounts the famous German Faust legend on *the* German creative medium par excellence, music, to produce virtually an allegory of Germany's cultural and political debacle in the twentieth century. Do Jews play a role in this novel so close to Jewish concerns? Only a rather minor one—yet one fraught with problems and controversies. In the novel's opening pages, its narrator briefly mentions the rabbi of the town where the novel's Faustian protagonist, Adrian Leverkühn, grew up. The few details offered here all reflect quite creditably on the Jewish figure. But in this context the name Breisacher already appears, an early foreshadowing of the "dismayingly unsympathetic" (*verwirrend antipathisch*) scholar, Dr. Chaim Breisacher, a leading figure in the Munich salon of intellectuals whose company Leverkühn later seeks out.

Chaim Breisacher, obviously Jewish, a polymath of fearsome proportions and, sure enough, a figure of "fascinating ugliness," epitomizes the novel's important theme of cultural atavism.[75] Sharing with the other members of the Munich circle a profound contempt for libertarian politics, democratic principles and "progress," Breisacher's reactionary extremism includes the notions, for example, that polyphony in music or prayer and social justice in religion signal unfortunate stages of cultural decline. The figures of this salon represent those intellectuals of the Weimar period whose supercilious resistance dug the grave of Germany's fledgling constitutional democracy and thus paved the road to National Socialism.

The novel's other Jewish character is the unctuous, garrulous impresario Saul Fitelberg, of French nationality, who makes a cameo appearance offering Leverkühn a lucrative tour with Europe's finest orchestras. The crassly mercenary and glib Fitelberg—especially when invidiously comparing Germans and Jews—cuts an unsavory and somewhat ludicrous figure. Subsequent literary scholarship has seen beneath the sleazy veneer even a sinister dimension: a devil figure whose temptations Leverkühn repulses with a proud "Apage Satanas."[76]

Objection to such blatantly offensive Jewish figures, without any countervailing example, seems to have surprised only Thomas Mann. By his own account,[77] members of his family warned him about precisely the kind of consternation these characterizations would certainly provoke when he would read to them from his manuscript-in-progress. Yet Mann would not budge. Nor do his efforts at self-exculpation, both in his letters and in *The Story of a Novel,* sound convincing. His claim that Fitelberg is a "charming, clever fellow"[78] and a "lovable figure"[79] is disingenuous; his pleas, with regard to Breisacher, that "the book demanded it,"[80] a specious subterfuge; his afterthought offering Kunigunde Rosenstiel[81]—a character of minuscule significance—as a positive Jewish counterbalance beneath even a word of contradiction.

But, in fairness to Mann, the issue of Breisacher requires one further word of explanation. The character and his ultra-reactionary views derive from a living prototype: Oskar Goldberg (1885–1952) and his book *Die Wirklichkeit der Hebräer* (1925),[82] which Mann considered "just plain Fascist" and "the work of a typical Jewish Fascist."[83] It is not unlikely that through Breisacher Mann was venting a good deal of the antipathy he harbored toward Jewish refugees who continued to love nostalgically the country that had humiliated them and, in extreme cases, even found rationalizations for Hitler and the Nazis. The occasional contemptuous references to "*Emigrantenpatriotismus,*" going back to the 1930s, when he already inveighed against Jewish "roadpavers for the anti-liberal turn," such as Oskar Goldberg (cited explicitly),[84] reach a crescendo of intensity in 1945, precisely the time when Mann was composing his Breisacher chapter (28) of *Doctor Faustus.*

One final issue invites consideration: Thomas Mann and Zionism. Unlike most of the sub-topics that fall within the purview of this study, Mann's relationship to Zionism has received recent scholarly attention in the form of two articles by Mark H. Gelber.[85] These accounts cover the ground admirably as far as they go, but, in omitting crucial Mann correspondence, published and unpublished, they leave one particularly glaring gap. Gelber rightly observes Mann's changes of heart over the years with regard to Zionism and the contradictions between his public and private utterances on this topic. Yet, through all these changes and discrepancies, one essentially consistent point stands out in relief right up to the establishment of the State of Israel: Mann's opposition to a full-fledged sovereign Jewish state to which Jews of all countries would emigrate, an opposition going back to his 1907 symposium response characterizing Jews as an "indispensable stimulus to European culture" (GW13:459). Thus, in 1928, more than two decades later, even while expressing warm support for Zionism, Mann maintained "as a German and man of culture," that he would "deeply bemoan" the loss of German and world Jewry to "the small oriental country," and repeated his conviction, in effect, that without Jews Germany would turn into a cultural wasteland.[86]

Mann's visit to Palestine in 1930 strengthened his support for Zionism and elicited excited admiration for the Yishuv's dynamic spirit and enterprise. "Everything is caught up in progress, the Jews are accomplishing beautiful work," he says in one interview.[87] Elsewhere he is quoted, "You know, it was a new as well as striking impression, when I saw for the first time free Jews in a free Jewish city, saw Jews uninhibited among themselves. They were changed people. . . . I realized Jews are drawn to Palestine so as to liberate and fulfill themselves spiritually."[88] But while exhibiting informal public enthusiasm of this sort, he refrained from similar expression in more formal terms. In that same year, 1930, he declined to write on Zionism for the *Neue Jüdische Monatshefte* with the plea that, since visiting Palestine, he had grown aware of the delicate problems and complexities and preferred to wait until the issues had further crystallized.[89] It is also important to note that several of Mann's interviews and public statements display sensitivity and understanding for the Arab side of the question; one of his characteristic private outbursts at Jews actually led him to compare Jewish treatment of Arabs in Palestine with Julius Streicher's behavior toward Jews in Nazi Germany.[90]

The enormity of Jewish suffering under the Nazis forced Mann to understand more keenly the importance of a Jewish homeland. Even so, he persisted in his earlier reservations about a bona fide independent national Jewish state drawing Jews from other countries. In 1932 he had stated, "It would be a misunderstanding to think that Zionism requires the mass return of the Jewish people to the traditional home of their race. Such a demand would be absurd, since the great majority of Jews are too firmly rooted in their occidental civilization and in the culture of their different home countries to break away and accustom themselves again to the ancestral land" (GW13:476-E). Ten years later, in the midst of the war, he repeated this sentiment in a letter, stating that for him Zionism should not aim at "the foundation of a Jewish national state," for he believed that Jews are "a cosmopolitan people who are of the greatest importance for the cultural life in general as a fermenting and stimulating element."[91]

Gelber correctly identifies a more positive shift in Mann's tribute to Chaim Weizmann of 1944, "An Enduring People" (GW13:502–507-E). Even so, Mann still wrote here of "the misunderstanding that Zionism aims to repatriate in Palestine all the Jews in the world . . . nor would it be in the interest of those so-called 'host' countries which owe so deep a debt of gratitude to the civilizing stimulus of the Jewish people," a "misunderstanding" that more accurately reflected Mann's idea of Zionism and *his* continuing hope that the well-settled Jews in the Diaspora, such as American Jews, would not flee en masse to Palestine. Yet, despite these reservations, Mann did lend his support, in the form of a statement, to the American Jewish Conference's battle in 1944 against the British White Paper limiting Jewish immigration to Palestine.[92]

In 1945 a new twist developed in Mann's thinking on Zionism—a development missing in Gelber's articles. Mann responded enthusiastically to a proposal from Isaac N. Steinberg (Russian revolutionary, and later, in the United States, a leader of the Territorialist faction) for an autonomous Jewish colony in Australia, a plan Mann considered "extremely desirable." Steinberg's plan appealed to Mann, first, in its pragmatic approach to the acute problem of homeless Holocaust survivors entangled in the political morass of a Palestine solution, and second, in "its non-political character," as it constituted "not a competitive movement to Zionism but an unpolitical supplement to it."[93] In another letter, reiterating his support for the Australian plan, Mann again emphasized the attractiveness of a solution "which does not contain the incendiary political elements no doubt inherent in Zionism."[94]

Yet, all these reservations did not prevent Mann from expressing public outrage in early 1948 when the United States, apparently in craven capitulation to Arab oil interests, suddenly withdrew its support for a Jewish home in Palestine. In a strongly worded statement for *Aufbau,* entitled "*Gespenster von 1938*" ("Ghosts of 1938") (GW13:515–516), Mann compared this American betrayal of Jewish aspirations to the infamous British and French abandonment of Czechoslovakia in 1938 in the face of Hitler's bluster, an "act of despicable and low expediency."[95] Repeated expressions of anger in Mann's letters prove that his *Aufbau* statement was no mere public posturing. Strangely, though, the establishment of the State of Israel in 1948 elicited no comment in Mann's letters—at least not until March 1949, when he remarked on Israel's "tremendous psychological significance for entire World Jewry" and expressed the hope—in keeping with his long-held concerns—that Jewish wisdom would keep "the newly strengthened Jewish consciousness from degenerating into a . . . vulgar nationalism."[96] Perhaps the next volume of diaries, which will include entries for 1948, will reveal Mann's private thoughts at the historic moment of Israel's birth.

The final years of Mann's life, 1949–1955, were filled with political controversy: his adamant refusal, for four years, to return to Germany;[97] his insistence, when he did finally return for the Goethe bicentennial in 1949, on visiting both West *and* East Germany; his increasing disaffection with the American scene in the McCarthy era; his feud with German critics who accused him of hypocrisy and treason during the war;[98] and his permanent return to Europe (Switzerland) in the early 1950s. But none of these issues has any significant bearing on Jewish matters. Hence, it is now appropriate to assess the data and attempt a comprehensive interpretation.

Quite obviously the picture is complex, ambiguous and changes decisively with key events such as the marriage to Katia, the visit to Palestine and, especially, the advent of the Nazis. A strain of negativism, however, remains constant and consistent from first to last. It never truly becomes outright antisemitism—such a charge would be a gross and unfair exaggeration—but neither do the facts confirm the philosemitism Mann claimed. Quite clearly he never managed to free himself from the anti-Jewish prejudices of his Lübeck childhood. In the closing pages of *Buddenbrooks,* Mann, as narrator, trots out hoary Christian canards about "the awful mystery, duplicity, obstinacy and jealousy of the Old Testament God."[99] More than forty years later, he still referred in one of his radio addresses to the "folk-bound Jewish race-God."[100] If the young Mann derisively referred to a first-night theater audience, with its substantial Jewish representation, as *"Premieren-Israel,"*[101] fifty years later, with the civilized world reeling from the shock of the Holocaust, the aging Mann was still caricaturing Jewish stereotypes in *Doctor Faustus.* Still, such things should not be confused with real antisemitism, namely, a deep hostility toward Jews and a willingness to see Judaism eradicated. No, Mann's persistent anti-Jewish streak belongs much more accurately to an ethnic snobbism. He felt *superior* toward Jews, especially in a social sense, and thus felt compelled to deride whatever he perceived as shortcomings: generally physical repulsiveness and social ineptitude. Such denigrations, spanning virtually his entire oeuvre, should not be underestimated; they plainly indicate a latent animus toward Jews. It is equally important, however, not to follow the example of Henri Peyre of Yale University, who unfairly attacked Mann in 1944 for statements made thirty years earlier as an overzealous German patriot.[102] Mann complained bitterly—and justifiably—about "disjointed quotations gleaned here and there" and "the inappropriateness of tripping up with the cudgel of ancient quotations."[103] So, too, here: one must beware of attaching undue importance to remarks made privately in a moment of pique or impatience but without truly malicious intentions.

Not untypically, Mann tended to identify individuals, as his diaries constantly indicate, by ethnic derivation. If a writer or professor or journalist who happened to be Jewish visited him, Mann invariably referred to him as a "Jewish writer" or "Jewish professor" or "Jewish journalist." Hence it can come as no surprise that friends who happened to be Jewish were "Jewish friends" and, more significantly, enemies who happened to be Jewish—like Kerr and Lessing—were "Jewish enemies" and that attacks on them focused, at least in part, on their Jewishness. This is, after all, a classic example of a familiar psychological phenomenon.

Mann held definite ideas about negative Jewish traits and types, as his fictional characters indicate. The Aarenholds, Naphta, Breisacher and Fitelberg all arouse repugnance or invite ridicule. Beyond physical and social shortcomings already mentioned, one may discern two other negative themes: a crass and aggressive acquisitive nature (the Hagenströms, the senior Aarenhold, Fitelberg) and a no less aggressive as well as arrogant intellectual extremism (the young Aarenholds, Naphta and Breisacher). He harbored no less definite notions about positive Jewish types but created only one wholly admirable Jewish character: Dr. Sammet. (To adduce Joseph as a second positive example raises problems since Mann conceived him originally as a "con-man.") The balance here clearly tips on the negative side.

For the favorable side of the ledger we must look elsewhere: to Mann's personal life and his public activity beyond his fiction. His genuine admiration of Jewish

"Geist," of Jewish receptivity to the world of art and intellect, brought him close together with Jews, an association he welcomed and fostered. Not once, as far as I can see, did he ever evade an intellectual or artistic relationship on ethnic grounds; on the contrary, examples abound of Jews he helped in times of difficulty, although he did not care for them or their work.

Not only did Mann share Goethe's appreciation of Jewish "Geist," he also adopted Goethe's view—and this emerges as another theme—of a certain affinity between Germans and Jews. Erich Kahler has argued—and Mann seems to have accepted his argument—that this affinity, to some extent intellectual–creative, to some extent spiritual–ethical, accounts for the antagonism between the two communities that developed into an unfathomable horror.

Above all, though, towers Mann's vigorous activity on behalf of two major Jewish causes of this century: their fight against Hitler and their battle for national independence. One can quibble all one wants about minor details; the fact remains that few other non-Jewish personalities of renown supported these Jewish causes so generously and energetically.

In short, then, no neat label or clear-cut definition fits Thomas Mann when it comes to his relationship to Jews and Judaism. He falls short of the lofty standard established by his illustrious eighteenth-century German predecessor, Gotthold E. Lessing. Yet, in spite of insensitivities and sometimes jarring lapses, Mann rallied to the Jews' support when it counted most.

Notes

The author gratefully acknowledges permission of Professor Golo Mann and the Thomas Mann Archives, Zurich, to quote from unpublished letters nos. 72, 93, 96.

1. Letter no. 146 in the year 1939, as registered in *Die Briefe Thomas Manns. Regesten und Register,* ed. Hans Bürgin, Hans-Otto Mayer and Yvonne Schmidlin (Frankfurt: 1980), vol. 2 (1934–1943). Volume 1 of this series covers the years up to and including 1933; volume 3 covers 1944–1950; and the just-published volume 4 covers 1951–1955 as well as addenda to all previous volumes. All documentation in the text of this article bearing the prefix R refers to the letters registered in these volumes. A two-digit number preceding the colon indicates the year of the letter (i.e., 39 = 1939) and a number following the colon indicates the number of the letter within that year. An E after the reference indicates English as the letter's original language. The Goethe quotation comes from his conversation with Eckermann on 23 October 1828.

2. Kurt Loewenstein, "Thomas Mann zur jüdischen Frage," *Bulletin des Leo Baeck Institute* 10 (1967), 1–59; Jacques Darmaun, "Thomas Mann und die Juden—eine Kontroverse," in *Auseinandersetzungen um jiddische Sprache und Literatur—die Assimilationskontroverse,* ed. Walter Roll and Hans-Peter Bayerdörfer (Tübingen: 1986), 208–214. (Volume 5 of *Kontroversen, alte und neue. Akten des VII. Internationalen Germanisten-Kongresses.* Göttingen, 1985.)

3. Martin Flinker, *Thomas Manns politische Betrachtungen im Lichte der heutigen Zeit* (The Hague: 1959), 151–169.

4. Peter de Mendelssohn, *Der Zauberer* (Frankfurt: 1975).

5. For details about the Jewish community in Lübeck see David A. Winter, *Geschichte der jüdischen Gemeinde in Moisling Lübeck* (Lübeck: 1968); and S. Goldman, "Geschichte der jüdischen Gemeinde in Moisling-Lübeck," *Zeitschrift für die Geschichte der Juden* 6 (1969), 159–164.

6. De Mendelssohn, *Der Zauberer*, 69.

7. This is Mann's own characterization (see R21:109) for his piece ["On the Jewish Question"]. See Thomas Mann, *Gesammelte Werke in dreizehn Bänden* (Frankfurt: 1974), vol. 13, 466–475. I shall use and cite, wherever possible, published English translations of Mann's works. However, when, as in this case, no translation exists, I shall translate the German text and cite its source in the original—wherever possible in the definitive thirteen–volume edition of Mann's collected works just cited. All documentation prefixed with GW refers to the volume and page numbers of this edition. Titles given in brackets, as in this case, are editorial inventions in the absence of Mann's own titles. As with the letters, an E following the reference indicates English as the original language.

8. Mann erroneously names his classmate Ephraim Carlebach. Loewenstein persuasively demonstrates that Mann actually means Ephraim's brother Simson. See Loewenstein, "Thomas Mann," 20.

9. See Manfred Hahn, "Heinrich Mann und *Das Zwanzigste Jahrhundert,*" *Weimarer Beiträge* 13 (1967), 996–1019.

10. In a gross exaggeration, Hahn finds "antisemitic tendencies" in ["Kritik und Schaffen"], one of Thomas Mann's short pieces in *Das Zwanzigste Jahrhundert* (GW13:519–522). The essay contains but a single passing Jewish reference: where Mann refers to Georg Brandes as a "quite uninteresting free-thinking Jew."

11. *Buddenbrooks,* trans. H. T. Lowe-Porter (New York: 1924).

12. The last three titles appear in *Stories of Three Decades,* trans. H. T. Lowe-Porter (New York: 1938). "The Will to Happiness," a story as yet untranslated into English, appears in GW8:43–61.

13. Ernest M. Wolf, "Hagenströms: The Rival Family in Thomas Mann's *Buddenbrooks,*" *German Studies Review* 5 (1982), 47.

14. For details of this episode see Marie Walter, "Concerning the Affair *Wälsungenblut,*" *Book Collector* 13 (1964), 463–472; Klaus Pringsheim, "Ein Nachtrag zu *Wälsungenblut,*" in *Betrachtungen und Überblicke zum Werk Thomas Manns,* ed. Georg Wenzel (Berlin and Weimar: 1966), 253–268; and de Mendelssohn, *Der Zauberer,* 652–668.

15. De Mendelssohn, *Der Zauberer,* 589.

16. See *Stories of Three Decades.*

17. *Sang Reservé* (Paris: 1931).

18. *Briefwechsel 1900–1949/Thomas Mann: Heinrich Mann,* ed. Hans Wysling (Frankfurt: 1984), 40–43.

19. Including a rumor that had Alfred Pringsheim forcing his son-in-law at gunpoint to retract his story. See K. Pringsheim, "Ein Nachtrag zu *Wälsungenblut,*" 255.

20. *Royal Highness,* trans. A. Cecil Curtis (New York: 1926).

21. See Mommsen's essay "Auch ein Wort über unser Judentum," in *Reden und Aufsätze,* 3rd ed. (Berlin: 1912), 410–424.

22. Wysling, *Briefwechsel,* 27.

23. See Katia Mann, *Unwritten Memories* (New York: 1975), 15–107.

24. See Mann's letter to James Laughlin, dated 4 November 1940, in Thomas Mann, *Briefe 1937–1947,* ed. Erika Mann (Frankfurt: 1963).

25. See Paul F. Proskauer, "Thomas Mann und Alfred Kerr," *Aufbau,* 19 September 1975 (*Der Zeitgeist* supplement), 11.

26. Katia Mann, *Unwritten Memories,* 11.

27. A full account appears in de Mendelssohn, *Der Zauberer,* 821–834. For Mann's attack on Lessing, see "Der Doktor Lessing," GW11:719–731.

28. *Reflections of a Nonpolitical Man,* trans. Walter D. Morris (New York: 1983).

29. Mann coins this term for the liberal intellectuals of the period, followers of his brother Heinrich, writers who espoused the liberal democratic traditions of France and Italy and, thus, did not merit the (for him) more substantial Germanic appellation of *Dichter.* Mann devotes an entire chapter to this topic in his *Reflections.*

30. *Diaries 1918–1939,* trans. Richard and Clara Winston (New York: 1982), 19–20.

31. A full account appears in Loewenstein, "Thomas Mann."

32. *The Magic Mountain,* trans. H. T. Lowe-Porter, 10th ed. (New York: 1953).

33. See Hermann J. Weigand, *The Magic Mountain: A Study of Thomas Mann's Der Zauberberg* (Chapel Hill: 1965), 96–139.

34. For an incisive discussion of the character Naphta and his Jewish background see Herbert Lehnert, "Leo Naphta und sein Autor," *Orbis Litterarum* 37 (1982), 47–69. As is well known in Mann scholarship, Naphta is partially modeled on Georg Lukács. For a full account of this relationship see Judith Marcus-Tar, *Thomas Mann und Georg Lukács: Beziehung, Einfluss und "repräsentative Gegensätzlichkeit"* (Cologne: 1982).

35. *Tagebücher 1918–1921*, ed. Peter de Mendelssohn (Frankfort: 1979), 223.

36. An extensive account of the Mann brothers' relationship appears in Nigel Hamilton, *The Brothers Mann* (New Haven: 1979).

37. See *Order of the Day*, trans. H. T. Lowe-Porter (New York: 1942).

38. De Mendelssohn, *Tagebücher 1918–1921*, 280.

39. See for example Mann's letter to Ernst Bertram in *Letters of Thomas Mann 1889–1955*, trans. Richard and Clara Winston (New York: 1971), 156.

40. See *Essays of Three Decades*, trans. H. T. Lowe-Porter (New York: 1948).

41. See Erika and Klaus Mann, *Escape to Life* (Boston: 1939), 6, 87–88.

42. The best examples are to be found in his essay "An Appeal to Reason" and in his interviews for newspapers. See especially the interviews "Thomas Mann and the National-Socialists" in the *Berliner Montagspost* (20 October 1930) and "Thomas Mann on Adolf Hitler" in the *Wiener Allgemeine Zeitung* (17 March 1932). Both appear in *Frage und Antwort. Interviews mit Thomas Mann 1909–1955*, ed. Volkmar Hansen and Gert Heine (Hamburg: 1983), 173–175, 186–188.

43. See *Stories of Three Decades*.

44. See Klaus Mann, *The Turning Point* (New York: 1942), 261–265.

45. R33:49 and R33:53.

46. The text of the letter and names of the signatories appear in Klaus Schröter, *Thomas Mann im Urteil seiner Zeit* (Hamburg: 1969), 199–200.

47. *Tagebücher 1933–1934*, ed. Peter de Mendelssohn (Frankfurt: 1977), 276.

48. See *Diaries 1918–1939*, 150.

49. *Ibid.*, 153.

50. R33:63.

51. The whole matter actually began with Schwarzschild's insinuations in his weekly journal in exile, *Das Neue Tagebuch*, namely, that Gottfried Bermann Fischer, son-in-law of Samuel Fischer and then director of the famous publishing firm, had negotiated a secret deal with Joseph Goebbels allowing the Jewish-owned firm to continue to publish in Nazi Germany. (No other publishing firm with Jewish ownership had such rights.) See *Das Neue Tagebuch* 4 (11 January 1936), no. 2, 30–31.

Two weeks later a protest against Schwarzschild's insinuations, signed by Mann, Hermann Hesse and Annette Kolb, appeared in the journal, followed by Schwarzschild's "Answer to Thomas Mann," which included inter alia the assertion with regard to the contemporary German literary scene. See *Das Neue Tagebuch* 4 (25 January 1936), no. 4, 82–86.

52. See *Letters of Thomas Mann 1899–1955*, 244–249.

53. "Deutsche Literatur im Emigrantenspiegel," *Neue Zürcher Zeitung*, 26 January 1936. The relevant Schwarzschild texts cited in n. 51 and the Korrodi article all appear in Schröter, *Thomas Mann im Urteil seiner Zeit*, 259–267.

54. See the famous "Exchange of Letters" in *Order of the Day*, 105–113.

55. It appeared later in English translation as *The Jews Among the Nations* (New York: 1967).

56. *Tagebücher 1937–1939*, ed. Peter de Mendelssohn (Frankfurt: 1980), 64.

57. *Ibid.*, 590–591.

58. *Ibid.*, 47.

59. No better example illustrates Mann's generosity than his efforts on behalf of Max Brod, for whom he wrote many letters and for whom he finally landed a job (at Hebrew Union College)—but by this time Brod had already emigrated to Palestine. See R38:401; R39:105, 117, 141, 301, R41:127; R42:348.

60. *Tagebücher 1940–1943*, ed. Peter de Mendelssohn (Frankfurt: 1982), 293, 847.

61. *Ibid.*, 117.

62. See n. 39.

63. The entire tetralogy appears in a one-volume English translation as *Joseph and His Brothers*, trans. H. T. Lowe-Porter (New York: 1948).

64. *Ibid.*, 106.

65. *Ibid.*, 377.

66. See Ludwig Lewisohn's review in *New Palestine* 34 (15 September 1944), 519–520.

67. See R35:216 and "Thomas Mann und sein Joseph-Zyklus," *Aufbau*, 8 August 1975.

68. See, for example, Walter Laqueur, *The Terrible Secret* (London: 1980).

69. *"Listen Germany!"* (New York: 1943), 69.

70. Mann prepared this speech at the behest of the U.S. Office of War Information (OWI) to disseminate the grisly details of the liberated death camps among the German people.

71. See *Tagebücher 1944–1946*, ed. Inge Jens (Frankfurt: 1986), 194–195.

72. R49:441.

73. *The Story of a Novel*, trans. Richard and Clara Winston (New York: 1961), 38.

74. *Doctor Faustus*, trans. H. T. Lowe-Porter (New York: 1948).

75. I have discussed this theme in some detail in my article, "Leverkühn, the Mermaid and Echo," *Symposium* 42 (1988), 1–13.

76. See Gunilla Bergsten, *Thomas Mann's Doctor Faustus*, trans. Krishna Winston (Chicago and London), 199.

77. *Story of a Novel*, 202–204.

78. *Letters of Thomas Mann 1889–1955*, 560.

79. R48:674-E.

80. *Letters of Thomas Mann 1889–1955*, 560.

81. R48:674, 675.

82. See Stéphane Moses, "Thomas Mann et Oskar Goldberg: une exemple de 'montage' dans le *Doktor Faustus*," *Études germaniques* 31 (1976), 7–24.

83. R42:144, R48:567.

84. *Tagebücher 1933–1934*, 473–474.

85. Mark H. Gelber, "Thomas Mann and Zionism," *German Life and Letters*, 37 (1984), 118–124; *idem,* "Thomas Mann and Judah Magnes," *Midstream* 30, no. 4 (April 1984), 46–50.

86. "Thomas Mann über das Judentum," *Selbstwehr*, 23 November 1928.

87. *Frage und Antwort*, 160.

88. From a conversation reported in Manfred Georg, *Theodor Herzl* (Berlin, Vienna, Leipzig: 1932), 8–9.

89. R30:176.

90. R35:198.

91. Quoted in Gelber, "Thomas Mann and Zionism," 122. See also R42:177.

92. See the appendix to *Tagebücher 1944–1946*, 798–801, for Mann's text.

93. R45:413-E.

94. R45:583.

95. An English version of this piece, in the form of a letter to the editor, appears in *Nation* 166, no. 17 (24 April 1948), 451.

96. R49:207.

97. For Mann's public statement on his refusal to return to Germany after the war see his open letter to Walter von Molo, "Warum ich nicht nach Deutschland zurückgehe" ["Why I don't return to Germany"], 1945 (GW12:934–935).

98. For a compact collection of the various elements in this controversy see *Die Grosse Kontroverse*, ed. J. F. G. Grosser (Hamburg, Geneva, Paris: 1963).

99. *Buddenbrooks*, 577.

100. "Listen Germany!" 12.

101. *Briefe an Otto Grautoff 1894–1901 und Ida Boy-Ed 1903–1928,* ed. Peter de Mendelssohn (Frankfurt: 1975), 18.

102. See Peyre's letter to the editor in *Atlantic Monthly* 173, no. 7 (July 1944), 26.

103. See Mann's response to Peyre, "In My Defense," *Atlantic Monthly* 173, no. 10 (October 1944), 100, 102.

The Distinctive Path
of German Zionism

Hagit Lavsky
(THE HEBREW UNIVERSITY)

The Zionist movement in Germany in the Weimar period was marked by three well-defined characteristics. It was Palestinocentric; its predominant political philosophy was radical-national, oriented toward socialist *étatisme* in the socioeconomic sphere; and it pursued a moderate course in the diplomatic or geopolitical sphere that sought compromise with Arab nationalism. By virtue of these positions, the German Zionist movement in the 1920s functioned as a sort of Weizmannist ruling faction in the World Zionist movement. Signs of the distinctiveness of the movement in Germany had emerged in the years prior to the First World War. The impact of the war helped to make these special features the hallmark of Zionism in interwar Germany.

Between East and West:
The Roots of Palestinocentrism

The West European brand of Zionism took a largely philanthropic approach, and its relation to Palestine might be called platonic. What set such Zionists apart from other Jews with whom they shared many concerns was their belief that the Zionist solution to the East European Jewish problem also represented a solution to their own dilemmas of self-identification. Thus, German Zionists asserted that ties of national unity bound them to their Russian and Polish Jewish brethren and they recognized Palestine as the focus of Jewish national aspirations. In doing so, they implicitly qualified their own bond with the land of their birth. Such qualifications, however, remained largely theoretical. In their everyday social and intellectual lives, they remained anchored in German Jewish society and culture.

Yet, additional factors in the formation of the German Zionist movement differentiated it from this typically Western pattern and linked it more closely to the type of Zionism that arose in Eastern Europe. German Zionism came into being against the background of a rising tide of German antisemitism in the last decades of the nineteenth century. In addition, it was heavily influenced by the wave of East European Jewish emigration that not only passed directly through Germany, but also created a large East European Jewish settlement there.[1] Many German Jews felt that this development lent momentum and focus to the antisemitic movement and some were drawn to a reappraisal of themselves as Jews and as Germans. Both processes—the emergence of a modern, organized, political and intellectual antisemitism and the influx of East European immigrants—profoundly influenced German Jewry and gave it a distinctive character among the West European emancipated Jewish communities.

Moreover, both processes had a special impact on the German academic world. It was at the universities that Jewish students faced these two processes most directly. The antisemitic movement was largely organized at the time through university-related and student groups. As for the Eastern immigration, students from the East played a very special role in Germany.

German culture generally and German Jews in particular held a special fascination for Central and East European Jews undergoing sociocultural change. Since the second half of the nineteenth century, Germany had been the recognized center of sophisticated European culture, the country where the main currents of contemporary thought and science were defined and confronted one another. Thus, Germany also acquired preeminence as a center of modern Jewish thought and scholarship. The German language was the medium of communication between the cultures of Eastern Europe and the West. German universities attracted students from across Europe and proved doubly attractive to Jewish students from Russia, who found it difficult to gain entrance to universities at home.

The arrival of students from the East took place concurrently with the rapid academization of German Jewry, a stage in the socioeconomic transition in the latter half of the century that brought many Jews into the middle class and some into the upper strata of the bourgeoisie. The sons of merchants became students, and the proportion of academic, liberal and white-collar professions in the Jewish middle class steadily increased.[2] At the university, young German Jews encountered manifestations of antisemitism and were bound, as young intellectuals, to react to them and to frame their weltanschauung in light of them. It was here, in the formative years of their lives, that they met numerous Jewish students from Eastern Europe, and this heightened their need to take a stand concerning the Jewish question. Among the Russian students were those who promoted Zionist ideas, who pressed for the creation of nationalist Jewish student unions and who were in the forefront of the unions' activities. These unions came to constitute the backbone of the Zionist movement in Germany and produced its younger leadership echelon. Russian Jewry, then, had a direct influence on the emergence of German Zionism, and during the 1880s groups of Hovevei Zion were organized in Germany that were closely linked to their sister groups in Russia.[3]

Thus, German Zionism was shaped by a unique juxtaposition of influences: emancipation and a degree of integration, the nurturing setting of the academy, antisemitism and the East European influx. In its very first generation, German Zionism articulated a more radical critique of Jewish life in the Diaspora and a more vigorous Palestine orientation than were found elsewhere in the West. It was absolutely opposed to fighting antisemitism in the manner of the *Centralverein deutscher Staatsbürger jüdischen Glaubens,* the representative body set up to defend German

Jewry against discrimination and defamation. The Zionists were also opposed to organized Jewish involvement in German politics.[4]

Close and solid bonds with Palestine were strengthened by virtue of the central role played by German Zionists in the formation of the World Zionist movement. Even before Herzl had rallied the Zionists, Berlin had overtaken Vienna and its Kadima Union as the center of Jewish nationalism in the West. In Germany, Herzl found an already organized group of supporters and there the first steps were taken to establish the World Zionist Organization (WZO). German became the first official language of the Zionist movement. The main newspapers of the movement— headed by *Die Welt*—were published in German, and the organ of the German Zionist Federation, the *Jüdische Rundschau,* was widely read by Zionists outside Germany. Naturally, most of the contributors to these papers were German Zionists and the leaders of German Zionism became the exponents of Zionist thought and activity. The same trend could be observed in the composition of the personnel in the Zionist Organization's main institutions. Max Bodenheimer (1865–1940) was at one and the same time the chairman of the German Zionist Federation (*Zionistische Vereinigung für Deutschland*—ZVfD) and of the Jewish National Fund (JNF). David Wolffsohn (1856–1914), one of the founders of the German federation, was the first president of the Jewish Colonial Trust.[5]

Of course, we must not exaggerate. The fact is that German Zionism in its first decades took the attitude that Palestine was a political-philanthropic solution for the Jews from Eastern Europe, while its critique of Diaspora life was little more than academic. The first German Zionists saw themselves as loyal citizens of Germany, born and bred in German culture.[6] The seeds of a different posture, already sown at the beginning of the twentieth century, put down roots and bore fruit only when they were reinforced by later developments.

National Radicalization
on the Eve of the First World War

Changing conditions in Germany and, above all, the entry of a new generation of German Zionists into the activist circle in the last decade before the First World War led to a further development toward a Zionist movement that focused on Palestine rather than on issues related to the German Jewish milieu.

What matters for us here is the process that shaped the ideas of this second generation. Born during the last two or three decades of the nineteenth century, they, too, came to Zionism as university students in their early twenties. It was they who provided the ideological and political leadership of the movement in Germany in the decade after the First World War. Among them were Kurt Blumenfeld (1884–1963), Felix Rosenblüth (1887–1968), Richard Lichtheim (1885–1963), Julius Berger (1883–1948) and others.

Coming of age just after the turn of the century, they, like their predecessors, encountered in the universities East European students on the one hand, and anti-semitism on the other. This led them to the same process of self-reappraisal and to the same conclusions reached earlier by German Zionists. But, unlike those who had come before them, they did not start from the hopeful premise of emancipation and thus had fewer illusions about the Jews' place in German society. The experience of antisemitism led many of this generation to more radical and less abstract conclusions regarding their own individual lives in Germany.

Furthermore, unlike the first generation, the young newcomers to the movement at the turn of the century were more completely estranged from the Jewish religious tradition, and could no longer see in it an alternative model of Jewish spiritual survival for the Diaspora. They necessarily sought another path of return to their people and their heritage. For their elders, Zionism was a positive reaffirmation of their Jewishness in the face of antisemitism. The younger Zionists found in nationalist ideology an answer to their profound need for a redefined Jewish identification. For them, Zionism was both an alternative to assimilation in German society and a new form of identification with Judaism.[7] Their needs were not adequately met by a philanthropic Zionism that presented no cogent alternative to merging with German society and culture. The second generation demanded a Zionism that would mean breaking with and uprooting (*Entwurzelung*) oneself from German society and culture while sinking new roots (*Verwurzelung*) in the national soil of Palestine in the immediate future.[8]

This new generation was drawn to the Zionist factions and trends that challenged "classical" Herzlian Zionism. Among these were the group around Ahad Ha-Am, the "Democratic Faction" founded by Chaim Weizmann, Leo Motzkin and Martin Buber, the advocates of "practical" and "synthetic" Zionism who emerged from the Russian Hibbat Zion tradition, and the labor organizations of the Second Aliyah in Palestine. All of them were East European in origin and following, but they struck a responsive chord among young Zionists in Central Europe. What they had in common was a call for Zionist radicalism on two levels. First, they sought an all-embracing, definitive statement of Zionist aims that would transcend the "mere" construction in Palestine of a Jewish political framework. They argued that the aim of Zionism was the construction of a new kind of national society in Palestine committed to social, cultural and economic renewal. Second, they believed that the Zionist program of activity in Palestine and in the Diaspora ought to be extended well beyond mere diplomatic and organizational efforts so as to advance the process of national renewal.

East European Zionist ideas found fertile soil among the young German Zionists. The main enterprise of the "Democratic Faction," the *Jüdischer Verlag* publishing house, was established in Berlin in 1902. Ahad Ha-Am was well received in German translation, mainly through Buber's mediation. The process of radicalization was also apparent in the *Blau-Weiss* youth movement. It was already commonly agreed among young Zionists in this period that they ought to renounce any aspiration for professional advancement in Germany and should seek training in a field more suited to Palestine. The youth were asked to abstain from participation in German politics. This included what were regarded as futile campaigns against antisemitism. It was not worth wasting one's energies either at the personal or the public level on defending an exilic existence that had to be superseded if a national renaissance were to be achieved.[9]

German Zionism's pivotal position magnified its exposure to the new ideas and alternative trends within Zionism. The students and university graduates played the role of an avant-garde in echoing and disseminating currents within East European Jewish nationalism, including a Palestinocentric pragmatism. Their impact on the movement at large was heightened by the fact that after Herzl's death, the top Zionist leadership was based first in Cologne and afterward in Berlin, strengthening the centrality of German Zionism. David Wolffsohn became president of the WZO and in 1911 was succeeded by Otto Warburg (1859–1938). Arthur Hantke (1874–1955), chairman of the ZVfD since 1910, was a member of the Inner Actions Committee of the WZO. The political transition from Herzlian diplomacy to "practical" Zionism was concretely expressed in the opening of the Palestine Office by Arthur Ruppin (1876–1943), and was symbolized by the transfer of the WZO central office and presidency to Berlin in 1911. During the last decade before the war, young German Zionists such as Julius Berger, Martin Rosenblüth and Kurt Blumenfeld held leading positions in the WZO administration.

Under pressure from these young activists, headed by Blumenfeld, the German Zionist conferences in Posen (1912) and Leipzig (1914) adopted radical Palestine-oriented resolutions. These called on the Zionist movement to demand of its members a full Zionist commitment—settling in Palestine—and to encourage the absolute uprooting of exilic Jewish existence. These resolutions prompted some first-generation Zionists such as Franz Oppenheimer (1864–1943) to cease their active involvement in the movement or to leave it entirely.[10]

German Zionism thus reached a stage that had no parallel in the world of Western Zionism. The outbreak of the war, however, prevented German Zionism from putting its new program to the test. The war itself, its course and its consequences, profoundly altered the German Zionist frame of reference and was to pose new challenges for the radicals in Germany.

The Test of National Radicalism in the First World War

The First World War strengthened the tendencies described here. On the one hand, the Jewish soldiers' encounter with the Jews of the German-occupied countries to the East sharpened their longing for the full, complete Jewish life that they felt was lacking in their own acculturated milieu. On the other hand, manifestations of German antisemitism at home and at the front shattered their last illusions of ever gaining acceptance in German society, even through national loyalty to Germany and the wartime fraternity of arms. Here was practical confirmation of the contention that there was no solution to the question of antisemitism other than to uproot the Jews from the Diaspora. In the coming years, the young German Zionists headed by Blumenfeld would argue over and over again that since antisemitism was endemic to the Jews' exilic existence, there was no point in trying to combat its manifestations.[11] The war also opened up new possibilities of fulfilling the Zionist aim in Palestine. Radical German Zionists now called for completing the rupture with the German environment and turned still more single-mindedly in the direction of Palestine.

If the war reinforced Palestinocentrism among the younger generation, it also held new challenges for the older generation. Veteran Zionists, who did not go through a process of prewar radicalization and who did not serve at the front, were naturally less likely to be influenced by encounters with German antisemitism or by Jewish life in Eastern Europe. The war affected the veteran leaders of German Zionism mainly by breaking the barriers between Zionists and non-Zionists, who were now able to cooperate on projects to enhance Jewish solidarity. At the beginning of the war, senior Zionist figures such as Franz Oppenheimer and Adolf Friedemann together with representatives of the B'nai B'rith and the *Centralverein* had established the *Komitee für den Osten* (Committee for Eastern Jews) to assist Jews in the occupied enemy territories. This was an institution of Jewish solidarity that emphasized patriotic service in the German national interest, under the protection of the German military. Trends of this kind grew more significant during the course of the war and reinforced the principle of German Jewish cooperation.[12]

A fresh incentive for relief activity on behalf of Eastern Jews was the mass influx from the East during and at the conclusion of the war. The *Zentralwohlfahrtsstelle der deutschen Juden* (Central Welfare Bureau of German Jewry) was opened toward the end of 1917 to centralize relief activities, coordinate the reception of immigrants and facilitate job placement for them. The German Zionists viewed these activities as a means for bridging social, cultural and ideological divisions among German Jews and for strengthening their own Jewish consciousness, on the one hand, and the immigrants' awareness of Zionist activities, on the other. Such activity was also encouraged by the German authorities' cooperative attitude.[13]

The Balfour Declaration prompted the German government to issue its own pro-Zionist declaration, which challenged non-Zionist Jews in Germany to define their stand on Zionism. The changed and much improved international status of the Zionist movement required the clarification of Jewish goals and the creation of Jewish representative bodies in preparation for the peace conference. Toward the end of 1917, the Zionists met with such organizations as the *Centralverein* and the *Hilfsverein der deutschen Juden*, thus further eroding the non-Zionists' policy of non-recognition of, and non-cooperation with, the Zionist movement. These developments strengthened the veteran Zionists' desire to enhance German Jewish cooperation. After all, in the prewar period nearly all of them had earnestly sought an influential and honored status for the Zionist position in the Jewish and general German arenas. From the Zionist point of view, the war had legitimized Jewish nationalism, had placed the Zionist movement in the forefront of Jewish affairs, and had encouraged its hopes and aspirations regarding Palestine. These factors heightened Zionist self-confidence generally and bred the hope that the Zionist philosophy could serve as a programmatic platform uniting Jewish activity on a national basis.[14]

Finally, the new Weimar Republic redefined the Jewish communities in Germany as "corporations by public law," establishing them on the basis of general and democratic membership. The communities were now able to reorganize and to develop activities in the spheres of religion, education, health and welfare. This created a new area for Zionist activity, with new prospects of winning influence.[15]

Thus, not only radical Palestinocentric Zionism gained ground as a result of the war. More traditional Zionism, with its Diaspora orientation, could also look forward to a new, favorable climate. It no longer faced a struggle for legitimacy and it could announce a platform of full cooperation between Zionists and non-Zionists.

After the War:
Victory of Radical Palestinocentrism

The postwar reorganization of German Zionism entailed a confrontation between two generations and two outlooks. But from the beginning, the younger generation enjoyed a considerable advantage. The war had strengthened the popularity of their radical view and attracted new young adherents to their cause.[16] The Balfour Declaration and the consequent political developments had a crucial impact here. The Zionist movement now faced the challenge of practical realization, of translating aspirations into a broad-ranging and realistic program and of shaping the means of its implementation.

Amid the uncertainties of the situation immediately following Germany's defeat and in the midst of the revolutionary disturbances rocking the country, the fifteenth German Zionist Conference met in Berlin in December 1918 to discuss the Zionist future in Palestine. The hundreds of delegates and observers seemed almost oblivious to what was going on in Germany. Indeed, soon afterward, in May 1919, a special meeting was convened in Berlin—the *Palästina Delegiertentag* (Palestine Conference)—devoted exclusively to the question of settling Palestine and deliberately ignoring all discussion of Diaspora-related activity.[17] But the road to an exclusive Palestinocentric orientation had to pass through three stages of development as other alternatives were eliminated.

The first stage was the initiative to establish a unified nationwide Jewish framework. The fifteenth conference, meeting about a year after German Zionists and non-Zionists had first discussed the possibility of creating a joint representation to deal with international Jewish affairs, approved a resolution calling for the convening of a German Jewish Congress. Such a body was to be a constituent member of the World Jewish Congress then being proposed by American Zionists and would also officially represent German Jewry on the national German scene. Partners in this initiative were the veteran Zionist leaders Alfred Klee (1875–1943) and Gustav Witkowski, together with young radicals such as Kurt Blumenfeld and Nachum Goldmann (1894–1982). The whole idea was launched by Arthur Hantke, who chaired the conference. The conference accordingly established a committee to draft a Zionist platform for a national German Jewish congress. But the initiative was doomed to certain failure, stamped as it was with such explicitly Zionist features. It was strenuously opposed by the *Centralverein,* and within two months it was shown to be unfeasible.[18]

The second alternative to exclusive Palestinocentrism was activity at the Jewish communal level. Ever since the days of Herzl, German Zionists had wanted to transform the Jewish communities into democratic, national-secular bodies, but they had had only limited success in putting this subject on the agenda of the ZVfD. The results of the First World War increased the attractiveness of this idea and its prospects for success. Activity on behalf of the newcomers from the East within the community framework promised to provide a broad field for strengthening the national spirit, developing an autonomous national life in Germany only marginally dependent on Palestine and—not least—for recruiting "the masses" into the Zionist fold.

Alfred Klee and Max Kollenscher (1875–1937), who had for years worked toward this goal, established the *Jüdische Volkspartei* (Jewish National Party—JVP) in 1919 to represent the Zionist cause in the Jewish community and to contend for the leadership at the local level. In addition, it was to represent those Jews from Eastern Europe who still lacked voting rights in German Jewish communities.[19] The establishment of a separate party for this purpose was, in fact, a compromise. The veteran leaders were able to realize their ambitions for political activity in Germany, but only outside the framework of the ZVfD as such. From its inception, the party's activity was not an integral part of the federation's activities and budgets.

The third and last stage of eliminating alternatives was most problematic owing to the close connection between Palestinocentrism and cooperation between Zionists and non-Zionists on behalf of projects in Palestine. This was possible in the framework of the fund-raising arm of the Zionist movement, the Keren Hayesod (Foundation Fund), established in 1920. Given the desire shared by many non-Zionists to cooperate in the economic development of Palestine, veteran Zionists fought their last rearguard action over the Fund. Their aim was to set up a framework for overall Jewish cooperation in which Palestine would be only one of several areas of endeavor and that would appeal in non-ideological fashion for general Jewish support. In this fight, they went so far as to establish a separate faction, called *Binyan ha-Aretz* (Building the Land), which threatened to split the federation. Paradoxically, this, in turn, contributed to the formation of the radicals' "National Unity Bloc," which crystallized the latter's position. The Bloc achieved electoral victory at the Zionist Conference in Hanover in May 1921, which marked a political turning point. Leaders of the defeated faction turned almost completely to activity within the *Jüdische Volkspartei*; from then on, the ZVfD was dominated by the radicals.[20]

Palestinocentrism

The heart and soul of the Zionist movement—from its inception—had been the Jewish national link with Palestine. This was true by definition. The centrality of Palestine to the Zionist program and to Zionist activities varied, however, from country to country and from one period to another. The nature of Zionist plans for Palestine and of Palestine-related work was also subject to processes of development and change. This remained the case even in the interwar years, when Palestine was officially defined as the Jewish National Home. The relative priority that Palestine as such held, in practice as well as in principle, for the various Zionist organizations and institutions and the ways in which these responded to the challenges presented by Palestine—the type of activities undertaken for Palestine, attitudes to life in the Diaspora and the consequent character of activities planned for the Diaspora—all varied from country to country. These differences developed because of the influence of local conditions in the interwar period and because of historical factors in the development of each Zionist movement.

"Palestinocentrism," when used to label a Zionist ideological or political tendency, rests on three separate definitions. In one sense, Palestinocentrism implies a personal commitment to the settlement and building of Palestine as the Jewish National Home and imposes on members a duty to settle there themselves, sooner or later. In the second place, Palestinocentrism defines building the land and promoting its development as the key priority for the Zionist movement as a whole. And third, it implies a negative attitude in principle to efforts directed toward the maintenance of Jewish life in the Diaspora. In mobilizing for the sake of building Palestine, the Zionist movement (in this view) ought to focus on that task and that task alone.

Although the conditions created in the aftermath of the First World War tended to give practical efforts for Palestine new significance as a vital part of the Zionist agenda, different Zionist movements responded in different ways to the question of Palestinocentrism. The desire to personally emigrate to Palestine may have been conditioned by the degree of social, economic and political pressure against Jews in each local context; but those very pressures led some Zionist movements to embrace a program of political action *in the Diaspora*. The outstanding example of this duality is the Zionist movement in interwar Poland. During the 1920s and 1930s, this movement represented the largest single reservoir of potential Zionist immigration. No other Zionist movement, however, was as much dedicated as the Polish one was (under the leadership of Yitshak Grünbaum) to a program of political activity in and for the Diaspora.

In contrast, there was a duality of a different nature in the affluent Jewries of the West, where Zionists were notably apathetic toward the possibility of their own emigration to Palestine. Their lives were not subject to the kind of social, economic and political pressures evident elsewhere. Yet—and perhaps *because* of those conditions of freedom—Western Zionists did not develop a national political agenda for their own Diaspora communities. They focused, instead, on Palestine's political and economic needs. Still, this Western Palestinocentrism was a limited one, and not only in the sense that it omitted the ingredient of personal immigration. The Zionists of England and the United States maintained throughout a positive attitude to Jewish life in their own countries and to Jewish integration in society at large in a manner indistinguishable from the non-Zionists.[21]

In comparison with both Western Zionism and Polish Zionism, German Zionism in the 1920s was preeminently Palestinocentric. Its devotion to the cause of building the National Home, on the one hand, and its pessimistic attitude toward Diaspora Jewish life, on the other, set its order of priorities and determined the character of its political, organizational and educational programs.

On the subject of emigration to Palestine, German Zionists took a more activist posture than did other Western Zionists. In their public debates, German Zionists concentrated largely on issues directly connected with the National Home such as the crucial questions of economic policy that were raised in the early 1920s and those related to Arab-Jewish relations in the wake of the disturbances of 1929.[22]

On the level of daily organizational activity, the members of the German Zionist movement and its local branches devoted most of their energy to strengthening Keren Hayesod and, through it, public interest in Zionism and Palestine. The achievements of the ZVfD in this field in terms of the funds collected far exceeded its relative size in the world movement, and this raised its standing in the eyes of Jews and non-Jews alike.[23] German Zionists successfully recruited non-Zionists for propaganda activity and material support for Palestine. The German Keren Hayesod was headed by the non-Zionist banker, Oskar Wassermann. The Fund also served as an important bridgehead for the *Pro Palästina Komitee* set up in Germany in 1926 and later, in 1929, for the enlarged Jewish Agency, with Wassermann as one of its heads.[24]

Work for the development of Palestine succeeded in attracting wide support in Germany and this success aroused the apprehensions of the anti-Zionists, leading to a vociferous attack by the *Centralverein* on the ZVfD and on the Keren Hayesod. German Zionist leaders persisted in carrying the debate into the opposing court. The conflict, if anything, strengthened both the Paslestinocentric orientation of the Zionists and their standing within German Jewry.[25]

Yet another field of Palestine-directed activity was education and preparation for emigration. These were largely entrusted to the *Kartell jüdischer Verbindungen* (Union of Jewish Student Associations) and to the Zionist youth movements. The aim of this activity was to detach young people from their German social environment, persuade them to remain aloof from political life in Germany and to forgo professional training for the German market. In the student union and the youth movements, young Zionists were immersed in Jewish and Hebrew culture and their individual daily lives were dominated by Zionist social activity. They were counseled on how to plan their education and professional training with a view toward their future integration in Palestine.[26]

Weimar society, with all its vicissitudes and with all the opportunities it offered for political and cultural participation, was no concern of the Zionist movement. As for the campaign against antisemitism, German Zionists were conspicuously absent from this fight until 1930.[27] The communal-political (*Gemeindepolitik*) front was left to the *Jüdische Volkspartei* until the end of the 1920s, when the movement began to include this work as an integral part of its activity.[28] The sole non-Palestinocentric sphere of activity was the work conducted among East European Jews in Germany. It must be stressed, however, that this field was largely left to the youth movements, to the Zionist parties and to individual initiative, and it was of less concern to the federation as such.[29]

The Socioeconomic Aspects of Radical Palestinocentrism

German Zionism's postwar orientation was marked by a special concern for the social and economic problems in the development of Palestine. The first postwar conferences of German Zionists were largely devoted to discussing these issues, as were leading articles in the Zionist press in 1919 and 1920.[30] True, this was a central theme in virtually all Zionist discussions after the Balfour Declaration, and not only in Germany. All the same, no other national Zionist federation devoted itself to the matter quite so consistently and intensively or at so early a stage.

One of the reasons for this concentration lay in the German Zionists' sense of general responsibility for the development of the Zionist enterprise, a product, perhaps, of their central role in the world movement before the war. The great majority of the postwar leaders, including Kurt Blumenfeld, Richard Lichtheim, the brothers Felix and Martin Rosenblüth, the brothers Julius and Alfred Berger and veterans such as Arthur Hantke, Otto Warburg and Max Bodenheimer were all involved in—and their perspectives were shaped by—the world Zionist central establishment. The question of economic and social planning for Palestine was then uppermost on the Zionist agenda. Moreover, the radical Palestinocentric outlook that was so influential among the younger generation led them to an emphasis on the process of Jewish national socioeconomic restructuring, which they saw as the single most important question facing postwar Jewish nationalism.

An additional factor was the social composition of this group, most of whom were university trained. Their intellectual capabilities and their education predisposed them to deal with theoretical questions, to articulate a social philosophy and to focus on such issues as economic planning and equity in the social system. The social sciences were well developed and flourishing in the German academic world well before the war. Social and economic questions engaged the attention of political thinkers in Germany, and Germany was the breeding ground of the main social and economic schools of thought. Zionists in Germany, educated in this milieu, gravitated toward this field almost naturally. One encounters this in the careers of Otto Warburg, Arthur Ruppin, Franz Oppenheimer and many others who occupied themselves with planning and implementation at various levels.[31]

The social outlook prevailing in the academic middle class was shaped by the *Verein für Sozialpolitik,* an offshoot of the Historical School that evolved in Germany in the nineteenth century. A national socioeconomic theory based on *étatisme* —the view that designated the state as the central force for economic management and growth—developed in Germany against a background of aspirations for national unification and industrialization. This school of thought tended to subordinate private or individual interests to the general social interest and influenced the shaping of social policy in Germany both in the prewar years and afterward. State intervention in the economy was favored not only for the sake of the national interest in the international arena, but also for the sake of internal social stabilization. This gospel was preached in the universities by the so-called *Kathedersozialisten* (chair socialists), who included Max Weber and Werner Sombart. Many leading German Zionists were their disciples.[32]

For the Zionists, it was natural to see the applications of this national-*étatisme* to Palestine and the Zionist endeavor. The national aim was interwoven with the vision of a new, more equitable society. The deliberate, systematic development of the country opened possibilities for an accelerated and expanded program of immigration and socioeconomic construction.[33]

This trend was accompanied by a moderate socialist viewpoint. The war and its consequences had also strengthened the social radicalism of young Zionists. The overthrow of the old regimes, the socialist revolutions in Russia and Germany and the establishment of democratic governments in Central and Eastern Europe fostered new hopes and exerted a special influence on the younger Zionists. These young people (as we already know) assumed that no political or social solution existed for Jews in the Diaspora; thus, they did not dream of working for a new socialist order in Europe. But they infused their Zionism with a longing for a new and just society, and the postwar awakening inspired in them a desire to link their Zionism to a socialist ideal. This synthesis was conceived in moderate, revisionist socialist terms that spoke of gradual reform within a given national framework rather than of Marxian, revolutionary class struggle. The younger generation in German Zionism was drawn further in this direction through its encounter with immigrants from the East, many of whom brought socialist ideas with them or were radicalized by their poverty and immigrant experience in Germany.[34]

The link between socialism and Zionism was embodied in the establishment of the autonomous Ha-Po'el ha-Za'ir group in Germany in 1917. Its founders came from Eastern Europe—Haim Arlosoroff and Israel Reichert—but it grew rapidly and spread throughout Germany, attracting many young and older Zionist activists and intellectuals. Among them were Martin Buber (1878–1965), Kurt Blumenfeld and the new editor of the *Jüdische Rundschau,* Robert Weltsch (1891–1982). In January 1919, Ha-Po'el ha-Za'ir began to publish fortnightly *Die Arbeit,* which was highly regarded in Germany and constituted a forum for clarifying Zionist positions on the socioeconomic future of the Jewish National Home. At the Palestine Conference of German Zionists in May 1919, Ha-Po'el ha-Za'ir was represented by thirty-nine delegates. Together with fourteen other socialist delegates, they constituted about a quarter of all the participants.[35]

The moderate socialism that was so popular among the youth had much in common with the views held by most other German Zionists. The close connection between German *étatisme* and the needs and aspirations that were linked to the Zionist return to Palestine, created a broad common ground and allowed for the adoption of a platform that might be called leftist *étatisme,* which directed German Zionism throughout the 1920s.

National Radicalism and Political Moderation

Interwar German Zionism was marked by its political moderation that stemmed from the liberal humanism of the enlightened bourgeoisie of Central Europe. German Jews were drawn to the social stratum that stood for this liberalism. German Zionists, whose leaders came from the universities and belonged socially and professionally to the intellectual bourgeoisie, tended even more to share this political culture. It was characterized by a critical political posture, openness to new ideas and progress and a social sensitivity that eschewed overly narrow definitions of self-interest.

Moreover, German Zionists were predisposed to regard the social and economic spheres as the main field for Zionist fulfillment, more so than the political sphere. Their prewar gravitation toward radical Zionist thought also led them to adopt a peace-affirming, humanist nationalism preached by the disciples of Ahad Ha-Am and by the Bar Kochba circle of Prague.

We have indicated how the First World War strengthened radical trends among the

Zionists. Yet the impact of the war added new dimensions to radical attitudes in the political sphere. Germany's defeat, with its political and economic consequences, intensified aggressive nationalism and xenophobia and threatened the new political and social fabric of the nascent republic. Within the general reaction that this nationalism evoked among German Jews, German Zionists felt the need to develop their own nationalism in an ethical direction that would bear no resemblance to German nationalism.[36]

The impact of the war on German Zionists in general was more distinctly evident among the younger generation of nationalist radicals, who were also more susceptible to the winds of socialist ideas that were sweeping through the new Europe. The result was the crystallization of a moderate socialist-national synthesis. The Ha-Po'el ha-Za'ir party (whose growth right after the war has already been mentioned) expressed this synthesis, which typified a growing trend in German Zionism even beyond the ranks of that party.[37]

Such political moderation was bound up with considerations related to the Arab question and to the humanist-ethical issues of national self-determination. There was a great deal of apprehension over the possibility that the realization of Zionist aims would lead to armed conflict. In Germany, therefore, Zionist views tended in the direction of a binational solution. There, as in Palestine, a *Brit shalom* group formed, and the well-known organ of German Zionism, the *Jüdische Rundschau,* became its mouthpiece. There was a relatively high consonance between *Brit shalom* and the moderate Zionist consensus in Germany.[38] Only there did the Arab riots of 1929 lead to the founding of an *Arbeitsgemeinschaft für zionistische Realpolitik* (Working Group for a Realistic Zionist Policy), set up to influence Zionist policy in the direction of a binational solution.[39]

The Political Role
of German Palestinocentrism

German Zionism in the 1920s was characterized by a broad consensus on most issues, and it is legitimate to label it generally leftist in the social and economic sense and anti-chauvinist in the political sense. This broad measure of agreement, unique to German Zionism, was incorporated in the movement's political and organizational structure. Unlike Zionist movements in other countries, Zionism took shape in Germany as a nonpartisan camp with a clearly defined and unified program.[40] Moreover, insofar as the Zionist parties did secure a foothold in Germany, it was their underlying similarity as much as their distinctiveness that seemed to matter. The relatively strong parties—Ha-Po'el ha-Za'ir at the beginning of the decade and Mizrachi in its second half—had moderate pro-Left platforms. For Ha-Po'el ha-Za'ir, which first developed in Palestine, it was precisely its moderate socialist line that enabled it to make impressive gains in Germany.[41] As for Mizrachi, in Germany it stood closer to the labor-oriented Ha-Po'el ha-Mizrachi of Palestine than to the world Mizrachi, whose main centers in America and Poland were right-wing in orientation.[42]

The right-wing Revisionists were completely outside the basic consensus of German Zionism and, therefore, never took firm root in Germany. The only leader to join them was Richard Lichtheim (in 1926). His affiliation remained an isolated phenomenon and in large measure led to his ostracism within German Zionism. At the time of their greatest popularity, in late 1929, the Revisionists elected only 12 of the total 149 delegates to the Jena Conference of the Zionist Federation.[43]

A climate of ideological consensus insulated German Zionism from the fissures and factionalism that marked other Zionist federations, especially in Poland. This unity overcame the threat of a split at the beginning of the 1920s when conflict over the Keren Hayesod almost led to the resignation of the *Binyan ha-Aretz* group and the establishment of a rival Zionist federation.[44] At the end of the decade, as well, when a sharp controversy developed between supporters of *Brit shalom* and their opponents, the leaders of German Zionism were on the brink of resignation, but eventually unity prevailed.[45] Although partisan recruitment did increase toward the end of the decade, the tone of German Zionism, set by the General Zionist wing, permitted the federation to retain its ability to function as a united, nationwide framework. Virtually all ideological trends were represented on its executive board for most of the period in question. These cooperated among themselves and took it upon themselves to lead the federation in the General Zionist direction even when the General Zionists lost their primacy.[46]

To be sure, the World Zionist movement's problems led to the same conflicts in German Zionism as they did elsewhere. Nevertheless, on the basis of its unity of outlook and organization, and by virtue of the type of ideas comprising this unity, German Zionism in the 1920s acted as a bastion of "Weizmannism." Like many German Zionist leaders, Weizmann was a product of the radical Zionist school representing the disciples of Ahad Ha-Am and was a leading member of the "Democratic Faction" at the beginning of the century. He, too, assigned top priority to the economic development of the National Home and to the formation and implementation of an economic policy based on the spirit of national rebirth and social renewal. That was why he encouraged a far-reaching partnership between the Zionist leadership and the labor movement in Palestine.

Weizmann's political outlook was also markedly moderate, even if not always perfectly clear. From the beginning of the 1920s, he shared a broad range of ideas with the new leaders of German Zionism. German Zionism became a sort of laboratory for testing his ideas and translating them into policy. German Zionists thus played a central role in establishing and shaping the Keren Hayesod, which crystallized the social and economic policy to be followed for Palestinian development and, in addition, drove Brandeis, Weizmann's rival, from the arena.[47] German Zionism became the bulwark against the various "bourgeois" parties that challenged the pro-labor settlement policy (to the point of threatening Weizmann's leadership in the mid-1920s) and above all, against Revisionism.[48] The movement's function in this regard reached its height in 1927, when German Zionist leaders founded the *Linkes Zentrum* (Left Center) as a representative faction of the ZVfD.

But this was also a turning point, and in the late 1920s things began to change. The growing importance of quasi-party activity came to undermine consensus politics and also revealed the limits of Weizmann's own accommodation of radical positions. The first crisis came at the end of 1927 when the emergence of the

German *Linkes Zentrum* led to the expulsion of the labor representatives from the WZO Executive.[49] The basis for joint political action was again damaged when open conflict erupted in 1929 between Weizmann and the *Brit shalom*.

There was also the cumulative effect of the severe economic crisis in Palestine. Palestinocentrism came under attack. By 1928 German Zionism had begun to devote a considerable part of its time and resources to Diaspora-oriented activity, such as education and political action in the Jewish communities.[50] Finally, the Nazis' gains in the 1930 Reichstag elections and the dark prospects facing the Jews of Germany forced the Zionists to turn their attention to the anti-Nazi front. Although even now their support for the *Centralverein* was only temporary, they worked to strengthen Jewish resilience through intensified education and by fostering national pride. At the same time, they worked to effect the emigration of German Jewry to Palestine.[51] This new synthesis was instrumental in the attainment by the ZVfD of the decisive place in German Jewish affairs, a role for which it had been preparing ever since its formative prewar period.

Notes

This essay is based on a paper presented at the International Colloquium held in Jerusalem in March 1985, "The Zionist Movement in Various Countries Between the Two World Wars." In developing the present version, I profited from comments and questions raised by my colleagues at the Institute of Contemporary Jewry, especially Ezra Mendelsohn and Jonathan Frankel.

1. Jehuda Reinharz, *Fatherland or Promised Land? The Dilemma of the German Jew, 1893–1914* (Ann Arbor: 1975), 13–39.
2. Abraham Barkai, "Die Juden als sozio-ökonomische Minderheitsgruppe in der Weimarer Republik," *Juden in der Weimarer Republik,* ed. Walter Grab and Julius Schoeps (Stuttgart and Bonn: 1986), 330–346.
3. Reinharz, *Fatherland,* 90–107. See also Moshe Zimmerman, "Mivneh ḥevrati veẓipiyot ḥevratiot baẓiyonut hagermanit lifnei milḥemet ha'olam harishonah," *Umah vetoldotehah. 2: Ha'et haḥadashah,* ed. Shmuel Ettinger (Jerusalem: 1984), 177–200.
4. Jehuda Reinharz, "The Zionist Response to Anti-Semitism in Germany," *Leo Baeck Institute Year Book* 30 (1985), 105–140; Jacob Toury, "Organizational Problems of German Jewry—Steps Towards the Establishment of a Central Organization (1893–1920)," *Leo Baeck Institute Year Book* 13 (1968), 57–90.
5. As regards German Zionists and the main trends in Zionist ideology at the time, I prefer rather to consider this as an interaction in which German Zionists played the role of exponents, if not more, rather than passively reacting to the initiatives of others, as implied by Jehuda Reinharz, *Dokumente zur Geschichte des deutschen Zionismus, 1882–1933* (Tübingen: 1983), xxxi.
6. Jehuda Reinharz, "Three Generations of German Zionism," *Jerusalem Quarterly* 9 (Fall, 1978), 95–110.
7. Kurt Blumenfeld, *Erlebte Judenfrage: Ein Vierteljahrhundert deutscher Zionismus* (Stuttgart: 1962); Richard Lichtheim, *Rückkehr: Lebenserinnerungen aus der Frühzeit des deutschen Zionismus* (Stuttgart: 1970); Reinharz, "Three Generations."
8. Kurt Blumenfeld, "Ursprünge und Art einer zionistischen Bewegung," *Bulletin des Leo Baeck Instituts* 4 (1958), 129–140.
9. Jehuda Reinharz, "Achad Haam und der deutsche Zionismus," *Bulletin des Leo Baeck Instituts* 61 (1982), 3–73; *idem,* "Martin Buber's Impact on German Zionism Before

World War One," *Studies in Zionism* 6 (Autumn 1982), 171–183; Ernst Simon, "Martin Buber vehayahadut hagermanit," *Perakim mimorashtah shel yahadut germaniah,* ed. A. Tarshish and Yochanan Ginat (Jerusalem: 1975), 15–69; on the radicalization in the youth movement, see Haim Shatzker, "Tenu'at hano'ar hayehudit begermaniah bein hashanim 1900–1933" (Ph.D. diss., The Hebrew University, 1969).

10. Richard Lichtheim, *Toledot haẓiyonut begermaniah* (Jerusalem: 1951), 108–109; Steven M. Poppel, *Zionism in Germany 1897–1933: The Shaping of a Jewish Identity* (Philadelphia: 1977), 50–62; Reinharz, *Dokumente,* xxxiii, and docs. 51, 65 (pp. 106, 132–142).

11. Reinharz, *Dokumente,* xxxv–xxxvi; Blumenfeld, "Innere Politik," *Der Jude* 1 (1916–1917), 713–717.

12. Toury, "Organizational Problems," 79–80.

13. Trude Maurer, *Ostjuden in Deutschland 1918–1933* (Hamburg: 1986), 508–522.

14. Toury, "Organizational Problems," 80–82; Reinharz, *Dokumente,* 203–206 (docs. 98–99). See also Hagit Lavsky, "Hamaavak 'im *binyan haareẓ* begermaniah—hakbalah lamaḥloket Brandeis–Weizmann?" *Divrei hakongres ha'olami hateshi'i lemad'ei hayahadut* (Jerusalem: 1986), Division B, vol. 2, 101–108.

15. Esriel Hildesheimer, "Der Versuch zur Schaffung einer jüdischen Gesamtorganisation während der Weimarer Republik," *Jahrbuch des Instituts für deutsche Geschichte* 8 (1979); Max Birnbaum, *Staat und Synagoge: Eine Geschichte des preussischen Landesverbandes jüdischer Gemeinden 1918–1938* (Tübingen: 1981) 355–364; Maurer, *Ostjuden,* 587–644.

16. For example, Ernst Simon, "Unser Kriegserlebnis," *Brücken: Gesammelte Aufsätze* (Heidelberg: 1965), 17–23; Alfred Landsberg (1887–1964) also became a devoted Zionist as a result of his war experience: interview with his daughter, Mrs. Havah Peltz, 6 November 1981, Ramat Hasharon.

17. *Protokoll des XV. Delegiertentages der Zionistischen Vereinigung für Deutschland, Berlin 25–27 Dez. 1918* (Berlin: 1919); "Palästina Delegiertentag," *Jüdische Rundschau* (hereafter cited as JR), 27 May and 6 June 1919.

18. Toury, "Organizational Problems," 83–88. Toury's assessment of the repercussions of the congress idea in the *Centralverein* is exaggerated. It relies mainly on the account of one individual, Alfred Apfel, who shortly afterward became a devoted Zionist. See also Donald L. Niewyk, "The German Jews in Revolution and Revolt, 1918–19," *Studies in Contemporary Jewry* 4 (1987), 41–66.

19. Reinharz, *Dokumente,* 82. See Maurer and Birnbaum on the various functions of the JVP. The whole question of the organizational and political links between the JVP and the ZVfD, between the JVP and the Poale Zion party, the status of Poale Zion and its functioning as a separate agent in community politics but as an integral part of the ZVfD requires further research.

20. Lavsky, "Hamaavak" sheds light on the position of Arthur Hantke, chairman of the ZVfD until 1920, as a pivotal figure who worked both for Diaspora-oriented activity and for setting a high priority on Palestine-oriented activity. His resignation of the chairmanship was connected to his move to London and his work in establishing the Keren Hayesod.

21. See Ezra Mendelsohn, *Zionism in Poland: The Formative Years, 1915–1926* (New Haven and London: 1981); Yonatan Shapiro, *Leadership of the American Zionist Organization, 1897–1930* (Champaign: 1971); Allon Gal, *Brandeis of Boston* (Cambridge, Mass.: 1980).

22. Hagit Lavsky, "Darkah hara'ayonit vehapolitit shel ẓiyonut germaniah batenu'ah haẓiyonit ha'olamit 1918–1932" (Ph.D. diss., The Hebrew University, 1985): see ch. 1 on the German Zionists and the shaping of the socioeconomic policy for Palestine and ch. 8 on Weizmann and the German Zionists in the critical year of 1929.

23. Lavsky, "Tekufat hainflaẓiah begermaniah vehamashberim shebe'ikvotehah (1922–1926) minekudat mabat ẓiyonit," *Haẓiyonut* 12 (1987), 165–181.

24. *Ibid.;* see also Josef Walk, "Das deutsche Komitee Pro-Palästina 1926–1933," *Bulletin des Leo Baeck Instituts* 15 (1976).

25. Lavsky, "Tekufat hainflaẓiah."

26. This is the impression created by many participants' testimony, both written and oral. The matter of training and aliyah from Germany in the 1920s calls for separate research, and I plan to deal with it in a separate essay.

27. Reinharz, "Zionist Response to Anti-Semitism." Reinharz points out that the Zionist position changed in 1923–1924 in the wake of antisemitic disturbances in Germany. But this refers only to a brief period of two to three months at the end of 1923 and early 1924 and does not reflect longer trends.

28. See Birnbaum, *Staat und Synagoge,* and Maurer, *Ostjuden,* on the activities of the JVP; see Reinharz, *Dokumente,* 428ff., on the ZVfD in the *Gemeindepolitik* from 1928 on.

29. Maurer, *Ostjuden,* esp. 610–717. The link between the Zionist parties and the Eastern Jews in Germany requires further elaboration. It is not clear, for example, that Maurer's claim that Ha-Po'el ha-Ẓa'ir was made up mainly of Eastern Jews is justified. There has been no research into the dynamics of development in either Poale Zion or Mizrachi.

30. See n. 17. Lichtheim's address on economics to the fifteenth conference was published in pamphlet form, *Der Aufbau des jüdischen Palästinas* (Berlin: 1919). The JR, the official organ of the ZVfD, and *Die Arbeit,* organ of Ha-Po'el ha-Ẓa'ir, devoted numerous articles and discussions to economic issues.

31. The main fruits of this experience may be seen in Arthur Ruppin, *Der Aufbau des Landes Israel* (Berlin: 1919). On the reception of this book and the reputation of its author, see Jacob Metzer, *Hon leumi lebayit leumi, 1919–1921* (Jerusalem: 1979), 69.

32. J. A. Schumpeter, *History of Economic Analysis* (Oxford: 1954), pt. 4, chap. 4, "*Sozialpolitik* and the Historical Method"; *International Encyclopedia of the Social Sciences,* vol. 4, s.v. "Economic Thought" (The Historical School). As to the Zionist students of Weber and Sombart, see Blumenfeld, *Erlebte Judenfrage,* 146–148.

33. This was stressed by Hantke and Lichtheim in their addresses to the fifteenth German Zionist Conference. See also Metzer, *Hon leumi.*

34. Robert Weltsch, "Deutscher Zionismus in der Rückschau," (1962) *An der Wende des modernen Judentums* (Tübingen: 1972), 51–64; Gershom Scholem, *Miberlin liyerushalayim* (Tel-Aviv: 1982), 80–102; interviews with Robert Weltsch, 21 February 1980, with Ernst Simon, 16 and 23 March 1982. Barukh Ben-Avram, "Ha-Po'el ha-Ẓa'ir hagermani—parashah shel kevuẓat intelektualim 1917–1920," *Haẓiyonut* 6 (1981), 49–95. On the role of German Jews in the German socialist movements, see H. H. Knütter, *Die Juden und die deutsche Linke in der Weimarer Republik* (Düsseldorf: 1971). There is a great deal of material on the connection between Jewish socialist movements and Jews from the East in Maurer's *Ostjuden.*

35. Ben-Avram, "Ha-Po'el ha-Ẓa'ir." Maurer's claim regarding the East European dominance within Ha-Po'el ha-Ẓa'ir has already been questioned (n. 29). As for the composition of the delegates to the Palestine Conference, see JR, 13 June 1919.

36. Weltsch, "Deutscher Zionismus"; see also the interviews cited in n. 34. Endless accounts in retrospect of the special Zionist reactions to German nationalism are to be found, for example, in the discussions of the national leadership of the ZVfD after the disturbances at the beginning of September 1929: Central Zionist Archives (hereafter cited as CZA) Z4/3567/III; A. Landsberg to Weizmann, 18 November 1929, Weizmann Archives. Evidence of this kind also emerged from an interview with M. Flanter, 9 May 1982, Jerusalem, and with P. Jacoby, 11 January 1981, Jerusalem.

37. Ben-Avram, "Ha-Po'el ha-Ẓa'ir"; Ernst Simon, "Martin Buber."

38. For example, the support for the attitudes taken by JR at the German Zionist conference in Erfurt, August 1926. Protocol of the conference in JR, 27 August 1926.

39. The founding meeting on 16 September 1929, Weltsch Archive at the Leo Baeck Institute, New York, 7185/3/2. The memorandum presented to the Zionist Executive, 16 September 1929, CZA S25/3122.

40. Lavsky, "Nisyonah shel politikah a-politit baẓiyonut: haẓiyonut hagermanit vehamerkaz hasemali, 1925–1927," *Umah vetoldotehah,* pt. 2, 261–284.

41. Ben-Avram, "Ha-Po'el ha-Ẓa'ir."

42. Lavsky, "Politikah a-politit"; session of the central committee of the German Mizrachi, JR, 14 October 1929; Reinharz, *Dokumente,* 438–439.

43. JR, 7 January 1930; Francis R. Nicosia, "Revisionist Zionism in Germany (1)— Richard Lichtheim and the *Landesverband der Zionisten-Revisionisten in Deutschland, 1926–1933,*" *Leo Baeck Institute Year Book* 31 (1986), 209–240.

44. Lavsky, "Hamaavak."

45. At the German Zionist conference at Jena, December 1929: JR, 3 and 7 January 1930.

46. Lavsky, "Politikah a-politit"; and see the discussions of the German Zionist conference at Breslau and its resolutions, JR, 1 and 5 June 1928.

47. Metzer, *Hon leumi.*

48. Lavsky, "Politikah a-politit"; see editorials in JR, 3 July, 7 and 14 August 1925, before the fourteenth Zionist Congress.

49. Lavsky, "Politikah a-politit."

50. See the discussions of the Breslau conference (n. 46); Reinharz, *Dokumente,* 405, 407ff., 428ff.

51. The headlines and editorials in JR of 7 March, 19 September and 2 December 1930. On the change from the Palestine front to the German scene at the German Zionist conference in Frankfurt, see JR 9 and 16, September 1932. See also Avraham Margaliot, "Hateguvah hapolitit shel hamosadot vehairgunim hayehudiim begermaniah lenokhaḥ hamediniyut haanti-yehudit shel hanaẓionalsoẓialistim bashanim 1932–35" (Ph.D. diss, The Hebrew University, 1971); K. Loewenstein, "Die innerjüdische Reaktion auf die Krise der deutschen Demokratie," in *Entscheidungsjahr 1932,* ed. W. E. Mosse (Tübingen: 1965), 349–403.

Ritual, Ceremony and the Reconstruction of Judaism in the United States

Charles S. Liebman
(BAR-ILAN UNIVERSITY)

Until very recently, observers of American Jewish life have noted a steady decline in ritual observance. This observation has been challenged in recent years[1] and was one of the points of contention in two recently published papers on the quality of Jewish life in the United States.[2] Each author assumed that the question of whether Jews were observing more, the same or less Jewish ritual than they had in the recent past was a critical dimension in assessing the quality of Jewish life in the United States. I wish to argue that the issue was improperly formulated. In the first place, insufficient account was taken of the distinction between ceremony and ritual. Second, too much emphasis was given to whether a particular ritual (or ceremony) was performed and inadequate attention was paid to the context in which it was performed and, therefore, the manner in which it is understood.

Ceremony and Ritual

Although the terms "ceremony" and "ritual" are used interchangeably in popular discourse, many students of religion distinguish between them.[3] Such a distinction is very relevant for understanding the religious behavior of American Jews. For our purposes, the comment by Zuesse in *The Encyclopedia of Religion* is especially appropriate. He notes that "some social anthropologists distinguish between 'ritual'—stylized repetitious behavior that is explicitly religious"—and ceremony, which "is merely social even in explicit meaning." Ritual not only involves "intentional bodily engagement,"[4] which is necessarily more stylized than ceremonial behavior, but it is also believed to be efficacious. It is directed toward a particular goal and becomes, among other things, a mechanism for achieving those goals. Religious ritual connects the participant to some transcendent presence. It provides a bridge to God by engaging the participant in an act that God has commanded. At the very least, it is efficacious in the sense that it is pleasing to God or avoids God's displeasure. But it only produces the desired results when performed correctly.

In ceremony, aspects of the social and cosmological order find representation. Participation in the ceremony affirms the individual's membership in this order. But since the ceremony is not deemed to be commanded by God, it need not be performed in as precise or stylized a manner as ritual. Because it is a consciously social act and a representation of a social order, it is more amenable to change than ritual. Precisely because it is not perceived as preordained, those in charge are held responsible for its suitability and appropriateness.

Ceremony is symbol. It, too, may be cloaked in an aura of mystery—participants may derive a variety of meanings from the ceremony, and the specific connections between the ceremony and the social order it represents may be sensed rather than articulated. But even the "sense" of the participants allows them to judge the content of a ceremony as unsuitable or inappropriate or poorly done. Ritual is both more resistant to change (though by no means invulnerable), and less amenable to criticism of its content.

In Judaism, it seems to me, most *mitzvot* (sing.: *mitzvah:* commandment), fit the definition of ritual. They are believed to be commands, ordained by God, that the Jew must perform in a prescribed manner. For example, before Jews eat bread, they must recite a blessing. Before reciting this blessing they must wash their hands and recite a blessing over this act. Even the manner in which the hands are to be washed is prescribed—the kind of utensil to be used, the order in which the hands are to be washed and the number of times each hand is to be washed are clearly spelled out. Within the Jewish tradition, questions are raised about whether the individual who performs a ritual in an improper manner has fulfilled his obligations. But indifference to the manner in which the ritual is performed is certainly inappropriate. It may render the blessing one recites prior to performing the mitzvah a "superfluous blessing," which itself is sinful. Ritualism, as Mary Douglas has observed, therefore, is the opposite of ethicism, which attributes primary importance to intention and devalues the precise manner in which an act is performed. "The move away from ritual is accompanied by a strong movement towards greater ethical sensitivity," she observes,[5] although her own study indicates how ultimately self-defeating this may become. If we understand ritual in this respect, there can be little question that there is an increase in ritual behavior among Orthodox Jews in the United States[6] and a decline among the non-Orthodox. The latter comprise close to ninety percent of American Jews.

On the other hand, ceremonial behavior flourishes. This is most noticeable within the Reform movement, which has embraced Jewish symbols and encourages its members to partake of ceremonial activity that it often (mistakenly in our terms) calls ritual. Its synagogues are far richer in Jewish ceremony than they were in the past. But this, too, should not be confused with ritual. The Sabbath service in a Reform synagogue may not include reading from the Torah (the central point of the traditional Sabbath service) or may include reading only a few lines rather than the entire weekly portion, but it will include a rather elaborate ceremony in which the Torah scrolls are taken out of and returned to the highly ornamented ark in which they are kept. A bar mitzvah ceremony in a Reform synagogue might have the rabbi removing the Torah scroll from the ark and handing it to the parents of the youngster whose bar mitzvah is being celebrated. The parents, in turn, hand the Torah, in this case a symbol of the Jewish tradition, to the bar mitzvah celebrant. In traditional Judaism, the only purpose for taking the Torah scrolls out of the ark is to read from them. Indeed, Jewish law is rather strict in proscribing other uses of the scrolls because of their sanctity. Hence the elaboration of the ceremonial in which the Torah scrolls are handled is certainly "ritually" inappropriate. But we are dealing with ceremony rather than ritual. The congregants do not believe that what they are doing was commanded by God, that it must only be performed in a prescribed manner or that its proper performance is efficacious. They are partaking of ceremonial behavior, that is, symbolic behavior, whose social nature in this case seems fairly explicit. The ceremony symbolizes the ties between parent and child in a Jewish context; the centrality of generational continuity and the special role of the parent–child relationship in transmitting the Torah (i.e., tradition); the almost proprietary rights Jews have with respect to the Torah; and the central role of the rabbi. The ceremony clearly projects a certain representation of the Jewish social order and affirms the participants' membership in this order.

The ceremonial service need not necessarily be contrary to ritual in order for us to appreciate what is and what is not being celebrated. A good example is the recent flourishing of *havdalah* services. At the close of the Sabbath, but as late as midweek if he forgets to do so, a Jew is commanded to recite three blessings that distinguish the Sabbath from the rest of the week. The *havdalah* service, as performed by most Orthodox Jews, is recited immediately on conclusion of the Saturday evening prayers. Its recital takes no more than two or three minutes. There is hardly a Jewish meeting, conference, seminar or event of any kind that has taken place during the last decade and held on the Sabbath that has not included the *havdalah* ceremony. Indeed, among the non-Orthodox this ceremony tends to be far more elaborate than among the Orthodox. The ceremony may conclude with all those present forming a large circle, holding hands, singing together and, quite often, kissing one another. While most of the participants are unlikely to perform *havdalah* in their own homes, they seem to look forward to the ceremony when performed under organizational auspices. The ceremony may be performed in a ritually correct manner, but from the point of view of Orthodox Judaism, it is not acceptable to conduct a *havdalah* service while omitting the evening prayers that precede it. It seems reasonable to suggest that the *havdalah* service described here is more appropriately defined as ceremony than as ritual.

The popularity of *havdalah*, along with other ceremonials we have mentioned, suggests a ceremonial renaissance among American Jews. Even this would not have been anticipated by students of Jewish religious life in the United States a generation ago. Those observers suggested that the steady decline in ritual and ceremonial behavior among American Jews (the two forms of behavior were not distinguished) foretold their approaching assimilation. That may or may not be true. But the situation is more complex than was suggested. American Jews are not abandoning Jewish ceremonials, nor are they substituting non-Jewish for Jewish ritual. Instead, they are transforming Jewish patterns of behavior into American ones. The very emphasis on ceremony and de-emphasis of ritual illustrates this pattern. Ceremony, in addition, lends itself—far more than ritual—to reconstruction, and it is this reconstruction that is so critical to understanding contemporary developments in the religious life of American Jews.

Religious Reconstruction

In his study of Jewish life in a wealthy suburban community first published in 1967, Marshall Sklare detected a development that is now identifiable as a major trend in American Jewish life. "I feel Judaism is changing," says one of Sklare's suburban respondents. "Some people only think of religion in terms of ritual. I don't."[7] How then do Jews think of Judaism? I suggest four central components, really two sets of two components each, that distinguish the manner in which American Jews conceive of their religious tradition and represent the tools for reconstructing that tradition. These are: personalism and voluntarism as one set of components; universalism and moralism as the other. They are all interrelated but, for heuristic purposes, are best discussed separately.

Personalism and Voluntarism

Personalism is a philosophical perspective in which "person is the ontological ultimate and for which personality is thus the fundamental explanatory principle."[8] Personalism is reflected in the observation by Sklare that "the modern Jew selects from the vast storehouse of the past what is not only objectively possible for him to practice but subjectively possible for him to 'identify' with."[9] Sklare is referring to the performance of mitzvot, or Jewish ritual, but personalism is imposed on all aspects of the religious tradition. Personalism refers to the tendency to transform and evaluate the tradition in terms of its utility or meaningfulness to the individual. "The best assurance of Jewish survival," Cohen and Fein say, "is the development of a community that offers its members opportunities for personal fulfillment not easily found elsewhere";[10] that is what American Jews appear intent on doing with their religious tradition.

Voluntarism refers to the absence or devaluation of *mitzvah*, or commandment. The individual is urged, encouraged, cajoled into performing certain acts of a ceremonial nature and is constantly reassured that what one does is legitimate if that is what one chooses to do. Personal choice is endowed with spiritual sanctity and is in all cases (contrary to past tradition) considered more virtuous than performing an act out of one's sense of obedience to God. While subtle distinctions exist between personalism and voluntarism, they are interrelated, and the examples offered here illustrate both these principles.

The new Conservative prayer book, *Siddur Sim Shalom,* includes among its selected readings a statement by Edmund Fleg (1874–1963), the French author and essayist, who only affirmed his Jewishness in mid-life. He wrote, "I am a Jew because [among other reasons] Judaism demands no abdication of my mind." This statement was reprinted and formed a central reading in a Sabbath prayer service at the Conservative movement's Pacific Southwest convention of synagogues in 1986. (We shall return to Fleg's affirmation because his formulation of "Why I am a Jew" foreshadows many aspects of contemporary Judaism.) Prayer, as it is transformed by personalism, ceases to become a medium of communication between people and God. Rather, asks one writer, "How, practically, can Jewish prayer function to help one confront anger and utilize it for personal transformation and social change?"[11] Another author says, "As we begin to focus on issues of importance to us, perhaps our Jewish traditions will evolve in ways to help us sustain our efforts. We have learned over the past 5000 years that things do not change overnight. But we have also learned that if we do nothing, they do not change at all."[12]

What we have here is the belief that tradition should be made compatible with the needs of the individual Jew. This, given the emphasis on voluntarism, is hardly surprising. Personalism and voluntarism are incompatible with ritual, that is, behavior performed in a specified, stylized manner undertaken because this is believed to be God's command. It is not, however, incompatible with ceremonial.

Siddur Sim Shalom, first published in the mid-1980s, offers a number of alternative services or prayers for different occasions. It has been argued that each of the alternatives in the Conservative prayer book, unlike the Reform prayer book, has a basis in Jewish law. However, the Union for Traditional Conservative Judaism, representing the more traditionalist wing within the Conservative movement, has published a responsum (legal opinion of Jewish law) that concludes, "although *Siddur Sim Shalom* may be used as a resource work, it should not be used for the purpose of fulfilling one's prayer obligations" because, among other reasons, some of the alternatives are not the services that the tradition prescribes.[13] Whatever the case, offering the worshipper a variety of choices reflects the spirit of personalism and voluntarism to which we have alluded.

The Conservative Temple Beth Ami in Reseda, California, proud of its efforts to encourage what it takes to be "ritual observance," prepared a booklet on the topic that it distributed to other Conservative congregations. The program was conceived and developed by a faculty member of the University of Judaism, the west coast rabbinical seminary and institution of higher education of the Conservative movement. The synagogue program is built around a voluntary group patterned on Weight Watchers. Each member of the group undertakes to perform certain "rituals" and to report back to the monthly meeting of the group on his or her progress. Members fill out a "12-Month Goal Sheet" in which "they should determine which rituals they would like to involve themselves in during the coming year. The members should understand that the goal of this program is not to make them become any more Jewish than what they will be comfortable with."[14]

No less interesting is that a number of these "rituals" have no great significance in Jewish law, others are customs rather than mitzvot and still others are probably contrary to Jewish law. However, their functions are quite obvious in contributing to a sense of family harmony and personal fulfillment. For example, among the eighteen Sabbath rituals we find: "playing shabbat music to set mood," "blessing children," "blessing wife," "blessing husband," "have a special Shabbosdick meal," "using a white tablecloth and good dishes" and "singing shabbat songs around the table."

Consistent with our understanding of personalism and voluntarism, we would expect that the definition of who is a Jew and the boundaries between Jew and non-Jew would become increasingly flexible. Jews, in keeping with these principles, are those who choose to call themselves Jews, and they are free to incorporate into their religious behavior whatever it is within a broadly and freely defined Jewish tradition that they find personally fulfilling. It would be an overstatement to say that the majority of American Jews affirm the applications of these principles in their extreme form, but it would not be an exaggeration to say that some of them do so and that most of them seem to be moving closer to, rather than further away from, the more extreme applications of these principles.

The recent decision of the Reform movement to include within the definition of a Jew someone whose mother is non-Jewish but whose father is Jewish is one such effort. This decision simply legitimated practices that have been employed for many years in many, if not most, Reform synagogues. This, in turn, is attributable to the rising number of mixed marriages (the marriage of a Jew and a non-Jew when neither partner converts to the other's religion) and, no less important, the desire of the couple to affiliate with a synagogue and raise their child within a Jewish framework. In other words, what we are witnessing is a process whereby the Jewish spouse, married to a non-Jew who may remain a believing Christian, not only demands legitimacy of Jewish status for himself/herself and children, but even, to some extent, for the Christian partner. As the authors of a study on conversion point out, over half of the non-converts in their sample "felt that one could be part of the Jewish people and community without undergoing a formal conversion process."[15] The point is brought home in articles by converts to Judaism who remain married to non-Jews, a condition facilitated by an increasingly tolerant Jewish community.

Thus, a potential convert to Judaism writes, "*Chanukah* and Christmas will probably both be observed, simply because the family ties my husband associates with the mid-winter holiday are too significant to abandon."[16] And another says:

> I am very fortunate because my husband supports my decision to convert to Judaism. . . . His main concern was that I might expect him to convert also, or that the rabbi might expect it. [Apparently the rabbi did not.] Tom is a very spiritual person and I had no expectations that he would have to take the same journey. I knew that we could still share much of Judaism as a couple and as a family.[17]

And later, describing her synagogue:

> At Beth Shalom there are many non-Jewish spouses and so there is a great deal of concern that these non-Jewish family members feel accepted and a part of the community. Our religious school also is very supportive of the children who have a non-Jewish parent or relative and every effort is made to make those children feel that they belong.[18]

And:

> I refuse to let my religious choice cause strife in my family. I made a personal religious choice and if I expect people to honor my choice than I must honor theirs.[19]

Or, as another writer says:

> As for synagogue and community involvement, I do not see a need for the gentile spouse to feel excluded. While there are definite honors from which one would be excluded, there are plenty of meaningful opportunities to involve the non-Jew in synagogue life and congregations should do that. Though these people may not be Jewish, that does not mean they do not want our synagogue and organizational activities to be successful. Because their families are involved, they do want to see us reach our goals.[20]

A recent book entitled *Raising Your Jewish Christian Child: Wise Choices for Interfaith Parents* is advertised as "how to give your children the best of both heritages" and urges readers to "act now to enrich your children's spiritual lives. This year's holidays can be the richest, most harmonious ones your family has ever celebrated."[21]

A book on the topic, even when published by a large commercial house, is only a straw in the wind. But the book, advertised in *Commentary* magazine, carries a blurb written by the then-president of the Association for the Sociological Study of Jewry, who calls the book "An endearing message on a thorny subject . . . both a ray of hope and a helping hand to families such as her own, who wish to celebrate the duality of faith and culture."

Universalism and Moralism

Universalism refers to the sense that the Jewish tradition has a message for all people, not only for Jews, and that it is also open to the messages of other traditions and cultures. As we have seen, Judaism can even be construed at times as open to non-Jews who may develop a variety of partial affiliations with the Jewish people. The *Commentary* ad that suggests how the child of an interfaith marriage can benefit from the "best of both heritages" is a good illustration. Moralism is another term borrowed from Sklare. He defines it as the notion that "religious man is distinguished not by his observance of rituals but rather by the scrupulousness of his ethical behavior."[22] Recent emphases in American Jewish life (as already suggested) continue to invoke the term ritual but convert ritual to ceremonial and reinterpret its meaning in moralistic terms. Jewish symbols are retained in their particularistic form, but the referent or meaning is explained as a moral or ethical imperative. Since ethics are generally viewed as universal, examples of universalism and moralism tend to overlap.

One of Edmund Fleg's reasons for being a Jew—"because the promise of Judaism is a universal promise"—suggests moralism as well as universalism. At the 1986 Conservative synagogue convention referred to earlier, a second selection entitled "The Essence of Judaism" was read immediately before the recital of the *Sh'ma,* a central point in the religious service. The selection (author unknown) begins by affirming that Jews are united by a four thousand-year-old bond that has "sensitized the Jewish individual to the needs of the group" and then states, "From one group to one humanity has been our goal. From our early teachings came the ideas of a society where individuals will treat each other with dignity and respect. These ideas are the essence of Judaism."[23]

Thus, the essence of Judaism is contained in three ideas: group (i.e., Jewish) needs, the integration of the group into one humanity and the treating of all individuals with dignity and respect.

The meaning of universalism and moralism is also illustrated in a newspaper article by a Conservative rabbi who writes on the topic *Golus* (or *Galut*), which means exile. He refers to the exile of the Jewish people from the Land of Israel. Within the Jewish tradition, especially its mystical wing, one can also find a metaphysical meaning attributed to the term. But it is strange to find a rabbi writing:

While *Golus* is a Jewish word it is not only a Jewish issue. It is a human issue as well. *Golus* in 1986 is children going to sleep hungry night after night. It is approximately 30 armed conflicts raging around the globe. It is the continuing deterioration of our habitat and ecosystem. . . . And most alarmingly, it is thousands of nuclear warheads ready at this moment to annihilate us all.[24]

In a sophisticated and carefully balanced discussion of the topic of Biblical particularism and universalism, Jon D. Levinson makes the following statement, which is very relevant to our concerns:

For Jews in the post-Enlightenment West, where ideas of human equality and democratic government hold sway, there is a temptation to stress the instrumental dimension of Jewish chosenness and to deny or ignore the self-sufficient dimension. We are sometimes told that the "chosen people" means the "choosing people," as if passive and active participles were not opposite in meaning. Judaism is presented as a commitment to some rather amorphous "Jewish values," which, on inspection, turn out to be *universal* values, in which Jews and gentiles alike ought to believe. Convenant, if it is mentioned at all, appears only as the basis for a warm, meaningful community life. The fact that the Covenant distinguishes sharply between insiders and outsiders—although both are God's—is ignored.

In large measure, such attitudes are dictated by the exigencies of living as a minority in a mixed society with a high degree of openness. It is simply not prudent to affirm a distinctiveness of ultimate significance based on heredity, and what is not prudent to express publicly often loses credibility, becoming peripheral or taboo even in private discourse. In addition, the contemporary theology in question represents a cognitive surrender to a Kantian theory of ethics in which morality entails universalability: if the behavior cannot be advocated for everyone, it cannot be moral. On Kantian principles, Jewish ethics—a norm for one group only—is a contradiction in terms. Hence the common substitution of ethics for Torah. "Ethics," writes Michael Wyschogrod, "is the Judaism of the assimilated."[25]

The moralization of Judaism is most pronounced on the Jewish political Left. Arthur Waskow is a major representative of this tendency. He serves as executive director of the Shalom Center located at the Reconstructionist Rabbinical College (but with a board of directors and advisory council that includes three Orthodox rabbis). Here, for example, is an excerpt from a recent fund-raising letter:

Across the US, Jews will celebrate the harvest festival of Sukkot from October 17 to 25 as *Sukkat Shalom*—the Shelter of Peace. The fragile Sukkah, open to wind and rain, is the exact opposite of a fallout shelter or of a "laser shield." It symbolizes that in the nuclear age, all of us live in a vulnerable Sukkah. *Our only real shelter is making peace.*

The theme of Sukkat Shalom is "From Harvest Booth to Voting Booth." Urge your congregation or Jewish group to press your members of Congress *to end all nuclear testing.*

Rosh Hashanah is the birthday of the world. As the new year turns and returns, *let us look our children and all the world's children in the eye and say—*

"We did our best to choose life for you and us this Rosh Hashanah!"

Universalism and moralism is not, however, confined to the Jewish Left. In his book *Sacred Survival,* Jonathan Woocher demonstrates how moralism comprises a basic component of what he calls the "civil religion" of American Jews, although what he actually describes is the civil religion of the Jewish lay leadership. He quotes one Jewish leader as saying, "Charity and working for social justice—Tzedakah and Mitzvos—are not options for Jews. They have the force of articles of faith. They are duties and requirements."[26]

What is remarkable in this quotation is the assumption that the terms "Mitzvos" and "Tzedakah" are accurately translated by the term "working for social justice," although both have a technical meaning within halakhic tradition. But this is a commonplace among American Jews, at least among their leaders. As another leader says, "For us, social justice—Tzedakah in its full meaning—has always been indivisible—for all." And yet another proclaims, "It has always been Jewish doctrine that social justice cannot be limited to Jews alone: Jews are dedicated to social justice for all mankind. 'Love the stranger as thyself,' the Bible taught."[27] The citation, taken out of context, confers on the passage a meaning that Bible scholars would find somewhat forced. Be that as it may, in the conception of American Jews (or at least their leaders), as long as Jews remain a people committed to these values, "Jewish survival is not a chauvinistic conceit, but a requisite for the continued fulfillment of the Jewish role as an exemplar of human values."[28]

Moralism, universalism and even a dash of personalism are reflected in contemporary American Jewish transformations of the holiday of Purim. Purim is unique among the holidays of the Jewish calendar. It is a holiday of joy and laughter in which drinking (even to excess) and revelry are encouraged. Despite its location within the catalogue of "religious" festivals, Purim is generally considered the most secular of holy days. It has been suggested by traditional rabbis as well as anthropologists that it is an inversion of Yom Kippur, the most sacred of all Jewish holidays. During Yom Kippur the community celebrates its relationship to God and locates itself as part of the sacred order.[29] Purim, on the other hand, reaffirms the secular order through the mitzvah of exchanging gifts among peers and of giving charity to the needy, thereby identifying one's social place. In addition, the popular custom (rather than mitzvah) of satirizing community leaders, including scholars, reflects the practice that anthropologists refer to as "inversion." This is another device to reaffirm the social order by permitting and marking off its periodic violation. In keeping with the spirit of the holiday, there is a remarkable degree of flexibility in its celebration. Customs include masquerading (most often as characters from the Biblical book of Esther) and the production of skits and plays of a humorous and satirical nature. The prescribed *mitzvot* include the two we have mentioned—charity to the poor and gifts to one's friends—and, in addition, partaking of a Purim feast and hearing a ritual reading of the story of Esther from a scroll. The story of Esther, after recounting how Mordechai and Esther save the Jews (God makes no appearance whatsoever in this rather extraordinary tale located in ancient Persia), goes on to tell of the punishments inflicted on the Jews' enemies. Haman—the archvillain of the story and the prototype of all antisemites—and his sons are hanged by order of the gentile king. In addition, multitudes of other non-Jews are killed by the Jews with permission of the king.

The holiday (as I indicated) has undergone an interesting transformation in the United States. Masquerading and public revelry are activities ill-suited to a minority group living as part of, rather than segregated from, a majority culture in which it seeks acceptance. Until recently, Purim, if celebrated at all, tended to be celebrated within the synagogue itself or in the home. It was, however, generally devalued among American Jews. This is less true today. Part of the reason, no doubt, rests on the insistence of many Orthodox Jews in displaying Jewish traditions to the general public. But the fact is that the non-Orthodox have acquiesced in this display, participating in it rather than shunning it. This, itself, may be a function of the increased legitimacy accorded to ethnicity in the United States. The reasons, however, are not of primary concern here. The question is, what have American Jews done with the festival in the last few years?

For one thing, although they now publicize Purim, it ceases to be an exclusively Jewish celebration. Rather, non-Jews are invited to partake as well, in which case, as we shall see, the holiday assumes somewhat different dimensions. According to a report in the *New York Times,* 1987 was the first year in which a sidewalk Purim parade was organized in Manhattan. But, says the writer:

> Its organizers hope that someday it will grow into an event like the Queens parade, which last year drew some 50,000 people.
>
> In Queens on Sunday, more than 10 blocks of Main Street will be closed for the parade. . . . It is a fully ecumenical event, according to Mitchell Mann, the chairman of the parade, and includes Jewish groups of every branch as well as Roman Catholic school marching bands and black cowboys on horseback. . . . Among the others marching are: mounted police and motorcycle escort, the United States Marine Corps Color Guard, St. Benedict's Fife and Drum Corps and the Mitzvah tank of the Lubavitcher Hasidim.
>
> At the end of the march, there will be a street fair and concert. . . . Among the attractions on the street will be a ferris wheel, rides on elephants and camels, a petting zoo and a wide variety of foods, both Jewish and not-so-Jewish.[30]

Universalizing the celebration of Purim involves not only changing who participates, but also what the holiday comes to represent. So, according to Orthodox rabbi and popular hasidic singer Shlomo Carlebach, as quoted in the same article, "Purim is a holiday of children." But he goes on to say, "this doesn't mean you have to be a child to enjoy it, just that you have to begin to believe in the world again like on the first day you opened your eyes." Implied, although unstated in this description of Purim, is that you certainly don't have to be Jewish.

Overtones of "personalism" mix with a universalism of style in the following report of a Purim celebration at a Conservative synagogue in Connecticut. According to the rabbi:

> The Hebrew text will be wrapped around with song, dance and narrative in musical revue format—a folk art pageant involving the entire congregation. . . . We present Purim in this way in order to bring out its ever-current as well as its ancient meaning. . . . A point like this is brought out through the songs of such composers as Spike Jones, Cole Porter and George Landry, late voodoo chief of New Orleans.[31]

An explicit example of the transformation of Purim in moralistic terms is its celebration at the largest Conservative synagogue in the New Haven area. The Congregation printed a pamphlet called *Purim Service* for its members. The *Purim Service* is read aloud as a replacement of, rather than addition to, the Biblical story of Esther. It is an abbreviated version, almost entirely in English, organized in the form of responsive readings, a style designed to involve the audience. What is especially striking about the reformulated story is the excising of any violence. Haman is not hanged on a gallows. Instead, "When the King found out that Haman plotted against the people of Esther, the Queen, he removed him from office and appointed Mordekhai in his place." The moral of the story is thus formulated as: "Our story is important because it is about people who had courage and who risked their lives to help others. That's what we celebrate on Purim."[32]

Conclusion

The failure by scholars to distinguish between ritual and ceremonial has resulted in an inadequate understanding of developments taking place among American Jews. It would appear that the former is declining while the latter may even be on the rise, a development indicating the Americanization of American Judaism. The term "Americanization," however, may be a misnomer because colleagues have observed similar developments taking place among Jews of Western Europe. Furthermore, these developments in the United States are not peculiar to Judaism. William D. Dinges, for example, notes that opposition to the radical change in Catholic liturgy in the 1960s, aside from charges of mistranslations, focused on the shift in understanding of the Mass from "propitiatory sacrifice" to "communal meal," in diminishing emphasis on the "Real Presence" and on tendencies "emphasizing love of neighbor and edification of the laity and on the new liturgy's alleged 'Protestant' and 'ecumenical' character."[33] The opposition, in other words, was disturbed by the very same trends we find taking place among American Jews.

Two sets of central values, I believe, animate the reconstruction of Judaism taking place in the United States: personalism and voluntarism is one and universalism and moralism the other. These values, by themselves, are the antitheses of ritual; it is no surprise, therefore, that their ascendancy also marks the decline of ritual observance. None of these aspects or values are entirely new, much less alien to Judaism: all of them are to be found within the tradition itself. What is new is the emphasis they have received and the fact that together they have become major dimensions or instruments through which American Jews interpret and transform the Jewish tradition.

Notes

1. Steven M. Cohen, *American Assimilation or Jewish Revival?* (Bloomington: 1988).

2. Steven M. Cohen and Charles S. Liebman, *The Quality of Jewish Life in the United States: Two Views* (New York: 1987).

3. Bobby C. Alexander, *The Encyclopedia of Religion*, vol. 3, s.v. "Ceremony," 179–183.

4. Evan M. Zuesse, *The Encyclopedia of Religion*, vol. 12, s.v. "Ritual," 405–406.

5. Mary Douglas, *Natural Symbols* (New York: 1973), 41.

6. Charles S. Liebman, *Deceptive Images: Toward a Redefinition of American Judaism* (New Brunswick: 1988).

7. Marshall Sklare and Joseph Greenblum, *Jewish Identity on the Suburban Frontier,* 2d ed. (Chicago: 1979), 77.

8. John H. Lavely, *The Encyclopedia of Philosophy,* vol. 5, s.v. "Personalism," 110.

9. Sklare and Greenblum, *Identity,* 48.

10. Steven M. Cohen and Leonard J. Fein, "From Integration to Survival: American Jewish Anxieties in Transition," *Annals of the American Academy of Social and Political Science* 480 (1985), 88.

11. Jeffrey Dekro, "Prayer and Anger," *Response* 46 (1984), 73.

12. Rebecca Alpert, "Sisterhood Is Ecumenical: Bridging the Gap Between Jewish and Christian Feminists," *Response* 46 (1984), 15.

13. Union for Traditional Conservative Judaism, *Tomeikh kahalakhah: Responsa of the Panel of Halakhic Inquiry* (1986), 12.

14. Temple Beth Ami, "Hevrat Mitzvah Program" (n.d.).

15. Egon Mayer and Amy Avgar, *Conversion Among the Intermarried* (New York: 1987), 9.

16. Amy Richards, "I Wish to Be a Jew: My Husband Doesn't," *Sh'ma* 17, no. 326 (1987), 41.

17. Anne Anderson, "My Support Is Real—So Are My Memories," *Sh'ma* 17, no. 326 (1987), 42–43.

18. *Ibid.*

19. *Ibid.*

20. Sharon Haber, "Gaining a Faith But Not Losing My Family," *Sh'ma* 17, no. 327 (1987), 51.

21. *Commentary* 84 (1987), 78.

22. Sklare and Greenblum, *Identity,* 89.

23. United Synagogue of America, Pacific Southwest Region. *Supplementary Prayer Book "Guardian of Israel"* (1986).

24. Cited in Liebman, *Deceptive Images.*

25. Jon D. Levinson, *Jewish Perspectives: The Universal Horizon of Biblical Particularism* (New York: 1985), 12.

26. Jonathan S. Woocher, *Sacred Survival: The Civil Religion of American Jews* (Bloomington: 1986), 85.

27. *Ibid.*

28. *Ibid.*

29. Shimon Cooper, "Inversion and Paradox in Purim Celebration." Paper delivered at the 1987 meeting of the American Anthropological Association.

30. *New York Times,* 13 March 1987, C34.

31. *Connecticut Jewish Ledger,* 12 March 1987, 13.

32. Congregation B'nai Jacob, *Purim Service* (n.d.).

33. William D. Dinges, "Ritual Conflict as Social Conflict: Liturgical Reform in the Roman Catholic Church," *Sociological Analysis* 48 (1987), 144.

Heroine or Traitor? The Controversy over Manya Vilbushevich-Shohat and Her Links with Zubatov

Yaacov Goldstein
(UNIVERSITY OF HAIFA)

Early in 1921 the newly formed General Federation of Workers in Eretz Israel—the Histadrut—decided to send a delegation to the United States. This decision, which was implemented later that year, represented the first step in the development of a long-standing relationship between the Histadrut and the Jewish trade unions in America, which eventually expanded to embrace American labor generally.

In the context of the times, it was understandable that the nascent Jewish labor movement in Palestine should try to win the support and goodwill of its counterpart in the United States. The European economy, and especially the European Jews, had suffered enormously from the effects of the First World War. The World Zionist Organization (WZO), with its popular base in war-torn Eastern Europe, was also adversely affected. The extensive Zionist organization in Russia was in the process of being liquidated by the Soviet regime. In Poland, the movement was deeply divided and engaged in a political struggle on several fronts at once: against the Jewish polonizing integrationists, against the anti-Zionist socialists of the Jewish Workers' Bund and against the anti-Zionist Orthodox camp. Elsewhere in Eastern Europe, the Zionists were no better off; in Central and Western Europe, they constituted only a small minority within the local Jewish communities. Together with the Zionist leadership in general, the labor movement in Palestine felt impelled to seek support from American Jewry.[1]

Links between the Poale Zion labor group in Palestine and its sister organization in the United States had been established prior to the First World War.[2] These links were continued by the new labor party, Aḥdut Ha'avodah, when it was formed in 1919 (through a merger of Poale Zion and the "non-party" group). The Ha-Poel ha-Ẓa'ir party similarly sought an American connection through the Tseire Zion. All such contacts, however, remained restricted to a small circle within American Jewish labor. For the most part, the unionized Jewish workers in America had no contact with the labor movement in Palestine or the Zionist movement. The minority of Zionist-oriented unions had failed to capture the imagination of American Jewish workers and their leaders, many of whom took a non-Zionist or even anti-

Zionist position.[3] For its part, the Palestine labor movement had no regular contact with American labor at large.

On November 9, 1917, a week after the Balfour Declaration (which was supported by President Wilson), the convention of the AFL approved a resolution that recognized "the legitimate claims of the Jewish people for the establishment of a national homeland in Palestine on a basis of self-government." This turn of events took many observers by surprise and, indeed, represented a major shift for the organization. Most of the Jewish union leaders within the AFL had opposed such a resolution. It was only the support of a non-Jewish majority, marshaled by Samuel Gompers, that led the AFL to take a pro-Zionist position. The labor federation's resolution reflected its general support for Wilson's policy and for America's entry into the war against the Central Powers.

The Jewish unions had always been characterized by a certain duality, embracing both Jewish causes and socialism. There was an obvious tension here because socialist internationalism could be construed to negate Jewish particularism. But the end of the First World War coincided with a distancing of the unions from doctrinaire socialism, on the one hand, and a heightened sense of Jewish commitment, on the other. This reflected socioeconomic trends in the Jewish population, which was evolving into a middle-class group. The process also reflected trends in American society at large that lent American labor its distinctive, pragmatic character. The collective Jewish awareness that came to the fore during the First World War had swelled Zionist ranks. The same trend had impelled the Jewish unions (as well as the American Jewish Committee) to join the new American Jewish Congress, even though this umbrella organization had been formed largely through Zionist initiative and could be expected to support Zionist positions.

In February 1919 a Congress of Jewish Labor convened in New York. It had been jointly organized by the socialist Zionist Poale Zion and the internationalist unions. A majority of the five hundred delegates were identified with the non-Zionists. The two central issues on the agenda were the Jewish struggle for civil and national equality in Europe and the Balfour Declaration. Although a compromise formula supporting the Balfour Declaration without reference to Zionist principles was reported out of the resolutions committee, it was defeated in the plenum (largely through the efforts of I. B. Salutsky-Hardman).[4]

Nevertheless, the support that non- and anti-Zionists gave the resolution cannot be dismissed lightly. Equally significant was the resolution adopted by the International Ladies' Garment Workers' Union (ILGWU) in 1920, in which the largest Jewish union expressed its appreciation to the British Labour party for supporting the Jewish National Home in Palestine. Yet another resolution in favor of the Balfour Declaration was passed by the other large Jewish union, the Amalgamated Clothing Workers of America (ACWA).

The Jewish unions were undoubtedly influenced by Zionist gains in the world arena and on the American scene. The weakening of the radical socialist ideology in favor of a more pragmatic approach was an added factor in this process. The same trend had led the Jewish unions to support the pro-war policy of the AFL, for example, as opposed to the pacifist, anti-war policy advocated by the American Socialist party to which many Jewish unionists belonged. Trade union solidarity proved stronger than abstract ideology. The Jewish unions' anti-Zionism had, by and large, been a legacy of their Marxist–Bundist ideological roots. The ascendancy of pragmatism over socialist dogma would, therefore, tend to favor Zionism.

Moreover, one ought to take into account the impact on the Jewish unions, as part of a minority ethnic group, of official American sympathy and support for the Balfour Declaration and the Zionist cause. American Jews tended to seek conformity with general American trends and opinion. Jewish support for Zionism was naturally enhanced by the pro-Zionist response of the American government.

Nevertheless, this process was only beginning to take effect in the immediate aftermath of the war. Bundist and general socialist radical tendencies were still quite strong in the Jewish labor movement, prompting it to eschew making common cause with bourgeois Jewish nationalist organizations. That was why an outside group—the Histadrut—was needed to appeal to this sector. The Histadrut claimed the support of fellow socialists for the vision of a new, humanistic and autonomous Jewish society in Palestine. It is largely to the Histadrut's credit that lengthy efforts finally succeeded in allaying Jewish labor's indifference toward and suspicion of the Zionist enterprise. This gradual process succeeded in eliciting support for labor Palestine, and, by extension, for Zionism. The first modest step in this campaign was taken in 1921.

Proposals for a Labor Zionist delegation to the United States had been aired before the founding of the Histadrut, but these had spoken of a party delegation to sister groups in America, not to the non-Zionist Jewish labor constituency in general. The new Histadrut organization took a larger view of the possibilities of such a mission, a view that reflected its non-party character. At its founding conference in Haifa in December 1920, the Histadrut voted in favor of "establishing contact with all institutions, organizations and parties, both Jewish and non-Jewish, both in Palestine and abroad, that may help to strengthen the position of the Hebrew worker and the construction of a labor Palestine. Such contacts shall be only of a practical nature."[5] Two weeks later, at the first meeting of the Histadrut council, a proposal to send a representative to the United States was discussed and approved. According to Berl Katznelson, the proposal was raised by Yitzhak Ben-Zvi.[6] Katznelson himself was his party's choice for undertaking a mission to the United States, but it was thought best that he be sent by the Histadrut as such rather than by only one of its constituent groups. The Histadrut executive council, in its session of January 9, 1921, decided that Katznelson should indeed go as part of a broader delegation.[7]

The events of May 1921 in Palestine, involving the first Arab riots to take place under the British Mandatory administration, shocked the Jewish community and the Zionist movement. This only heightened the importance of sending the delegation to American Jewish labor. (It would appear that in this case, as in so many others in Labor Zionist history in Palestine, it took an external event to prod the movement into implementing steps already decided in principle but somehow left in the planning stage.) The events of May 1921 fostered an atmosphere of urgency and the delegation was finally created. It consisted of Berl Katznelson, Yosef Baratz and Manya Shohat. The Histadrut was to fund the mission.[8]

One of the central objectives of the delegation was to sell shares of the financial arm of the labor movement, the Bank Hapoalim (Workers' Bank).[9] Other, more long-range objectives were of wider import: eliciting support for Labor Zionism and establishing regular communication with American labor.

We may divide the story of the Histadrut delegation into two stages: the first, from November to mid-December 1921 and the second from then until Berl Katznelson left the United States in the summer of 1922, the last of the delegates to do so. During the initial stage, the feeling among the delegation members was one of optimism and achievement. Despite the difficulties they faced, they felt they were succeeding in winning over new sympathizers and that both the short-term and the long-term goals of their mission would be fulfilled. The American Poale Zion rendered them inestimable assistance in organizing their work. Particularly gratifying was the support they encountered among non-labor Zionists, the most prominent among them being Judah Magnes.[10] This was largely the work of Manya Shohat. Through Magnes, she was also able to establish friendly relations with Max Pine of the United Hebrew Trades and Joseph Schlosberg of the Amalgamated. A similar feather in their cap, they thought, was the contact they had established with the influential Yiddish daily, the *Forverts,* and its editor, Abraham Cahan. The delegation believed that it had persuaded Cahan to moderate his paper's critical editorial line on Palestine, perhaps even to adopt a favorable position.[11]

A provisional administrative committee was set up in the United States to work with the delegation. It was composed of Max Pine, H. Ehrenreich and A. Braunstein. Judah Magnes served as treasurer. Afterward, on December 7, an official public committee was formed, the American Workers Committee for the Workers' Bank in Palestine. The committee immediately decided to hold a large public gathering to kick off its campaign for Jewish labor support.[12]

This early momentum was stymied by a critical letter by the Bundist leader, Vladimir Medem,[13] published in the *Forverts* on December 14, 1921, which created a stir and provoked a polemical exchange. The letter attacked the Zionist labor movement in Palestine and Manya Shohat personally.

Medem, who had immigrated to the United States shortly before the arrival of the Histadrut delegation, had been a leading figure in the Bund in prewar Russia. His considerable prestige gave his view rapid currency among Jewish labor circles in America. Medem was upset at the "favoritism" entailed in seeking massive support for the "tiny group" of Jewish workers in Palestine at the expense of hundreds of thousands of needy Jewish workers in Eastern Europe. Those in Palestine certainly deserved American Jewish support, based on Jewish class solidarity, but, he contended, such aid should be strictly proportional to the number of workers involved. By these criteria, the Labor Zionists had already received their fair share and more. Jewish labor must not, he argued, contribute to the Palestine workers' claim to preeminence. Only a commitment to Zionism could justify that claim, and the American Jewish labor movement was far from such a consensus or commitment. As for Manya Shohat, Medem accused her of having at one time collaborated with Sergei Zubatov, a higher-ranking functionary of the Tsarist secret police (the *Okhrana*), in organizing a legal, anti-radical trade union in Russia and of supplying information on her comrades.[14]

Manya Vilbushevich-Shohat, who thus stood accused of working with the hated

Okhrana, was already something of a legend in her own time. Since her days of radical activity in Russia, she had been known as one of the young leaders of the revolutionary movement. The halo of awe that surrounded her had been enhanced by tales of her heroism in Palestine as one of the leaders of the Bar-Giora and Hashomer self-defense organizations.[15] This background will explain the seriousness of Medem's accusation and its dramatic impact. In the ethical world of the revolutionary movement, there was nothing worse than being called a traitor or an informer. In this case, Manya Shohat stood accused of being both.

Manya Shohat challenged Medem to face her before a socialist tribunal of comrades (which did not, however, take place). She herself was not primarily an orator or writer—her strength lay more in deeds than in words—and she did nothing further to follow up the incident. Moreover, her colleagues in the Histadrut mission, Katznelson and Baratz, were not recruited to defend her in the local press, as might have been expected. Among the local figures, it was Yitzhok-Ayzik Hourwich, a prominent member of the American labor movement, who took up the cudgels on her behalf.[16] He continued the debate with Medem in a series of articles in the *Forverts,* in the course of which Medem added further details to his charges. The Poale Zion organization also defended Manya. But the labor Zionist press in Palestine was notably silent on the affair.

The memoirs of Pinhas Shneurson, an active member of Hashomer and a veteran of Aḥdut Ha'avodah, raise a serious charge against Berl Katznelson in this affair. According to Shneurson, the Zionist socialist Nachman Syrkin sent a letter from the United States expressing incredulity at the silence of the Labor Zionist movement and the Histadrut in the face of Medem's allegations. Manya Shohat had, after all, been sent to represent the Histadrut. Syrkin was particularly surprised at the reticence of Katznelson, who was also Shohat's party comrade. Syrkin's letter was discussed in the central committee of Ahdut Ha'avodah, at which Shneurson was present. It was decided to dispatch a telegram of "indignation and support to Manya" in the name of the party, the Histadrut, the Labor Battalion (Gedud Ha'avodah) and Kfar Giladi, Manya's kibbutz. Ben-Gurion took this task upon himself. Shneurson, who was treasurer of Kfar Giladi, states that he supplied money for this purpose; when no telegram was sent, he was left with no choice but to resign from the central committee.[17]

Berl Katznelson's position on the controversy emerges from his letters as well as from the "American diary" that he kept at the time. He claimed to have foreseen, or at least suspected, that the Bundists and other anti-Zionists in the labor movement would exploit Shohat's past in order to pillory the Histadrut mission.

> I told Manya before we left, I begged her not to go, but she just laughed and brushed it off, with that absolute, childish, naive and stupid self-confidence of hers. Now I have no idea how the affair will end. In America it is very hard to establish one's innocence."[18]

Katznelson wanted to hush the matter up and to protest Shohat's irresponsible behavior. As he saw it, she had played right into the hands of the enemies of Zionism: "This is an excellent gimmick [for the Bundists] to bury us in the public eye. . . ."[19]

Medem . . . pulled this trick out of his hat, which is based on the information in Michalevich's book.[20] . . . It is immaterial whether or not Medem himself believes it. It is the old Bundist [ideological] hostility coming out. . . . I do not believe that after ten years of silence the facts can be fully determined and the stain removed.[21]

The allegations about Shohat were based on a series of events that began at the end of 1899 when the nineteen-year-old Manya Vilbushevich, as she was then, was arrested and sent to a Moscow prison. There she encountered Sergei Zubatov, a leading figure in the *Okhrana*. During the course of their discussions, they spoke of the role that legal trade unions might legitimately play in Russian society. They could, Zubatov argued, improve working conditions—shorter hours, more hygienic conditions and higher wages—as long as they kept out of politics. Zubatov guaranteed that the government would not oppose the struggle of such unions against their employers.

On her release from prison in July 1900, Manya Vilbushevich undertook to form the Independent Jewish Workers' Party. Its founding conference, held with official government approval, took place in Minsk in July 1901 Vilbushevich was a prominent leader of the group and a member of its central committee. The organization was acive for two years, until the authorities reneged on their previous commitments and took steps to liquidate it.

Manya Vilbushevich-Shohat remained convinced of the sincerity of Zubatov's intentions and of his sympathy for the goals of the Independent Jewish Workers' Party. She stuck to this view even when, after the Bolshevik Revolution, documents were published that showed that Zubatov had submitted reports to his superiors on his contacts with her, including details of her and her comrades' activities that she had supplied to him.

It was this episode, lasting from 1900 to 1903, that Medem had dredged up. In point of fact, there was no argument over Manya's contact with Zubatov. The polemics centered on the question of whether she, in her role as witting or unwitting informer, had transmitted information that was detrimental to the workers' movement and its leaders. This charge was difficult to prove or refute with any clarity, so that each side remained fixed in its own position. The affair served as ammunition for Medem and his supporters to snipe at the Labor Zionists in general and at the Histadrut mission—as the representative of labor Palestine—in particular.

I present here eight documents—excerpts from articles that appeared in the *Forverts* and *Di Tsayt* (the Labor Zionist daily edited by David Pinsky) from 1921 to 1922—which shed light on this affair and convey its highly emotional and ideological character. It is also a colorful illustration of the deep and bitter divisions that characterized the Jewish labor movement, divisions going back at least to the Russian Pale of Settlement in the 1890s, which were still very much alive in New York in the 1920s.

Documents

1. The *Forverts*, 14 December 1921

Some Remarks About the Zionist Workers' Delegation

BY VLADIMIR MEDEM

Several months ago a delegation from Palestine arrived with the intention of collecting funds here, in America, for a workers' bank.

Zionists from Palestine coming to Zionists in America—how cozy! What they do is their own business, of course. We have no interest in that. But now they have found a platform from which to address the socialist public at large. Dr. Magnes has written a letter to the *Forverts* endorsing his Zionist friends and calling upon the Jewish labor movement in this country to "give them a hearty welcome," hear them out and support them. This cannot pass without comment.

Dr. Magnes is, as he puts it, a "lover of Zion." Eretz Israel appeals to his "historical and religious sensibilities." Had he simply addressed himself to those who share these sensibilities, who feel the same love and aspirations, this would, again, have bothered nobody. But for that kind of appeal he would not have received space in the *Forverts*. What he goes on to say is that he is not presenting an appeal on Zionist grounds, but simply on the grounds that workers from Palestine have come to speak to workers in America, whose help they deserve. "This is not a matter of Zionism or anti-Zionism" [he states].

I myself am an opponent of Zionism. But that does not mean that I wish to punish the few Jewish workers in Palestine for their Zionist sympathies. I do not place them in any separate category: they are workers like all others and should be treated like all others. What I find objectionable in Dr. Magnes's appeal is that he, indeed, places his Palestinian friends in a separate category.

When American Jewish workers send help to their brothers overseas, that is a worthy, important and necessary act. This task, though, must be implemented rationally and with a sense of fairness. There should not and must not be a privileged group of haves and an underprivileged group of have-nots. Across the Atlantic there are hundreds of thousands of Jewish workers who need assistance. Who should receive that assistance? All of them. In what amounts and in what proportions? There can only be one answer to that: help must be sent according to the criteria of need and the numbers of people involved. How many Jewish workers are there in Palestine? Dr. Magnes quotes a figure of ten thousand. This is an exaggeration, but let us grant him the ten thousand. That still represents a negligible percentage of the European masses. Do they deserve first consideration when it comes to [American] assistance?

What is actually involved here? When the People's Relief[22] allocates funding, the Palestinians always receive a disproportional amount. I wouldn't begrudge them the money but for the fact that each extra dollar that goes to them is taken away from others, and this is an injustice. That, however, is not the end of the matter. During the past year the local Poale Zion, with the help of our own People's Relief, have carried out a campaign to raise funds for farm implements for Eretz Israel.[23] I do not know the precise amount that was sent to Palestine, but it is surely greater than the total amount sent to Europe in the same period. Ten thousand people received more than hundreds of thousands did. Where is the fair play in this? And still they are not satisfied. Again they arrive to pass around the alms box, and yet again they want to appeal to our labor organizations for aid to Eretz Israel. What about the masses of workers in Poland, Lithuania, Latvia, Romania and Russia—in those countries which contain the vast majority of the Jewish people and of the Jewish working class; in those countries where the workers' organizations are doing such wonderful work and are on their last legs because American aid has lately become so limited and grudging?

Ten thousand workers: that is equivalent to the labor force of one medium-sized European city. What would one say if such a to-do were constantly made about just one city and tens of thousands of dollars were always being demanded for this handful of people? One would say that this was madness. But apparently it is thought quite acceptable to speak and write about the few Palestinians! And this is not a matter of Zionism or anti-Zionism? . . . It most assuredly is!

Let the Zionists go to the Zionists. The American labor movement, however, has no stake in this matter. The American labor movement must assist those who need it the most. The Palestinians account for perhaps two or three percent [of all Jewish workers]. They have already received several hundredfold of what is their due. It is time to call a stop. It is time to fulfill our obligations toward those in the European countries.

These brief comments might have sufficed had not Dr. Magnes also made a point of speaking of the persons who comprise the Zionist delegation. I am perforce obligated to make a statement about one of them.

Among the Zionist delegates is a certain Manya Vilbushevich. Older members of the [Jewish labor] movement will recall the Zubatov episode. Zubatov was in charge of the Okhrana in Moscow and led the legion of spies and gendarmes who flooded the Jewish cities in an attempt to uproot the Jewish workers' movement. He arrested Manya Vilbushevich, he lured her into his net, she became his partner, his helper. Never mind that while in prison she "spilled the beans" about everything she knew. He [Zubatov] had her freed, sent her off to Minsk and there she served him for many months. The public knew that her politics had become warped, but it was not known how far she in fact had gone. People trusted her and she took advantage of that trust to send Zubatov detailed reports [*mesires*] about conspiratorial matters about which she had learned.

After the revolution of 1917 her letters to Zubatov were published, and that was when it was discovered that she had been an agent provocateur. Her "record" is now known. If it should be required, I would be happy to provide the details.

[In due course] she left for Palestine. She was forgotten and no one would care now to dig up ancient history, had she kept a low profile in some obscure corner.

Someone with that kind of chapter in her life ought to know her place. Let her do what she wants, go where she wants, but let her not climb onto the public stage—not among the workers.

I am sure that Dr. Magnes has no concept of these facts. I am equally sure, however, that the local Poale Zionists are well aware of them. And the Poale Zionist press welcomed her in the warmest terms as "the best spokesperson the Palestine workers could wish for." That is not only nonsense, but downright cynical [illegible in all copies checked—Y.G.].

2. The *Forverts,* 16 December 1921

A Letter from Manya Vilbushevich:
She Demands that Medem Face Her
Before a Court of Honor

Worthy Editor—In the *Forverts* of 14 December Vladimir Medem accused me of provocation on the basis of my letters to Zubatov.

It has been no secret that during the period of the Independent Movement[24] (the so-called "Zubatovshchina") I, as a leader of that movement, corresponded with Zubatov.

That was done with the knowledge of the central committee of the party, many members of which now belong to communist and socialist parties.

I publicly state before the entire socialist world that the accusation against me is *absolutely false*. It is impossible, however, to fully explain the matter in polemical articles and letters. I therefore demand that Vladimir Medem be brought before a court of honor of socialist leaders so that the entire truth can be examined.

Yitzhok-Ayzik Hourwich would represent me at such an occasion. His address is 110 West 40th Street, New York.

> Respectfully,
> Manya Shohat-Vilbushevich

Mrs. Shohat (Vilbushevich) brought this letter to our editorial offices and we are printing it exactly as she wrote it. Still, we do not quite understand why Mrs. Vilbushevich wants to summon Mr. Medem to an honor court over this kind of question, which is . . . of a purely public nature. The question is: did she in fact write to Zubatov, then the head of the gendarmerie in Russia? Did she or did she not [write] such a letter in which [secrets] of the revolutionaries were revealed? If she did, then Mr. Medem has nothing to answer for, since his criticism was simply that a person who had done such a thing ought not to be [in a position] dealing with workers.

To our own question she made the following reply:

The charges against her were made in the Russian revolutionary journal, *Byloe*[25] three years ago. The charge is a grave one, indeed. Names are mentioned of revolutionaries whom, according to *Byloe,* she gave away to Zubatov. It is also charged that she revealed the existence of a secret printing press.

"Finally I shall have an opportunity to explain this affair once and for all. I have waited for this chance for twenty years. But it is difficult to explain matters before the public at large. The public is not acquainted with many details which must be explained and would not be readily understood. For those few people who are well acquainted with the circumstances, I will be delighted to provide this explanation."

When we asked why she did not issue this explanation three years ago when *Byloe* published the charges, she answered: "That was just at the high point [i.e., the worst point] of the war when such explanations were impossible." She then added the following words:

"It is only natural that Medem should hold the opinion he does, but I do not understand why he chose to air his views in this form."

In conclusion we should like to note that in her words, "that was done with the knowledge of the central committee of the party, many members of which now belong to communist and socialist parties," she is referring to the party founded by Zubatov.

Many Bundists say that among those accused is someone who is now active as a communist in Russia, but that he had been pardoned by the Bund and accepted once again in their party [after the Zubatov episode].

Among the charges against Mrs. Vilbushevich is that she reported that the fourth conference of the Bund would take place in Bialystok, and he [Zubatov] promptly dispatched spies, but they were unable to discover the exact whereabouts of the meeting. . . .

The Editor

3. The *Forverts,* 20 December 1921

Mr. Medem Responds:
A Reaction to Mrs. Vilbushevich's Offer to Meet Him
Before a Court of Honor

In my article published in Wednesday's *Forverts* I acquainted the socialist public in America with Mrs. Shohat (Manya Vilbushevich) and stated that she was a former co-worker of Zubatov, not only in the political sense but in police matters as well. . . . Now Mrs. Vilbushevich has published a letter to the Editor of the *Forverts* in which she declares that this accusation is "absolutely false." Indeed?! Then allow me to point out some facts.

A few quotes from a letter that she wrote on August 2, 1900 to Zubatov, published in 1917, will suffice. I have before me the full text of the letter, as it appears in B. Michalevich's book, *Memoirs of a Jewish Socialist.* The letter is too long to be reprinted in full (it takes up nine pages in the book). I shall cite only a few selected excerpts.

1. "I had a long, involved conversation with Gershuni. . . .[26] When I asked him what his plans were, he answered that he would use every opportunity for legal activities that you [Zubatov] would provide, but at the same time, parallel with that, he would continue to carry on illegal activities, though in Central Russia rather than among the Jews."

2. "I should also note that you have made a grave mistake in speaking so freely with people (though you may have done so deliberately, I cannot know this). You have let everyone know our most important matters. Since they do not know that I am the chief 'traitor', they are accusing each other of talking too much, or even, some of them, charging others with being provocateurs."

3. "Since I had not met S. in Minsk, I decided to stop and see him in Vilna for a few hours. . . . When Zhenya Hourvich[27] and Ruderman found out, they gave me the following message: 'Don't tell [him?] anything' (they are wary of him, though why they trust me I don't know). They said that I should only ask him to take me to see someone close to the movement in Vilna. When I'd made contact, I should tell him to relay the message that Evgenii Gorelik is being closely watched, and that spies are following him everywhere he goes."

4. "If I am ever convinced that you are not what I took you for, then I will confess to one and all that I was a provocateur."

Twenty years have passed since the day that letter was written. The author of that letter must certainly have become convinced since then that Zubatov was not what she "took him for." She has had ample time to fulfill her pledge and confess that she was a provocateur. Instead, she brazenly denies the whole thing. So, I took it upon myself to make the promised announcement for her. . . .

4. *Di Tsayt*,[28] 2 February 1922

V. Burtsev[29] *on Manya Shohat*

BY M. ANIUTIN

I was revolted by the ugly, jesuitical defamation issued by comrade Medem against comrade Manya Shohat. Is his hatred for Palestine and Zionism so powerful that it overwhelms his sense of decency and any moral scruples?

The least particle of objectivity would have prevented Medem from defaming a woman whose only crime was her unbridled enthusiasm.

The Zubatovshchina[30] is well enough known by now. We know who its leaders were, including the Jewish ones. Volin[31] became a Syndicalist. He wrote pamphlets, and no one attacked him as an agent provocateur. Chemeriskii[32] returned after the Zubatovshchina to activity in the Bund. At present, he is quite active among the Communists in Russia, and no one accuses him of having been a provocateur. This should apply as much if not more to Manya Vilbushevich, who retained the trust of even those who opposed her and regretted her involvement. Even Michalevich, author of *Memoirs of a Jewish Socialist*—himself an anti-Zionist and a Zionist-baiter—even he did not go so far as to level such a charge against her. He writes that Zubatov exerted a "magnetic power" over Manya Vilbushevich, and that she developed a "passionate" belief in him. Regarding the letter which Medem has cited, Michalevich writes that it does not reveal the entire story of the secret relations between the "exalted young girl from Minsk and the inveterate Moscow superspy. It is full of hints and innuendoes which may be *variously* interpreted. . . ."

That is the verdict of an anti-Zionist who still wishes to retain some degree of historical perspective.

Medem, however, is a partisan demagogue, and will stoop to any level to besmirch Zionism, even to using dirty methods.

I wish to report to the readers of *Di Tsayt* the views expressed by Vladimir Burtsev on the subject. Regardless of one's feelings about Burtsev's position, he is still the acknowledged expert in this field. He examined the records of the police section, and had contact with Zubatov himself after the revolution.

Here is his statement, transcribed word for word:

This is the statement given by Vladimir Burtsev to Mr. M. Yarblum in the presence of Dr. Pasmanek regarding Manya Vilbushevich.

—*Yarblum:* Do you believe that Manya Vilbushevich was a provocateur?

—*Burtsev:* We never thought of Manya Vilbushevich as a provocateur. We did not include her in that category. We knew that she had worked with Zubatov, and that Zubatov was a provocateur. We regretted that Manya Vilbushevich worked with him. She agreed with his approach, opposing the political revolutionaries by setting up legal economic organizations with the permission and assistance of the police. By doing this she interfered with and brought harm to the revolutionary movement.

—*Yarblum:* Did she betray revolutionaries to the police?

—*Burtsev:* No. We don't know of a single instance of that. It is quite possible that in her dealings with Zubatov she spoke of and described people, criticizing their activities, etc. However, that was done not to betray them to the police, but only in the context of discussing the issues and pointing out her opposition to their methods. In any case, she was no provocateur. Just as Lev Tikhomirov was no provocateur, though he was also a supporter of police socialism. The only reproach against Manya Vilbushevich is that she dealt with Zubatov, who was a provocateur.

—*Yarblum:* Were the copies [of documents] found in the police records always identical to the originals?

—*Burtsev:* Almost always identical, though there were exceptions, when the copies appear to have been tampered with a bit. In the case of Manya Vilbushevich, I recall that there were some doubts about the copy, but I cannot recall precisely.

5. The *Forverts,* 4 February 1922

Myth and Fact About the Famous Spy Zubatov

BY V. MEDEM

Over the last month I have received letters from several friends and acquaintances, asking me why did I not reply to the Poale Zion pack of vilifiers. The readers of the *Forverts* probably are unaware of the fact that after I trod on Zionist toes by revealing the truth about the sad case of the notorious Manya Vilbushevich, that whole crowd has been screaming for my blood. I have kept my peace, and I have no intention of entering into a polemic with that bunch. To do so would dignify their wild ravings.

If you are accosted by a drunken goy while crossing the street, or if a common fishwife shouts something coarse at you, or if a [Nachman] Syrkin tries to bite you on the heel (because that is as high as he can reach), or if some other trash sticks to your shoes—you would not stop to argue with them over it. You just go on your way, and that's that. And that is what I have done and will do in the future.

Some interesting aspects have nevertheless come to light as a result of all this, and deserve mention. Also, several honorable people, with whom I do not hesitate to enter into a discussion, have written accounts of the events as they remember them and have reminded us once again of the entire almost-forgotten "Zubatovshchina." Their descriptions contain a few inaccuracies, which deserve to be pointed out and corrected. That is what I propose to do.

Two of my former compatriots have recently published articles about the episode—A. Litvin in *Di Tsayt* and S. Rabinovich in *Der Veker*—and both fall prey to the same error. Litvin somehow has turned the Zubatovshchina into a kind of giant, a phenomenon that embraced "tens of thousands of people." And Rabinovich has turned Zubatov into a veritable sorcerer, a creature with almost demonic powers.

Rabinovich writes:

"Zubatov was tall, lean, dark-haired and had piercing eyes. He was quite young at the time, and women certainly found him attractive." And this "handsome devil" bewitched "many self-respecting Bundist activists, from branch committee members up to [members of] the central committee."

As you can see, this borders on the legendary: a portrait of a charismatic figure who developed an entourage of thousands, all of whom trumpeted his gospel over that of the Bundist committees and leaders. A figure of heroic proportions indeed!

It is psychologically fascinating to see a myth take shape before one's very eyes, to see human memory become enthralled by sheer fantasy.

One minor detail, perhaps, but one worth noting nonetheless: the honorable Mr. Rabinovich has radically transformed Zubatov's appearance. The picture he paints is diametrically opposed to the facts.

I knew Zubatov by sight. I have spoken with him on two occasions, and I have an excellent memory for faces and for people's looks. But, just to be sure, I checked with someone who spent a year and a half with Zubatov, and he absolutely confirmed my own remembered impression. Zubatov was not tall, not lean and not dark. He was neither handsome nor young. He was of medium build, blond, with blond mustache and side-whiskers. His face was pasty-gray, ordinary—the face of an average middle-level bureaucrat. His age may be judged from the fact that in the eighties already, some fifteen years before the period that concerns us, he was active as a provocateur.

He never had tens of thousands of supporters. The entire "Independent" party consisted of a handful of *polu-intelligenty* [half-educated intelligentsia] in one city alone—Minsk. Not one of the central activists of the time was bewitched by him, let alone members of the central committee, all of whom, without exception, considered him a dangerous gendarme. Among the branch committee members, whom Rabinovich mentions, only two were placed under arrest at the time. Zubatov was completely unsuccessful at wooing the first of them. He did actually worm some scrap of paper out of the second, in which he undertook to discontinue his activity—but he was never a Zubatov-man. No one in the Zubatovshchina was in a leading position of any kind in the Bundist movement. They were either ex-members or other camp followers. At the time, I myself was on the Minsk committee, and I knew all the people there.

Litvin cites a passage from Michalevich's memoir, where he speaks of Gershuni and the latter's attitude to Zubatov:

"Gershuni (we read there) was greatly impressed by Zubatov, and for some time after his release in 1901 still dreamed that Zubatov was sincere about his plans."

Gershuni's good name is too dear to me, I cannot let this pass. Michalevich is simply mistaken; he was not even in Minsk at the time. I was there and was on close friendly terms with Gershuni. On the day after his release from prison (by the way, this was not in 1901 but in the summer of 1900—by early 1901 he had left Minsk, gone underground, had no further dealings with Zubatov), Gershuni came to see me at the "cottage" (a few *versts* outside of town) and told me at length his impressions of Zubatov. He had no delusions about that man. He told me that Zubatov was dangerously clever. That is all. There could not have been any question of his believing in Zubatov's supposed sincerity.

Soon afterward, in fact, the Bund published its famous proclamation against Zubatov. With the exception of a handful of callow youths, all honest revolutionaries shunned him completely and gave him a wide berth.

That is point number one. Now about a second point, which has a direct bearing on the Vilbushevich matter.

From the very first my point has been, not that she was among those infected by Zubatov's ideas: one may forgive false consciousness, if the person involved repents of it afterward (though to this very day I have no idea whether or not she feels any remorse). Rather, I pointed out that she was not merely an ideological follower of Zubatov the politician, Zubatov the monarchist, but also a partner of Zubatov the agent for the Okhrana. She submitted secret reports about the revolutionary activity of the Bund, and thus helped him in his police work.

And this is the interesting part. Normally, if a member of a party is caught doing that sort of thing, even if there is only a hint of suspicion that that person is a provocateur, the party is duty-bound, quite understandably, to take the necessary steps against her. For the party this is a matter of simple honesty and integrity.

Just a few days ago I read the editorial in *Di Tsayt* of 28 January, which states:

It is customary that when someone in a position of trust is charged with graft, and an investigation is launched, the accused is temporarily suspended. He is under a cloud of suspicion, and as long as he has not been cleared he cannot remain at his post. If he is innocent, he will return with honor; if he is guilty, then he ought to have been removed anyway. That is the accepted norm in the honest world.

Yes, indeed, that is the norm in the honest world. And not only in cases of alleged corruption, but certainly also—perhaps most of all—in a case of alleged provocation. But how has *Di Tsayt* behaved in the Vilbushevich matter? Precisely the opposite. It has taken the accused under its protective wing, enshrined her as a heroine, bathed in waves of affection a person who has been publicly charged with having been a provocateur. In four years, no one has denied this.

You say that these people do not believe in her guilt? Oh, they believe it alright. If they did not believe it, they would at least have to follow their own advice and "suspend" her until the charge was fully investigated. But they know full well that the charge is true.

Though any honest socialist with healthy revolutionary feelings must feel his gorge rise in such a case, this feeling is totally alien to them. What do they know of revolutionary traditions? What do they have in common with revolutionary ethics? How can people who inhabit a mental world of Zionist adventurism understand socialist morality? All that they know is Zionist "unity."

It is . . . interesting. Only a few weeks ago there was the affair of the pact between the Zionist leader Jabotinsky and the blood-stained Petliura,[33] of which *Di Tsayt* wrote in friendly, comradely terms. At *Di Tsayt* they do not even agree with Jabotinsky, but they could not find in their lexicon even one courageous, blunt word to properly label this criminally disgusting act by one of their generals. But when it comes to a socialist who has denounced an act of provocation, he becomes a ready target for their invective; because Jabotinsky the Zionist, the loyal officer of the king of England, is one of their own, and Medem the socialist belongs to an alien, hostile world.

I prefer it that way. I am proud of their enmity. But this small incident should show everyone exactly what these people are. And it is high time that the Jewish workers' movement came to appreciate how such people are trying to take a free ride at its expense. These uninvited guests have no place among Jewish workers.

In the last few weeks the smear-campaigners at *Di Tsayt* appear to have wearied of barking at me. Maybe they have exhausted their supply of spleen and slime. Too bad. Perhaps with these few remarks I will be throwing them a new bone. So go ahead and bark!

6. *Di Tsayt*, 25 February 1922

Statement by the Central Committee of Poale Zion Regarding Medem's Accusations Against Manya Shohat

On 6 February there appeared in *Di Tsayt* a long account by Dr. Y. A. Hourwich regarding Manya Shohat's conflict with Vladimir Medem.

Since then, our comrade Manya Shohat has appealed in writing to the central committee of the Poale Zion party, asking that we assemble a court of honor to investigate the entire affair.

We herewith present comrade Shohat's letter and our reply.

MANYA SHOHAT'S LETTER:

8th February 1922

To the central committee of the Jewish Socialist Workers' Party "Poale Zion" of the United States and Canada, honored comrades:

As you know, V. Medem has categorically refused to submit his complaint against me to a court of honor. However, since the repercussions of his complaint have interfered with the work of the Eretz Israel Workers' Bank, I appeal to you as a fellow-member of Poale Zion, and ask that the central committee take the initiative and set up a nonpartisan tribunal to deal with the charges imputed to me.

I am sure that my explanations will put an end to the legend that I betrayed revolutionary comrades to the tsarist regime, and so forth.

Should you accept my proposal, I will send a letter of resignation to the workers' movement in Eretz Israel, which sent me here.

Respectfully yours,
Manya Shohat

The reply of the central committee of Poale Zion:

New York, 15th February 1922

To comrade Manya Shohat, New York

Dear and esteemed comrade Manya Shohat,
The central committee, in its meeting of Monday, 13th February, has read your letter of 8th February in which you ask the committee to undertake to set up a nonpartisan tribunal to deal with the charges made against you by Mr. Medem.

The central committee of the American Poale Zion party must turn down the proposal that it take the initiative to establish a court to deal with your case, for the following reasons:

For ourselves, we require no trial. Neither the central committee nor the party needs to have further proof of your political integrity and purity. You have worked for our cause over the course of eighteen years and we are thoroughly cognizant of your devotion, your cooperative spirit and your heroic efforts on behalf of the interests of the Jewish proletariat.

For the rest of the public, we also see no need for a trial, because public opinion in America knows full well that V. Medem has not cast aspersions upon you as such, but upon the Jewish workers' movement in Eretz Israel. You only served as a pretext for him to attack the Workers' Bank and the work for Eretz Israel.

A court of honor to judge between yourself and V. Medem would be appropriate, as Dr. Y. A. Hourwich has on several occasions proposed. But Mr. Medem has for various reasons declined to participate in such proceedings.

We therefore categorically refuse to hold a trial over your case and we reject the false accusations made against you by V. Medem.

The central committee, speaking in the name of the entire Poale Zion party, expresses its full confidence in you and respect for you as a member of our movement and as a comrade-in-arms in the struggle for the great ideal of Jewish and workers' liberation.

With our greatest regard, for the central committee of the Jewish Workers' Party "Poale Zion" of America,

A. Hemlin
General Secretary

7. The *Forverts*, 6 April 1922

In Conclusion: The Question of Mrs. Vilbushevich

BY V. MEDEM

The material which I submitted in my two previous articles should have made the Vilbushevich affair abundantly clear. I have now only to add a few observations.

I have just received a letter from Russia. I had written to several acquaintances who work at the Museum of the Revolution in Petrograd. One of them is in fact Zaslavsky,[34] the same man who first published the material about M. Vilbushevich in *Byloe*. He tells me that he is prepared to make an official affidavit, and that he will send it to me shortly. In the meantime, he writes as follows about Mrs. Vilbushevich:

Her excuses are simply absurd. It was not just one isolated letter from her to Zubatov that came to light. The journal (*Byloe*) had in its possession the entire Zubatov correspondence with the police: dozens of letters, documents, telegrams. The copies did not arouse any cause for doubt. They bear the notations made by Zvoliansky [director of police—V. M.] and the other high-ranking spies. Only a demented person would suggest that these are false or imaginary. In no case have they been published exactly word for word. . . . I would take upon myself full responsibility for the article about Vilbushevich. Unfortunately I am far from America. . . . You are suffering [the consequences] and reaping the "compliments" which by right should be directed to me.

The Poale Zion's role in this has been ugly. Without investigating the matter—having no intention of doing so—it has declared its solidarity with its "comrade." Now they must share her ignominious position.

All is out in the open. Dr. Hourwich has said something to the effect that . . . Vilbushevich was not . . . an "ordinary" provocateur. An "ordinary" one—that is, a paid one. I have never said that she took money from Zubatov for the work she did. She did not do it as a job; she served gratis. In my first article, in the *Forverts* of 14 December, I stated the following:

He arrested Manya Vilbushevich, he lured her into his net, she became his partner, his helper. Never mind that while in prison she "spilled the beans" about everything she knew. He [Zubatov] had her freed, sent her off to Minsk and there she served him for many months. The public knew that her politics had become warped, but it was not known how far she in fact had gone. People trusted her and she took advantage of that trust to send Zubatov detailed reports about conspiratorial matters about which she had learned.

Zaslavsky's materials show black on white that this description is absolutely accurate. There is no reason to believe that Vilbushevich accepted money from Zubatov for the work she did. There is even mention of a "debt": in a letter dated the 18th August she asks him [Zubatov], "Did they bring you my debt?" On another occasion he gave her 100 rubles for the purchase of literature (that is what he stated in his report to the police for the month of November), but this is not a clear indication of anything. She actually worked for nothing, but that does not change the nature of that work. She literally dropped huge numbers of names and addresses, with notes added:

"This one is an agitator; that one is a propagandist; this one writes proclamations, he has an illegal lithograph machine; that one should be arrested; that one should be arrested as soon as possible. . . ."

If these are not denunciations, if this is not provocation, then nothing is. This woman was in up to her neck in the police slime.

After I had revealed these discoveries to the American public, the Zionist gang took up the cudgels in defense of their "comrade." They poured heaps of offal over me. They made me out to be a liar. Their intention has been quite clear. But they have made the swindle too obvious, and it won't hold water. Any honest person knows what to believe.

One would only ask: will not a solitary soul in the Zionist camp show a healthy, human sense of decency and be nauseated by the whole affair? One expects nothing from the Zionist writers and the Zionist politicians—they are too far gone. They have to back up one of their own. There may be those who simply do not comprehend what I am asking of them, who see nothing wrong in Vilbushevich's "innocent" letters. That is understandable. For such people, betrayal and denunciation is a praiseworthy occupation. But is there among all of them not one person who feels the need to speak the truth?

I believe that this concludes the matter.

8. *Di Tsayt,* 14 February 1922

A Crime Motivated by Enmity to Zionism

BY DR. N. SYRKIN[35]

Seldom has the public witnessed a deed as ugly as the slander by that Zionist-baiter, Medem, against the Jewish socialist, Manya Vilbushevich. And the more the public demands that justice be done, the deeper, morally and spiritually, the slanderer sinks; the wider he spreads his net of lies and slanders, the viler and more arrogant become his despicable opinion and pose.

Medem naturally knows quite well that Manya Vilbushevich is no provocateur, that she betrayed no one, that she was only a victim of a political situation that led thousands of others astray as well—half of the Bund in a number of cities. Medem's slander, however, is directed against Zionism. It is meant to blacken the name of the workers in Eretz Israel, to poison the unfortunate minds of his unwitting readers, whom Medem and his friends have been driving for years into spiritual isolation.

Medem is invited to have his day in court, he is given the dignity of a chance to present his case before being judged; but Medem fears going before a court, because in such a forum all his lies will melt away and disintegrate. In attempting to free himself from this challenge, he spins further lies.

Manya Vilbushevich, the liar and slanderer claims, has already been convicted, she has been revealed long ago as a provocateur: how can he, as a socialist, stand with her before a court of honor? Ask him where, when and by whom was Vilbushevich accused of being a provocateur? Isn't it the case, in fact, that the Russian socialists and Medem's own documents leave the impression that Vilbushevich was led politically astray but that she was an honest and pure socialist? Medem replies: You make me laugh. I am not afraid of you, so bark, Jew-boys, bark! When a Jewish hoodlum turns renegade, is baptized and dons a police uniform, he also faces Jewish society and says: you make me laugh, I am not afraid of you, so bark, Jew-boys, bark! Thus, we have a deeper understanding of Medem and his pedigree.

Medem bases his slander against Manya Vilbushevich on her own exculpating letter to Zubatov written in 1900. The letter was translated in volume 2 of Michalevich's memoirs (Warsaw, 1921). From this letter, if indeed Vilbushevich wrote it the way it appears (which any honest person can see is a valid question), Medem takes out of context a few quotations and reads into them the product of his own miserable mind. Were he honest, a true defender of the public, he would have reported how Michalevich himself characterized Vilbushevich and the entire Zubatov movement. This, of course, he is afraid to do, because if he did that his entire slander would fall to pieces.

Medem the Honorable, who fights for the Truth, will certainly have no objection if we reproduce part of Michalevich's description of the events. . . .

Michalevich writes about Vilbushevich's relationship to Zubatov as follows:

> The practiced Moscow provocateur exercised a truly magnetic power over her. He played the role of a martyr, of someone who suffers because of his ideas. He would complain to her that he was caught "between two fires." His young interlocutor would be literally melted by his honeyed words. Her belief in Zubatov became a passion. She took him for a great man who had been called to save Russia.

Manya Vilbushevich was not the only one who was led astray by Zubatov. Gershuni, a talented revolutionary, also became a strong believer in Zubatov. This is what Michalevich writes:

> Even as practical a personality as Grigori Gershuni [later the leader of the Socialist-Revolutionary party] was greatly impressed by Zubatov, and for some time after his release still (in 1901) believed that Zubatov was sincere in his plans (*Memoirs*, p. 6).

Michalevich describes the impact that Zubatov had in leading masses of Bundists astray, all of whom truly hoped that through political neutrality they would achieve legalization for the Jewish workers' movement. The legal unions movement spread rapidly throughout southern Russia, but led to mass demonstrations and arrests. Zubatov's experiment quickly fell out of favor in high places, and Plehve ordered Zubatov sent under police supervision to one of the central Russian provinces. After the Kishinev pogrom, when the political climate became overheated, there was no longer any latent support for legal unionism.

The "Independents," as the Zubatovites used to call themselves, liquidated themselves, publicly declaring their own dissolution in July 1903. The Minsk committee of the Bund issued an appeal to them to return to the ranks of the Bund. Among the leaders of the Zubatov movement were Y. Volin, who became a Syndicalist, and Mashe Chemeriskii, who returned to the Bund and served on the Bund's committee in Lodz.[36] Manya Vilbushevich left for Palestine and became active in Aḥdut Ha'avodah (*Memoirs*, pp. 1–21).

But what does Medem the Honorable do? He mentions none of this entire truthful account. He covers up the fact that the Bund accepted the whole Zubatovite party back again into its ranks; that the Zubatovite leader Chemeriskii was later a member of the Lodz committee of the Bund; that no one ever accused these leading Zubatov supporters of having been provocateurs; that there is no record of a single case of any of the Zubatov supporters having betrayed people to the police. In the entire literature to be found in *Byloe*, Vilbushevich is nowhere mentioned as a provocateur, even though this was after the entire Zubatov episode was investigated.

Burtsev, the expert in these matters, states openly that Manya Vilbushevich had, according to all the revelations regarding the Zubatov movement, nothing to do with provocation. But Medem the Truthful, in his slander-mongering, has seized upon a letter written by Manya Vilbushevich to Zubatov in 1900, which appears in the memoirs. It is a dramatic letter by a struggling soul, no longer sure whether she can still believe in Zubatov or whether he is no more than a careerist and a swindler. She asks him to tell her the whole truth. She writes that she had come close to killing him in her worst moments of doubt.

The letter is naive, trusting, but also threatening, making it clear that there would be a price to pay for manipulating her. One sees in that letter the suffering of an honest, misled child, wrestling with an onslaught of doubts, possibilities, desires. She mentions people—Gershuni, Zhenya Hurvich, Ruderman, Shachanovich—but these are all people with whom Zubatov had already had dealings, who were personally in touch with him.

There is about this letter the air of a purely personal outpouring. It is dominated throughout by a spirit of moral restlessness. Anyone who reads it even once gains the strongest impression that in all that soul-baring, there is not the slightest whiff of betrayal.

Let honest people read the letter and Michalevich's account, and they will reject with moral revulsion that interpretation, according to which Vilbushevich was a traitor. It is quite clear that the Bund never considered the Zubatovites traitors. It accepted the great mass of them back into its organizations. . . . Indeed, the Bund never even made an accusation against Manya Vilbushevich. . . . Even Michalevich does not say, in explaining the letter, that Vilbushevich ever betrayed anyone to the police. The great Zionist-baiter did not seize upon this blameless letter (which is not yet proven genuine). The Zionist-baiter Michalevich makes no complaint against the Aḥdut Ha'avodah activist on the basis of this letter. He writes that this letter is "full of hints and innuendoes which may be *variously* interpreted. . . ." (*Memoirs,* p. 22).

But Medem the Honest did not choose to "interpret" this blameless letter written by a suffering young girl "variously"; instead, stooping as low as he could go, he uses it in order to charge her as a provocateur. Medem, however, is the only one in the whole socialist movement who has made this accusation; and Vilbushevich . . . is the only one of the entire Zubatov party against whom this accusation is made.

This is a trick we all can understand. The hoodlum cannot bear it that Jewish workers in America might be interested in Jewish socialism in Palestine. Pinochle and packages for Jewish workers are closer to Medem's heart than a great socialist idea. His poor little business is in danger. He weasles out of a court of honor. He holds his "interpretation" to be a conviction so he has no need for any further formal proceeding. Supposedly in the name of socialism!

But a socialist is not a liar, not a slanderer, not a slighter of honor. . . . The "socialist" Medem [advises] the Poale Zion to put Manya Vilbushevich on trial. Poale Zion has as little grounds for doing so as the Bund had when it installed Chemeriskii in its Lodz committee. The difference between the Bund and the Zionist-Socialists is that the Bund used the Vilbushevich incident as a pretext for attacking Zionism, while the Poale Zion would not have sought an opening for slander to serve its political purposes. That is the political side of the question.

Socialist Zionism has constructed an edifice of ideas, of thought, of desires, which will grow ever greater and more powerful, until a new consciousness enters the minds of the Jewish proletariat. The Bund would seek to destroy this edifice with lies, silly jokes, anecdotes, gossip, slander and helpless anger. Medem the Bundist has been following me around for twenty years, collecting my good and my bad jokes, recounting all sorts of anecdotes and feeling no shame in publishing them. Instead of learning something, finding something out about socialism, about Zionism; instead of listening to my ideas; all he does is crawl around in my spitoon, where he evidently feels quite comfortable. And if you poke him with your stick, he screeches.

Notes

1. *Igerot Ben-Gurion,* 2d ed. Yehuda Erez (Tel-Aviv: 1972), covers the years 1919–1928. See p. 13, letter to the central committee of Poale Zion in America, dated 10 October 1919, from Jaffa.

2. *Ibid.*, 22: Ben-Gurion to Shlomo Kaplansky, London, 25 September 1920. See also *Igerot Sprinzak* 1 (1910–1929), ed. Yosef Shapira (Tel-Aviv: 1965), 228.

3. Zvi Even-Shoshan, *Toledot tenu'at hapo'alim beereẓ yisrael*, vol. 2 (Tel-Aviv: 1966), 23. In the United States at the time there were about half a million organized Jewish workers. According to Even-Shoshan, these represented the largest single organized and unified Jewish force in the country. But for years, this force had been under the influence of Bundists and anti-nationalists of various sorts and, therefore, inimical to Zionism. Poale Zion in the United States tried for many years without success to penetrate this constituency.

4. Melech Epstein, *Jewish Labor in the U.S.A., 1914–1952* (New York: 1969), 66.

5. See n. 3.

6. *Igerot Berl Katznelson 1919–1922*, 178ff., Katznelson to Ben-Gurion, Jaffa, vol. 5, January 1921.

7. *Protocols of the Secretariat of the Histadrut Executive, January–December 1921*, meeting 4 January 1921.

8. Regarding the final discussion of the delegation's composition, see minutes of the Histadrut secretariat meeting of 14 June 1921, 139ff.; *Igerot Berl Katznelson 1919–1922*, 199ff., Katznelson to the World Union of Poale Zion in London, 24 January 1921.

Manya Vilbushevich-Shohat (1880–1961). Revolutionary, member of the Second Aliya, one of the founders of "Hashomer," she was born in the Grodno province of Russia and was drawn in her youth to the workers' movement. She left her fairly affluent family and devoted her time and energy to revolutionary work. She was active in the All-Russian Social-Revolutionary party, but was also involved with the Jewish Workers' Bund. She was arrested in 1899. After her release, and under Zubatov's influence, she helped to found the Independent Jewish Workers Party. In 1904 she visited Palestine, where the idea of workers' settlement collectives took root in her mind. She returned to Russia and was once again active in revolutionary ranks, but in the summer of 1907, she returned to Palestine. There she made contact with the Bar-Giora group and helped to found the collective settlement at Sejera. She was among the founders of the Hashomer self-defense group and, after 1909, one of its leaders. During the First World War, she and her husband, Israel Shohat, were deported to Turkey. She returned to the country in 1919, where she was a leading member of Poale Zion and among the founders of the General Workers' Histadrut. When the Hagana was founded, she was among its active members. She was a longtime member of Kibbutz Kfar Giladi. During the 1930s, she was active in the Jewish-Arab Brotherhood League. During the Second World War, she was a leader of the V League, which stood for closer ties with Soviet Russia. In 1948 she joined the Mapam party.

Joseph Baratz (1890–1969) was a founder of the labor movement in Palestine and a member of the Second Aliya. He was a founder of the first *kvutsa*, Degania, in 1910, and a lifelong member there. He was a founder of the General Workers' Histadrut.

Berl Katznelson (1887–1944), a founder of the labor movement in Palestine, a leading intellectual and guiding spirit. Born in Bobruisk, Russia, he arrived in Palestine in 1908 and worked as an agricultural laborer. He was a founder and leader of the Histadrut, editor of the Aḥdut Ha'avodah party organ, *Kuntres* and, starting in 1925, founding editor of the daily *Davar*. He was a founder and leader of the Mapai party (1930).

9. *Protocol of the Histadrut Executive*, meeting of 14 June 1921, 139ff.: Berl Katznelson's remarks.

10. Judah Leon Magnes (1877–1948), born in San Francisco, and ordained a rabbi by Hebrew Union College in 1900. From 1905–1908, he served as secretary of the Federation of American Zionists and settled in Palestine in 1922. He collaborated with Chaim Weizmann on the founding of The Hebrew University of Jerusalem.

11. *Igerot Berl Katznelson*, vol. 5, *1921–1930*, 18, 23; see p. 98 for Katznelson's observations on the addition of Magnes, Fein and Schlosberg.

12. *Ibid.*, 108–109, 441.

13. Medem's letter appeared in the *Forverts* under the heading "Some Remarks About the Zionist Workers' Delegation."

Vladimir Medem (1879–1923) was born in Liepāja (Libau) in Russian Courland. His father was a high-ranking officer in the Russian army, an assimilated Jew who had his young son baptized. Medem was drawn to Jewish activities in Minsk, where he lived after his expulsion from Kiev University for participating in a student strike in 1899. In Minsk, he joined the Bund. After fleeing to Switzerland, he became a central figure in the Bund leadership and was considered the party's most important ideologue in Poland during the First World War. He immigrated to the United States in 1921.

14. Sergei Vasilievich Zubatov (1863[4?]–1917). During the period 1896–1902 he commanded the *Okhrana* in Moscow. He championed the idea of dealing with the workers' economic grievances without reference to political issues. This idea produced the Independent Jewish Workers' Party, which existed from 1901–1903. In 1903 Zubatov was transferred to Saint Petersburg, and then dismissed by von Plehve. Exiled to Vladimir, he lived on a government pension. After the abdication of Nicholas II in 1917, Zubatov committed suicide. See Jeremiah Schneiderman, *Sergei Zubatov and Revolutionary Marxism* (Ithaca and London: 1976).

15. Bar-Giora, the first underground Jewish organization in Palestine, was formed in Jaffa in 1907. It aimed to create a countrywide self-defense organization. Hashomer was established in 1909 by members of Bar-Giora.

16. Yitzhok-Ayzik Hourwich (1860–1924), a Russian-trained lawyer who immigrated to the United States in 1890, where he earned a Ph.D. in economics and briefly taught at the University of Chicago. Afterwards he served as a government statistician in Washington. From 1912 to 1914 he was a leading official to the ILGWU. He was a well-known writer and editor, and during the 1920s became fiercely anti-Communist.

17. Pinhas Shneurson, "Bagedud ha'avodah," in his *Bashurah harishonah* (Tel-Aviv and Merhavya: 1978), 103.

18. *Igerot Berl Katznelson, vol. 5, 1921–1930,* 38–39: Berl to Leah Miron-Katznelson, 17 December 1921.

19. *Ibid.*

20. Beinish Michalevich (1876–1928), pseudonym of Iosif Izbitsky, a leading figure in the Bund.

21. *Igerot Berl Katznelson, vol. 5, 1921–1930,* 36, letter dated 15 December 1921; see also *ibid.,* 116: "American Diary," 16 December 1921.

22. People's Relief Committee was an organization established by labor movement circles in American Jewry in 1915 to aid refugees and other East European Jews hurt by the war. It existed until 1925.

23. A campaign organized in the United States in 1920 by the Poale Zion.

24. The Independent Jewish Workers' Party, founded in July 1901 (see n. 14).

25. *Byloe,* a periodical devoted mainly to the publication of historical documents, memoirs and articles relating to the Russian revolutionary movement. It appeared sporadically beginning in 1900.

26. Grigorii Andreyevich Gershuni (1870–1908), Russian-Jewish revolutionary and a legend in his own time, he was a founder and leader of the terrorist arm of the Social-Revolutionary (SR) party. Arrested and tried in 1903, his death sentence was commuted to life imprisonment. He escaped from Siberia via China and Japan to the United States. He later died in Switzerland.

27. Evgeniia (Zhenya) Hourwich (Yitzhok-Ayzik Hourwich's sister), radical and Bundist activist. She translated Marx's *Das Kapital* into Russian. She remained in Russia after the Revolution but did not join the Communist party.

28. *Di Tsayt,* the daily newspaper of the Poale Zion in America, published by David Pinsky between September 1920 and April 1922.

29. Vladimir L. Burtsev, editor of *Byloe* for many years, was considered a member of the populist wing of Russian radicalism. He devoted a great deal of time to unmasking undercover agents of the *Okhrana* and other government agencies.

30. See n. 14; see also: Shmuel Galai, *The Liberation Movement in Russia, 1900–1905* (Cambridge: 1973), indexed references to "Zubatovshchina"; Ezra Mendelsohn, *Class Struggle in the Pale* (Cambridge: 1970), 139–141, and the chapter on "Opposition Movements" generally.

31. Iulii (Yudl) Volin, a Bundist who was drawn to Zubatovite ideas and was a leader of the Independent party. See Schneiderman, *Sergei Zubatov* (index).

32. Aleksandr Chemeriskii, member of the Bund in Minsk, and later a leading figure together with Manya Vilbushevich, Iosif Goldberg, Iulii Volin and others in the Independent party. See Schneiderman, *Sergei Zubatov* (index).

33. The reference is to discussions between Vladimir Ze'ev Jabotinsky, while he was still a member of the Zionist executive, and Slavinsky, a minister in the Ukrainian independence movement's government-in-exile led by Semyon Petliura. Petliura was ostensibly planning to recapture the Ukraine from Soviet forces. Jabotinsky reached an agreement with Slavinsky over the establishment of a Jewish police force to protect Jews. This aroused a storm of controversy in the Jewish world because it was regarded as collaboration with a notorious pogrom-monger.

34. David Zaslavsky (1880–1985), Russian Jewish journalist and writer, trained as a lawyer at Kiev University, and a member of the Bund. In 1920, in an open letter, he recanted his anti-Bolshevik past. He became a member of the Communist party in 1934.

35. Nachman Syrkin (1868–1924), one of the leading ideologues of Socialist Zionism and a leading figure in Poale Zion. Educated in Berlin and Zurich, he attended the first Zionist Congress in 1897. He immigrated in 1908 to the United States, where he lived for the remainder of his life.

36. I have been unable to locate any other reference to Mashe Chemeriskii. Perhaps Syrkin meant to refer to Aleksandr (Sasha?) Chemeriskii (see n. 32).

Review Essays

Zionist History Reconsidered

David Vital, *Zionism: The Crucial Phase*. Oxford: Clarendon Press, 1987. 276 pp.

This is a sequel to the author's *The Origins of Zionism* (Oxford: 1975) and *Zionism: The Formative Years* (Oxford: 1982), and as such it is welcome. Professor Vital is an accomplished writer and few can rival his literary talents. However, this time he has overreached himself. His sentences are so convoluted (some extend for no less than eight to ten lines!) and contain such a labyrinth of clauses and sub-clauses that, at times, one can hardly penetrate their inner meaning. But since Vital's narrative is more descriptive than analytical, economy of words is not his concern. Perhaps some readers will delight in this kind of presentation, but when words cease to convey thought one's patience wears thin.

This defect is compounded by a visible lack of discipline. The author is so carried away by his own reflections that the examination of documentary evidence takes second place. He is overly selective and prone to value judgments. In vain does one search for an analysis of cause-and-effect relationships and for an attempt to answer the indispensable questions: *How?* and *Why?* He simply moves from one episode to another, ignoring the sequence of events, let alone chronological order. He is very good at the characterization of his dramatis personae but, on the whole, the book strikes one as a historical essay rather than a solid piece of research.

The book deals with an important subject that covers a crucial phase in Zionist history (1914–1920). The subject has previously been dealt with thoroughly by the late Leonard Stein in his book *The Balfour Declaration* (London: 1961), and in my two books: *The Question of Palestine, 1914–1918: British-Jewish-Arab Relations* (London/New York: 1973); and *Germany, Turkey and Zionism, 1897–1918* (Oxford: 1977). If one hopes to find striking new discoveries in Vital's book, one is bound to be disappointed. With the exception of some French (and certain other) sources, most of the documents examined will be familiar to readers of previous works on the subject, although the uninitiated reader may be led to believe that Vital is the first to research these sources. Vital's failure to properly acknowledge his predecessors' contribution is ungenerous and unbecoming, to say the least.

My main concern with Vital's book, however, is substantive. I regret that I found much with which I must take issue. At the very beginning of the book, one is struck by a curious statement, "The decision of the Zionists to concern themselves exclusively with Erez-Israel had led the movement into a trap" (p. 6). Did he expect them to fare better in Uganda, the Argentine or Mesopotamia? And was Zionism at all possible without Zion? The Jewish Territorial Organization (ITO) had tried its hand in a number of countries, only to fail.

It is true that the Turks were strongly opposed to Jewish immigration and settlement in Palestine, but the numerous prohibitions (which incidentally were not applicable, as Vital claims), "specifically and uniquely to Jews" [p. 7] never constituted an insuperable obstacle to Jewish colonization. Given the venality of Turkish officials and the protection afforded by foreign consuls, it was always possible to bypass Ottoman laws, however stringent. In practice, the Turkish "monumental stone wall" (p. 6 and the heading of chap. 6) was nonexistent. Nor is it true that "none of the four Jewish members of the new Ottoman parliament [in 1908] . . . were inclined to sympathy for Zionism" (p. 75). With regard to three of them, the evidence points the other way. It would have been useful to consult the contemporary dispatches of Victor Jacobson and Vladimir Jabotinsky in this matter.

Vital should know that in 1912–1914 a drastic change took place in Turkish policy. As Dr. Brode, the German consul general in Jerusalem, reported, "The Turkish authorities, who had originally regarded Zionist activities with suspicion, subsequently treated them with goodwill." Talaat Bey, minister of the interior, was particularly friendly and instructed the Ottoman authorities in Palestine to grant the Jews special privileges and extend the scope of their autonomy. Restrictions on freedom of immigration were also abrogated and discriminatory ordinances with regard to the purchase of land were modified. As a result, in the period immediately before the war, over six thousand Jews entered the country and urban development continued unhampered.

This change was partly due to the prudence of the Zionist Executive in Berlin, which suppressed politics in favor of colonization and made loyalty to Turkey the cornerstone of its policy. Vital's contention that the "practical" form of Zionism proved "illusory," that it was "fated to arouse . . . the misgivings of the Turks, and therefore the Zionists [were] to be cast back into a *political* arena" (p. 85), is, therefore, unfounded. Contemporary Zionist records as well as German consular reports belie this conclusion. Nor does his assertion that, in the prewar period, the Zionists "had no clear idea where they wished to go" (p. 50), stand up under careful examination. Indeed, Vital himself states two pages later that "this was the direction in which the Zionist Organization now strongly tended to move" (p. 61). However, the direction was not the one Vital points to—namely, toward the creation of "a centre for the *spirit* of Israel" (p. 60)—but rather toward the creation of a material infrastructure for a future Jewish entity in Palestine. Even Ahad Ha-Am, when revisiting Palestine in 1912, admitted that a miracle had taken place. Viable Jewish agriculture, only a vision thirty years earlier, had become a reality.

It was the pioneers of the Second Aliya (1904–1914) who brought about the revolutionary changes in the new Yishuv and the country as a whole. Their contributions to the creation of a Jewish working class, to a cooperative system of farming (a unique feature in the history of modern colonization), to Jewish self-defense (the Ha-Shomer), to the emancipation of women and to the idea of "ingathering of the exiles" (encouraging of the immigration of Yemenite Jews) are passed over in silence.

Vital seriously misrepresents German policy toward Zionism in that period when he says there was "no sign of political interest in Zionism on the German side" (p. 124). On what grounds does he state with such confidence that there is no hard evidence that the Germans ever attempted to press the Turks to soften their position and that "there is no real likelihood that if they did they would succeed" (p. 287)? There is, in fact, overwhelming evidence to show that these assumptions are false.

Nor is he fair to German Zionist leaders. His statement that the ability of Otto Warburg and his associates in Berlin, of Richard Lichtheim in Constantinople and of Arthur Ruppin in Jaffa "to protect and sustain the Yishuv proved to be severely limited" (p. 126) is contrary to fact. If the German government was helpful, it was largely owing to the persuasiveness of Otto Warburg, Arthur Hantke, Victor Jacobson and Richard Lichtheim. Lichtheim in particular distinguished himself as a superb diplomat. During his stay in Constantinople, he cultivated warm friendships with successive German and American ambassadors whose goodwill proved of inestimable value. He was also successful in eliciting from the German embassy instructions to the consulate in Jerusalem (November 22, 1915) in which, with the *Auswärtiges Amt*'s prior approval, it was stated, inter alia, that "it is politically advisable to show a friendly attitude towards Zionism and its aims."

German protection proved invaluable for the preservation of the Yishuv during the war. On November 15, 1917, Jacob Thon, Ruppin's successor, acknowledged, "We would have suffered irreparable harm had the mighty hand of the German Government not protected us in our hour of danger." Events fully vindicated the policy of the Zionist Executive in Berlin. Passive neutrality, let alone a one-sided pro-entente orientation as advocated by its opponents, could have proved fatal to the settlement in Palestine. Vital's criticism on this score is unjustified. He asserts that the Executive was "inert" and "had no choice but to sit out the war and hope for the best" (p. 136). Documentary evidence shows that this is far from accurate. The Executive rejected the concept of passive neutrality bordering on inactivity. Its members were determined to secure international support and this in no way ran counter to their principle of neutrality or reflected any proclivity for one or another power.

Nor was this principle the product of the war or a caprice of some German Zionist leaders, as Vital implies. Zionist neutrality was conditioned by the international character of the movement. The Jewish question that it aimed to solve was of international dimensions; it was, therefore, imperative to win the support of all the powers concerned, not to chain it to one power exclusively. This policy, which originated with Herzl, was followed by the "practical" Zionists and endorsed publicly by the Eleventh Zionist Congress in the summer of 1913.

Moreover, far from reducing the chance for a serious hearing at the Peace Conference after the war (p. 129), a multi-lateral and international-oriented policy, if anything, placed Zionism on the diplomatic map. The German Zionist leaders, strange as it may seem, did have some indirect influence on the publication of both Jules Cambon's statement to Nahum Sokolow and Balfour's letter to Lord Rothschild. By maintaining good relations with German officials and the German press, they inadvertently created an atmosphere of competition among the powers, thus indirectly accelerating the decision-making process in Paris and London.

This point escapes Vital. His strictures (1) that the Executive was "entirely devoid of strength" and acted "without authority," casting the Zionist movement worldwide into "disarray" and bringing its institutions to the point of "virtual collapse" and (2) that it was "timid" and, therefore, was "reduced to a cipher" (pp. 129, 136, 165, 227 and *passim*) reflect his own biases rather than the true state of affairs. He echoes the wrath of Vladimir Jabotinsky and Meir Grossman, who were at loggerheads with the Zionist Executive over the creation of a Jewish Legion in the Allied forces. Such a fighting unit, if posted to Palestine to fight the Turks, would have seriously compromised the principle of neutrality and gravely jeopardized the safety of Palestine Jews. It was with good reason that Jabotinsky and Grossman were denounced. Even Sir Mark Sykes, of the British Foreign Office, a staunch supporter of Jabotinsky's project, sounded a note of warning. In April 1917, noting the failure of the British offensive in Gaza and the wholesale evacuation of Jews from Jaffa–Tel-Aviv by Djemal Pasha, he cabled to London from Cairo that Jabotinsky's scheme should not be pursued lest the Turks deliver a deathblow to the Jews as they had done to the Armenians. Vital quotes this document (p. 250), but he conspicuously refrains from drawing any conclusion from it.

Aaron Aaronsohn's contribution and that of his "Nili" spy ring to the British conquest of Palestine and to the creation of a favorable atmosphere among British officials prior to the publication of the Balfour Declaration was far greater than that of Jabotinsky. And yet, save for a footnote (p. 250), his name is not mentioned even once. By contrast, Jabotinsky earns about thirty pages in Vital's book.

Vital is no more enlightening on Britain's Near Eastern policy than he is on Anglo-Zionist relations. Few of his statements stand up to rigorous examination; some are not supported by documentary evidence; others are self-contradictory. It is a fallacy to believe, as he does (pp. 89–90), that the dismemberment of the Ottoman Empire was the predetermined goal of British policy. The Asquith–Grey administration was disinclined to undertake new imperial responsibilities, particularly in Palestine. In April 1915 a special interdepartmental committee (the de Bunsen Committee) was appointed to consider the nature of British interests of Turkey-in-Asia. It rejected the idea of partition and recommended maintaining an independent Ottoman Empire, but with a decentralized system of administration. This document testifies to the non-annexationist character of British policy. With regard to Palestine, the committee maintained that it was an international concern and therefore "must be the subject of special negotiations, in which both belligerents and neutrals alike are interested." The desirability of Palestine's neutralization and internationalization was diametrically opposed to the Samuel–Weizmann proposals.

Vital deals with the de Bunsen report (pp. 98–101), but he either fails to grasp its meaning or misreads it, claiming that Palestine was "slated from the very beginning to be brought under the new [i.e., British] Government." Nor is he correct in saying that Samuel's January 1915 memorandum, as well as the possibility of "a *Jewish* Palestine, was easily forgotten in exalted circles" (pp. 93, 98, 189). Foreign Minister Edward Grey's sponsorship in March 1916 of the idea of a joint Allied pro-Zionist declaration is evidence to the contrary. The draft proposal conjured up the prospect of eventual Jewish self-government in Palestine. It surpassed the Balfour Declaration in this regard.

Furthermore, it is not true that there is no evidence of ministerial intervention in this move. Edward Grey and Lord Crewe, Vital tells us, "had simply agreed with what had been put up to them by the officials" (p. 189). But Grey was definitely involved. He overruled objections raised by Sir Arthur Nicolson, the permanent under secretary of state, but because of illness, invited Lord Crewe to deputize for him at the Foreign Office. Contrary to what Vital states, Crewe sympathized with Zionism, and it was he who drafted the cables to Petrograd and Paris of March 11, 1916. French objections led the British to drop the proposal. Even so, Sir Maurice de Bunsen was confident that the interest of Jews in Palestine "will not be over-looked" and concurred with the suggestion that eventually they might undertake the management of their restored national life there.

If Samuel and Weizmann, as well as Sokolow, failed to get their message across in 1915–1916, it was not (as Vital would have it) because of any indifference to Zionism per se in official circles, but because their plan was inextricably linked with a British-protected Palestine that, at the time, was impractical. It was not until early in 1917 that their doctrine began to appear relevant to British strategic interests.

Lloyd George became prime minister in December 1916, thus altering the picture radically. Palestine was one of his primary objectives. He had been advocating its annexation since the outbreak of the First World War; to him British and Jewish Palestine were almost synonymous. He had a long-standing interest in Zionism and Samuel's memorandum strongly appealed to him. It also fit in well with his strategic and political concepts. During his administration, Asquith–Grey's non-annexa-tionism was abandoned and the recommendations of the de Bunsen Committee ignored. Vital's assertion that under Lloyd George "British desiderata, policy and expectations in the Near East underwent no change" and that "the thread of ideas . . . leading from the de Bunsen Committee . . . remained unbroken" (p. 209) does not square with documentary evidence. However, elsewhere he hints at the "reordering of purposes and priorities by Lloyd George's new Government" (p. 232) without noticing that he thereby contradicts himself. In no case does he explain what these "purposes and priorities" were, nor does he document any of the above statements.

It is true that the need to extricate Britain from the 1916 Asia Minor agreement, popularly known as the Sykes-Picot agreement, made Zionism more attractive both to Lloyd George and Sir Mark Sykes, although the motive for this agreement was entirely different from that mentioned by Vital (p. 199). But to claim that this was a "crucial [element] upon which all else hinged, and from which . . . all subsequent developments [i.e., the Balfour Declaration] flowed" (p. 228) is erroneous. This theory is as old as the Balfour Declaration itself. Had this been the case, Jules Cambon's statement of June 4, 1917 would have stampeded the British into outdo-ing their competitors by an even stronger commitment. The fact remains that they did not. Neither Sir Ronald Graham, assistant under secretary for foreign affairs, in any of his notes, nor Balfour, during cabinet meetings, urged the necessity of countering the Quai d'Orsay. Sykes himself realized, while in Paris, that it was premature for the British to press for revision of the agreement and believed that no prominence should be given to Zionist desiderata before French ambitions in Syria were satisfied. Time and again he emphasized the indivisibility of the entente; the role ascribed to him by Vital is imaginary.

It was not until the Peace Conference in 1919–1920 that full use was made of Zionism to undo the 1916 agreement and ensure sole British trusteeship of Palestine;

when the Balfour Declaration was originally discussed this consideration was hardly taken into account. Its publication in 1917 has to be seen within the context of the global British–German confrontation. In March 1916 the mere possibility that Jews might opt for a German protectorate of Palestine sufficed for Grey to approve unequivocally a far-reaching formula proposed by Hugh J. O'Beirne and Lord Crewe. And it was only after reports reached London in 1917 that Germany intended to capture the Zionist movement that Balfour invited Rothschild and Weizmann to submit a draft formula. Vital implies that Balfour's motive was to spur the process of easing the French out of Palestine (p. 169), yet he also admits that Balfour assured the cabinet that "so far as the French were concerned, all was well. Cambon's letter to Sokolow was produced and read, and the Cabinet was satisfied" (p. 284). Balfour was anything but anti-French and the war, it should be remembered, was with Germany, not with France.

The link between British strategic interests and the principle of self-determination, which was the *raison d'être* of the compact with Zionism, seems to escape Vital completely. And it is absurd to claim that "the British decision to couple Palestine with Zionism was one to which the Zionists themselves had made no direct contribution" (p. 236, also p. 90) and that Weizmann was merely the "epitome . . . of the alliance . . . [rather] than its engineer" (p. 223). For we read elsewhere in Vital's book that it was Weizmann who did more than anyone else "to persuade the British that the Zionists would . . . serve their purposes" (p. 261) and that he and Sokolow not only demonstrated goodwill and efficacy but "seemed to validate the fundamental assumption on which the association of the Zionists with British interests ultimately turned" (p. 262, also pp. 252, 260 and *passim*).

It takes two to make an alliance. The British and the Zionists played into each other's hands: Britain used Zionism to legitimize its position in a vital strategic area and the Zionists, too, derived enormous benefits. The Balfour Declaration was a watershed in modern Jewish history. To term this declaration merely "an act of British foreign and imperial policy in wartime" (p. 298) is an interpretation that the British statesmen who sponsored this policy consistently denied. Vital will find few historians to subscribe to his view that, although of "great moral importance," the practical value of the Balfour Declaration was "very doubtful" (p. 308). The triumph of Zionism in 1917 belies his basic contention that the Zionist movement suffered from "a dearth of effective leaders and, above all, the inability of those who claimed to lead it to formulate an effective policy" (p. 89).

It is impossible to comment on all the book's errors, lacunae and inconsistencies. In sum, having examined this book thoroughly, I am bound to say that it does little justice to its title let alone to the subject itself.

ISAIAH FRIEDMAN
Ben-Gurion University
of the Negev

Medicine and Murder

Robert Jay Lifton, *The Nazi Doctors, Medical Killing and the Psychology of Genocide*. New York: Basic Books, 1986. 576 pp.

Doctors stood guard over the killing process at Auschwitz, and now Robert Lifton has set himself the task to discover why and how physicians coming from a profession dedicated to healing were transformed into mass murderers. The commitment of these doctors to mass murder also raises wider questions about the social role of medicine and its guardianship of public health and morals. For Auschwitz brings into focus and to a climax many trends and tendencies of the modern age: here as in a prism we can see the potential dangers inherent in certain ideas and social structures that were either ignored or only dimly perceived at the time. The role that medicine played in society for a century before the Holocaust provides one example of such a trend. This did not have to lead to the Holocaust but, in fact, it helped to define the attitudes of the Nazi doctors toward their victims.

An in-depth examination of how these doctors saw their task and how their victims perceived it is essential before the wider implications of their involvement in the death process can be assessed and the actual workings of the camp fully explained. Robert Lifton has done so in his excellent and exciting book, largely through interviews with two groups of people: twenty-eight physicians and one pharmacist who were directly involved in the killing and former Auschwitz prisoners who had worked on the medical block, over half of them doctors. The interviews are set within a wider context, that of Nazi ideology, science and Auschwitz itself—a self-contained polity, detached from the rest of society, governed by its own rules of life or death.

Robert Lifton points out that the reversal of healing and killing stands at the heart of his book.[1] Indeed, the first two parts—one dealing with euthanasia, the other with Auschwitz—are headed, respectively, the "Genetic Cure" and the "Racial Cure," thus setting the tone for the analysis of how doctors became killers. The third and last part of the book deals with the psychological means that enabled the doctors to carry on with their grisly task. Though Lifton has much that is interesting to say about euthanasia, including in-depth portraits of the doctors involved, the focus of the book is Auschwitz. When, on their own initiative, doctors continued the euthanasia program that had been officially stopped—deciding who should live or die—they began to play a role that would end at the gas chamber.

Crucial to the author's analysis, and particularly insightful, are the portraits of three Auschwitz doctors—Josef Mengele, "Ernst B" and Eduard Wirths—and the presentation of the complex relationship between the prisoner-doctors/nurses and their masters. The discussion of the attitudes of the individual doctors toward their task raises crucial questions about their participation that can be answered only through such in-depth analysis. All these doctors came from a respectable medical background; nothing had predisposed them for Auschwitz. It was a prisoner who told Robert Lifton that, were it not for Auschwitz, Josef Mengele might have had a successful professional career: he could have been a "slightly sadistic German professor."[2] Wirths, the chief doctor at Auschwitz, figures as a correct bureaucrat, a fatherly man plagued by bouts of conscience, who had been a good physician in the past. "Ernst B" was the exception: he was acquitted after the war, and in Auschwitz he was perceived by many prisoners as "a human being in S.S. uniform." And yet this physician, who treated prisoners as his equals, referred to Josef Mengele as the most decent colleague he had met in Auschwitz.

The performance of actions that plumb the depth of evil by so-called normal people is by now commonplace to those who study the Final Solution, and no historian can any longer take the easy way out when confronted by this phenomenon by resorting to the demonic or the abnormal as an explanation. Eduard Wirths was a loving family man, capable even of deep human relationships with inmates. Rudolf Hoess, the commandant of Auschwitz, next to Wirths the most important person in the camp, exemplified this pattern when he stood at the gas chamber and thought of his wife and children without, so he tells us, connecting them in any way with what he was witnessing.[3] Lifton's explanation for this moral bifurcation is what he terms "doubling": the formation of two relatively separate functioning selves at moral odds with each other. This is, no doubt, a correct diagnosis of such attitudes and behavior. The principal factors that bridged the two selves and kept such people functioning effectively, according to Lifton, were the integration of these men into Auschwitz through peer pressure, opportunism—seeing a chance to further their careers—and, most important, belief in Nazi ideology. These physicians saw themselves as "biological revolutionaries," rejuvenating the Volk. They killed Jews in order to cure the nation. For Lifton the major finding of his study was the success of ideological commitment in transforming healers into killers.[4]

The basis of Nazi ideology was racism, and it was this commitment that distorted the doctors' view of their science and the nation—indeed, of all that was public— without affecting their private relationships with family or colleagues. Racism facilitated "doubling," indeed, demanded it, at least until the enemies of the superior race had been obliterated. The militancy built into racism and projected onto the stereotype of the Jew led Mengele, for example, to look on Jews as wholly evil; his belief that the Aryan must protect the norms of society made him call the Jews, according to Lifton, "some sort of freaks." The fact that racism claimed to conserve society's standards was crucial (so it seems to me), in facilitating the Nazi doctors' transition from healers to killers. The Jews were not only anti-national, they were diseased, corrupting respectable society. Lifton addresses this racism, although I might have given it greater weight as it infuses almost all that the doctors told him. Thus, "Ernst B" stated that his colleagues were really not ideological at all, and yet they all affirmed their commitment to racial biology. "Ernst B", for all his supposed humanness, admitted to belief in the existence of a "Jewish problem" that had to be solved.

Auschwitz was the triumph of racism as an ideology, its ultimate consequence. It is all the more distressing that so many contemporary historians write about National Socialism as if its racism were a minor point. In their preoccupation with social structures or pragmatic politics, they are apt to forget a fundamental aspect of the movement. Thus, in the recent dispute among German historians concerning how to integrate the Nazi past into a German national identity (the so-called *Historikerstreit*), racism is ignored and Nazi killings are compared to other non-racist massacres in recent history—or parallels are implied between the murder of the Jews and the destruction of Prussia in the Second World War.[5] The strength of racism, unlike wars and revolutions, lies in its appeal as a faith beyond the anxieties of daily life, an appeal that enabled it to survive all vicissitudes and to maintain a potential presence long before and after National Socialism. Racism greatly facilitated the rise of National Socialism; without this ideology, there would have been no Final Solution. *The Nazi Doctors* is crucial in demonstrating the overriding significance of racist ideology for those who were involved in the killing process.

To be sure, other important factors joined racism in easing the doctors' transition from healing to killing: the Auschwitz environment, the pressure from other doctors working there and, last but not least, the numbing effect after the first shock, aided by the ritual nature of the killing. The test newly arrived doctors had to pass was selection at the ramp; some tried to escape this task while others were shamed by their colleagues into deciding over life and death. Alcohol also served to dull the senses of the doctors; heavy drinking was a central element in the process of numbing. However, one additional dimension must be added to the list of factors that helped create Auschwitz doctors, one I have already mentioned at the beginning of this essay: the social role of physicians in the past must have predisposed these men to fulfill the task assigned to them in Auschwitz. From their traditional function as guardians of public health as well as morals, they passed to that of guardians of the race and nation. *The Nazi Doctors* is concerned with the immediate killing process and its psychological roots, and to go wider afield would have prejudiced the in-depth analysis. Nevertheless, the historical dimension is an important part of the picture, and it must include the functioning of physicians in society together with the influence of both world wars.

The social role of physicians in the nineteenth and early twentieth centuries has been well documented: their function in socializing the working class and—of special relevance for their task under National Socialism—their central role in defining and stigmatizing those who stood outside the generally accepted norms of society. The medical concept of health came to include the proper standard of morality and behavior.[6] Michel Foucault's thesis that the doctor often replaced the priest during the nineteenth century as the guardian of morals may be somewhat exaggerated, but it remains true that physicians increasingly performed this function for many individuals and for the nation. The stereotypes of the insane or the homosexual are medical constructs, and the Jewish stereotype, much older, was also at times subsumed under the powerful principle of health and sickness. For a century before Auschwitz, the so-called outsiders had been thought sick (e.g., Jews were believed subject to nervous diseases), with the all-important difference that here physicians were still healers and believed that such illnesses might be cured.

Doctors were grossly overrepresented in the Nazi party; they were a Nazi-prone group from the very beginning.[7] These were, of course, only a small percentage of all the doctors practicing in the Reich (it has been estimated that some three hundred to four hundred doctors took part directly in crimes against humanity).[8] In their Nazi party membership, economic hardship and fear of Jewish competition surely played a role. Nevertheless, Michael H. Kater, who studied those Nazi doctors who joined the movement early on, found that they were motivated by nationalism and commitment to ideology rather than by economic factors.[9] Later, opportunism, no doubt, played a part as so many rushed to join the triumphant Nazi party. The continuity in attitudes between the early Nazi physicians and the Auschwitz doctors is obvious and raises the question why doctors were attracted to Nazi ideology more than other professionals. This problem cannot be solved here, but a study of the history of the profession of medicine from this particular vantage point seems essential in order to understand fully why doctors were the driving force in the "euthanasia" program in general as well as in Auschwitz in particular.

If the history of the medical profession could have had some influence in facilitating the actual conversion of Nazi doctors from healers to killers, then the two world wars also served to make their task easier. Most of the doctors at Auschwitz were too young to have served in the First World War; however, "Johann S," for example, a man deeply involved in the "euthanasia" program—but who himself had never fought—sought to recapture the "mystical frontline experience" as against Germany's degradation and defeat.[10] The revitalization of the Aryan race was part of an ongoing war that was meant to make Germany victorious in spite of defeat. The First World War as the initial encounter of most men with mass death had its numbing effect at the time. But as a myth that informed the postwar world, it stood for heroism and sacrifice, "walking through a sea of corpses," in order to save the nation. Echoes of this myth are present in the self-justification of Auschwitz doctors: they also were fighting in the trenches with mass death all around them, not only that of their own making, but also that of other Germans falling at the front. "Ernst B" recounts that one way to persuade a reluctant doctor to take part in the selection process at the ramp was to tell him: "What do you do in war . . . in battle, don't you have to select there as well?"[11] The reference was to the examination of wounded during the First World War in the first-aid stations directly behind the front. There physicians had to select those wounded they could still treat under such conditions and leave others to die. That war had also been seen at the time as affording a unique opportunity for medical experimentation given the existence of an undernourished German population available for nutritional experiments.[12]

The First World War with its refinement of the enemy's stereotype had also served to brutalize the politics of a defeated Germany. It was no coincidence that soon after the war, in the midst of the postwar crises that followed defeat, the physician Alfred Hoche and the lawyer Karl Binding advocated taking the life of all those who were unproductive—useless to society and the nation—parasites in racist terms.[13] The First World War together with the social use of medicine enabled Auschwitz doctors to seek the security of already-existing traditions.

The Second World War made use of the myths of the First as Nazi doctors saw themselves "on the battlefield of the race war" (as one doctor put it) and sought among themselves—sometimes even with prisoner-doctors—to reconstitute a ca-maraderie of the trenches. Lifton writes that there was some truth to the Nazi image that saw Auschwitz as the moral equivalent of war.[14] But if this were so, then what we see today as "doubling" was for the doctors a consistent moral position; sus-pending all moral restraints when it came to fighting the enemy was legitimized, so to speak, by racism and by the First World War and its propaganda. From the beginning of modern warfare, the dehumanization of the enemy was paired with the claim that wars were fought in order to rescue morality from its foes. When "Ernst B" called Hoess a man of integrity and Mengele a decent human being, he may have assumed, not without some historical justification, that doing one's duty and obey-ing orders in wartime, however terrible, was part of any normative definition of human decency and integrity. Nazi doctors could not and would not draw a distinc-tion between mass murder and war; nor were they totally mistaken in this case, for it was one of Germany's mainly unspoken war aims to annihilate the Jewish people. Robert Lifton fully understands the importance of such factors in facilitating the conversion from healer to killer. They are a constant presence in the book, even if there is no space to make all the connections.

Within the constant encounter with death at Auschwitz, the discussion of the relationship between Nazi doctors and the prisoner-doctors/nurses is of special interest. There is no room here to even begin to discuss this relationship in all its complexity. However, the favorable comments of the prisoner-doctors about their Nazi masters, given in interviews so long after the event, startle the reader. Thus a Communist prisoner, who today is still a dedicated Communist, calls Wirths (who must surely be rated as one of the worst mass murderers of all time), "a man of rare nobility," while several prisoner-doctors perceived Mengele as educated and culti-vated. These prisoner-doctors were not the collaborators to whom Lifton devotes a special section (these were mainly antisemitic Polish doctors, with one Jew included in this category). The prisoner-doctors who made favorable comments about Nazi doctors fully realized the crime being committed and the essential role that the doctors played in the killing process. The book provides several explanations for the bond between victim and criminal. One prisoner-doctor likened this bond to that formed under extreme coercion by terrorists and their victims. Lifton sees a certain amount of "doubling" among the prisoner-doctors themselves, for they, with their vicarious control over life and death, could also appear as saviors of individual lives. The book does not address this relationship as thoroughly or conclusively as that of the Nazi doctors to Auschwitz, its main theme; yet it provides important new evidence for those who have analyzed the victims' behavior in death and concentra-tion camps.

Lifton's book not only adds a new dimension to our understanding of the death camp, but it also—through its concentration on the complicity of respected mem-bers of the medical profession—addresses problems of the socialization of medicine as well as of the "medicalization" of outsiders. History may not be a seamless web, but the very magnitude of the Jewish Holocaust demonstrates the extent to which the past served to aid the implementation of the Nazi program. The connection between this past and Auschwitz needs further exploration. Meanwhile, this book provides a crucial analysis of what the physicians themselves thought they were doing and how the prisoner-doctors perceived them. The work also proves, once again, that National Socialism without its ideology might simply have been a right-wing dictatorship of the kind that, though deplorable, would not have led to Auschwitz or perhaps even to the Second World War.

GEORGE L. MOSSE
University of Wisconsin
and The Hebrew University

Notes

I am most grateful to Michael H. Kater for sharing with me some of the insights of his forthcoming book on Nazi doctors.

1. Robert Jay Lifton, "On Investigating Nazi Doctors: Further Thoughts," *Psychohistory Review* 1987, 59.
2. Robert Jay Lifton, *Nazi Doctors* 377.
3. Rudolf Hoess, *Kommandant in Auschwitz,* ed. Martin Broszat (Munich: 1963), 133–134.
4. Lifton, "On Investigating Nazi Doctors," 62.
5. Hans-Ulrich Wehler, *Entsorgung der deutschen Vergangenheit? Ein polemischer Essay zum Historikerstreit* (Frankfurt on the Main: 1988).
6. See especially Alfons Labisch, "Doctors, Workers and the Scientific Cosmology of the Industrial World: The Social Construction of 'Health' and the 'Homo Hygienicus," *Journal of Contemporary History* 20, no. 4 (1985), 599–617; George L. Mosse, *Nationalism and Sexuality: Respectability and Abnormal Sexuality in Modern Europe* (New York: 1985), chap. 7.
7. Michael H. Kater, *The Nazi Party. A Social Profile of Members 1919–1945* (Cambridge, Mass.: 1983), 73.
8. *Der Spiegel,* 16 January 1984.
9. Michael H. Kater, "The Nazi Physicians' League of 1929, Causes and Consequences," in *The Formation of the Nazi Constituency 1919–1933,* ed. Thomas Childers (London and Sydney: 1986), 156.
10. Lifton, *Nazi Doctors,* 132.
11. Lifton, *Nazi Doctors,* 196.
12. Johanna Bleker, "Vom 'Sortiergeschäft im Grossen' zur 'Triage.' Das Problem der Krankensichtung im Krieg," in Johanna Bleker and Heinz-Peter Schmiedebach, eds., *Medizin und Krieg. Vom Dilemma der Heilberufe 1865–1985* (Frankfurt on the Main: 1987), 211. Some physicians also took a leading part in the Turkish massacres of Armenians during the First World War, and here their nationalism also determined their use of medicine. Vahakn N. Dadrian, "The Role of Turkish Physicians in the World War I Genocide of Ottoman Armenians," *Holocaust and Genocide Studies* 1, no. 2 (1986), 175, 178.
13. Karl Binding und Alfred Hoche, *Die Freigabe der Vernichtung Lebensunwertes Lebens* (Leipzig: 1920). Neither Binding nor Hoche used racism as an argument but based their book on considerations of the common good; George L. Mosse, *Towards the Final Solution, a History of European Racism* (New York: 1978), 216.
14. Lifton, *Nazi Doctors,* 431.

The Meaning of Exile

Arnold M. Eisen, *Galut: Modern Jewish Reflections on Homelessness and Homecoming*. Bloomington and Indianapolis: Indiana University Press, 1986. xx + 233 pp.

Arnold M. Eisen's work is a fine example of the excellent scholarship in Jewish studies currently flourishing in America, scholarship that has been enriched by exposure to Israeli learning. Characteristic of the American ambience—but in this respect contrasting somewhat with the tendency of Israeli scholarship—is the daring sweep shown by the author who, although essentially a scholar of modern Jewish religious thought, also ventures to mine the classical sources in this evocative study of the meanings for Jews, past and contemporary, of the concept Galut (exile).

The justification for Eisen's broad scope, which reaches as far back as Genesis, Deuteronomy and the Talmudic tractate Avodah Zarah, is his contention that Biblical and rabbinical notions exercised a crucial influence on the shaping of modern reflection on exile and return and that the contemporary debate cannot be comprehended in isolation from these classical sources. He shows that even the various intellectual leaders of the Zionist rebellion against the Galut condition continued to invoke and deploy the traditional Jewish resonances associated with the idea of Galut. One example is A. D. Gordon, the Labor Zionist thinker, who inveighed against the use of Arab labor and the imitation of European cultural modes, calling them *avodah zarah* (the rabbinic term for idol worship). Others are Yehezkel Kaufmann and Jacob Klatzkin, both extreme negators of the Galut, yet much of whose writing, according to Eisen, "can be read as a virtual midrash on the Bible." Already in his gloss on the wanderings of the patriarchs in Genesis, Eisen discerns a distinction, seminal for his entire study, between the political and metaphysical dimensions of homelessness. The metaphysical appears in the banishment of Adam and Eve from the Garden of Eden, the political in the condemnation of Cain to perpetual wandering. Eisen's examination of Deuteronomy probes the traditional images of home, temporarily achieved, while his consideration of the Mishnaic tractate Avodah Zarah adds a layer of rabbinic reflection upon the unfortunate state of exile.

The main thrust of Eisen's enterprise, however, is in the second part of this book. With real stylistic flair, he leads the reader through a broad selection of thinkers (notably Benedict Spinoza and Moses Mendelssohn), who, he argues, brought to pass the underlying intellectual transformation—the demystification, universalization and politicization of the traditional conception of Galut—that made the Zionist revolt against it possible. The Zionist thinkers receive the greatest attention, for, as

Eisen says, "nowhere have the lessons of exile and homecoming been pondered more keenly, or more paradoxically, than among Zionists who sought to harness the tradition in order to bring it to an end."

Eisen's method throughout is the analysis and comparison of selected texts of thought focusing on the concept of Galut. Often with remarkable incisiveness and always with eloquence and perspicacity, his analysis encompasses a bountiful selection of Jewish thought on his chosen theme. He draws out the relevant contributions of Franz Rosenzweig, Martin Buber, Ha-Rav Kook, Jacob Klatzkin, Abraham Heschel and many others. Moreover, the scope of his analysis covers important contemporary thinkers ranging from Ben Halpern and Arthur Hertzberg in the United States to Nathan Rotenstreich and Eliezer Schweid in Israel.

In a sense, Eisen follows in the tradition of two illustrious predecessors, Yehezkel Kaufmann who produced the monumental but overly discursive *Golah venekhar,* and Yitzhak Baer, who wrote a smaller work entitled Galut. Much as they did, Eisen not only analyzes and explicates the thought of others, but he also engages in an ongoing critique of his subject matter, thereby making a further contribution of his own to Jewish reflection on the subject. For example, although highly respectful of Yehezkel Kaufmann's majestic work and concurring with his demolition of Ahad Ha-Am's notion of *ḥefeẓ hakiyum* (the will to live), Eisen, in turn, discerningly subjects Kaufmann to criticism. The latter had argued that not a putative will to live but rather Jewish religion rooted in faith explains Jewish survival in Galut. On this Eisen comments perceptively, "The obvious problem with this explanation is that most, if not all, the cultures in which Jews lived were also religious; faith had been no less important a force in these societies than amongst the Jews themselves. . . . Why had other faiths not managed to preserve other societies as Judaism had saved the Jews?"

The choice of the term "reflections" in the title of this work is appropriate since it is not a systematic history of ideas. Indeed, it tends to treat ideas almost as if they had a self-contained, ethereal existence of their own, their logical nexus at times automatically translating into a causal one. Thus Spinoza leads to Moses Hess, and Hess to Ahad Ha-Am with a facility that might well raise some objections from historians accustomed to the meticulous documentation of causal interconnections between events and ideas.

It is perhaps the same sparseness of historical context that weakens part of Eisen's critique of Ahad Ha-Am. He all-too-lightly dismisses that important thinker's distinction between "subjective" and "objective" negation of the Galut, commenting that in this connection Ahad Ha-Am's terminology is "unusually laden with jargon." To this reader, at any rate, it is Ahad Ha-Am's meaning that remains crystal clear, and his distinction is a profound contribution to Zionist thought on Galut, whereas what seems befuddled is Eisen's criticism, especially his judgment that "Ahad Ha'am engaged in fantasy when he pictured a diaspora infused with the culture of its center in Eretz Israel." Eisen comments, "The fact that there was no alternative to diaspora existence does not make such existence possible" (p. 78).

It may well be possible to label as fantasy Ahad Ha-Am's vision of a cultural center without any foreign admixture and obeying a national morality, but was his belief in the objective possibility of Diaspora existence equally a fantasy? After all, within the historical context of Ahad Ha-Am's thinking (especially before the First World War), it was highly feasible to anticipate a viable Diaspora life based on at least a modicum of the Jewish cultural autonomy advocated by Simon Dubnow, within the multi-national Russian and Austro-Hungarian empires (which encompassed the larger part of world Jewry). To be sure, Ahad Ha-Am did not hold that this would be sufficient, and on that score he differed from Dubnow. However, his assumption that given a relationship with a creative cultural center in Zion such a Diaspora might be viable was not unrealistic in his own time.

Apart from this point, Eisen's treatment of Ahad Ha-Am's contribution is both penetrating and balanced. At one level of discourse, he sides with Micah Josef Berdiczewski's critique of the master, contending that the separation Ahad Ha-Am sought to effect between the moral content of Jewish tradition and its religious garb was unconvincing. With Yehezkel Kaufmann, he faults Ahad Ha-Am for relying on a blind and romantic faith in *hefez hakiyum* of a national Jewish spirit and "for staking Jewish revival on a dubious theory about religion's natural evolution into ethics and culture" (p. 77). On the other hand, Eisen admits that Berdiczewski's contrary attempt to condemn the Galut and jettison the Jewish past was even more problematic in its implications.

In the last two chapters, "Between Homecoming and Redemption" and "Between Homeland and Diaspora," the author adeptly compares, contrasts and criticizes a wide range of Israeli and American Jewish thought, from Amos Oz and Yeshayahu Leibowitz to Jacob Neusner and Ben Halpern. In this reviewer's opinion, however, Eisen's treatment of Eliezer Schweid's ideas does not do justice to that important Israeli thinker. He overstates Schweid's views all the better to criticize them. In his *Judaism and Secular Culture* (published in Hebrew in 1981), Schweid advocated a deepening of the shared Jewish *parhesia* (public or civic space) of Israeli society and called for derivation of civil legislation from Jewish law wherever possible. At the same time, he appealed for greater adaptability of the rabbinate to the circumstances of life in a sovereign Jewish state. This is a far cry from advocating "some form of halakhic state" (p. 137) as Eisen misleadingly describes it.

Similarly, Eisen distorts somewhat the demand made by Schweid (whose thought he calls "quasi-religious Ahad Ha'amism") that Judaism "be a full content for life, a complete human existence," of which Eisen says that it is "a norm in search of an authority" (p. 153). Why he should say this eludes me, especially since he goes on to provide the answer, which not only Schweid but any secularist who is positive about his Jewish identity would give to the question "Why be Jewish"? namely, that being oneself and seeking self-fulfillment within the framework of the people and culture into which one was born is a natural and authentic pursuit. What Schweid calls for is an integral Jewishness that does not distinguish between Jewish and human concerns, that draws sustenance from the entire range of the Jewish cultural heritage and that functions within the ambience of the Hebrew language, that is, a society of Jews and the homeland of the Jews—all of this in contrast to the cultural dualism that perforce characterizes Diaspora Jewries.

Eisen is at his best in analyzing American Jewish thought. He shows that its normative position followed the lines of Mordecai Kaplan's contribution, which "became the effective creed of American Zionist thought." It has, he notes, "never conceived of the return to the Land as a homecoming, or of America as a province of the age-old exile" (p. 149). Among the exceptions on either extreme of this normative position he points to Jacob Petuchowski, the Reform thinker who, in *Zion Reconsidered* (1966), bluntly repudiated the claim that Israel constituted a spiritual center for all Jews. On the other side, Ben Halpern and Arthur Hertzberg continue to insist on the relevance of the term "Galut" to the American Jewish situation, notwithstanding the special qualities that have made it so attractive for Jews. Of Jacob Neusner, Eisen says that he wavers between the Kaplanist consensus and Halpern's Zionist deviation. However, since the publication of Eisen's book, Neusner has taken his position to an extreme that distances itself not only from Halpern, but even from Kaplan (see his article in the *Washington Post,* March 10, 1987).

Throughout this stimulating book, it is abundantly evident that the author himself shares in the anxiety over the choice between homecoming in Israel and at-homeness in America. He notes that Israelis are loath to concede the analogous claim by the American Diaspora that their situation (like Israel's) is unprecedented. Israel is a homecoming; America is at-homeness; both inhabit the space between Galut and *geulah* (redemption) (p. 175). At the time of the book's publication, Eisen taught Jewish philosophy at Tel-Aviv University, having not long before fulfilled a "homecoming" to Israel. Since its publication, he has moved back to a teaching post in the United States. In the introduction he tells us that "I have over the years found myself on both sides of this conversation: an 'Israeli' among American Jews, an American among Israelis; at once in exile and at home among both. The present study developed out of a search for middle ground."

In the light of this statement of purpose one looks with interest for the outcome of his search in his rather oscillating and agonizing conclusion. What does Eisen offer as the middle ground? On the one hand, he makes clear his view as to where the center of gravity of Jewish life lies. "There is a focus to the Jewish world and Jewish history some forty years after the Holocaust and statehood," he avers, "and that center of gravity is not America" (p. 175). He states rather harshly that in America there is "self-deception, attenuation of commitment, impoverishment of learning" and that American Jews "lack an independent Jewish culture, an unequiv-ocal Jewish identity" (p. 177). He also says, "One can survive in the meantime, somewhere else, and one can even thrive. But one is not home" (p. 183).

On the other hand, one senses his disillusionment or dissatisfaction with "home," at any rate with the present condition of the State of Israel, since it now seems to him that simply removing the Jews from exile and gathering them in a sovereign state protected by the force of their own arms can remake neither the Jewish spirit nor the Jewish destiny. To him Israel as just another normal state is neither desirable nor possible.

One of Eisen's conclusions appears to be that none of the conventionally touted metaphors—such as center and periphery or two foci of an ellipse—can cope with the complexities of the contemporary Israel-Diaspora relationship they are meant to describe. "Better to abandon the search for a controlling metaphor altogether," he advises, "and to turn directly to the several matters at issue between Israel and American Jewry." At the same time, Eisen offers contemporary Jews a spectrum of distinctions ranging between Galut on the one side and *geulah* on the other.

At the one extreme there is "homelessness," meaning the condition of those Jewries still suffering distress and persecution. This is obviously an undesirable condition that one must seek to overcome and end, presumably by opting for either of the next two options on the spectrum—"at-homeness" in America or "home-coming" in Israel. Since Eisen's view of the Diaspora is extremely American centered, one is not sure whether other Jewish communities that also enjoy real emancipation—the Jews of Britain, for example—fall into the same category of "at-homeness." Or is this reserved purely for the United States? Given the fact that American Jewish "at-homeness" functions within the reality of a coexisting Israel, and benefits from it, Eisen appears to accredit it with equivalent value to that of "homecoming" in Israel. However, he evades the consequences of this dualism by taking refuge in the final terminological distinction on the spectrum—metaphysical homecoming. This ultimate condition is contrasted with the merely political home-coming embodied in Israel and is said to elude all Jews whether at home in America or having come to Israel. Eisen writes, "The conclusion is well-nigh inescapable, to be a Jew, now as always, is to be in exile from the world" (p. 186).

GIDEON SHIMONI
The Hebrew University

Pinsk and Washington

Ben Halpern, *A Clash of Heroes—Brandeis, Weizmann, and American Zionism.*
New York and Oxford: Oxford University Press, 1987. x + 301 pp.

The clash mentioned in the title of this book refers to what is known in Zionist historiography as the Brandeis-Weizmann struggle from 1919 to 1921, one of the great internal crises in the history of Zionism. It reached a dramatic climax at the Cleveland Conference of the Zionist Organization of America (ZOA) in early June 1921 when the Brandeis administration was forced to retire from the leadership of the American movement.

There is certainly no living historian better equipped than Ben Halpern to write about that controversy. He is served by a deep knowledge of the two trends and the two men who came into fierce collision: Chaim Weizmann representing European Zionism, Louis D. Brandeis leading the American movement. Furthermore, Halpern has reflected on the theme for decades. Now we have the opportunity to share in his conclusions.

The structure of the book is simple, but elegant: it opens with a short statement about the author's approach. He describes it as historical-sociological, although here, as in his former works, Halpern comes through as very much the historian. Then there are two independent chapters about the personal and Zionist developments of Brandeis and Weizmann. Both men met for the first time in London in August 1919, and they disagreed on the issue of the formation of a Jewish Council. From there on, the steps of Weizmann and Brandeis are described and analyzed together. Their second encounter was at the difficult London Zionist Conference of July 1920. The issues discussed there were the character of the future activities of the Zionist Organization (whether political, or only economic and administrative); the character of the Foundation Fund (Keren Hayesod) created at the conference; and subsequent to both, the character, tasks and composition of the new Zionist leadership. Brandeis and Weizmann diverged on each one of these topics, a strong personal element of rivalry and mutual antipathy coloring their discussions. The outcome was the personal breach between the two leaders. Later, during Weizmann's visit to the United States, they barely met.

After London, the scene was set for the grand collision between the two sections of the movement in America. Halpern describes in detail the unfolding of these events, providing much insight into their background. He concludes his analysis with a long chapter (actually, two chapters in one). The first part is a succinct and useful description of the developments until 1930 when members of the Brandeis group returned to the leadership of the ZOA; the second part contains Halpern's concluding comments.

Halpern's book is very much a book for the historian: calm and reflective, served by a fingertip knowledge that goes far beyond familiarity with all the printed sources and enables him to give to each event its proper weight in the overall picture. But for this impatient reviewer, Halpern's serene detachment is frequently unsettling. After all, we are dealing here with one of the most dramatic events in the history of Zionism. It is a difficult task to comment on a book that is so professionally correct and on so high an intellectual level—but where, somehow, the colors are paler than they ought to be. Under Halpern's steady microscope, all the issues are well understood and explained. But too much of the throb of the action gets lost, too many of the darker motivations of the leading actors are only implied (since they are undocumentable) rather than stated and explored.

The outstanding example is Halpern's treatment of Brandeis. To me, it seems that Halpern is too "soft" on Brandeis. Brandeis's behavior among the Zionists was quite different from his conduct in general, be it as lawyer, as adviser to presidents or as Supreme Court justice. Among the Zionists, a dimension of his personality was released that had been kept under strict control among his professional peers—and quite a dimension it was!

The time was crucial. Zionism's great opportunity expressed in the Balfour Declaration was being translated into hesitant and partial facts. The Jewish community in Palestine had been ruined by the war, its numbers reduced by one-third. The Zionist movement, its ranks in disarray and its organizational structure weakened because of the war and the subsequent pogroms in Eastern Europe, had difficulties coping with such a sequel of mixed opportunities and problems. Delicate political negotiations were going on in Europe between the Zionists and the British and with the other members of the Entente. British policy regarding Palestine wavered between a pro-Zionist formulation of the Mandate and the much more restrictive intentions embodied in the Churchill Memorandum, first drafted in 1921. Herbert Samuel was the first high commissioner of Palestine. He was a Jew and a pro-Zionist, but faced with stiff Arab opposition he was changing his mind.

At that unsettled and complex moment, Brandeis entered the arena of European Zionist politics, about which he knew precious little, like an elephant in a china shop. His performance in Europe and in the United States, from 1919 to 1921, was invariably aggressive, arrogant and totally uncompromising. Whoever opposed him or his Zionist ideas, most of them half-baked in any case, was immediately classified as a moral cripple. To compromise was immoral, too—at least in matters Jewish or Zionist. Brandeis possessed a well-developed capacity to remember his opponents and a vindictiveness of remarkable dimensions. He had humiliated the great Jacob Schiff, who in his old age had been honest enough to change his mind about his past ideas and had tried to find a personal way toward Zionism. He came to despise Louis Lipsky, to whom American Zionism owed much more than to him. He ridiculed Weizmann, on whose shoulders lay an infinitely heavy burden of Zionist problems and responsibilities.

Brandeis's Zionist performance from 1919 to 1921 had a disturbing personal dimension that is difficult to ignore. It was as if long pent-up tensions found release in an astonishing ego trip. It may be significant that the one opposing figure on the Jewish scene whom Brandeis treated with care was Louis Marshall. Marshall was a public figure and possessed the kind of forceful personality that, apparently, justi-fied caution.

Undoubtedly, Brandeis was a personality of very large dimensions. One may wonder if the harm he did to the Zionist cause was not equally large. But did he really cause harm? Several generations later, how do we evaluate the historical importance of the Brandeis-Weizmann confrontation?

A comparison much heard of in the Weizmann camp in the spring of 1921 was with the Uganda controversy of 1903. Many of Weizmann's companions were veterans of that epic confrontation, and it seemed to them that a quite similar situation was replaying itself in America. They were right, up to a point. There was something comparable in the tension characteristic of both events as well as in the lining up of East Europeans versus West Europeans. Nevertheless, the similarities were more of form than of substance.

Two of the results of the Uganda debate significantly influenced the history of Zionism. First, after the controversy there was never again any doubt that the Zionist movement led to Zion. The second result was more subtle: the 1903 crisis established the dominance of a certain ideological approach in Zionism that was to remain dominant later on. Russian Zionists suffered from the pogroms of 1903–1906 like Russian Jews in general. There was an apparent contradiction in the Zionists' reaction: in spite of the pressure of the deteriorating situation of Russian Jewry, they were less ready than West European Zionists to give way and to adopt pseudo-Zionist solutions that were apparently faster and easier than the difficult path leading toward the Land of Israel. Consequently, Zionism as a long-range idea, as a movement attuned to larger historical trends more than to short-term necessities, was decisively affirmed as a result of the Uganda controversy.

What about the results of the Weizmann-Brandeis struggle? Independently of how we evaluate the ideas of Brandeis and his associates concerning the economic development of Palestine or their plans for the reorganization of the Zionist organi-zation, theirs represented a serious attempt to participate in the leadership of the world Zionist movement and perhaps even to take it over. It was something that had never happened before in American Zionism: a group with the will to lead the whole movement, armed with a well-articulated plan and, especially important, with an impressive array of human talent to man the firstline positions in the world organi-zation. Figures like Louis D. Brandeis, Jacob de Haas, Julian W. Mack, Stephen S. Wise, Felix Frankfurter, Benjamin V. Cohen, Bernard Flexner, Robert Szold and others, embodied intellectual and professional qualities that stood out even in a talent-rich movement like the Zionist one.

The defeat of the Brandeis group at the Cleveland Convention in 1921 had several negative consequences, in general Zionist terms. Halpern mentions the disarray of the American movement in the 1920s. In addition, the Zionist movement returned to the old pattern of relationships between its European and American branches that had been established before the First World War: the Europeans fulfilled the politi-cally leading role and American Zionism, in spite of its potential, limped behind.

Apparently, there were no positive results, for either side. The struggle that had shaken the very foundations of American Zionism and had seemed to threaten the unity of the Zionist movement caused little more than a ripple at the Twelfth Zionist

Congress, which took place at Carlsbad in August 1921, only two months after the Cleveland decision. No member of the Brandeis group deigned to participate in the Congress. It was left to Julius Simon to make a well-intentioned presentation explaining the American case. He was listened to, but the matter generated little interest. The delegates turned quickly to the urgent business at hand, namely, how to set up the Jewish national home in Palestine.

All this still leaves the crucial question of how to explain the reasons for the defeat of the Brandeis group in the spring of 1921. Halpern shows that the Americans' case had a strong logic of its own and that in several crucial matters the positions of Weizmann and Brandeis were quite close. In addition, there were moments during the debates when Mack and his colleagues had a clear tactical advantage over Weizmann.

One possibility is that a certain intrinsic weakness of American Zionism, more than the actual struggle itself, explains the outcome of the confrontation. Weizmann had his own explanation for that weakness, as he had written a year before to Herbert Samuel:

> The leaders of American Zionism are not nationalist Jews. To them Zionism is not a movement which gives them a definite viewpoint of the world, which gives them a definite outlook on Jewish life. Zionism is to them largely a movement which tends towards the building up of a country with which they themselves have not much in common but which they are ready to accept, because it makes an appeal to the Jewish masses of which they know nothing.

This opinion, which expresses in a nutshell what many European Zionist leaders thought about the Brandeis administration, does not quite stand the test of historical fact. For Brandeis and his friends, Zionism *was* connected with a "viewpoint of the world," albeit an American point of view—or more exactly, American Zionist. The Palestinocentric face of the American movement was not a matter of Brandeis's personal views or tactics but part of a position elaborated in American Zionism in the years before Brandeis's appearance in the movement.

The internal development of American Zionism had followed stages that were different from those of European Zionism, although it took place at more or less the same time—the first decade of the twentieth century. Unlike the Europeans, the Americans had not evolved from the Uganda decision to the Helsingfors resolutions and from there to the Zionist synthesis that had begun at the Eighth Zionist Congress in 1907. Matters like the role of Zionism in the Diaspora and its participation in the life of Jewish communities in Eastern Europe had very limited meaning under the conditions prevailing within American Jewry. Zionism in the United States came to mean something quite diverse from its significance in Europe. To quote Israel Friedlaender's felicitous definition, its emphasis was on "Zionism plus Diaspora, Palestine plus America."

There are no indications that Brandeis and his associates, who represented a new group (indeed, even a new phenomenon) in American Zionism, were aware of these former ideological developments. Nonetheless, unknowingly they were continuing an ideological line that had a logic of its own, not necessarily connected with a certain figure or a given group in the American Zionist leadership.

This is why the "Summary," the detailed (even if rather confused) statement prepared by the Brandeis-Mack administration in February 1921 deserves careful attention. In its principles, it was the first and last attempt to translate the ideological premises of American Zionism into a political platform.

The "Summary" had little chance (if any) of becoming a blueprint for an actual reorganization of the whole Zionist movement. First, because Weizmann refused to consider it as a basis for negotiations, rightly claiming that it dealt with matters that were beyond his mandate and belonged within the realm of a Zionist Congress. Second, because the "Summary" signaled a retreat in American Zionist ambitions: no longer to lead the world movement but to argue for its reorganization in a way that would make it possible for the American Zionists to guard their own turf. This was a hopeless proposition. And last because, as explained, the conception underlying it made some sense under American Jewish and American Zionist conditions, but none under the ideological and political realities of the European-minded World Zionist Organization.

Perhaps, we should reconsider our accepted evaluation regarding the significance of the Brandeis-Weizmann struggle. With all the passion and sorrow it caused, the Brandeis-Weizmann confrontation was and remained an internal affair of American Zionism. From a historical perspective, we are led to conclude that unlike the Uganda controversy, it did not (and apparently could not) rise to the category of a Zionist crisis of worldwide proportions. But it certainly weakened the Zionist movement. It brought about the neutralization during the 1920s and 1930s of one of its largest sections, a result that certainly influenced negatively the balance of Zionist achievement.

Everyone who studies the Brandeis-Weizmann controversy is left with the feeling that there are still elusive elements in the ultimate understanding of that historical episode. It is Ben Halpern's lasting merit that he has produced the best description and analysis of that issue. He compels us all to reconsider again the primary and secondary significance of that important event in Zionist and in American-Jewish history.

EVYATAR FRIESEL
The Hebrew University

Book Reviews

Antisemitism, Holocaust and Genocide

Leonard Dinnerstein, *Uneasy at Home: Antisemitism and the American Jewish Experience.* New York: Columbia University Press, 1987. xi + 281 pp.

Lecturers who warn Jewish audiences of the persistent dangers of antisemitism in the United States never need to worry about ending up on the *New York Times* list of "100 Neediest Cases." For public opinion polls reveal that Jews tend to believe that there is more antisemitism than there really is; fewer gentiles harbor negative feelings about Jews than Jews seem to realize.

But the paradox goes even deeper. Leonard Dinnerstein, who is probably the preeminent historical authority on the subject, also believes that it suffers from neglect rather than exaggerated concern. "Antisemitism as a factor in American Jewish history has been to a considerable extent overlooked by other historians" (p. ix), he writes in justification of the republication of his articles, which are largely devoted to the expressions of such bigotry in the American South, in the federal government in the 1930s and 1940s and in the black community. Though he promises, in collaboration with others, to deliver a full-scale history of American antisemitism, scholars should welcome *Uneasy at Home,* especially since some of the essays are the standard interpretations. The apparatus of endnotes and bibliography is also ample enough to tempt other scholars to pursue his leads.

Although this collection advertises itself as revisionist, the author is actually a rather old-fashioned historian, unencumbered by the avant-garde methods of social history. He does not try to deconstruct such pivotal texts as Henry Ford's *The International Jew* nor delve into the intricacies of psychoanalytic theory to account for the persistence of such bigotry. The book offers precious little theory at all, serving up so much meat and potatoes that nowhere is a definition of antisemitism offered, although no reader is likely to dispute Dinnerstein's categorization of the Leo Frank case and of the riot at the funeral of Rabbi Joseph Jacob as illustrations of the phenomenon.

Uneasy at Home does note that antisemitism becomes more acute during periods of social and economic crisis, a generalization that the author does not attempt to prove. That is convenient. Crises can be found almost anytime in modern society without being correlated to antisemitism, the history of which is punctuated with incidents that can be seen as episodic rather than as the convulsions of a society erupting against the Jews. Terming the Frank affair "a Dreyfus case in Georgia" is not helpful—except as a contrast—since it was so aberrant. Dinnerstein blames the lynching on the fears of modernization and industrialization, which leaves unexplained the concurrent election of Atlanta's most prominent Jewish lay leader to head the local Chamber of Commerce. No other Jews were harmed nor did mobs storm through the streets chanting the Southern equivalent of *"À bas les juifs."*

Part of the problem with Dinnerstein's perspective is that it is not comparative. Acquaintance with antisemitism elsewhere would underscore how mild its American form has been. His account of the "savage" bigotry unleashed during the Civil War would puzzle the chronicler of East European Jewry, for example. No serious historian has denied the presence of antisemitism in the United States; in moral terms, the existence of even one artifact or proponent of it is bothersome. But how strong a case has Dinnerstein made that the subject has been unduly neglected? How should such scholarly imbalances be rectified? A book of essays—none of which employs a comparative method—devoted mostly to discrete topics is simply inappropriate for the construction of an actual argument because such a volume conveys no genuine sense of proportion, no marshaling of all relevant and significant evidence in order to strike the right balance.

Dinnerstein justly praises the historiography of Jonathan Sarna, including his 1981 *Commentary* article on American antisemitism, while ignoring a key feature of Sarna's argument: that all sorts of institutional checks spiked antagonism to Jews. Dinnerstein points to Oscar Handlin's tricentennial history of American Jewry, *Adventure in Freedom* (1954) as an example of the sort of approach he wishes to correct. But even Handlin devoted dozens of pages in his survey to discrimination, including three pages on the Frank case. And what would Dinnerstein prefer to call a general history of American Jewry—*The Ordeal of Prejudice?* Does that do justice to the main features of life in a country that has not imposed religious restrictions on Jews and that has harbored the most affluent and powerful and free Diaspora community in history? Dinnerstein's chapter on the East European Jewish immigration acknowledges that the descendants of these immigrants "can live where they like, work almost any place they have the necessary skills, and worship—or not—in any manner that pleases them." This "almost total freedom" includes "formal barriers (by federal and state government) against wanton bigotry" (pp. 37–38), thus bolstering the scholarly orientation that Dinnerstein elsewhere derides.

The reader of an anthology such as this should not expect the classic Aristotelian unities to be maintained. The first two chapters focus on the East European immigration and its emphasis on requiring the advantages of education, the sort of adaptation and adjustment that the introduction claims constitutes too narrow a reading of the American Jewish past. The South is given so much attention (four chapters) largely because Dinnerstein has devoted his considerable energies of research to the region, but his emphasis on hostility is rather unconvincing. He emphasizes the apparent paralysis of Southern Jews during the desegregation crisis of the 1950s and 1960s, aptly noting that their eagerness for acceptance and for the abrogation of distinctiveness reflected anxieties about antisemitism. But in the absence of evidence that white Southern society was pervaded with hostility to Jews, such anxieties may mean nothing other than a capacity to be easily intimidated. Dinnerstein assumes that Jewish fears were empirically warranted. But he misses an intriguing feature of the South's public culture. Historically permeated with racism, with xenophobia, with nativism, with filiopietistic reverence for tradition and social hierarchy, with expectations of conformity, it lacked an ideology of Jew-hatred. Despite the homogeneity of the white community, acceptance of Jews was widespread and specific antipathy to Jews was uncommon. The wild racist demagoguery of the region only rarely (as with Tom Watson and John Rankin) targeted Jews. No wonder then that Dinnerstein wisely leaves unchallenged a 1966 generalization by Charles Stember that, according to early public opinion polls, "the South appeared less antisemitic than other areas" (p. 244).

Dinnerstein often refers to "American" attitudes toward Jews, when he really means the views of gentiles. Although the practice is common enough in, say, German Jewish historiography, the slip is an odd one in the American context because it concedes the extreme antisemitic position that Jews are not really Americans. But there never was a "Jewish problem" in the United States because the full rights of citizenship were never really disputed (unlike Germany, where they had to be won through the struggle for emancipation). Dinnerstein insists that "neither Jewish, nor American Jewish, history can be understood without an extended analysis of how others have reacted to Jews" (p. 6). That is incontrovertible. But then why equate gentile reactions so exclusively with antisemitism? His formulation of the topic excludes any interest in the phenomenon of philosemitism, or what forces (beyond the Jewish defense agencies) might have resisted antisemitism; and even his interest in ambivalence toward Jewry (when the admiration can be sneaky) is scant. At best, this is a volume about only one form that gentile attitudes have assumed toward Jews in the United States. The emphasis is peculiar—and paradoxical—at a time when other Jewish scholars, especially sociologists, are worried that so many gentiles and Jews are falling in love with one another that the perpetuation of a vibrant community may be imperiled.

However much American Jews still feel that they are *supposed* to worry about latent as well as overt hostility to them, they do not live with their bags packed. Howard Morley Sachar has recalled bringing American Jewish students studying in Israel to meet David Ben-Gurion who would ask them whether they could really identify with "ancestors" like the Puritans and the early colonists, whether they were not really more at home in Israel. The students tended to respond that they experienced no estrangement at all, that they felt at home in both countries.

STEPHEN J. WHITFIELD
Brandeis University

Judith E. Doneson, *The Holocaust in American Film*. Philadelphia: The Jewish Publication Society, 1988. viii + 262 pp.

When *Judgment at Nuremberg* was first broadcast in the United States as a television drama in 1959, four or five references in the original script to the Nazi gas chambers were deleted out of respect for the sponsor, the American Gas Association. These sorts of imperatives within popular culture would not seem to encourage a suitable presentation of the history and meaning of the Holocaust. But the effort to make sense of the senseless, to make mass murder intelligible to a mass audience, is, nevertheless, the subject of Judith E. Doneson's cogent book, an incarnation of her doctoral dissertation at The Hebrew University of Jerusalem. Dealing with films from *The House of Rothschild* (1934) through NBC-TV's *Holocaust* (1978), the author evinces a primary interest in the range of interpretations of the Holocaust, usually depicted either as an instance of universal suffering or as a distinctly Jewish phenomenon. Without developing her position, she herself leans toward the latter interpretation as historically and morally more correct. But *The Holocaust in American Film* suggests how uneasy the makers of most of these works were with particularism and peoplehood, with the unique ordeals of the history of the Diaspora. For both the antecedents to genocide and the *Shoah* itself tended to be shown to American audiences under the auspices of universalism.

For example, Anne Frank wondered, "Who has made us Jews different from all other people? Who has allowed us to suffer so terribly up till now?" This covenantal echo is posthumously transformed in George Stevens's film of *The Diary of Anne Frank* (1959), as in the earlier play. "We're not the only people that've had to suffer," Anne (Millie Perkins) is made to say. "There've always been people that've had to. . . . Sometimes one race. . . . Sometimes another." (pp. 70–71). In Charlie Chaplin's *The Great Dictator* (1940), the inhabitants of the ghetto are merely proletarians, stripped of any distinctive Jewish traits or features. As Doneson points out, these United Artists Jews are not joined together by a common religion or heritage but are bound to one another only by their status as victims. The director-scenarist-star reinforces this depreciation of separatism, for Chaplin plays both the Jewish barber and the dictator Hynkel.

Doneson is also interested in how the unprecedented and incomprehensible character of the Holocaust had to be accommodated to American audiences. Again, consider *The Diary of Anne Frank*. The film ended on an optimistic note ("In spite of all, I still believe men are good"), instead of at Bergen-Belsen where she died (a scene that a sneak preview audience rejected). And audiences did not seem to realize that the film was based on the actual experiences of the family in the Amsterdam secret annex, apparently assuming that what they were viewing was fictional. Such ignorance was perhaps corrected with the appearance of NBC's *Holocaust,* a nine-and-one-half-hour series that 120 million Americans watched—almost one citizen in two. The original script featured a lower-middle-class Polish family named the Levins, who ranged from Orthodoxy to Zionism. But the typical American TV addict could not be expected to identify with such a family, which was thereupon converted into an upper-middle-class Berlin family, the Weisses, headed by a distinguished physician. The actors in *Holocaust* could hardly have been expected to be as wretchedly emaciated as the inmates of the camps. But did they have to be shown keeping their suitcases and family pictures in Auschwitz?

In her chapter on this particular made-for-TV film, Doneson is a trifle defensive, conceding the perils of "trivialization" but denying that they scuttle the value of

Holocaust, which had a tremendous popular impact elsewhere as well. (The final moments of the original, in which Rudi—the sole surviving Weiss—goes to Palestine, were cut in the West German version, however, with the explanation that "any apologetics for the Jewish homeland would have been undesirable.") Critics of *Holocaust,* such as Elie Wiesel, are quoted as denouncing the inaccuracies and insensitivities of the TV work; but Doneson is clearly sympathetic to the view that such compromises and failures are dwarfed by the extraordinary educational impact that *Holocaust* exerted. She credits the film with raising the consciousness of politicians and ordinary citizens—without apparently noticing how glib and obtuse its analogies to contemporary evils often were.

In retrospect, it is puzzling how slowly and rarely the Holocaust itself had been broached, a mystery that the author obscures by devoting so much attention to films about far milder sorts of antisemitism, like *Gentleman's Agreement* (1947), or by opening her book with *The House of Rothschild* (1934), as though 20th Century Fox were somehow anticipating the genocide to come. The first major American film after the Second World War to confront head-on the destruction of European Jewry was *The Diary of Anne Frank,* which stops short of the camps, of course. And Otto Frank himself realized that audiences responded as much to the pathos of adolescent struggle and yearning as to the horror awaiting the family outside. Doneson misses, I think, the virtual uniqueness of the film—in the decade and a half after V-E Day— in disseminating information about the *Shoah.*

In the following year, Adolf Eichmann was captured in Argentina and Wiesel published *La Nuit* in an English translation; yet, only in 1965 did Hollywood make another film about the Holocaust—Sidney Lumet's *The Pawnbroker* (not counting Stanley Kramer's *Judgment at Nuremberg* [1961], in which *none* of the major or even minor actors plays a Jewish character). From the mid-1960s, however, the subject is occasionally faced—from *Ship of Fools* (1965) to *Cabaret* (1972) to *Voyage of the Damned* (1976) to *Julia* (1977). In a sense, the climax of Doneson's book is the treatment of NBC's *Holocaust,* in which finally the Jewish dimension is unflinchingly addressed.

Although Doneson quotes liberally from various critics and authorities, not once in her text does she refer to Annette Insdorf's *Indelible Shadows: Film and the Holocaust* (1983), which is listed in the bibliography. This earlier work is broader in scope (embracing European and Canadian films), but scarcely less incisive, even though Insdorf's summaries often come at the expense of analysis or the development of an overall theme. Because *The Holocaust in American Film* goes into greater depth, although it deals with fewer films, it may be ultimately a bit more satisfying as a guide to the serious reader and interpreter of film.

But the one-dimensional quality of Doneson's approach is to be deplored. The formal properties of the cinema seem of no interest to her, even though casting, composition, lighting, montage, and so on, are bound to affect responses. In several instances Doneson has not dug very deeply into the background of movie production. Her efforts to get beyond the staples of historical explanation and causality (e.g., citing the salience of race and violence in America in the 1960s) are perfunctory. Nor does the author wonder why several of the films she has selected are not really directly, or maybe even indirectly, about the Holocaust at all. Given the ethical acuity and aesthetic sensitivity that are necessary in tackling this topic, Hollywood's reluctance to imagine the unimaginable may be just as well.

STEPHEN J. WHITFIELD
Brandeis University

Richard Hovannisian (ed.), *The Armenian Genocide in Perspective*. New Brunswick: Transaction Press, 1986. 215 pp.

The Turkish denial of the Armenian genocide weighs heavily on this volume of articles, most of which were contributed to the International Conference on the Holocaust and Genocide held in Tel-Aviv in 1982. Israel Charny, one of the organizers of the conference, describes the pressures exerted by the Turkish government to remove the Armenian topic from the agenda and the response of the Israeli government, which succumbed to these pressures. It is to the great credit of the organizers that they, nevertheless, held the conference under these most difficult conditions of government intervention and foreign threat.

Richard Hovannisian, the distinguished historian and editor of this volume, refers in his foreword to the intense campaign of denial and refutation consistently waged by the Turkish government in its determination that the Armenian question never again become a subject for international consideration. In a later article, he analyzes the historiography of the denial of the Armenian genocide, tracing its different phases. He describes the anguish of the survivors and the descendants of the victims as they are thrust into a defensive position from which they are required to prove time and again that they have indeed been wronged, individually and collectively. And he inquires whether there is "any just and practical alternative to the dictum 'might makes right.'"

This is the theme, too, of the introduction by Terrence Des Pres, "Remembering Armenia," in which he comments that the challenge "this volume of essays rises to meet . . . is nothing less than power versus truth, [a] struggle of memory versus forgetting." He argues that the Enlightenment emancipated the educated elite from open service to their political masters, but that at the present time "the repoliticization of knowledge seems to be gaining momentum." This is, of course, highly relevant to the co-opting of some academics as active propagandists for the Turkish government's denial. And it is also highly relevant to Armenian terrorism as an anguished response to the "current collusion with the perpetrators of the crime."

Marjorie Dobkin also reflects on the denial from a different perspective in her article "What Genocide? What Holocaust? News from Turkey, 1915–1923: A Case Study." She documents media reporting and eyewitness accounts explicitly denouncing the "unprecedented crimes" and "crimes against humanity." Then she notes that suddenly the Turkish denial gained press coverage. One of the more chilling commentaries on morality in international affairs is her analysis of this transformation under the pressure of commercial interests. It recalls the attempts of the independent experts from the United States and Belgium to sabotage reference to the Armenian genocide in the most recent updating of the report on genocide by the Human Rights Subcommission, reflecting, one supposes, concern for the effect on the NATO alliance.

Finally, Vigen Guroian is concerned with this issue in his analysis of the content of Turkish denials, which consist of the customary justifications and excuses invoked by other governments in defense of their genocidal massacres of vulnerable groups. He also raises the issue of collective responsibility, arguing that when a nation's leadership consistently refuses to remember its past conscientiously, "it risks burdening itself and its citizens with an uneasy conscience and inflicts upon the nation a deformation of character that will severely hinder its capacity to act rationally and responsibly." This would be relevant to the Austrian refusal to acknowledge its active and willing participation in the Holocaust, but it may be a doubtful proposition, a projection from individual psychotherapy.

A second major theme is the exposition of the Armenian genocide itself. Richard Hovannisian opens the section with a discussion of the historical dimensions of the Armenian question from 1878–1923. His analysis of the commitment of the Western powers to the establishment of an Armenian state and the abandonment of that commitment under pressure of national self-interest, international rivalries and the Turkish resurgence under Kemal Atatürk is linked to Marjorie Dobkin's account of the commercial incentives in the United States that encourage historical revisionism. The final paper is a creative contribution by Robert Melson entitled "Provocation or Nationalism." Melson's major emphasis is on the causative significance of narrow Turkish chauvinism in the context of an Armenian renaissance and the disastrous campaigns of the First World War, with the threat of the further disintegration of the former empire. In a comparative article, Hrair Dekmejian identifies the basic characteristics of twentieth-century genocides.

Two papers discuss the psychosocial responses of survivors to the overwhelming traumas. Levon Boyajian and Haigaz Grigorian deal mainly with survivor guilt, anxiety symptoms and reactive depression, with poignant examples of survivor vulnerability that are heightened by the continued Turkish denial. Donald and Lorna Miller contribute their preliminary observations based on a long-term project in oral history—interviews with survivors—which promises to be an important contribution.

The remaining papers consider the literary responses to the Armenian genocide. They are complementary. Leo Hamalian provides a detailed analysis of the "Armenian Genocide in Literary Imagination." Vahe Oshagan deals more generally with the impact of the genocide, concluding that "almost seventy years after the catastrophe, the Armenian literary imagination has still not been able to grapple with the reality of the pain and of death and has not formulated the human message."

All in all, this is a most valuable contribution to scholarship on the Armenian genocide and an excellent text for college students.

LEO KUPER
University of California,
Los Angeles.

Eberhard Jaeckel, *Hitler in History*. Hanover and London: University Press of New England, 1984. 115 pp.

Ian Kershaw, *The "Hitler Myth": Image and Reality in the Third Reich*. Oxford: Clarendon Press, 1987. 297 pp.

Hans Speier, *German White-Collar Workers and the Rise of Hitler*. New Haven: Yale University Press, 1986. 208 pp.

Hans Speier's book, an English translation of the German revised and expanded edition published in 1977, is a detailed and comprehensive contribution to our understanding of Weimar society. This macro-sociological analysis was actually completed in 1932, but it could not be published at that time. Using the archives of various trade unions and interviews with trade union officials and politicians, Speier analyzes German society from 1918 up to the collapse of the Weimar Republic. Other related studies on modern German social history deal with the old established middle class, independent merchants and craftsmen. Speier focuses mainly on the new middle class—the white-collar workers: clerks, civil servants of low and middle rank, commercial employees and foremen.

The author clearly demonstrates that the social status of the new middle class was endangered from both the old middle classes and the new industrial blue-collar workers. Borrowing concepts from Weberian sociology, he argues that the half-educated white-collar workers were dissatisfied with their social position. They feared proletarization as a threat to their social ambitions and they supported their claims to social prestige with a nationalism that was distinct from that of the old bourgeoisie. Nationalism compensated them for the social disadvantages that they believed they were suffering compared to the blue-collar workers, whose prestige and status improved after the First World War. Speier found that the majority of white-collar workers were antisemitic nationalists. Volkish and conservative ideas found enthusiastic support in unions like the German National Association of Commercial Clerks (DHV).

How receptive were the white-collar workers to the Nazis? A study dating from 1940 examined social stratification of Nazi voters in various communities in Baden and Hesse and found an overrepresentation of white-collar workers in the Nazi party: twenty percent of the Nazi party (NSDAP) in 1933 were salaried employees. The implication of this and other studies is that such people were prime Nazi voters. Newer studies, however, tend to dispute these conclusions. Thomas Childers and Richard P. Hamilton have shown, through detailed electoral analyses for Hamburg and Berlin, that Nazis did best in upper-middle-class districts. Many white-collar workers evidently had more in common with the working-class milieu from which they came than with the bourgeoisie, and they voted for the socialist parties.

Kershaw's study is another well-researched and illuminating contribution by the leading British historian of the Third Reich, which should be read in conjunction with his other works on public opinion under the Nazi regime. It is a totally new version of his *Hitler-Mythos: Volksmeinung und Propaganda im Dritten Reich* (Stuttgart: 1980). While the German version concentrates on Bavaria only, this study covers all of Germany. The author has also added an important chapter on

Hitler and the Jewish question that summarizes his conclusions from previous work on German public opinion and Nazi antisemitism. The present book, written in Kershaw's usual flowing and elegant style, is based mainly on the sources he has used in his previous works: secret reports prepared periodically by German security agencies as well as reports by Social Democratic exiles—the *Sopade Berichte*. In his view, there were affinities, but not identity, between Hitler's visions and the expectations of the German public. Such, for example, was the case with the concept of *Lebensraum* and with the Jewish question. Hitler did not win popularity and support because of the Jewish issue. Kershaw's analysis of the election propaganda of 1930 shows that antisemitism was not the main theme but that it served as background for the Nazi propaganda. In his view, other issues, not antisemitism, dominated the image of the NSDAP in the eyes of its pre-1933 membership. The rush to the party was not because of Hitler's antisemitism, which was a secondary component in its appeal.

After his assumption of power, Hitler deliberately distanced himself from anti-semitic rhetoric and violence, although he continued to approve of them. He advocated, rather, legal discriminatory steps, which enjoyed widespread approval. This guided his approach in the April 1933 boycott and during the riots of the spring and summer of 1935. In those years, his few pronouncements on the Jewish question were only vague statements. In the war years, the public maintained a studied disinterest in the fate of the Jews—an unpleasant topic. The Jewish issue, as a result, was not as conspicuous as other issues. Kershaw concludes that antisemitism was of secondary importance in cementing bonds between Hitler and the German public. For the Nazi radicals, however, popular antisemitism was a springboard for activating governmental antisemitic measures.

The great value of this remarkable book is that it is the best account we have on the relationship between Hitler and the German public, showing the vital integrative power of Hitler's image in the Third Reich. This makes it obligatory reading for any student of Nazi Germany.

Jaeckel's study is based on a series of lectures he delivered at the Tauber Institute of Brandeis University and should be read in conjunction with his earlier book, *Hitler's Weltanschauung* (Middletown: 1969). As he explained in this study on the Führer's worldview, Hitler had two fundamental goals: territorial conquest and elimination of the Jews. In the present book, Jaeckel investigates the circumstances and means of implementation of these objectives. He argues that the German war of expansion is to be seen in the wider context of the expansionist policies of Italy and Japan. Within this context, Hitler's plan coincided with other geopolitical ambitions of the time. The expansionist plan was disclosed gradually; Hitler did not confide his ultimate aims even to his closest collaborators. In foreign policy, he followed a plan of territorial expansion designed in the 1920s, whose essence was the conquest of the Soviet Union. Its implementation was to take place in three stages: first, consolidation and rearmament; second, the defeat of France; third, war against Russia. In a detailed analysis of the reasons for German's declaration of war on the United States, he argues that this decision was not a result of Japan's attack on Pearl Harbor. Hitler feared that, as in the First World War, America's entry on the side of the Allies (and the supposed "Jewish stab in the back") would halt Germany's thrust toward the east. To avoid this, the Jews were to be eliminated in the extermination policy and the Americans would be kept busy by Japan. In Hitler's calculations, a war with Japan would prevent American intervention in Russia's favor, diverting its forces to the Pacific.

In the chapter devoted to the Holocaust, Jaeckel argues against functionalist interpretations that describe the Holocaust as the result of improvisations. In his opinion, there was no single killing order but a variety of orders extending over several months. In the spring of 1941, Hitler granted Himmler the power to kill Jewish officials in the Soviet Union and to incite pogroms. Later, during July and August, he extended this order to include all Russian Jews and later on to all of European Jewry.

Jaeckel's treatment of Hitler's assumption of power is tinted with a sort of Bonapartist interpretation. Hitler came to power when a political stalemate that stemmed from a lack of sociopolitical consensus paralyzed the Weimar Republic. In this power vacuum, when the reins of government were transferred to him, he instituted a monocracy supported by various groups, playing them off against each other, flattering all of them and promising everything to everybody. Jaeckel's book is an outstanding attempt at historical synthesis of the major topics relating to Hitler and the Third Reich.

DAVID BANKIER
The Hebrew University

Francis R. Nicosia, *The Third Reich and the Palestine Question.* Austin: University of Texas Press, 1985. 319 pp.

As the author points out in the preface, this book is primarily an analysis of German policy toward Palestine in the prewar years, and only indirectly a study of the Palestinian question itself (ix–x). Hence, it is narrower in scope than the available studies of Nazi Germany's policy in the Middle East, which Nicosia mentions, as well as the study in Hebrew by David Yisraeli, *The Palestinian Problem in German Politics 1889–1945* (Ramat Gan: 1974), which he does not mention.

Nicosia has gone through a wealth of archival material, although he seems to have overlooked relevant files, notably in the holdings of the Central Zionist Archives in Jerusalem; he also failed to consult the Deutsche Zentral Archiv in Potsdam and the Hagana Archives. However, using material from archives in three European countries, the United States and Israel, he has made a useful contribution to the subject.

To a degree, Palestine policy in the early years of Nazi rule was a continuation of the policy of Imperial Germany, whose extensive interests in the Middle East were linked to its global ambitions. But to a greater extent the Nazis continued the policy of the Weimar Republic which as a defeated country striving to reestablish its position pursued only limited economic, religious and cultural aims. Nicosia may overstate the case in attributing a strong Zionist component to German policy during the Weimar years (pp. 12–13), but he shows that under the Nazis, Germany's economic interests in Palestine increased through the Haavara agreement, which was part of the Nazi effort to rid Germany of the Jews.

At the same time, the Nazi treatment of the Palestine question in the prewar period set the stage for what followed. The Final Solution was already foreshadowed in the ideas and practices that emerged in the 1930s. By this we mean the Nazi view that Jewish emigration could not solve the Jewish problem for Germany, a view that crystallized in connection with the Peel Commission's plan to partition Palestine and was accompanied by the increasing brutality of their anti-Jewish measures. The Palestine policy was also a portent of developments in another direction. The increased power of Germany—a power bent on the destruction of the post-First World War settlement, made her attractive to Arab nationalists who felt that this settlement had frustrated their ambitions. The threat to partition Palestine and to create a Jewish state on its soil activated contacts between Nazi Germany and the Arabs, not only with the mufti of Jerusalem and other Palestinian leaders, but also with Arab elements in Syria and with the governments of Iraq and Saudi Arabia. These contacts were expanded during the war years. Hostility both to the Jewish National Home and the Jews, in general, became a central feature of Nazi Germany's Arab policy during the war, indeed, its most constant and credible component. Germany's other promises to the Arabs were riddled with ambiguities and reservations since other European powers' interests in the Arab world took precedence over the demands of the Arab nationalists.

At first, the German policymakers felt they had to take account of British interests; after 1938, those of Italy; after 1940, those of France and Turkey as well. Moreover, Nazi ideology dictated racial contempt for the Arabs who were regarded as objects of European domination.

The year 1938 was, in many aspects, a watershed for the Nazis. Nicosia mentions that in March the *Anschluss* handed over control of the Jews and Jewish emigration in Austria to the SS and SD and, after Kristallnacht, they became dominant in these spheres in the Reich proper as well (pp. 153–156). In 1938 anti-Jewish measures were intensified and tightened. These developments were in line with the overall strengthening of the Nazi grip on power; this came about through the removal of top personnel from the armed forces and the reorganization of its command and the appointment of Ribbentrop as foreign minister. Furthermore, the Czechoslovakian crisis—provoked by the Nazis—brought Europe to the brink of war; Hitler was ready to step over the line. It was in these circumstances that the Middle East policy formulated in 1937 in connection with the Peel Partition Plan began to be implemented. The Nazis embarked on a more positive policy toward the Arabs; they showed more interest in fomenting unrest in Palestine and Syria and in arms transactions, and they established diplomatic relations with Saudi Arabia. All this did not mean that the Nazis had abandoned Palestine as a useful outlet for Jewish emigration but, practically, it assumed relatively less importance in this respect.

Another issue tackled by Nicosia is that of Jewish responses to Nazi policies. He is right to say that there was a fundamental incompatibility between Nazi Germany and Zionism (pp. 24–25), even though the Nazis saw Zionism as a means of facilitating the removal of Germany's Jewish population. However, Jewish and Zionist responses were not generally based on the recognition that the Jewish position in Germany was irrevocably lost (p. 41). In the 1930s there was no feeling that the Jews had to flee for their lives. The Jewish leadership, including mainstream Zionist leaders, did not countenance the total liquidation of the Jewish German community but supported the orderly emigration of certain groups who could be absorbed into other countries, including Palestine. To some Jewish and Zionist leaders the acceptance of total liquidation was tantamount to repudiating emancipation and turning back the tide of history. Nicosia does not try to elucidate the position among the Jews or even that within the Zionist camp itself. There were right-wing Zionists such as Jabotinsky who saw no future for the Jews in the Diaspora but opposed Haavara, whereas pragmatic left-wing and center leaders supported it. It is also difficult to agree with Nicosia's sweeping description of the Zionist concept of nationhood as *völkisch,* related to the traditional German meaning of the term and other *völkisch* nationalist movements in Eastern and Central Europe (pp. 17, 194).

L. Hirszowicz
Institute for Jewish Affairs, London

David M. Szonyi (ed.), *The Holocaust: An Annotated Bibliography and Resource Guide.* New York: Ktav Publishing House for the National Jewish Resource Center, 1985. xiv + 396 pp.

The profusion of Holocaust literature in recent decades has led to a spate of Holocaust bibliographies. Last year there even appeared a book that includes a small "bibliography of bibliographies" of the Holocaust: Morton H. Sable, *Holocaust Studies: A Directory and Bibliography of Bibliographies* (Greenwood, Florida: Penkevill, 1987). Sable's flawed but interesting attempt is the only one I have seen that includes books in Hebrew and Yiddish; he even includes Nazi organizations and other "Holocaust deniers." Another recent effort is the second edition of *The Holocaust: An Annotated Bibliography* by Harry James Cargas (Chicago and London: American Library Association, 1985), which is a copiously annotated list of some five hundred English-language books recommended for libraries. Cargas, who calls himself a "post-Auschwitz Catholic" obsessed by the Holocaust, also participated in the work under review. The most extensive English-language bibliography on the Holocaust to date, however, is the unwieldy and insufficiently annotated volume by Abraham J. Edelheit and Hershel Edelheit, *Bibliography on Holocaust Literature* (Boulder and London: Westview Press, 1986). It includes over nine thousand books and articles in English on the Holocaust, Holocaust instruction and Holocaust-related literature.

Holocaust-related literature is defined by every Holocaust bibliographer as he sees fit. It tends to include such topics as Jews in the Allied armies, European Jewry in the last pre-Holocaust generation, Nazism and antisemitism in general. In the work under review, the concept is extended to take in modern Jewish history as well as Nazi attempts to exterminate non-Jewish groups.

Szonyi's book, in which he was assisted by fifteen specialists, can hold its own in what has become a quite developed field. The running heads on every page assist the reader in finding the material since the book has no index. Coverage, as usual, is limited to material in the English language, with articles included. Annotations are normally provided; they are briefer but more critical than those in Cargas's book, which are too generous in some instances. For example, in the book under review, the largest section, written by Szonyi himself ("Scholarship, Memoirs, and Other Nonfiction on the Holocaust") has notes pointing out the faults of *The War Against the Jews* by Lucy Dawidowicz (p. 37) and of *The Extermination of the European Jews* by Raul Hilberg (p. 39); for Hilberg's important book, the differences between the various editions are also shown.

Other, smaller sections include "Literature (Belles-lettres) of the Holocaust: A Select Bibliography" by Jeffrey Hirshberg and David G. Roskies; and "Bibliographies on the Holocaust for Young People" by Bea Stadtler.

The last half of the book is aimed primarily at those who plan Holocaust commemorative programs in the United States and Canada. Here the reader finds, inter alia, addresses of organizations, audiovisual materials and where to get them, monuments and their location, how to conduct interviews, how to program. A sample program is included, which has some Hebrew and Yiddish readings.

AVRAHAM GREENBAUM
University of Haifa

Communal History

Chimen Abramsky, Maciej Jachimczyk and Antony Polonsky (eds.), *The Jews in Poland*. Oxford: Basil Blackwell, 1986. xii + 264 pp.

The articles collected in this volume present selected problems in the history of Jews in Poland from the beginning of the Polish state in the tenth century until events in 1982. They were prepared as papers for the conference on Polish Jewish studies held in Oxford in September 1984 and can be considered not only as a step forward in historical studies, but also as an important stage in contemporary Polish Jewish discussions.

This was the second major conference on the history and culture of Polish Jews and Polish Jewish relations. The previous one was held at Columbia University in March 1983, with the participation of only a few Polish historians. In April 1986 another meeting was organized by the Tauber Institute of Brandeis University. In September of the same year, a conference on the history of Polish Jews before the partitions of Poland was held in Cracow, and in February 1988 the biggest of all these meetings was held in Jerusalem. The papers presented during all these conferences, save for the one at Columbia, will be published.

Each conference was marked by vivid discussion of the various topics, not always of purely academic interest. It is important to note that these exchanges of opinion were not fruitless. Comparing papers presented at the first of the conferences with those presented subsequently indicates that progress toward resolving certain issues has taken place, while other problems are now more clearly defined. At the same time new issues, which will have to be discussed in the future, have surfaced.

The volume under review comprises seventeen articles. Aleksander Gieysztor opens with the beginnings of the Jewish settlement in the Polish lands. Daniel Tollet, Jacob Goldberg, Gershon Hundert and Andrzej Ciechanowiecki discuss problems concerning the history of Jews in the Polish Commonwealth (sixteenth to eighteenth centuries). Stefan Kieniewicz, Daniel Beauvais, Ryszard Bender and Frank Golczewski consider Polish Jewish relations in the nineteenth and early twentieth centuries. Joseph Lichten comments on the problem of assimilation in the nineteenth and twentieth centuries. Interwar Poland is the topic of articles by Ezra Mendelsohn and Jerzy Holzer. Teresa Prekerowa, Władysław Bartoszewski and Yisrael Gutman analyze Polish Jewish relations during the Second World War, and

Michal Borwicz and Łukasz Hirszowicz end the volume by discussing postwar Polish Jewish relations. The editors have added very useful maps.

The volume ably presents the scope and variety of topics discussed during the Oxford conference. The articles convey much important material and formulate some interesting hypotheses. However, they should be viewed as a stage in a developing dialogue. This is especially important in the case of studies concerning contemporary history, but is valid for the other articles as well.

A. Gieysztor considers the names of villages such as "Kozary" to be proof of Khazar settlement in Poland. However, at the Cracow conference this view was disputed and other possible origins of these names were suggested. The explanation of the political sources of antisemitism in the peasants' movement in Galicia before 1914, proposed by F. Golczewski, is valid, but—I think—insufficient. The author neglects the economic differences between the Jewish market town (shtetl) and the virtual subsistence economy of the majority of peasants. This was a source of intense social conflict that was transformed into ethnic strife. Similar situations are well known in countries where ethnic minorities other than the Jews have played a similar economic role.

E. Mendelsohn asks in his study if interwar Poland was "bad or good for the Jews." I had the opportunity to discuss this question (*Polin,* vol. 1) and I hope that the author will continue the exchange of views. The discussion presented in this volume concerning Polish Jewish relations during the Second World War was extended at subsequent conferences and is far from being resolved. Documents and studies recently published in Poland suggest that the pogrom in Kielce in 1946 may not have been a provocation of the security organs (a hypothesis mentioned by M. Borwicz), and cast new light on the shameful wave of official antisemitism in 1968 (this is discussed by Ł. Hirszowicz). I hope that further documentation will come to light to afford a deeper insight into the causes and effects of these events.

The articles herein present a fair range of facts, views and opinion. I would hope that these might influence popular attitudes and stereotypes, and that future studies may offer explanations for many questions raised by the authors. This is an important work because its role in provoking renewed discussion will certainly influence the course of further research.

JERZY TOMASZEWSKI
Warsaw University

"Amilat," *Judaica Latinoamericana: Estudios historico-sociales.* Jerusalem: Magnes Press, 1988. 265 pp.

Amilat is the Israeli society for research on Latin American Jewry. In Hebrew, the word implies "toil." And the editors of this volume—Margalit Bejarano, Rosa Perla Raicher, Silvia Schenkolewsky and Leonardo Senkman—have toiled to good effect, presenting nineteen brief studies, twelve in Spanish, seven in English. Out of eight non-Israeli contributors, three are Latin American, three from the United States, one an Oxonian and one a Pole. These papers were presented in Jerusalem in 1985 at the Ninth World Congress of Jewish Studies. However the printed proceedings of that congress were synoptic, whereas *Judaica Latinoamericana* offers full or expanded versions.

Lacking colonial-era and nineteenth-century studies, the book focuses squarely on twentieth-century Jewish immigrants and their adjustment to Latin America. The process has been precarious. As Haim Avni points out in his introduction, Jewish survival remains threatened by Latin America's monolithic cultural tradition and explosive social polarization.

Though uneven, this anthology contains several outstanding items. Through periodicals and interviews, Margalit Bejarano has traced the transformation of Cuban Jewry under Gerardo Machado and Grau. David Bankier has analyzed the successful popular-front tactics of German Jewish Communists in Mexico. Leonardo Senkman has plowed through Argentine, U.S. and UN archives to demonstrate Argentina's blatantly anti-Jewish immigration policy just after the Second World War. Ignacio Klich has cast a wide net to clarify Peron's Jewish policy as part of his rapprochement with the United States and has illuminated intramural politicking among U.S. diplomats and Jewish notables. To Nelson Vieira we owe a delightful, if naive, sketch of Jews and Jewish themes in recent Brazilian letters.

Judaica Latinoamericana illustrates the extraordinary variety of investigative endeavor on the Jewish condition in Latin America. But the authors have failed, alas, to take cognizance of one another's work. Senkman and Klich might have served as mutual correctives, likewise the various researchers into community and school organization; while the secondary sources of some of these pieces are badly missed in others. For this the editors are blameless. The lack of a bibliography and an index is another matter. Then, too, the proofreaders have been rather sleepy, and there are some missing footnotes. But these are minor failings. In the immediate future, until several of these chapters quite naturally grow into books, this should remain a useful reference for the Jewish historian dealing with Latin America as well as for Latin Americanists in general.

FRED BRONNER
The Hebrew University

Michael Brown, *Jew or Juif? Jews, French Canadians, and Anglo-Canadians, 1759–1914*. Philadelphia: The Jewish Publication Society, 1987. xii + 356 pp.

Jew or Juif? is an insightful and well-written history of Jewish integration in Canada up to the outbreak of the First World War. More specifically, the volume examines the reasons for the almost total Jewish identification with Anglo-Canada and, conversely, Jewish alienation from French Canada. Montreal serves as the primary, but not sole, focus for the study because it was the oldest, largest and wealthiest Jewish community in Canada. "In fact," notes the author, "in many respects, and for a very long time, to speak of Canadian Jewry meant, in large part, to speak of Montreal Jewry."

The pattern for Jewish identification began in 1760 when the first Jews arrived in Canada with the conquering British army. Until then, the French regime had prohibited Jews and other non-Catholics from settling or even visiting the colony. Conditions changed under the British. The Naturalization Act of 1740 considered Jews equal to Christians in the British colonies (although not in England), and this toleration continued and expanded through the eighteenth and nineteenth centuries. Britain's policy of welcoming the persecuted of other lands; its respect and reverence for the rule of law; its open sympathy for the Jews of Russia; its later support for Zionism, and its positive feelings toward Jews as a consequence of a Protestant affinity for the Bible, fostered strong feelings of attachment for England on the part of Jews.

The admiration Jews felt toward England was transferred to its colonial possessions. One of Canada's chief attractions for Jews was the fact that it was a British possession. Nevertheless, Jewish immigration to Canada during most of the nineteenth century remained small: in 1881 Canada contained only 2,443 Jews. To a degree this stemmed from a lack of knowledge about Canada on the part of Jewish immigrants and from the greater attraction of the United States. After 1881, Russian and Romanian oppression increased immigration to Canada, and the Jewish population rose to 75, 681 by 1911. Canada attracted these immigrants primarily because it was a "British country" and offered them freedom and economic opportunity.

Once in Canada, Jewish immigrants did their best to make themselves "British" in their institutional and personal lives. They did so because of their admiration for things British and because they wanted to be accepted by Anglo-Canadians. Thus, they adopted the language, customs, social and behavioral patterns of the ruling majority.

At the same time, Canadian Jews found the United States both fascinating and attractive. This led numbers of them to move across the border. Some went in search of a better livelihood, others because of the greater intellectual, cultural and educational opportunities available to Jews in places like New York City. Because of proximity and the growing ease of travel and communication between the two countries, the larger and more dynamic American Jewish community exerted a strong influence on Canadian Jewry. Canadian Jewish cultural life drew heavily on American Jewish cultural institutions, such as the American Jewish and Yiddish press and the Yiddish theater. The Canadian Jewish pulpit became largely Americanized by the twentieth century, the work of rabbis who came from the United States; and American Jewish religious movements, especially Conservative Judaism, found adherents in Canada. Most American Jewish charitable, fraternal and national organizations of the period established Canadian branches, and two of Canadian Jewry's major institutions, the Federation and the Canadian Jewish Congress, were modeled after their American counterparts. Although Canadian Zionism developed independently of the American movement, both organizations maintained close links. Consequently, Canadian Jews increasingly felt and acted as if they were Americans.

This might have conflicted with their loyalties toward Great Britain. It did not,

Michael Brown argues, because ongoing commercial relations and ties of language, culture and sentiment promoted among the English, the Canadians and the Americans the feeling that they were part of an increasingly integrated North Atlantic "Anglo-Saxon" civilization. This permitted Canadian Jews to reconcile their two ideals and their English and North American loyalties.

If the nineteenth century saw Canadian Jews becoming more attached to England and the United States, their feelings about France could best be described as ambivalent. Jews had enjoyed few rights in ancien régime France, and the emancipation they gained during the French Revolution deteriorated under Napoleon. The French Catholic church continued to be hostile to Jews and Judaism throughout the nineteenth century and anti-Jewish prejudice figured prominently in French intellectual life. The founder of modern racial antisemitism was the French aristocrat le Comte Joseph Arthur de Gobineau, and the climactic event of nineteenth-century antisemitism, the Dreyfus affair, occurred in France.

French Canadians exhibited many of the same attitudes about Jews as their coreligionists in France. The Catholic Church transferred its hostility toward Jews to the New World, while French Canadian literature and the French Canadian press disseminated French antisemitism. Moreover, French Canadian nationalists found Jews to be convenient scapegoats for much of what they resented and opposed. These attitudes left Jews uneasy and disinclined to live with French Canadians. Only in British-controlled Montreal, where the language of the government and business was English, did Jews feel comfortable enough to live with the French.

As Canadian Jewry grew, it established a variety of institutions to serve its religious and social needs. These organizations together with the Jewish desire to live in "Jewish" neighborhoods led to the creation of an almost autonomous Jewish life in Montreal, Toronto and other places in Canada. This autonomy was also encouraged by the fact that Jews were non-Christians in a "Christian country." While in many respects Jews were considered part of the Anglo-Canadian community, so long as they were not Protestants they could never be fully Canadian in all senses of the term. Although Jews achieved a strong measure of integration into Anglo-Canada, they never quite lost their sense of insecurity and nervousness regarding their status during the period covered by this study. In a postscript, Brown notes that although today's Canadian Jews are an integral part of the Canadian social mosaic, the rise of French Canadian nationalism has revived their previous insecurities.

The author has sifted through a wealth of primary and secondary sources in English, French, Hebrew and Yiddish. The result is a perceptive and thoughtful study of the Canadian Jewish experience. One small lapse is that Todd Endelman's fine study on the Jews of Georgian England does not appear to have been consulted by the author in his discussion of the attitude of eighteenth and nineteenth century Englishmen toward Jews. This, however, in no way detracts from the value and importance of Brown's work.

ROBERT ROCKAWAY
Tel-Aviv University

Frances Malino and Bernard Wasserstein (eds.), *The Jews in Modern France*. Waltham: Brandeis University Press, 1984. 354 pp.

What is one to make of a collection of essays on modern French Jewry that begins with an article by a prominent French historian who suggests that Alfred Dreyfus's disgrace resulted from his lack of sociability and argues that, for most Frenchmen in the nineteenth and twentieth centuries, the Jewish issue "was a minor question, or no question at all"? The editors of *The Jews in Modern France* may simply have wanted to be provocative, but Eugen Weber's dismissal of the significance of French Jewry is a telling indication of a sharp tension that is manifest throughout the volume between French Jewish historians and French generalists over the place of the Jewish community in modern France. For while historians of Franco-Judaica such as Paula Hyman, Yerachmiel (Richard I.) Cohen and Nancy Green are at pains to emphasize the problematics of French-Jewish relations, the specialists on France such as Weber, Patrice Higonnet and Stanley Hoffmann insist that Jewish issues have been of little consequence in modern French society and that the antisemitism manifested in the Dreyfus affair and in the Vichy era are only aberrations in French history. Unfortunately, despite the best intentions of Bernard Wasserstein and Frances Malino (the editors of the volume who cochaired the conference on Jews in Modern France at Brandeis University in 1983 from which many of the articles are taken), there is little significant interchange between the two groups. Although the two perspectives are often counterpoised, the overall impact is that of a *dialogue de sourds*.

The root cause of the problem and the fundamental weakness of the volume is the fact that neither group seems capable of developing a satisfying interpretative model on which to base Jewish historical development in France. Thus, the Jewish historians tend to limit their approach to the specifics of thought and behavior in the Jewish community during periods of crisis and often ignore general factors that fostered integration into the larger society. The French historians, in turn, seem strangely on the defensive, obsessed with reaffirming the values of French assimilationism and minimizing more recent scholarship that raises serious questions about the impact of cultural monolithism on French thought and behavior.

There are exceptions, of course. Nancy Green's article on East European Jews in Paris before the First World War incisively describes the dynamics and problematics of immigrant acculturation in France, while Zeev Sternhell's provocative essay on antisemitism in the Third Republic highlights the ambiguities of the left–right division in modern French history. Unfortunately, the issue that might have bridged the barrier between Jewish and French historians by breaking down both groups' convenient stereotypes—the role of a resurgent contemporary Jewish community in an increasingly pluralistic France—is limited to Shmuel Trigano's tendentious argument for inevitable marginalization. At times, the division between the two camps in the volume transcends the issue of the significance and the acceptance of a distinctive Jewish presence in France and becomes a debate over the future of French Jewry itself. Thus, while the generalists see the continued existence of the

Jewish community as only incidental to the concerns of the larger French society, the Jewish historians emphasize the attempt by French Jewry in the modern period to balance the often-conflicting demands of group survival and loyalty to the larger society. The most dramatic reflection of the divisions between the two groups is Patrice Higonnet's inclusion of Michel Debré, the Catholic grandson of a chief rabbi and spokesman for DeGaulle's anti-Israel policies, in his list of successful French Jews.

Under the circumstances, it is quite remarkable that anything useful emerges from the discussion. And yet there is much of value in the volume. Paula Hyman's overview of French Jewish historiography not only masterfully summarizes the relevant literature, but also attempts to trace the growing interest in French Jewry in the context of developments in both Jewish historiography and communal development. Yerachmiel Cohen's careful study of French Jewish responses to Vichy as well as the previously mentioned essays by Green and Sternhell are valuable synopses of their monographs. Michael Marrus's impressionistic analysis of contemporary antisemitism is a dispassionate discussion that serves as a valuable counterpoint to the emotion-filled treatment of the topic by both Frenchmen and Jews.

In the end, however, the reader is left dissatisfied. The editors certainly are to be commended for bringing the much-neglected subject of Franco-Judaica to a wider readership. Yet the underlying methodological and ideological conflicts remain without resolution. Despite a reasoned effort by David Landes in one of the final essays to find common ground between the interests of France and of its Jewish community, his vapid conclusion that everyone ultimately "would be poorer" if French Jewry disappeared serves only to highlight the conceptual gap that continues to exist between French and Jewish scholarship and self-consciousness in the contemporary era.

DAVID WEINBERG
Bowling Green State University

Jonathan Reider, *Canarsie: The Jews and Italians of Brooklyn Against Liberalism.*
    Cambridge: Harvard University Press, 1985. 290 pp.

Canarsie is a vivid re-creation by a Yale University ethnologist of a powerful moment in the early 1970s when the phenomenon of white ethnic backlash erupted in metropolitan centers across the United States. The official battle cry of this conservative turn among previously liberal, urban, middle-class whites was a fear of "black crime." This cry became especially acute when Afro-Americans attempted to move into previously all-white neighborhoods or when liberal administrators proposed school busing programs that would increase the enrollment of blacks in majority-white schools.

The turn to the right was also an expression of frustration about profound shifts in American culture that had occurred during the previous several years. The most

distressing of these changes were the sexual and cultural revolution of the young, the defeat of the United States in Vietnam and the signs of an increasingly uncertain economic future punctuated by President Nixon's 1971 wage-price freeze.

One of the most sensational events of the "backlash" period occurred in the fall of 1972 in Canarsie, New York, a lower-middle-class residential area with seventy thousand residents in Brooklyn. When thirty black students were bused into a neighborhood school, a portion of the Italian and Jewish population rose up in a display of racism that also included some violence. For three days, hundreds of Canarsie parents formed a jeering mob around John Wilson Junior High School in an attempt to intimidate the black students and keep them from entering.

The strength of Reider's book is that he dramatizes with an impressive ring of authenticity the voices and outlook of many lower-middle-class Italians and Jews as they rationalized behavior and opinions they would have abhorred had the targets been their own ethnic group. With a knack for eliciting and capturing racy speech and with an impressive sense of drama, Reider skillfully structures the book to allow the residents to depict the world as they see it. For many of those interviewed, the story they have to tell is relatively consistent.

According to the white ethnics, they are mostly descended from immigrants who started at the bottom and industriously worked their way up. Like the blacks, they, too, faced discrimination and hardship, but their ancestors chose to obey the laws and practiced sexual restraint. As a result, they managed to build solid families, acquire nice homes and create safe communities. Moreover, most of the interviewees did not consider themselves to be racists. Some claimed to have been active on behalf of the Civil Rights movement. Nevertheless, they were now faced with an invasion of black "animals." If the interlopers had been decent, middle-class blacks, who also had stable families and kept their property in good shape, there would have been no problem. But a violence-prone, promiscuous, amoral and lazy underclass was threatening to transform their paradise into hell.

If this version of the story of Canarsie is to be believed, then it was not the Canarsians who altered values in their switch from the support of liberal Democrats to that of conservative Republicans. Rather, liberalism itself was no longer the New Deal doctrine that put the interests of the common people first. Instead, liberalism had transmogrified into the elitist instrument by which soft and sanctimonious "limousine liberals" of the Mayor John Lindsay type could make the Canarsians pay the price for the social problems of others.

Throughout the presentation of this story and its variations, Reider indicates that he is skeptical of the self-justifying analysis that his interviewees collectively present. On occasion, he even interpolates countervoices from within the Jewish and Italian ethnic communities. He also includes brief insights about the socioeconomic underpinnings of the Canarsians' mode of perception by drawing on a variety of social and cultural theorists such as Max Weber, Erving Goffman and Michel Foucault. But his skepticism has crucial limitations.

First, Reider rarely presents documentation to prove how widespread any particular opinion might be, outside of some voting tabulations and poll results culled from secondary sources that deal with the broader Brooklyn community. Few local statistics are provided; it is not even clear, for example, whether Jewish participation in particular racist mobilizations was all that significant. Names and other facts are altered to prevent identification of sources. The reader simply must have confidence in Reider's degree of objectivity because there are no controls on his data. But how can the reader's confidence be sustained when Reider fails to challenge seriously the opinions he hears in order to determine their degree of accuracy? It is likely that an angry and embittered person will invent or significantly embellish a personal history simply to make his or her present feelings of betrayal appear more justified. It is also likely that the world the Canarsians made was not really as stable and healthy as it is made to appear in order to contrast it to the "black jungle." In his interviews, Reider never raises the possibility that some Canarsians, who are morally outraged by the "promiscuity" of blacks, may not always have dutifully controlled their sexual appetites; perhaps they expressed them in ugly forms that are never mentioned.

Moreover, even though Reider repeatedly looks to culture as an important explanatory factor, his analysis is thin in comparison to the richness of an earlier comparative study, Stephen Steinberg's *The Ethnic Myth: Race, Ethnicity and Class in America* (1981). Reider's Jews are depicted as drawn to universalism in contrast to the particularism of the Italians; they tend to look more to the state and less to the ties of family; and, for unexplained reasons, they are more successful in accruing money and education.

Black Americans are truly the elusive and fearful "other" in this narrative, not only for the Canarsians, but for Reider as well. The reality of their history and culture is reported only through the eyes of their antagonists. We are told only that they have suffered "historic brutalization" (p. 9), a sign of Reider's apparent sympathy for the highly controversial "damaged culture" school of thought. To re-create that life experience with sensitivity would probably undermine the implicit thesis of the book, namely, that the sociology of Afro-America can be usefully discussed—by Canarsians or their ethnologist—in the general context of the immigrant experience.

There is no doubt that *Canarsie* is a powerful text. But the tragic worldview that it creates for us is remarkably similar to that of Saul Bellow's 1970 neo-conservative novel, *Mr. Sammler's Planet*. This is peculiar, for Reider professes "practical liberalism" (p. viii), and neither Bellow nor the fictional Mr. Sammler (a scholar who lives on the West Side of Manhattan) are typical Canarsie residents. Is it possible that Reider has unconsciously shaped his material by bringing to it a perspective that shares the underlying assumptions of those neo-conservative *Commentary* writers who claim to be "liberals who have been mugged"? In fact, part of the reason for *Canarsie*'s power is that it confirms—indeed, it offers a superficial cogency to—ideas, attitudes and reactions that have been selectively picked up and transmitted by the mass media. Therefore, the reader might ask, to what degree are the formulations and perspectives of the Canarsians themselves shaped by a larger cultural apparatus? To what extent are such perspectives unique and based on genuine experience and to what extent are Canarsians singing the "same old song" that one has heard over the years from all groups under stress who choose to blame those beneath them?

Unfortunately, the answer to these queries cannot be found in Reider's book, for we learn little about his methodology and have little means for verification. He confronts us in lucid, fast-moving prose with a terrible reality, but he offers few means of measuring its scope. The book mainly adds details and some intelligent musings to received stereotypes of "white backlash" and "black crime."

Astonishingly, *Canarsie* ends with a call by the author for liberal Democrats to capture the conservative agenda of denouncing welfare cheats, strengthening law and order and promoting a tougher foreign policy. Throughout much of the book, Reider has tended to neglect the task of carefully and scientifically approximating social reality, instead substituting the passionately rhetorical mental world of a select group of Canarsians. Now, at the end, he urges that anti-racists ignore effective programs and policies—ones that see violence and crime as symptoms, not merely as problems—for the sake of winning votes. Could it be that, in the course of his research, the liberal Reider became infected with the very conservative disease that he set out to diagnose?

ALAN WALD
University of Michigan

Neil C. Sandberg, *Jewish Life in Los Angeles: A Window to Tomorrow.* Lanham: University Press of America. xii + 211 pp.

This is a welcome addition to the sociological literature on the Jews in the United States. Although there have been a number of national and community surveys of American Jews in the 1970s and 1980s, the two most thorough and analytical studies have been based on surveys of Boston Jews: Steven M. Cohen's *American Modernity and Jewish Identity* (1983) and Calvin Goldscheider's *Jewish Continuity and Change* (1986). A book-length study of the Jews of Los Angeles, whose half-million Jewish population is the second largest one in the United States, should provide a more balanced overall picture of the present state of American Jewry. However, although Sandberg's subtitle, *A Window to Tomorrow,* would appear to indicate that he sees Los Angeles Jewry as representing the future of American Jewry as a whole, he does not himself make any detailed comparisons with other community studies. Sandberg's study is also less analytical or informed by a theoretical focus than the studies of Cohen and Goldscheider. This may be because Sandberg has a more explicit concern with community policies and is directed to a readership not only of social scientists, but also of Jews who are involved in community decision making.

The general message presented recently by a number of American Jewish sociologists, and in a more popular form in Charles Silberman's *A Certain People,* is that the pessimistic forecasts of the assimilation of American Jews are wrong and that there is little cause to be concerned about the demographic future of American Jewry. Sandberg's position is somewhat difficult to decode. He does, at a number of points, express grave concern about the future of Los Angeles Jewry, and his policy suggestions are intended to remedy a situation in which 55 percent are unaffiliated to any Jewish organization. On balance, however, he opts for an optimistic evaluation of the future. This is based on comparisons that he makes among the generations, especially between the third and fourth generations.

In his generational comparisons, Sandberg discusses Marcus Lee Hansen's "law of return" of the third generation, but he does not review the extensive literature which was generated by Hansen's thesis. He does not even mention Herberg's "three generations thesis," which was a significant extension of Hansen and provided the focus for subsequent discussions. Sandberg questions whether it is meaningful to refer to a "return of the third generation," and he argues that the revival of ethnicity in the late 1960s and the 1970s occurred in all the generations, especially in the second generation. With respect to the future, however, the focus is on the fourth generation. Here Sandberg's findings are very mixed; although he refers to a revival in this generation, he is unable to demonstrate a clear pattern.

Sandberg found that the difference between the third and fourth generations in synagogue affiliation is very small (24.6 percent and 28.1 percent, respectively). As for religious observance, among the affiliated there is a slight increase in some observances (e.g., fasting on Yom Kippur), but among the unaffiliated, who constitute more than two-thirds of the total, the decline in religious observance continues in the fourth generation. Sandberg argues that the "renaissance" of the fourth generation is a selective one: they demonstrate strength in ethnic and cultural indicators rather than in religious indicators. But his data do not provide unambiguous support for this statement. With respect to identity with the Jewish "nation" and some nonreligious cultural aspects of identity, there is a slight increase in the fourth generation as compared with the third, but the generational decline in the membership of Zionist groups continues in the fourth generation, and the differences among the generations regarding attitudes toward Israel and Zionism are not significant. The percentage of non-Jewish spouses increased from 28.8 percent in the third generation to 43.5 percent in the fourth, and Sandberg notes that the intermarried provide their children with less Jewish education and are more disposed to social interaction with non-Jews. He questions Silberman's argument that intermarriage will increase the size of the American Jewish community.

Sandberg argues that the continuation of Jewishness in Los Angeles rests mainly in the informal areas of family and friendship, but his data to support a fourth-generation "renaissance" are based on small attitudinal differences and not on behavioral indicators. Rather than a "renaissance," it would be more accurate to say that the statistics show a stabilization in a number of indicators of Jewish identity and behavior. It might be risky, however, to draw any conclusions from Sandberg's statistics, and this for two reasons. First we are not told how many of the total sample of 413 were from the fourth generation. Since this was a representative sample, the number from the fourth generation was possibly only about 50 or 60 persons. Second, there is no standardization for age, and it is very important in this field to show whether differences are among generations or among age cohorts. We will have to wait for a study based on a larger sample that allows for such analyses before we can answer with more confidence the questions raised in this book.

STEPHEN SHAROT
Ben-Gurion University of the Negev

Rosaline Schwartz and Susan Milamed, *From Alexandrovsk to Zyrardow: A Guide to YIVO's* Landsmanshaftn *Archive*. New York: YIVO Institute for Jewish Research, 1986. xi + 96 pp.
Michael R. Weisser, *A Brotherhood of Memory, Jewish* Landsmanshaftn *in the New World*. New York: Basic Books, 1985. xiii + 290 pp.

In 1938 a group of Yiddish writers published a collection of articles on the *landsmanshaftn*—immigrant associations—entitled *Di yidishe landsmanshaftn fun nyu york*. Since that time, the world that produced the *landsmanshaftn* has been turned upside down. The passing of the immigrant generation, the concomitant decline of immigrant culture, the rise of the welfare state and, finally, the Holocaust changed forever the conditions in which Jewish immigrant associations had flourished.

Recent attention to social history has pointed the way toward a new kind of research about the immigrant experience: one that concentrates on the particular experiences of local groups, neighborhoods, women in the labor force and at home and so on. The *landsmanshaftn* were, if anything, the epitome of particularism and localism on the Jewish social scene.

By the 1970s it was clear that the number of active *landsmanshaftn*—once numbering six thousand in New York City—was rapidly dwindling. Record books, banners, correspondence, constitutions, memorial books and newsletters—all precious sources for the kind of social history that might offer new insight into the immigrants' world—were being stored in basement closets, left in a warehouse of the New York State Insurance Department Liquidation Bureau or discarded. It was becoming increasingly difficult to locate founding-generation members to provide oral histories of their own particular societies.

New York's YIVO Institute—the premier scholarly institution devoted to the study of East European Jewry—undertook to rescue and collect as much as possible of these important forms of documentation and to house them in a *Landsmanshaftn* Archive. The archive's catalogue, published by YIVO, presents in summary form the results of the project, which lasted from 1979 to 1981 and collected material and interview questionnaires from over eight hundred societies. In addition to brief descriptions of the holdings, the *Guide* contains an appendix listing Jewish cemeteries in New York City and environs, an alphabetical index of societies and a map of Jewish communities in Poland (1921–1939) where free-loan associations existed, partly supported by *landsmanshaftn* in New York. The existence of the archive should greatly facilitate research into this little-appreciated facet of Jewish immigration history. Indeed, one doctoral dissertation has already been written using some of the archive's resources: "Communication and Ethnic Community: The Case of *Landsmanshaftn*," by Hannah Kliger (University of Pennsylvania, 1986). Let us hope that the material—some of it kept with loving care over three generations—will inspire practitioners of the new social history to research this core experience of the first and second generations of New York Jews.

Although Michael Weisser tries hard to capture the flavor of *landsmanshaft* life, he eschews social history for what he terms "*bubbe mayse* [old wives' tale] history." I suppose that what he means to convey by this is that his account is heavily anecdotal. This releases him from the irksome task of having to "prove a point or render a judgment" (p. ix) about what he writes.

Yet, Weisser is not altogether candid about this, for he does, in fact, have a thesis. He tells us:

> In essence, the *landsmanshaftn* formed an impermeable "underground" of immigrant culture and immigrant identity whose links extended back to the most vital roots of East European life (p. 173).

> People who joined a *landsmanshaft* and kept it at the psychic core of their existence were . . . rejecting the larger society and resisting its opportunities for assimilation (p. 5).

> These societies came into existence because their members could only respond to the opportunities of America in the most limited terms (p. 42).

> The primary impulse that often kept people within their *landsmanshaft* circle was fear: fear of the outside world, fear of the unknown, fear of doing anything that might leave them vulnerable to another wave of violence, dislocation, and decimation (p. 30).

> To the extent that the landmanshaftn helped their members acclimate to the demands of a new society, they contributed to their members' survival, but survival was not the same thing as success. If anything, adherence to the ideals of the *landsmanshaft* became an obstacle to the process of learning how to . . . cope with a new way of life (p. 28).

In short, Weisser sees the *landsmanshaft* members as those Jews who remained outside the mainstream of American life and failed to "make it" in the New World.

Weisser has dipped into the YIVO *Landsmanshaft* Archive, selecting a few illustrative examples of *landsmanshaft* activities. But had he done the job more thoroughly and relied a bit less on the *bubbe mayse* method, he might well have revised his judgment. The *landsmanshaft* did give newcomers the basic tools for coping with their new environment: a social network that showed them the ropes in housing and employment; social benefits such as sick funds, unemployment benefits and life insurance ("death benefits" in *landsmanshaft* parlance); a stake in a community of manageable proportions; and a means of maintaining contact with the old home.

But the *landsmanshaft* provided much more, in addition to such basic survival aids (yes, survival was not necessarily the same as success, but it surely did not preclude or prevent success!). The *landsmanshaft* constitutions and minutes clearly show the effects of acculturation—more than Weisser admits. English was more in evidence in younger and second-generation groups. The fraternal society model, with its regalia, rituals, rules and regulations provided an animated social form that was much more part of America than of shtetl society. Arguments over finances, splits along generational lines, elections of officers and fund raising provided the context for political acculturation on an intimate level. The everyday life of the *landsmanshaft* was more about proper democratic procedure, concern for the integrity and loyalty of elected officers and the gradual equalization of women's roles in public life than about "fear of the unknown" (let alone fear of violence and decimation). The balls and banquets were more about the passage from working-class to business and white-collar status than about "rejecting the larger society and resisting its opportunities for assimilation."

It is much fairer to say that if the *landslayt* feared one thing, it was anonymity. A Jew without a sense of belonging was lost in mass, urban American society. The desire to be buried among one's own, in the *landsmanshaft* cemetery plot, is eloquent testimony to the strong hold of "belongingness," and it affected those who "made it" and their children just as much as it affected those who were less successful.

Weisser does a good job on matters related to the links of *landsmanshaftn* to their hometowns, especially with regard to relief work after the First World War and work for displaced persons (DPs) after the Second. Here he has stuck closer to plain history, leaving the *bubbe mayses* for someone else. He also has some worthwhile things to say about shifting neighborhoods and cemeteries.

All in all, the history of the *landsmanshaftn* might have been better served—and Weisser might have written a better book—had he done a bit more research and devoted more attention to the full range of *landsmanshaftn* holdings at YIVO.

ELI LEDERHENDLER
Tel-Aviv University and
The Hebrew University

Demography, Economics and Sociology

Steven M. Cohen and Paula E. Hyman (eds.), *The Jewish Family: Myths and Reality*. New York and London: Holmes & Meier, 1986. 242 pp.

It is commonly believed, and obviously true, that the Jewish family plays an important role in the survival of the Jewish people. But only limited research has been carried out to establish how, when and under what circumstances the Jewish family actually executes its functions. The compilation under review makes an important contribution to the clarification of these issues.

This collection of essays resulted from an interdisciplinary conference on the Jewish family convened in 1981. It addresses itself to aspects of the Jewish family that come under scrutiny in five disciplines: history, sociology, anthropology, demography and literature. The book has four sections: "Jewish Families in Traditional Societies"; "Jewish Families in the Transition to Modernity"; "Images of the Jewish Family" and "Demographic Variations in Contemporary Jewish Families." Two epilogues round out the presentation of the pertinent issues.

The considerable length of the period under discussion—the seventeenth to the twentieth century; the comprehensive geographical range—Western and Eastern Europe, America, the Middle East and Israel; and especially the interdisciplinary range do not seem conducive to a full integration of the disparate materials. However, the central topic, namely, the phenomenon of the family as such, does provide a common denominator that holds the sections together.

The family is a universal social framework that exhibits common features such as a gender- and age-oriented role division. Research, in general, emphasizes four main tasks of the family: procreation, maintenance, socialization and social placement of its members. Research on the Jewish family also attempts to identify the particular—possibly unique—traits of the Jewish family as a core group and as a societal institution that sustains Jewish communities wherever they are.

The intertwining of history and creed in the Jewish religion and Judaism as a system of religious observances are major factors in Jewish life. Accordingly, some authors attempt to analyze the role of the family as a focus for the observance of religious laws and as a pivotal factor in the performance of religious activities. Gershon Hundert and Shlomo Deshen relate to religion as a code of norms that affects family behavior. Gershon Shaffir and Chava Weisler deal with the coordination of religious practice in the family and in other communal groups such as the *havurah* and the hasidic courts. Marion A. Kaplan discusses religion as a stabilizing force in Jewish family life in a context of assimilation.

Other contributors to the volume consider the interaction between the family and the wider community. This ongoing interaction has a noticeable effect on the family itself. The response of Jewish families to situations of social isolation, to the challenges and the very process of assimilation and to changes brought about by migration and integration into new societal frameworks is a recurrent theme; Deshen describes the influence of Islamic culture on the Jewish family. Moshe Shokeid investigates the dynamics of change in the Moroccan family in the process of integration into Israeli society. David Biale analyzes the historical impact of the Enlightenment on the structure of the Jewish family in Europe. And Kaplan reviews aspects of role division in the Jewish family in Germany under the impact of assimilation.

There is a consensus among the authors concerning the decisive role that women play in the life of the Jewish family. Deshen, Shokeid, Kaplan, Susan A. Slotnick and Gladys Rothbell speak of the Jewish woman as wife; Deshen, Kaplan and Rothbell describe her status and functions as mother; Biale reviews her status and tasks as mother-in-law.

The section in which demographic factors are discussed is well integrated and provides interesting and useful data for a comparison of family structure in the Israeli society with the structure of the family in Diaspora communities.

The various essays brought together in this volume are of an unequal quality. Some seem to be based on insufficient source materials (Anita Norich), or appear to be lacking in adequate data and appropriate field research (Hundert, Weisler). Others display new insights and open up new avenues for further research. Kaplan's analysis of the role of the Jewish woman in the process of assimilation and Biale's depiction of the young groom who comes under the authority of his mother-in-law in traditional East European families stand out because of their innovative approaches to the problem of family role division. Deshen and Shokeid's investigation of Jewish families in a Moslem milieu each open up new vistas for future comparative family research.

All in all, and notwithstanding its diversity, this collection of essays has considerable merit. It issues a call for incisive and thorough research in this field of Jewish studies and highlights the relevance of family research for Jewish studies. As Paula Hyman writes, "Studying the Jewish family enriches our understanding of such critical phenomena of modern Jewish history as acculturation, Jewish identity and Jewish mobility."

PENINA MORAG-TALMON
The Hebrew University

S. N. Eisenstadt, *The Transformation of Israeli Society.* London: Weidenfeld & Nicolson, 1985. xiv + 590 pp.

Although this book deals mainly with modern Israeli society, perhaps a more appropriate title would be "Jewish Civilization and the Development of Modern Israel." I suggest this because both in reality and in terms of Eisenstadt's own analysis, modern Israel is rooted in ancient Jewish civilization and the Diaspora developments of the Jewish people.

If the title of the book is somewhat misleading, Eisenstadt, who is one of the foremost sociologists in the world today, cannot be faulted in the way he handles this broad and intricate subject. The historical background, which he presents in Part I, is masterfully condensed into eighty pages. He goes on, with equal success, to analyze the development of modern Israel. He presents the whole gamut of social development in Israel through his well-known structural-functionalist theoretical perspective. The old Yishuv and the period of the British Mandate, the new state up to the Six Day War, the Yom Kippur War and the more recent periods serve as bench marks in a lively analysis of the intricate interplay between the major variables of demography; the Holocaust; political and economic factors; religious versus secular influences; relations between the *'edot* (ethnic communities) and between Jews and Arabs, Israel and the Diaspora; security and foreign relations; and the emergence of new social problems. The story that unfolds assumes a certain unity through Eisenstadt's insistence that there is a continuous process of crystallization of institutional molds. In other words, change and transformation in society is possible and likely not through sudden destruction but rather through the slow reconstruction of social institutions.

Eisenstadt highlights this process most effectively when he discusses the ways in which the center and the periphery of Israeli society influence each other. Changes in, and new interpretations of, the overall Zionist vision of national–cultural renaissance have led to ideological conflicts and shifts in values and symbols; these, in turn, have produced changes in the collective Israeli identity. Despite ongoing problems of national security that sometimes create a fortress mentality and despite the special problems of a small society, a pluralistic social framework has developed.

This unique story is still evolving. Ultimately, it is about "the very survival of Israeli society and in many ways also of the Jewish people and civilization." In an almost desperate mood, Eisenstadt concludes by quoting from a Talmudic text included in the closing prayer of Yom Kippur, the *Ne'ilah,* "The people's needs are large, their knowledge broken; their wants and wishes they can scarce express." He is, nonetheless, hopeful that Israel will develop institutional frameworks and symbols that will lead to creativity and overcome tendencies toward anarchy and stagnation. This is the challenge of Israeli society.

ERNEST KRAUSZ
Bar-Ilan University

Elizabeth Ewen, *Immigrant Women in the Land of Dollars: Life and Culture on the Lower East Side, 1890–1925.* New York: Monthly Review Press, 1985. 320 pp.

Elizabeth Ewen's innovative comparative study of Italian and Jewish immigrant women in New York City during the era of mass migration draws on a remarkable collection of oral histories—conducted by the City University Oral History Project—of women who were members of the International Ladies Garment Workers Union. The book shares the strengths and weaknesses of its primary sources. The former include a measure of intimacy and directness unavailable in traditional written records, especially those concerning women. Ewen often successfully drives home a point in her argument through a powerful direct quotation. She also explores with considerable insight the dynamics of the process of acculturation, especially in areas such as social mores and consumption patterns, that have generally eluded previous historians. Her chapters on changing immigrant attitudes toward dating, sex and marriage and on the attractions of popular culture offer fine insights into immigrant women's hesitant and uneven entrance into American vernacular culture.

But there are also problems that result from relying on oral recollection. Although Ewen generously supplements the interviews with material drawn from novels, autobiographies and social surveys, she does not always succeed in convincing her reader of the general applicability of her argument. Reference to more traditional sources such as the foreign-language press or Yiddish etiquette books for women explaining American customs would have lent greater depth to her portrait of a generation and an era.

Immigrant women also organized. Often they participated actively in religious worship. Indeed, their lives extended into many of the public areas of activity until recently characterized by historians as male. Yet Ewen does not discuss many of these aspects of immigrant women's lives, with the important exception of their involvement in the labor movement.

As a result, Ewen paints an effective but two-dimensional portrait of immigrant women on the Lower East Side. Although she sensitively devotes two chapters to women's Old World experience, her approach to the role of Jewish or Italian culture in the lives of immigrant women minimizes its specificity and maximizes its working-class universality. Compare, for example, her treatment of food riots on the Lower East Side in the chapter, "The Land of Dollars," with Paula Hyman's analysis of the 1904 kosher meat boycott.* Hyman uses the Yiddish press and her knowledge of Jewish religious culture to situate the riots within the context of Jewish women's activity, pointing to their ability to blend traditional behavior with radical socialist rhetoric. Ewen argues that "consumer resistance flowed from the women's role in the family, their relationship to the marketplace, their ties and relationships to each other and their neighborhoods" (p. 183). In Ewen's discussion the question of whether Italian women drew on a different cultural compass to orient their rioting than Jewish women does not arise. To her, gender, class and the immigrant experience alone serve as the context of women's behavior.

Nonetheless, Ewen contributes significantly to our understanding of immigrant women's lives and helps to redress the balance that has tilted heavily toward men's activities as paradigmatic for all immigrants. Her conceptualization of daily life as an arena of cultural conflict between the generations should stimulate future social

*Paula Hyman, "Immigrant Women and Consumer Protest," *American Jewish History* 70 (September 1980), 91–105.

historians to devote greater attention to the many topics embedded in the round of mundane living. Similarly, her attention to consumer capitalism and changing immigrant consumption patterns as a battleground of assimilation has anticipated a number of more recent studies that suggest this may be the new cutting edge of immigrant scholarship.

DEBORAH DASH MOORE
YIVO Institute for Jewish Research

Arcadius Kahan, *Essays in Jewish Social and Economic History.* Edited by Roger Weiss with an Introduction by Jonathan Frankel. Chicago and London: University of Chicago Press, 1986. 208 pp.

Comparing Kahan's article, "Impact of Industrialization on the Jews in Tsarist Russia," with a pirated copy of the paper as it was originally given at a conference in Los Angeles years ago revealed only one difference. In the original, footnote 30 reads, "I intend to have the calculations for income of the owners of real estate, money capital and large-size industrial and trading firms for the final version of this paper." In this collection of Kahan's essays, the footnote is gone. In a way that sums up the nature of this collection. As in all posthumous works, Arcadius Kahan was not able to revise these papers and they have to be treated with this in mind.

It can be safely said that few of these essays could have been written by anyone else today. Together they form the most important collection of studies on economic history of the Jews of Eastern Europe in the modern period. This does not mean that there is a lot of competition. This is a field that has been neglected for a number of reasons—not the least of which is that it requires special academic and linguistic skills. Luckily Kahan had both and produced a series of studies that would stand out in a crowded field as well.

In all of these studies, Kahan combined a sensitivity to the humanity of his subjects together with a commitment to analysis and quantitative measures. His economic training here is crucial. In the same study on industrialization and Russian Jewry, he points out the critical importance of vertical integration as a tool of economic survival. This point, which is clear as soon as it is pointed out, has many consequences; it is one that (to the best of my knowledge) was never clearly enunciated before. Similarly, his economic analysis of life in a ghetto under Nazi rule (also never previously published) combined intimate knowledge with careful analysis to create a paper that is just as moving as a memoir of someone who actually lived through the experience, which Kahan did not (he was in the Red Army), while retaining the precision and explanatory power of objective analysis.

There is no doubt that had Professor Kahan lived to edit the book himself it would have been much fuller and the references to the relevant literature would have been more complete and up-to-date. There is currently no better volume devoted solely to the social and economic history of the Jews in Eastern Europe and we are highly unlikely to see such a volume in the near future.

SHAUL STAMPFER
The Hebrew University

Judith E. Smith, *Family Connections: A History of Italian and Jewish Immigrant Lives in Providence, Rhode Island, 1900–1940.* Albany: SUNY Press, 1985. 228 pp.

Prolific research in American immigration and ethnic history accumulated over the last decade has demonstrated the inadequacy of the two formerly dominant paradigms in this field of study: (1) "assimilation," conceived of as the disappearance of preindustrial, traditional values and behavioral patterns characteristic of the immigrant cultures in the face of the challenges of modern society and (2) "individual achievement," Horatio Alger–style, as a common path of socioeconomic advancement for new Americans. New concerns and emphases have emerged in recent writing on the immigrants and on ethnic communities in the United States. Three themes seem to have had the greatest impact. First, the focus on the dynamic interplay of traditional and new elements in the immigrant families' adaptation to the host society and on the active role they played in this process, responding to as well as creating the circumstances of their lives. Second, the emphasis on the collectivist, kin- and group-embedded rather than individualistic, "self-made" strategies of the immigrants, starting in the migration process itself and in their subsequent adjustment to the new environment. And third, the acknowledgment of the importance of the broader, structural context (at the national as well as local level) of their incorporation into the American economic and social systems, "interacting" with individual and group resources the immigrants brought with them or developed in America.

Family Connections, a study of the lives of Italian and Jewish immigrants and their children in Providence, Rhode Island, in the period from the turn of the century until the Second World War, is part of this new social historiography, embodying all three of the above concerns in its conceptualization and interpretation of evidence.

The book consists of four chapters. Chapter 1 outlines the historical conditions immigrants faced in Europe at the time of their migration and in Providence from the years of their arrival through the 1930s. Chapter 2 traces the relationship between family and work in terms of economic cooperation and "reciprocity" among the household members. Chapter 3 charts the original setting and later modification of kinship and neighborhood networks of support and assistance. Chapter 4 is devoted to immigrant mutual-aid associations—their emergence, operation and changing role in the course of the first four decades of this century. The study's major thesis is that during that period, under the impact of forces originating in the larger American society (e.g., suburbanization, growth of large corporations and of the service sector of the economy and of the spread of mass education, consumption and recreation), the immigrant "ethos of reciprocity" based on close economic and social cooperation had weakened, giving way, in the second generation, to other kinds of bonding, with the immigrant's ethnic sense and expressions redefined to fit the changed historical conditions.

The book is well and vividly written, and it is illustrated with interesting old photographs and maps of Jewish and Italian neighborhoods. The narrative effectively blends quantitative analysis of data from various local sources (manuscript schedules of the population censuses and city directories, birth and marriage transcripts, real estate records) with ethnographic material from oral life histories of immigrants and their children. Particularly engaging as an outcome of this combined methodology is the chapter dealing with the family culture of work, grounded as it was in the old-country experience. The author describes the ingenious cooperative strategies of pooling the resources and contributions of all available members and the efficient planning and operation of kin and friendship networks of informal mutual assistance in the immigrant neighborhoods.

Most illuminating, since many studies of this type deal with a single ethnic group, is the comparison between Jews and Italians. As Smith shows, faced with similar external circumstances, first in Europe (widespread poverty and social dislocation) and then in the city of Providence, these two groups responded with basically similar coping and adaptation behavior. Both migrated from Europe and settled in Providence in "chains" of families or *landslayt* and *paesani*. In their work and residential settings, both groups relied, too, on the crisscrossing kinship and associational networks of assistance. There were also important differences, however, in their respective modes of entry and the subsequent position of Jews and Italians in the local economy. The former were concentrated from the beginning and throughout the period under investigation in the trade and service sector, the latter mostly in manufacturing production. Interestingly, the Italian family ties appear to have been more extended, close and enduring over time than those of the Jewish family.

A few reservations should be mentioned. Following what has unfortunately been the rule in the discussions of the East European Jewish background as found in American ethnic studies, Smith limits her discourse to presenting the situation in the Russian Pale of Settlement even though the Providence immigrants also came from Galicia, Hungary and Romania where conditions were different. Some statistical tables concerning immigrant kin-networks and work locations (e.g., on pp. 77, 100, 108) are based on numbers much too small to support her otherwise convincing conclusions, whereas others (e.g., pp. 48, 64) present data sets combined in single figures for the whole period studied and do not illustrate the changes she describes. Similarly, Smith's conclusion (p. 72) that the majority of second-generation Providence Jews and Italians entered employment in large industrial and commercial companies is asserted rather than empirically demonstrated. A comparison of the occupational codes listed in the appendix with the appropriate tables (pp. 67–70) suggest, rather, that they—especially second-generation Jews—mostly worked in small retail and craft establishments owned, if not by their parents or relatives, quite probably by other Jews. Lastly, although there is nothing wrong in using interviews with immigrants from other cities as illustrations for the Providence story, a closer inspection of annotations reveals that a great deal—almost half—of the study's ethnographic material has actually come from the WPA survey conducted in the 1930s in Bridgeport, Hartford and New Haven in nearby Connecticut.

Resulting perhaps from the ambiguity of the data, a certain hesitation underlies the author's interpretation of what exactly happened with "immigrant lives" during the half-century preceding the Second World War. Was it, as she repeatedly claims (particularly at the beginning and the end of her study), that changes that had occurred in the larger American society and in the city of Providence "dramatically altered" the shape of kin- and ethnic-networks by the 1930s? Or was it, rather, as Smith herself points out occasionally (e.g., pp. 24, 82, 122, 159), that the developments she analyzes were in "ascendancy," forming and gathering strength, to become new qualities that consolidated only in the postwar decades? The evidence presented in the study suggests that the latter interpretation is historically and sociologically more accurate.

A good example and application of new perspectives and insights offered by recent writing in the social history of American immigration, *Family Connections* should be on the reading list of all those interested in this and related topics.

Ewa Morawska
University of Pennsylvania

Language, Art and Literature

Mikhail Agursky and Margarita Shklovskaya, *Maxim Gorkii, 1868–1936. Iz literaturnogo naslediya: Gorkii i evreiskii vopros.* Jerusalem: Center for Documentation and Research of East-European Jewry, The Hebrew University of Jerusalem, 1986. 535 pp.

It was an excellent idea to publish a work on Gorky and the Jewish question as a contribution to the study of Russian Jewry. The idea has been admirably implemented in this volume.

Gorky was unique in the Russia of his time both for his range as a writer and publicist and for his sympathetic and knowledgeable interest in Jews as people as well as in the Jewish question. Until the last years, when Stalin's system was closing in on him, he maintained an independent mind while remaining devoted to the socialist ideal.

There is a great deal of material on the subject of Gorky and the Jews. The editors state that the aim of this selection is to include the items that most clearly show Gorky's views in this field. In the nature of things a precise criterion of selection would be difficult to formulate. The work consists of three main parts: an informative introduction by the editors; Gorky's writings; and recollections by others about Gorky and his views.

The main part, Gorky's work, is arranged by period: 1906–1913, 1914–1921, 1922–1928 and 1929–1936. Among the first items is the famous story "Kain (Chaim) and Artem." This story is easily available elsewhere, but the collection would not have felt right without it. There are more selections from Gorky's correspondence and essays than from his literary works, which in any case are all now available in the latest Soviet edition. The third part, "Recollections, Encounters, Reactions," contains some of the most interesting material, written mostly but not only by Jews and originally written in various languages.

The 162 items, many of which are not easily accessible and some of which are published here for the first time, are fully annotated, bibliographically and biographically, and each is furnished with a commentary. The standard of scholarship is all that could be desired. There is a generous selection of photographs, including those of the people whose recollections comprise the third part as well as of Gorky at various stages of his life. The covers, incidentally, are in the style of a Soviet edition of Gorky with no reference to the Jewish topic.

Browsing in this book, as much in the annotations as in the materials themselves, strengthened the reviewer's impression that the basic change in Russia came less in 1917 than in the mid-1930s when the system of trying to control everything from above was firmly set by Stalin. For Russian Jewry, 1917 was in some important respects a new but ephemeral era of opportunity, while the mid-1930s represented an obvious deterioration as the Jews came to be seen as a suspect element inside the new order. The period covered by Gorky's active life could be seen as the last forty years of a historical process that led to the new order rather than as twenty years on either side of a pivotal change. It is perhaps ironic that one of Gorky's preoccupations in his last years, during the real change, was the preparation of a collection of his writings on the Jews, which was never published.

JACOB MILLER
Glasgow

Bibliography of Hebrew and Yiddish Publications in Poland Since 1944 (Polish Jewry: Bibliographical Series 3). Collected by Dvora Zeichner and Ajzyk Szechter. Recorded by Dvora Zeichner. Bibliography prepared for publication by Dalia Kaufman. Edited with an introduction by Jacob M. Kelman. Jerusalem: Center for Research on the History and Culture of Polish Jews/Center for Research and Documentation of East-European Jewry/The Hebrew University of Jerusalem, 1987. (82) + (2), 102 pp.

After a lengthy gestation, the third publication of the Polish Jewry Bibliographical Series has most welcomely appeared. Post-Holocaust Polish Jewish history is laid bare here in the uncannily paradigmatic story of Yiddish and Hebrew publishing. Close to a half-century after the liberation of Lublin by the Soviet army in the summer of 1944, we now have a comprehensive (though inevitably incomplete), accurately recorded and clearly presented bibliography of Yiddish and Hebrew imprints in Poland from that pivotal year until today. Were this bibliography to give nothing more than a full and reliable description of over five hundred Yiddish publications, we would be grateful. It provides, however, much more: Jacob M. Kelman's able introduction, virtually a concise monograph (and almost as long as the bibliography itself), places the items in their historical and institutional contexts.

As Kelman makes clear, post-Holocaust Yiddish-language publishing in Poland[1] began in 1944 with notices posted on community bulletin boards. Survivors were then searching for one another and groping for ways to piece together their shattered lives. Suddenly, there was a future to plan for. In those halcyon days of ideological pluralism, every grouping in Polish Jewry—Zionist and anti-Zionist, Communist and Bundist, Orthodox and secularist—stenciled a bulletin or a pamphlet for its slowly reemerging membership (many of these early publications, handwritten or stenciled on shoddy wartime paper, have not been preserved). Despite material obstacles, more Yiddish (and Hebrew) publications (forty-three percent of the total of 566 items) appeared in Poland between 1944 and 1949 than during any of the other three periods into which Kelman logically divides post-Holocaust Jewish publishing in Poland. Most of these first-period imprints were informational and were technically as deficient as they were humanly impressive.

Unable or unwilling to return to their former homes, survivors together with returnees from the Soviet Union responded zealously to the Polish government's plan for resettlement in the former German lands of Lower Silesia. By the late 1940s, over half of Polish Jewry was living in this region where a fine Yiddish theater, a lively press, schools, libraries and youth clubs—to mention only the cultural and educational networks—were functioning. With the hindsight of the 1980s, this enterprise may seem quixotic, but Kelman rightly describes the Polish–Jewish effort at cultural renewal with admiring sympathy. He mentions, for example, Shoylik Ferdman, who prepared most of the language texts and anthologies for the rebuilt Yiddish school system. Shoylik Ferdman now works on the *Great Dictionary of the Yiddish Language* in Jerusalem. Both projects were formed by the impulse to serve Yiddish culture.

By 1948 only the Communist party and its allies were allowed to operate freely in Poland and most of the Zionists had by then left for Israel. During the "black years" (1950–1957), the center of Jewish cultural life in Poland moved to Warsaw where it could be more easily controlled and supervised. Yet, 186 publications appeared during this time, almost a third of the entire 566. Wladyslaw Gomulka's return to power at the end of 1956 augured liberalization for Poles but not for Jews, whom Poles blamed for Bolshevizing Poland. Between 1958 and 1967 (a calamitous year for Polish Jews), only 122 items (twenty-two percent) appeared. The great experiment of rebuilding Jewish life in Poland was over. In 1967 and 1968 even Jews remote from Jewish life and in full agreement with the regime were forced to leave the country. However, even after most of the Jews had left, the regime continued its token Jewish cultural activities such as the Warsaw Yiddish theater, which provided simultaneous interpretation from Yiddish for Polish gentiles and other spectators. Since 1968 the number of publications in Yiddish and Hebrew has declined to a mere trickle. The 1986/1987 Jewish calendar is virtually all in Polish. The percentage of Jews in Poland who read the Yiddish section of the bilingual *Folkshtimme* decreases steadily.

Precisely because he is so aware of the tightrope that editors of Jewish publications in Communist Poland have had to walk, it is strange that Kelman has not provided better guidance regarding the reliability and integrity of the Warsaw editions of Emanuel Ringelblum's *Ksovim fun geto* and other published works from the "Oneg Shabat" Archives such as Perets Opotshinski's *Reportazhn fun varshever geto,* edited by Ber Mark (Warsaw: 1954). As is clear from the number of entries for him in the bibliography (only Leyb Olitski and Dovid Sfard are as prolific), Ber Mark was a central figure in the history of post-Holocaust Jewish publishing in Poland, particularly with respect to Holocaust literature. Warnings to use Mark's works with caution have often been sounded;[2] in a recent essay on Opotshinski, Joseph Kermisz wrote that Mark's 1954 Opotshinski edition does not follow even the most elementary principles of editing.[3]

There is so much valuable information in the introduction to this bibliography that it should be indexed and one index should serve the entire work; initials of given names should be resolved throughout.

The bibliography proper is the product of discrete contributions (collecting, recording, preparing for the press and editing) by all four of the project's participants. There is nothing mechanical about making good bibliographies, even in the age of computers and data bases. Many hands have somehow managed to make a fine pie (despite the adage about "too many cooks . . ."). But, in particular, we must thank Kelman, who not only introduces the work skillfully but has edited it ably as well. Editors, like bibliographers, are too often taken for granted.

LEONARD PRAGER
University of Haifa

Notes

1. Although Hebrew is given pride of place in the slightly misleading title, only 22 of the 566 items listed are in this language, 6 of which are Polish textbooks of Hebrew for the Roman Catholic clergy.

2. See, for example, Gershon David Hundert and Gershon C. Bacon, *The Jews in Poland and Russia, Bibliographical Essays* (Bloomington: 1984), 205.

3. Joseph Kermisz, "Umbakante bleter fun Perets Opotshinski: Varshever geto-kronik," *Di goldene keyt* 124 (1988), 139.

Sarah Blacher Cohen (ed.), *Jewish Wry: Essays on Jewish Humor.* Bloomington: Indiana University Press, 1987. ix + 244 pp.

I sometimes feel that almost everything that can be said about Jewish humor has been said—too often and at excessive length—and Miss Cohen goes far toward confirming my view by using four essays (out of the fourteen in her collection) that have already appeared elsewhere and by including one or two others that should not have appeared at all. But the book has its saving moments.

There is a delectable piece on Stanley Elkin by Maurice Charney and another on Mordechai Richler by Michael Greenstein, while Alan Cooper has some perceptive things to say about Philip Roth. Some of the contributors, however, approach their task with undue gravity, and there is no detail so insignificant that they will not make a meal out of it. In an otherwise admirable essay on Woody Allen, for example, Gerald Marsh alights on his glasses, which, he believes, link him immediately with Harold Lloyd, Groucho Marx and Jerry Lewis. He also wears trousers, which, it could be argued, must link him with Buster Keaton, Charlie Chaplin, W. C. Fields, Laurel and Hardy, Abbott and Costello, the Three Stooges and Popeye. But Mr. Marsh presses on regardless, "Glasses suggest three male stereotypes in movies and in our culture: the blindness of childhood naiveté . . . the sophistry of intellectual dexterity . . . or the clumsiness of physical weakness." The one thing it does not seem to suggest to Mr. Marsh is imperfect vision.

Esther Fuchs tries to prove that Israeli literature abounds in humor, but the harder she tries the more she shows that it doesn't. She feels, for example, that the plays of Hanoch Levin "elicit a frightened laughter," but I would say any laughter they elicit is embarrassed rather than frightened: Levin, though gifted in other respects, somehow manages to be grotesque and obscene without being funny. There is, of course, Kishon—and Kishon at his best is one of the funniest men alive—but Miss Fuchs quotes him at his worst. What is perhaps more to the point, his humor is Hungarian even when his subject matter is Israeli, and he reads better (and sells better) in German than he does in Hebrew.

Most of the contributors to this volume seem to approach their task in the belief that if the humor is Jewish, it must be good; I rather fear that in this respect Cohen herself is the worst offender. In a chapter headed "The Unkosher Comediennes," she analyzes the humor of Sophie Tucker, Belle Barth, Totie Fields and Joan Rivers with the earnest concern of a scholar weighing up the humor of Jane Austen. Tucker had some fairly amusing numbers but is better remembered as a singer ("the last of the red-hot mommas") than as a comedienne. Barth and Fields I have never heard of, which, to judge from their humor as quoted by Cohen, is a mercy. Rivers one hears of too much. She can, I will reluctantly admit, be funny, but she can also be consummately unfunny and to compare her, as Cohen does, to the "*shtetl yente*" is an insult both to the *shtetl* and the *yente,* and the measure of her success tells one less about the character of Jewish humor than about the health of American society. She is a pioneer of Tampax humor and explores areas—gynecology and obstetrics—left untouched by others; but if all humor deadens one's critical faculties, Miss Rivers comes near to deadening one's sense of disgust. She has given obscenity a bad name and if she is to be held up as an example of Jewish humor, then Jews have a lot to answer for.

Chaim Bermant
London

Yael S. Feldman, *Modernism and Cultural Transfer: Gabriel Preil and the Tradition of Jewish Literary Bilingualism.* Cincinnati: Hebrew Union College Monograph Series, no. 10, 1986. 224 pp.

When Gabriel Preil first began to publish his poetry in the United States in the mid-1930s—at first in Yiddish and subsequently in Hebrew, too—he embarked on a unique literary career. The appearance on the Yiddish scene in America of a young, new writer was no common occurrence by that time, to say nothing of a bilingual poet. Preil's position has grown increasingly conspicuous over the years as linguistic assimilation among American Jews took its toll on both Yiddish and Hebrew publishing. With an unexpectedly forceful, modernist drive, he has dared to defy the cultural and linguistic reality around him. His work has lost none of its freshness and, in marked contrast to his depressing role as "the last Hebrew poet in America," he has sometimes been dubbed "grand duke of New York."

Preil is best known today as a Hebrew poet who, like Judah Halevi of medieval Spain, finds himself "at the [W]est's furthest edge," while his readers are for the most part in the "[E]ast"—that is, in Israel. Indeed, since the 1950s, the best representatives of the younger generation in Israeli literature have displayed a great deal of interest in Preil's poetry. Yet Preil has kept up his output in Yiddish as well. Alongside his eight volumes of Hebrew verse (the first was published in 1944), he has also collected his Yiddish works in one volume (*Lider,* 1966). His Yiddish poems written since then have not yet been published in collected form. This second voice of the poet has been a sort of terra incognita to most of his readers in Israel, and it has been brought to renewed attention mainly through the efforts of Yael Feldman.

Feldman's present study, in fact, focuses on the complex nature of the linguistic duality in Preil's oeuvre. Although his earliest poems in both languages were published virtually at the same time, they were quite different in both thematic content and style. While his early Yiddish poems fit easily into the modernist wave that was then reaching its peak in American Yiddish letters, his Hebrew works were thought to hark back to literary models that even then were considered outdated. Yael Feldman's nuanced and sensitive analysis helps to illuminate the inner struggle in the young writer's consciousness between the two languages and the two distinct literary traditions: on the one hand, modernism with its avant-garde forms of expression, on the other hand, the more classical Hebrew style that was shared by many well-known figures in the generation that followed Bialik. Preil began early on to reshape his Hebrew work by borrowing literary models from the Yiddish world, and this is what determined his unique place in contemporary Hebrew literature. Feldman demonstrates how Preil's bilingualism becomes the linchpin for understanding his work.

In her wide-ranging theoretical introduction, Feldman discusses previous research on bilingual literary creativity, in general, and on the interrelationship between Hebrew and Yiddish literature, in particular. The close symbiosis between Hebrew and Yiddish belles lettres that exited up to the First World War had been based on the activity of East European writers, most of whom devoted themselves to writing prose. Within the realm of poetry, however, bilingual creativity had been rather more restricted, so that it becomes difficult to formulate any general theory.

The analogy that Feldman draws between Gabriel Preil, the American Hebrew–Yiddish poet, whose work represents one of the last links in the bilingual tradition, and the nineteenth-century father figure in that tradition, the bilingual Jewish writer par excellence, Mendele Mocher Sforim (Shalom Abramovich), is therefore most illuminating (pp. 36, 67). Despite the vast differences between them and despite their separation in time, she discovers a certain common ground. Just as Yiddish provided Abramovich with a powerful tool to modernize Hebrew prose, so did it allow Preil to do the same thing (on a smaller scale) for Hebrew poetry. There is even a striking parallel in the manner in which critics received their works. Just as fanatical Hebraists tried to ignore Abramovich's extensive Yiddish oeuvre (and extreme Yiddishists did likewise regarding his Hebrew work), so have Hebrew literary critics tended to disregard Preil's Yiddish poetry and consider him only a Hebrew poet. In Preil's case, however, the reason is not so much a deliberate avoidance as a lack of knowledge. Feldman's book serves a valuable purpose in bridging this gap.

After having presented her general thesis, she proceeds to a more specific analysis. The book, thus, contains a most welcome balance between various aspects of literary criticism: theoretical, historical and descriptive poetics. Feldman unfolds a masterful exposition of the complex and all-important relationship between the dual roots of Preil's work. She analyzes at great length (at times, possibly more than necessary) some of Preil's most important early poems, also drawing on some later, autobiographical poems to shed further light on the growth of the young artist. For example, she uses the later works to discuss the influence on Preil of various literary figures. Preil's ambivalence toward the work of Zalman Shneur, as expressed in a poem of the late 1940s, forms a springboard for a discussion of the romantic basis of Preil's earliest Hebrew works. On the other hand, Feldman cites a poem in which J. L. Teller, the Yiddish modernist poet, appears in order to discuss the role Teller played as the young Preil's literary mentor.

In this manner, the author weaves a fascinating and many-layered account of how the young, bilingual poetic novice in America picked his way amid the literary crosscurrents of his time. His attraction to Hebrew, a legacy of his parental home in Lithuania, meets and mingles with a second factor: his close contact with Yiddish poets in America, who helped him to publish his first works. Yet, in addition, one must be cognizant of the potent, if less apparent, influence of "big brother"— English. English was both the voice of the surrounding culture and the third literary tradition that nourished Preil through his reading of the great English poets, both romantic and modernist. Preil thus developed a mature and distinct "romantic imagist" poetry that found a new and attentive audience in Israel.

Feldman's book focuses mainly on Preil's early poems, summarizing only briefly his later work. One can only hope that she will eventually expand her research along the lines that are suggested by the analysis she has offered here. Hebrew literature in America, its poetry in particular, still awaits other descriptive analyses such as this one as well as a more comprehensive appreciation of its achievements amid very special complicating but also fructifying conditions.

In the meantime, we have gained a most valuable contribution to the literature on bilingual, Hebrew–Yiddish creativity. Feldman has tested accepted literary theory by applying it to the remarkable and rare case represented by Gabriel Preil's poetry.

AVRAHAM NOVERSHTERN
The Hebrew University

Jakob Hessing, *Else Lasker-Schüler: Biographie einer deutsch-jüdischen Dichterin.* Karlsruhe: von Loeper, 1985. 220 pp.

The fingers of one hand amply suffice to count women poets of renown in the annals of pre-World War Two German literature. Indeed, the only woman always represented in the standard anthologies of German poetry (not including the postwar period) is Annette von Droste-Hülshoff, and even she remains virtually unknown outside the German-reading world. Else Lasker-Schüler (1869–1945), who could claim no more than a minor reputation in the Weimar era, has rapidly gained in stature to the point where today she ranks among the most distinctive and powerful voices of her generation.

But perhaps more than a German poet, Else Lasker-Schüler was a *Jewish* poet—in many ways even more profoundly so than her more celebrated countrymen, Heinrich Heine and Richard Beer-Hofmann. Heinz Politzer, who knew her personally in Jerusalem, rightly characterized her oeuvre as "Hebrew poetry in German," adding with keen perception that "she dreamt Hebrew visions, but the only words she could clothe them in were German." The critics of the last four decades have, of course, recognized this special component of Lasker-Schüler's work, a recognition that actually goes all the way back to her close friend, the (non-Jewish) poet-essayist Peter Hille, who called her the Jewish poetess par excellence, to be compared with the Biblical Deborah.

Although the title of Jakob Hessing's recent study of Lasker-Schüler announces a biography, it offers much more than a mere account of the poet's life. More accurately a critical biography, the book focuses on and explicates those works of Lasker-Schüler that reflect the poet's Jewish sensibilities and together represent a truly unique combination of Jewish-secular spirituality expressed with exquisite poetic imagination in the German language. Hessing's study possesses a number of strengths. Whereas other analyses place Lasker-Schüler's writings in a general cultural and literary context, this one locates them, much more illuminatingly, within the German Jewish context, providing a succinct account of the intellectual currents swirling through the German Jewish community of the poet's time. In focusing on the Jewish mind behind Lasker-Schüler's work, Hessing retrieves it from the Christian and aestheticist interpretations that have dominated the critical reception of the last decades and have badly misunderstood and distorted the Jewish component. For example, virtually every critic has read a kind of sentimental ecumenicism into the conclusion of *Arthur Aronymus,* which depicts Jews and Christians sitting down together at a seder. Hessing alone rescues the real point here: not a fusion of Judaism and Christianity, but a recognition of, and respect for, the separate and independent strength and validity of both religions.

Hessing illuminatingly weaves together the (mainly painful) facts of Lasker-Schüler's life—her dropping out of school, her two failed marriages, her close relationship to Peter Hille, the devastating loss of her son, her poverty and homelessness and her final difficult years in Palestine—with her major works of Jewish import: the early poem *Mein Volk,* stories such as *Der Prinz von Theben, Der Wunderrabbiner von Barcelona, Arthur Aronymus,* the travelogue *Das Hebräerland* and some of the late oeuvre, including the posthumously published *IchundIch.* Significant relationships with prominent Jewish figures, for example, Buber, U. Z. Greenberg and Agnon, receive their due at appropriate junctures. Through all of this, Hessing brings out cogently the dual themes of assimilation and isolation and the dialectical tension between them that characterize Lasker-Schüler's relationship to her German environment, indeed, much of what was transpiring in the background between the Jewish community and its German hosts. The felicitous integration of biography and literary criticism also elucidates and helps us to understand Lasker-Schüler's extraordinary private imagination and her inability (refusal?) to distinguish between fact and fantasy.

Yet, for all these undeniable virtues, Hessing's book possesses, in my view, two regrettable flaws. The lesser one is the book's lack of formal documentation. The informal and rather arbitrary approach to the citation of sources reduces the book's value as a scholarly contribution—and this is no mere pedantic quibble. A more substantive failing, I believe, is Hessing's unwillingness to traverse and confront previous scholarship on Lasker-Schüler's Jewish persona and its poetic expression. The uninitiated reader would not guess from reading Hessing that several scholars have already addressed this topic and a few, in fact, have even anticipated some of his observations. The author's failure to perform such a review vitiates to some extent his own considerable accomplishment; moreover, in barely mentioning, for example, Sigrid Bauschinger's admirable comprehensive study of Lasker-Schüler, the author appears to be somewhat ungenerous.

Still, in spite of these lapses, Hessing's book not only contributes very significantly to a more accurate understanding of Lasker-Schüler scholarship, but also, on a broader scale, provides keen insight into the fateful German Jewish relationship of the pre-Hitler era.

ALFRED HOELZEL
University of Massachusetts, Boston

David Rosenberg (ed.), *Congregation: Contemporary Writers Read the Jewish Bible*. New York: Harcourt Brace Jovanovich, 1987. 526 pp.

To read *Congregation* in Israel requires suspending one entire range of possible modern Jewish responses to Scripture in favor of another. Each of the contributors to this book—all native or naturalized North Americans—has chosen one book of the Bible as a catalyst for his or her personal wrestling with the *textus receptus*. Such individualized commentaries or confessions assume a very different resonance in the country where the Bible has once again become a primary political resource and referent of transcendent authority for the social contract. Israelis are engaged in a war of citations resembling nothing so much as the medieval *disputatio*, each side mobilizing prooftexts to substantiate its own worldly agenda. I quote from the Book of Isaiah, you quote from Joshua; I cite, "Remember that you were strangers in the land of Egypt"; you retort, "Remember what Amalek has done to you." It is a phenomenon fraught with public consequence. Presuming the fixity of meaning, it has a literalizing effect on social as well as hermeneutic activity.

The American Jewish writers in this volume are for the most part engaged in a very different, very personal dialogue with Scripture that reflects the American mode of peaceably incorporating divergent traditions into democratic vistas while respecting their inviolability within the private domain. The aggregation of particularistic readings creates a community of readers that becomes a shared, if not authoritative, resource. Playfulness and open-endedness as interpretive strategies are applied to the sacred text with all the vigor and boldness that these writers and critics—representing nearly every gradation of familiarity with traditional sources and the widest possible range of literary sensitivity and philosophical rigor—can command. David Rosenberg introduces the volume by asserting, "The concept that best includes all our contributors . . . narrows down to one of personality, of individual integrity and creative openmindedness." Freud often preempts the rabbis as the mediating presence in this process.

There is an arrogance here that is by turns endearing and annoying. Granted, the peculiar accessibility of Scripture is such that through the hermeneutic discourse the text is brought to address each interpreter on his or her own grounds. Nevertheless, this familiarity, loosely identified with the midrashic mode, is in these essays often in danger of degenerating to the point where it is no longer predicated on what Gerald Bruns calls, elsewhere, the "secrecy" that is a "quintessential feature of sacred writings, . . . [the] hiding of the light that enables us to know its presence." When modern authors are asked to approach the "original biblical authors as fellow creators of story and verse" (Introduction), what can emerge is a kind of cozy intimacy that makes Job a household word and Balaam's ass a domestic pet. Transparency and over-familiarization are the price paid in a number of these essays for the mandate to participate in a cultural reform, in an unfettered renegotiation of the classical texts. The peculiar ironic edge that characterizes much of American and Canadian Jewish fiction, that anecdotal verve that feeds on incongruity and presumption, becomes trivial in this context as God is recast as the creator of holes for bagels and the stern or nagging prototype of one's own father. Quaint tales of snot-nosed kids and greasy *melamdim* in *ḥeder* were superseded fifty years ago by Henry Roth's consummate rendering of the immigrant Jewish vernacular that somehow managed to preserve the possibility of transcendence in the encounter with the Scriptures, so that certain moments became, simply, non-negotiable:

> "*Veeshma es kol adonoi omair es mi eshlach.* . . ." The rabbi tapped his pointer on the table. "But when Isaiah saw the Almighty in His majesty and His terrible light. . . . Woe me! he cried, What shall I do! I am lost!" The rabbi seized his skull-cap and crumpled it. "I, common man, have seen the Almighty, I, unclean one, have seen Him. Behold, my lips are unclean and I live in a land unclean—for the Jews at that time were sinful"—
> —Clean? Light? Wonder if—? Wish I could ask him why the Jews were dirty. What did they do? Better not. Get mad. Where? (Furtively, while the rabbi still spoke, David leaned over and stole a glance at the number of the page.) On sixty-eight. After, maybe, can ask. On page sixty-eight. That blue book.
> —Gee, it's God.

The most powerful essays in the present volume do succeed in moving us back behind the veil of secrecy that both obscures and affirms the luminosity of Scripture—without relinquishing the slantwise vision of the restless post-Enlightenment Jew. Daring interpretive leaps balanced by an inhibited intimacy characterize the contributions of Geoffrey Hartman, Leon Wieseltier, John Hollander and a few

others. Wieseltier tackles Leviticus through positing both revelation and the past-
ness of revelation as givens in this encounter. He offers the idea of belatedness as a
governing mode:

> The pastness of God's presence, at least to the senses, is responsible for the centrality of
> history in Western theologies. The faith of the Jew is premised upon the denial of
> contemporaneity with revelation. . . . Coming too late, . . . the Jew is never more than
> a mock contemporary. He is the one who can almost see, almost hear, almost taste.
> Coming too late, he has nothing but time.

Yearning for experience, proximity, the Jew finds limited consolation in tradition
and textuality.

Elaborating a different sense of belatedness that corresponds to stages of accessibility to the original text, John Hollander recapitulates his childhood encounter
with the King James version of the Psalms ("The Lord is my shepherd," as familiar
to the schoolboy as the Star-Spangled Banner, with "goodness and mercy" personified in a systematic misreading as "good Mrs. Murphy" who "follows me all the
days of my life"). He then traces his discovery of the Vulgate in the repertoire of his
school and college choirs ("generally it was *singing* the Latin psalms rather than
listening to them, which brought yet another psalter into my possession") and,
finally, his more mature grappling with the Hebrew verses. These are not simply
stages in the gradual approach to the authentic text, but milestones in the growth of
poetic sensibility:

> Re-entry into the original . . . in no way makes the poem shed its outer garments for
> the sake of a naked linguistic truth, and the various translations and versions and
> misprisions all coexist and inhere in every phrase. . . . The problems and puzzles of the
> psalms will remain eternal occasions for the reader's negative capability as well as for
> the interpretive wit that turns every reader into a poet, if only momentarily.

The "interpretive wit," which is the struggle between belatedness and the presumption of authenticity or originality, is brazenly exhibited in Harold Bloom's
essay. Applying his own hermeneutic strategies to the "J" strand of the Book of
Exodus, he sets about to transcend "the present state of Biblical scholarship" in
order to recover a primary voice: "J's freedom from belatedness rivals Shakespeare's, which is to say that J's own originality is as intense as Shakespeare's." J as
author or as a narrative stance is characterized by his portrait of Yahweh as "uncanny" (in the Freudian sense of sublime) yet *heimlich,* agonistic yet familiar. Performing a midrashic act while claiming to identify an original source, Bloom is
privileging his own narrative activity. The hubris that makes the critic the belated
coauthor of any text permits acts of revisionism that argue for missing sections of
the *Akedah* story, that identify Joseph as a Davidic figure—that would, above all,
challenge the integrity and authority of the received text:

> What precisely is the Bible? Genesis, Exodus, and Numbers are, for me, the J writer,
> and *not* the composite text in which the redactors have had the last word. . . .
>
> An awareness of J's strength gradually leads one to the realization that normative
> Judaism is an extremely strong misreading of the Hebrew Bible that was concluded
> eighteen centuries ago in order to meet the needs of the Jewish people in Palestine under

Roman occupation. . . . It is Western culture's largest irony, in our very late time, approaching the year 2000 C.E., that we still need to recover the vision of God that was seen so vividly by the uncanny writer, J, who was our origin.

The other voices in this sometimes inspiring, sometimes exasperating cacophony of solo refrains include more or less official spokespersons for American Jewish culture (Elie Wiesel, I. B. Singer), prominent writers (Cynthia Ozick, Herbert Gold, Mordecai Richler) and critics and interpreters (Stephen Mitchell, Grace Schulman).

The Hebrew Bible, bedrock of Jewish consciousness from the time of its canonization, was largely lost in the general amnesia that attended the acculturation of East European Jewish immigrants into American civilization. It reenters in the last quarter of the twentieth century mainly through the mediation of the critical and scholarly encounter; the poetry and fiction of American Jews remain for the most part devoid of that allusive layer that continues to inform even the most secular Hebrew imagination. In recent years, the noise of the disputations in the Israeli marketplace has all but drowned out the ironizing voices of the Hebrew poets who might have acted as a link between the two communities of readers, helping to free the one from oversubjectivization, the other from overdetermination. In the meantime, the elevated status of free interpretive acts partly accounts for the new yearning for Scripture that brings one group of disparate writers together as a provisional, latter-day congregation.

SIDRA DEKOVEN EZRAHI
The Hebrew University

Alexander Scheiber, *Essays on Jewish Folklore and Comparative Literature.* Budapest: Akadémiai Kiado, 1985. 453 pp.

Alexander Scheiber was among the most renowned scholars of Jewish folklore in Europe. His many publications in German, French and English in such journals as *Fabula, Journal of American Folklore, Acta Antiqua* and *Enzyclopädie des Märchens* established him as a central figure in this field. If to these are added his abundant publications in two "esoteric" languages (most important, however, for Scheiber himself), Hebrew and Hungarian, the great achievements of this scholar during his fifty-year career are manifest. The present collection of some of his most important work on Jewish folklore facilitates an assessment of his contribution to the field. A three-volume collection of Scheiber's articles in Hungarian was published several years ago:[1] however, he himself emphasized the importance of collecting and publishing his studies in other European languages and in Hebrew.[2]

For about forty years, Scheiber was director of the Rabbinical Seminary of Budapest, a position that symbolized his two basic interests: the Hungarian culture in which he lived and created and Jewish *Wissenschaft,* to which he devoted his intellectual efforts. Scheiber considered himself the disciple of the great Jewish

Hungarian scholars—David Kaufmann, Ignaz Goldziher, Samuel Krauss, Emmanuel Löw and especially Bernhard Heller. Like them, he was a product of the great European tradition of scholarship with the depth and historical-philological interests of nineteenth-century Jewish *Wissenschaft*. Like them, he had a special interest in the relationship between Jewish learned culture—historiography, philosophy, halakhah, poetry and Biblical interpretation—and Jewish folk culture and its links to international folklore. In his article on Bernhard Heller, whom he considered his teacher and mentor, he emphasizes the three layers of his work: Jewish studies, the study of *aggadah* and folktales, and comparative literature. As is common in such appreciations, Scheiber characterizes here his own interests no less than those of his teacher.

The present collection of articles was published in journals and *Festschriften* between 1940 and 1984. The material is very heterogeneous: it includes articles (or series of articles) of impressive length as well as dozens of brief notes published as reactions to other scholars' publications.

The breadth of Scheiber's interests can be demonstrated through the two long series of articles that occupy the central part of this book. The first one is called, "Antike Elemente in der Aggada," and was published as a series of articles in *Acta Antiqua* between 1961 and 1978. The thread that ties the separate parts of this work together is the discovery and comparative study of parallel themes in Talmudic-midrashic *aggadah* and in the literature of the classical world. Such tale types as the "Matron of Ephesus," the princess locked in the tower, the treasure of the wise man (he takes with him only his wisdom); such narrative motifs as running on the heads of wheat plants, God-fearing animals, death as a result of joy, the burning bush; such proverbs as "the lie has no feet," and many others are all examined and compared in relation to their sources, development and different appearances in rabbinic *aggadah* and Greek and Roman writings. Using dozens of examples, Scheiber proves that rabbinic *aggadah* belonged in many respects to the Hellenistic world in which it grew and developed, but also that there were essential differences in the uses to which folkloric materials were put in Jewish and Hellenistic sources.

The second long series of articles, "Alte Geschichten im neuen Gewande," was published in thirteen parts between 1966 and 1984 in *Fabula* (except for the last one, which appeared in the *Festschrift* for Dov Noy). This series discusses no less than eighty (!) themes. Each one of these brief and concentrated studies opens with one folkloric unit-motif, custom, narrative pattern or simile in modern literature and exposes, by a digressive method, the sources of this folkloric unit in world folklore and ancient literature.

Scheiber shows, for example, how narrative episodes in the novels of the Polish writer Julian Stryjkowski—the rabbi and *melamed* (children's tutor) who saves children from the werewolf—are taken from sources in hasidic literature and international folklore. This series of "notes," in particular, demonstrates Scheiber's breadth of reading and erudition in European literature. It also points to his broad cultural approach: he does not devote his studies to folklore alone or belles-lettres alone, but makes enormous efforts to define and prove the cultural continuity between the learned, artistic culture and its folk and popular layers. This series of studies serves to show, it seems, how artificial and incorrect such a dichotomy really is. It also proves Scheiber's deep roots in Hungarian, non-Jewish culture. Poems, stories and other writings of Hungarian writers are the main starting point of these studies.

Hungarian culture was also the central theme of other studies in the book. Here Scheiber uncovers the Hungarian parallels to such popular themes as the *golem* of Prague, the Wandering Jew, the folksong "Who Knows One," the Bar Kochba games and many others. Like Moses Gaster before him, who devoted so much work to the study of Romanian folklore that he is considered the founder of Romanian folkloristics (though that did not prevent his expulsion from Romania for Zionistic activity),[3] Scheiber devotes most of his work to the discovery, analysis and publication of a culture known very little outside its own borders.

The study of the legend of the Wandering Jew in Hungary (pp. 134–160) illustrates Scheiber's special tendency. The dissemination and forms of this legend in most of world culture have been studied before. Scheiber sought to bring to the attention of international scholarship the special form of the legend in Hungary. With great erudition, he sets out its various appearances in Hungarian literature from its beginnings to the last fascist manifestations; he also notes its appearance in many genres of Hungarian folklore: proverbs, folksongs, folktales and rituals. An important (and innovative) chapter is the detailed study of the function of the chapbook in the dissemination of this legend in Hungary. With his keen folkloristic instinct, he sensed the importance of this medium of transmission for the legend of the Wandering Jew and for folklore in general.[4]

The series of articles entitled "Samson Uprooting a Tree" (pp. 70–80) opens with the same theme of Hungarian folklore connected with Jews. A strange and obscure twelfth-century sculpture in the cathedral of Pécs, depicting a hero uprooting a tree, is the starting point for a detective-like search. After analyzing the elements of the sculpture, Scheiber reveals the sources of the motif in Jewish *aggadah,* its transmission to Hungarian culture and its variant forms in literature. This study demonstrates Scheiber's scholarly interest in the relationship between folk art, folk literature and belles lettres. He engages in a similar analysis of the narrative elements that compose a painting or sculpture in the article on "The Smoke from Cain and Abel's Sacrifices," the fish island (the tale of Rabba bar-bar-Hanah), and the "Donkey on the Ladder" (an excellent study of a philological-artistic puzzle appearing in colophons of medieval Hebrew manuscripts). This type of study gives clear expression to Scheiber's gravitation toward interdisciplinary areas, eliminating barriers between different fields of humanistic and social sciences.

"A Donkey on the Ladder" is typical of Scheiber's inductive investigatory method—a method that has attracted students of folklore since the beginning of the discipline. Here the folklorist presents an obscure and hitherto unknown custom, folk belief or narrative motif. In a digressive manner, the history of the theme is reconstructed together with its cultural context. This method of mosaiclike reconstruction is used by Scheiber in several other studies: on the custom of swearing an oath by holding the *ẓiẓit* (fringes) or by holding the ring of the synagogue doors and the custom of blowing the *shofar* (horn) in burial rites of great men.

Scheiber's studies are in many cases short, comparative notes that present material and seldom analyze it. The two series of articles mentioned earlier are, as a matter of fact, collections of such fragmentary brief notes. His tendency to collect material and describe its chronological and geographical setting is in full accord with the historical-geographical or comparative school in the study of folklore.[5] Scheiber also sought the sources of the folkloric theme in order to construct what he believed to be the *ur-text*. Although Scheiber started his scholarly work when this school was already fading, it still had major influence on many scholars, especially Scheiber's teacher, Bernhard Heller.[6]

The major weakness of Scheiber's work is demonstrated in one methodological article, "The Study of Jewish Folklore in the Periodical *Revue des études juives*" (pp. 204–222), which sets out to describe the contribution of this central French Jewish publication to the study of Jewish folklore. Scheiber opens with a general survey of the field from Grunwald's *Mitteilungen* up to the Hungarian scholars. This section is totally unsatisfying. He divides the main discussion into sections on rabbinic *aggadah:* folktales and folkloric collections, publication of texts, folksongs, proverbs, folk customs, magic and amulets. The problem is that the discussion does not analyze or describe the contribution of these essays to Jewish folklore studies, but merely gives a brief bibliographical description that hardly goes beyond the style of an annotated bibliography. What the author has missed is an opportunity to give a methodological survey of the development of Jewish folkloristics since the end of the nineteenth century as reflected in this central journal. Moreover, no attempt is made to characterize the approaches and methods of such seminal figures as Israel Lévi and Bernhard Heller, most of whose publications appeared here.

In spite of the fragmentary character of so many parts of this book, due credit must be given to some central and comprehensive essays. The works on *Eshkol hakofer* of Yehuda Hadassi, the satirical poems of Emmanuele of Rome, the Wandering Jew in Hungary, the Sacrificial Smoke of Cain and Abel, and the choice of the place for the Temple (but why was this essay published twice here, once in French and again in Hebrew?) are major contributions to the study of Jewish folklore. These works possess that breadth of perspective, synthesis of different facets of culture and the overview of Jewish folklore within European culture, that were so typical of a scholarly tradition of which Alexander Scheiber was one of the last representatives.

ELI YASSIF
Ben-Gurion University
of the Negev

Notes

1. *Folklòr és tàrgytörténet*, vols. 1 and 2 (Budapest: 1974); vol. 3 (1984).
2. *Ibid.*, Introduction, 15.
3. Cf. B. Schindler (ed.), *Occident and Orient, Gaster Anniversary Volume* (London: 1936); Moses Gaster, *Studies and Texts in Folklore, Magic, Medieval Romance, Hebrew Apocrypha and Samaritan Archaeology,* 3 vols. (London: 1928).

4. Eli Yassif, "The Folk Book—Folklore or Popular Culture?" *Jerusalem Studies in Jewish Folklore* 1 (1981), 117–133; *idem,* "What is a Folk Book?" *International Folklore Review* 5 (1987), 20–27.

5. Of the abundant literature written on this school, see R. M. Dorson, "Concepts of Folklore and Folklife Studies," in *Folklore and Folklife,* ed. R. M. Dorson (Chicago and London: 1972), 12–20; J. Hautala, *Finnish Folklore Research 1828–1918* (Helsinki: 1968).

6. Heller wrote the chapter on Jewish and Arabic folk literature in one of the cornerstones of the comparative school: Bernhard Heller, "Das hebräische Märchen," in *Anmerkungen zu der Kinder—u. Hausmärchen der Brüder Grimm,* ed. J. Bolte and G. Polivka (Leipzig: 1930), vol. 4, 315–364.

Leonardo Senkman, *La identidad judía en la literatura argentina.* Buenos Aires: Editorial Pardes, 1983. 500 pp.

The opening statement of this lengthy study announces its main objective: to analyze the Jewish presence in Argentina as reflected in literary works written mainly by Jewish Argentine authors. The first section of the book is devoted to the processes of rural and urban immigration, with the accompanying issue of acculturation, and to the national ideological framework that resulted from the immigrants' integration into (or temporary rejection by) the Argentine mainstream. The second part centers, quite aptly, on Alberto Gerchunoff as the paradigmatic figure of the immigrant dreamer who is destined to witness the collapse of the liberal policies on which he placed his initial hopes. The focus then shifts to the fundamental problems of Jewish identity in Argentina faced by the younger generation of poets, playwrights and fiction writers. The final section deals with the Jewish presence in the works of two Catholic writers, Manuel Gálvez and Leopoldo Marechal. As Senkman himself admits, these last two analyses are better suited for the promised second volume of this project, which will center on the Jew in Argentine non-Jewish literature.

Written by a sociologist with a deep understanding of history and literature, who is at home with the appropriate methodological tools, the book emphasizes the Jewish content of the texts more than literary concerns per se. Senkman's search for the issues raised by authors who confront the complexities of integration, acculturation and assimilation involved taking a risk: the selection of many texts whose literary value is minimal but, as cultural artifacts, contribute to the elaboration of a continuum. At one end of the range, Senkman finds an integrationist approach—with assimilation as the final goal. Next along the continuum come critiques of the values of both the Argentine national social order and the Jewish community (particularly its emphasis on material success as a path to, and measure of, social recognition). Finally, there is the most recent critical literature that poses serious and perhaps unanswerable challenges to communal organizations and records the bankruptcy of state policies.

We have here a process that starts with the timid hope for acceptance and recognition of the newly arrived and ends with the knowledge that rootedness grants rights of assertiveness. Senkman asks whether Gerchunoff and Mario Szichman could be seen as representing polar opposites of the immigrant experience—from elegiac praise of the New Zion to mordant view of vaudevillian urban characters. The transition from the dream that called for a Jewish renaissance through working the land to the reality of urban life hints at a trajectory of failure: not only of the Jewish communal leadership, but of the entire Argentine nation whose inner contradictions have exploded into violence.

After briefly discussing several texts by Gerardo Mario Goloboff and Alejandra Pizarnik (both Argentines), Brazilian Clarice Lispector and Mexican Esther Seligson, Senkman finds that these works form part of a wide arch that spans the generations. Their writing incorporates local national references and allusions in an attempt to produce a recognizable national literature, while also alluding to traditional Jewish motifs with strong links to the ancestral past. Moreover, Senkman suggests, the Jewish references are not facile or faddish. Instead, there is a subtler recalling of historical markers, registering and rendering a consciousness of change that reaches toward a richly textured and varied definition of the Promised Land. Origins, exile, the land, the people and hopes for historic fulfillment play important thematic roles.

Gerchunoff's presence is felt throughout the book. Almost everyone is measured against this writer: from César Tiempo to more recent writers such as Marcos Aguinis and Ricardo Feierstein. Gerchunoff inspired a process of defining and balancing the options outlined by the integrationism of Jewish liberalism. Younger authors framed radical queries about the feasibility of the total and thorough integration of Jews into Argentine culture. Efforts to legitimize the existence of the Jewish community and the practice of a particular identity within the national mainstream underscore an enduring vulnerability and a problematic resolution of integrationist formulas. This is one of the key themes brilliantly elucidated by Senkman in the writings of so many Jewish Argentine authors.

Some readers may find Senkman somewhat repetitious in tracing the treatment of similar motifs by different writers. There are also other, possibly unavoidable, minor flaws in this ambitious undertaking. Because of its broad scope, however, Senkman's study far surpasses all other studies hitherto made of this subject. It joins that select list of obligatory reading for anyone interested in Jewish identity in Argentine literature and for those seeking an understanding of the problems faced by minority cultures in their attempts to survive within a dominant culture.

SAÚL SOSNOWSKI
University of Maryland

Sol Steinmetz, *Yiddish and English: A Century of Yiddish in America*. University, Alabama: University of Alabama Press, 1986. 172 pp.

Yiddish and English, having lived on intimate terms for more than a century, are now having their relationship reexamined. The connections between the two languages have long been the subject of serious sociolinguistic study, theoretical speculation and bad jokes. Lexical and syntactical borrowings and influence have been documented, raising intriguing questions about the cultural or historical significance we ought to attach to the contact between the two languages. How, if at all, does this reciprocal borrowing differ from that involving English and other immigrant languages? What is the effect of such intimacy on the poetry and prose of either language? Why is the symbolic significance of Yiddish still so great in Jewish American literature, even when most of today's authors have no knowledge of the language? Why have so many Yiddish idioms, patterns of speech and slang expressions penetrated into popular English discourse?

The subject of Sol Steinmetz's book encourages such questions, but *Yiddish and English* does not attempt to address them. Urging what he calls a "balanced view" of Yiddish in America, Steinmetz delights in pointing out how wrong are the doomsayers who have long predicted the imminent demise of Yiddish, but cautions against the unrealistic view that sees it as thriving. He posits, instead, the existence of a vibrant new Jewish language—or at least dialect. Culminating in an appendix with a glossary of some twelve hundred words, phrases and idioms that he argues constitute this "Jewish English," Steinmetz's book is a testament to the language spoken mostly by members of the modern Orthodox community in America. Their primary language may be English, but in discussing any of the elements of traditional Jewish life—rituals, family, culture, history, study—they rely on a different language in which Yiddish or Hebrew loanwords carry the burden of meaning with English serving as the grammatical vehicle. This language, which has been called Yinglish or Judeo-English by others, is now used as an alternative to Yiddish. It is an "insider's language" used by the Orthodox as "a natural way of expressing Jewish values and concepts, as merely another expression of *yidishkayt* (p. 84)." One of the myriad examples Steinmetz offers will suffice as illustration: "My host bought an aliya for me, but I didn't know about it until the shammus, according to the minhag of the yekkis, handed me a silver-plated aliya card" (*Jewish Press,* July 4, 1975).

It is not really clear why such a sentence, with its four loanwords (aliya, shammus, minhag, yekkis), is accorded a status denied the awful Yiddish-English mixture patterned, decades earlier, on the speech of unlettered immigrant Jews. That perversion of Yiddish Steinmetz calls "potato Yiddish," joining others in suggesting what has yet to be rigorously analyzed: that the New York *Jewish Daily Forverts* used this mixture of bad English and worse Yiddish as an encouragement to acculturation and thus helped bring about the decline of Yiddish letters in America. The following sentence with its five loanwords is a typical example: *Der loyer in mayn bilding geyt mufn tsum beysment flor.* If either of these examples is an accurate reflection of the state of Yiddish or of Jewish speech in America, one can only add *okh un vey* (defined by Steinmetz's glossary as "alas; woe") to the speakers of Yiddish, English or any mixture of the two that is in the making!

There is much fascinating material in this book concerning the roots of popular Yiddish and English idiomatic expressions. Steinmetz's footnotes cite the original contexts for such words as *moyshe kapoyer* and *yakhne* as well as the more familiar yenta and shlemiel. (The latter is a particular gem, deriving from a Talmudic figure who is unlucky enough to have his name associated with an even more hapless prince killed while in the act of making love to a Midianite woman.) He cites the source for "the bottom line" (from the Yiddish *di untershte shure,* which made its way into commercial circles thanks to New York Jews), and of "son-of-a-gun" (from criminal slang via the Yiddish word for thief, *ganef*). Such derivations, interesting examples of the Yiddish influence on English, rely on the work of other scholars. The theoretical underpinnings of Steinmetz's own work relies primarily on the scholarship of Joshua Fishman, whose sociolinguistic research in Yiddish is the base for all subsequent study. Steinmetz is a lexicographer, a meticulous collector of words and phrases that he culls from an extraordinary range of sources, including *Time,* the *New Yorker, Jewish Life, Jewish Parent* and many other popular magazines as well as Jewish professional journals and classics of English and American fiction, including Joyce's *Ulysses.* His text often consists of a series of examples with too little commentary; it reads like a transcription from index cards collected painstakingly and indiscriminately over many years. The range and sheer number of examples is more impressive than the theoretical framework or explanations that have been offered for them.

A footnote to the book's introduction points out that "a comprehensive linguistic study of Yiddish-English contact has often been called for, but apparently a great deal of preparatory fieldwork needs to be done before such a study becomes feasible." Yiddish scholars are still waiting for just such a linguistic and cultural study.

ANITA NORICH
University of Michigan

Religion, Thought and Education

Mordechai Breuer, *Jüdische Orthodoxie im Deutschen Reich 1871–1918. Die Sozialgeschichte einer religiösen Minderheit*. Frankfurt on the Main: Jüdischer Verlag of Athenäum (Publication of the Leo Baeck Institute), 1986. 525 pp.

The historiography of German Jewry has been preeminently "Whig": despite their obvious differences, both "assimilationist" and "Zionist" historians concentrated on virtually the same subjects, that is, the victorious, if vexed and bickering, protagonists in the drama of emancipation and assimilation. Those elements of German Jewry seemingly excluded from the drama—rural, East European immigrant and especially Orthodox Jews—are only now being rediscovered. For this reason, Mordechai Breuer's *Jüdische Orthodoxie im Deutschen Reich, 1871–1918* is an invaluable contribution. It is the first scholarly study of German Orthodoxy and surveys uncharted territory: page after page is filled with topics that even the most assiduous reader of postwar scholarship would merely have glimpsed. And Breuer treats his subject with an intelligence and erudition informed with equal measures of compassion and criticism. Yet this important pioneering effort, paradoxically enough, sustains the prevalent "Whig" conception of German Jewish history it intends to overturn.

Breuer sets out to account for Orthodoxy's survival. He asks, "What were the factors which both favored the continued existence of an Orthodoxy that was at odds with the developments of the time and even allowed that Orthodoxy to acquire a considerable inner resilience?" (p. 6). His answer is that in the Hirschian ideology of *Torah 'im derekh erez*, German Orthodoxy evolved a flexible posture that enabled it to select the best of what the contemporary world offered without abjuring any of the heritage that it deemed to be binding. Because it was not a petrified fundamentalism, German Orthodoxy could appropriate the forms of modern life suitable to a religious minority and fill them with its own contents. Orthodox Jewry created a public realm (*Öffentlichkeit*) of journals, pamphlets, sermons and novels that promoted its self-understanding; founded voluntary associations and organizations such as the *Freie Vereinigung für die Interessen des orthodoxen Judentums* (1885) to further its political and social interests; and established a rabbinical seminary, a teachers' seminary and schools to educate its leaders and its laity.

At the same time that German Orthodoxy utilized these modern forms, it also set definite limits to its accommodation. Most important, Orthodox Jews renounced the social dimension of Emancipation: they claimed the right to pursue their own purposes separately rather than integrating with non-Jews. (Nevertheless, Orthodox Jews felt that an observant Jew had greater affinities with a believing Catholic than with a liberal Jew, and they preferred non-Jews to liberal Jews as business associates—particularly when the association hinged on keeping Sabbath working hours—and as teachers of secular subjects in Orthodox schools.) Similarly, Orthodox Jews never propounded an ideology of German nationalism, although they readily professed their patriotism and did not hesitate to lobby the local or national authorities on issues such as Sabbath attendance of schools, Sunday work hours in offices or conditions for Orthodox conscripts. Their "Deutschtum" was circumscribed, first, by their conviction that the Jews were a people (*Volk*), even though for tactical political purposes they argued the Jews were a "confession" (especially in the *Austritt* controversy), and, second, by their expectation of redemption: they were German until the coming of the Messiah (*bis dahin*).

In his account of the consolidation of Orthodox institutions and culture in the Wilhelmine era, Breuer does not neglect failures and shortcomings. Scrupulously chronicling the discrepancies between aspirations and achievements, he shows, for example, that a non-practicing Orthodoxy existed whose members espoused a notion of vicarious (the rabbi's) observance; that Orthodox schools fell short of their goal of imparting a religious as well as a secular education, in part because of governmental pressures but also because of parental ones; and that the Hildesheimer Seminary remained narrow in its cultural horizons and unsatisfactory in the Talmudic knowledge of its students. He also points to the community's predominant "petit-bourgeois" (*kleinbürgerlich*) mentality, which made it a cultural consumer rather than a cultural producer. Hirsch's ideal served more as a shield against secular culture than as a spur to constant reconsideration of it. Finally, in an excellent concluding chapter, Breuer examines the fin-de-siècle "new orientation" when a group of young intellectuals (Pinchas Kohn, Josepf Wohlgemuth, Eduard Biberfeld, Issac Breuer) mounted a fundamental critique of the Hirsch–Hildesheimer tradition. They revived mysticism and Talmud study (*lernen*), rehabilitated the image of East European Judaism and turned toward Zionism.

Breuer is an obvious master of his subject (his analysis of halakhic developments in chap. 5 is especially enlightening). But despite a backdrop of contemporary and classic German sociological theory, Breuer's study is largely internal in its conception. It is unduly focused on the person of Hirsch and the city of Frankfurt. The second chapter, for example, is primarily devoted to a detailed explication of Hirsch's *Bildungsideologie*. Breuer introduces the other variants of German Orthodoxy (Bamberger, Hildesheimer) only by way of comparison. But was Hirsch's position predominant? Who was more representative? Or was regionalism a factor? These questions are not resolved—in part because of Breuer's method. Breuer's *Sozialgeschichte* does not equal "social history" in its current Anglo-American usage. Breuer does not get much beyond an anecdotal and impressionistic account of demographics, residential patterns, occupational and social structure and the like. As a result, his excellent analyses of ideology, institutions and politics are not properly contextualized.

Breuer's study is internal in an additional sense. He has effectively made into a presupposition of his study the Orthodox commonplace that Orthodox Jews were further removed from liberal Jews than Catholics from Protestants. With the notable exception of politics, Breuer does not compare the Orthodox and liberal German Jewish communities. Yet, he repeatedly shows that Orthodoxy consistently responded to developments in liberal Judaism and that such "reactive behavior" (p. 252), as he calls it, was fully in keeping with Orthodoxy's origins in the "interaction between emancipation on the one side and Reform on the other" (p. 30). He demonstrates that Orthodoxy's most successful institutions imitated, and competed directly with, liberal ones: the press, the schools, Hildesheimer's seminary and the *Freie Vereinigung*. Moreover, Orthodox Jews shared many of their attitudes with liberal Jews: an attachment to early nineteenth-century German culture, the veneration of Moses Mendelssohn, the denigration of Eastern Jews. Thus, Breuer's evidence suggests the factors that united liberal and Orthodox Jews might have far outweighed those dividing them.

Breuer's pioneering study now makes it indefensible to write a "Whig" history that excludes Orthodoxy from German Jewry. Historians should also reject the other side of the "Whig" coin by henceforth refusing to exclude the rest of German Jewry when writing the history of German Jewish Orthodoxy. Moreover, just as "Whig" historians are now aware that it is no longer analytically productive to rely on the categories of the "Zionism-assimilation" conflict, so perhaps it is also time to reconsider the utility of categories derived from the "liberal-Orthodox" one.

David Sorkin
Oxford Centre for Postgraduate
Hebrew Studies, St. Antony's College, Oxford

Arthur Cohen and Paul Mendes-Flohr (eds.), *Contemporary Jewish Religious Thought*. New York: Scribner's, 1987. xix + 1163 pp.

It is a pleasure to be able to report that *Contemporary Jewish Religious Thought* does, indeed, deal with contemporary Jewish religious thought. This is no mean accomplishment. Encyclopedias produced in the last decades under Jewish auspices have tended to the concrete rather than the spiritual. It has been commented, for example, that one misses the Bible for the stones in the Hebrew *Enẓiklopedia mikra'it*. So the ambition of Cohen and Mendes-Flohr to focus precisely on the ideological and philosophical rather than on the institutional or sociological is commendable. Second, this book does contain a considerable amount of "contemporary thought": that is to say, the thought of the contemporaries who wrote the various articles rather than surveys of what the ancients or the medievals thought or even pieces on the history of this or that idea (though these do appear, of course—and are even welcome). Needless to say, Jewish thought will never cut loose of its sources, but it is clear that many of these essays attempt to continue the process rather than merely summarize the past. The measure of freshness gained is well worth the historical scope that may be lost. This reader found many pieces intelligent and suggestive, although easier read by dipping here and there and following one's own interest than by consuming them in order from A to Z.

That is how the book is put together: one hundred essays in alphabetical order, from Aesthetics (Steven Schwarzschild) to Zionism (Ben Halpern). In between, one can find pieces on, say, Apocalpyse (Nahum Glatzer), Chosen People (Henri Atlan), Conscience (Steven Schwarzschild), Dogma (Menahem Kellner), Eschatology (Arthur Cohen), Ethics (Shalom Rosenberg), Hasidism (Arthur Green), Heresy (Ze'ev Gries), History (Paul Mendes-Flohr), Imagination (Geoffrey Hartman), Jerusalem (Shmaryahu Talmon), Memory (David Roskies), Music (Moshe Idel), Natural Law (Jeffrey Macy), Oral Law (Jacob Neusner), Peace (Aviezer Ravitzky), Political Theory (Ella Belfer and Ilan Greilsammer), Reason (Eugene Borowitz), Religion and State (Aharon Lichtenstein), Secularism (Ben Halpern), Suffering (David Hartman), Torah (James Kugel), Woman (Blu Greenberg). The list—and this is but a random selection—indicates that, despite the term "religious" in the title, a rigorously defined theological approach did not serve as the organizing principle; rather, we have reflections on how Jewish spirituality confronts different concerns. "Torah" is taken broadly and imaginatively, sweeping from Bible to Rosenzweig, Kaplan, Soloveitchik and Buber. The medieval Maimonides (to judge from the index) is currently considered Judaism's most seminal thinker, although it would be wise to recall that—as was the case in earlier centuries—the portrait drawn of Maimonides is often a mirror image of its author. Many of the topics, to be sure, are the grist of standard tomes on Judaism, but a considerable number contend with a distinctively contemporary agenda. The interpretative process, the very textuality of Jewish expression itself, is at the crux of articles such as Gesture and Symbol (Josef Stern), Midrash (David Stern), Torah (James Kugel), Sacred Text and Canon (David Stern). Other essays reflect the recognition of community and, indeed, politics as subjects for analysis; and Mysticism (Moshe Idel) takes its place alongside Medieval Jewish Philosophy (Jacob Agus). Halakhah, as a standard of definitive norms, is not directly central to any of these concerns, but both the dynamic process of halakhah and its concretizing thrust do underlie many of the discussions.

The authors of these hundred essays represent the cream of contemporary Jewish scholarship, although most are more than academics. There is a nice blend of senior eminence and promising youth, of non-Israelis and Israelis (although many of these are Western immigrants to Israel). One even gains the impression that an international conversation is taking place, an encouraging contrast to what often seems to be the divisive reality of Jewish life. A sense of confidence pervades the whole. Judaism, it implies, has the intellectual substance to engage moderns. One also gets a useful synopsis of major theses by their protagonists: Yeshayahu Leibowitz on Idolatry, Arnold Eisen on Exile, Gershom Scholem on Judaism. And these summaries are not, on the whole, tired rehashes of the old material. Many essays are well conceived; confined to relatively few pages, authors crafted pieces that both focus and span the central problematic of their topic, although a few, naturally, are narrowly idiosyncratic. One can, I think, enter one minor disappointment as to the spectrum of authors and positions. Jewish thought is presented across the range, from the secular to the Orthodox, with much in between. The Orthodoxy represented, however, tends clearly to the left: David Hartman discusses Halakhah and Emmanuel Rackman writes on Orthodox Judaism. But Jewish life today has seen the rise of much that is clearly to the right of their positions, and the readership of *Contemporary Jewish Religious Thought* should have been given a whiff of that Judaism, too. Did the editors consider that perspective unappealing or dull? Or, alternatively, did its representatives refuse to participate in a pluralistic volume such as this?

All in all, though, the book before us is almost always useful and insightful—and occasionally profound. It should be in all Jewish libraries.

G. J. BLIDSTEIN
Ben-Gurion University of the Negev

A. Roy Eckardt, *For Righteousness' Sake: Contemporary Moral Philosophies.*
Bloomington and Indianapolis: Indiana University Press: 1987. xi + 365 pp.

For Righteousness' Sake is an extraordinary book that warrants not only reading, but also rereading by all who are concerned with formulating a religiously based philosophy of moral living. It is of importance to both Christians and Jews since it bases itself on their traditions without invidious comparisons and provides the soundest foundation for mutual respect and accommodation that this reviewer has ever encountered.

Although the style is often informal and colloquial, this is not an easy book for the casual reader to understand. Perhaps it would be better to speak of an individual style since it reflects the author's unique way of thinking and writing. He does not hesitate, for example, to use Hebrew terminology or Greek concepts. He deliberately alternates genders when speaking of God in order to make a point. The subtlety of thought and the richness of material from Jewish, Christian, Greek, European and Eastern philosophical thought makes this a work for those with professional interest and background. For that audience, this is a many-textured approach that is uncommon in professional books, as is the combination of technical points and prophetic passion, of scholarly objectivity and ethical concern. Thus it is a work both for those who would seek to understand modern currents of moral philosophy and for those to whom this is not merely a matter of interest and understanding, but of guidance for practical paths of living. It is to be hoped that it will influence others who will translate its message into terms that are understandable by masses of believers as well.

Dr. Eckardt belongs to that small but important group of Christian scholars for whom Judaism is an integral part of their Christian belief. Indeed, major sections of this book are devoted to Judaism itself, whereas large parts of the discussion of Christianity focus on the Jewishness of Jesus, the departure from Judaism of Paul and others, the relationship of Christianity to Judaism today, the responsibility of Christianity toward the Jewish people and toward the State of Israel in the light of historic Christian antisemitism and the Shoah and the call for the Judaization of Christianity. It would be fair to say that the concern with Judaism is central to this book.

When discussing liberation theology, for example, the author expresses great concern that many adherents of this view are not sympathetic to the State of Israel and ignore the fact that if there is any group to whom the principles of such liberation should apply, it is the Jews. "If God is not the God of the rich, not a white racist, not a sexist, then neither is she an antisemite. It is sad that in an epoch when God has become poor and black and female, she has not yet become Jewish" (p. 293). This is part of his total concern with the Shoah and Eckardt's conviction that Jewish powerlessness today is out of the question, a fact that must be recognized by all Christians, who bear a great measure of responsibility for the Shoah.

On the other hand, it would be misleading to think of this as a Jewish book. A Jew could not have written it in view of the strong Christian base upon which it is built. The very framework of the book, for example, is taken from H. Richard Niebuhr's typology of "Christ and Culture." Eckardt, however, has transformed this and expanded upon it, making the two basic components into "Faith and History." Niebuhr's five possibilities become eight "Normative Images," and it is very much to Eckardt's credit as a scholar and thinker that he is able to present each of these alternative images in objective terminology, doing them full justice while also presenting their shortcomings.

The eighth image, "history transforming faith," is dealt with in the final four chapters of the book in great detail, and it forms the heart of his concern. This eighth image represents Eckardt's own point of view and thereby changes the nature of the book from a scholarly overview of contemporary moral philosophies into a creative pattern of life advocated by the author, to which the other seven viewpoints have provided the necessary prologue. They are necessary not merely for an under-standing of the eighth viewpoint, but also because many parts of them can be accepted into that viewpoint and because pluralism dictates that no one Christian viewpoint can claim exclusivity.

"People of eight," as Eckardt calls them, are advocates of a "Christian theocentric historicism" (p. 225), a post-liberal approach that does not cast aside the positive values of liberalism but adds to them the realism and transcendence that enable it to serve as a bridge between "a certain spiritual past and the moral challenges and agonies of humankind today, to point the way responsibly to the future (p. 226). The history of Christianity on which this is based dictates both "Christian moral responsibility to the people Israel" and "lessons for Christians from the people Israel" (p. 269). Living in an unredeemed world, the paradigmatic historical event remains the Exodus from Egypt, which symbolizes all future liberation. There is to be no spiritualization of faith, which must work morally and responsibly *within* the world and *within* history. Eckardt does not accept a simplistic view of history as always revealing the will of God. On the contrary, it is difficult to discern patterns of righteousness and morality in history. Although there may be no redemption within history, human beings are called upon to act responsibly within history. To be involved in the actions needed to transform the world by righteousness in accord with the will of God, is to be "upon the side of God's future" (p. 262). Our faith tells us what it is that God would accomplish. Now the problem is to find people who will "help her bring it off" (p. 262).

Among other questions that confront the author and his "people of eight" are many concerning Christian belief and doctrine. For example: How is the resurrection to be understood? Can it ever be purified of antisemitism without eliminating the doctrine altogether? While enumerating numerous problems and hesitations, Eckardt opts for the position that the resurrection is to be seen within the context of Judaism as a vindication of the Pharisaic position as opposed to the Sadducean and not as a triumph of messianism or of the Church over Judaism (p. 312). This accords well with his discussion of Jesus, in which he states that Jesus is not a false Messiah, but both a failed Messiah and a terribly mistaken Messiah (p. 67). Eckardt is as forthright in his questioning of God as he is of human beings and of religious belief. He brings his book to a conclusion with a discussion of the trial of God based upon the Shoah, and states that the ultimate responsibility for such evil is God's, not because of his direct will, but because God created this world as it is. God is, so to speak (Eckardt's term) "the ultimate klutz" who is stuck with the world he created (p. 324).

It is impossible to do more than hint at the richness and depth of Eckardt's thought. Obviously, there are many Christians who will not be able to accept the approach he advocates. From the Jewish point of view, that is a pity, because it is the only approach I am aware of that permits a Christian to retain the individuality of being a Christian and at the same time relate positively to the basic beliefs of Judaism. Eckardt's Christianity is rooted in morality and ethics, in this-wordliness, in faith and in post-liberal reality, eliminating even the smallest amount of anti-Judaism and Christian triumphalism, affirming faith and yet leaving room for doubt and for pluralism.

REUVEN HAMMER
The Jewish Theological
Seminary of America (Jerusalem Campus)

Zev Garber (ed.), *Methodology in the Academic Teaching of Judaism*. Lanham: University Press of America, 1986. 284 pp.

Debates concerning the role and place of Jewish studies in the academy, so pronounced during the 1950s and early 1960s when Judaism was decidedly the "outsider" in the academic world, centered on issues such as belief versus knowledge and ethnicity as opposed to academic inquiry. The appearance of this anthology, edited with great care, devotion and skill by Zev Garber, marks Judaism's coming of age in the academy. There are those, it is true, who still cling to the old and somewhat artificial distinctions, but the complexity and sophistication of Jewish studies in their manifold expression seems to have outpaced all but the most tenaciously obstinate arguments.

Focusing on the relationship of Jewish studies to the humanities, the text aims to acquaint college and university educators with "the rich diversity of Jewish studies, to suggest ways Jewish studies can successfully be integrated into humanities classes, and to provide substantial and imaginative materials to assist them in that pursuit" (p. 1). These tasks are presented in four sections: "Theory and Method," "Teaching Judaica Across the Disciplines," "Teaching Judaism to Non-Jews," and "Innovation" (or, in Garber's words, a "wild card" or "open end" section). The unifying thread that links the fourteen essays and Garber's thoughtful introduction can be stated in the form of a question: What has a revealed tradition (the past) to tell contemporary people?

Garber draws the reader's attention to several crucial issues such as the relationship of professor to student—advocating a student-centered one that is not patronizing; the use of audiovisual materials to engage students on the cognitive as well as affective levels; and the highly desirable but elusive goal of pursuing knowledge for its own sake. He openly states that a teacher of Jewish studies "should see his/her role beyond the normal academic one."

Dan Breslauer's fine essay, "Jewish Literary Themes in the Teaching of Judaica," is a masterful presentation of how Jewish narratives can enhance the study of history, myth and psychology. Herbert Basser's contribution, "Approaching the Text: The Study of Midrash," contains a wealth of useful material concerning the teaching of midrash to students of diverse backgrounds. The essays by Eugene J. Fischer and James F. Moore (two non-Jewish contributors), "Theological Education and Christian-Jewish Relations" and "Team Taught, In-Class Dialogue: A Limited but Promising Method in Teaching Judaism," respectively, correctly stress the importance for both Judaism and Christianity of informed interfaith exchange.

The last section contains an imaginative piece by Arthur Waskow, "Wrestling with Torah, God and Self," in which he observes that the shift from a modern to a post-modern worldview provides an excellent opportunity for "renewing, reinventing Judaism—instead of restoring Judaism as it was before the modern era" (p. 242). The final essay in this section, "Reflections on a New Integrated and Interdisciplinary Approach to Undergraduate Studies: Jewish and Western Civilizations," is a useful summary of how the authors (Steven Lowenstein, Joel Rembaum and David Stern) integrated the teaching of Jewish and Western cultural expressions. Interesting pedagogical issues are raised such as the relationship between the students and the text, and education and value formation.

Combining methodological strengths with a wealth of classroom experiences and management techniques, the essays in this volume are of great use both to students and teachers.

ALAN L. BERGER
Syracuse University

Robert Gordis, *Judaic Ethics for a Lawless World.* New York: The Jewish Theological Seminary of America, 1986. 179 pp.

The author, editor of *Judaism* and professor of Bible at The Jewish Theological Seminary of America, attributes the ills of modern civilization to "the loss of a system of moral values." Relief, however, cannot be expected to come from religion because "modern man will not accept a dogmatic basis for morality," while the old dichotomy between facts and values effectively excludes morality from the realm of scientific inquiry. The author proposes, instead, a modified version of the doctrine of natural law, which he defines as "a moral order which is in harmony with human nature." The doctrine assumes that human nature, while changing, is somehow constant in time and universally uniform to the extent that it is knowable. Gordis then goes on to present certain sources in Judaism that seem to affirm natural law and to claim that an overwhelming majority of men and women should be able to give their allegiance to such a moral order "though it rests upon a substratum of religious faith."

In the judgment of this reviewer, Gordis's modified natural law doctrine does not constitute a philosophically credible ethical theory. It can hardly be expected, therefore, to be the answer to the world's need for a believable system of moral values. To begin with, his notion of a "human nature" that changes but remains constant is never adequately explicated. After all, if what makes "natural law" natural is its being grounded in the nature of the human being, then, as with all empirical matters, we must insist on a scientific explanation of that nature. But, alas, that has always eluded us. Furthermore, Gordis has adulterated his natural law doctrine with religious notions. Having admitted that modern man will not easily accept a dogma-based morality, why should he then think that modern man would find one based on "religious faith" any more acceptable just because it is non-denominational?

However, if we put aside his natural law thesis, we can profitably regard the last two thirds of the book as an insightful exposition of various aspects of Judaism. Here Gordis is at his best as Biblical scholar. In a remarkably concise chapter, the author sums up the moral and religious teachings of Genesis and correctly concludes, "If all the rest of the Bible were to be lost it would be possible to reconstruct the fundamentals of religion and ethics from the opening chapter of Genesis" (p. 70).

Gordis then treats what he calls "three challenges to the basic faith underlying natural law": (1) the implications of evil, particularly of the Holocaust; (2) the rise of fundamentalism in all religions, which (according to Gordis) leads to the downgrading of ethical values; and (3) the Kierkegaardian interpretation of the '*akedah* (the story of the binding of Isaac) as the teleological suspension of the ethical, which (Gordis correctly points out) is a misreading of the Biblical account of Abraham's trial.

In the final section of the book, Gordis attempts to demonstrate that the world has much to learn from the Judaic tradition in the areas of ecology, religious pluralism, democracy and world peace. According to the author, the ideal of freedom of conscience consists of three phases. The first is the right of a group to practice its own faith—a right which the Jews, as the eternal minority, have most consistently defended. The second is the freedom extended by one group to others who differ in belief and practice. Here again, Judaism—by virtue of its belief that the Torah in its present form is meant for Jews only—has no special difficulty. The third level of religious liberty involves the willingness of a group to grant freedom of thought and action to dissidents within its own ranks. Gordis, in this connection, traces the history of sects in Judaism and treats the problems Conservative and Reform Judaism are currently experiencing in Israel. While his analysis of this subject is quite thoroughgoing, it is not at all clear that he makes good his contention (p. 125) that the Hebrew tradition has a significant contribution to make to a theory of pluralism de jure and not merely de facto. In regard to the ideals of democracy and world peace, Gordis makes out a much more persuasive case that their origins are to be found in the Jewish tradition.

Once again, and to our good fortune, Robert Gordis has proven himself to be an insightful and articulate expositor of the Biblical and rabbinic traditions, particularly in terms of the important issues confronting contemporary society.

SHUBERT SPERO
Bar-Ilan University

Joel Roth, *The Halakhic Process: A Systemic Analysis.* New York: The Jewish Theological Seminary of America, 1986. 398 pp.

Joel Roth is a scholar of Jewish law and this volume is obviously the result of years of study and thought. His book is a welcome addition to the increasing number of erudite works in the English language dealing with the halakha such as those by Louis Jacobs, Jacob Neusner, Aaron Schreiber and others. Roth is chiefly interested in a systemic analysis of the halakhic process—as the title of his work clearly shows. According to the author, "systemic principles fall into two categories, explicit and implicit. Explicit principles are those that have been stated in the legal literature, while implicit principles are those that can be deduced from the legal literature." Many of the topics covered by the author have been discussed extensively by others such as *d'oraita* and *d'rabanan,* custom, precedent and, in general, the sources of the legal system.

In addition to these basic subjects, which must be examined in any serious book analyzing the halakha, Roth considers at some length topics that are not always referred to by others such as what he terms "extra-legal sources within halakha." These include the consideration by halakhic authorities of medical-scientific data, sociological data, economic data and ethical-psychological data. If anyone had doubts about the direct or indirect influence of the aforementioned in the halakhic decision-making process, Roth effectively dispels them.

On reading this volume, one is impressed with the erudition of the author, who brings an extensive number of examples from the sources to make or prove his point. However, three things bother this reader. First, while this volume is in essence a work of objective scholarship and not a polemic, there is an undercurrent throughout the book of the Conservative approach to halakha. When one finally arrives at Chapter 10, near the end of the volume, the cat is out of the bag and the author honestly and forthrightly states his own subjective, Conservative view of the halakhic process.

Second, in introducing his theses, the author relies exclusively on Menahem Elon for general legal theory; Elon, in turn, relied very much on Salmond. It is reasonable for Elon to quote editions published in the 1960s when his work came out in 1973; but when Roth, whose work was published in 1986, quotes those same sources (Salmond, Allen), he is way off the mark. In fact, it is quite clear that in spite of his attempt to place the halakha in the perspective of general legal theory, Roth is unaware of the literature on the subject. It is also obvious that he has had no general legal training.

Finally, very few secondary sources are referred to. Much has been written on the topics under discussion, but the author delves into his source material as if no one else has ever worked on his subject. Where the author does refer to secondary sources, he does not always accurately pass on to the reader what was actually written by the authors. For example, in discussing borrowings from other legal systems, he refers to the writings of Saul Lieberman and Boaz Cohen. However, anyone who has carefully read these authors knows that Roth's statements about Lieberman's view of "the pervasive Greek influence on Jewish law" or Cohen's view regarding Roman law's influence on Jewish law, are unfounded. In fact, Lieberman is actually somewhat perplexed by the evidence of interaction of Greek ideas and the *aggadah,* on the one hand, and the *lack* of Greek influence on Jewish law on the other hand.

The above reservations do not detract from the value of the book as a whole. There is a wealth of information and analysis in this volume, and the author is usually correct in his keen observations about the source material. He is undoubtedly right that *yirat shamayim* (fear of God) is a sine qua non of halakhic authorities; that it is what "motivates halakhic authorities in their commitment to the integrity of the system they govern."

The author rightly points out and convincingly demonstrates that the halakhic system contains within it principles that could and did lead to far-reaching amendments of the law itself. These include: "It is time to act for the Lord, they have violated your Torah"; "It is better that one letter of the Torah be uprooted"; "There are times when the amendment of the Torah is its establishment"; "One should live by them, not that he should die by them." However, one may get the wrong impression that these statements were widely applied. Roth's examples of putting these principles into practice are taken almost exclusively from the Talmud. However, the Jewish legal system was a living, vibrant way of life for the Jews throughout the ages—until the present—and when one studies the history of the law in post-Talmudic times one receives a much more evenhanded picture. Over the centuries, these existing principles were not extensively applied as a means of developing and amending the law. As Justice Holmes has said, "the life of the law has not been logic: it has been experience." The experience of the halakhic system does not end with the Talmud; it only begins with it.

SHMUEL SHILO
The Hebrew University

Zionism and Israel

Michael J. Cohen, *The Origins and Evolution of the Arab-Zionist Conflict*. Berkeley, Los Angeles and London: University of California Press, 1987. xiv + 183 pp.

This slim volume aims at fulfilling the real need for a brief, non-partisan, historical introduction to today's Arab-Israeli conflict for the undergraduate student or the "educated general reader." As the author rightly notes, most serious scholarship on the subject is not accessible to this audience because it is either too narrowly focused or too detailed, whereas there are no current popular works that incorporate recent archival revelations.

While the concept of this book is a sound one, the result is not as successful as it might have been. One would have expected a person of Michael Cohen's background to be the ideal choice for undertaking the tasks of overview, synthesis and popularization of the specialist literature. Quite unexpectedly, the first two chapters—dealing with areas not previously covered by Cohen's own research or writing—are more successful than the last two, which deal with a number of subjects about which he has written many articles and four well-received books.

Like Fred Khouri's *Arab-Israeli Dilemma,* which first appeared in 1968 (3d, updated ed., 1985), Cohen's book begins with a two-pronged approach that discusses the birth of Arab nationalism and British promises (chap. 1) and the origins of Zionism and the Balfour Declaration (chap. 2). The author's smooth and skillful presentation is based on important original works by George Antonius, Sylvia Haim, Elie Kedourie, Leonard Stein and others, to which he adds glosses based on revelations in more recent studies.

The link between the two opening chapters is the British wartime "promises" made to each movement. What Khouri did sketchily in seven introductory pages, Cohen now covers in fifty-seven, and he succeeds in offering the reader a fair presentation of the historical controversy surrounding the nature and extent of British pledges to the two national movements—concluding with a comparative assessment of the Balfour Declaration and the Hussein–McMahon correspondence. At times, his judgments may appear overstated, for example, when he describes Britain behaving as "an imperial power that was unconscionably willing . . . to scatter promises to minor actors . . . with little or no thought for future consequences" (p. 28). Yet Cohen is usually at his best when he is discussing British policy-making on Palestine in its imperial, military or domestic contexts.

In what is otherwise a very disappointing chapter, the strongest parts of "Mandatory Problems 1920–1945" (chap. 3) are Cohen's discussions of Zionist decision making and the Anglo-Zionist struggle (e.g., the Zionist request for a Jewish Division and Ben-Gurion's final disillusionment with Britain over the latter's rejection of the scheme). In a less satisfactory sub-chapter, the author relies heavily on the work of Joel Migdal and Kenneth Stein on land sales and the socioeconomic dynamics of leadership in the Palestinian Arab community in order to suggest that the Palestinians were largely the authors of their own misfortune.

Cohen's treatment of the cycle of disturbances, commissions of inquiry and British white papers leaves much to be desired. The Peel Commission surely deserves to be treated as a pivotal episode in the history of the Mandate. The submissions made to it, its deliberations and recommendations and the reactions to its report merit a more detailed analysis than the author has chosen to give. On another level, there are too many factual errors and imprecisions to consider this chapter good, careful history. For example, Cohen refers to the rioting of March 1920 (pp. 65, 68, 69), when, in fact, there were (largely non-violent) demonstrations on March 8, a prelude to the serious riots that broke out in Jerusalem between April 4 and 6, 1920. On page 85, Cohen seems to have mixed up his Zionist congresses: it was not in 1929, but in 1931, that Vladimir Ze'ev Jabotinsky demanded "in the congress plenum, that the movement declare as its final goal the establishment of a Jewish state in Palestine." Hence, Cohen cannot use this as an explanation of the revisionist leader's contribution toward "alarming" the Arabs who rioted against the Jews of Jerusalem, Hebron and Safed in late August 1929. For an indication of Jabotinsky's real contribution toward raising the political temperature around the Western (Wailing) Wall issue, one has to look not at Jabotinsky's Zionist Congress speeches but rather at his activities during his brief residence in Palestine from October 1928 to July 1929. These activities (and his very physical presence, it seems) were considered so provocative by the British that they were unwilling to grant him a visa to reenter Palestine for several years following the 1929 rioting.

One would have expected chapter 4 to have been an easy one for Cohen to write since it summarizes his *Palestine and the Great Powers, 1945–1948* (1982). Unfortunately, "From Mandate to Independence, 1945–1948" offers a narrative that is not as lucid or as smoothly written as other parts of the book. The main weakness of this chapter lies in its structure and organization, which necessitate several overlaps, repetitions and chronological leaps forward and backward in the narrative (e.g., Truman's speech of October 4, 1946 on p. 111 and again on p. 116; a jump backward from fall 1946 on pp. 111–112 to summer 1946 in the middle of p. 112). The chapter's title might have benefited from more objective wording so as to avoid the specific Israeli perspective and to live up to the book's proclaimed evenhandedness.

The book's usefulness is enhanced by excellent maps, a glossary and a brief selection of suggested readings. However, the book's documentary section is less useful and seems to have been appended as an afterthought. Most of the fourteen documents are readily available in Walter Laqueur and Barry Rubin's *Israel–Arab*

Reader (revised, 1984). Some of the documents (the Azouri extract or even the well-known Faisal–Weizmann agreement) have no direct connection to the author's earlier discussion; neither is the reader ever specifically informed during the course of Cohen's narrative that the text of a relevant document may be consulted by turning to the appendix.

The book's usefulness might also have been enhanced by more systematic footnoting. While fully appreciating the conscious decision of author and publisher to limit the number of footnotes for a popular work of this kind, many readers will nonetheless feel shortchanged by the dozens of unattributed quotations or ideas. This is not merely a legalistic question affecting the credibility of the author's presentation; fuller footnoting would also have given the reader a greater understanding of the sources of Cohen's material and would be an accurate pointer as to where further reading might be done.

On the whole, *Origins and Evolution* is a well-conceived project that was, unfortunately, not so well executed. Careful revision would be needed to render this a truly useful and reliable book.

Neil Caplan
Vanier College, Montreal

Simha Flapan, *The Birth of Israel: Myths and Realities*. London: Croom Helm, 1987. 227 pp.

Simha Flapan, director of Mapam's Arab affairs department for eleven years, and founder-editor of *New Outlook,* has written an unabashedly political polemic in condemnation of the Israeli establishment that, Flapan claims, since 1948 has deliberately averted its eyes from peace and denied the Palestinian Arabs the right to a homeland of their own.

The "myths" that Flapan claims to debunk are: in 1947 Israel accepted the UN Partition Plan and the Palestinian Arabs, following the call of the mufti, launched a jihad that forced Israel to seek a military solution; the Palestinian Arabs fled Israel in answer to the calls by Arab leaders, despite the efforts of Jewish leaders to persuade them to remain; the Arab states invaded the newborn state in 1948 and made the 1948 War inevitable (Flapan maintains that the Arabs were ready to compromise and that war was not inevitable); tiny Israel triumphed against overwhelming military odds and ever since the Arabs have consistently rejected Israel's hand extended in peace. All these, Flapan insists, are the products of what he terms "Israeli propaganda."

This is a damning indictment, but one that the author, notwithstanding his three years of research at Harvard, had obviously determined many years ago. Abdullah of Transjordan shares with Ben-Gurion the dubious distinction of being the central villain of Flapan's piece. Together, they colluded to prevent the rise of a Palestinian Arab state on the West Bank.

There has always been a utopian aspect about the fringe elements of the Yishuv and later of the Israeli left, which over the decades has engaged in the elusive search for a responsible Palestinian Arab negotiating partner. Since meaningful negotiations never got off the ground, inconvenient questions (such as the Arab terms for accepting Israel) have never had to be faced. Yet Flapan himself agrees that a Palestinian state could never have emerged in 1948 except in economic union with Israel, "which would provide substantial income from customs and federal services and allow for the participation of the more industrially advanced Jewish state in joint development programs" (p. 41). In other words, Israel was supposed to subsidize a nation that had steadily refused to recognize its national legitimacy and had fought its growth since 1920! Flapan also concedes that the Palestinians consistently opposed all UN plans for Palestine.

And who was to head that Palestinian state if not the mufti of Jerusalem, recently fled to Cairo from Europe, where he was wanted for collaboration with the Nazi regime since 1941? Again, Flapan concedes that the mufti's reputation among his own people was "untarnished" by this collaboration (p. 65). On the morrow of the Holocaust were the Jews to ignore the mufti's record? There was not a single serious observer of the Middle East in 1948 who would have subscribed to a mufti-led Palestinian state on the West Bank, and only intellectual dilettantes can write years later that it was "a real possibility" (p. 47).

Flapan holds Zionist "terror" equally responsible with the Arab Higher Committee for having prevented the emergence of a truly representative Palestine leadership. Historically, this is simply incorrect, as Flapan must know. The Husseinis' hegemony over the Arab community, achieved during the 1920s, and their reign of terror against the Nashashibis in the late 1930s, were carried out before Jewish terror assumed any significance whatever. Although Flapan has plenty to say about the opportunities for peace missed by Israel and Israeli terror against the Arabs, he has nothing whatever to say about Arab terror against innocent Jewish and Israeli citizens.

On the question of borders, Ben-Gurion is depicted as the Machiavellian tactician, accepting the UN plan as a feint but determined all along on military expansion. Again, Flapan indulges in the luxury of academic hypothesis rather than giving serious consideration to the absurdities of the hourglass frontiers proposed by the UN. Could any state, whose very existence was denied by its neighbors, have existed for long with such borders? Here, too, Flapan contradicts himself. Almost hidden away is his later concession that the Palestinians' opposition to partition and Israeli statehood made their fears of Israeli expansion self-fulfilling (p. 49).

Flapan relies largely on Ben-Gurion's own war diary, quoted selectively, and on Israel's published foreign ministry documents, both available, presumably, at Harvard. It is a shame that he did not research the numerous archives now open, and of course, as he is the first to realize, no researcher has the benefit of entry to Arab archives. One of the few Arab books used by Flapan—and at length—is *The Secret of the Catastrophe* (1955) by Nimr al-Hawari, a Palestinian Arab refugee. Al-Hawari, as Flapan informs us, was a doubtful character, who wrote his book after returning to Israel and accepting a judgeship under Israeli rule. Thus he collaborated in imposing Israeli military rule against his own people, who called him a traitor for doing so. It is on a translation of this book that Flapan rests much of his dubious case that "responsible" Palestinians were ready to recognize and make peace with Israel in 1948.

There is much more to comment on in this somewhat enervating book, but space does not permit. In dealing in depth with the numerous talks and negotiations that were forever going on behind the scenes, Flapan makes no serious attempt to analyze the status of the negotiators within their own camp—if he had, he would have been forced to conclude that the leaders who controlled policy, on each side, were seldom transmitting on the same wavelength—except, of course, for Israel and Abdullah. The deeper, underlying problems are never hinted at: Israel's need for borders with some military logic; the presence of a culturally European Jewish state in the midst of an Islamic Arab world; Arab fears of Jewish economic dominance and exploitation; the numerous schisms and feuds within the Arab world and the Palestinian camp itself.

Perhaps the greatest distortion resides in Flapan's superficial comparison between the 1948 War and the 1982 Lebanese War. He willfully ignores the difference between a war for survival (1948) and a preemptive war to crush a terror base in a neighboring state (1982)—or so the majority of the Israel population and cabinet were led to believe.

Coming to the present day, Flapan perceives "signals and indications from the PLO of a readiness to negotiate a political solution to the conflict." Yet again, Flapan shoots himself in the foot, as he himself quotes from the PLO Covenant of 1964, which declares the 1947 partition to have been "illegal and false" and recognizes the rights only of those Jews already in Palestine before 1948 (by now, a small minority of the Israeli population).

Herein lies perhaps the crux of the whole problem. Israel undoubtedly has committed many deeds (most of them in the heat of war) that the majority of its population would rather forget—though in contrast to the Arabs, Israelis have never cheered atrocities committed by its "freedom fighters." (Mass Arab support for terrorist atrocities has had a deep psychological effect on Israelis that cannot be exaggerated.) But before there can be any meaningful negotiations, the Palestinians have to convince the Israeli mainstream that it has given up the illusion of a united Arab Palestine and that it recognizes the right of Israel to exist within viable borders.

MICHAEL J. COHEN
Bar-Ilan University

Andrew Handler, *Dori: The Life and Times of Theodor Herzl in Budapest (1860–1878)*. Alabama: University of Alabama Press, 1983. xiii + 161 pp.

While not in accord on all issues, recent studies of Herzl are generally agreed on certain fundamental points. Andrew Handler takes issue with the consensus as found in Amos Elon's *Herzl* (1975), Desmond Stewart's *Theodor Herzl: Artist and Politician* (1974) and David Vital's *The Origins of Zionism* (1975) and *Zionism, the Formative Years* (1982).

All these accounts agree that the great influences shaping Herzl before his conversion to Zionism had been the liberal German nationalism of his university years in Vienna, Austro-German liberalism and Viennese aestheticism. Indeed, Germanic influences even extended to his childhood years in Budapest, when he, typically, celebrated Martin Luther in a youthful poem as the father of modern liberty. Further, all are in accord that Herzl transferred these values into his vision of Jewish nationalism, which was liberal, secular and cosmopolitan. The Jewish state was to be a model of European progressivism. For these reasons, Herzl was hostile to the Hebraic revival promoted by Russian Zionists; he viewed Judaism merely as a source of nationalist symbols and liturgy to be harnessed to the ends of secular nationalism.

Exploring Herzl's childhood years in Budapest, where he lived almost until the age of eighteen at which time the family moved to Vienna, Handler insists that Herzl was both more affected by Judaism and by Hungarian influences during his years in the capital of Hungary than we have thought. The idea is an intriguing one, but the basis for this argument is so flimsy that in the end we are back where we started, with the prevailing consensus. Handler's assertions are based on hypothetical events, insignificant events and non-events.

The author is chiefly concerned with establishing that certain alleged experiences in Herzl's boyhood, judged insignificant or hypothetical by other scholars, did occur and were significant. For example, Handler insists that "the spiritual impact of Judaism" was an important ingredient of Herzl's early adolescence. He criticizes the "uncritical and unsubstantiated" underestimation of Herzl's religious training and knowledge, which he asserts, "has been a matter of compulsive repetition" (pp. 21, 70). On what evidence does he draw in support of this categorical assertion? Only that from age six to ten Herzl attended a Jewish elementary school where for the most part he received good grades in his Jewish subjects. The evidence pointing to a contrary conclusion is either dismissed or ignored. For example, neither Herzl nor anyone else ever mentioned his bar mitzvah. Handler speculates that there may have been no bar mitzvah because of the cholera epidemic in Hungary at the time. He goes on to guess that Herzl never alluded later in life to a bar mitzvah because he was so "bitterly disappointed" over its cancellation (p. 55). The author sustains his conviction about the importance of Judaism in Herzl's upbringing on the basis of surmise. Similarly, none of the adolescent Herzl's numerous literary essays were on Jewish themes, as Handler acknowledges, "In fact, having read the compositions, one may be hard put to identify their author as a Jew" (p. 67). This does not shake the author's belief in the profound impact of Judaism on the young Herzl.

Handler believes that Herzl's first exposure to Zionism had a religious source in the teachings of the religious proto-Zionist Rabbi Judah Alkalai (1798–1878). Alex Bein made a passing, speculative reference to the Alkalai connection fifty-five years ago in his classic biographical study of Herzl. The sole evidence here is the annual visits of Herzl's grandfather, Simon Loew Herzl, an observant Jew, to the Herzl home. No evidence is cited that Simon Loew even shared Alkalai's views, only that he was from Zemun, outside of Belgrade, where Alkalai was rabbi of the Sephardic community. Here, too, the far greater weight of evidence to the contrary is shrugged off. The author states, "That Herzl should make no mention of any aspect of the relationship with his pious grandfather is puzzling" (p. 27). That none of Herzl's youthful essays contain a reference to Alkalai is "puzzling and inexplicable" (p. 140). Of course, none of the evidence, both on the young Herzl's relation to Judaism and his alleged exposure to Alkalai, is at all "puzzling and inexplicable" if we abandon the author's thesis.

Other conclusions are equally shaky. First, that Herzl "showed great enthusiasm for and profound understanding of Hungarian nationalism" (p. xii). This assertion is based on two youthful essays celebrating ancient Magyar heroes who fought the nation's enemies. The effects or the influence of this enthusiasm on Herzl are not identified or traced.

Finally, we are told, Budapest and not Vienna was the seedbed of modern political antisemitism and modern political Zionism. The author claims, "The diverse manifestations of anti-Semitism in Hungary in the mid-1870s, predating those in Austria, and exceeding them in intensity and demagoguery" must have had a significant impact on the young Herzl (p. 11). The evidence here consists of two speeches in the Hungarian Diet, one in 1875, the other in 1878, made by the Liberal deputy Gyozo Istoczy. In his first speech, Istoczy opposed the government's policy of encouraging Jewish assimilation, charging that Jews were engaged in a conspiracy for world domination. In the second speech, Istoczy proposed that the European powers take diplomatic action to promote a Jewish state in Palestine and force Europe's Jews to go there. Apparently he was called to order by the Speaker and the proposal was not debated. Handler admits that Istoczy was "a leader without followers" (p. 116). He insists, however, that Herzl "was surely aware" of the speech, though he made no mention of it (p. 111). It is on the basis of this thin reed that the author argues that both the impact of antisemitism on Herzl and the idea of political Zionism can be traced to his Budapest years.

None of the standard works on European antisemitism support the claim that Hungarian antisemitism during Herzl's boyhood was more virulent than antisemitism in Vienna when Herzl resided there—quite the contrary. In his study of European antisemitism, *From Prejudice to Destruction* (1980), Jacob Katz points out that Istoczy was an isolated figure, the butt of a "derisory reception," and that "his listeners were more amused than impressed by his proposal" (pp. 240, 274). Ironically, Katz argues that it was the outbreak of political antisemitism in Germany in the early 1880s, championed by such prestigious figures as the court preacher Adolf Stöcker and the historian Heinrich von Treitschke, that helped boost antisemitism in Hungary and Istoczy's fortunes as well. But by then the Herzl family had moved, and Herzl was studying law at the University of Vienna. It was in Austria that late nineteenth-century European antisemitism enjoyed its greatest political success, with the election of Karl Lueger, the Christian Social leader, as mayor of Vienna in 1897.

The author supports each contention—that Herzl was influenced by Judaism, by Magyar nationalism and by political antisemitism in Hungary—by unearthing facts considered insignificant by previous researchers. Are these facts significant? Can one identify the traces of Judaism, Magyar nationalism or Hungarian antisemitism in the later Herzl? The author makes no case for this. Herzl's ignorance of Judaism is well known. On the other hand, pride in a long history of victimization and steadfastness and loyalty to the camp of the persecuted led him to identify with Jews. As for Magyar nationalism, the author points to no sign of its influence as detected in the later Herzl. Last of all, Herzl was certainly aware of antisemitism before the 1880s. But to all indications, antisemitism in Hungary in the 1870s, as yet an insignificant force, had no salience for him. By his own account, anti-semitism first troubled him during his university years in Vienna in the early 1880s. His first recorded discussion of antisemitism was in his diary in February 1882, and he pointed to its symptoms in Tsarist Russia, imperial Germany and in Austria—not mentioning Hungary.

The author displays a sure hand in describing the pace of Magyarization among Budapest's Jews. One would like to know more about how the particular dual German–Magyar cultural mix shaped Jews and the effects of the transition from German to Magyar loyalties. Certainly—and this applies not only to Herzl—the influence of childhood experiences on later life is decisive. But Handler's foray into Herzl's boyhood in Budapest does not increase our knowledge of the man nor provide any reason to alter our view of him.

JACQUES KORNBERG
University of Toronto

Norman Rose, *Chaim Weizmann: A Biography.* New York: Viking, 1986. xvi + 520 pp.

Many biographies and collections of biographical memoirs of Chaim Weizmann were printed at different stages of his long career. They ranged during his lifetime from celebrations by his admirers to caustic attacks by his foes, and the same type of discussion continues after his death. But with the career long ended and the record reasonably complete and accessible, it is time for a more dispassionate and sober accounting of a remarkable life. Norman Rose's biography attempts to provide such an account in the form of a one-volume biography.

It may be said at the outset that any compact biography of so complex a life story as Weizmann's, ranging over so wide and various a panorama of locales, social settings and modes of action, can hardly hope to do justice to the totality of its subject. Weizmann has been presented primarily—and understandably—as a diplo-matic virtuoso, with some attention to his life as a scientist, mainly in the same context. His private life (always well known but usually mentioned only in passing) will certainly some day be treated by psycho-historians, academic or popular, in the same way that Herzl or Freud have recently been treated.

Rose's biography is far from being that kind of book. He does include one chapter that gives an interesting account of Weizmann's domestic situation and from time to time makes the usual observations about the style of his subject's encounters and relationships with others. But the book is mainly a summation of Weizmann's public career, especially in the context of British politics. A full consideration of Weizmann's public life would obviously have to enter into the tangled thickets of Zionist and general Jewish politics of the time. Rose deals with these subjects—for example, Weizmann's stormy relations with American Jewry, with Polish Jewry, with German Zionists and above all with the Yishuv—only very sketchily, usually by brief references that rely on the reader to possess prior knowledge. But these are, of course, subjects that need further cultivation and, in some cases, are being developed in new studies that Rose was not able to use.

Rose's account of Weizmann's lifelong relationship with the framers and functionaries of British foreign policy is based on his earlier extensive research. For an analysis of the relationship that is more fully documented and explicitly argued than is possible in the present volume, the author refers the reader to his book on *The Gentile Zionists* (1973). He was also able to use, in addition to the extensive Weizmann archives, the extraordinary diaries of Blanche Dugdale, of which he edited and published pertinent excerpts in a previous work. The benefits of this accumulated mastery of British foreign and domestic political history are clear in the easy control and sure touch of the author's discussion on this aspect of Weizmann's activity, which is, of course, the one that more than any other demanded Weizmann's continuous attention.

Given the way this biography is focused on Weizmann's orientation to British politics, it is natural for the plot of the narrative to fall into two parts: a rising curve up to his departure from the Zionist leadership in 1931, after successfully holding off the threat of the Passfield White Paper; and a descending curve from the time he reclaimed the leading role in 1935 until his relegation to the ceremonial presidency of Israel. The impression of rise and fall is, of course, largely an effect of the concentration on the strength or weakness of Weizmann's ties to British policy of the period and the degree of confidence he could place on the conformity between Zionist aims and British interest. Even this perspective does not justify such a detailed picture of the specific history of Zionist encounters with British officials. But, viewed in the larger frame, it enhances comprehension as well as dramatic effect. It was in the later period that Weizmann himself complained that he now had to deal with British officers who "no longer knew Joseph."

A less explicit, but perhaps more interesting, reflection on Weizmann's career among the British is inherent in the author's exposition and occasional comments concerning the methods by which Weizmann influenced, or failed to influence, British policy. Weizmann's own view, at least on certain occasions, was that when he appealed to British conscience and values he was more effective than when he argued in terms of British interests. The biography at hand, without at any time explicitly stating it, provides striking evidence that this assessment was accurate— perhaps more so than was intended.

It would be more precise to say that when Weizmann was able to appeal to both conscience and interest—interest, as perceived at the time by the British officials themselves—he could achieve positive gains; when he could appeal to conscience alone—because the British officials did not perceive their national interest in the way Zionists tried to present it—he could register no positive gains but was sometimes able to fend off or delay imminent dangers. If his career can be plausibly presented as a drama of rise and decline, it is because, in general, the clash of conscience and interest (to use the common Zionist perception of the events) was less marked in British official circles during the first period of Weizmann's Zionist leadership than it was in the second.

If one looks more closely at particular episodes, this observation applies to variations within the general picture as well. Rose does not attempt an independent assessment of Weizmann's role in obtaining the Balfour Declaration but briefly recounts the usual report of lobbying and persuasion as the major explanation of the historic achievement; such an approach is almost inevitable in a study primarily biographical. But the strategies of middle-range bureaucrats like Mark Sykes and Leopold Amery as well as the needs of wartime propaganda perceived by ministers obviously were essential for the success of Weizmann's efforts. Once the declaration was issued, it was a moral commitment that Weizmann and his colleagues could appeal to when some officials no longer perceived British interest to be served by the Zionist connection.

The first signs of active Arab opposition to the Zionist "invasion" were enough to make British authorities wary of bearing the onus of the Zionist burden, not only during the military administration but soon after its replacement by the civil administration of the Palestine Mandate. Herbert Samuel, a Zionist himself, who came in as the first high commissioner, was led by the experience of Arab riots to favor sharp revision of the British commitments he had earlier helped to elicit. A similar change of heart took place when Ormsby Gore and Malcolm MacDonald, Zionist sympathizers, each became responsible, in turn, for Palestine as head of the Colonial Office and had to contend with the inconveniences of Zionism for Britain. If the 1920s seem in retrospect an era of political success and the 1930s a period of decline in Weizmann's influence among British leaders, this was largely the effect of the impact of heightened Arab militancy and other international complications in the latter years on British perceptions of their national interest.

Nevertheless, some of the most noteworthy demonstrations of Weizmann's diplomatic prowess were achieved precisely in the face of adversity. Perhaps the most striking came at the very end, when President Truman was persuaded to support the retention of the Negev for the Jewish part of partitioned Palestine—a decision contrary to what the U.S. State Department felt to be the American interest and one that followed an interview Truman granted Weizmann as a gesture of personal respect. Other diplomatic successes in Weizmann's record include his appeal to Lloyd George and Balfour in 1921 against Samuel's pressure to disavow explicitly the intention to build a Jewish state—a subject that has been lucidly expounded by Evyatar Friesel. Another diplomatic feat carefully elucidated by Rose in his several studies is the campaign to offset the Passfield White Paper in 1930–1931, which yielded the MacDonald letter and left the way open for the renewed rapid advance of Zionist settlement in the 1930s. Common to all these cases, however, was that they were defensive reactions, and they succeeded in good part by holding British leaders to past commitments, made in many cases to Weizmann himself.

Appeals to conscience against interest or to past commitments against present pressures could not hold the line forever. Nowhere was this more clearly shown than in the Peel Commission report, which conceded flatly that the Mandate was written primarily in the Zionist interest, but held that the obligation assumed was simply unworkable. On the other hand, the Commission proposed partition, which would give the Zionists the assured authority, through state sovereignty, that alone could make their task of ingathering and resettling the desperate refugees of oppressed Jewries possible. The sense of decline in Weizmann's political fortunes in the late 1930s, as Rose depicts the unfolding events, was not only due to the breakdown of the defenses he erected with such virtuosity; it derived still more from his inability to advance the Peel Commission proposal of partition as a positive replacement for the discredited Balfour Declaration. British leaders did not believe that their interest would be well served by it.

Partition was ultimately carried out and the Jewish state was born—but not through the agency of Britain or with Weizmann at the helm. Thus, what in Jewish history is a tragic triumph is viewed in the framework appropriate for this biography as a classic tragedy.

BEN HALPERN
Brandeis University

Shabtai Teveth, *Kinat David,* vol. 3, *Hakark'a habo'er.* Tel-Aviv: Schocken, 1987. 501 pp. (English edition: *Ben-Gurion,* vol. 3, *The Burning Ground, 1886–1948.* Boston: Houghton Mifflin, 1987.)

The third volume of Shabtai Teveth's biography of David Ben-Gurion deals with the years 1932–1943, a period that began with his great campaign to "conquer Zionism" and ended with the realization that much of European Jewry, the natural reservoir for settling the country and strengthening the political power of the Zionist movement, had been exterminated. The reasons for the volume's title, *The Burning Ground,* are twofold. The first is Ben-Gurion's premonition, the sense that never left him throughout this period, that the very ground was, indeed, burning and that a catastrophe was imminent for the Jewish people and for the Zionist movement. The second reason is the supremacy he accorded this premonition in his political outlook and his priorities, for which he was prepared to sacrifice important and cherished principles.

This sense of emergency—heightened by the worsening condition of European Jewry and by the Revisionist movement's increasing influence—caused Ben-Gurion, in the early 1930s, to demand publicly and vociferously that his party, Mapai, take over the leadership of the World Zionist Organization. That view was not shared by all of his colleagues. His opponents, headed by Yitzhak Tabenkin, argued that taking such a position would force Mapai to compromise its values in order to attract the votes of the masses. Thus, the movement would be transformed from a socialist labor movement into a popular party "fit only for elections" (p. 25). Thus, a schism was created in the newly founded Mapai party between the backers of "ideology" and those in favor of "seiz[ing] the political hour"; between those for whom the time factor was crucial and those for whom the integrity of socialist values was more important.

Teveth argues that Ben-Gurion's sense of urgency led him to define the situation as one involving drastic choices, "either the rapid fulfillment of Zionism, or its annihilation" (p. 14). He was driven by fear that the Arabs might destroy the Yishuv—a fear instilled by the riots of 1929—and that violent incidents would prevent Jews from coming to settle in Palestine. This anxiety was compounded by fear that Britain would renege on its commitment to the Balfour Declaration and the Mandate. Finally, to these factors in his thinking was added a serious sense of unease over the swift rise of the Revisionist movement.

Ben-Gurion's attitude toward aliyah, for example, was largely determined by this belief that time was running out. By the early 1930s, he parted ways with the idea of selective immigration. In a meeting of the Mapai Council in 1933, he maintained that immigration under auspices other than those of the He-Halutz (Pioneer) movement also contributed to building the country. At this time, the overwhelming majority in his own party disagreed with the idea of nonselective immigration.

Ben-Gurion also stirred up controversy in his party through the agreements he reached in London with Revisionist leader Vladimir Ze'ev Jabotinsky. Ben-Gurion and his supporters, whom Teveth terms "the peace party," saw these agreements and the internal political peace they were meant to guarantee as a means to maximize Jewish-Zionist benefits in a time of auspicious circumstances (p. 110). For that reason, this political détente was more important to them than the dictates of party program. In the opposition were the overwhelming majority of the United Kibbutz Movement (Ha-Kibbutz ha-Meuhad) and a large number of urban Mapai members led, again, by Tabenkin, a group dubbed by Teveth, "the party of values." The latter, zealous defenders of the socialist faith, demanded that the agreements be submitted for ratification by all Histadrut members and not by the Mapai leadership alone. The vote took place in 1935. Sixty percent rejected the agreement, dealing Ben-Gurion a bitter disappointment.

Another divisive issue was the controversy over the Partition Plan of 1937. Ben-Gurion supported the plan since he was obsessed by the thought that "the time allotted by history to the Zionist movement would come to an abrupt end" (p. 213). He saw the plan as a unique opportunity to fulfill the immediate goals of the Zionist movement—above all, saving Jews from the looming disaster in Europe. Once again, Tabenkin rejected Ben-Gurion's conception and continued to support the policy of gradual development, summed up by the phrase "one settlement at a time." In Teveth's opinion, the opposing stands taken on this issue epitomize the absolute disagreement between those to whom ideological values were primary and those who were "alert to the winds of change and obey the necessities of the hour" (p. 221).

According to Teveth, Ben-Gurion was a master at turning apparently disastrous situations to Zionism's advantage. The riots of 1936 serve as an example. The riots resulted in a food shortage and caused Arab workers to stay away from Jewish employers, leading to a scarcity of workers and bringing about the closure of Palestine's two ports, Haifa and Jaffa. As a result, many factories had no raw materials. Teveth finds that Ben-Gurion, unlike those who feared that the events would mean the collapse of the Jewish community in Palestine, reacted quite positively, as though it were a heaven-sent opportunity to turn adversity into advantage. He worked to transform the separation between Jewish and Arab populations in Palestine, caused by the riots, into a means to strengthen the Jewish population as an independent national economic unit. He built up the Jewish defense forces and managed to utilize the riots themselves—in particular the Arabs' strategy of indiscriminate murder—as a means of winning over British public opinion.

Ben-Gurion's approach to Yishuv-Diaspora relations also reflects his belief that catastrophic situations could be put to some good use. His basic formula was that the pressures faced by the European Diaspora would help to strengthen the Yishuv and that utilizing the deteriorating situation of the Jews in Central and Eastern Europe was the only means to force the issue of free Jewish immigration to Palestine; "He always viewed the suffering of the Jews as a source of strength. This was at the root of his Zionist philosophy," Teveth writes (p. 438). In the summer of 1939, Ben-Gurion stated, "We would like Hitler to be destroyed, but as long as he exists, we must take advantage of it for settling [Jews] in Palestine" (p. 318).

Examples abound from the 1930s and early 1940s of Ben-Gurion's conviction that a stronger Yishuv would emerge in the wake of the Jews' need to leave Europe en masse. Thus, the Biltmore Program of 1942, which called for Jewish statehood in Palestine, was founded on the assumption that masses of refugees would be stranded in Europe after the war and that this would justify the establishment of a Jewish commonwealth in Palestine. At the outset of the Second World War, Ben-Gurion viewed it as "a rare opportunity to achieve the 'Zionist solution,' the only true solution to the problem of the Jewish people" (p. 376).

Teveth suggests that Ben-Gurion viewed the relations between Palestine and the Diaspora as one undergoing a dialectical change. As their situation worsened throughout the late 1930s, the Diaspora Jews were transformed from supporters of the Yishuv to people in need of support, from those giving aid to those receiving it. However, in order for the Yishuv to render aid on a massive scale, it had to be strengthened. The purpose of the slogan "benefiting from the catastrophe" was to burst the vicious cycle in which the Yishuv was caught—not being able to offer aid to the Diaspora without first being aided by it.

What of Ben-Gurion's attitude to the extermination of European Jewry? In the final chapter of the book, Teveth finds that here, too, the principle of benefiting from the catastrophe prevailed. Although he states that Ben-Gurion ceased speaking about the problems of the Yishuv for three years once the enormity of the Holocaust became clear in the fall of 1942 (p. 441), Teveth also quotes Ben-Gurion, speaking at the end of 1943, saying that the Holocaust would win world support for the Zionist movement. In fact, Ben-Gurion did not speak of benefiting from the catastrophe during the first half of 1943 because he feared that the catastrophe would be total and would wipe out the Zionist achievements in Palestine and the Yishuv itself, in addition to European Jewry. His silence stemmed, therefore, from his fear that no benefits would be salvaged from the ruins. Teveth himself notes that by the end of

1943, at a time when it was perfectly clear that the Yishuv was incapable of organizing large-scale rescue operations, Ben-Gurion maintained that the only course left was to further the political aspirations of Zionism. "It is better for the Jewish people to gain a state from the Holocaust than to gain nothing from the Holocaust," he wrote (p. 442).

This book is not without its faults. Among them is the author's exaggerated identification with and admiration for his subject (see, for example, p. 384); the insufficient attention paid to Ben-Gurion's role as leader of Mapai; and the insufficient treatment of Ben-Gurion's ideological transformations during the period in question. However, all in all this is a fascinating, insightful, well-documented book.

YEHIAM WEITZ
The Hebrew University

Avner Yaniv, *Dilemmas of Security: Politics, Strategy and the Israeli Experience in Lebanon*. New York and Oxford: Oxford University Press, 1987. 355 pp.

Avner Yaniv, a political scientist at Haifa University, has made an attempt to remain dispassionate while analyzing Israel's involvement in Lebanon during the period 1982–1985. He seeks neither to reproach nor to condemn those responsible for a policy that apparently went awry, and he maintains that no judgment is called for since Israel behaves similarly to other states. In essence, every country pursues its own power interests, and the author focuses on what he terms the "harsh realpolitik assumptions." He is therefore ethically neutral, as indicated by his use of the word "experience" in the title as opposed to the more value-laden "intervention" or "invasion."

Yaniv's theoretical construct is workable, although not profound. Basically, he argues that Israel is constantly faced with security dilemmas that force it to choose between accommodation and decisive preemptive action. Almost always, Israel acts on the basis of its vision of a worst-case scenario, and this leads to its implementation of the second option. Strategic interests are paramount, but in the Lebanese case a threat to the Jewish state's security was not as demonstrable as in previous instances when Israel resorted to the use of military force. The PLO had observed a cease-fire along the Lebanese border since July 1981, Syria was coexisting with Israel along the Golan and Lebanese fronts, Egypt had already implemented its peace treaty with Israel and Iraq was diverted by its conflict with Iran. Nevertheless, Israel decided that conditions dictated a major strike at PLO positions in southern Lebanon and a Pandora's box of calamities was thus opened.

The author introduces his concept of "security dilemma" in the first chapter, where he also presents four alternative hypotheses to explain Israel's behavior. He avers that each hypothesis contains "more than a grain of truth" but that a security dilemma had been developing for fifteen years and was the overriding motivating factor in 1982. After this promising analytical framework is established, it recedes to the background for the remainder of the book, as Yaniv concentrates on what may be viewed as an illuminating and detailed diplomatic history of the Israeli role in Lebanon. Military deployment, command structure, logistics, technology and weaponry are not discussed to the same degree, although Yaniv served in a combat unit for ten years and was a civilian consultant to the planning division of the general staff. Also relegated to a secondary tier of interpretation is the Arab side of the conflict. Lebanon and its disparate ethnic militias seem acted upon more than actors in their own right, and the same holds true for the PLO. Yaniv clearly wants to focus on Israeli policy and he, therefore, does not use any Arabic sources, not even translations of articles from the Arab media. He does cite some English-language publications by Arabs, but he does not try to delve into PLO behavior by making use of Rashid Khalidi's informative study (which is listed in the bibliography but not mentioned in the voluminous notes). No indication is given as to whether Yaniv was given access to PLO documents secured by the Israelis in southern Lebanon, as were Yossi Olmert, Rafi Yisraeli and other scholars.

Yaniv must be commended for his accuracy, clarity and ability to delve beneath the surface of political actions. He does not describe Israeli policy simplistically but views it rather as a mélange of sub-policies emanating from individuals or interest groups. Many motivations may be simultaneously germane and it is interesting to note how minor a role is ascribed to Prime Minister Begin. Among the most illuminating sections of the book are those dealing with Israeli-Lebanese relations prior to 1982, the formulation of Israel's plans to intervene in June of that year, and the gestation of Shiite resistance to the Israeli occupation. Yaniv's study is certain to remain a fundamental source for future scholars owing to the insights provided on these and other critical subjects.

Although well documented and detailed, some tantalizing statements included in Yaniv's treatise could surely benefit from further elucidation. For example, it is claimed that Begin knew in advance that Phalangists would move into Sabra and Shatilla, that Syrian President Assad ordered the car-bomb attack on the U.S. Marines' compound in October 1983, that Syrians arranged for the assassination of Druse leader Kamal Jumblatt and that the PLO encouraged Libya to abduct the Shiite cleric Imam Sayyid Musa al Sadr. It is also implied that Syria planned the murder of Lebanese President-elect Bashir Gemayel. Some further comments on these points would certainly have been helpful.

Yaniv's monograph is carefully prepared and includes a good bibliography, useful index and excellent maps. On the other hand, too many typographical errors appear and some names are constantly misspelled (namely those of Chaim Weizmann, Zbigniew Brzezinski and Nicholas Veliotes). Factual accuracy is at a high level, but there are some exceptions. Haj Amin al Husseini's supposed death prior to 1968 is, indeed, premature, as he lived until July 1974. Also, the Democratic Front for Peace and Equality (which includes Charlie Biton) is not the Communist party but rather an electoral coalition whose major component is Rakah, Israel's Communist party.

Yaniv believes that Israel's Lebanon "experience" caused rifts within the Israel Defence Forces (IDF), produced unacceptably high military casualties and divided the Israeli public on an issue related to security. He also argues that underestimating the potential hostility of southern Lebanese civilians toward Israelis represented a major intelligence failure. No heroes emerge from this study, and Ariel Sharon and Bashir Gemayel seem to be portrayed in the most negative light, even though the author tries to adhere to his non-judgmental stance. In the end, Syria strengthened its hand and the Palestinian problem remained as unresolved as ever. Nonetheless, and paradoxically, the years of turmoil in Lebanon may have led inadvertently to the accomplishment of Israel's initial goal, as the PLO has been weakened in Lebanon and the rising power of the Shiites may serve to counter any Palestinian effort to reestablish a base of operations south of the Litani River.

ARTHUR JAY KLINGHOFFER
Rutgers University

Recently Completed Doctoral Dissertations

Sylvia Bernice Fleck Abrams　　　　Case Western Reserve University, 1988
"Searching for a Policy: Attitudes and Policies of Non-governmental Agencies Toward the Adjustment of Jewish Immigrants of the Holocaust Era, 1933–1953, as Reflected in Cleveland, Ohio"

Esther Benbassa　　　　Université de Paris III, 1987
"Haim Nahum Efendi, dernier grand rabbin de l'empire ottoman (1908–1920): son rôle politique et diplomatique" (Thèse d'Etat)

David Breakstone　　　　The Hebrew University, 1987
"Hadinamikah shel yisrael behayei hayehudim beamerikah. Nituah shel kelim hinukhiim behezkat 'tekstim tarbutiim' " ("The Dynamics of Israel in American Jewish Life. An Analysis of Educational Means as Cultural Texts")

Susan Canedy Clark　　　　Texas A&M University, 1987
"America's Nazis: The German American Bund"

Hava Eichler　　　　Bar-Ilan University, 1983
"Ziyonut veno'ar behungariah bein shtei milhamot ha'olam" ("Zionism and Youth in Hungary Between the Two World Wars")

Elvin Sanford Gabriel　　　　George Washington University, 1987
"Philosophical Antecedents of Freudian Psychoanalysis"

David Howard Goldberg　　　　McGill University, 1987
"Ethnic Interest Groups as Domestic Sources of Foreign Policy: A Theoretical and Empirical Inquiry"

Steven Frank Greffenius　　　　University of Iowa, 1987
"Patterns of Response in a Dyadic Relationship: Flexibility and Reciprocity in the Egyptian–Israeli Conflict"

Erich Edmund Haberer　　　　University of Toronto, 1987
"The Role of Jews in Russian Revolutionary Populism: 1868–1887"

Dvorah Hacohen　　　　Bar-Ilan University, 1986
"Mediniut haklitah shel ha'aliyah hagedolah beyisrael bashanim, 1948–1953" (Absorption Policy and the Mass Immigration to Israel, 1948–1953")

Hagit Halperin　　　　Tel-Aviv University, 1987
"Yesodot statiim vedinamiim beyezirot Alexander Pen" ("Static and Dynamic Elements in the Works of Alexander Pen")

Eyal Kafkafi　　　　Tel-Aviv University, 1987
"Tmurot baideologiah shel hakibbutz hameuhad bitekufat hamilhamah

hakarah, 1944–1954" ("Ideological Change Within Ha-Kibbutz ha-Meuhad in the Cold War Period, 1944–1954")

Ava F. Kahn   University of California, Santa Barbara, 1988
"Pragmatists in the Promised Land: American Immigrant Voluntary Associations in Israel, 1948–1978"

Elvira Maler   Columbia University, Teachers College, 1987
"The Adjustment of Three Generations of Soviet Immigrants from Riga, Latvia, to Life in the United States" [Ed.D.]

Donald James McKay   University of Illinois, Chicago, 1987
"Soviet Jewish Emigration to Chicago, 1970–1980"

Yaakov Meir   Bar-Ilan University, 1983
"James MacDonald vehaplitim, 1933–1946" ("James MacDonald and the Refugees, 1933–1946")

Gad Opaz   Tel-Aviv University, 1987
"Zikat hakibbutz limekorot hayahadut bemaḥshavat ḥug shdemot" ("The Kibbutz's Tie to Jewish Sources as Expressed in the Thought of the Shdemot Group")

Haim Peles   The Hebrew University, 1988
"Hahityashvut hadatit beereẓ-yisrael bishnot ha'esrim" ("Religious Zionist Settlement in Eretz Israel in the 1920s")

Derek Jonathan Penslar   University of California, Berkeley, 1987
"Engineering Utopia: The World Zionist Organization and the Settlement of Palestine, 1897–1914"

Lawrence Perlman   Brandeis University, 1987
"Abraham Heschel's Idea of Revelation, Phenomenologically Considered"

Aviel Isaiah Roshwald   Harvard University, 1987
"Estranged Bedfellows: Britain and France in the Levant During World War II"

Shuly Rubin Schwartz   The Jewish Theological Seminary of America, 1987
"The Emergence of Jewish Scholarship in America: The Publication of the *Jewish Encyclopedia*"

Lance J. Sussman   Hebrew Union College, 1987
"The Life and Career of Isaac Leeser (1806–1868): A Study of American Judaism in Its Formative Period"

Marcia Shoshana Walerstein   University of California, Los Angeles, 1987
"Public Rituals Among the Jews from Cochin, India, in Israel: Expressions of Ethnic Identity"

Yagil Weinberg   Yale University, 1987
"Situational Structures: The Relations Between the United States and Israel"

Yehiam Weitz   The Hebrew University, 1988
"'Emdot vegishot bemifleget po'alei ereẓ-yisrael klapei shoat yehudei eiropa, 1939–1945" ("Positions and Attitudes in the Mapai Party Toward the Holocaust of European Jewry, 1939–1945")

STUDIES IN
CONTEMPORARY JEWRY

VII

Edited by Jonathan Frankel

417

Dvorah Hacohen, Ben-Gurion and the Second World War: Plans for Mass Immigration to Palestine

Dalia Ofer, Illegal Immigration to Palestine During the Second World War

David Rechter, The *Gezerd* Down Under

Review Essays

Marcus Arkin on Jews in the nineteenth-century German economy

Michael Brown on American Jews in the halls of academe

Richard I. Cohen on the temptations of conversion

Steven Kaplan on Ethiopian Jews

Shlomo Slonim on the establishment of Israel and the Arab world

Robert Wistrich on Habsburg Jewry

. . . Plus reviews and a listing of recent doctoral dissertations